PROPHETIC RELIGIONS AND POLITICS

Religion and the Political Order

PROPHETIC RELIGIONS AND POLITICS

Religion and the Political Order

Volume One

Edited by Jeffrey K. Hadden

and Anson Shupe

A New ERA Book

Paragon House
New York

Published in the United States by
Paragon House Publishers
2 Hammarskjold Plaza
New York, NY 10017

A New Ecumenical Research
  Association Book

"Modern Islamic Sociopolitical Thought"
  by John L. Esposito
    © John L. Esposito, 1984

Designed by Paul Chevannes

Library of Congress Cataloging-in-Publication Data
Main entry under title:

Religion and the Political Order.

  (Sociology of religion series)
  Vol. 1 edited by Jeffrey K. Hadden and Anson D. Shupe.
  "A New ERA book"—V.
  Includes bibliographies and index.
  Contents: v. 1. Prophetic religions and politics.
  1. Religion and politics—Collected works. I. Hadden, Jeffrey K. II. Shupe, Anson
D. III. Series.
  BL65.P7R433 1986 291.1'77 85-21663

Prophetic Religions and Politics.

  (Religion and the Political Order; v. 1)
(Sociology of Religion Series)
  Papers presented at an international conference, held in Nov. 1984, in Martinique.
  "A New ERA book."
  Includes bibliographies and index.
  1. Regligion and politics—Congresses. I. Hadden, Jeffrey K. II. Shupe, Anson D.
III. Series. IV. Series: Sociology of religion series.
  BL65.P7R433 1986 vol. 1 291.1'77 s 85-21664
  ISBN 0-913757-63-2 [291.1'77]
  ISBN 0-913757-53-5 (paperback)

Contents

Acknowledgments   *ix*
Introduction
Jeffrey K. Hadden and Anson D. Shupe   *xi*

PART I—THE PROPHET IN THEORY AND
ACTION   *1*

1. Prophecy, Charisma, and Politics: Reinterpreting the
   Weberian Thesis
   Theodore E. Long   *3*

2. The New Fundamentalism: Rebirth of Political
   Religion in America
   Wade Clark Roof   *18*

3. Charismatic Leadership Trajectories: A Comparative
   Study of Marcus Garvey and Sun Myung Moon
   Michael L. Mickler   *35*

4. Ran Mohan Roy: Pioneer of Indian Freedom
   Cromwell S. Crawford   *52*

PART II—PROPHETIC RELIGION EMERGING
AT THE GRASS ROOTS   *71*

5. Liberation Theology in Latin America: Sociological
   Problems of Interpretation and Explanation
   Roland Robertson   *73*

6. Religion and the Legitimation of Violence
   William R. Garrett   *103*

7. Indigenous Religions and the Transformation of
   Peripheral Societies
   Paget Henry   *123*

PART III—PROPHETIC RELIGION IN THE
SERVICE OF NATION BUILDING   *151*

8. Modern Islamic Sociopolitical Thought
    John L. Esposito   *153*

9. What Is Islamic Fundamentalism?
    Nader Saiedi   *173*

10. *Dakwah Islamiah:* Islamic Revivalism in the Politics of
    Race and Religion in Malaysia
    Zulkarnaina M. Mess and W. Barnett Pearce *196*

11. Religion and Politics in Post-World War II Poland
    Karol H. Borowski   *221*

PART IV—PROPHETIC RELIGION AND THE
POLITICS OF ACCOMMODATION   *233*

12. Militancy and Accommodation in the Third
    Civilization: The Case of Japan's Soka Gakkai
    Movement
    Anson D. Shupe   *235*

13. Historical Perspectives on Religion and Regime: Some
    Sociological Comparisons of Buddhism and
    Christianity
    Randall Collins   *254*

14. Comparative Perspectives on Religion and Regime in
    Eastern Europe and the Soviet Union
    Jerry G. Pankhurst   *272*

15. Prophetic Christianity and the Future of China
    Frank K. Flinn   *307*

16. Pentecostals and Politics in North and Central America
    Margaret M. Poloma   *329*

17. Egypt's Islamic Militancy Revisited
    Saad Eddin Ibrahim   *353*

PART V—CONFLICT AND
INSTITUTIONALIZATION   *363*

18. Prophets, Priests, and the Polity: European Christian
    Democracy in a Developmental Perspective
    John T. S. Madeley   *365*

19. Some Elementary Forms of Authority and
    Fundamentalist Politics
    John H. Simpson   *391*

20. Protestantism and Politics in Scotland and Ulster
    Steve Bruce   *410*

21. Prophecy and Ecstacy: Religion and Politics in the
    Caribbean
    Stephen D. Glazier   *430*

    Contributors   *447*

    Index   *449*

ACKNOWLEDGMENTS

Coordinating an international conference on the beautiful island of Martinique, logistically speaking, was no mean feat. Our efforts at recruiting scholars from diverse disciplines and backgrounds formed only part of the overall enterprise. Without the help of many other persons we could not have managed the enormous number of practical but necessary details involved.

We are particularly grateful to the New Ecumenical Research Association which made funding for the conference possible. David S. C. Kim, though unable to attend, once again displayed his commitment to intellectual integrity by encouraging us to develop themes and topics as we saw fit. A special thanks also to John Maniatis, Executive Director of New ERA, for encouraging us to submit our conference proposal and for providing able staff support. Jolanda Smalls handled preconference arrangments and Herb Mayr managed conference logistics in Martinique. To these two persons we are grateful for performing yeoman service in handling all the mundane but indispensable details associated with transporting, feeding, and lodging the two dozen conferees who gathered in a remote corner of the Caribbean.

Richard Quebedeaux and Frank K. Flinn, consultants to New ERA, were also participants in the conference and contributed to its interdisciplinary flavor. Jack Kiburz, Editor of New ERA Books, and his able staff were helpful in the task of transforming conference papers into an integrated volume.

Our deepest debt goes to the conference participants themselves. By preparing their papers in time to be circulated before the conference, they provided a rich array of intellectual substance which both leavened and gave focus to lively discussions. Each participant also provided written critiques of two or more conference papers. This was an invaluable contribution to us as editors and to participants who rewrote papers. And, finally, conference participants were punctual in producing edited or rewritten manuscripts. We learned much from each of the participants and their cooperation made our job so much easier.

This conference was the first in a series aimed at gaining closure on religious and political developments that are reshaping the world. All of the above persons have helped to make this ambitious task seem more realizable.

Jeffrey K. Hadden
Charlottesville, Virginia

Anson Shupe
Arlington, Texas

Introduction

JEFFREY K. HADDEN

AND

ANSON SHUPE

A Legacy of Secularization

HE publication of Thomas Kuhn's *The Structure of Scientific Revolutions* (1962) sensitized members of the scientific world to the fact that their ideas, indeed the grounding of their thought processes, are shaped by the scholarly communities in which they labor. "Normal science," as Kuhn conceived it, occurs within a generally taken-for-granted conceptual, or paradigmatic, framework. No paradigm is inclusive of all questions that might be raised about a subject matter, but paradigms do focus the structure of attention while simultaneously excluding other questions. Paradigm shifts tend to be infrequent, and when they occur the process is akin to social revolutions.

Leaving aside the question of whether Kuhn intended to include the social sciences in his analytical scheme, it is clear that social scientists have found his work useful for thinking about their work (e.g., Freidrichs 1970; Mullins 1973; Ritzer 1975). If we can also duck questions relating to the specific content of a social science paradigm, Kuhn's notion of a paradigm is *at least* a useful metaphor for thinking about major ideas that have dominated social science thought.

Hammond (1985, 1) has recently observed that Western thought is dominated by a linear image which views society as being transformed through time from somewhere to somewhere else. Born in the *zeitgeist* of evolutionary thought in the nineteenth century, the social sciences developed a complex, and at least loosely connected, set of concepts to characterize this process of societal transformation. *Modernization, rationalization, bureaucratization, industrialization* and *urbanization,* Hammond notes, are but a few of the concepts developed to describe and analyze this "one-directional" process of social change.

"In the social scientific study of religion," Hammond notes, "this dominant linear image is expressed chiefly in the term *secularization,* the idea that society moves from some sacred condition to successively secular conditions in which the sacred evermore recedes (1985, 1)." The theory postulates a strong and casual relationship between the forces of modernization and the vitality of religious belief and religious institutions. As modernization sweeps across the globe, religion gradually loses its grip on culture and any sway it may hold over the individual will be radically transformed. The concept secularization, thus, is used to describe the process whereby modern societies are removed from the domination of religious institutions.

There are many variations on the theory, but each is undergirded by this powerful linear image of history. Accounting for the persistence of religion in the midst of the secular takes on the character of "normal science" in Kuhn's framework—a "mopping-up" operation wherein scholars fill in the details of the theory and account for anomalies. The notion of the *privatization* of belief is one such conceptual mop-up operation. According to this conception, religion becomes a personal matter in the modern world, anchored in individual consciousness, rather than a cosmic force. Religion may be capable of maintaining its traditional function as a mechanism of social control among "the poor and unwashed masses" and even of fostering a "residual of good will" in highly secular societies. But scholars who take seriously the idea of secularization discount the significance of religion as an earth-moving force.

This volume was born out of a gnawing skepticism about the efficacy of secularization theory to account for all the apparent anomalies of religious influence in the modern world. The role of religion in the Civil Rights movement in America during the 1960s caught the attention of Hadden (1969), and Shupe, as a student in Japan, was moved to study the rise of Soka Gakkai Buddhists to political power. Later, we both contributed to the literature assessing the ascendancy of the New Christian Right in America (Hadden and Swann 1981; Shupe and Stacey 1982; Bromley and Shupe 1984).

More important than our own research was the ever present awareness that religious influence around the globe simply refuses to go away. The near simultaneous birth of the Moral Majority in the United States and the stormy rise to power of Shi'ite Muslims led by Ayatollah Khomeini in Iran gave us cause to join with others (e.g., Marty 1980) to consider whether we were experiencing world-wide revolutionary tide of religio-political fundamentalism. Indeed, when we first started discussing the collaboration on the topic of religion and politics, we frequently spoke of the phenomenon of "global fundamentalism."

We still find some compelling arguments for thinking about fundamentalism as a global phenomenon—and we may yet seek to focus attention solely on this issue—but the concept is too narrow to serve as an organizing framework for assessing the impact of religion in the political affairs of the citizens of this planet.

As Toffler (1970), Naisbitt (1982), and so many others have noted, we are bombarded with news—*one glitch at a time*. And the half-life of our awareness of all those glitches is not long. We can watch Protestants and Catholics in Northern Ireland do battle on the evening news for weeks on end, but when the cameras shift to the United States Embassy in Teheran, where Shi'ite youth are holding Americans hostage, we quickly forget the struggle that goes on in the streets of Belfast. When the cameras shift to Lebanon, so also does our consciousness. And on and on.

Our exposure to many religio-political conflicts, thus, tends merely to be episodic rather than cumulative. We have only a vague awareness of multiplying episodes of religious struggle. Yet in the United States and around the world developments attest almost daily to the explosive potential of religious ideology. Consider the following as illustrative:

In the United States the politics of abortion and the pro-family movement, the deep entanglement of Roman Catholic bishops in the nuclear arms debate, the movement to defy the government by providing sanctuary to political refugees from Central America; the revolutionary movements grounded in 'liberation theology' in Latin America, Africa and Asia; the revival of Islamic fundamentalism in over sixty-five nations from Morocco to Malaysia; intrareligious conflict between Sikhs and Hindus in India, Buddhists and Tamils in Sri Lanka, and Protestants and Catholics in Northern Ireland; the resistance of the Catholic church to authorities in Poland and of Muslim militia to the Soviets in Afghanistan; the struggle of the South African Council of Churches against apartheid; the rise of new cults and sects all over the world . . .

These events, and many more, point increasingly to religion as a phenomenon to be taken seriously if one is to understand national and world developments.

But do these many discrete developments call for a reassessment of the conceptual foundations of theories of religion in the modern world? Until recently few (e.g., Hammond 1985) have ever questioned the proposition that secularization is a very long process. Even on such an overall linear trajectory should we not expect intermittent revivals of fundamentalism as well as other forms of religious expression?

The answers are still far from clear. Even though a number of scholars with diverse perspectives are currently converging toward a rejection of simplistically invariate secularization process, we nevertheless want to avoid settling for premature closure on the issue. Reassessment of the dominant assumptions and models of every field of social science as well as the humanities is required, and the necessary data on much-publicized but surprisingly little understood religio-political developments must be drawn together.

We agreed in early 1983 to work together toward the achievement of this goal. We organized a New ERA-funded conference on "Prophetic Religion and Politics," which convened on the island of Martinique in mid-November 1984, as a promising first step toward such a gigantic, even intimidating, task. There an interdisciplinary group of scholars who had conducted research and field work in regions as diverse as the Americas (North, Central, and South), Eastern Europe, the Indian sub-continent and the Far East, the Caribbean, and the Middle East met to begin critical reflection on dominant analytic modes and to contribute case and comparative studies for an as-yet inadequate data base.

Our decision to hold this conference grew out of a largely fruitless search for the needed contemporary scholarship. Some years earlier the religio-political interface had been a topic of comparative inquiry (see, e.g. B. L. Smith 1976; D. E. Smith 1966, 1970, 1974; Lewy 1974), but for our purposes these analyses were flawed for several reasons.

First, the overwhelming proportion of these studies uncritically incorporated the linear secularization/modernization/functionalist theoretical models of the 1950s and 1960s along with the subtle ethnocentrism in them.

Second, a primary focus of these studies was on religion as a dependent variable with secularized nation-building, mostly in the Third World, as the independent (political) variable. The industrialized nations of the West and the Far East were largely ignored, perhaps because it was assumed that religion there had run its course as a significant factor in social change.

Third, since the publication of even the best of these sources (e.g., Lewy 1974 and D. E. Smith 1970) so many dramatic events involving religion and social structural/political change have occured even in the so-called "secularized" industrial nations that the need for a new assessment on a global scale has become glaringly apparent.

Our own hunch is that rather than some single linear trend of secularization, we are currently riding the crest of a cyclical process in which progressive forces of secularization generate the alienation and discontent that facilitate intermittent religious revival and revitalization. Still the sheer magnitude of such activity worldwide cautions us to keep a healthy skepticism toward any conclusions just yet.

The sheer magnitude of religio-political activity presented us with the practical dilemma of how to begin considering the more generic relationship between religion and the political. Should our initial foray into the subject include various cultural traditions and world regions, or should we forego the richness of comparative cases and settle instead for closure within only one tradition, such as Islam or Christianity? Should we consider only those most dramatic situations where political revolution has occurred, or do we want a broad range of potential outcomes that can result when the religious institution and the polity meet?

Our ultimate goal is conceptualization and theorizing. Our strategy for achieving this goal is at once pragmatic and programmatic. We decided to preserve a multi-cultural approach (which necessitated a multidisciplinary team of scholars). But we also made the decision to narrow our focus to one specific dimension of religion. We selected the prophetic, or change-oriented, elements of religion because, at least on the face of it, they appear to be so often involved in the social upheavals and transformations occurring all around us.

From an early date, our quest had two pathways. First, we felt the problem sufficiently important that we were willing to make a long term career commitment to the task. Shortly after we began working together on the project, Hadden was elected President of the Society for the Scientific Study of Religion. Shupe agreed to be Program Chair for the 1985 Annual Meetings of the Society. By identifying "Religion and the Political Order" as our Program Theme, we hoped we could entice some of our colleagues to pick up our quest.

Clearly, it was a matter of selecting the right theme at the right time. Our call for papers produced thematic titles far beyond our expectations. Further, a positive assessment of the Martinique conference on "Prophetic Religion and Politics" resulted in the New ERA funding a second conference on the general theme of religion and politics. Thus, as we complete this volume, we are working simultaneously on the SSSR Annual Meeting program and a second New ERA conference. By the time we complete these two meetings in the fall of 1985, we will have engaged over one hundred scholars in the preparation and delivery of papers related to our inquiry into the relationship between religion and politics.

In some instances we can document that our initiative "seduced" colleagues to pick up our agenda within the context of their own scholarly competency. But, in large measure, what we seem to have accomplished was to locate and channel energies already directed toward expanding knowledge about religion and politics.

In organizing and preparing for the conference we were very conscious of the need to locate a delicate balance between an integrative theme and the individual scholarly interests of participants. We felt that if we tried to bend people too far away from their own interests, there was a real danger that we would stifle their creativity and turn the challenge into a mere "assignment"—as in a high school homework assignment. On the other hand, we felt that giving people no more direction than "do something on religion and politics" would likely produce a collection of perhaps interesting but unrelated papers.

Our decision was to pursue a middle ground. We sought out those we knew to share our interest in religion and politics and invited them to write a paper on the change-oriented or prophetic aspects of religions within the context of their own research and scholarly expertise.

We were not surprised that some chose to ignore the thematic charge altogether. To the contrary, we were surprised by the number of those who did, in fact, pick up on the theme of prophecy and religiously conceived change. The volume will be much more satisfying to those who seek to broaden their understanding of the links between religion and social change than it will be for those seeking great depth in the analysis of the concept of prophet. Only Theodore E. Long ("Prophecy, Charisma, and Politics: Reinterpreting the Weberian Thesis"), at our request, explicitly addresses the utility of the concept prophet in the Weberian tradition. His work helps focus on the limits and possibilities of that idea in the work of several other contributors.

As conveners of the conference, we were interested in exploiting the considerable talents of the colleagues we recruited. We are satisfied that our understanding of the problem has been significantly enhanced by their efforts. By this personal measure, our first step toward understanding the broad and complex ways in which religion intersects the political order has been a success. The broader measures of success will be whether (1) others agree that the contributions to this volume are illuminating of the issues raised and (2) they stimulate others to join in the quest to understand the dynamics and power of religion in modern political process.

The Sociology of Prophetic Religion

Any sociological understanding of prophecy as a phenomenon must begin with its classic definition and analysis by Max Weber. Unfortunately, as Theodore Long reports in this volume, most sociologists do not go beyond Weber in conceptualizing the prophet and his or her pivotal role in helping transform values, undermining authority or overthrowing regimes. Too often, Long argues, sociologists simply equate the prophet with charismatic authority. It is true that the prophet "is the exemplar of charisma, its purest embodiment and perhaps its very model." But the prophet is not completely defined when we say he or she has charismatic authority.

Weber's meaning of the prophet's charisma was a uniquely personal one. Such charisma derived from the prophet's unique person and talents or was presented to him or her by some suprahuman agency. It was not simply a form of counter-establishment authority pertaining to a marginal leader and legitimated by others who were also disaffected with *status quo* institutions.

The importance of this reassessment of Weber's theory of the prophet rests in how we anticipate and interpret prophets empirically. For one thing it means that prophets can arise within "routine structures" and establishment institutions. Prophets need not be "marginal men" or without "legitimate" credentials or resources. They can just as likely emerge from a bureaucracy as from a wilderness, from times of societal disorganization or crisis as much as from times of relative stability.

This reassessment also means that the "prophet" can become a conceptual tool applicable to a wider range of situations. For example, we are under no obligation to think of the prophet in strictly *nominal* terms, i.e., where a prophet is reduced to a *type* with a narrow set of characteristics of which charismatic authority is paramount.

Instead, prophetic behavior can be conceptualized as a *continuum*, a variable value that in principle could even be quantified and measured in other than either/or terms. Thus, non-prophetic persons or even organizations could, on occasion, behave prophetically.

This broader understanding of the prophets and the prophetic values they advocate will be necessary if we are to move beyond the image of Old Testament Israelite prophets that figure so importantly in Weber's theory. This collection of essays demonstrates all too well that there are simply too many situations worldwide where religious leaders and groups are acting in a prophetic mode without approximating the classic elements of charismatic authority: from base communities in Latin America to Hindu nationalists to the Roman Catholic church in Poland. We may have to redo our theory and concepts, however venerable, to make better sense of real developments, but that is the nature of the scientific enterprise.

The Organization and Content of This Volume

The five sections of this volume group essays into clusters presenting distinct issues in the prophetic religious-political relationship. Part one offers a theoretical reassessment of Weber's classic theory of prophetic action (Theodore E. Long, "Prophecy, Charisma, and Politics: Reinterpreting the Weberian Thesis") and examples of real-world prophets. Long's essay we have discussed above.

Notwithstanding Jerry Falwell's claim that the Moral Majority is a broad-based political movement embracing persons of every faith, geographical region, and economic class, the evidence does not support these claims. The Moral Majority is substantially a Baptist phenomenon (Liebman 1983) and the broader phenomenon known as the New Christian Right is largely a fundamentalist movement. But fundamentalism is in the midst of some rather significant changes.

Wade Clark Roof ("The New Fundamentalism: Rebirth of Political Religion in America") traces fundamentalism in the United States from its birth in the late nineteenth century through the emergence of a "new" fundamentalism during the present decade. Contrary to popular stereotypes of fundamentalism as a rigid, closed system, Roof argues that fundamentalism shows much evidence of being open, flexible, and adaptive. In pursuit of their aggressive "politics of morality," for example, they have been open to partnerships with groups which were arch enemies of the old fundamentalism.

Roof skillfully analyzes structural and demographic changes in society which help explain this transformation. As liberal Protestantism continues to lose the grip it once held in shaping American culture,

Roof sees the fundamentalists rushing in to fill the vacuum. But in the process of ascending to power, the "strong centralizing tendency in American life" is likely to transform fundamentalism in the direction of ever greater moderation and tolerance.

Michael L. Mickler's essay ("Charismatic Leadership Trajectories: A Comparative Study of Marcus Garvey and Sun Myung Moon") compares the leadership ascent of Jamaican-born Marcus Garvey and Korean-born Sun Myung Moon, both of whom drew widespread attention and criticism for importing their movements to the United States.

Mickler conceives a leadership trajectory in three stages that form an emerging process through which first the prophetic figure, and later the larger society, come to see the prophet as moving from the periphery of society towards centers of power. The result is that power holders move to protect their threatened interests by repressing the given prophet. As the experiences of both Garvey and Moon demonstrate, there emerges gradually a definition of the prophetic leader as a criminal. Other examples, such as Father Divine in the United States, during the Depression, come to mind. Mickler's essay offers a theologian's view of what sociologists term a "labeling perspective" on the social construction of deviance and criminality.

Cromwell Crawford ("Ram Mohan Roy: Pioneer of Indian Freedom") offers a case study of prophetic leadership in a religious tradition (Hinduism) frequently thought of as priestly and unchanging. Ram Mohan Roy, a precursor of later Indian heroes such as Mohandas T. Gandhi, illustrates the fine line sometimes difficult to draw between religious prophet and civil religious patriot.

Prophets, Crawford reminds us, do not always confine their role to an occasional foray from the wilderness into this-worldly activities, and their styles can be pragmatic as well as abrasive and bellicose. Sometimes they even conduct their prophetic role on a daily basis in conventional social structures. This application of the term "prophet" expands the entire prophecy concept, perhaps a necessity if "prophet" is to be meaningfully applied outside Western religions and cultural traditions.

Part two presents three papers exploring how prophetic religions work from the grassroots. Liberation theology has become a rubric for a variety of change-oriented versions of Christianity (both Protestant and Catholic) in Central and South America, Europe, Asia, and Africa. Roland Robertson's essay ("Liberation Theology in Latin America: Sociological Problems of Interpretation and Explanation") on Catholic forms of this phenomenon serves as a primer on the key elements in the liberation theologies of Latin America: their histories, ideologies, and political implications.

More importantly, Robertson deals with a sociology of knowledge issue: how "insider" (i.e., advocates) and "outsider" (i.e., non-Latin American social scientists) can analyze and explain liberation theology apart from either the older functionalist models of modernization or value-laden liberationist ideology.

Robertson further raises important social and demographic questions about Catholicism in Latin America. For example, what are the implications of the oft-ignored fundamental fact that only relatively small numbers of Latin Americans are "meaningfully christianized"? Such basic demographic realities, Robertson argues, may limit, shape, or even determine the future of liberation theology in Latin America.

William R. Garrett ("Religion and the Legitimation of Violence") echoes many of the concerns raised by Robertson about where liberation theology may be leading. Garrett notes that while violence in the name of faith is not a new phenomenon, the late twentieth century has witnessed a significant rise in efforts to inspire men, in the name of their faith, to "beat their plowshares into swords." He identifies three distinct types of radical religion: (1) Right, (2) Democratic Center, and (3) Totalitarian Democratic Left. All three types have established ties to resurgent nationalism around the globe. Liberation theology, an example of Totalitarian Democratic Left, is the most puissant of the contemporary religious movements. The grounding of knowledge in *praxis,* Garrett argues, surrenders theological analysis to political dogma. He does not question the good intentions of liberation theologians, but is concerned that the fruits of their labor may be "uncritical religious legitimation of revolutionary violence."

Paget Henry ("Indigenous Religions and the Transformation of Peripheral Societies") taps yet another potent dimension of grassroots religions. Henry writes from the theoretical perspective of dependency theory. During colonialism religion was used to legitimate central dominance of the periphery. In the period immediately following colonialism, peripheral societies continued to be dominated in nearly every respect by the cultural systems of the center societies, and religion continued to serve the interests of center societies. But, Henry argues, in the post-colonial era, religious ideologies may arise which undermine and, hence, delegitimize center dominance.

To develop this argument, Henry analyzes three geographical regions where religion, in different ways, has served to undermine center dominance. In the Caribbean, Rastafarianism is a "new religion" which has been an impelling force, far beyond its numerical strength, challenging the values of the societies which long dominated the island nations. In Latin America liberation theology is a movement transforming a religion imposed upon indigenous people centuries ago. In the third case, Islamic revival is recovering a heritage as it proclaims Western dominance of Muslim cultures illegitimate. While the cultures of these three case studies are very different, in each the process of *delegitimizing* the once dominant value systems is integral to the emergence of new values.

Prophetic religions may also function in the service of nation-building, although not always in the way we might expect. This is the subject of four papers in Part three. The colonialization of the Islamic world in the nineteenth century by European Christian nations presented a two-pronged crisis which was both political and religious. First, the conquest interrupted twelve centuries of unbroken expansion of Islamic power and cultural influence without a single incidence of loss of sovereignty to a non-Islamic power. This historical fact dealt a devastating blow to Muslims' perception of history, which constituted the second prong of the crisis. The political defeats were interpreted as a loss of divine favor and guidance from Allah.

John L. Esposito ("Modern Islamic Socio-political Thought") traces the response of Muslims to this crisis, with emphasis on the period since 1945. Three patterns of response, each advocating a "return to Islam," are identified: (1) conservative, (2) fundamentalist, and (3) modernist. Esposito's categories vary from popular conventional use and, hence, the critical distinctions should be noted. Conservatives, who essentially represent the religious "establishment," find the classical formulation of Islam quite adequate. Their goal is to return to this tradition as it has been preserved in Islamic law. Fundamentalists share these goals *except* they "claim the right to go back to the fundamental sources of Islam to reinterpret *(ijtihad)* and reapply them to contemporary needs." Within this assumptive framework, the Ayatollah Khomeini is a conservative while Libya's Colonel Muammar el-Qaddafi and the Saudi Arabian leaders are fundamentalists.

Islamic modernists have learned from the West without aspiring to westernize their cultures. They are open to fairly wide-ranging reinterpretation of the sacred documents. The struggle between these several factions, Esposito concludes, is to be interpreted as an indicator of the continuing significance of Islam in the political affairs of the followers of Allah.

Nader Saiedi ("What Is Islamic Fundamentalism?") locates Islamic fundamentalism in historical perspective and then identifies the basic cultural, political, and economic characteristics of this religious movement. Islamic fundamentalism, according to Saiedi, is not properly understood as a rejection of westernization, modernization, and capitalism. Rather, it is a reaction to the failures of Islamic liberalism in the nineteenth and twentieth centuries. Further, Islamic liberalism is not an adaptation to Western influence but has an independent tradition tracing back to the seventeenth century. Western influence, thus, confounds rather than defines the social, political, and economic dilemmas of Middle Eastern Islamic societies.

Saiedi is an Iranian Baha'i who took political refuge in the United States following the Khomeini revolution. This may account for the fact that there is sometimes a thin line between his analysis and an ideological statement. Still, Saiedi dissects Islamic fundamentalism with great skill. His categories of analysis suggest a framework for comparative analysis of fundamentalism in world religions. And if he occasionally crosses the line between analysis and moral judgment, the analytical categories he develops will serve well the task of separating the two.

Prophetic strains in religious traditions can serve as the locus for nation-building. Paradoxically, however, they can fuel attempts to unify a pluralistic culture as well as work against such unification by dividing competing minorities further. Mess and Pearce's study of the *dakwah* movement in Malaysia *("Dakwah Islamiah:* Islamic Revivalism in the Politics of Race and Religion in Malaysia") illustrates the political impact that a prophetic brand of Islam—calling for a narrow version of a theocratic Islamic state—may have.

Mess and Pearce suggest that even if the government resists turning itself into a theocracy, it may be forced to use religious rhetoric and deal with issues in religious terms. The religious movement may, in fact, achieve at least a partial victory just by pressuring the government to consider its theocratic agenda. This is particularly true if the government wishes to co-opt the prophetic movement in an attempt to maintain stability and unity.

The Catholic church has played an important prophetic role in the conflict between the Polish government and the Solidarity workers' union. That a church best known for its priestly hierarchy and ritualistic/theological complexity could act prophetically is the theme of Karol H. Borowski's analysis ("Religion and Politics in Post-World War II Poland"). Tracing the polity's relations with the church (vascillating between toleration and repression) since World War II, Borowski hypothesizes the conditions under which an indigenized church has come to challenge prophetically a communist regime.

An emigré, Borowski clearly holds strong—even partisan—views of the Polish situation. Nevertheless, his essay importantly underscores the clash of two cultural systems each of which makes exclusivist "truth" claims as well as demands for ultimate sovereignty over temporal affairs. Traditional Old Testament conceptions portray the prophet as spitting against the wind. But in our revised conception, one might expect the prophet to work in conjunction with the "establishment" in the pursuit of social change; or if not in conjunction, within a framework of accommodation. Part four offers a variety of angles on this theme.

The slippage between the lofty aspirations and high flung rhetoric of "world-transforming movements" and their actual accomplishments is a subject well researched in the sociology of religion (e.g., Wilson 1981; Bromley and Shupe 1979). This process of a change-oriented millennial group "accommodating" to secular values and operating styles, Anson Shupe ("Militancy and Accommodation in the Third Civilization: The Case of Japan's Soka Gakkai Movement") argues, is actually accelerated when the group seeks entry into the arena of interest groups and political parties of liberal democracies.

Shupe examines the case of the Soka Gakkai, an organization closely affiliated with the militant Nichiren Shoshu sect of Japanese Buddhism, and how it began to lose much of its revolutionary character and abandon real pursuit of its *ultimate* goals through having to adopt the pragmatic style of that larger political arena (i.e., seeking more mundane, *proximate* victories).

The implication is that when a group espousing absolutist religious ideology enters into the world of political negotiation and compromise, the former faces strong inevitable pressures to bend to the latter. This is a lesson as pertinent to the emerging New Christian Right in the United States as it is to Islamic fundamentalists seeking theocracies throughout the world.

Using a broad range of historical examples, Randall Collins's essay ("Historical Perspectives on Religion and Regime: Some Sociological Comparisons of Buddhism and Christianity") examines the alternative ways religion may relate to the state and then posits conditions under which it may garner the greatest political power.

Collins challenges the linear assumption of secularization theory, which presumes that increasing secularism in politics, and concludes (similar to Simpson elsewhere in this volume) that the maximal potential for religion's political influence is actualized when religion is most extensively organized independently of the state. Thus, such mass movements of a religious nature as are occurring worldwide may be a permanent structural feature of modern politics and not merely anomalies.

The implication of this development is that the international community may have reached a critical point at which technology, the diffusion of theologies and ideologies, and the rising expectations of mass citizenries now interface to fuel an awakening of change and revolution which we are just beginning to anticipate.

The intertwining of Roman Catholic faith and Solidarity banners in public demonstrations in Poland, the stubborn resistance of *Mujahedeem* (Islamic "holy warriors") to Soviet oppression in Afghanistan, and Billy Graham's speaking to large crowds in Moscow as the KGB watches on are symbols of the fact religion is alive in communist nations. But just as certainly, each symbolizes the reality that communism is a jealous mistress who does not jauntily share the divided loyalties of her subjects.

Jerry G. Pankhurst ("A Comparative Perspective on Religion and Regime in Eastern Europe and the Soviet Union") examines the relationship between religious faith and state dominance in the several Eastern European communist regimes. He approaches the subject from the perspective of *interest group competition*. The state has a monopoly on resources of coercion as they endeavor to replace religion with politics. Still, religious institutions are not without resources which can aid or impede the efforts of the state to achieve legitimacy and efficacy in their task of nation building. Pankhurst provides a fascinating conceptual framework for understanding the ongoing chess game between religion and regime in the Eastern European nations. He concludes with ten hypotheses, based on variable structural-demographic features, which are quite useful in assessing the degree of social influence religious groups in communist nations may be expected to exercise.

Frank K. Flinn ("Prophetic Christianity and the Future of China") examines the latent developments in an area that has had little recent scholarly exposure—the resurgence of religion in the People's Republic of China. Post-Maoist government sympathies for a benevolent, tolerant policy toward religion, many of them specific forms imported from the West, have led to important changes in the role of religion in mainland China.

Religion has not disappeared under the communist regime, but in fact its various adherents have continued to multiply. Moreover, they see a role for themselves in the as yet unfinished internal revolution of China, not simply sacramentalizing the neo-Marxist order but prophetically serving as a crucible to generate and channel discontent. This is particularly true for Christian churches of assorted Catholic and Protestant denominations which have weathered years of official hostility, if not persecution, now to enjoy resurgence.

Pentecostals, perhaps more than any Protestant Christian group, have a tradition of other-worldliness. This is the last group we would expect to be involved in the political arena. But is there evidence that Pentecostals may be hearing voices from on high instructing them to become involved in politics? For a short while in 1982 Rios Montt, a convert from Catholicism to a pentecostal tradition, heeded the call to serve as president of Guatemala. Pat Robertson, founder to the Christian Broadcasting Network, and Jim Wallis, leader of the Sojourners community, stand as politically engaged charismatics on nearly opposite ends of the political spectrum. And in 1984 *Charisma,* a respected conservative magazine in the pentecostal tradition, endorsed Ronald Reagan for president.

Margaret M. Poloma ("Pentecostals and Politics in North and Central America") examines the evidence and concludes that these apparent anomalies are just that—anomalies. Poloma draws from a wide array of experience and data, including a recent study she conducted. Although she admits the data are not without "signs of ambivalence," Poloma concludes that Pentecostals are likely to remain generally passive to politics in both the United States and Latin America.

Contemporary Islamic faith is not normally thought of in the same breath with political accommodation. Saad Eddin Ibrahim ("Egypt's Islamic Militancy Revisited") is a respected sociologist from American University in Cairo who has studied Muslim militants in Egypt for a long time. By pursuing a policy of moderation and accommodation, while remaining steadfast in the face of violence, Ibrahim thinks that President Mubarak may have found a middle ground to stay the tide of militancy. He skillfully identifies and analyzes the key organizations and actors in post-Nasser Egypt. Sadat's demise was moving too fast on too many fronts.

It may be some time before we know whether Mubarak's early success in dealing with militants can be attributed to his astute prowess, or a respite while militants regroup following the Sadat assassination. For the moment, Ibrahim's thesis of accommodation stands as a provocative suggestion that there may be grounds for dealing with Islamic militants other than the bloody confrontations that have characterized recent years in the Middle East.

Social structures, as every sociologist knows, but all too frequently neglects, are powerful forces in shaping social and cultural life. Part five presents four stimulating comparative studies which demonstrate the power of social structure to shape and give direction to religious conflict.

Contemporary secular scholarship tends to accent the importance of *interests*—particularly economic interests—in the political arena while discounting the importance of *values* as the foundation for action. Hence, conventional wisdom holds that Christian Democratic parties in Europe are merely one among many groups driven by the pursuit of self-interest and competitive advantage.

John T. S. Madeley ("Prophets, Priests, and the Polity: European Christian Democracy in a Developmental Perspective") believes modern scholars underestimate the degree to which Christian Democrats have been motivated by the desire to apply democratic techniques and Christian principles to the resolution of temporal problems. This is not to say that Christian Democratic parties do not act out of self interest. They do. But Madeley sees an important tension between the "priestly" interest-claims and "prophetic" value-demands of the Christian Democratic tradition. In the end, Madeley concludes, "the electorally most successful parties have proved truly inadequate vehicles for the prophet, if trusty chariots for the priest and politician." Still, the tension between the priestly and prophetic has played an important role in shaping the face of modern Europe.

Prophetic or change-oriented religion requires more than charismatic versions or enthusiasm to flourish. Societies' structural conduciveness toward tolerating or encouraging interest groups (including religious ones) is also a critical factor.

On this theme, John H. Simpson ("Some Elementary Forms of Authority and Fundamentalist Politics") compares the contextual or "exogenous," conditions of both the United States and Canada which have promoted a proliferation of politically oriented religious movements (i.e., the "politics of morality") in the former country and a noticeable lack of such in the latter. These conditions, Simpson argues, are independent of the phenomenon of modernization so often touted as an explanation for them.

Simpson's provocative analysis provides additional ammunition for the proposition that social science theorizing needs to break out of the confines of the "modernization" paradigm and consider more generic variables in social structure.

Steve Bruce ("Protestantism and Politics in Scotland and Ulster") compares the religio-political histories of Scotland and Ulster, the former having seen relatively little Protestant-Catholic conflict while the latter has been notorious for it, to separate out the necessary from the sufficient ingredients shaping religious conflict.

An important element as to whether or not religion becomes a rallying point for political conflict, Bruce observes, is the theological and economic homogeneity of the populations in questions. Conflict expressed religiously in change-oriented or prophetic terms is often the result of a complex interweaving of economic and demographic patterns as well as the varying rates of modernization.

As much as any essay in this volume, Bruce's analysis shows the need for a thorough appreciation of the historical antecedents of modern conflicts. In the case of Northern Ireland and surrounding countries, little meaningful understanding can be achieved without references to the tides of nationalism and religious hatred spanning the past several centuries.

Accommodation among some former "religions of the oppressed" in the Caribbean region is the theme of Steven D. Glazier's essay ("Prophecy and Ecstasy: Religion and Politics in the Caribbean"). An anthropologist with broad field work experience in the Caribbean, Glazier examines three prophetic ex-slave movements: (1) Ras Tafari, (2) vodun, and (3) the Spiritual Baptists. He examines their social organization, beliefs, and members' upward social mobility in order to understand their mixed fortunes when engaging in politics.

Glazier criticizes many past analysts for using outmoded data and theoretical models, concluding that various leaders whose religious authority has stemmed from their prophetic role have been willing to enjoy the benefits of allying with politicians even at the expense of losing their appeal to lower-class adherents. The absorption of these religious groups into mainstream institutions and a radical transformation of their membership compositions are the likely consequences, Glazier believes. Elsewhere in this volume, Paget Henry, a native of Antigua, challenges this interpretation, at least with respect to the Rastafarian movement.

These brief introductions give the reader some sense of the breadth of substantive and theoretical inquiry pursued by the contributors to this volume. In a few words it is impossible to capture the depth of perceptive insights. We invite you to share the rich and rewarding experience we shared at Martinique and again in editing these papers.

References

Bromley, David G. and Anson Shupe. 1979. *Moonies in America: Cult, Church and Crusade.* Beverly Hills, CA.: Sage.
Bromley, David G. and Anson Shupe, eds. 1984. *New Christian Politics.* Macon, GA.: Mercer University Press.
Friedrichs, Robert W. 1970. *A Sociology of Sociology.* New York: Free Press.
Hadden, Jeffrey K. 1969. *The Gathering Storm in the Churches.* Garden City, N.Y.: Doubleday,
Hadden, Jeffrey K. and Charles E. Swann. 1981. *Prime Time Preachers.* Reading, MA.: Addison-Wesley.
Hammond, Phillip E., ed. 1985. *The Sacred in a Secular Age.* Berkeley, CA.: University of California Press.
Kuhn, Thomas S. 1970. *The Structure of Scientific Revolutions.* Chicago: University of Chicago Press, 2d ed.
Lewy, Guenter. 1974. *Religion and Revolution.* New York: Oxford University Press.
Marty, Martin E. "Fundamentalism Reborn: Faith and Fanaticism," *Saturday Review,* May (1980), pp. 37–42.
Mullins, Nicholas C. 1973. *Theories and Theory Groups in Contemporary American Sociology.* New York: Harper and Row.
Naisbitt, John. 1982. *Megatrends.* New York: Warner Books.
Ritzer, George. 1975. *Sociology a Multiple Paradigm Science.* Boston: Allyn and Bacon.
Shupe, Anson and William A. Stacey. 1982. *Born Again Politics and the Moral Majority.* New York: Edwin Mellen Press.
Smith, Bardwell L. ed. 1976. *Religion and Social Conflict in South Asia.* Leiden, The Netherlands: E.J. Brill.
Smith, Donald Eugene, ed. 1966. *South Asian Politics and Religion.* Princeton, N.J.: Princeton University Press.
Smith, Donald Eugene. 1970. *Religion and Political Development.* Boston: Little, Brown and Company.
Smith, Donald Eugene, ed. 1974. *Religion and Political Modernization.* New Haven, CT.: Yale University Press.
Toffler, Alvin. 1970. *Future Shock,* New York: Random House.
Weber, Max. 1974. *The Theory of Social and Economic Organization.* Trans. A. M. Henderson and T. Parsons. New York: Free Press.
———. 1952. *Ancient Judaism.* Trans. H. Gerth and D. Martindale. New York: Free Press.

———. 1963. *The Sociology of Religion,* Trans. E. Fischoff. Boston: Beacon.

———. 1978. *Economy and Society: An Outline of Interpretative Sociology,* Ed. by G. Roth and C. Wittich. Berkeley, CA.: University of California Press.

Wilson, Bryan, ed. 1981. *The Social Impact of New Religious Movements.* Barrytown, N. Y.: Unification Theological Seminary.

PART ONE
THE PROPHET IN
THEORY AND ACTION

1

Prophecy, Charisma, and Politics: Reinterpreting the Weberian Thesis

THEODORE E. LONG

R ELIGIOUS prophecy seems to become entangled with politics almost inevitably. Unlike the administrators of society who operate as agents of established authority, prophets stand outside existing structures making claims on behalf of transcendent powers. Whatever their content, prophetic claims raise the issue of social authority, creating opportunities for and stimulating action to transform or undermine existing regimes. By its very nature, religious prophecy appears to carry great political relevance.

Sociological understanding of prophecy and its political relevance relies heavily on Max Weber's historical and theoretical work. His study *Ancient Judaism* highlights the role of the prophets in Israel's religious and political development. In his *Sociology of Religion* (also chapter 6 in *Economy and Society*) Weber elaborates the sociological nature of prophecy, and his analysis of social domination in *Economy and Society* links prophecy to politics through the concept of charisma (chapters 1, 3, and 14; also *Theory of Social and Economic Organization*, chapters 1 and 3). Though some disagree with specific aspects of Weber's analysis, most scholars use it as a springboard, for it offers a formidable approach to the most pivotal issues surrounding prophecy and politics:

3

1. What is the *sociological character* of prophecy, especially in relation to charisma?
2. What is the *social location* of prophecy?
3. What is the *social and political relevance* of prophecy?

The complexities of Weber's work notwithstanding, contemporary scholarship seems to have settled on a fairly crisp and straightforward interpretation of his position on these issues. As exemplified by several standard textbook treatments of the topic, prophecy is conceived as a special form of leadership which gains significance as an agent of social change (Hargrove 1979; McGuire 1981; Roberts 1984; Wilson 1978).

1. Prophecy is the *prototype of charismatic authority* and leadership.
2. Prophecy arises *outside the routine institutional order* as a political response of the alienated to societal crisis.
3. Prophecy is a *revolutionary force* which challenges existing authority to institute major socio-political changes.

That interpretation of Weber's ideas on prophecy is not without merit, but it is misleading and incomplete on a number of points. A careful rereading of his work, together with the insightful suggestions of some recent critics and scholars, will serve not only to unpack this tight summary, but also to fill in its gaps and correct its mistakes.

The foundation for this revised analysis is a reconsideration of the defining link of prophecy with charisma, which conventional wisdom has overextended toward the equation of prophecy with charismatic authority. Returning to Weber's more precise conception of prophecy as personal charisma will enable us to see that prophecy is primarily a religious phenomenon, not a political one, and that its main relevance to religious and political life is cultural, not organizational. In consequence the direct effects of prophecy on political life are often limited, but it has more indirect and long-term import as a resource for culture formation and societal change through the development of religious world-views. It is this clarification of the nature of prophecy that will help us sort out the complexities of religious ferment and its relation to politics in the world today.

Prophecy and Charisma: Matters of Definition

There is no question that Weber's conception of prophecy is yoked to his master view of charisma, for he explicitly defines the prophet as a "bearer of charisma" (Weber 1963, 46). What is not so clear is the nature of the relationship between the two phenomena. Approaching the question through Weber's sociology of religion, it appears that prophecy is simply an example or instance of charisma, a more general term which serves as a starting point for classifying the prophet sociologically. As one among many particular instances of charisma, prophecy is neither completely defined by it nor always engaged as its representative. When we enter the relationship first through the analysis of charismatic authority, though, prophecy seems more the exemplar of charisma, its purest embodiment, and perhaps its very model. It serves as a prototype of charisma, constantly employed to display its definitive features. Sociological analysis has favored the latter interpretation, thereby promoting the equation of prophecy with charismatic authority.

That equation has led the conception of prophecy toward an organizational emphasis on group leadership, the exercise of which involves the prophet in political challenge to authority and radical societal change. As Weber conceives it, charismatic authority is the power of leadership claimed by one of exceptional powers and recognized as exemplary by a group of followers (Weber 1947, 359). By virtue of its exceptional quality, it is "sharply opposed both to rational . . . and to traditional authority" (Weber 1947, 361) as a "revolutionary force" (Weber 1947, 362) which seeks to establish "*new* obligations" (Weber 1947, 361). Accordingly, prophetic exemplars of charisma are seen as leaders of revolutionary groups seeking to institute a new social order. Even if they are ultimately unsuccessful, their action creates considerable political turbulence. Their impact on political change is therefore natural, inevitable and profound.

There is no reason to deny prophecy its potential for authoritative leadership of challenging groups, but it is a mistake to make it a matter of definition. Weber's own study of Hebrew prophecy exposes the empirical flaw in such an equation. The great pre-exilic prophets of Israel found little social support, and they never were able to claim a following they could lead, among kings or peasants (Weber 1952, 278ff.). They were "peculiar men" (Weber 1952, 286), even pathological in some respects, who

> . . . did not think of themselves as members of a supporting spiritual community. On the contrary. Misunderstood and hated by the mass of their listeners, they never felt themselves to be supported and protected by them as like-minded sympathizers as did the apostles of the early Christian community. Hence, the prophets spoke at no time of their listeners or addresses as their "brethren" (Weber 1952, 292).

Unlike Muhammed, the Israelite prophets led no political movements; unlike Jesus, they did not even have religious disciples. As deviant doomsayers they wore the mantle of charisma, but no one recognized their charisma as a valid claim on social authority. Petersen thus correctly points out that Weber's studies "do not justify the 'effectual' definition of the prophet as charismatic authority or agent of change" (Petersen 1979, 136).

That conclusion has important implications for the issue of prophecy's social and political relevance, which I consider later. The more immediate and logically prior question it raises, however, concerns the meaning of Weber's connection of prophecy with charisma. Petersen concludes that the connection is simply faulty because "the typology of authority (charismatic leader) and the classification of religious performer (prophet) may not be fully interchangeable" (Petersen 1979, 136). Rather than abandoning Weber's formulation, though, we can make sense of it by exploring the meaning of charisma a bit further than Petersen has taken it. When we do so, it becomes apparent that Weber's discussion of charismatic authority incorporates a more primitive conception of charisma consistent with both his theoretical and historical analyses of prophecy.

Just as Weber built his definition of social action on the more primitive conception of action (Weber 1947, 88), so he constructed the idea of charismatic authority around a more nuclear phenomenon: *personal charisma.* "The term 'charisma' will be applied to a certain quality of an individual personality by virtue of which he is set apart from ordinary men and treated as endowed with supernatural, superhuman, or at least specifically exceptional powers or qualities" (Weber 1947, 358). In this most fundamental sense, charisma is a special personal quality which distinguishes one as gifted, not just in the sense of being talented, but in the sense of having unusual powers beyond ordinary human capacity. It is by virtue of social recognition of those gifts that charismatic claims to authority are validated and the charismatic individual is treated as a leader.

Because he was concerned primarily with the problem of domination, Weber's discussion tends to elide the distinction between the *quality* of charisma and the social *role* proffered in recognition of it. He speaks as if the social recognition of charisma automatically and simultaneously authenticates the existence of charismatic gifts and confers social authority on their bearer. Indeed, that may often be the case. Logically, however, Weber leaves open the possibility that the gifts of charisma may be acknowledged without also bestowing leadership on their bearer. His own recognition of the many ways in which charisma can be attached to and embedded in other routine authority structures (Weber 1978, 1121ff.) constitutes *de facto* recognition of that distinction.

Weber often relies on prophets as *examples* of charismatic authority, but they are *exemplary* only of this more fundamental category of charisma as a personal gift. He defines the prophet as "a purely individual bearer of charisma, who by virtue of his mission proclaims a religious doctrine or divine commandment" (Weber 1963, 46). The criterion of prophecy is not social authority but simply the presence of charismatic qualities in the individual. It is not, of course, just any old charisma that makes a prophet but a divine gift employed as part of a religious mission. What distinguishes prophecy from ordinary life and other charisma is its backing; in God it claims the ultimate sponsor, the prototypical source of charismatic gifts. And while others may not cede social authority to prophets, they still have supernatural power at their disposal to advance their mission. Many other charismatics require social authority to make much headway, but prophets have a transcendent source of power at work, whatever the social response. All that is required of the prophet, then, is to proclaim a doctrine or commandment (or in the case of exemplary prophets, to display a way of life). Implementation of the doctrine is beyond the prophet's control in divine power and social response. In some cases, prophecy may become the social vehicle for implementation, but it is no less prophetic—or charismatic—if the message falls on deaf ears, as did that of the Israelite prophets Weber analyzed.

The Social Location of Prophecy

Conceiving of prophecy as personal charisma rather than as charismatic authority calls for revisions in our understanding of the social location of prophecy, some of which have already been suggested by empirical studies. It implies first that *prophecy may arise within established groups and institutions* rather than just among the alienated and marginal. Second, and partly in consequence of the first, it leads us to the conclusion that *prophecy need not always await internal societal crisis* but may also arise as an expression of group solidarity. Third, converging with the first two insights, the revised conception alerts us that *prophecy is primarily a religious phenomenon, not a political one,* originating in and primarily directed toward the religious life of a people.

Sources of prophecy: The conception of prophets as charismatic leaders of challenging groups is biased toward an image of them as social outsiders. Established officeholders and solid citizens are almost logically excluded as potential prophets by virtue of their ordinary qualities, professionalism, and loyalty to established institutions (Weber 1978, 1112). But *if it is personal charisma alone which defines the prophet, then it becomes possible for prophecy to arise within the routine social structures of ordinary life*. Most simply, the gifts of the spirit and the call of the divine may be bestowed on the ordinary citizens of the realm, such as Jesus of Nazareth, the respected son of a carpenter. More formidably, *prophetic charisma may also arise within the established structure of power*, in two ways. First, a person who holds or gains organizational power may later be recognized as a prophet by virtue of unusual acts. Second, prophetic action can be institutionalized, built into the ordinary functioning of religion (and politics). Barnes's research confirms this variety of sources for prophecy for a sample of fifteen prophets of the great religions (Barnes 1978, 1–18).

To some extent, Weber himself acknowledged these possibilities, but he did not fully accept them, in part because of what appears to be faulty empirical sources. Certainly his provision for the routinization of charisma incorporates such a possibility, but Weber gave little theoretic attention to how the routine might generate or incorporate prophecy. His review of Jewish history identifies "war prophets" of the Israelite confederacy and royal prophets of the king's court as established and conventional sources of prophecy, but he portrays the pre-exilic prophets as socially detached intellectuals opposed to the established order (Weber 1952, 109; 279). On the basis of new biblical scholarship, Berger (1963) has suggested instead that those new prophets arose from a professional class of prophetic figures (Nabis) and performed cultic functions. He goes so far as to suggest the notion of "charismatic office" to fill in Weber's theoretical structure as a counterpart to the "charisma of office" that develops after charisma is routinized. Without denying the alienative sources of prophecy, we have solid grounds to add the possibility that prophecy may also take root within established orders.

The conditions of prophecy: In the same fashion, we must elaborate conventional impressions that prophecy is a natural, even cyclical product of internal societal decay and crisis. Weber's conception of charismatic authority posits an alternation between charisma and the routine forms of authority, traditional and legal. Charismatic leaders emerge in "extraordinary" historical "moments of distress" to meet the critical needs of individuals and society (Weber 1978, 1111–12). To Weber's credit on this matter, Barnes found that the social environment of prophetic leaders has almost uniformly been "a period of social upheaval" (1978, 12). That does not exhaust the possibilities, however, for Barnes only examined successful major leaders/founders of world religions, and he relied on biographers' interpretations of the times. Even bracketing the latter problem of reliability and accepting the affinity of upheaval and charismatic authority as Weber posited, a great many more possibilities come into view when we consider the conditions of personal charisma, some of them brought forward by Weber himself.

The natural cycle of institutionalization and challenge is a dialectic of authority which governs the conferral of leadership on prophets, but it does not restrict the appearance of personal charisma and prophecy itself. *Just as it can arise most anywhere in the social order, so prophecy can also find fertile ground in various social conditions.* Thus prophets may be found in times of tranquility, as the royal prophets of the King's court in Israel. More precisely, Weber identifies two other specific variations in social conditions cultivating prophecy.

First, the Jewish prophets found many of the occasions for their proclamations in the shifting tides of world politics, not internal societal conditions: "Except for the world politics of the great powers which threatened their homeland and constituted the message of their most impressive oracles, the prophets could not have emerged. . . . Free prophecy developed only with the rising external danger to the country and to the royal power (Weber 1952, 268)." Similarly the earlier war prophets, almost in professional fashion, took their cue from the conflicts between peoples, rising to make their declarations on the occasions of the confederacy's military adventures and challenges.

Second, it also appears from Weber's observations that prophecy may be called forth in the service of social solidarity, routinely as well as in extraordinary times. However cynical they may have been, the royal prophets flourished as oracles of cohesion, and the war prophets found their calling in the unusual requirements of solidarity in time of war. Not just an extraordinary phenomenon, then, prophecy can arise anytime, even under routine conditions of social life. Not just an internal matter, prophecy is responsive as well to the currents of global inter-societal relations. Not just a response to times of trial, prophecy can grow as an expression of social solidarity.

The institutional locus of prophecy: In the classic conception of prophecy, it is almost redundant to say that the prophetic leader is a political actor both within a group and on the larger societal stage. Moreover, even those prophets without followers, such as the prophets of Israel, were "objectively political" in their "manner of functioning" (Weber

1952, 275), especially because of their ethical concerns. But it is just as clear from Weber's analyses that while they are *in* the world of politics, they are not *of* it; they are relevant to politics without taking up residence in that realm. Of those same Israelite prophets, Weber concluded:

> . . . subjectively they were no political partisans. Primarily they pursued no political interests. Prophecy has never declared anything about a "best state" . . . nor has it ever sought . . . to help translate into reality social-ethically oriented political ideals through advice to power holders. The state and its doings were, by themselves, of no interest to them. Moreover, unlike the Hellenes they did not posit the problem: how can man be a good citizen? Their question was absolutely religious, oriented toward the fulfillment of Yahwe's commandments (Weber 1952, 275).

Whatever political relevance Israelite prophecy had, it was "purely religiously motivated through Yahwe's relationship to Israel" (Weber 1952, 319). *First and foremost, prophecy is a religious phenomenon; whatever political significance it may have is secondary to and derivative from its religious mission.*

When we think of prophecy primarily as personal charisma, that conclusion is perfectly sensible. The prophet receives a call from God and proclaims a divine revelation. Whatever the form and implication of the prophet's message, that revelation "always contains the important religious conception of the world as a cosmos which is challenged to produce somehow a 'meaningful,' ordered totality" (Weber 1963, 59). Prophecy's call is not to reform the political realm, but to unify all of life around a religious principle, such as Israel's covenant with Yahwe. The "decisive hallmark of prophecy," Weber declares, is "the proclamation of a religious truth of salvation through personal revelation" (Weber 1963, 54). That religious message is often implicated in political issues of the day, and its very proclamation may actually become a political phenomenon. But those are contingencies of prophecy, not constitutive of it. It is for the sake of religious mission that the prophet claims attention, not for political aims, and if prophecy enters politics, it is only through religious action for the sake of salvation.

The Social and Political Relevance of Prophecy

These considerations lead directly to the question of prophecy's social and political relevance, and together with the conception of prophecy as personal charisma, they force us to confront the issue from a new direction. While we cannot abandon Weber's global conception of prophecy as a revolutionary force, we must reinterpret it and specify its meaning. For if prophets are not necessarily political leaders, what kind of force is prophecy? If its political relevance is only contingent, when and where in social life is its relevance felt? And what actual consequences does it have for the world, if any? I want to suggest that prophecy is a cultural phenomenon which makes its revolutionary force felt as a diffuse resource of a community, often through religious organizational vehicles. Rarely are its consequences felt directly in social structure in the short run; instead, it works primarily to build or reconstruct cultural communities over the long run.

The revolutionary force of prophecy: As a bearer of charisma, the prophet is an agent of revolutionary change. Weber's accounts are unequivocal on that point, but they are often given a misdirected interpretation which emphasizes political revolution and organizational change. Uncoupling prophecy from charismatic authority makes it difficult to sustain that view and suggests instead a *cultural* interpretation. That Weber himself conceived this revolutionary force in cultural terms there can be little doubt. In his general discussion of charisma he declares: ". . . in a revolutionary and sovereign manner, charismatic domination transforms all values and breaks all traditional and rational norms . . . (1978, 1115); and:

> Charisma, in its most potent forms, disrupts rational rules as well as tradition altogether and overturns all notions of sanctity. Instead of reverence for customs that are ancient and hence sacred, it enforces the inner subjection to the unprecedented and absolutely unique and therefore Divine. In this purely empirical and value-free sense charisma is indeed the specifically creative revolutionary force of history (1978, 1117).

The revolutionary force of prophetic charisma lies in the area of values, norms, and sacred customs; its power is symbolic, not social. Indeed, among the politically engaged Israelite prophets, the prototypical act was a verbal one of declaring God's judgment and enunciating his commands. What political impact they had came precisely from proclaiming the new religious and ethical obligations of Yahwe.

Injecting this powerful force into the social order clearly constitutes a challenge and opposition to existing authorities, but not as part of a struggle for political or organizational power. Rather, *prophecy challenges the legitimacy of existing orders,* first by standing outside routine administrative control with competing legitimacy and second, by asserting the "unprecedented and absolutely unique" cultural claims of the divine. The sharp opposition of prophecy to existing authority owes to its "extraordinary" nature (Weber 1978, 244), that is, from being "outside the realm of everyday routine and the profane sphere," as Parsons put it in his earlier translation (Weber 1947, 361). Later, discussing prophetic revelation as the prototype of charismatic justice, Weber notes that "in its pure type it is the most extreme contrast to formal and traditional prescription and maintains its autonomy toward the sacredness of tradition as much as toward rationalist deductions from abstract norms" (Weber 1978, 1115). It is thus the cultural autonomy of prophecy which constitutes the challenge to established orders, for it cannot be brought under their control, and it competes for the subjective allegiance of the people governed by those orders.

How prophecy gains relevance: Even without followers, the Israelite prophets became visible actors in the political process. Though they were not theorists of social reform (as was the nonprophetic Ezekiel), they were distinctly concerned with it (Weber 1963, 51). And while they did not seek kingly power, they oriented their proclamations to that political center of power (Weber 1963, 58). Their pattern of involvement reflects two conditions, one ideological and the other structural, which help us understand how the revolutionary cultural force of prophecy makes itself felt.

On the ideological side, the prophets were utopian, both politically and religiously (Weber 1952, 297). Their messages were absolutist, admitting no possibility of compromise or variation, and they held out a standard of perfection which even the most resolute follower would have had difficulty achieving. Relevant to political issues these doctrines were, but practical they were not. "The prophets were demagogues, and anything but practical politicians or political partisans" (Weber 1952, 319). Their interest in politics was not to implement a specific program but to articulate "a unified view of the world derived from a consciously integrated and meaningful attitude toward life. . . . To this meaning the conduct of mankind must be oriented if it is to bring salvation" (Weber 1963, 59). The relevance of prophecy, then, is felt through the development and articulation of a systematic world-view. To the extent that the prophets are successful, they create a general and somewhat diffuse resource which individuals and groups may use to articulate social claims, allocate interpersonal rights and responsibilities, and legitimate organizational efforts and arrangements.

On the structural side of the relevance question, it must be noted that the Israelite prophets had easy access to the political realm. The differentiation of religious and secular institutions had scarcely begun, and prophecy had been institutionalized in the royal court for some time. In those circumstances, prophecy became political because that was the only way it could be religious. Had there been no established role for prophets in the political realm, and had religious institutions been already well developed, prophecy well may have been encapsulated far more within the religious realm. Indeed, among prophets in general (Weber 1963, 60ff.) and among the Israelite prophets in particular, the social yield of prophecy is the creation or elaboration of religious community, not political success. It appears that the primary (though by no means exclusive) vehicle for prophecy is religious organization, for that is where prophecy finds its greatest relevance and the greatest receptivity to divine commands.

The consequences of prophecy: We know fairly well what lies in the historical wake of prophecy. Consistent with the conception of the prophet as a bearer of personal charisma, many prophets have had little success, political or religious. A small number have found some political and military success, but of those whom we might call successful, *the most visible result of their work is the creation of religious communities* (cf. Barnes).

These communities have developed in two directions, sometimes overlapping. In the most obvious case, *prophecy stimulates the development of "new religions,"* spawning specific faith communities which take the prophet as founder and perhaps savior. Included in this group are the great world religions and a host of less prominent and successful faiths. Less obvious, but perhaps even more crucial, *prophecy has created a resource for the formation of whole cultures:* The Hebrew prophets are a case in point, according to Weber. When the tenuous political association of the Israelite tribes broke apart after the fall of Jerusalem, the pariah people of Israel reconstituted their community in exile on the basis of a common allegiance to Yahwe. The pre-exilic prophets had created the resource for culture-building in their call to maintain the covenant with God. Though it had fallen mostly on deaf ears before, that proclamation planted the cultural seed that was cultivated in captivity and grew to sustain a nation which otherwise would not have been. Only after the prophets are gone do the effects of their prophecy become manifest in the ". . . subjective or internal reorientation born out of suffering, conflicts, or enthusiasm. . . . in a radical alteration of the central system of attitudes and directions of action with a completely new orientation of all attitudes toward the different problems and structures of the 'world' (Weber 1947, 363)." If we look for the short term effects of prophecy, in direct modifications of the social and political structure, we will miss its most profound effects, the "inner subjection" of peoples to a transcendent meaning system which may guide their action for centuries.

Religion, Prophecy and Politics: Sorting Out the Connections

It is not so important that our views be true to Weber, nor even that our views of Weber be true, though both conditions are virtuous in their own right. Rather, the primary aim of this exercise has been to refine our conceptual tools for use in analyzing religion's engagement with society, especially the tremendous political thrust of religious movements today. I undertook this excavation of Weber's work because that is where the foundation of our conception of prophecy and politics lies. And the reinterpretation of that conception outlined here not only corrects our view of Weber but of prophecy as well. Properly employed, that more precise view provides a sorting mechanism for discriminating among the various religious movements and their political outcroppings that will advance our understanding of religious movements, political dynamics, and societal change.

The conventional idea of prophecy and politics highlighted one specific connection between the two, albeit a very important one. In that formula, prophecy issued naturally in change-oriented political movements, challenging existing authorities by promoting a radically new social order. By making prophecy and politics mutually defining, that conception blinds us to the multi-faceted interactions of religion and politics, either by rejecting other empirical possibilities by conceptual fiat or by assimilating all aspects of religious politics to the model of prophetic challenge. When we separate prophecy and politics conceptually, however, we gain analytic power and open up new lines of inquiry in the studies of both religion and politics.

As the charismatic proclamation/demonstration of divine claims and judgments on human life or institutions by one called to that mission, *prophecy carries a variety of possibilities*. Which of them it realizes is a matter of empirical contingency. Prophecy may or may not yield a movement, and if it does, that movement may well be religious rather than political. Whatever its vehicle and realm of action, moreover, prophecy may align itself with reigning powers more to build up solidarity than to disrupt or radically transform it. Further, the focus and impact of prophecy may center on culture as much or more than on social organization. And its consequences, whatever they are, may appear at one or more levels of social life—individual, group, institutional, societal, or global. How prophecy develops, and the specific course it takes, will depend on historical and situational factors operating at the time, as well as the emergent trajectory of and response to the prophetic effort itself. Ironically, this broad range of empirical possibilities comes into view only by applying the narrower and more precise conception of prophecy developed here.

This revised conception can also be employed profitably in the investigation of religious politics. Most fundamentally, we can now make more careful distinctions among various types of religious political action, sorting out the truly prophetic efforts from those which are not. Instead of assuming that political religion is prophetic, as the conventional notion did, we submit it to empirical examination and set aside those examples without prophetic grounding. But as we thereby reduce the number of prophetic movements, we also may replace them in our catalog by identifying prophetic politics in places we had not previously looked, such as movements which focus on culture rather than organization or those which build a society rather than challenging one. In this instance, we recognize the multiple empirical connections of prophecy to social and political life which had gone unattended under the aegis of conventional assumptions. Such sorting not only gives us more precise empirical units to analyze but also pushes us to more careful theorizing and interpretation of religious politics. Different religious types of political action can be expected to take different courses in the political process with different sets of potential consequences. That these variations have not yet been systematically identified or classified testifies to the lack of analytic fecundity in conventional assumptions about prophecy.

Applying this revised conception of prophecy to phenomena already thought of in other terms has its hazards, of course. It could deteriorate into an arbitrary exercise in semantics fueled by quibbling over the status of various movements as prophetic or not. Or it could lead to some confusion between old and new meanings so that the term "prophetic" might serve us even less well than it has previously. It could also paralyze analysis for want of conceptual terms for nonprophetic religious political action or become irrelevant because habit and convenience accommodate us to the conventional idea of prophecy. Finally, because this new conception is more narrow than the one currently in use, it may be rejected as a threat to the analytic potency of the idea of prophetic politics.

I have already exposed the mistake in this last view by showing that the narrow conception actually generates more analytic opportunities than the broad definition which assumes too much and allows for too little. And if we are stopped by intellectual habit, convenience, or laziness from using such a productive revision, it is certainly not the fault of the new conception. Confusion in the use of terms is certainly possible, but that semantic confusion is minute compared to the inherent conceptual confusion carried in the conventional concept. Even if people use the term "prophetic" for movements or activities which are only partly so, that will cause little trouble so long as scholars are careful to make clear how they are using the term. Only the problem of arbitrariness is real, but it need not undermine the utility of the revised conception. We ask of the idea of prophecy only that it be productive of insight, not that it be "true" or "real." It is the distinctions which are important, not the terms, and if arguments over classification yield greater insight in the long run, they are worth it.

Conclusion

The abstract character of these reflections notwithstanding, they illustrate the potency of the concept of prophecy understood in terms of personal charisma. Such a conception extends the limited frame of organizational leadership within which prophecy had been bound to a wider sphere where prophecy enjoys multiple opportunities. While untangling it from authority analytically has made its political and societal relevance more problematic, linking prophecy with cultural revolution and religious world-views has actually enlarged its potential relevance and impact. And even as it points out potential limits of religious charisma, it helps us identify more specifically the various places where religion continues to enjoy opportunities for shaping the social order. Finally, that prophetic religion continues to be a fertile area both for social action and scholarly analysis testifies once more to the prescience and power of Weber's analysis.

What remains is a formidable task of exploiting Weber's conceptual insights to analyze prophecy and politics. The challenge is two-pronged: empirical and theoretic. Empirically, we could profit simply by applying the new conception to case studies and comparisons as we take them up. In addition, an historical and comparative review of prophecy and religious politics would yield a more systematic and complete codification of what we know about prophetic politics, thus understood, and what we still need to discover. Theoretically, we need to use those cases and codifications to identify the variables that fuel prophecy, link it to politics, guide its direction, and generate its influence. In short, we need a true theory of prophecy and politics. Second, we need to apply such a theory to particular historical circumstances, especially to the contemporary world, to develop our understanding and to gain a purchase on the future possibilities of prophecy in political action. Finally, having separated prophetic religious politics from other types, we need to consider how we might conceive what remains, developing definitions and theories in those related areas as well.

References

Barnes, Douglas F. 1978. Charisma and religious leadership: An historical analysis. *Journal for the Scientific Study of Religion* 17, no. 1 (March): 1–18.

Berger, Peter L. 1963. Charisma and religious innovation: The social location of Israelite prophecy. *American Sociological Review* 28, no. 6 (December): 940–50.

Hargrove, Barbara. 1979. *The Sociology of Religion: Classical and Contemporary Approaches.* Arlington Hts., Ill.: AHM Publishing.

McGuire, Meredith. 1981. *Religion: The Social Context.* Belmont, CA.: Wadsworth.

Petersen, David L. 1979. Max Weber and the sociological study of ancient Israel. *Religious Change and Continuity: Sociological Perspectives,* ed. Harry M. Johnson. San Francisco: Jossey-Bass, 117–49.

Roberts, Keith A. 1984. *Religion in Sociological Perspective.* Homewood, IL.: Dorsey.

Weber, Max. 1952. *Ancient Judaism.* Trans. H. Gerth and D. Martindale. New York: Free Press.

———. 1978. *Economy and Society: An Outline of Interpretive Sociology.* Ed. G. Roth and C. Wittich. Berkeley, CA.: University of California.

———. 1947. *The Theory of Social and Economic Organization.* Trans. A.M. Henderson and T. Parsons. New York: Free Press.

———. 1963. *The Sociology of Religion.* Trans. E. Fischoff. Boston: Beacon.

Wilson, John. 1978. *Religion in American Society: The Effective Presence.* Englewood Cliffs, N.J.: Prentice-Hall.

2

The New Fundamentalism: Rebirth of Political Religion in America

WADE CLARK ROOF

N OT since the Scopes trial in 1925 has there been so much public attention focused on religious fundamentalism in the United States. Emerging as a movement in the late 1970s, the "new fundamentalism" became increasingly visible in the 1980s in the form of a resurgent religious traditionalism coupled with a political activist stance: popular television preachers armed with moral agendas; ideological clashes over abortion, prayer in the schools, pornography, and the like; new alliances of conservative Protestants and Catholics calling for a return to traditional values; and finally, the embrace of Ronald Reagan by the "New Christian Right" in the 1984 presidential election as defender of God, country, and all that is good.

All this has brought about a growing awareness of the conservative religious presence in the country and raised concerns about its role in the political process. In 1925 fundamentalism was retreating in the face of modern science and thought, and thus could be written off as a force of any consequence; now, however, there is less certainty about its inevitable demise. Recent flexing of the "old time" religious muscle and a new surge of religio-political fervor raise the possibility—and perhaps, the specter—of an emerging "right-wing" force capable of shaping the nation's destiny in the remaining years of this century.

18

This resurgence of fundamentalist politics caught many by surprise. Americans knew, of course, that conservative religion existed, but it was assumed that people holding to such beliefs and attitudes generally kept silent in public and were predisposed against direct political involvement. They were supposed to be preoccupied with personal piety, with strict belief, and with moral uprightness, certainly uninterested in, and untarnished by, the practicalities of political life. After all, for almost a half century, fundamentalists had been withdrawn from public life and were anything but "noisy" in politics. Indeed, social scientific research gave every reason to dismiss them as engaging, civic-minded persons concerned with the public issues. Throughout the 1950s and 1960s many studies documented that conservative Protestants were passive in attitudes toward most social concerns and much less inclined toward political activity than were their more liberal counterparts.[1] The prevailing scholarly opinion held that fundamentalists adhered to a narrow, sectarian theology which was at odds with a public posture and, thus, it seemed quite likely they would remain a marginal and non-politically oriented religious movement in modern society.

Against this background of apathy and withdrawal, the rebirth of religious politics poses something of a quandary: Why has religious fundamentalism surged in visible popularity in the 1970s and 1980s? Why has it taken a political posture? And what are the distinguishing features of the new fundamentalism as compared with the old? To answer these questions, this essay reviews the historic development of the movement, and demonstrates how recent events and changes in American life have rejuvenated aspects of its heritage that have remained dormant throughout most of this century.

Rediscovery of a Heritage

Americans are rediscovering fundamentalists and finding that many of their long-held views do not fit very well. Much of the confusion stems from a lack of historic understanding of the movement, and its incredible diversity and flexibility in relating to the culture. The media contribute to the confusion by perpetuating stereotypes and generalizations that are often outdated and distorted. Currently the term fundamentalism is used both for describing a reactionary religious movement and a coalition of conservative movements. "Fundamentalist" and "evangelical" are used almost interchangeably, obscuring historic differences between them and glossing over the rich varieties of belief systems found within the conservative Protestant heritage.

Evangelicals comprise the larger constituency in America today. Indeed, perhaps not more than one-third of evangelicals could be considered hard-core fundamentalists.[2] Even within the fundamentalist wing we find an amalgamation of many differing traditions, often inherently contradictory in their attitudes toward culture and politics—resulting in, as George M. Marsden says, a movement "frought with paradoxes that have made it sociologically mystifying" (Marsden 1983, 151).[3] Without some understanding of these paradoxes, and the long-standing tensions in the relations of fundamentalist belief and culture, we are unlikely to grasp why it has once again surfaced as a force of some consequence in contemporary America.

Fundamentalism as an identifiable religious movement emerged in the late nineteenth century. It arose out of a growing sense of concern about theological and cultural trends, brought on by religion's confrontation with modernity at just the time when Protestantism's hold upon American life was beginning to wane. From the very early days Protestantism had been based largely in rural and small-town America, but by the turn of the century it was facing unprecedented challenges. Moral and religious views were increasingly harder to sustain in the rapidly expanding urban and industrial centers. New social ministries were called for in the cities, old interpretations of the Scriptures were challenged by new insights of higher criticism, and Darwinian views advanced by the educated classes contradicted many of the older notions about creation. Moreover, religion's historic role in the culture was itself undergoing a transformation. Protestantism was in the early throes of what Robert T. Handy describes as the "second disestablishment" (Handy 1971)—facing the realities of a growing immigrant Catholic population and of religious pluralism, thereby undermining its power and influence in the society.

For all these reasons, divisions within Protestantism intensified between liberals and conservatives, or as Martin E. Marty says between "public Protestants" and "private Protestants" (Marty 1970). Whereas the former were concerned with adjusting to modern circumstances in the form of new ministries and interpretations, the latter were inclined to hold firm to traditional supernatural formulations and to stress personal faith and morality. By the turn of the century, the Protestant revivalist tradition had given birth to several new religious movements: the *holiness movement,* with an emphasis on perfection and strict personal ethics; the *pentecostal movement,* stressing experiential faith and life in the Spirit; and the *fundamentalist movement,* which called for right doctrine (the "fundamentals") and the divinely revealed literal truth of the Bible over and against worldly accommodations in religion and in the culture. All three movements shared such traits as the importance of individual conversion, an upright moral life, and the authority of the Bible, but what distinguished fundamentalism most from the others was its strong "truth-orientation"⁴ and more militant posture toward modernist religious and cultural trends. In comparison to holiness and pentecostal enthusiasts, fundamentalists were far more defensive and aggressive in trying to maintain the old moral and religious order in the face of so many new challenges.

Yet from the beginning there was a deep-seated ambivalence in the movement's relation to popular culture and politics. Arising out of the revivalist tradition, there was, of course, great emphasis placed upon winning souls to Christ and individual regeneration. This is the strong "privatistic" side of fundamentalism which is generally known. But there was also another side of the tradition, deeply concerned with preserving the culture-dominating ideals of the old religious order. Throughout the nineteenth century evangelical Protestantism was the dominant religious force in America, so strong it held forth as a virtual establishment shaping the mores and values of the nation. Calvinism had left a dual legacy: a theocratic tradition of subordinating the civil order to the church, and a more voluntary, separatist tendency lifting the individual conscience above such authority. Both theological strands are to be found in fundamentalism. Indeed, as recent historical scholarship has shown, the two strands have competed for fundamentalist allegiance from the early days of the movement; and from time to time the movement has shifted in its emphasis between a theocratic, politically activist stance and a separatist withdrawal from public involvement.⁵

Its strong theocratic tendencies were apparent when the movement first coalesced in the crisis-ridden years following World War I as an organized holy war against modernism. America's destiny and the moral and religious future all seemed to be tied up with global events. George Marsden captures the climate of the times:

The spectacle of Germany, the cradle of Protestantism, having succumbed to the barbaric "might is right" evolutionary philosophy of Friedrich Nietzsche suggested that America's alleged Christian heritage was a tenuous legacy. Preachers made the most of such analogies after the war when the nation seemed threatened by labor unrest, a "Red menace," and revolutionary outbreaks of public displays of sexuality in new dances, movies, tabloid newspapers, and advertising. Worse still, some Protestant denominations were embracing these modern trends. Such apostates were virtually dispensing with the Bible as a norm for modern people, incorporating evolutionary doctrines into their theologies and looking for the Kingdom of God in the social and political progress of modern culture. (1983, 152).

As fundamentalists saw it, the future of civilization was at stake. They were cast into the role of defending a Christian America against the threats of a growing religious diversity, urban and industrial challenges, and modernist interpretations of the Scriptures. Preserving a religious order took precedence over pietistic withdrawal; hence, during this period the movement was highly visible in its battles with the Social Gospel, Biblical higher criticism, and Darwinism. Involved were dimensions of religion, culture, and power in a holy war against the ways of the world.

But its early activist phase was short-lived. The movement largely faded from national attention after the heavily-publicized Scopes trial in 1925, about the same time it became evident that the conservatives' campaigns to fight modernism in the churches had lost. Fundamentalist thinking did not of course dissolve or disappear; dissident conservatives either grew silent in the pews of the mainstream churches or else they founded new, oftentimes "nondenominational," churches. Having lost the theological battle for control over the ecclesiastical mainstream, generally speaking conservatives "submerged" from public life and instead turned inward. They did not forego the public arena altogether. For example, between 1921 and 1929, thirty-seven anti-evolution bills were introduced in twenty state legislatures. But sensing themselves to be outsiders, they increasingly drew upon their separatist heritage which encouraged personal piety and distance from worldly powers. To be sure, there were some political rumblings in the 1950s targeted against communism and fears of worldwide conspiracies against the United States, but generally fundamentalists left politics alone and concentrated their efforts upon saving souls, building schools, and expanding their ministries to all those who would believe. Growing belief in "dispensational premillennialism," or the view that things would get worse as history approached a final calamity when Christ would return with avenging armies, served to legitimate their withdrawal from public life and a more sectarian stance.

Old Themes, New Themes

Now in the 1980s the movement has surfaced again, somewhat more reminiscent of the old-style, pre-1925 active fundamentalism than that which Americans came to know during the intervening decades. A new fundamentalism has emerged which breaks with years of separatist withdrawal and civic apathy in favor of a more theocratic, or establishmentarian, stance toward culture and politics. James A. Speer (1984, 40) is undoubtedly correct in suggesting that over the long course fundamentalism has followed a "church-to-sect-to-church" pattern of relating to the society: first a political activist phase, then withdrawal and distancing from the culture, and recently to a more engaging, reform-oriented posture once again.

The old themes of biblical authority and personal redemption are still to be found. Beliefs in the Second Coming and biblical inerrancy have always been crucial to fundamentalist theology. But the old sectarian themes have taken on new meanings. Contrary to popular understanding, fundamentalist belief systems are flexible and lend themselves to rich and varied interpretations, depending on the cultural context. In the present situation the content and meanings have become newly charged politically. The imagery surrounding the Second Coming is now frequently cast in terms of a nuclear holocaust and linked in the militarized theology of the new religious right as support for a strong national defense. The doctrine of biblical innerancy, or the old-style basing of claims upon "the Bible says," is infused with new ideological overtones. The new fundamentalism uses the Bible as an economics textbook, a political handbook, and a family reference guide. Texts cited concern not just salvation and spiritual matters, but also ways to bolster "Christian economics," the traditional family, and the American Way of Life. The Scriptures get interpreted through an ideological filter, resonate with contemporary "New Right" concerns. The new fundamentalists denounce the food stamp program and welfare; they revel in free enterprise capitalism and the work ethic. Few say it more pointedly than Jerry Falwell in *Listen, America!*: "Ownership of property is biblical. Competition in business is biblical. Ambitious and successful business management is clearly outlined as a part of God's plan for His people" (1980, 11–12).

Perhaps the most distinctive departure from the old sectarian fundamentalism lies in its *aggressive "politics of morality"* stance. What is so striking is not simply the stress on moral reform but also the strong reliance upon the tactics of professionals for organizing a supportive constituency—the role of lobbies, political action committees, blocvote organizers, think tanks. Since the late 1970s various well developed electorate-organizing groups have flooded the mails, taken to the media, registered voters, raised funds, and courted legislators. The

Moral Majority, Inc. is perhaps the best known of these, but there are others with a distinct religious tone including Religious Roundtable, Christian Voice, Christian Freedom Foundation, and Coalition for Traditional Values. Strategies include the computerized targeting of audiences known to be concerned about specific issues (e.g., gun control) and preparing "Christ-centered" responses to them or "report cards" on the views of public officials and candidates for elections. This has led to the manipulation of one-issue politics and to attempts at forging religious solutions to meet stated group concerns—what Kevin Phillips aptly describes as "The Balkanization of America" (1978, 37–47; Jorstad 1981). Such efforts appear to have made a difference in senatorial and congressional contests in several states in the 1980 election, and were a factor of some importance in Ronald Reagan's landslide 1984 second-term victory.[6] Perhaps their greater influence lies in getting certain kinds of bills before legislative bodies, state and national, and in mobilizing support for translating them into law—on issues like abortion, prayer in schools, and the teaching of creationism in high school.

Another departure is its willingness to form partnerships with groups which the old fundamentalism often derided including Roman Catholics, Mormons, and Jews. Rather than attack these groups it seeks alliances with them, in creating broad support for a moral agenda. Nowhere is this more obvious than in the religious affiliations of many of the "New Christian Right" leaders—Richard Viguerie and Phyllis Schafly are Roman Catholics, Orrin Hatch is Mormon, Paul Weyrich is an Eastern Rite Catholic, Howard Phillips is Jewish. The enemy is no longer Catholicism or even liberal Protestantism, although occasionally there are outbursts against those who do not believe as hard-core Protestant fundamentalists do.

The enemy has shifted—from church and seminary to community, state, and national politics. Now the target is "secular humanism," an ideology which directly clashes with fundamental belief in God, biblical righteousness, and the traditional family and school. Believers who in the past were never able to agree on matters of demonology and the Rapture now seem to have found a rallying call. Writes Carole Flake: "For the fundamentalist crusader, secular humanism had become the source of all the sins of America, the multiformed beast of modern liberalism: the cold idol of godless science; the brazen serpent of pornography and homosexuality; the unpainted temptress of women's liberation; the meddling giant of big government" (1984, 218).

Because of this great threat to American life, fundamentalists find it necessary to soft-pedel strict religious belief to make room for others, of whatever religious background, who share similar concerns. Unity lies not in theology but in moral crusade. Their passion for reform draws upon both of the Calvinist theological strands that have long informed fundamentalism: a neo-Puritan demand for discipline, law and order, combined with a revivalist call for national repentance.

An aggressive moral stance and a new spirit of creating alliances point to what may be the most striking difference of all—a more open attitude toward the culture. For most of its history, conservative Protestantism has exemplified sectarian behavior; its posture was one staunchly of "Christ *against* culture." Today there is a distinct difference. Surely, the new fundamentalism criticizes the culture and wants to change things, but it does so less from the outside, much less abrasively, and more in the manner of a reform movement. Its accommodating stance is apparent in its entrepreneurial and cultural expressions: Christian sex manuals, Christian money guides, Christian soap operas, Christian bumper stickers, etc. It comes through in the popular psychologies of positive thinking, how-to-succeed and turning your "scars into stars" themes, attention to self-realization and the rewards of faith. The message is conveyed in the media by means of polished, smooth-talking televangelists utilizing the most sophisticated electronic equipment and production techniques available today. The "electronic church" encompasses diverse types of religious broadcasting, but much of what is included—e.g., the *PTL Club* and the *700 Club*—freely utilizes entertainment techniques from secular television.[7] Personalities like Pat Robertson and Jim Bakker have broken out of the old roles of television evangelist and have found ways of linking the old verities of righteousness to the personal concerns and immediate needs of their viewers in an atmosphere of spontaneity and surprise, sharing and smiling.

While a war is waged with the prevailing moral and cultural trends, especially those identified as emanating from secular humanism, the style and manner in which it is often done is accommodating of the culture in many respects and can hardly be described as deeply alienated from it or belligerent in its rejection thereof. Such figures as the Rev. Jerry Falwell and Senator Jesse Helms are much at home in the halls of Congress, the National Press Club, and political party gatherings. Indeed, Falwell himself is an interesting case-study in the emergence of the new fundamentalism: Over the past fifteen years he has mellowed considerably in his views, from a non-accommodating, non-political to a more engaging public role.[8]

The New Demographics

Accommodation toward culture and politics arises out of the new social and demographic base for conservative religion in America today. Still disproportionately Southern and of small-town origins, poorly educated and of lower socio-economic status, yet their profiles have changed significantly in the past couple decades. The social and lifestyle changes are more striking than the continuities. Evangelicals and fundamentalists have achieved greater respectability and far more visibility in the nation as a whole—as evidenced by the testimonies of entertainers, athletes, beauty queens, even Presidents. The movement is less identified with the South and less associated with economic deprivation; by the end of the 1970s conservative Protestants had come a long way from revival tents, backwoods camp meetings, and Bible-verse billboards. This being the case, they can hardly still be thought of as illiterate and marginal in the ways that H.L. Mencken and others portrayed them in earlier times.

Perhaps the most significant change is the upward shift in socio-economic status. Fundamentalist and evangelical religious groups in the 1960s and 1970s benefited greatly from expanding educational and job opportunities. Whereas in 1960 only seven percent of members of evangelical and fundamentalist denominations had attended some colleges, by the mid-1970s that figure was twenty-three percent—a rate of increase that exceeds that of any other major religious group. (Hendricks 1977, table 5). These gains stand out when compared with liberal and moderate Protestants whose educational base hardly changed at all in these decades. Catholics also made striking gains in education, occupations, and income in this period but not equal to those of conservative Protestants. In large numbers they began to taste affluence, becoming middle class, Republican, suburban, and well connected in business, social, and political circles. Increasingly represented in the lower–middle eschelons of American life, conservative Protestants gained entrance into the mainstream during this period and came to enjoy greater respectability, social and economic standing, and a new self-esteem.

A second important demographic change concerns the shifting age structure. Once a phenomenon of older, highly marginal persons, today there are many young, successful Americans found within the evangelical and fundamentalist communities. This greater acceptance among the young reflects a remarkable diffusion of religious beliefs and attitudes, and is of considerable long-term significance. Recent analysis of the religious subcultures in the United States shows that evangelical and fundamentalist Protestant bodies have considerably younger memberships than do liberal and moderate Protestants. Younger memberships translate into higher birth rates. Both the proportion of women in their child-bearing years and the number of children per woman are noticeably higher in the conservative faiths (McKinney and Roof 1982). Not surprisingly, themes of the traditional family and conventional sex roles have taken on such symbolic significance in this sector. The new fundamentalism is aggressively pro-family, in part because of the fit between ideology and membership constituency; it is within this collectivity—compared with other religious groupings—that the traditional family is most intact in contemporary America and traditional family values are most widely accepted.

Why Political Rebirth Now?

Having examined the changing themes and shifting social and demographic bases, we are now better able to address the question as to why there has been a rebirth of political fundamentalism. That is, why fundamentalists, have after a lengthy period of keeping silent in public, begun making noises again? Or to cast the question in terms of the theological strands within fundamentalism described earlier: Why has a theocratic, establishmentarian stance reemerged?

Certainly we cannot dismiss the importance of the television media and conservative Protestantism's use of it. Religious broadcasting has of course long been an arm of outreach for religious groups, but televangelists like Falwell, Bakker, Robertson, and Swaggert rediscovered its potential in the 1970s. A culturally accommodating style combined with the popularization of religious themes of country and patriotism helped in creating the new climate.

Recharging the old symbols of civil religion was especially important in the aftermath of the Vietnam War, and the television preachers were adept at infusing them with apocalyptic urgency in the cause to "save" America—to restore the nation's might and morality. They could explain how America's international humiliation was God's punishment for its moral decline, but that in time the nation would rise to great

28 WADE CLARK ROOF

strength again, drawing off the old convenantal tradition emphasizing the abiding relationship between God and people.

Far more important than the media, however, was the perceived moral crisis of the nation itself. The resurgence of politicized evangelicalism must be viewed against the backdrop of the 1960s. The decade of the 1960s was a period of radical turns in morality and the culture, a time when as historian Sydney E. Ahlstrom notes "the old foundations of national confidence, patriotic idealism, moral traditionalism, and even of historic Judaeo-Christian theism, were awash. Presuppositions that had held firm for centuries—even millennia—were being widely questioned" (1972, 1080). The counter-culture, anti-war protests, drug usage, rock music, and especially altered family arrangements through divorce, abortion, homosexuality, equal rights for women, and children's rights, all provided "evidence" of moral decay gripping the country as a whole. Added to this were court decisions declaring abortion legal and prayer in school unconstitutional. Abortion would prove to be the most wrenching, and still unresolved, moral and religious issue facing Americans for generations and thus, highly symbolic of the revolutionary changes occurring in the lives of women and in the family. Prohibiting school prayer would also touch a deep nerve of traditional piety, and come to be viewed as the moral and spiritual sabotage of an American sacred institution by secularists.

In this climate of perceived moral collapse, a new politicized fundamentalism arose to meet the national challenge. The times called for establishing private schools for educating the young in the time-honored tradition, for a return to active involvement in political affairs—in effect, for an all-out effort to bring America back in line with its religious foundations. As John H. Simpson puts it: "Surrounded by a flood of puzzling and disturbing events—assassinations, riots, campus discontent, Vietnam, liberation movements (Chicano, Native American, women, and gay)—and, finally, the hostage incident in Iran, the Evangelical/Fundamentalist persuasion was something that survived, relatively unchanged, from the less puzzling past. As such, it provided a strong source for a sense of cultural continuity" (1983, 202).

Two aspects of the moral crisis are worth examining, one noting continuity with fundamentalism's earlier period of activism and the other a distinct break with it. The first is that the 1960s brought about a confrontation with global cultures: Eastern mysticism, strange new cults, radical Jesus movements, the revival of the occult. Then came the expanded war in Vietnam, the hostage crisis and other international humiliations. Somewhat reminiscent of World War I days, this configuration of global exposures and events aroused nativistic fears and activated deep-seated anxieties about the nation's future. It seems altogether reasonable that this set of experiences was important in provoking strong religio-political sentiments. It is still perhaps too soon to adequately judge, but the Asian influence on American religiosity which occurred in this period will likely have a lasting and quite significant impact.

The second is that we should not underestimate the enormity of moral and cultural disjuncture in this period. Up until the 1960s the moral views held by fundamentalists were, by and large, those *shared* with most other Americans. Even if they did lose the theological battle in the 1920s, there was no great perceived gap in the decades that followed between fundamentalist views on morality and those of the populace at large. But this would change with the 1960s.[9] The discontinuities in the tradition became so acute as to constitute a major breakdown in the historic patterns. Commenting on this very point Phillip E. Hammond observes: "It was one thing to know that some people got divorced because their marriages were unhappy, for example, but it became something else to be confronted by an ideology rejecting marriage and promoting single parenthood. It was one thing to know that homosexuality exists but another to see a Gay Caucus at the Democratic Party. Abortions carried out illegally in a back alley was one thing; abortion publically funded and openly advocated as a means of birth control was another" (Hammond, 1985, 10–11).

Finally, we must take note of fundamentalism's newly-achieved social and political standing. As we have seen already, the new fundamentalism is positioned in the culture such that it is capable of expressing far greater establishmentarian sentiment than ever in the past. Surveys show that even more Americans subscribe to views consistent with the socio-moral platforms of fundamentalists than actually belong to such organizations. That is, many who cannot accept the fundamentalist belief system, nonetheless, endorse views similar to those who are religiously committed.[10] One might speculate that despite the enormity of the moral breakdown of the 1960s, had religious conservatives not had an increasingly affluent, lower middle-class clientele and well-heeled, smooth leaders, the "New Christian Right" would not have become what it is, or aroused the great concerns that it has. The fact is that the alleged moral crisis which occurred, was perceived as such by Middle America—a sector sometimes described as insecure in its standing, but hardly as marginal in contemporary society. What was at stake was a way of life—*their* way of life—and with their recently acquired symbols of status and greater purchase on power, they were mightily prepared to go to battle in its defense.

Conclusion

As this overview of recent developments implies, there is a new fundamentalism in the United States that is clearly distinguished from its earlier forms. Fundamentalism is hardly a closed belief system characterized by a few simple doctrinal items and easily predictable political expressions. Rather it is a religious system embodying many symbolic themes, ambivalent attitudes toward the culture and tensions among theological motifs, but for this very reason amazingly adaptable to changing social conditions. Far from being an outlook bound to wither in the face of modernity, the belief system shows considerable "staying power" as evidenced by its capacity to engender a plausible world-view to many Americans today whose life-situations and social circumstances are quite different from those of earlier subscribers.

This evolving, adaptable character of American fundamentalism is important in the context of worldwide expressions of political religion today. One can point to surface similarities of fundamentalist themes in this country with those found elsewhere on the globe, yet the fact is that religious dynamics in a democratic, voluntaristic tradition typically follow a course peculiar to their own.

In religion as in politics, there is a strong centralizing tendency in American life. Centripetal forces run deep—that is, the tendency for sectarians to become more churchlike, for groups to move from the periphery toward the middle; as John Murray Cuddihy observes, America "tames" its fanatic faiths into a more bland, tolerant "religion of civility" (1978). Fundamentalism is hardly immune to these forces; indeed, with its heritage of deep concerns for social order and revivalist outlook, it is a prime candidate for a religious transformation. Theologically, socially, and culturally, fundamentalism in this country is set on a course of accommodation and coalition politics, which mitigates any long-standing militant posture toward American culture. In contrast to the more fiercely anti-modernist revivals in Islam, or the more authoritative Sokà Gakkai in Japan, or the embittered and class-entangled religious conflicts in Northern Ireland, American fundamentalism is tame.

There is also the broader religious situation in the country today, which augurs against a militant sectarianism as well. Liberal Protestantism has lost much of its force in shaping the culture, and secular currents run stronger than ever—both of which have helped to create what is described as the "naked public square" (Neuhaus 1984), or the lack of a strong public religious presence. Conservative and fundamentalist forces are now rushing in trying to fill this vacuum and are contending with others to become culture-shaping influences in American life. What this situation encourages is neither separatism nor rigid exclusiveness, but rather accommodation and inclusiveness. While often the rhetoric within the fundamentalist community appears otherwise, a posture of inclusiveness and pluralism is the only way that it can become a broadly based normative faith. Progressive-minded fundamentalist leaders know this, and are not about to turn their backs on opportunities they now have for expanding their power and influence in the larger society.

This is not to suggest there will not be conflict and confrontation in the years ahead, but rather that the general drift will be toward a moderating public religious presence. One is hesitant to try to predict the future, considering how the tradition has followed such a curious path of rather abrupt and precipitous shifts in the past. It is not inconceivable that with a symbolic victory of some sort—for example were the pro-life crusade to overturn the legalization of abortion on demand—the religious support underlying the "New Christian Right" could become diffused. Already there are signs from among Falwell supporters of a willingness to negotiate further on the abortion issue, in the interest no doubt of bringing about a broadened pro-life consensus. It is even more likely that hard-core fundamentalists will break away and call for new moral agendas. Growing levels of accommodation may provoke new schisms as has been so often the case in the past. But rather than prolonged polarization or intense warfare between groups, we can expect the emergence and shaping of a new religious and cultural mainstream reflecting more fully the moral values and concerns of the current religious constituencies.

Notes

1. The literature on religion and politics implicitly or explicitly advancing this view is voluminous. An influential study on religion and prejudice making such assumptions is Stark et al. (1971). For a good review of much of this literature, see Wuthnow (1973, 117–32).
2. In 1984, the Gallup Poll estimated that evangelicals comprise twenty-two percent of the adult American population. Evangelicals are defined as those who (1) describe themselves as "born-again" Christians or have had a "born-again" experience; (2) have encour-

aged other people to believe in Jesus Christ; and (3) hold a literal interpretation of the Bible. See Princeton Religion Research Center (1984).

3. For a more extended discussion, see Marsden (1980).
4. Samuel S. Hill, Jr. notes that fundamentalists are "truth-oriented" as compared to more "conversion-oriented" evangelicals, "spiritually-oriented" devotionalists, and "service-oriented" ethical types (1981).
5. Several historical interpretations have pointed to the importance of this dual legacy in fundamentalism. See Speer (1984) and Chandler (1984).
6. According to a New York Times/CBS News poll, 81% of white "born-again" Protestants voted for the Reagan-Bush ticket in 1984, as compared to 58% of white Catholics, 69% of other white Protestants, and 32% of Jews. See New York Times, 25 November 1984.
7. For a general treatment of televangelism currently, see Hadden and Swann (1981).
8. Jerry Falwell at the National Religious Broadcasters Convention in Washington in February 1985 was quoted saying "Our people are more pluralistic today than they were 10 years ago." Not only is this probably true, Falwell appears to be quite pleased that it is true. See coverage of the convention carried in the Los Angeles Times, 9 February 1985.
9. For further elaboration on this point, see Hunter (1983, chap. 7).
10. Grassroots support for the Moral Majority, Inc. as an organization is nowhere as strong as is support in the general population for a position on the issues (or at least many issues) that is consistent with Moral Majority views. See Shupe and Stacey (1982).

References

Ahlstrom, Sydney E. 1972. A Religious History of the American People. New Haven, CT.: Yale University Press.

Chandler, Ralph Clark. 1984. The wicked shall not bear rule: The fundamentalist heritage of the new Christian right. In New Christian Politics. Ed. David G. Bromley and Anson Shupe. Macon, GA.: Mercer University Press, 41–58.

Cuddihy, John Murry. 1978. No offense: Civil Religion and Protestant Taste. New York: Seabury Press.

Falwell, Jerry. 1980. Listen America! New York: Doubleday.

Flake, Carol. 1984. *Redemptorama: Culture, Politics, and the New Evangelicalism*. Garden City, N.Y.: Anchor Press.

Hadden, Jeffrey K., and Charles E. Swann. 1981. *Prime Time Preachers: The Rising Power of Televangelism*. Reading, MA.: Addison-Wesley.

Hammond, Phillip E. 1985. *Political Evangelism: The Anglo-American Comparison*. Unpub. manuscript.

Handy, Robert T. 1971. *A Christian America*. New York: Oxford University Press.

Hendricks, John Stephen. 1977. *Religion and Political Fundamentalism: The Links Between Alienation and Ideology*. Ph.D. diss. University of Michigan.

Hill, Samuel S., Jr. 1981. The shape and shapes of popular southern piety. In *Varieties of Southern Evangelicalism*. Ed. David E. Harrell, Jr. Macon, GA.: Mercer University Press, 89–114.

Hunter, James Davidson. 1983. *American Evangelicalism: Conservative Religion and the Quandary of Modernity*. New Brunswick, N.J.: Rutgers University Press.

Jorstad, Erling. 1981. *The Politics of Moralism*. Minneapolis, MN.: Augsburg.

Marsden, George M. 1983. Preachers of paradox: The religious new right in historical perspective. In *Religion and America*. Ed. Mary Douglas and Stephen M. Tipton. Boston: Beacon Press, 150–68.

———1980. *Fundamentalism and American Culture*. New York: Oxford University Press.

Marty, Martin E. 1970. *Righteous Empire*. New York: Dial Press.

McKinney, William and Wade Clark Roof. 1982. A profile of American religious groups. In *Yearbook of American and Canadian Churches 1982*. Ed. Constance Jacquet. Nashville, TN.: Abingdon Press, 267–73.

Neuhaus, Richard John. 1984. *The Naked Public Square*. Grand Rapids, MI.: Eerdmans.

Phillips, Kevin. 1978. The Balkanization of America. *Harper's* (May): 37–47.

Princeton Religion Research Center. 1984. *Emerging Trends* 6, no. 8 (October).

Shupe, Anson and William A. Stacey. 1982. *Born-Again Politics and the Moral Majority: What Social Surveys Really Show*. New York: Edwin Mellen.

Simpson, John H. 1983. Moral issues and status politics. In *The New Christian Right*. Ed. Robert C. Liebman and Robert Wuthnow. New York: Aldine, 188–205.

Speer, James A. 1984. The new Christian right and its parent company: A study in political contrasts. In *New Christian Politics*. Ed. David G. Bromley and Anson Shupe. Macon, GA.: Mercer University Press, 19–40.

Stark, Rodney, Bruce Foster, Charles Y. Glock, and Harold C. Quinley. 1971. *Wayward Shepherds: Prejudice and the Protestant Clergy*. New York: Harper & Row.

Wuthnow, Robert. 1973. Religious commitment and conservatism: In search of an elusive relationship. In *Religion in Sociological Perspective: Essays in the Empirical Study of Religion*. Ed. Charles Y. Glock. Belmont, CA.: Wadsworth, 117–32.

3

Charismatic Leadership Trajectories: Two Case Histories

MICHAEL L. MICKLER

Introduction

BOTH popular and formal discussions of charismatic leadership illustrate the futility of imposing hypothetical "ideal types" on dynamic historical reality. For example, in the "attribution of charisma to leaders of any and all sorts, and to those who are no more than colorful or exhuberant personalities," popular treatments invariably tend toward loose, unqualified, and "vulgarized" usages (Wilson 1975, viii). On the other hand, systematic attempts to refine, quantify, or critically examine the concept typically conclude that "charisma would seem to be a very rare quality, if it exists at all" (Cohen 1972, 304).

In short, such discussions alternate between the poles of theoretical ambiguity and empirical irrelevance. In order to avoid either of these extremes, this paper suggests that charismatic leadership be reconceptualized not as an ideal type but as a set of processes referred to here as charismatic leadership trajectories. Although such trajectories can be conceptualized in a variety of ways, this paper develops a particular trajectory to assess charismatic eruptions within modern settings. Utilizing data from this trajectory, I suggest why charismatic leaders frequently have greater impact when the organizations they head disintegrate rather than survive.

To develop these points, the paper is organized into several sections. The first reviews the theory of charisma, its application, and its current revision in order to point out basic inadequacies and to suggest the alternative approach outlined above. The second section, which makes up the bulk of the paper, utilizes Marcus Garvey and Sun Myung Moon as "cases in point" to generate a trajectory of *self-stigmatization, dramatization,* and *criminalization.* Here, the attempt is to explain how charismatic leadership emerges, proliferates, and is checked within modern settings. (Lofland 1977, 342; see also Glaser and Strauss 1967). The concluding section compares the post-criminalization "career" of Marcus Garvey with current trends in Sun Myung Moon's Unification church in order to assess the ambiguities of "success" as applied to charismatic leaders.

The Theory of Charisma

As Max Weber noted, "the concept of charisma ('the gift of grace') is taken from the vocabulary of early Christianity" (1968, 47) and prior to his usage had been adapted by church historians, notably Rudolph Sohm from whom he adopted the term. Nonetheless, the development of charisma as a theory begins with Weber who detached the concept from its Christian roots and applied it to political life. Following Weber's lead, the theory has been utilized within the field of comparative politics and eventually, though in dilute form, became popular among lay audiences. Recently, as a result of popular "debasement," some sociologists have sought to rehabilitate and in some cases revise Weber's original formulation.

Weber's formulation: It is impossible to review Weber's theory of charisma without setting it within the context of his general theory of society and social change. Charisma, here, is one of three "pure types" of legitimate authority, the others being rational-legal and traditional. Put differently, Weber posited that "men obey willingly" out of self-interest, custom, or in the case of charisma, out of "devotion to the specific and exceptional sanctity, heroism or exemplary character of an individual person" (1968, 46). The other major distinction Weber drew among these three types of authority is that while rational and traditional structures have permanence in common as institutions of daily routine, "the provisioning for all demands that go beyond those of everyday routine . . . has a charismatic foundation. . . . "In this sense," charisma is essential to Weber's system of analysis as the basis for the explanation of social change" (Friedland 1964, 19).

A problem, however, arises in that Weber distinguished between pure and routinized forms of charisma. In its pure form, Weber noted, "Charisma knows only inner determination and inner restraint. The holder of charisma seizes the task that is adequate for him and demands obedience and a following by virtue of his mission. His success determines whether or not he finds them" (1968, 20). And elsewhere he noted, "Within the sphere of its claims, charismatic authority repudiates the past, and is in this sense a specifically revolutionary force. It recognizes no appropriations of power by virtue of the posession of property . . . The only basis of legitimacy for it is personal charisma, so long as it is proved; that is, for as long as it is able to satisfy the followers or disciples. But this lasts only so long as belief in its charismatic inspiration remains" (1968, 52).

Unlike pure charisma which is highly unstable and disdainful of "normal family relationships" as well as "everyday economizing," routinized charisma consists of a "permanent routine structure." This, in part, is due to the desire of original disciples or administrative staff to see their social and economic positions legitimated. It, also, is due to the disappearance of the personal charismatic leader and the problem of succession which inevitably arises. In these cases, routinized charisma normally moves in an authoritarian direction and becomes either traditionalized (hereditary) or rationalized (official) or both. In certain circumstances, however, Weber recognized that the charismatic principle might develop in an anti-authoritarian direction. Here, an "elective principle" is introduced and the traditional position of the leader is held to be dependent on the will of those over whom he exercises authority.

Applications: With the possible exception of his work on prophecy, Weber never developed an extended application of his theory. Instead, at various junctures he alludes to "a variety of different types as being endowed with charisma" (1968, 48). These include the Byzantine "berserker" who, in war-like passion, "bites his shield like a mad dog," the "shaman" who "in the pure type is subject to epileptoid seizures as a means of falling into trances," and a number of more bizarre examples, both quasi-criminal and counter-cultural. Weber's usage here, though undeveloped, contrasts vividly with subsequent applications of his theory that characterize charisma as "inspirational leadership" at best and mere "popularity" at worst.

Within academic settings, Weber's theory has been applied most widely in comparative politics and has been utilized to explain such diverse phenomenon as the development of ex-colonial "new states" (Apter 1963, 1965, 1968; Runciman 1963; Friedland 1964; Willner 1965; Bendix 1966; Rustow 1968; Perinbanayagan 1971), the rise of totalitarianism (Fagan 1965; Schram 1967; Tucker 1968; Nyomavky 1976), and the preservation of democracies during times of crisis (Ratnam 1964; Lowenstein 1966; Tucker 1968). In other words, charisma presumably has been the answer to the question: "What do Nkrumah, Nyrre, Lumumba, Nehru, Gandhi, Sukarno, Ataturk, Hitler, Lenin, Mao, Castro, Kim Il Sung, Roosevelt, Churchill, and De Gaulle have in common?" Such indiscriminate application of Weber's theory has led not only to conceptual "stretching" and "straining" but to the reduction of charisma from the "rare and magical" to the familiar and, in some cases, to the reassuring. This latter tendency is well illustrated in the attribution of charisma to Dwight D. Eisenhower during the 1952 election campaign (Davies 1954), an application rivaled only by the more recent attribution of charisma to IBM (Vinson 1977).

It is a short step from these treatments to the popular usage of charisma which has become wholly detached from its Weberian roots and come simply to mean popularity, stage-presence, or sex appeal. These latter usages were particularly prevalent during the presidency of John F. Kennedy and have since generalized beyond politics to cultural life in general. Thus, "a football player or musician who doesn't have charisma won't make it to stardom. Favorite ministers and professors are said to have charisma, and in some of the most bureaucratic churches there is an active charismatic movement" (Swatos 1981, 123). Put another way, "Charisma is now merely for fun; its public is of fans rather than of followers" (Wilson 1975, 125).

Revisions: Given what has been described as the "debasement" of charisma, scholars from a variety of methodological and ideological perspectives have advocated abandoning the term altogether. Third World scholars have critiqued its usage as the "easy way out" of more exacting explanations of politics in new states (e.g., Ratnam 1964). Marxist scholars "reject charisma as atavistic, irrational mystification which needlessly obscures, with infantile and romantic fancies, the 'real' factors at work in social development, and the 'real' principles of social organization" (Wilson 1975, 106). Western scholars such as Arthur Schlesinger (1960, 6–7) have characterized charisma as "the most mischievous of Weber's contributions—a specific feature of the world of myth and sorcery . . . prophetic, mystical, unstable, irrational and incapable of dealing with the realities of modern industrial society."

Confronted with stiff critiques, some sociologists have attempted to revise Weber's formulation. In general, these revisions have gone one of two ways. The first has been to *broaden* Weber's definition of charisma in order to accommodate its popular usage. The second has been to *narrow* the definition of charisma so as to restrict its indiscriminate application.

The foremost exponent of a broadened definition of charisma, that is, toward a definition making explicit what is already implicit in its current usage, has been Edward Shils (1975). In several articles later collected together as part of a single volume, Shils supplements Weber's pure and routinized forms of charisma with a more far-reaching "charismatic propensity" diffused throughout the entire organization of a society. Elaborating this idea through his notion of "center and periphery," Shils defines charisma as the "awe-arousing centrality" animating modern society's corporate bodies (including secular, economic, governmental, military, and political) and empowering them to keep the social periphery in order. However, since Shil's argument notes that charisma also resides in the opposition to each of the major dimensions that contain it, the utility of his analysis is open to criticism. As Benson and Givant (1975, 589) point out, "a theory or concept that explains equally a phenomenon and its opposite explains nothing."

If Shils has been the leading exponent of a broadened definition of charisma, Bryan Wilson (1975, vii–xi) has been the most articulate advocate in favor of narrowing Weber's formulation. For Wilson, charisma is not to be conceived in "the dilute sense in which some contemporary writers employ it," but in "the stronger sense of divinely inspired power." In support of this, Wilson argues, "Weber gave first place to the supernatural in his characterization of charisma, and the term itself stands in direct continuity with its Christian theological sense of gift of divine grace." Having, then, redefined charisma in a more restricted theological sense, Wilson develops a second premise: "supernatural belief is fully and widely credible only in premodern societies." Based on these two premises, his conclusion follows that charisma is "an anachronism in the modern world."

Wilson's revision, however, is just as extreme as Shils's. Rather than explaining *everything* about modern social organization and development, Wilson argues that charisma explains *nothing*. In this sense, both revisionist trends expose the futility of imposing ideal types on dynamic historical reality. Weber attempted to avoid this dilemma by differentiating between pure and routinized forms of charisma, a distinction that has led to confusion in subsequent applications of his theory and in the current revisionist efforts that tend toward either the routinized (Shils) or pure (Wilson) sides of Weber's discussion. A more promising line of development would be to treat both as component parts of more basic charismatic leadership trajectories. The following case studies illustrate a particular trajectory adapted to charismatic eruptions in contemporary settings.

Two Case Histories

At first glance a comparative analysis of Marcus Garvey and Sun Myung Moon seems incongruous. Aside from their disparate origins, Jamaican-born Marcus Garvey (1887–1940) emerged in the United States during the decade immediately following World War I and headed a fraternal organization preaching a "Back to Africa" gospel of Black nationalism, while Korean-born Sun Myung Moon (b. 1920) emerged in the United States during the 1970s as the head of a religio-social movement proclaiming interracial, intercultural, and interreligious unification. Despite these ostensible differences, however, the two exhibit similarities at three points relevant to this study. First, though originating in Third World contexts, both self-consciously chose the modernized West and, in particular, the United States, as the focus of their activities. Second, both developed politicized followings and exemplified typical charismatic disregard for both traditional and rational-legal authority structures. Third, both provoked widespread societal reaction and thereby afford the opportunity of examining modern mechanisms of social control.

Based on these points of contact, it is possible to generate a common charismatic leadership trajectory applicable to both figures. Briefly, its stages may be identified as (1) *self-stigmatization:* the process whereby individuals or groups labeled in negative or deviant terms subsequently identify with their negative attributions and in so doing come to understand themselves as set apart for a particular mission; (2) *dramatization:* the process by which previously marginalized self-stigmatizers move from social peripheries toward centers of power and by revolutionary acts seek to fulfill their claims and validate their new-found identities; and (3) *criminalization:* the process by which societies define these intrusions as not merely deviant but criminal and thereby justify active repression.

Self-stigmatization: For the concept of self-stigmatization, I am indebted to a discussion of Wolfgang Lipp (1977) who attempted to combine the theory of charisma with insights derived from the sociology of deviance. Although complex, his development is worth summarizing as the basis for this analysis. Grounding his treatment in the premise that social life is a process in which "grades" or "marks" are continually awarded "as praise or reproof, admiration or contempt," etc., Lipp notes when labeling processes primarily distribute negative values, punitive measures, and social guilt, a condition of stigmatization exists and individuals or groups become recipients of negative attributions. Such "actors," Lipp argues, are likely "in search of escape or evasion" but may, paradoxically, "react by capitalizing on their supposed defects . . . re-evaluate . . . and present them as positive elements" (1977, 66). This strategy Lipp calls "self-stigmatization"—a "crucial bridge to charismatic processes" which he describes as "the decisive turntable on which forms of behavior, originally classified as deviant by society are transformed into activities quite central to society, enjoying their own rules and producing innovations in social structure." Although these innovations are not specified, it is, nonetheless, the case that "Devotion, discipleship and all kinds of dynamic collective movements attach themselves to 'self-stigmatizers' who have alone or proto-typically have dared to enter the dangerous areas of social discrimination . . . stigmatization, self-sacrifice, and contrastigmatization" (1977, 74).

In the context of Lipp's discussion, Marcus Garvey and Sun Myung Moon may be depicted as self-stigmatizers who managed to reverse negative identity attributions and generate active followings. Garvey, for example, has been credited not only for having "brought the Negro people, for the first time, a sense of pride in being Black," (Powell 1945, 50) but also for having "built up the largest black mass movement in Afro-American history" (Martin 1976, ix). The Reverend Moon, on the other hand, has sought to revivify Korean national identity by parleying its stigmatized status as a "divided" nation into an international religious organization proclaiming unification. Although space limitations hinder full development, I will summarize briefly the process of self-stigmatization as applicable to both figures.

In Marcus Garvey's case, the general stigmatized status of Blacks in the Western hemisphere was aggravated both by British class traditions in his native Jamaica and by his travels as a quasi-journalist in the Caribbean basin which confirmed for him the exploitation of blacks in the region. These two factors combined to produce acute motivational tensions that simmered until an apparent conversion experience. As Garvey described it: "I read *Up From Slavery* by Booker T. Washington, and then my doom—if I may so call it—of being a race leader dawned upon me . . . I asked: 'Where is the black man's government? Where is his King and his kingdom? Where is his President, his country, and his ambassador, his army, his navy, his men of big affairs?' I could not find them, and then I declared, 'I will help to make them.'" (Garvey 1925, 126). Based on his vision of "uniting all the Negro peoples of the world into one great body to establish a country and a Government absolutely their own" (126), Garvey found both his life's work and the source of his appeal. As biographer David Cronon put it:

> Garvey attracted attention chiefly because he put into powerful ringing phrases the secret thoughts of the Negro world. He told his listeners what they most wanted to hear—that a black skin was not a badge of shame but rather a glorious symbol of national greatness. He promised a Negro nation in the African homeland that would be the marvel of the modern world. He pointed to Negro triumphs in the past and described in glowing symbols the glories of the future. When Garvey spoke of the greatness of the race, Negroes everywhere could forget for a moment-greatness of the race, Negroes everywhere could forget for a moment theshame of discrimination and the horrors of lynching (1955, 4).

In a number of important respects, Sun Myung Moon's experience approximates that of Garvey. First, the stigmatized status of Koreans in northeast Asia was aggravated for Reverend Moon both by Japanese colonial policies in his native Korea and through his own sojourn in Japan as a student and erstwhile leader in an abortive Korean liberation movement. Second, as with Garvey, these factors produced acute motivational tensions that were resolved by a dramatic experience; in Reverend Moon's case, a series of revelations convinced him of his destiny as an instrument of divine providence. Third, Reverend Moon's call was linked to his oppressed homeland in such a way that Koreans could identify with even the most shameful and stigmatizing national experiences as confirmations of, even qualifications for, their own messianic calling. For example, Korean domination under the Japanese is deemed, "not less severe than that which the 'First Israel' and 'Second Israel' suffered respectively in Egypt and the Roman Empire," and subsequent partitioning of the peninsula into communist North and democratic South is an "offering of sacrifice as a nation placed on the line for universal salvation" (*Divine Principle* 1973, 523–4). In this sense, oppressions and deprivation are not a source of shame but rather of a transformed national consciousness. That is, "The historical course of untold misery, which the Korean people have gone through, was the necessary way for them to walk as the people of God's elect." Finally, rather than apologize for cultural borrowings and indigenous syncretisms, it is argued, "All aspects of culture and civilization must bear fruit in this nation" *(Divine Principle* 1973, 526, 530).

Dramatization: Dramatization refers to the process by which marginalized self-stigmatizers move out from social peripheries and into engagement with centers of power and influence where by revolutionary (though, of necessity, often symbolic) acts they seek to actualize their claims and validate their new-found identities. While this development is, perhaps, straightforward enough, in order to effectively dramatize their claims, would-be charismatic leaders must possess at least three sets of "dramaturgical" skills. First, they must be able to capture an audience; that is, amid general populations, they must be able to recognize and effectively win a constituency. Second, among those mobilized, charismatic leaders must be able to create and sustain high levels of tension and dramatic conflict. Typically, they do this through charismatic "scripts" or ideologies that: (1) personify the world, that is, people it with heroes, villains, and fools, and (2) contrast their own potency as representing an unstoppable "wave of the future" over against the short-run reality of being hemmed in by powerful opponents. Yet, because the prospect of endless conflict is too foreboding to attract many enthusiasts, a third dramaturgical skill required of charismatic leaders is an ability to blend in elements of catharsis. Charismatic leaders normally do this by generating rituals and organizational structures that not only mirror their visions but which are an actual foretaste of ultimate fulfillment (see, e.g., Merelman 1969).

Based on this analysis, both Marcus Garvey and Sun Myung Moon may be credited as having dramatized their claims. Coming to the United States from peripheral locales and with limited resources, each was able to be heard, provoke dramatic conflicts, and built impressive organizations. In so doing both showed themselves to be accomplished strategists, propagandists, and organizers capable of evaluating contemporary trends, manipulating public opinion, and marshalling available resources to maximum effect. Again, though space limits detailed development, I will elaborate on the above-described dramaturgical skills as they apply to both figures.

Capturing an audience: In several important ways Marcus Garvey and Reverend Moon were fortunate in encountering relatively favorable conditions for dramatizing their claims. In Garvey's case, a ready pool of disaffected blacks was available as a result of post-World War I race riots, a revival of the Ku Klux Klan, the great migration of Southern rural blacks into Northern cities and because other "colored" organizations had ignored teeming black masses in favor of their "talented tenth." In Reverend Moon's case, post-countercultural disillusionment among American youth not yet ready to join the "system" but freed from pressures of military conscription was, likewise, helpful. Nonetheless, it is equally important to recognize the way in which both figures quickly sized-up the situation and seized the initiative. Garvey, for example, originally came to the United States to raise money for a Jamaican school, but on seeing a "growing mood of frustration and despair," immediately began propounding his ideas on race redemption. Similarly, though touring the United States in 1965 and 1969 when conditions were not favorable, Reverend Moon noted conditions had changed by 1972 and immediately launched coast-to-coast evangelical tours.

Maximizing dramatic conflict: In one sense, a Black man leading a mass movement in the 1920s and a Korean at the head of a middle-class American youth movement in the 1970s both had built-in dramatic possibilities. These, however, were only by-products of larger dramatic tensions that animated both leaders: that is, the tense alignments of global, almost mythic, forces locked in mortal struggle over against which both saw their respective organizations playing pivotal roles. According to Garvey's script, though he "frequently disclaimed any animus against the white race" (Cronon, 184), the villains clearly were white colonial interests, its heroes were embattled Black nationalists, and its fools the powerful Black interests pushing notions of accommodation and social equality. Thus, although 400 million "Negroes of the World" would not be denied, Garvey as their champion was ringed about by enemies and prospects hung in the balance. For Reverend Moon, communism, the villain over against which the Western democracies have played the fool, is portrayed as a threat most directly against the Republic of Korea but also against divine providence. In this sense, though God will prevail, God's immediate champions may not, and a reign of darkness is an ever-present possibility.

Structuring catharsis: In addition to capitalizing on social discontent and personalizing global conflicts, both Garvey and Reverend Moon balanced high levels of tension with positive emotional outlets. They did this by structuring their organizations in such ways that both evoked and embodied their respective visions of ultimate fulfillment. In this context, Garvey's Universal Negro Improvement Association (UNIA) was not an organization in the usual sense but rather *the aegis under which an independent Black nation was already emerging.* This was readily apparent in proliferating newspapers, political unions, factory corporations; in development of the African Orthodox Church; and, most profoundly, in the mammoth international conventions held annually in and around Madison Square Garden and Harlem during the early 1920s. Replete with parades, flags, honorary orders, titles, mottos, consultations, official declarations (including demands for representation in the League of Nations), and presided over by Garvey as "Provisional President of the African Republic," these month-long meetings had all the trappings of a government-in-exile. In addition to annual conventions, the other great cathartic outlet for "Garveyites" (as well as Garvey's main fund-raising and promotional vehicle) was the Black Star Steamship Line (BSL) which was intended to "link the colored peoples of the world." In much the same way, Reverend Moon's Unification Church has not been a church in the normal sense but, for Moonies, the framework within and through which a unified world has already begun to take shape. As with the Garvey movement, this has been apparent in the church's organizational proliferation (now encompassing metropolitan newspapers, maritime, and other industry, cultural exchanges, and cross-disciplinary academic meetings) conceived and implemented on an international scale. It has also been apparent in the church's ritual life, most dramatically in its massive international marriages.

Criminalization: Criminalization in this model is the process by which societies define intrusions of charismatic leaders as not merely deviant but criminal and thereby justify active repression. This, however, is an extremely subtle process in advanced, liberal-democratic, and pluralist societies for two reasons. First, such societies are both ideologically and structurally committed toward maximizing toleration and, thus, are able to sustain relatively high degrees of tension. Second, because stigma and charisma are "in actual social reality . . . related [and] . . . may pass over into one another" (Lipp, 72), societies must be wary that stigmas not attach themselves to their agencies of social control. For these reasons, any repressive measures taken must be carefully legitimated. In particular, they must have the appearance of being prosecution and not persecution. Thus, regardless of public demand, modern agencies of social control are not likely to enact official sanctions against charismatic leaders unless they can get an indictment. This, however, is not difficult in technical societies given charismatic leaders' typical disregard of formal procedures, especially with regard to finances. Moreover, once indicted, it is extremely difficult for charismatic leaders to avoid (or reverse) convictions as these procedures tend to be vehicles for irrational societal grievances.

Given this analysis, it is obvious that, justifiably or not, both Marcus

Garvey and Sun Myung Moon were subject to a process of criminalization. Both not only provoked social controversy but both were indicted and subsequently convicted by the United States government. Garvey, along with three associates, was indicted on twelve counts of mail fraud in connection with raising funds for the BSL in 1922, was convicted in 1923, was denied on appeal, entered Atlanta Federal Penitentiary in 1925, and was deported as an "undesirable alien" in 1927. The Reverend Sun Myung Moon, with one aide, was indicted on thirteen counts of tax evasion in 1981, was convicted in 1982, and having exhausted all judicial appeals, began serving an eighteen-month jail term at Danbury Federal Penitentiary, Connecticut in 1984. Although complex, I will sketch briefly the criminalization process at work in both cases.

In Garvey's case alleged irregularities in the sale of BSL stock were the means by which United States attorneys focused a variety of public grievances against the flamboyant Jamaican. The government was successful in prosecuting the case for two reasons: First, Garvey's BSL was managed poorly. This was partly due to Garvey's preference for "unquestioning personal loyalty over business competence in his associates" and partly to Garvey's own impulsiveness in plunging into inadequately researched business ventures. Second, and more importantly, Garvey blurred the distinctions between promotional and business aspects of his enterprises. As biographer Cronon points out, "With messianic fervor, Garvey apparently believed that funds raised for any aspect of his redemption program could be used wherever he decided they were needed" (1966, 79). While this perogative was not a problem for Garvey's supporters and may have been necessary to maximize his organization's impact, "the result could only be financial chaos in the books of the U.N.I.A. and the B.S.L." Furthermore, a combination of business failure and continued promotion enabled the government to argue that Garvey and his codefendents "had knowingly and with criminal intent used the mails to promote the sale of Black Star stock after they were aware that the financial condition of the line was hopeless" (Cronon 1966, 114–15).

Although the issue was tax evasion, the government successfully pressed its case against Reverend Moon basically for the same reasons that had worked against Garvey. First, Reverend Moon's tax liabilities were managed poorly. This was, in part, due to Reverend Moon's reliance on personal aides and, in part, to those aides' determination to shield him from outside scrutiny. Second, Reverend Moon's style of church leadership blurred the distinctions between personal and church funds. Despite the fact that Reverend Moon's case, unlike Garvey's, was complicated by First Amendment questions and exemptions, the government overrode those considerations by treating him no differently than "any high ranking business executive," that is, "without consideration of his religious beliefs."[1] Thus, a combination of efforts to protect Reverend Moon from investigation and a confused morass of church finances enabled prosecutors to win a conviction on conspiracy to defraud the United States government.

Conclusion

Criminalization is by no means a terminus to the trajectory outlined in this paper, and it remains to assess the effects of charismatic leadership. Such assessments, however, are subject to a pervasive irony. That is, because charismatic-led movements hold competing (even contradictory) elements in dynamic tension, they may upon collapse be coopted by a variety of successor movements to legitimate programs deviating from the original vision though ultimately more consequential. On the other hand, when charismatic organizations hold themselves together and routinize, dynamic tensions work themselves out among competing internal factions, thereby blunting any social impact at least in the short-run. Paradoxically, then, charismatic leaders tend to have more immediate impact when the organizations they led disentegrate rather than survive. This irony is apparent when comparing the post-criminalization career of Marcus Garvey to current trends in the Reverend Moon's Unification Church.

In Garvey's case, despite late support from "Garvey Must Go" advocates, his imprisonment and deportation had devastating consequences on the UNIA for two reasons: First, Garvey's severe castigation of enemies within to the extent of blaming his imprisonment on machinations of associates sparked resentment among American leadership. Second, and more significantly, his deportation generated conflict over the location of organizational headquarters and led to a 1929 schism splitting the UNIA into two rival associations. Further, as Cronon notes, "A Negro world that had been able to support Garvey's million-dollar business ventures in the prosperous twenties found his ambitious global projects too expensive a luxury to maintain in the hardship years of the thirties" (1966, 167). In short, despite efforts to revive the work, first in Jamaica and later in England, the once-proud UNIA had collapsed by the time Garvey died in 1940.

Given the transience of his organization, Garvey's impact has been surprisingly significant. This is primarily because "Garveyism" itself was a volatile mix of Bookerite "up by the bootstraps" economic philosophy, mass organizational, and promotion techniques, "Back to Africa" nationalism and black messianism which on dissolution could be appropriated by a variety of groups incorporating some elements and disregarding others. Thus, Garveyism has been cited as a major source for such diverse ideological groupings as the Rastafarians, Black Muslims, the United States civil rights movement, Black power advocates, and African nationalist leaders Kwame Nkrumah and Jomo Kenyatta. In Jamaica, where Garvey was not received sympathetically in life, it was argued ten years after his death that "Garveyism lies at the heart of the modern political movements through which West Indian nationalism is seeking to express itself" (King 1950, 15). On the other hand, Garveyism has not been invoked solely for revolutionary purposes. For example, in the current renaissance of Garvey scholarship, revisionist Afro-American historians have sought to remove him from the aberrant fringe toward mainstream respectability (Clarke 1974; Martin 1976; Burkett 1978; Davis and Sims 1980).

It is possible that Reverend Moon, in similar fashion, might be a future source of revived Asian or Korean racial and national consciousness. This, however, is unlikely for two reasons: First, the current Asian situation is not comparable to that of the black world nor has Reverend Moon attempted or demonstrated any significant appeal among Asian or even Korean-Americans. Second, and more importantly, his Unification church has a greater chance of holding itself together than Garvey's UNIA. Although this assertion is hazardous given the unforeseeable character of future trends, the Unification church has one distinct advantage over Garvey's movement: its ethos as a "church" with common beliefs, ethical norms, and, most significantly, a common ritual life suggests a greater likelihood of corporate cohesiveness and survival capability.

That the Unification church should hold together and routinize does not imply, however, that its social impact will be enhanced. In fact, the reverse is more likely. This is basically because Unificationism as a charismatically congealed admixture of corporate capitalism, social-gospel idealism, anti-communism, and Korean messianism tends, unavoidably, toward internal factionalization. Varying orientations have emerged within the Unification Church: avoidance of dissension among its bureaucratic and business-class constituencies; its immigrating and upwardly mobile foreign nationals; its liberal intelligentsia; its ex-radical, black, feminist and European socialist element; its anti-communist cadre; its less educated grassroots membership. And likewise, its Korean elite and mainstream Japanese leadership will require a careful process of internal compromise, restraint, and mutual accommodation. Ironically, however, the very procedures facilitating organizational consolidation may work to impair the broader impact of the Unification church at least in the immediately foreseeable future.

Notes

1. These are the comments of U.S. prosecutor Jo Ann Harris and Judge Gerard L. Gottel. See "Transcript of Hearing," *United States of America v. Sun Myung Moon*. United States District Court Southern District of New York, 81 Ct. 0705(GLG) (Foley Square, N.Y.: Southern District Reporters, U.S. Courthouse, 16 July 1982), 27, 35.

References

Apter, David E. 1968. Nkrumah, charisma and the coup. *Daedalus* 97: 757-92.

———. 1966. *Ghana in Transition*. New York: Atheneum.

———. 1955. *The Gold Coast in Transition*. Princeton, N.J.: Princeton University Press.

Bendix, Reinhard. 1968. Reflections on charismatic leadership. In *State and Society*. Boston: Little, Brown, 616–29.

Bensman, Joseph and Michael Givant. 1975. Charisma and modernity. *Social Research* 42: 570–614.

Burkett, Randall K. 1978. *Black redemption: Churchmen Speak for the Garvey movement*. Philadelphia: Temple University Press.

Clarke, John Henrik, ed. 1974. *Marcus Garvey and the Vision of Africa*. New York: Vantage Books.

Cohen, D.L. 1972. The concept of charisma and the analysis of leadership. *Political Studies* 20: 299–305.

Cronon, David E. 1966. *Black Moses*. Madison: The University of Wisconsin Press.

Davies, James C. 1954. Charisma in the 1952 Campaign. *American Political Science Review* 48: 1083–1102.

Davis, Lenwood G. and Janet L. Sims, 1980. *Marcus Garvey: An Annotated Bibliography*. Westport, CT.: Greenwood Press.

Divine Principle. 1973. New York: The Holy Spirit Association for the Unification of World Christianity.

Fagan, Richard, 1965. *Charismatic authority and the leadership of Fidel Castro. The Western Political Quarterly* 8: 275–84.

Friedland, William H., 1964. For a sociological concept of charisma. *Social Forces* 43: 18–26.

Garvey, Marcus, 1925. *Philosophy and Opinions of Marcus Garvey.* Ed. Amy Jacques Garvey. New York: Arno Press.

Glaser, Barney G. and Anselm L. Strauss. 1967. *The Discovery of Grounded Theory.* Chicago: Aldine Publishing Company.

Lipp, Wolfgang, 1977. Charisma—social deviation, leadership and cultural change. *The Annual Review of the Social Sciences of Religion* 1: 57–77.

Lofland, John. 1977. *Doomsday Cult.* Enlarged Edition. New York: Irvington Publishing.

Martin, Tony. 1976. *Race First.* Westport, CT.: Greenwood Press.

Merelman, R.M. 1969. The dramaturgy of politics. *The Sociological Quarterly* 10: 216–41.

Nyomavky, Joseph. 1967. *Charisma and Factionalism in the Nazi party.* Minneapolis: University of Minnesota Press.

Perinbanayagan, R.S., 1971. The dialectics of charisma. *The Sociological Quarterly* 12: 387–402.

Powell, Adam Clayton. 1945. *Marching Blacks.* New York: Dial Press.

Ratnam, K.J. 1964. Charisma and political leadership. *Political Studies* 12: 341–54.

Runciman, W.G. 1963. Charismatic legitimacy and one-party rule in Ghana. *Archives Europennes de Sociologie* 4: 148–65.

Rustow, Dankwart A. 1968. "Ataturk as founder of a state." *Daedalus* 97: 793–828.

Schram, Stuart. 1967. Mao Tse-tung as a charismatic leader. *Asian Survey* 2: 383–88.

Shils, Edward. 1975. *Center and Periphery.* Chicago: University of Chicago Press.

Swatos, William H., Jr. 1981. The disenchantment of charisma: A Weberian assessment of charisma in a rationalized world. *Sociological Analysis* 42: 119–36.

Schlesinger, Arthur. 1960. On heroic leadership. *Encounter* 15: 3–11.

Tucker, Robert C. 1968. The theory of charismatic leadership. *Daedalus* 97: 731–56.

Vinson, Donald E. 1977. Charisma. *International Journal of Contemporary Sociology* 14: 269–75.

Weber, Max. 1968. *On Charisma and Institution Building*. Ed. S.N. Eisenstadt. Chicago: The University of Chicago Press.

Willner, Ann Ruth and Dorothy Willner. 1965. The rise and role of charismatic leaders. *The Annals of the American Academy of Political and Social Sciences* 358: 77–88.

Wilson, Bryan R. 1975. *The Noble Savages*. Berkeley: The University of California Press.

4

Ram Mohan Roy: Pioneer of Indian Freedom

CROMWELL S. CRAWFORD

ABRAHAM Lincoln once remarked that the world has never had a good definition of the word liberty. The problem is that to define liberty is to limit it. But while liberty cannot be defined, it can be demonstrated; and one of the finest demonstrations of liberty is the life and labors of Raja Ram Mohan Roy (1772–1833). Like Lincoln, he had an intense passion for liberty which was the key to his whole life. One can see this pursuit in all areas of his life—religious, moral, social, political, and intellectual.

Roy was a pioneer of Indian freedom. Modern historians of India now refer to him as "the prophet of the new age." He drew a blueprint for political agitation along constitutional lines which, fifty years later, helped to bring about the birth of the Indian National Congress. His political views have a modern ring and "in essential features represent the high-water mark of Indian political thought of the nineteenth century."[1]

Portions of this essay are adapted from the author's book: *Raja Ram Mohan Roy: His Era and Ethics,* forthcoming.

Ram Mohan Roy and Emergent Nationalism

Nineteenth-century India was in the grip of unprecedented tumult. The Charter Act of 1813 marked a new attitude of "trusteeship" on the part of the British rulers. However, while the government was secure in its view that Providence had entrusted these benighted natives to its tutelage, there was difference of opinion as to the principles on which the establishment of order was to be based. There were three primary divisions with the Conservatives (e.g., Edmund Burke) and Liberals (James Mill) at the poles, with the Great Administrators (e.g., Mount Stuart Elphinstone) taking a middle path.

The new Indian middle-class was organized around three groups—Orthodox, Radicals, and Liberals. The Orthodox were determined that political submission must not be followed by cultural submission, so they used old traditions, such as the caste system, as protection against foreign encroachments. The Radicals, chiefly student Anglophiles, debunked Hinduism as productive of an effete culture by joining beef-eating and beer-drinking clubs, and by receiving Christian baptism. Roy was the chief architect of the Liberal response to the Western challenge. He rejected the cultural isolationism of the Orthodox and the cultural abdication of the Radicals. Instead, with the wisdom of the Buddha, he chose the middle path. He was joined on this course by a small but influential group of Indians who could no more eat beef than crawl into cultural cocoons. These he drew into the growing cult of nationalism which had no precedent in Indian history. For this Indian to have brought about something so un-Indian, Roy has been deservedly described as "the greatest creative personality of the nineteenth-century India."[2]

These social forces which contended to decide the direction of British welfare toward the Indian people gave shape to Roy's prophetic role. Roy's ideas did not germinate in a vacuum, and the British impact constituted one area in which Roy did his thinking and carried out his reforms. This cultural assimilation was inevitable given the synthetic and encyclopedic character of the Raja's mind. Like a hungry man he devoured everything he read in the newspapers pertaining to European politics, society, and education. He incorporated the thinking of Western philosophers and was considered a member of the Benthamite school. He drew heavily on the research and translations of the

Orientalists, and openly declared his indebtedness to Western religious influences, both of the Trinitarians and Unitarians. Thus, when Ram Mohan speaks, we must listen for the accents of Burke, Hastings, Jones, Bentham, Mill, Munro, and a host of others. It is his speech, but the stress and pitch of these personalities lend it peculiar prominence.

Yet while admitting the above, "the talents and labors" of all Western benefactors must be set in their proper time frame. Chronologically, they are subsequent to the two earlier influences of Persian and Vedantic thought. Only after he had drunk at the well of Perso-Arabic thought with its Islamic and Aristotelian blends, and had imbibed the heady elixir of Advaitic monism, did he then turn to the fountains of the West.

In the short span of time covering his Calcutta years (1815–1830), he laid the blueprint for the Indian national movement. His approach was philosophically progriotic but not simply eclectic. Says one English observer: "His attitude toward the West was neither that of surrender, or withdrawal, or conflict. It was one of comprehension. The new world from the West was not to be a substitute but a supplement to the old. Synthesis, which is different from syncreticism was his remedy for the predicament of Hinduism."[3]

The means by which he sought to bring about this synthesis was a reason which he discovered in the Upanishadic literature of ancient Hinduism. In his new world-istic loyalty to Hindu values, traditions and reform, or in functionalist terms, "modernization" could go hand in hand.[4]

In this new approach to the problem of emerging Indian Nationalism, Ram Mohan was able to supply the rising Westernized class with what they sorely wanted, but which neither Orthodox nor Radicals could deliver, namely: to be Westernized without being de-Hinduized. Whereas the Orthodox offered a past that had no future and the Radicals offered a future that had no past, the Raja made possible a past that had a rich future and a future that had a rich past.

This background briefly introduces Roy as a central figure in the Indian political thought of the nineteenth century. He would have agreed with Aristotle that "the good of man must be the end of the science of politics." "Man" for him was not merely "Indian man" but "International man." But politics, like charity, begins at home, thus it is useful to begin with his activities on the national front and then examine the international area.

Ram Mohan Roy As Pragmatic Prophet

His English biographer hails him as the "tribune and prophet of the New India." The prospect of an India, educated and "approximating to European standards of culture, seems to have never been long absent from Rammohan's mind; and he did, however vaguely, claim in advance for his countrymen the political rights which progress in civilization inevitably involves."[5]

Most importantly, the Raja's political ideals were rooted in his religious view of man as "eternally free." This revelation based on the Upanishads was at odds with the caste-ridden beliefs and practices of the prevailing religion of India. In Roy's view, political reform therefore went hand in hand with religious reform. The intimate connection between religion and politics is clear from the following extract of one of his letters. He regrets to say:

> The present system of religion adhered to by the Hindus is not well calculated to promote their political interest. The distinction of castes, introducing innumerable divisions and sub-divisions among them, has entirely deprived them of patriotic feeling, and the multitude of religious rites and ceremonies and the laws of purification have totally disqualified them from undertaking any different enterprise. . . . It is, I think, necessary that some change should take place in their religion, at least for the sake of their political advantage and social comfort.[6]

Further, he believed that some of the very virtues of Hinduism had become political vices. Hindu civilization had produced an ethos of refinement and sociability which, carried to extremes, had proven politically emasculating. The metaphysical manners of his people had rendered them too docile to withstand their many conquerors. He lamented: "We have been subjected to such insults for about nine centuries, and the cause of such degradation has been our excess in civilization and abstinence from the slaughter even of animals."[7]

But in spite of the degrading effects of centuries, Roy was a firm believer that, in terms of their native capacities, the Indians were not inferior to the Europeans. He confronted racism directly, regarding no man his superior. He debunked the myth of "Asiatic effeminacy" and pointed out that almost all of the great personalities of antiquity were Asians.

The spiritual grounds for his conviction of racial equality, and indeed, the unity of the human race, originated in his belief in the essential oneness of the individual with the universal *Brahman* (Reality). That is, ignorance (or *maya*) impedes this consciousness of metaphysical Oneness, but perfectibility is a human birthright.

In Hindu religious tradition perfection was conceived as an individual enterprise involving renunciation, but Roy insisted that the spiritual cultivation of the individual can take place in and through society. The ascetical ideal of renunciation is maintained; however, it is not renunciation *of* action, but rather renunciation *in* action. Thus, the quietism of the East is synthesized with the activism of the West, and the result is an ethic of disinterested performance of duty. This ethical stance is identical with that of the *Gita*. In the spirit of the *Gita*, Roy emphasized that in order to realize *moksha* (liberation), one must not only practice *upasana* (duties of meditation and worship), but *nishkama karma* (disinterested social duties).[8] In the performance of *nishkama karma*, the actor is completely free of utilitarian motives. Happy in the possession of his true self, he works for the welfare of the world and thereby attains perfection.

Thus Roy, in the tradition of a Hindu philosopher-king, elevated work for the world, especially political activity, to the realm of *dharma* (religion). He demonstrated that one does not have to become a *yogi* and retreat to the forest to achieve self-realization. Work in the world is worship. The business of religion is to free people to become themselves and help create the family of man on earth. The world for the reformer was polymorphous. It included males and females, Christian and Hindus, Brahmins and Shudras, Asiatics, and Westerners.

In addition to the ideal of *nishkama karma*, the practical ethics of the Raja incorporated the Golden Rule of the Bible which teaches that man should do unto others as he would wish to be done by. This is not mere pragmatism; it is natural and spiritual law. As the common core of universal moral experience, "it is taught in every system of religion," and is "principally inculcated by Christianity."[9] Roy believed that "this simple code of religion and morality is so admirably calculated to elevate man's ideas to high and liberal notions of God," and that it is "well fitted to regulate the conduct of the human race in the discharge of their various duties to themselves, and to society."[10]

Shifting from practical ethics to social polity, Roy held that it is the duty of civil administration to secure for the citizenry their natural rights and freedoms. These included the fundamental rights of life and property and the freedoms of speech, opinion, conscience, and association. Together, these constituted "happiness," the goal of organized society conceived as a balance between individual rights and the common good. Obviously, the formulation of such socio-political concepts as the "natural rights of man" were Western. Among Western social and political theorists, Bentham in particular had a formative influence upon Ram Mohan's liberalism and rational critique of social and political problems. But while the formulas were foreign, the spirit of the principles was not alien to Hindu *dharma*, thus making it possible for Roy to insert "his humanitarian religion as a motive power to the organization of social polity."[11]

Roy's religious view invested his sense of being Indian with a sense of dignity and worth. Indians deserved all the benefits of freedom because they were the sons and daughters of God, and therefore could not be treated as inferior to the British. The only area in which the Europeans were superior to Indians was in respect to technological advancement and democratic institutions.[12]

To help bridge this gap Roy welcomed the British presence. He believed that England had a cultural and humanitarian mission to perform in India. The alliance, in his view, would introduce Indians to modern-world culture, establish institutions of democratic government, and bring the nation into the family of other free and enlightened peoples of the world. He conceived this British mission in almost messianic terms, referring to Englishmen as a "nation who not only are blessed with the enjoyment of civil and political liberty, but also interest themselves in promoting liberty and social happiness, as well as free inquiry into literary and religious subjects among those nations to which their influence extends."[13]

This statement should be taken as a mixture of hope and fact. While the future was open, he could look down the road and see certain possibilities. His remarks in 1832 on the settlement of Europeans in India reflect his maturing vision.

He first listed "Advantages" of the settlement of Europeans in India. They were reckoned as:

1. The introduction by Westerners of modern systems of agriculture, commerce, and mechanical arts;
2. Removal of superstitions and prejudices by the spread of communication;
3. Improvement of laws and the whole judicial system;
4. Protection against the abuses of power;
5. Diffusion of European arts and sciences, and the cultivation of the English language through schools and seminaries;

6. Multiplying channels of communication to enable managers of public affairs to collect authentic information about the country;
7. Military security against foreign invasion.

The complete text of the eighth and ninth items clearly show how Roy felt about India's connection with Britain:

8. The same cause would operate to continue the connexion between Great Britain and India on a solid and permanent footing; provided only the latter country be governed in a liberal manner, by means of Parliamentary superintendence, and other such legislative checks in this country as may be devised and established. India may thus, for an unlimited period, enjoy union with England, and the advantage of her enlightened Government; and in return contribute to support to the greatness of this country.
9. If, however, events should occur to effect a separation between the two countries, then still the existence of a large body of respectable settlers (consisting of Europeans and their descendants, professing Christianity, and speaking the English language in common with the bulk of the people, as well as possessed of superior knowledge, scientific, mechanical, and political) would bring that vast empire in the East to a level with other large Christian countries in Europe, and by means of its immense riches and extensive population, and by the help which may be reasonably expected from Europe, they (the settlers and their descendants) may succeed sooner or later in enlightening and civilizing the surrounding nations of Asia.[14]

Next, the Raja lists some of the principle "Disadvantages" that the settlement of Europeans might bring, along with the remedies calculated to prevent them from occurring. Mapping the future, he says: (1) Because of the common bonds between settlers and the ruling class, there is the possibility that Europeans may dominate the Indians and discriminate against them on the grounds of religion, color, and habits. The potential problem can be obviated by only allowing, for the first twenty years, the immigration of "educated persons of character and capital," and by the enactment of trial by jury; (2) Europeans could have the upper hand over the populace by having readier access to persons in authority. This should be remedied by placing Indian and European attorneys on the same footing before the judges.

The fourth point is of special interest: Ram Mohan argues that in certain quarters there is apprehension that "if events should occur to effect a separation (which may rise from many accidental causes, about which it is vain to speculate or make predictions), still a friendship and highly advantageous commercial intercourse may be kept up between the two free and Christian countries, united as they then will be by resemblance of language, religion and manners."[15]

This remarkable document gives us Roy's vision of the new India in a clear and concise way. He sees India as a country governed in a liberal manner, with Parliamentary superintendence, and all necessary legislative checks and balances. People of all classes and stations in life would have the same civil rights with jury trials—the juries being composed impartially of Europeans as well as Indians. The first European settlers, he envisaged (if, in hindsight, somewhat naïvely), would be of superior caliber, acting from motives of benevolence, public spirit, and brotherhood. Their presence would certainly serve as a social leaven, not only by raising European standards, but also emancipating Indians from ignorance and superstition, thereby securing their affection and loyalty.

The result would be an India, enlightened by European education with schools dotting the whole country, and the English language spoken far and wide. Economically, India would be strong, geared to the advanced technology and agricultural methods of the West. Politically, India would be safe from foreign invasion, protected by British power. Should the political ties between the two countries be severed, the European inhabitants of India would continue to raise the country's standards until it reached the level of the countries of Europe, and through India, surrounding Asian countries would similarly be modernized.

Prophetic Strategies

The above discussion makes it abundantly clear that while Roy believed that India needed to undergo a period of political tutelage, he also believed that India would one day come of age and become an independent nation in its own right. The settlement of British colonialists in India was only a means toward an end, namely, a free India in the foreseeable future. As he remarked to one French traveler: "India requires many more years of English domination so that she might not have to lose many things while she is *reclaiming her political independence.*" (Italics supplied.)[16]

In the meantime, Ram Mohan stood as watchdog over the British political establishment. He clearly understood both the light and dark sides of the British character and worked for the triumph of the one over the other. In the words of Rajani Kanta Guha: "The Government of India was in his day a benevolent despotism. Rammohun wanted that it should retain its trait of benevolence, but outgrow its irresponsible character, and steadily move towards a representative form calculated to fulfill the noblest political aspirations of the Indian people."[17]

To accomplish this goal, Ram Mohan was quick to seize upon the power of the press. This was to be the medium for furthering his prophetic message. Through the printed page he could not only keep his countrymen informed with useful knowledge, but also supply the rulers with authentic information about the facts of Indian life. He seems to have been guided by the Socratic principle that "knowledge is virtue"—that an enlightened government would somehow act more benevolently than one that was out of touch with the people.

It followed from this that the indispensable prerequisite of good government was a free press. But insistence on freedom of the press made him irritate the Achilles heel of British statesmanship which was "the unwavering faith of the Olympians at home in the infallibility of the man on the spot."[18] The Raja, however, was sceptical of all forms of infallibility—religious, rational, and most of all, the political infallibility of petty bureaucrats.

Ram Mohan entered the field of journalism soon after the government of Lord Hastings abolished press censorship in August 1818. From the time of the publication of Hicky's *Bengal Gazette* in 1780, the English Press had been in disfavor with the government because of its outspoken criticism of governmental mismanagement. When criticism went "too far," the government of Lord Wellesley clamped down with certain restrictive regulations issued in May of 1799. Editors held in violation of these regulations were to be deported to Europe.

Obviously, the above punishment could not be meted out to Indian editors also held in contempt. Therefore, in the name of fairness to European editors, and also because of his more liberal views, when Lord Hastings took the reins of government he restored free discussion to the press and only held the press responsible to the laws of sedition and libel.

After the Regulation of 1818, two towering figures make their appearance upon the stage of Indian journalism—J. S. Buckingham, the liberal voice of the Calcutta *Journal,* and Ram Mohan Roy (though while not the founder of native journalism, still its chief architect). Roy founded the *Sambad Kaumudi* (The Moon of Intelligence); the *Brahmana Sevadhi* (Brahmanical Magazine); the *Jam-i-Jahan Numa;* and the *Mirat-ul-Akhbar* (Mirror of Intelligence).

The *Brahmana Sevadhi* was the organ through which Roy defended Hinduism against the attacks of Christian missionaries. The *Sambad*

Kaumudi and the *Mirat-ul-Akhbar* dealt not only with social and religious issues, but were also politically oriented.[19]

The voice of the liberal press, both Indian and European, proved too strident and dangerous for the British administrators whose policies came under fire constantly. Two members of the Council in India, Adam and Bailey, wrote strong notes on the question of the freedom of the press. Bailey expressed official fear that an unleashed press could very easily foment insubordination, discontent, and infidelity among the native troops, which would seriously affect the stability of the British Empire. In point of fact, Bailey's true apprehension was that the Indians, though apathetic for the present, might be roused in the near future by the liberal press and begin making demands for political rights and privileges. As a staunch Christian, Bailey was also offended by the manner in which Christian missionaries were publicly censured in the *Brahmana Sevadhi* without regard for their position as members of the ruling class.

The theory which guided Bailey's policy was that laws must be suited (according to Social Darwinian assumptions) to the appropriate level of a society. England, he claimed, had a free press but also had complementary institutions of the same "evolutionary" accomplishment. Thus men were prepared to cope with the "exaggeration and misrepresentation which must ever attend freedom of publication."[20] Hindus, he assumed, had nowhere reached such an enlightened level.

The Anglo-Indian Press expressed similar misgivings about the Regulation of 1818, as did the Council. The *Asiatic Journal* warned about the perilous responsibility taken upon themselves by those who removed the censorship of the Indian Press, and anticipated evil times ahead unless the resident authorities acted with "resolution, constancy, union, and vigour." Among the publications blacklisted by the *Asiatic Journal* was preeminently the *Sambad Kaumudi*.

The Council finally made up its collective mind on the need to remove the dangers posed by the Regulation of 1818. The liberal press tried to argue that the free vernacular press was rendering yeoman's service to the government by acquainting it with the "real situation and sentiments of the whole population."[21] The Calcutta *Journal* raised the point that if "a spark of discontent" is kindled anywhere is it not best that it be immediately discovered by the Free Press, instead of being smothered in silence, "until it secretly extend far and wide, and then suddenly burst into unquenchable flame?"[22] But none of these arguments allayed the fears and suspicions of the Council.

The opportunity to act upon their trepidations was seized by Adam who officiated as Acting Governor-General upon the departure of Lord Hastings and expelled the editor of the Calcutta *Journal*. The expulsion of the editor was followed by the capricious promulgation of a Rule and Ordinance, dated March 14, 1823, that required newspaper owners to obtain licenses from the Chief Secretary of the Government who could, without appeal, rescind such "freedom of the press."

Ram Mohan was indignant. He raised a strong protest against this Ordinance, submitting a Memorial to the Supreme Court (in the company of five other Indian sympathizers, who together became known as the Memorialists). Roy furnished "proofs" of Indian loyalty to the British government since the preamble to the Rule and Ordinance had implied certain political apprehensions.

First, he noted that the natives of Calcutta had invested major capital with the government. Secondly, landholders had improved their estates and increased their productivity because of their faith in promises made by the government at the time of the Permanent Settlement in 1793. Thirdly, Indians had come to the assistance of the British during the last wars fought by them against neighboring powers. Fourthly, the Hindu community of Bengal was outspoken about the continual literary and political improvements that had enriched their lives under the prevailing system of government.

These unequivocal proofs of loyalty and attachment, Roy claimed, were tributes to the wisdom and liberality of the British government in the means they had adopted for the gradual improvement of social and domestic conditions, and for the establishment of institutions of learning and justice. At the same time, the vernacular and English press had contributed to the good of society by diffusing useful and political knowledge, and had never been socially or politically irresponsible. Yet, the government had seen fit to promulgate a Rule and Ordinance imposing severe restraints on the press through requirements of oaths and licenses.

The situation was serious because Hindus had an aversion to making any voluntary affidavit or oath, and therefore they would have preferred to leave the publishing field rather than obtain licensing. If this was to happen, the circulation of information which had significantly improved the general intelligence of the people would cease, Roy warned. A shutdown press would preclude Indians from keeping the government informed about the conduct of its executive officers; and by the same token, it would prevent them from communicating frankly with the King and his Council on the way the government was running British interests in India. Given the vastness of the area which must be combed for information, both King and local government would stand to lose should the vernacular press go out of business. Roy further argued that the moment the precious right of free speech, to which they had been accustomed since the establishment of British rule, was withdrawn, the citizens of Calcutta would no longer be justified in making the boast that Providence had placed them under the protection of the British nation.[24]

The Memorialists expressed confidence that the British government would not follow the political policy of Asiatic potentates who imagined rulers were best off when they kept their subjects ignorant about what was going on. The high ethical tenor of the Memorial is repeated in its concluding statement. Every good ruler, it maintained, who is aware of human fallibility and has reverence for the moral order, must know that serious errors can be incurred in the operation of so vast an empire. Such a leader will, therefore, "be anxious to afford every individual the readiest means of bringing to his notice whatever may require his interference." To achieve this end, the "unrestrained Liberty of Publication, is the only effectual means that can be employed."[25]

Yet the presiding judge, Sir Francis Macnaghten, "paid no regard whatever to the Memorial," having made up his mind before the hearing that he would rule in favor of the Government. Ram Mohan then appealed to the King in Council. The Appeal has justly been described as "one of the noblest pieces of English" composed by Ram Mohan.[26] But for all its moral and historical reasoning, the Appeal met with a similar fate as the Memorial. The Privy Council declined to intervene in the matter. Soon after the passage of the Ordinance, Roy ceased publication of the *Mirat-ul-Akhbar*.

Prophet Ram Mohan Roy And The Status Quo

Freedom was an ideal Roy deeply cherished, not only for Indians but for all the people of the world. He loved India, but was not a narrow patriot. He was a "nationalist-internationalist," i.e., his cosmopolitan sympathies made him look upon citizens of all nations as brothers and sisters, and he sorrowed for those who were unjustly oppressed.

Roy knew the history of Europe intimately and followed the rise and fall of freedom as if it were taking place in his own land. He was deeply anguished when he heard the Neapolitans, after forcing a constitution from their despotic king, were thrown back into servitude by the intervention of Austrian troops. So grieved was he that he canceled a social engagement with a friend. On the other hand, he was thrilled by the news of the establishment of a constitutional government in Spain and gave a public dinner party in the Town Hall to celebrate the occasion. He was similarly pleased to hear of the victory of the liberal party in the Portuguese Civil War. He wrote to Woodforde, August 22, 1833: "the news from Portugal is highly gratifying though another struggle is still expected."[27]

In connection with the French Revolution, when he received the report in Calcutta of the famous "Three Days" (July 27–29, 1830), it was reported that "so great was his enthusiasm that he could think and talk of nothing else!"[28] An outspoken advocate of Catholic emancipation, through the pages of the *Mirat-ul-Akhbar,* Roy even publicly criticized the British for their autocratic treatment of the Irish Catholics.[29]

The foregoing discussion clearly attests to the claim that Raja Ram Mohan Roy was "the first great modern International Ambassador."[30] In the schemes of lesser men, politics always divides, but with this world statesman, politics was a unifying force. He dreamed of a world united. In a letter to the Minister of Foreign Affairs of France, he revealed his plans for a Congress of all nations in which to settle international disputes. For Roy to conceive a "League of Nations" a century before the League of Nations became a reality, he had to be "a man of universal sympathies, profound interest in human destiny and far-sighted vision."[31] But at the root of it all was his deep commitment to liberty—liberty of social intercourse, of movement, of belief, of expression—and he was an undaunted champion of that liberty for his own land as well as those of Europe and the New World.

Yet how could a man with such sympathies for liberal and nationalist movements abroad reconcile these feelings with the political domination of his own homeland?

To answer this question several factors about the course Roy chose need to be emphasized. First, while Roy did not have the opportunity to choose his political circumstances, he did make every effort to liberalize those circumstances. Even his critics admit that within the colonial framework, Ram Mohan blazed the trail for several generations of moderate constitutionalist agitation and pioneered protest over such issues as Indianization of services, trial by jury, separation of powers, freedom of the press, and consultation with Indian landlords, merchants, and officials on legislative matters. Wrote one critic: "His critique of the zamindari system and plea for an absolute ban on 'any further increase of rent on any pretence whatsoever' strikes a sympathetic chord in progressive hearts even today."[32]

Given his circumstances, to call *this level* of agitation "moderate" lacks the historical appreciation that comes when Roy is judged in the light of his peers. For instance, the leaders of the Dharma Sabha found no cause for distress under the government, even when the government was reacting negatively towards its appeal in behalf of the practice of *sati*.[33]

By contrast, Ram Mohan was never quiet or willing to be silenced. He made so much political noise through his newspapers that he was branded a fomentor of public unrest. He not only agitated for good government, but also undertook his political reforms in the hope of the ultimate substitution of good government by *self-government*. The fact was that in Roy's day the Western system of education was an instrument by which an *elite*, allied to the British rulers, could be created, but British rulers knew there was a danger that the heady wine of Western thought might also produce social revolutionaries of one kind or another who would end up as political radicals. For this reason there was initial opposition by the British rulers to Western education, particularly when they realized that a small but self-conscious intellectual elite keenly desired it.[34] When the cause of Western education was won, Ram Mohan concluded "that the British rulers had opted for India's modernisation as a matter of enlightened self-interest."[35] There is little doubt that Roy anticipated that within a matter of two generations, under a benevolent and enlightened leadership, the historical forces nurtured by education would ripen and India would stand on its own political feet.

Roy's hope for independence was first religious and then political. The failure to read Roy's political ideas in their religious context makes it possible to assess him as a political moderate. But Ram Mohan was not a moderate. He was a modernizer because his Vedantic philosophy saw man as possessed of the same "natural rights" as were being published abroad in Europe under the impact of the French Revolution.

From the standpoint of hindsight, Ram Mohan's hopes for independence were misplaced. His admiration of the British and his reliance upon the system were so great that he failed to perceive the essentially acquisitive character of the colonial mind. Perhaps this was inevitable within the context of his time and place. But, whereas it took India two hundred years to win her independence, Roy was only prepared to wait forty or fifty years. What would he have recommended at the end of this period had freedom not been forthcoming? His answer is clear. *An India come of age* should have "the spirit as well as the inclination to resist effectually." India could prove "an ally of the British Empire or troublesome and annoying as a determined enemy."[36]

Ram Mohan Roy and Prophetic Authority

Roy illustrates the ageless quality of the prophet, for though he lived in the nineteenth century, he speaks eloquently to our times. His campaign for liberty provides a case study of prophetic religion and politics. A key factor in this case is the question of authority, internal and external.

A distinctive feature of prophetic consciousness is the "call" to ministry. At first glance it appears that the appellation of "prophet" is ill-suited to the Raja because, in the Judeo-Christian tradition, the call is attended by abnormal psychical characteristics. Hebrew prophets felt the call as an *external compulsion* often accompanied by visions, trances, and sometimes, cataleptic states. Within that culture, these served as their badge of authority.

Before we allow our Western cultural perceptions to identify these external and abnormal psychical elements as intrinsic to the prophetic consciousness, we must recognize that they can be sufficiently explained in terms of Hebrew psychology and theology, and that with the maturation of their religion, some of these phenomena diminished in the spiritual consciousness of the people.[37]

Vedantic psychology and metaphysics, with its conviction of the *internality* of the divine, did not lead Roy to claim that he was dramatically "called from on high" to campaign for liberty, but this does not deny that he, too, like Amos, Hosea, and the rest of the Hebrew prophets, felt an *irresistible compulsion* to carry through *an appointed task*. Freedom was his people's birthright, and he felt a humanitarian obligation, from which he could not extricate himself, to win back those rights. It was this obsession to stand up and be counted, even at the risk of his life, that invested his mission with an authority not of men.

A second factor contributing to the working of Roy's prophetic consciousness and reinforcing its conviction of internal authority was his communion with the divine and his sympathy with his fellow men, especially the downtrodden. As a result, Roy's writings are living monuments to religion and morality, and his life and labors bear witness to the influence of these ideals. People who fought beside him saw in him the embodiment of a profoundly humanistic religion. He was not just the *voice* but the *vehicle* of those ideals which began to stir the Indian giant to awaken from its long sleep of medieval darkness. He was able to kindle this national renascence because he translated his religion and morality to sympathy with the entire nation, even in the midst of denouncing its shoddier side, and thus served as an effective link between the demands of religion and the demands of the Raj. Hosea and Jeremiah, for similar reasons, forged similar bonds between Yahweh and Israel.

Turning from the man to his message, the question of authority emerged when Roy's interpretation of Hinduism clashed with the prevailing bastions of orthodoxy. Threatened by the incursions of the government and the missionaries, Hinduism became even more rigid, emphasizing the external marks of the faith. Roy found this preoccupation with caste and ritual superstitious, embarrassing, and hence made the characteristically prophetic move of returning to the source—to the pristine revelation of *Sanatana Dharma* (Eternal Religion). The slogan, "Back to the Vedas," so frequently on the lips of subsequent prophets, began with Roy's translation of the Upanishads. He explains: "This work will, I trust, by explaining to my countrymen the real spirit of the Hindoo Scriptures, which is but the declaration of the unity of God, tend in a great degree to correct the erroneous conceptions, which have prevailed with regard to the doctrines they inculcate."[38]

In somewhat similar fashion, the Hebrew prophets leaped the institutional hurdles by a return to the faith of Abraham, Isaac and Jacob. The prophet has little difficulty reading contemporary meanings into ancient times and texts because he believes he has tapped the sources of life and treats particular scriptures as the historical molds in which the Eternal Spirit has periodically and progressively poured forth of itself. Demands of humanity and justice thus loom larger than the dictates of custom and ritual. This clash of values inevitably creates a division in the household of faith (and Roy was piously pummeled by the Orthodox), but prophecy thrives on persecution.

Moving from the issue of internal authority to those of external authority, we find the prophet can be fast and flexible; both friend and foe. Roy was a friend of the British, honored by the king, and confidante of viceroys. He subscribed to the British policy of tutelage, and respected their religion and culture, especially their democratic institutions. But none of this admiration prevented him from public agitation. India might have been the jewel in the Crown, but Roy was the thorn in the flesh of its administrators. As friend, he identified with British ideals, but when they violated democratic principles, he used those very tools to attack them. In the case of censorship, the government tried to justify the infringement of the press on the grounds that Indians were not mature enough to handle freedom, but Roy reminded the Christian rulers that if there were any incapacity it was not due to lack of gifts but of opportunity. The underlying racism was a denial of religion which affirms a common creator and common humanity. He thus used the authority of religion to judge the authority of regime, and refused to grant to Caesar that which did not belong to Caesar.

Finally, prophetic religion, being transcendent, is global in its mission. Roy's dream went beyond India and Asia to a world united in peace and prosperity. He was a nationalist precisely because he was first an internationalist. Chronologically, nationalism precedes internationalism, but within the dynamics of prophetic religion the order is reversed. In the singular eye of the prophet, the One precedes the many, for the many exist in the One; are worthy of separate dignity and destiny because they proceed from the One; and are somehow blunderingly moving toward the One in spite of their ignorant prejudices.

Notes

1. R. C. Majumdar, H. C. Raychaudhuri, K. K. Datta, *Advanced History of India* (London: Macmillan, 1960), 813.
2. Vincent A. Smith, *The Oxford History of India*, 3d. ed., ed. Percival Spear (Oxford: Clarendon Press, 1958), 733.
3. Ibid.
4. Ibid.
5. Sophia D. Collet, *The Life and Letters of Raja Rammohun Roy*, ed. D. K. Biswas and P. C. Ganguli (Calcutta: Sadharan Brahmo Samaj, 1962), 303.
6. Ibid., 213.
7. *The English Works of Raja Rammohun Roy*, ed. Kalidas Nag and Debajyoti Burman, pt. 3 (Calcutta: Sadharan Brahmo Samaj, 1946), 137–38.
8. Ibid., pt. 2, 20.
9. Ibid., pt. 2, 3.
10. Ibid., pt. 2, 4.
11. Brajendranath Seal, "Rammohun Roy, The Universal Man," in *Father of Modern India,* ed. S. C. Chakravarti (Calcutta: Rammohun Roy Centenary Committee, 1935), 108.
12. *Works,* pt. 4, 71–72.
13. Ibid., pt. 7, 177–78.

14. Ibid., pt. 3, 82–83.
15. Ibid., pt. 3, 83–85.
16. Collet, 386.
17. Rajani Kanta Guha, "Rammohun and Politics," in *The Father of Modern India*, 301.
18. Guha, 302.
19. J. K. Majumdar, *Raja Rammohun Roy and Progressive Movements in India* (Calcutta: Art Press, 1961), 299.
20. Bayley, "Note on the Native Press", October 10, 1822, *Modern Review* (1928): 562.
21. *The Calcutta Journal*, 14 February 1823.
22. Ibid., 15 April 1823.
23. *Mirat-ul-Akhbar*, 4 April 1823, quoted by *Calcutta Journal*, 10 April 1823.
24. Collet, 428.
25. Ibid., 177.
26. Ibid.
27. *Works*, pt. 4, 93.
28. James Sutherland, "Reminiscences of Rammohun Roy," *India Gazette*, 18 February 1834, reprinted in *Calcutta Review* 57, no. 1, 61.
29. *Works*, pt. 4, 94.
30. Sarojini Naidu, "Tribute to Rammohun," *Father of Modern India*, 236.
31. Tara Chand, *History of the Freedom Movement in India*, vol. 11 (Delhi: Ministry of Information and Broadcasting, Government of India, 1967), 260.
32. Sumit Sarkar, "Rammohun Roy and the Break with the Past," in *Rammohun Roy and the Process of Modernization in India*, ed. V. C. Joshi (Delhi: Vikas Publishing House, 1975), 59–60.
33. Majumdar, 330.
34. B. N. Ganguli, "Rammohun: His Political and Economic Thought," in *Rammohun Roy: A Bi-Centenary Tribute*, ed. Niharranjan Ray (Delhi: National Book Trust, 1974), 48.
35. Ibid., 48.
36. Extracts from a letter to J. Crawford, 18 August 1828 in *Works*, 297.
37. H. Wheeler Robinson, *The Religious Ideas of the Old Testament* (London: Duckworth, 1947), 115.
38. *Works*, pt. 2, 11.

PART TWO
PROPHETIC RELIGION
EMERGING AT THE
GRASS ROOTS

5

Liberation Theology in Latin America: Sociological Problems of Interpretation and Explanation

ROLAND ROBERTSON

THE term liberation theology has acquired a wide range of referents. It is most closely associated in the minds of many intellectuals with the societies where it initially became, and has since become even more, conspicuous—namely, those of Latin America. It is important at the outset, however, to emphasize that since the mid-1960s there have developed liberation theologies outside the context of Latin American Catholicism. A number of branches of Protestantism have developed parallel, intersecting or alternative forms of liberation theology (while Latin American liberation theology has not been without Protestant input); there are theologies of liberation referring to racial groups (notably blacks); there are liberation theologies of continents other than Latin America and specific groups within continents (such as Asian Christians), as well as Third World theologies of liberation; there are feminist liberation theologies; and so on. Moreover, in the context of sociological as opposed to theological discussion *per se* it is of significance to note that

73

one of the major carriers of Latin American liberation theology—
namely, the base community—has parallels, *inter alia,* in Europe,
North America and South East Asia.[1]

Nevertheless my central concern here is with the characteristics,
growth, and significance of liberation theology as a movement in Latin
America. Even though, as I have indicated, liberation theology has
not been an exclusively Catholic concern in Central and South America, I will consider it and some of its carriers primarily in reference
to Latin American Catholicism. Notwithstanding the fact that Latin American liberation theology is part of a global trend toward "political religion" and political theology—as well as manifesting a global
concern with the problematic relationship between indigenous and
trans-societal or supra-societal forms of doctrine and ritual—there
is something very distinctive about its growth and impact since the
late 1960s. Moreover, because of the size of the Latin American
Church as a whole (for example, Brazil is the country with the
largest number and Latin America is the continent with the highest
concentration of professing Catholics in the world)[2] and the increasing significance of Latin America in world affairs (not to mention the fact that the most concentrated intellectual, political, and
social expression of theologies of liberation have emanated from
Latin America) there are obvious reasons for starting with that continent in any attempt to come to sociological terms with the contemporary phenomenon of liberation theology. I will discuss three
main issues: (1) the characteristics and recent history of liberation
theology in Latin America; (2) central problems of interpretation and orientation in analyzing the latter; and (3) major aspects
of the historical-sociological explanation of the rise and growth of
liberation theology as a loosely-patterned Latin American movement.

Characteristics and Manifest History
of Liberation Theology

What is liberation theology? Very simply, it can be defined as that set of
ideas which express in self-proclaimed theological terms: (1) that an
indifference to political concerns actually constitutes a political-
ideological choice and that thus all theology has been and is political;
(2) that churches have frequently been collaborators (at least by default)
with exploitative groups or quasi-groups, ruling classes, or agencies of
imperialism; (3) that religion in its essence is concerned with human
fulfillment; (4) that exploitation has drastically hindered the latter,

notably among the most materially impoverished, excluded or marginal; (5) that the conditions that sustain the latter must comprise a significant part of modern theology, which itself should systematically connect concern with spirituality to political, economic and social issues; and (6) that active attempts should be made to alter the circumstances which produce exploitation and alienation. Each form of liberation theology has manifested its own distinctive emphasis within this broad prospectus (which is *not* to say that the prospectus itself explicitly preceded the crystallization of the specific forms). In the case of the kind of liberation theology which has developed in Latin America since the mid-1960s, the following more specific claims may be found:[3]

(1)   That contemporary Latin America's circumstances of exploitation, oppression, and deprivation results from a long history of imperialist control, beginning with the Spanish and the Portuguese in the sixteenth century and culminating with the United States Americans in the modern period;

(2)   That the present Latin American, as well as the Third World circumstance as a whole, is a consequence of the operation of a world-system of economic and political exploitation (with some liberationists claiming that Latin America constitutes a global socio-theological vanguard in its attempt to change the world system);

(3)   That the traditional scholastic theological style has been fundamentally ahistorical and "eternalistic," whereas a concern with concrete circumstances of inter-societal and intra-societal exploitation demands an approach which is historical and (r)evolutionary;

(4)   That the Catholic church has—and not only in Latin America—tended to promote ahistoricity and inhibit concern with sociocultural (r)evolution and the history of mankind;

(5)   That, on the other hand, since at least the end of the nineteenth century the church has shown official interest in social questions and that, particularly since Vatican II, the teachings of the church have been oriented in the direction of a greater concern with the material condition of humanity (more specifically, the poor, marginal, and excluded);

(6)   That modern theology requires a hermeneutical format which, starting from modern circumstances of exploitation, reinterprets human—including religious—history in such a way as to both validate the interpretive starting point within the modern circumstances and the reading of history upon which it is based;

(7)   That it follows that theology should be existentialist rather than

essentialist, christocentric (although in some respects Moses is as paradigmatically significant as is Christ) and homocentric rather than theocentric, inductive rather than deductive, biblical and circumstantial rather than scholastically theological;

(8)   That a traditional doctrinal preoccupation with inner spirituality and personal sin has sustained the neglect of the idea that sin can and should be regarded as a structural property and that salvation should be thought of as collective and historical;

(9)   That dominant theologies commence with the challenge of the *non*-believer (which is an inappropriate category for Latin America) rather than from "the man who is not a man";

(10)   That theology should be directed, via "social-science analysis," to the promotion of concern with orthopraxis (itself a way of knowing) rather than with orthodoxy—concretely, an orthopraxis which favors the poor and sees the church as being constituted by "the people";

(11)   That the actions undertaken within the focus upon orthopraxis should be geared to the establishment of a terrestrial Kingdom of God;

(12)   That the envisaged Kingdom would take the form of—and thus that present actions should be directed at establishing—societies and a world system based upon principles of communality and egalitarianism (as opposed to exploitative hierarchy).

In stating the essential features of the crystallization and diffusion of liberation theology two main themes should be emphasized. First, there is the issue of the manifest, recent history of the latter; second, there is the matter of its organizational and social vehicles. Thus, leaving the more complex task of discussing the roots of liberation theology for later, the modern Latin American notion of theology centering upon the idea of liberation was first fully expressed by the Peruvian Catholic Gustavo Gutiérrez in the late 1960s—most elaborately in his *A Theology of Liberation* (1973), which contains a number of the ideas in the second (as well as the first) of the itemizations noted above. However, in the historiography of pro-liberationism almost equal status is often accorded to a non- (or in a special sense a pre-) theological work—namely that of the Brazilian educationist Paulo Friere, whose *Pedagogy of the Oppressed* (1970) has won him fame not merely among educationists across the world but also as a secular precursor and subsequently an ingredient of the liberation theology explicitly espoused by Gutiérrez. Moreover, it is not an exaggeration to say that apart from very specific questions—such as those concerning the political side of worship, the interpretation of the life of Christ, or the implications for personal faith of liberation theology—many of the major features of the ideational and praxiological side of liberation theology as a socio-cultural movement are to be found in the works of Friere and Gutiérrez. For the most part, other significant contributors have written as exegetes or elaborators, one exception to that generalization being those few who have been specifically preoccupied with the question of the relationship between liberationist Christianity and Marxist thought. Some Latin American Protestant theologians have added to the Gutiérrezian perspective by making special connections between aspects of Protestant thought and Catholicism-based liberationism; in any case, Protestant liberation theology in Latin America has not been entirely unautonomous.[4]

Two major, general trends have developed among liberation theologians, trends which have hinged considerably upon orientations to Friere's theme of *conscientization*, i.e., consciousness-raising with respect to the concrete circumstances in which individuals, particularly the oppressed, find themselves. The more conservative trend involves elaboration of the idea of liberation without linking it to the pedagogical and praxiological principle of conscientization. In other words, liberation theology remains in this perspective a matter of theological and historical reflection. At the more radical end of the continuum one finds the position presented by the Uruguayan Juan Luis Segundo in *The Liberation of Theology* (1976). Segundo's form of liberation theology in effect envisages the end of theology via the demythologizing processes of conscientization. Conscientization and the more scholarly processes of historicization involve, in that perspective, an end to abstract doctrines of human nature; for critical discourse must, as McCann (1981, 201) says, "be appropriate to the structures of meaning inherent in the historical moment." Clearly, it is this second strand of liberationism which is the more open to rapprochement with Marxist activism. However, only a small number of liberationist intellectuals (e.g., Berryman, 1984) have been publicly concerned with the *minutiae* of that issue.

Gutiérrez' earliest well-noted statement on the idea of a theology of liberation was presented at a conference immediately preceding the Medellín conference of Latin America episcopacies (CELAM) in 1968 (a year of expression of rebellious and revolutionary sentiment in many parts of the globe), although he had already made a significant impact at a conference organized by the social philosopher and articulator of radical Latin American thought, Ivan Illich, in 1964 and had followed that presentation with others at gatherings of Catholic intellectuals. The Medellín conference is by now well recognized as constituting a critical turning point in Latin American Catholicism. (It also may well come to be regarded as a critical juncture in Latin American history as a whole, conceivably in the history of the Catholic church and, thus, of the modern world.) The Medellín conference (which followed the inconsequential founding conference of national episcopacies in 1955) concluded that the Latin American continent was living in "a situation of sin." Class oppression, international imperialism, and "institutionalized violence" on the part of dominant classes were held responsible for the poverty and circumstance of exploitation of the lower classes and the excluded. It was agreed that special efforts should be made to promote the education of the poor and develop popular organizations, notably the base communities.

In spite of the expression of these ideas—stated mainly in three out of a total of sixteen sections—the final Medellín document was not in its overall textual sweep a greatly radical document. Penny Lernoux (1979, 12) has noted that in spite of the "strong social criticism and prophetic commitment" in the sections on justice, peace, and poverty, the document, even in its most critical passages "failed to analyze the causes of 'institutionalized violence' or offer an alternative, still holding out for a 'third way' between communism and capitalism" (which had been the policy of and the rationale for supporting Christian Democratic parties in Latin America). However, "once committed to official paper . . . words take on a life of their own, and so it was with the Medellín Conclusions, certain phrases of which, such as 'institutionalized violence,' were written into the Magna Carta of a socially activist Church."

Liberation, Marxism, and Base Communities

It is at precisely this interpretive juncture that a problem arises as to the link between liberation theology and Marxist ideology. While there can be no doubt that much writing under the banner of liberation theology have attempted to connect it—at least rhetorically—to Marxist thought (as have many of its opponents), the broader question arises as to whether study of liberation-theology as a *movement* should include analysis of trends in Latin American Marxism as such. In the present context such analysis is impossible. Nevertheless my own view is that a comprehensive understanding of liberation theology, both as a cultural phenomenon and as a loosely organized movement, requires wide-ranging discussion of both Latin American Marxist and socialist thought, on the one hand, and Marxist and secular socialist movements, on the other. Here I must heavily compromise by indicating a few of the more salient developments.[5]

While one can find examples of minor connections between radical

Catholicism and Marxist ideas following the beginnings of attention to Marxist writings among circles of Latin American intellectuals in the later years of the nineteenth century, it was not until the 1960s that there crystallized a wide perception of a problem as to a positive relationship between Catholicism and Marxism. During that period the idea of Christian Democracy—as pointing beyond both capitalism and communism—became thematized, and Christian Democratic political parties developed, only to be dealt a critical blow with the triumph and then overthrow of the democratically-elected Allende regime in Chile.[6] Moreover, partly under the influence of the example of Cuba and then in response to the installation of particularly authoritarian regimes in a number of Latin American countries in the mid-1960s there were signs of a shift towards a more Marxist-oriented priesthood, a major paradigmatic case being that of the Colombian, Camilo Torres. By the early 1960s Torres was insisting that Marxist revolutionaries need not be atheistic, that socialism is compatible with Christianity, and that Christians and Marxists should actively collaborate in order to promote societal change. Although he left the priesthood in a formal sense, Torres never renounced his Catholicism. He died fighting with the Colombian Army of National Liberation in 1966.

However, of greater significance than the mythic status of Torres, was the development of the Christians for Socialism movement in Chile (which he partly inspired). Developed in the late 1960s, and against the backdrop of significant relaxation of episcopal condemnation of Marxism, the Christians for Socialism movement (which included Protestants and was part of a wider international movement) grew rapidly after the election of Allende in 1970, although it lasted in a formal sense only from 1971 until 1973 in Chile. The position of its adherents involved a shift to the left, toward Allendean Marxism and away from the third-stance (i.e., between and beyond capitalism and communism) of the Christian Democrats. By the early 1970s as many as one Chilean priest in eight supported Christians for Socialism. The views expressed at the first international meeting of Christian Socialists in Santiago on issues of injustice, poverty, and suffering were close to the kinds of ideas developing in more professedly theological vein in pristine liberation theology. Indeed, Gutiérrez, Segundo, and other prominent liberation theologians went to Chile to advise Christians for Socialism and groups connected to the latter. Moreover, within the Christians for Socialism movement there was clear expression of opposition to the Catholic leadership and a tilting toward the Marxist idea that religion is embedded in the alienation of capitalist society (and thus that religious needs may disappear with the "humanization" which opposes alienation). Many Christians for Socialism echoed Castro's call for a strategic alliance between Marxists and revolutionary Christians. Like many other Latin American societies, Chile had experienced a large inflow of foreign priests and members of religious orders in the 1960s. That clerical group played a major part in the attempt to assimilate Marxism in the Allende years. In fact, of the eighty priests who openly heralded the Allendean transition to socialism in 1971, half were foreign-born (Smith 1982, 247-8).

Movements of the type, of which Christians for Socialism is the major example, emerged in various parts of Latin America in the late 1960s and early 1970s, notably the Movement for Third World Priests in Argentina and the National Office of Social Information (ONIS) in Peru.[7] Their significance is that they directed the concern of the more "socially-conscious" Latin American Catholics in an ideological direction and, at the same time, filtered socialist and neo-Marxist ideas—including dependency theories—towards the liberation theological position. They also exacerbated disillusionment with Christian Democratic tendencies which had seemingly been ineffective in stemming the tide of authoritarianism and class oppression and which had become associated with "modernization and development" theories (not least through the Alliance for Progress). Individual Christians for Socialism and members of related movements quite frequently became leaders of base communities.

Following the partial legitimation of liberationist ideas at Medellín, many Latin American theologians and left-oriented intellectuals were encouraged to believe that the Latin American church and perhaps the Catholic church as a whole could be pushed substantially in the liberationist direction. However, there were determined men in the Vatican, in European Catholic contexts, and within the Latin American church itself who were sufficiently disturbed by the Marxist overtones of liberation theology and/or the latter's implications for the structure of authority within the church to begin to mount a firm opposition. In the period of preparation for the third CELAM the battle lines were thus drawn. On the one hand, the conservatives attempted to impose, during the three years or so prior to the Puebla meeting of 1979, a "New Christendom" conception of Latin American Catholicism, which was a version of the old rejection of both capitalism and socialism but with particular emphasis upon the threat of Marxism. There were also attempts to characterize the base communities—which had been encouraged in the Medellín document and had grown considerably in number since that time—as vehicles of actual or potential Marxism. On the other hand, and not least because of the successful attempts to exclude them from Puebla, a number of the major liberation theologians and their supporters mounted a fierce defense of liberationism and the base communities.

The document issued at the conclusion of CELAM III actually condemned neither liberation theology nor the base communities. Moreover, it did not condemn Marxism. "The conservatives seem to have prevailed in the doctrinal sections, the progressives in the description of reality and in committing the Church firmly on the side of the poor" (Sandoval 1979, 41). However, in view of the lengths to which the CELAM secretariat and conservative European-church and Vatican officials had gone to stem the tide of liberation theology and its Marxian appurtenances, the liberationists and their North American and European supporters generally seem to have taken the view that Puebla constituted a strategic victory. Certainly the Puebla gathering concentrated attention on liberation theology in many parts of the world (in part because the Pope delivered the opening address). Sociologically speaking, Puebla led to the thematization (in a sense, the institutionalization) of "the problem of liberation theology." To that extent Puebla was certainly a victory for the liberationists (of whatever stripe).

Since Puebla there have been a number of dramatic developments of relevance to any consideration of liberation theology. The Vatican has attempted to bring a number of the more prominent liberation theologians into line and has attempted unsuccessfully to obtain the resignation of priests from the Nicaraguan revolutionary government. The base communities have increased in number—most notably in Brazil, Mexico, Peru, and Argentina—and have played a significant part in the Sandanistan revolution in Nicaragua and in the revolutionary movements in El Salvador and Guatemala. Catholic bishops (not necessarily liberationists in any strict sense) have adopted critical stances in relation to authoritarian regimes in El Salvador, Guatemala, Chile, Brazil (now on a democratic path), and elsewhere. Much more diffusely, there has apparently been an extension of lay involvement in the church across Latin America, as well as a marked increase in church-based discussions of social questions, often in modified forms of conscientization.

The base communities which have so rapidly increased in number (with a very heavy concentration in Brazil, where there may be as many as 60,000) began in the 1950s and early 1960s as experimental parish structures—notably in Panama and Brazil. Many of them developed in rural areas and particularly among the recent migrants to the *barrios* of large cities. The messages of Vatican II concerning the need for more evangelization, lay involvement, and greater emphasis upon social questions encouraged the growth of base communities, which were formally legitimated at Medellín and at Puebla, although the ideas lying behind base communities in Brazil largely predated the post-conciliar developments along such lines. In some Latin American locales the base communities were an outgrowth of the European worker-priest form of pastoral activity, while, in any case, all over the continent the long-standing shortage of priests (made worse and more evident by population growth and migration to the cities) stimulated the growth of base communities as well as the further importation of foreign priests. (In parts of Northeastern Brazil there is only one priest to as many as 150,000 people; in Bolivia as many as one-third of the priests are from overseas.)

Cleary (1985, 87–9) identifies three broad foundational forms of base community. The first of these is the most well-known and is largely post-Medellín (Brazil being a partial exception). It frequently involves a stress on direct use of the Bible, working for and with the poor, empowerment of the laity, consciousness raising, and development of the idea that the church is the people's church. Secondly, there is the form which has some of its roots in Catholic (and to a significant degree, Protestant) pentecostalism or charismaticism. This type of base community is more concerned with religious expression in strongly communalistic settings. The pentecostalists have been praised by church conservatives and condemned (for their other-worldly spiritualism) by liberationists. Finally, there is the *catechumenate,* the least prevalent form of base community and of Southern-European origin. Appealing more tó educated and middle-class individuals the *catechumenate* (originally in early Christianity a vehicle for baptismal preparation) facilitates what Cleary calls "intensive value-education for adults." It encourages discussion of values, comparison of values with actual behavior, and so on.

Within these three forms there is, however, considerable variation, as well as shading between them. It is the first and second forms which have received most attention as base communities and the former much more than the latter. (In fact some commentators reserve the category of base community exclusively for the first form.) In turn, the question has frequently been raised as to the degree to which theological and religious matters play a significant role in the operation of the communities and, if they do, whether and to what extent liberation-theological methods are employed. In regard to the first question, it is important to note that in some places—notably Nicaragua, Chile, El Salvador, and Guatemala—the base communities have often originated as or become purely secular-political or communal-economic collectivities, sometimes to the point of excluding those not dedicated to revolutionary principles.[8] With respect to the second question—the extent of application of liberation theology—there is, again, considerable variation. One has to be careful in linking the growth of liberation theology to the proliferation of base communities, for in areas of some South American countries, there has been little connection between the two developments, even with respect to the form of base community which is ongoingly concerned with concrete issues such as land tenure, water supply, and so on; while in others liberation theology has been closely applied and, indeed, liberation theologians closely involved, as in Peru (where many priests, nuns, and lay catechists are taught the techniques of organizing base communities by Gutiérrez and other liberation theologians).

Problems of Analysis and Explanation in Studying Liberation Theology

Relatively little has been written from a decidedly social-scientific point of view on Latin American (or other forms of) liberation theology, most of the rapidly growing literature on the subject being exegetic, theologically critical, or hortätory. Moreover, a large proportion, but certainly not all, of the favorable statements have been published by the Maryknoll publishing house, Orbis Books, which long ago adopted a heavily pro-liberationist position.[9] (Orbis has published at least seventy-five books of or on liberation theology.) In addressing liberation theology in a social-scientific vein, one is, for the most part, thus confronted by a field of polemical argument, so much so that in adopting a detached mode of analysis, one runs the risk of seeming insensitive to the undoubted sufferings of a large proportion of the Latin American people. I can only state that my aim here is to contribute to the establishment of a sense of "sociological proportion" in the understanding of liberation theology. Not only is such an aim intrinsically desirable from a scientific standpoint, it is also worth pursuing for the light it may, over the years, contribute to the amelioration of the conditions which liberationists rightly deplore.

When one comes to the specifics of the agreements and disagreements among self-consciously academic observers of the Latin American religious scene, one cannot but be struck by the extent to which a number of recent analysts of Latin American Catholicism and its relationships to societal—as well as broader continental and global—contexts find it necessary to distance, in varying degrees, their own writings from those of the most prestigious sociologist of Latin American religion of the years immediately before the clear-cut thematization of liberationist themes in the 1970s. I speak of Ivan Vallier. The most fundamental disagreement with Vallier hinges mainly on his commitment to a societal-modernization perspective (opposed, of course, by liberationists) which emphasized the development of Catholicism in Latin America with respect to its contemporary and future capacity to contribute to the making of a broad consensus on basic values in each society (Vallier 1970).

Vallier argued that the Catholic church in Latin America had passed through four main stages, prior to a fifth which he claimed was developing at the end of the 1960s. In the first stage the "church type" was *monopolistic*, in the sense that Catholicism was identified in the Iberian colonial period with the thrust of political society (the Christendom ideal). In the second stage—which occurred in the mid-nineteenth century, following the takeover of Latin American political systems by "liberal" rationalists from the forces of Spanish or Portuguese imperialism—the church became *political*. That entangled it in forging alliances with conservative or reactionary groups, against the largely anti-clerical political elites. The third stage was a *missionary* stage in which the church attempted, following "the failure of the political strategy to provide more than a temporary security," to combine the purposes of both insulating Catholics from secular society and engaging in missionary effort. That, in turn, led to another liability—namely, the establishment of the image of the church as authoritarian and domineering. The solution was seen to lie in a fourth strategy, that of *social development*, involving a reentry into the political realm by developing programs for social reform and change. The fifth stage constitutes in some respects a continuation of the latter. In this *cultural-pastoral* stage the church "assumes the role of spokesman for a higher moral order." It is involved in the promotion of programs of public service which are not the concern of existing governmental agencies. However, in a more discontinuous respect, the church is also, in the fifth phase, greatly concerned with activities at the local level that draw the individual into the church as a fully committed . . . layman. Thus religious and social needs, argued Vallier, are merged and the layman is, at least in theory, "able to live in a pluralistic, secular society as a Christian and a citizen simultaneously." Strategically speaking, "Catholic influence at this stage is intended to be most pervasive, yet the most subtle, consisting largely in a set of values and normative principles to guide individual actions." It is Vallier's image of the fifth phase which has particularly created controversy.

In announcing the arrival of the cultural-pastoral phase of Latin American Catholicism Vallier (1970, 79) went out of his way to isolate "a much publicized, and perhaps growing, pattern of Catholic activity that is assuming a radical revolutionary position . . ." He states:

> It may be that this growing wedge of Christian revolutionaries will gain a central position of power in the Church . . . In my judgment the key question is will their involvements in . . . political issues revive traditional ecclesiastical ambitions which, in essence, imply that "Catholics have all the answers"[?] If this occurs, religious cleavages and political cleavages will reinforce each other—a direction that can only exacerbate and prolong dissensions with *[sic]* societies that are already fragmented and hesitant. Consequently the Christian revolutionaries may be resurrecting an old strategy [i.e. that of monopolistic Christendom] instead of developing a new one.

In providing plausibility with respect to his prognosis concerning the contemporary period, Vallier indicated three trends of the late 1960s. First, he thought that the growth of other "religions," particularly Pentecostalism and communism, would push the church into greater religious specialization and at the same time into necessary innovations. The Catholic response to communism had been to encourage the development of Christian Democratic parties (notably, but not only, in Chile and Venezuela) in formal independence from the Catholic church; while the answer to the challenge of Pentecostalism (particularly in Brazil) had been an incipient trend in the direction of greater "congregationalism."

Second, Vallier saw hope in the growth of the industrial sector and in the process of rapid urbanization. These developments demanded attention from the church in the form of religio-moral engagement. Simultaneously the increasing significance of the urban poor and marginal status groups directed the church away from alliances with traditional elites and from commitment to traditional structures of organization. Third, and most important, was the constraint on the church to move away from "particularistic and confessional interests" to a concern with the human needs of all men and women and from defensive postures to organizational structures which stress long-term goals, flexible programs and the socialization of lay people in such a way as to combine secular and religious commitments. The church could no longer appeal to the poor and marginal purely in terms of supernatural salvation. Pentecostalist and spiritualist movements were taking over these functions. Catholicism's "burden" was "to underwrite, and if possible, give meaning to central secular values (Vallier 1970, 153).

The more recent commentators on Latin American religion and politics have, of course, written largely in reference to trends which were only in embryo at the time of Vallier's major contributions (Levine 1981, 1–55; Maduro 1982; Mutchler 1971, 3–18). More specifically, they have written with reference to the *increasing centrality* of "the Christian revolutionaries," the *relative failure* of Christian Democratic parties to find an institutional niche in Latin America; the *convergence* of Latin American "communism" and Christian revolutionism; and the strong shift to authoritarian corporatism in Latin America from the mid-1960s up to the very recent past. Moreover, even while there have certainly been major developments with respect to lay involvement in the church, the most striking form in which this has happened—namely, the base communities—does not straightforwardly conform to Vallier's image of their significance. This is most clearly the case with respect to those types of base community (major examples occurring in Chile and Nicaragua) which have emphatically involved fusion of theological and ideological issues, usually in strong favor of the latter, in relation to revolutionary praxis. Pentecostalism and spiritualism have, it is clear, spread remarkably widely in a number of Latin American societies since the late 1960s (sometimes with the encouragement of dictators). But, on the other hand, the division of functions between Catholicism and those movements concerned with introversional and *Gemeinschaft* spirituality is nowhere as neat as Vallier's prognosis suggested. In some areas there is mutual hostility between Pentecostalism and liberationism, while there is some evidence that Pentecostalism has been *an inspiration for* the base community with respect to the Pentecostalist emphasis upon the priesthood-of-all-believers and its "congregationalism." In the latter regard the emergent scenario would not be so much a division of religious functions but rather an ideologically conflictful duplication of such.

Both liberation theologians and their more directly ideological allies, as well as some recent "non-participant" social scientists, have firmly rejected the modernization theory to which Vallier subscribed. In its place has been put a world-systems or international-dependency theory of revolutionary societal change (with particular reference to the Third World, including Latin America) as well as rejection of the significance of the distinctions between the sacred and the secular and the religious and the political to which much modernization theory (and much of recent Vatican policy) has subscribed.

The first thrust entails, of course, rejection of so-called modernization theory's emphasis upon the relative autonomy of change at the societal level. To the neo-Marxist theorist of a world-systems or dependency persuasion, societal change is embedded in and largely the consequence of the operation of a capitalist world-system. That stance calls for the adoption, in praxiological vein, of what Wallerstein (1982, 289–300) calls anti-systemic strategies, i.e., strategies oriented toward *both* internal-societal revolutionary change and change of the world-system as a whole beyond its present capitalist circumstance. The second thrust denies the conventional liberal-democratic distinction between civil and political society. It substitutes for the liberal-democratic and modernizationist conception of consensus (which has in recent years been expressed in some forms of civil-religion theory) a more "compressed" image of the solidarity necessary both for revolutionary change and post-revolutionary stability. Whereas the liberal-democratic, modernizationist conception regards "consensus" as ideally "standing over" and constraining both religious and political spheres, the liberation-theoretic standpoint sees consensus as resting, in the undesirable past and present as well as in the revolutionary *and* post-revolutionary moments, on the *conflation* of the sacred and the secular and of the religious and the political. This is ironic since although "functionalism" has been rejected (often vehemently) by pro-liberationists, the conception of "religion" which they have adopted bears no small resemblance to the conflationary views of some *functionalists* that religion has to be defined in terms of its providing diffuse "models for and models of" action, interaction and organization (Robertson 1981).

In any case, the liberal-democratic and the liberationist conceptions of political systems and of the character of democracy clearly differ. While the former declares a commitment to differentiated realms of action and structure and veers away from notions of direct democracy and "totalistic" involvement in politics, the liberationists and their academic sympathizers adhere to what is sometimes called a "European" (more specifically, a Rousseauesque) as opposed to an "Anglo-Saxon" conception of democracy, one which stands against the differentiated, representational form associated with the "Anglo-Saxon" model.

It has been one of the points of some liberation theologians that, particularly since the injection of Aristotelian thinking into medieval Christian Catholicism, all of Western theology has been sociological. More, since the anthropologization and historicization of Western Protestant theology (notably in Germany) during the nineteenth century, Western theology has been severely constrained by the thematization of what may generally be called social problems and by the growing sense of the social and cultural grounding of theology and religion. The thematization of "social problems" can be traced, as far as the modern era is concerned, to the declining years of the nineteenth and the early years of the twentieth centuries. The Catholic church was constrained to focus on social problems by the rise of the labor movement, the developing clash between capitalism and socialism (especially of the Marxist variety), and "modernism"—although in the background stood the loss of the Italian papal states and the consequent circumstance of the transnational church having fully to confront (except in Vatican City itself) its position as a church operating in reference to the secular state. Within the Protestant churches in many parts of the world the same period saw increasing tension between those who sought, in the mode of *social* Christianity, to render Christianity socially relevant and those who, on the other hand, sought to emphasize the spiritual and more conservative side of Christian teachings and thus rejected the modern ethos. However, regardless of the particular stance adopted, the fact remains that "the social question" had been thematized and subsequent history has shown, as in the case of American fundamentalism, that initial opposition to concern with that issue leads inexorably to a direct, if reluctant, engagement with it.

Durkheim argued that, as modern consciousness manifested an increasing awareness of the social constraints upon and consequences of religion, the latter (and theology) would become increasingly sociological and political, notably with respect to issues of justice. Moreover, he daringly suggested that future innovations on the religious front would involve particular concern about the poor and underprivileged and concern on the part of the underprivileged about their lot (Pickering 1984, 476–99). That the working classes have, since Durkheim's time, been particularly religious, let alone innovatively so, on a global or even Christian-societal scale, is a thesis deserving of considerable skepticism. Nevertheless it is worth considering liberation theology in Durkheimian light. For, regardless of the question as to whether working class religiosity increases, there can be little doubt that concern *about* the latter *is* increasingly expressed in many modern religious forms. In any case, in Latin America popular, or folk, religiosity is extensive and susceptible to rapid and changing forms of mobilization. The *sociology* which is involved in attempts to mobilize the working class, the rural poor, and the *lumpenproletariat* in Latin America, in the name of "liberation," is particularly explicit. While it is the case that all sociological students of religious or ideological movements have to face the fact that the latter have their own "sociologies," the detailed explicitness of "liberation sociology" necessitates a degree of confrontation.

Insofar as theology and religion have become more explicitly and directly oriented to social matters it is, of course, inevitable that the issue of the nature and degree of *political* activity should arise and that in the process the sense of the secularity of the modern *state* will be sharpened. However, while there is a clear interest in the scope and power of the modern state among modern religious collectivities and movements there has been little sign of a serious political dimension emerging in modern theologies or religious doctrines. In fact, despite the crystallization of a conception (initially German) of political theology and the diffuse sense among liberationists that their theology suggests a non-liberal form of democratic government, precious little attention has been paid to the development of concrete images of political structure and process in a modern condition of the strong secular state facing widening religiomoral concern.

While many liberation theologians have come to reject the kind of political theology promoted in the German context—on the grounds that it fails to underwrite political *praxis* and is more concerned with abstract notions of identity and meaning of allegedly little relevance to the poor and oppressed of the Third World, they have not, in their advocacy of political engagement, done much more than provide extremely diffuse images of political process. Indeed, insofar as Latin American liberationists and their supporters have a theory of politics at all, it is largely characterized by its simple rejection of the corporatist policies advanced since the mid-1960s by the military on the pretext of national security in a large number of Latin American societies. In spite of the significance in liberationist mythology of the base community phenomenon, one is still left with the strong impression that the general thrust of liberation theology on its more political side is in the direction of a seizure of the state, with the structures of the latter being left more or less intact after the revolution but put to work for new ideological ends, in the name of "the popular state."

However, while it is an easy matter to fault liberation theology for its failure to develop a full-fledged conception of political process and structure, let alone a viable conception of political economy (Novak 1982, 298–314), the sociologist has to be extremely careful not to commit the fallacy of idealistic reductionism. Specifically, the sociologist should not consider liberation theology simply as a system of ideas—let alone regard the base community phenomenon *in toto* as an implementation of them. Liberation theology is located in a number of different Latin American (and other) *structural contexts*. It is simply bad sociology to assume that the only way to analyze the liberation movement is by confronting the ideas which it develops and promotes.

For Vallier (1970, 157) the analytical emphasis should have been put upon "the structural changes that are occurring between the Church (and its immediate institutional extensions) and the wider society," rather than "positive outputs flowing from manifest ideologies of change." This prescription suggests that in analyzing liberation theology as a movement we should be particularly sensitive to the specific ways in which it interacts with the church and with particular societal contexts rather than speaking as if it can only be "read" in terms of its own ideas and immediate practices. In this regard both pro- and anti-liberationists (Bruneau 1982, 1979; Smith 1982) tend to miss the mark.

What I am getting at is the need for a satisfactory analytical vantage point. Vallier's own position was clear. His overriding concern was with the contribution which the Catholic church in Latin America could make to processes of economic and political modernization, assuming the desirability of the liberal-democratic polity admired by Tocqueville (which formed the predicate for the type of functionalism upon which his own work was largely based). He was skeptical about the contribution which embryonic liberationism could make to the promotion of a form of autonomy-within-reciprocity in relation to the political, religious, and economic spheres. On the other hand, he did not live to witness the modern circumstance, nor did he, in any case, fully acknowledge the extent to which the state in Latin America (and in varying degrees across the world) has itself become, in modern times, a distinctively "moral"—or, indeed, quasi-religious—agency.[10] Thus those social scientists who have criticized Vallier for having too narrow a conception of "religion" and/or for being naive about the separability of religion and politics in our time certainly have a point. Nevertheless (not least because of the current shifts towards more democratic and responsive policies in South, if not in Central, America) the vantage point from which I suggest we should proceed is what might be called neo-Vallierian.

A neo-Vallierian standpoint with respect to the Latin American circumstance has the following basic features: It regards liberation theology as being *fundamentalistic* to the extent that it advocates the *conflation* of the political and religious realms (as well as a number of other conflations). In denying the autonomy of either realm—that is, in politicizing personal religiosity and religious doctrine, as well as in rendering politics as a realm for the working-out of absolute values—it encourages totalism in the face of societal complexity (be it all a complexity embodying not merely injustice but also a "heart of darkness"). On the other hand, liberationists have confronted a particularly (but perhaps not *the* most) formidable version of the modern, secular state, which itself has developed highly totalistic tendencies. They have, moreover, been operating within a church context which has traditionally been lacking in responsiveness to issues of human justice.

Thus the second main feature of what I am calling a neo-Vallierian perspective involves our regarding the current situation in Latin America as a very significant site for confronting one of the most pressing problems of the modern world: namely, the relationships between religion and politics, church and state, religious doctrine and political ideology, and ethics of absolute values and ethics of responsibility. In other words, rather than taking the political realm as given or conceiving it *solely* in the stereotypical terms of the liberal-democratic tradition, a neo-Vallierian stance allows for the emergence of new connections—technically, *interpenetrations*—between these domains. At the same time it does not fall into either the unreflective position whereby "the revolt of the oppressed" is seen as leading inexorably to a "higher" form of democracy and justice or, at the other extreme, the negatively critical position in which the ideas and "logical" implications of liberation theology are judged solely by their compatibility with idealized liberal-democratic conceptions of political process. Moreover, even though details cannot be provided here, such a stance involves regarding the state as a relatively independent actor, in rivalry with the church in the provision of "values."

A crucial aspect of the neo-Vallierian standpoint, as I have skeletally indicated, has to do with Vallier's own argument concerning structural changes in the relationship between the Latin American church and the wider society. One particularly interesting facet of the latter centers on the base communities; for there is a view held among non-liberationist Catholics (some of them, clearly, being in the Vatican) that the latter will long outlast and come to acquire much greater significance than liberation theology *per se* as a relatively distinct "revolutionary" movement. As I implied much earlier in this paper, we have insufficient knowledge of the base communities at the present time.[11] However, there is a reasonable possibility that they may indeed be contributing to the growth of citizenly, voluntaristic involvement in some South, if not Central, American polities in such a way as to attenuate severely the spiritualistic fatalism which has been so typical of the Latin American "masses" and, on the other hand, promote a relatively disciplined, indeed pragmatic, orientation to political activity. There are signs that such has already happened on a limited scale in Brazil (where there are links also between the base communities and the labor movement) and elsewhere. At the same time it may well be that the base communities' encouragement of lay involvement in church and extra-church activities and decision-making will provide the basis for a church which can (as Vallier hoped) remain disentangled from subservient collaboration with authoritarian regimes (or—as in the case of Mexico—promote a firmer basis than heretofore for value judgment upon the operation of the political system). Nevertheless one cannot completely ignore the view that, not for the first time, the Latin American church has legitimated a venture over which it has lost or will lose control. (The major previous occasion was the fascistic leanings of some Catholic Action groups in the 1930s and 1940s and the major modern possibility of such is Central America, notably Nicaragua, Guatemala, and El Salvador.) There is the further possibility that insofar as the trend, in evidence at this time of writing, away from political authoritarianism is sustained, the base communities will lose some of their *raison d'être* and thus their vitality or, as a variation on that possibility, a shift to either the more pietistic or the more pentacostalist form (or mixtures of both).

Finally, a more general and diffuse point concerning the sociological analysis of Latin American liberationism needs to be made, a point which has much to do with the fact that liberation theology has attempted to provide a thoroughgoing, partly social-scientific account of *its own* origins and *raison d'être*. One of the major tasks of the sociologists is (although a few deviant schools of sociology would deny this) to explain the rise of socio-cultural movements. The way in which such explanation will proceed is (positivism notwithstanding) greatly conditioned by the interpretive stance which is brought to the phenomenon in the first instance. The stance which I have attempted to justify involves steering beyond the external judgmental approach, on the one hand, and the internal, self-justificatory line, on the other. With that in mind I turn to outlining what I take to be the major ingredients of an historical-sociological explanation of the rise of liberation theology (as opposed to a comprehensive explanation *per se*).

Caveats on the Social Context of Liberation Theology

In a relatively brief overview of the emergence of liberation theology it is possible only to cite a few salient facts of Latin American history. In that connection I want to draw attention to a small number of issues of which serious Latin Americanists are aware but which, on the other hand, even relatively perspicuous writers on Latin America have frequently neglected.

Contrary to the diffuse conventional wisdom, it is misleading to characterize Latin America as a "Catholic continent." The facts are that: Central and South America are among the least evangelized areas of the world; the ostensibly dominant church collectivities in Latin America have had relatively little power with respect to most of the countries in which they have been situated; in spite of attempts to facilitate the power of Rome, Lisbon, or Madrid, the people of Latin America have often resisted organized Catholicism; and while it is true that much of Latin America was subject to a fusion of imperial-political and clerical-religious control prior to the series of successful moves toward independence from Spain (in the case of Brazil, from Portugal) in the nineteenth century, most Latin Americans have been subject for at least the last one-hundred-and-fifty years to a form of explicitly secular-state control. Throughout its history Latin America has suffered, by any standards, from a shortage of priests and so-called religions, with many rural areas (in more recent times, urban areas also) being virtually without an official church presence. Even where that has not been the case, Catholicism has either coexisted with—not infrequently been psychoculturally subordinated to—one or another form of Amerindian or Amerafrican folk religion or, as in Brazil stood beside thaumaturgical cults, many members of which have been nominal Catholics (see Wilson 1973, 106–31).

Thus when one is talking about the dramatic shift in Latin American Catholicism during the period of the crystallization and growth of liberation theology one has to keep firmly in mind that much of this shift has occurred in specific reference to a population which is, on average, only about twenty percent Catholic in the sense of active involvement in the life of the church. Moreover, this population has not been subject (in spite of a baptismal rate of about ninety percent) to disciplined internalization of Catholic doctrine (which until very recent times took a basically medieval, pre-Reformation form in Latin America).[12] This raises very important questions about the degree to which liberation theology and its appurtenances constitute an indigenous or an autochthonous development. Those questions fall into two main categories: On the one hand, there is a set of queries concerning the degree to which liberation theology as an intellectual product derives from distinctively Latin American culture and experience. On the other hand, there is a cluster of questions relating to the issue of the relationship between new religious thrusts in Latin America and pre-conquistador culture and experience.

As far as the first question is concerned, it should be noted that not merely did a considerable proportion of the more influential Latin American theologians receive academic training in Europe (particularly in the 1960s period of revitalized Marxism and radical theology), but that since the post-Vatican II interest in evangelization, "humanization," lay involvement, individual conscience, and openness to other religions increased. With respect to a rapidly growing and more urban population, many foreign priests went to work in Latin America (although that phenomenon was by no means new to the continent). It was along those lines that many of the hermeneutical, philosophical and Marxist-sociological ideas which have become so evident in Latin America in recent years were diffused. There is thus a supportable thesis to the effect that liberation theology is not a genuinely autochthonous movement (in the sense of having developed *de novo* in Latin America). However, it must be stressed that even though many of the analytical tools of liberation theology have been "foreign made," they have been put to work on distinctively Latin American themes (which, in turn, have been adapted to liberationism on other continents). Among the latter are the place of Latin America in world history and within the contemporary world-system. Latin America is regarded as a kind of continental vanguard in relation to the Third World, the place which leads human history in the direction of the Kingdom of God.

A special place in that historical scenario is sometimes found for the indigenous religions of Latin America—most notably those of the Incas and the Aztecs. In that respect it is important to note that not merely traditional Latin American Catholicism but also the Amerindian religions have for a long time manifested anti-capitalist sentiments.[13] Thus the anti-capitalism of liberation theology has deep roots in Latin American religion and does not derive in any facile sense from contemporary Marxism (which, many liberation theologians insist, provides mainly a *method* for uniting theory and practice in relation to the class barriers which inhibit the realization of genuine Christianity). Even more broadly speaking, liberation theology may be seen as a movement which seeks to provide an understanding of the entirety of Latin American experience (relative to the history of mankind) in such a way as to see the present circumstance as a long-term, delayed consequence of the Southwest European conquest of Latin America. Even though there are considerable dangers in generalizing across South and Central America as far as social conjunctions of church and state, the precise histories and societal orientations of national churches, and so on, are concerned, there is much less sociological risk involved in speaking relatively homogeneously of Latin American identity and global experience. Thus while a very circumscribed notion of "indige-nous" would involve the question of the degree to which pre-conquistador religion *per se* is a core feature of liberationism (a question which cannot be answered in the affirmative), a broader conception (which, on a continuum, veers towards autochthony) would raise the question as to the long-term continuity of Latin American experience and its manifestation in liberationism.

One major aspect of long-term continuity has to do with Latin American Catholic millennialism. The initial conquest of Latin America was perceived by many Spanish and Portuguese as a millennial mission to the West, following the expulsion of Islam from Iberia and the confinement of Protestantism to Northern Europe. It is not farfetched to see Latin American Catholicism in the late twentieth century as still constrained by this vision and the conflict within the Latin American church as being in part bounded by the kind of counter-Reformational Catholicism which has for so long prevailed in Latin America. A second major aspect of long-term continuity is directly related to the theme of Amerindian religion, notably the ways in which various cultic commitments—such as those involving shrines of the Virgin in Mexico and Paraguay—constitute rallying points with respect to the overthrow of oppressors, and manifestations of religious-nationalist sentiment. To some extent these cultic commitments are related to tensions within the Latin American church concerning the locus of authority. (In any case, it should be emphasized that there are currently two major, intersecting conflicts within the Latin American church and within the church as a whole *vis à vis* Latin America: one about Marxism and liberation theology, the other about episcopal and Vatican authority.)

A third theme within the perspective of long-term continuity is, perhaps, of even greater significance. This centers on the ways in and degrees to which modern Latin American "religion-society" relations are continuous with what Martin calls "the Latin Pattern." Martin maintains that the "South American (extended Latin) Pattern" has provided an opportunity for limiting the circumstance in which "massive religious beliefs, ethos and institutions [confront] massive secularist beliefs, ethos and institutions"—mainly because Latin Ameri-ca developed when European Catholicism shifted from the left to the center. Thus it is speculated that in the extended-Latin pattern there may arise "a substantial Catholic left ameliorating the secularist militan-cy of the left as a whole. At this juncture the organicist element in Catholicism may discover useful congruences with socialism" (Martin 1978, 6–7).

Use of this perspective would involve careful consideration of the possibility that the liberationist movement may be as much a restraint on Marxism in Latin America (at least in some societies) as it is a carrier of the conflict-producing, "scientistic materialism" so opposed by the Vatican and the Catholic right wing. It also draws attention to the problem of the degree to which there is a distinctive "deep-code" that shapes the operation of Latin American politics and, more broadly, the structures of authority in Latin America. In the latter regard Baum (1980, 85–7) has maintained that a major feature of societal functioning and change in Latin America is (as an extension of an Iberian tendency) commitment to the view that "whosoever gains supremacy, for however long, claims the role of promulgator of the interests of all." It was precisely this tendency which Vallier hoped could be broken by the church and yet which he feared would be exacerbated by the more radical forms of nascent liberationism.

Ever since the rise of the secular state in Latin America in the nineteenth century, the church has been under threat with respect to its influence and indeed, except for certain phases in the present century, the church has largely confined its ministrations to the comforting of the poor with respect to the rewards which they will receive in the afterlife. This became particularly problematic with the strong swing toward authoritarian corporatism in the 1960s and the ensuing development of the doctrine of national security which in effect put a number of Latin American societies on a military basis and made militarism a kind of state ideology. The sharp swing toward authoritarian corporatism occurred shortly after Vatican II, which has had a very significant impact on the shape of Latin American theology and religious practice. Indeed some commentators, and probably a number of Vatican officials, regard liberationism as a direct *product* of Vatican II, which is one of the reasons for the church reconsidering the message of the latter in 1985. With its advocacy of evangelization, its plea for concern with the human dimension of religious doctrine and practice, its underwriting of the need for more extensive forms of lay involvement in the running of the church, and its sensitivity to local cultures, the message of Vatican II struck deeply in Latin America. Moreover it was during the proceedings in Rome at that time that Latin American bishops had the opportunity to develop a continental solidarity which had been singularly lacking in the history of the Latin American church.

The concurrence of Vatican II, the problems created by rapid urban population growth and the authoritarian trend created the immediate matrix from which liberation theology emerged, although, as I have noted, it was the importation of revolutionary and quasi-revolutionary ideas from Europe which finally facilitated the crystallization of liberation theology. The attempt to create a "larger space" for Latin America within the Roman church occurred at precisely the point when there was a resurgence of ideas concerning revolution and historical interpretation, as well as the development of ideas concerning the relationship between internal-societal oppression and the structure of the world economic system.

Given the legitimating effects of Vatican II (as well as the development of Catholic ideas concerning the world-future of man, as in Chardin, and the turn to a more existential form of Catholic theology, as in the work of Maritain), and the nature of "the enemy" (the authoritarian rulers, their Catholic collaborators, and the capitalists of the "core countries" in the world system), it is (as we may now say with the benefit of hindsight) not particularly surprising that liberation theology has developed along the lines which it has. The most important sociological questions which can now be asked have to do with the implications and consequences of liberation theology as a diffuse movement, particularly but not only in Latin America.

All revolutionary movements—and I use that term loosely and very advisedly in relation to liberation theology—are to a significant degree held in what Hegel called the subliminal thrall of that which they oppose. In a major sense, then, liberation theology and its carriers are inevitably part-echoes of the regimes which they oppose, unless, of course, Latin America is now experiencing *its* "Reformation."

Notes

1. I use the term "base community" throughout my discussion in reference to that heterogeneous phenomenon which is referred to in Latin America as *Comunidade Eclesial de Base* and which many Latin Americanists translate as "Christian base community," or in such a way as to give a clearly religious gloss to the kind of collectivity in question. I prefer "base community" because it does not involve prejudging the issue of the degree to which the manifestations of the phenomenon should be invariably described as involving religiosity.

2. Severe qualifications must be added to these quantitative characterizations of Latin American and Brazilian Catholicism. The "pervasive influence" of the church may be confined to as little as 30 per cent of the Latin American people. See William V. D'Antonio,

"Democracy and Religion in Latin America," in D'Antonio and Pike (1964, 257). As far as Brazil is concerned, Bruneau's (1982, 30) observation that the phrase "the largest Catholic country in the world" hides as much as it reveals is of considerable importance. In Brazil (in particular) Catholic religiosity is frequently combined with, even subordinated to, spiritualistic and/or "popular," pre-Catholic religion. It is, however, of great significance that the latter was validated as "a people's [i.e., the Latin American people's] Catholicism" at the 1979 meeting of the Latin American Episcopal Council. See "Evangelization in Latin America's Present and Future," in Eagleson and Scharper (1979, 184–7).

3. The overall characterization which follows has been distilled from a large number of primary and secondary sources. Among the attempts to summarize or evaluate Latin American liberationism I have found the following particularly helpful: Cleary (1985, 43–82); Dussel (1976); McCann (1981); and Berryman's "Latin American Liberation Theology," in Torres and Eagleson (1976, 20–83).

4. The question of Protestant *antecedents* of Latin American liberationism (Catholic, Protestant or Catholic-Protestant) cannot be discussed here, nor can the related question of the degree to which it is an indigenous or autochthonous theology. On the latter opinions range from Latin American claims that it is of deep-historical Latin American—even pre-*conquistador*—origin to the arguments of Norman that liberation theology is a continuation of an older Latin American tendency to import European forms of critique. For the former, see Dussel (1976); for the latter see Norman (1979, 43–56) and Norman (1981, 1–93). Many aspects of the controversy are discussed, with a convincing tilt toward the anti-autochthony argument, in Neely (1978).

5. Even more important than the significant question of the strategic activities of communist and other Marxist organizations is the issue of *the kind* of Marxism which has been influential in Latin America. My own impression is that Leninism and a diffuse Gramsciism have predominated—the former because of its emphasis on anti-imperialism and organizational weaponry, the latter because of its interest in the undoing of ideological hegemony. For a survey see Sheldon B. Liss (1984). Latin America (nor, for that matter, Iberia) has not produced an innovative body of Marxist thought *per se* (Anderson 1976, 28–9). Whether the alignment between Marxism and liberationism in Latin America will produce innovation—

for example, with respect to new Marxist theories of strategy—is an interesting question. Insofar as Latin American Christian Marxism could make an innovative contribution to Marxist thought it would almost certainly center on the newly-found sympathy for Christian ideas in some materialist circles (Fuller 1984, 112–22). (There is no doubt that in some areas—notably Chile in the early 1970s—Marxist parties *directly competed* with the church for base-community loyalties.)

6. This period of Chilean history, which has had such a great impact in the shaping of the ideological morphology of modern Latin America is richly analyzed in Smith (1982). A good example of Christian Democratic ideology, including strong warnings about the "new religion" of Marxism is Montalva's essay, "Paternalism, Pluralism, and Christian Democratic Reform Movements in Latin America," in D'Antonio and Pike (1964, 25–40).

7. There were crucial differences between Christians for Socialism and other parallel movements, notably the Argentinian one—in particular, the Chilean movement challenged the church hierarchy and offered a clear-cut Marxist or neo-Marxist alternative to both the church and Christian Democracy. See Smith (1982, 230–80) and Dodson (1979, 111–34).

8. Smith (1982, 278) plausibly maintains that the traditional absence of "deep faith commitment" makes it likely that the Church will "suffer considerable losses among its constituency" when the laity attempts "to come to serious terms with Marxism."

9. The Maryknolls have, of course, been particularly active in Central America in the period of growth of liberation theology and the proliferation of base communities.

10. Norman (1981) places great emphasis on post-eighteenth-century Latin American Catholicism being explainable in terms of it defending itself against different forms of the increasingly secularly-moralistic state. Bruneau (1982, 7) not unpersuasively, maintains that liberationism is "accurate in its analysis, if not in its prescriptions." The Church has been more-or-less defenseless against the onslaught of the state and the economy.

11. Not merely do we not know much about the nature and variety of their activities, we do not yet have any satisfying measure of their extent. On the latter point commentators often fail to emphasize that an individual may belong to a number of base communities. Thus increase in the number of base communities is not indicative of growth in the number of Latin Americans involved in them.

12. For example, general reading of the Bible was prohibited by popes and Iberian monarchs until the end of the eighteenth century.
13. For controversial discussion of this with respect to workers on Colombian plantations and in Bolivian tin mines, see Taussig (1980).

References

Anderson, Perry. 1976. *Considerations on Western Marxism*. London: NLB.

Bastide, Roger. 1976. Sociology of Latin American religions: The contribution of CIDOC, *Cross Currents* 26, no. 3: 313–27.

Baum, Rainer C. 1980. Authority and identity: The case for evolutionary invariance. In *Identity and authority*. Ed. Roland Robertson and Burkhart Holzner. New York: St. Martin's Press, 61–118.

Berryman, Phillip. 1984. *The Religious Roots of Rebellion: Christians in Central American revolutions*. Maryknoll, N.Y.: Orbis Books.

———. 1976. Latin American liberation theology. In *Theology in the Americas*. Ed. Sergio Torres and John Eagleson. Maryknoll, N.Y.: Orbis Books, 20–83.

Bruneau, Thomas C. 1979. Basic Christian communities in Latin America: Their nature and significance (especially in Brazil). In *Churches and Politics in Latin America*. Ed. Daniel H. Levine. Beverly Hills, Calif.: Sage Publications, 225–37.

———. 1982. *The Church in Brazil*. Austin: University of Texas Press.

Castro, Americo. 1976. *The Structure of Spanish History*. Princeton, N.J.: Princeton University Press.

Cleary, Edward L. 1985. *Crisis, Change, and the Church in Latin America*. Maryknoll, N.Y.: Orbis Books.

D'Antonio, William V. and Fredrick B. Pike, eds. 1964. *Religion, Revolution and Reform: New Forces For Change in Latin America*. New York: Praeger.

Dodson, Michael. 1979. The Christian left in Latin American politics. In *Churches and Politics in Latin America*. Ed. Daniel H. Levine Beverly Hills, CA.: Sage Publications, 111–34.

Dussel, Enrique. 1976. *History and the Theology of Liberation*. Trans. John Drury. Maryknoll, N.Y.: Orbis Books.

Eagleson, John and Philip Scharper, eds. 1979. *Puebla and Beyond*. Trans. John Drury. Maryknoll, N.Y.: Orbis Books.

Frei Montalva, Edwando. 1964. Paternalism, pluralism, and Christian democratic reform movements in Latin America. In *Religion, Revolu-*

tion, and Reform: New Forces for Change in Latin America. Ed. William V. D'Antonio and Fredrick B. Pike. New York: Praeger, 25–40.

Freire, Paulo. 1970. *Pedagogy of the Oppressed.* Trans. Myra Bergman Ramos. New York: Seabury Press.

Fuller, Peter. 1984. The historical Jesus. *New Left Review,* no.146: 112–22.

Gutiérrez, Gustavo. 1973. *Theology of Liberation.* Trans. Sister Caridad Inda and John Eagleson. Maryknoll, N.Y.: Orbis Books.

Guitérrez, Gustavo and Richard Shaull. 1977. *Liberation and Change.* Maryknoll, N.Y.: Orbis Books.

Lernoux, Penny. 1979. The long path to Puebla. In *Puebla and Beyond.* Ed. John Eagleson and Philip Scharper. Maryknoll, N.Y.: Orbis Books, 3–27.

———. 1980. *The Cry of the People.* Garden City, N.Y.: Doubleday.

Levine, Daniel H., ed. 1979. *Churches and Politics in Latin America.* Beverly Hills, CA.: Sage Publications.

———. 1981. *Religion and Politics in Latin America: The Catholic Church in Venezuela and Colombia.* Princeton, N.J.: Princeton University Press.

Liss, Sheldon B. 1984. *Marxist Thought in Latin America.* Berkeley, CA.: University of California Press.

McCann, Dennis P. 1981. *Christian Realism and Liberation Theology.* Maryknoll, N.Y.: Orbis Books.

Maduro, Otto. 1982. *Religion and Social Conflicts.* Trans. Robert R. Barr. Maryknoll, N.Y.: Orbis Books.

Martin, David. 1978. *A General Theory of Secularization.* New York: Harper & Row.

Miranda, Jose. 1982. *Marx and The Bible.* Maryknoll, N.Y.: Orbis Books.

Mutchler, David E. 1971. *The Church as a Political Factor in Latin America.* New York: Praeger.

Neely, Alan. 1978. Liberation theology in Latin America: Antecedents and autochthony. *Missiology: An International Review* 6, no. 3: 343–69.

Nettl, J.P. and Roland Robertson. 1969. *International Systems and the Modernization of Societies.* New York: Basic Books.

Norman, Edward. 1979. *Christianity and the World Order.* Oxford: Oxford University Press.

———. 1981. *Christianity in the Southern Hemisphere.* Oxford: Clarendon Press.

Novak, Michael. 1982. *The Spirit of Democratic Capitalism*. New York: Simon and Schuster.

Pickering, W.S.F. 1982. *Durkheim's Sociology of Religion*. Boston: Routledge and Kegan Paul.

Robertson, Roland. 1981. Considerations from within the American context on the significance of church-state tension. *Sociological Analysis* 42, no. 3: 193–208.

Sandoval, Moises. 1979. Report from the Conference. In *Puebla and Beyond*. Ed. John Eagleson and Philip Scharper. Maryknoll, N.Y.: Orbis Books, 28–43.

Segundo, Juan Luis. 1976. *The Liberation of Theology*. Trans. John Drury. Maryknoll, N.Y.: Orbis Books.

Smith, Brian H. 1982. *The Church and Politics in Chile*. Princeton, N.J.: Princeton University Press.

Stevens-Arroyo, Anthony M. 1983. Popular religion in Latin America: The 20th century Irredentist vindication of 15th century Indo-European intercivilizational encounters. Brooklyn College, City University of New York, Unpub. paper.

Taussig, Michael T. 1980. *The Devil and Commodity Fetishism in South America*. Chapel Hill, N.C.: University of North Carolina Press.

Torres, Sergio and John Eagleson, eds. 1976. *Theology in the Americas*. Maryknoll, N.Y.: Orbis Books.

———. 1981. *The Challenge of Basic Christian Communities*. Maryknoll, N.Y.: Orbis Books.

Vallier, Ivan. 1967. Religious elites: Differentiations and developments in Roman Catholicism. In *Elites in Latin America*. Ed. Seymour Martin Lipset and Also Solari. New York: Oxford University Press. 190–232.

———. 1970. *Catholicism, Social Control, and Modernization in Latin America*. Englewood Cliffs, N.J.: Prentice-Hall.

———. 1972. Church "development" in Latin America: A five-country comparison. In *The Roman Catholic Church in Latin America*, ed. Karl M. Schmitt. New York: Alfred A. Knopf, 167–93.

Wallerstein, Immanuel. 1982. Socialist states: Mercantilist strategies and revolutionary objectives. In *Ascent and Decline in the World-System*. Beverly Hills, CA.: Sage Publications, 289–300.

Wilson, Bryan R. 1973. *Magic and the Millennium*. New York: Harper & Row.

Woodward, Ralph Lee, Jr. 1976. *Central America: A Nation Divided*. New York: Oxford University Press.

6

Religion and the Legitimation of Violence

WILLIAM R. GARRETT

"The United States shouldn't worry about the Soviets in Latin America, because they aren't revolutionaries anymore. . . . But they should worry about the Catholic revolutionaries, who are."[1] Fidel Castro

VIOLENT action undertaken in the name of religion is not a wholly new phenomenon in human affairs. Religiously legitimated wars, revolutions, pogroms, and crusades against a rival faith appear with uncanny frequency in the histories of both the Occident and the Orient. Mounting empirical evidence of the last two decades makes this conclusion incontestable: A rapidly increasing number of contemporary religionists are being inspired by the dogmas of their faith to beat their plowshares into swords.

Three salient features makes the recent resurgence of radical religious violence so noteworthy: (1) its extraordinary virulence at precisely that time when many interpreters were reporting a trend in international relations toward a burgeoning secularity, along with a corresponding increase in the level of civility by which major religious communities were interrelated; (2) the tendency among many exponents of contemporary radical religion to embrace a stance aptly characterized by J. L. Talmon[2] as "totalitarian democracy"; and (3) the momentous social

103

consequences which radical religion of a totalitarian democratic cast is capable of unleashing on believers and nonbelievers alike in the post-modern world.

The Diverse Forms of Contemporary Radical Religion

A definition of terms is called for at the outset. By radical religion, we mean that coterie of true believers who (1) subscribe to a fundamentalist or orthodox understanding of the basic tenets of their religion or sect[3]; (2) relate those religious constructs to a set of social conditions which are variously defined as exploitive, repressive, or immoral so that (3) a substantive reformation of the social order is given warrant on sacred grounds. This definition casts a sufficiently wide net to encompass Catholic members of the IRA, Druse militia in Lebanon, Sunni and Shi'ite combatants in the Iraqi-Iranian war, Catholic supporters of Solidarity's struggle in Poland, liberation theologians and their followers in Latin America and elsewhere, as well as the more activist branches of the New Religious Right in the United States.

Radical religion is not cut from the same bolt of cloth everywhere, even when it appears in different societies under the aegis of the same denominational organization: Catholic radicalism in Poland, for example, is vastly different from the Catholic radicalism in Brazil. Contemporary radical religion can be divided into three basic types: (1) a *totalitarian right*, (2) a *liberal, democratic centrist*, and (3) *totalitarian democratic left*.

These categories derive, in part, from Talmon's[4] perceptive analyses in *The Origins of Totalitarian Democracy*, where liberal democratic patterns are contrasted to those of totalitarian democracy and totalitarianism of the right is compared to totalitarianism of the left. Essentially, Talmon distinguished between liberal and totalitarian democracy *not* on the basis that one affirmed the value of liberty while the other denied it, but on the differing styles of political action designed to attain human freedom. He elaborates thus:

> The liberal approach assumes politics to be a matter of trial and error, and regards political systems as pragmatic contrivances of human ingenuity and spontaneity. It also recognizes a variety of levels of personal and collective endeavor, which are altogether outside the sphere of politics.

The totalitarian democratic school, on the other hand, is based on the assumption of a sole and exclusive truth in politics. It may be called political Messianism in the sense that it postulates a preordained, harmonious and perfect scheme of things, to which men are irresistibly driven, and at which they are bound to arrive. It recognizes ultimately only one plane of existence, the political. It widens the scope of politics to embrace the whole of human existence. . . . Its political ideas are not a set of pragmatic precepts or a body of devices applicable to a special branch of human endeavor. They are an integral part of an all-embracing and coherent philosophy. Politics is defined as the art of applying this philosophy to the organization of society, and the final purpose of politics is only achieved when this philosophy reigns supreme over all fields of life.[5]

Central to the totalitarian democratic stance is the stalwart conviction that the state must be utilized as an instrument of coercion in order to assure the collective liberation of the body politic. The paramount role assigned to the state in this political style is based on the presupposition that individual freedom can be realized only when a whole people is induced to conform, with lively enthusiasm, to a common will. In other words, modern totalitarian democracy is a "dictatorship resting on popular enthusiasm"[6] in which the state must take the lead not only in nurturing individual assent to the collective will but also in framing the substantive content given expression in that collective will.

Talmon traces the evolution of totalitarian democratic politics from the writings of Rousseau, to the Jacobin improvisation, the Babouvist crystallization, and finally to its culmination in communist single-party dictatorships which regard their governance as *ipso facto* commensurate with the will of the people—or more precisely with the will of the people rightly understood.

The tradition of the right stands in sharp juxtaposition, Talmon maintains, to that of the totalitarian left. Totalitarians of the right predicate their political action on historic, racial, or organic concepts which assert the superiority of one *Volk* over others, and thereby preclude the possibility of a universal order based on a value structure applicable to all humankind. Totalitarians of the right also resort readily to the use of force out of the conviction that it represents the only permanent way to preserve order among inferior peoples tainted with cultural or biological deficiencies.

When totalitarians of the left employ force, they do so in order to hasten the pace of a people's progress toward improved social conditions and ideological harmony. Totalitarians of the left embrace, therefore, a political messianic mission whose overriding goal is to usher in an eschatological age complete with a utopian social order, and all accomplished in the here and now rather than prorated into some distant hereafter—as would be typical for religiously inspired messianic movements. Accordingly, totalitarian democrats commonly regard revolutionary struggles as a necessary first stage in the long process of establishing a system of popular sovereignty in which everyone is forced to become free and, in that free state, compelled to will the common will.

Undergirding the theory and practice of the totalitarian democrats is an *idée fixe* of crucial importance with implicit anti-intellectual overtones. This premise states that the source of all valid knowledge pertaining to social affairs derives from sentiment rather than reason.[7] Rousseau[8] regarded the general will *(la volenté générale)*, for example, as a spontaneous emergent from the interaction (or collective effervescence) of citizens whose individual wills were, in the process, constrained solely by a generalized concern for the welfare of the total society. By driving an analytical wedge between the realm of will and the realm of knowledge, as well as by arguing that each realm was distinguishable by its own ends and the means for attaining those ends,[9] Rousseau relegated reason to a secondary role of supporting the moral order of society as expressed in the general will. When scientific or philosophic reason claims absolute primacy, however, it constitutes a real and present danger to social solidarity. What a political society requires is citizens who are capable of responding freely and spontaneously to the general will out of a deep-seated sense of obligation and loyalty. Reason tends to foster among citizens an interest in discerning objective truth and, thus, inspires criticism rather than commitment. Accordingly, Rousseau—ever the romanticist—devalued reason in favor of sentiment as the basis upon which moral will in social life was to be founded.

For somewhat different reasons, Marx, too, opted for an epistemological position which viewed valid knowledge as a direct product of the "real life process" or *praxis*.[10] Theoretical reason was an abstracted and falsified depiction of reality, in Marx's view, which only barely masked the class interests of the prevailing societal elites. Those ideas which ought to inform the restructuring of social life must derive out of the revolutionary struggles of the working class, for they alone can create a social order which transcends the exploitation and alienation of all previous societies. Within the Marxist framework, then, reason is denied an independent role insofar as the articulation of valid political knowledge is concerned. The basis for real knowledge—that is, politically useful knowledge—is practical-critical activity.

Embedded in the anti-rationalist stance of totalitarian democrats from Rousseau to Marx was an ancillary bias against the cultural tendencies of modernity which (1) widened the scope of "discretionary social behavior" for individuals, (2) established a rule of law in the public realm (which treated persons equally instead of attempting to "make them equal"), (3) differentiated between a public and private realm in the polity (and limited politics to the former sphere so that the whole of life was not politicized), and (4) elevated the individual to the status of the primary social actor rather than allocating primacy to the state, family, church, or some other corporate entity. What modernity had secured, according to the totalitarian democrats, was a measure of individual freedom bought at the high price of fragmented human relations set within alienated communities.

In part, this anti-modern bias reflects a nostalgic backward glance to an earlier era of romanticized *communitas*. For Rousseau,[12] the ideal societies were clearly the city-states of Sparta and Athens or, more recently, Geneva. He warns in Book Two of *The Social Contract* that a people should be wary of developing a social order which is too large to be well-governed, even though he must finally admit that one cannot *a priori* set territorial or population limits on the size of viable societies. Although Marx limited his comments on the new social order after the revolution to a few, fragmented comments, he does seem to imply that socialist society will include a succession of *Gemeinschaftlich* features, all of which presuppose a decentralized form of social organization and a preference for the milieu of the village rather than the ethos of urban regions.

The critique of modern society was highly selective among the totalitarian democrats. Technological and material advances which improved the life conditions over those which prevailed in the pre-modern era were certainly not to be jettisoned. None of the totalitarian democrats ever waivered in their conviction, however, that the material benefits of modernization could be appropriated without accepting its cultural presuppositions as well. This tradition has been vulnerable to the charge that, when confronted with this problem, its leaders have swiftly taken flight into schemes of utopian wish-fulfillment which pay far too little attention to what Peter Berger[13] has aptly described as that "calculus of pain" entailed in the revolutionary process.

My intent at this juncture is not to set up the utopian elements in the thought of Rousseau, Marx, and others in this tradition (Lenin, for example) as straw men which can be toppled by a mere puff of pragmatic realism. What is of crucial importance for the analysis developed below is this: Behind the mythic structure of the totalitarian democrat approach stands the fundamental premise that human freedom can only be attained through a collective political process wherein the commitment to modern individualism is transformed into an integrated ideological perspective governing the economy, polity, and culture. Furthermore, within this framework, the collectivity as represented in civil society ranks as the supreme good. The collective interest must, therefore, take precedence over individual interests, which are regarded by definition as partial, selfish, and hence misguided.

Totalitarian democracy in its pure form is predicated on a fundamental contradiction. It seeks to achieve human freedom through a process which molds individual wills into a harmonious and uniform ideological perspective. True freedom becomes, in short, the willingness to will the same thing. Liberal democracy in its pure form must cope with a different, but no less serious, contradiction, namely, the assumption that individuals in the pursuit of their discrete interests simultaneously produce the greater good for society as a whole. Empirically, of course, historic societies have struck any number of compromises to place them somewhere on a continuum between these two polar options. Nevertheless, it does make a difference whether societal members predicate their action on liberal democratic or totalitarian democratic presuppositions.

My primary concern in this essay is not to rehearse the differences between these two strategies for attaining a democratic order, but to lay the foundations for understanding the nature and purposes of radical religion as it has recently come to the forefront in world affairs. Briefly put, *my thesis is that a significant portion of the religiously legitimated movements engaged in militaristic or revolutionary actions today are a consequence of having wedded theological ideas to a totalitarian democratic stance.*

At first blush, totalitarian democratic theory might appear an unlikely consort for most of the world religions—especially those of a universalistic, monotheistic character. Certainly, the classical theorists of totalitarian democracy evidenced little sympathy—and often outright antipathy—for organized religions. Rousseau, it will be recalled, tolerated particular religions as the private opinions of citizens which were not matters of concern to the sovereign,[14] but he insisted that all citizens must subscribe to the civil religion of a society—and he regarded unfaithfulness to its tenets as sufficiently serious to warrant the punishment of death. Strictly speaking, civil religion was not a set of religious dogmas similar to Catholicism, Calvinism, and the like. Civil religion served a purpose which was at once secular and utilitarian, for it gave articulation to those tenets which were indispensable for participation in society.

Marx concurred with Rousseau on the need for a set of ideological beliefs to which all citizens must affirm their allegiance. Yet, Marx carefully avoided the use of religious language to describe these secular commitments, while he excoriated the churches for their role in perpetuating socio-economic privileges for the ruling class minority and misery for the masses. At root, however, the differences between Rousseau and Marx were more linguistic than substantive. What mattered in both instances was the collective ideology which required of all citizens that they embrace a posture of deep-seated obligation to civil society.

It should also be noted that there is no elective affinity between any of the theologies of the major world religions and the political stance of totalitarian democracy. Nevertheless, discrete movements within Roman Catholicism, Protestantism, and Islam have all embraced this political approach in recent years. Since this claim cannot be explored in all its ramifications in the limited space available in this essay, the major empirical focus in the discussion which follows will be on liberation theology, especially as this strand of political thought has developed among Catholics and Protestants in Latin America. The remainder of this essay, then, will be devoted to developing several propositions of a generalized nature which identify some of the crucial dimensions relative to the recent upsurge in radical religion.

Propositions Pertaining to Contemporary Radical Religion

The following propositions summarize several of the more salient characteristics of radical religion as this phenomenon has taken shape and form over the last few decades. Some propositions pertain to radical religion generally, while others relate specifically to radical religion in a totalitarian democratic mode. Each proposition is followed by a brief commentary.

Proposition One: Radical religious communities are emerging in the decade of the 1980s as the institutional structures wherein revolutionary sentiments are cultivated. This process is occuring in much the same manner as the universities nurtured revolutionary movements in the 1960s.

Social movements generally require some institutional base within which to mobilize human and ideational resources. In the recent past, and with increasing frequency, religious organizations have provided the institutional staging ground for critiquing extant societal arrangements and formulating strategies for correcting societal inequalities in the allocation of power, wealth, and social opportunities. In Northern Ireland, the churches on both sides of the dispute have provided support for the conflict for a long while. More recently there has been an effort to recast the interpretation of this warfare in terms of liberation theology and this may well help intensify church involvement.[15] Likewise, the revolution in Iran (where religious leaders have all but usurped governmental functions), the civil war in Lebanon, and the spiraling conflicts in Latin America have all been centered around religious organizations, and religious leaders have frequently provided overt legitimation for revolutionary violence.

Proposition Two: Contemporary radical religion can be differentiated analytically into three distinct types: (1) radical religion of the right, (2) radical religion of the democratic center, and (3) radical religion of the totalitarian democratic left.

Radical religion of the right tends to embrace a set of religio-ethnic prejudices which define other groups as inferiors. The use of force—or at least the threat to use force—by a strong central government is regarded as appropriate and necessary in order to compel persons to follow that definition of proper conduct endorsed by the religious right. Hence, radical religionists of the right strive to form a strong alliance with central governments so that the power of the state can be employed to attain religious ends. Perhaps the most extreme example of this type is the Islamic fundamentalism of Iran where the alliance between government and religious leaders has attained almost total fusion.

Tendencies in the direction of radical religion of the right—although not nearly as extreme—are evidenced in the efforts of Jerry Falwell and other neo-conservative Christians in the United States. Constitutional restraints have thus far inhibited several of the schemes concocted by neo-conservatives in this country—such as the reintroduction of prayer into the public schools, federal aid to religious schools, censorship laws relating to pornography and obscenity, the delegalizing of abortion, and the like—but the neo-conservatives have made some strides toward forming informal alliances with high-placed governmental officials for the purpose of affecting policy decisions. To be sure, these alliances may represent no more than efforts among officials in the Reagan administration to co-opt the religious right[16] and the real influence of the neo-conservatives may well be far less than its leaders claim.[17] Nonetheless, the aspirations of these neo-conservative Christians clearly reveal tendencies in the direction of the radical religious right as this stance has been defined within the context of the present typology. In Weberian terms[18] the danger attending this orientation is that the inherent tension between religion and the world is transcended by subsuming the world under the dominion of the religious community.

Radical religion of the liberal democratic center has admittedly a somewhat peculiar ring, since liberal democrats are by definition reformists who strive to achieve social change through peaceful democratic processes. Radical religionists of the center subscribe to a notion of human rights which is derived ultimately from their religious suppositions.[19] Their conception of human rights is employed as an instrument for critiquing the exercise of state power, especially when that state power is used as a means for coercing citizens to adopt the regime's interpretation of proper beliefs and behavior patterns.

Radical religion of the liberal democratic center has been most visible recently in countries aligned with the Marxist bloc—namely, East Germany, Hungary, Poland, and even in the Soviet Union. Radical religionists in these countries have been inspired by their faith and convictions to assert a claim to such freedoms as free speech, assembly, conscience, legal due process, and the like in defiance of governmental efforts to suppress such rights. East Germany, for example, is experiencing a rapid growth of base communities *(Basengruppen)* which are challenging monolithic governmental policies that strive to suppress any deviation from "the omnipresent state ideology."[20] Radical religionists in socialist societies are not so much committed to overthrowing the regimes in their respective countries as they are to opening up the social structure through a series of reforms to allow for greater "discretionary social behavior." Again, in Weberian terms, radical religionists of the liberal democratic center strive to create and/or maintain a dynamic tension between religion and the world, so that each is afforded some degree of autonomy in relation to the other.

Radical religion of the totalitarian democratic left represents a fusion of theological ideas with some variant form of Marxist social theory. The liberation theologies of recent years constitute the best examples of this sort of religious radicalism. Religion is regarded, given the rubrics of this third type, as primarily concerned with the liberation of people *qua* people from material want and political dependency.[21] It locates the source of valid theological-political ideas in the praxis of struggle against exploitation and repression. And it acknowledges (with varying degrees of reluctance) the necessity for using violence and entering into revolutionary conflicts as the only feasible means for uprooting entrenched structures of social injustice. (Further elaboration of this type appears in propositions four, five, and six below.) Finally, it should be noted that this third type also tends toward a fusion of religion and world, with religion relegated to such a subordinate position that it stands in danger of losing its social influence altogether once it has provided legitimation for a totalitarian democratic regime (see proposition four below).

Proposition Three. Radical religion of all three types has forged powerful links to a resurgent nationalism in almost all contemporary societies. This linkage has redoubled commitment to a struggle often defined as an effort to escape from the economic or political hegemony of a foreign power.

Explicit expressions of nationalistic aspirations were prominent in the Islamic fundamentalist revolution in Iran. Similar sentiments appear in the writings of liberation theologians in Latin America,[22] South Africa,[23] Ireland,[24] and elsewhere. In somewhat more muted forms, the stirrings of nationalistic fervor suffuse the religious radicalism in Poland, East Germany, and Hungary. Even in the United States, the Moral Majority has integrated an ultra-nationalistic political agenda into its overall religious program. The result has been a mutual reinforcement of radical religion and nationalistic sentiments, along with a sharp rise in the tendency to historically and ethnically contextualize theological formulations.

Proposition Four: Radical religion of the totalitarian democratic type, to the extent that it couches its analyses of the socio-economic situation in Marxist or neo-Marxist dependency theories, precludes the likelihood that alternative policy options to the "revolutionary solution" will even be considered. By the same token, the theological component is allocated but one role in relation to the social scientific infrastructure of liberation theology, and that is to provide religious legitimation for the diagnosis and strategy through which liberation from economic, political, and class oppression is to be achieved.

The thrust of this proposition is to suggest that the partnership between theological and social scientific constructs in liberation theology constitutes a markedly unequal partnership. That perspective which functions to define the situation thereby acquires inordinate power over the selection process through which appropriate responses for rectifying that situation are sorted out. The decision to incorporate the "secular sciences, particularly the social sciences, in theological thinking"[25] has been made quite self-consciously by liberation theologians. However, only one theoretical perspective from the variety afforded by contemporary social science has been attractive to liberation theologians, and that is the Marxist paradigm. This perspective portrays the plight of the Latin American masses in the familiar terms of inevitable class conflict, oppression of the poor, economic dependency (largely as a function of policies inflicted on Latin America by multinational corporations based in the United States), and political repression from indigenous elites (with the support again of the United States and its military might). Following the lead of Guitérrez[26] and Segundo,[27] theology is regarded by liberation theologians as the "second step," following the analyses of the social situation laid down by that select group of social theorists considered authoritative.

What is not clear is the extent to which liberation theologians have grasped the implications of their decision to place their religio-moral precepts in a subservient relationship to the Marxist analytical paradigm. The whole case for liberation theology hangs perforce on the cogency and validity intrinsic to the Marxist diagnosis of the situation. If that social interpretation is misguided or mistaken, then liberation theologians may well have legitimated a demonic political strategy whose revolutionary practices will exact a bloody toll on precisely those masses whom they wished to liberate and they may well have ushered in dictatorial regimes more repressive than the national security states all too prominent on the Latin American landscape today.

All theological systems, of course, carry along with their doctrinal rubrics certain social presuppositions. The point to be made with respect to liberation theology, however, is that the concrete social theory appropriated in this instance is much more conducive to the acceptance of revolutionary violence than alternative social theories patterned on reformist presuppositions.

For a number of reasons, liberation theologians have not been motivated to focus their critical scrutiny on the Marxist infrastructure which informs their religio-political stance. Harsh criticism has been forthcoming from other quarters, however. Peter Berger[28] recently concluded that: ". . . the most important criticism to be made of the new Christian leftism is not that it promulgates false norms, nor that it is theologically mistaken, but that it is based on demonstrable misperceptions of empirical reality. Put differently: What is most wrong about 'liberation theology' is neither its biblical exegesis nor its ethics but its sociology." In face of such charges, liberation theologians have typically responded by rhetorically asserting the validity of the Marxist paradigm as the "only social theory which begins with the class structure of the global economy . . ." and adequately comprehends our "world histori-cal situation."[29]

There are, no doubt, a number of background factors in the Latin American and Third World social experience which condition this uncritical acceptance of the Marxist myth that the only viable develop-ment strategy is armed revolution and the construction of a socialist society.[30] This judgment on the part of liberation theologians is not predicated on a critical appraisal of the empirical evidence in support of the Marxist interpretation, however, or a dispassionate evaluation of the outcomes from other socialist revolutions. It is rather a "leap of faith" with respect to matters on which there is at least some empirical evidence to guide decision-making.

The reluctance to critique the theoretical suppositions of Marxist analyses portends what will most likely be the role of liberation theologians once the revolution has begun. That is to say, if liberation theologians are unwilling to exercise critical judgment with respect to socialist theorizing, then it is doubly unlikely that they will be able to exercise critical judgment with respect to the use of force as the revolutionary social practice gets underway.

The fact that the theme of violence resurfaces time and again in the writings of the liberation theologians indicates they are uneasy about the potential for abuse of military might. Some have addressed the issue of the forms and limits of permissible violence,[31] while others have sought to reconcile the historic repugnance of Christian thought to the use of violence with the revolutionary agenda.[32] The overwhelming judgment on the part of liberation theologians is, however, that revolutionary violence is, on the one hand, almost certainly inevitable[33] and, on the other hand, therapeutic in the sense that it creates new structural conditions for the experience of grace.[34]

The alacrity with which liberation theologians have endorsed pro-grams of revolutionary violence has revealed the extent to which this movement is motivated by exceptionally strong utopian sentiments. In spite of the talk about the need for critical, empirically-based, historical-ly focused analysis as the starting point for theological reflection and political action, this movement manifests a remarkable naïveté. This is so both with respect to the positive contributions of revolutionary violence and the ability of socialist societies to deliver on their promises of a more humane order. I have in mind here, of course, those Marxist, Marxist-Leninist, and Maoist societies and not the socialist democratic orders *à la* Sweden.

Few movements in the church have forged so close a "Christ of culture" alliance as the liberation theologians, to use Niebuhr's famous categories, and thereby identified the mission of the church so completely with the fortunes of a program for political transformation. Not only is the tension between church and world vitiated, but so too is the ability of the church to speak prophetically against actions undertaken in the name of the revolutionary cause.

Probably it could not have been otherwise. Marxist ideology is a jealous mistress which tolerates no other competitors. This feature Marxism shares with other forms of totalitarian democratic thought— even Rousseau was compelled to invent the notion of civil religion in order to assure a resonance between religious ideals and the demands of the general will. Rousseau's ideas never really were put to an empirical, historical test through institutionalization in a concrete societal system.

The same cannot be said for the Marxist paradigm—although it has been argued that no Marxist society thus far has really been faithful to the fundamental premises laid down by Marx himself. Nonetheless, the experience of the East German regime can be instructive of the way in which competing ideological systems—like religious dogmas—relate to the political ideology of the state. The Party in East Germany— operating as the vanguard of the communist order and in keeping with Lenin's[35] embellishments on the Marxist notion of the dictatorship of the proletariat—holds to the view that Party ideology represents a dynamic manifestation of the will of the people. Accordingly, party needs and interests take priority over universal statements pertaining to human rights or even legal statutes enacted by the state.[36]

In other words, the Party reserves the sole right to determine the prevailing ideology for the body politic and allocates no social space to other groups or agencies to articulate an alternative point of view. There is no reason to believe the East German experience is idiosyncratic among Marxist regimes. The repressive measures undertaken against the Solidarity movement in Poland would appear to be simply another instance of trying to silence claims made in the name of the people which are independent of the Party apparatus.

Insofar as liberation theology in Latin America is concerned, then, all of this suggests that its role will be severely restricted once the revolutionary struggle has begun. Liberation theology may well be crucial in supplying motivational support for and legitimation of the revolutionary cause. But once the revolution is underway, there can be little room for criticism. Even if liberation theologians were willing to raise objections to the social analysis or practices of the revolutionary cadres, they would have to be suppressed in order to assure the success of the emergent revolutionary order and to assure that only one agency—the party—speaks for the people in this new order. Consequently, we can predict that the social space needed by the churches or other social groups to voice alternative ideological perspectives from that enunciated by the party would simply not be made available in the sort of totalitarian democratic regime which liberation theologians currently have endorsed.

Proposition Five: Radical religion, especially of the totalitarian democratic type manifested in liberation theology, represents a form of chiliastic thought as a consequence of its emphasis on praxis *as a revelational source of knowledge.*

This proposition helps explain why liberation theologians display so little interest in empirical knowledge of and rational reasoning about which sorts of regimes—capitalistic or Marxist—have the better record in stimulating economic growth, fostering political freedom, and nurturing cultural creativity. The answer lies in part, I believe, in the peculiar sort of chiliastic mentality which is pervasive in the outlook of liberation theologians. The concept of the chiliastic, utopian mentality derives from Mannheim's[37] seminal explorations of utopian thought. He distinguished chiliastic utopianism as a movement originating among the lower classes who are suddenly awakened to their potential political power. Religion and politics are subsequently fused into one ongoing process where the "new" and the "impossible" spring into existence in the immediate present as a consequence of transcendent intervention into the normal course of affairs. In this model, rationality gives way to enthusiastic insight, and optimism soars to new heights in the expectation that the Absolute will intervene at any moment to disclose new truth.

To be sure, liberation theology does not attain close approximation to the pure chiliastic utopian mentality of a Thomas Münzer, but there are stark indications of chiliastic utopian tendencies in the movement. The first such indicator inheres in the claim that praxis constitutes the source from which theological ideas are given shape and form. As Harvey Cox[38] notes, "what the members of the base communities are doing is the praxis of which liberation theology is the theory." Along the same lines, Segundo[39] argues that commitment represents the first step in theologizing, for commitment brings one into solidarity with the masses through concrete acts of engagement in their struggles, suffering, misery, and need. Out of this historically concrete struggle for liberation, the liberating message of the Bible becomes manifest. Thus, it is the praxis which gives meaning to liberation theology and not liberation theology which gives meaning to praxis. Gutiérrez[40] strikes a similar theme in language which has an even more distinctly chiliastic tone to it:

> To reflect on the basis of the historical praxis of liberation is to reflect in the light of the future which is believed in and hoped for. It is to reflect with a view to action which transforms the present. But it does not mean doing this from an armchair; rather it means sinking roots where the pulse of history is beating at this moment and illuminating history with the Word of the Lord of history, who irreversibly committed himself to the present moment of mankind to carry it to its fulfillment.

Moreover, the criterion by which the adequacy of theology is to be measured should no longer be the rational specifications of truth in orthodoxy, Gutiérrez[41] insists, but the doing of the truth in *orthopraxis*.

One of the abiding traits of all chiliastic movements has been their unpredictability once "whirl becomes king." This would appear to pose a serious problem for liberation theologians, namely, how can the chiliastic tendencies of their movement be reconciled with their political expectations based on the Marxist paradigm? The answer given to this dilemma by liberation theologians is reminiscent of the tack taken by Marx when he expounded on the nature of that political society the proletariat would create when they became free of the false consciousness imposed on them by bourgeois society. Marx argued that, given what we know about human nature and man the producer on the basis of scientific materialism, the basic dimensions of socialist society can be explicated, without delineating all the specific arrangements eventually adopted. Liberation theologians respond in a similar fashion by asserting that their participation in *praxis* thus far is sufficient to convince them that socialism remains the ideology most compatible with the teachings of Jesus and the Gospel.[42] Accordingly, liberation theology retains a chiliastic fixation on praxis as the source for valid theological meanings while simultaneously holding on to the telic elements in the Marxist myth pertaining to the sort of societal system the revolution will eventually be responsible for creating.

Proposition Six: Radical religion of the totalitarian democratic type represents a de-modernizing force in world affairs.

The classical architects of totalitarian democratic thought were all, in their own ways, profoundly opposed to modernity. Harvey Cox[43] points out, for example, that Rousseau was the first who used the term *moderniste* in the pejorative sense often associated with modernity or modernism today. Cox[44] also reminds us that those who first rejected modern theology were Third World theologians who were "despisers of the modern world itself." What members of this tradition find offensive in modernity is not the improved standard of living accompanying it, but its bureaucratic rationality, consumerism, the quest for the maximization of profit, the omnipresent influence of science and technology, its devastation of the natural environment, the shallowness of its mass culture, and its trivialization of religion.

Many of these characteristics of the modern world are also severely criticized by liberal democrats and totalitarians on the right. The revolution in Iran, for example, carried virulent anti-modern sentiments. Nonetheless, modern bourgeois society must be judged by more than its popular rock musicians, its Three Mile Island disasters, and its proliferation of computers. The crux of the anti-modern argument centers on the issue of individual freedom: Should individuals have the right to accumulate and dispose of wealth and property within certain broad guidelines (say, the Declaration of Human Rights of the United Nations)? Should the expression of individual points of view which deviate from governmental policy be regarded as a *de facto* failure to fulfill one's obligations to the political community? Should individuals consume culture on the basis of personal preference or should culture serve as an instrument for molding human character and consciousness in terms of certain politically prescribed norms?

The anti-modernists among liberation theologians almost unanimously support collective means for the distributing of wealth, the identifying of individual obligations, and the directing of culture. In addition, they also call for individual societies to eschew the pursuit of self-interests alone in their foreign policies in favor of a broader concept of national obligations to the poor and dispossessed of the world, whatever their country of origin may happen to be. There is, indeed, a globalization of concerns with respect to the correction of injustices, suffering, and human want which many anti-modernists regard as problems directly traceable to the actions of societies, corporations, and individuals operating within the modern, bourgeois framework.[45]

Certainly, one cannot fault the moral logic which asserts that world powers—capitalist or communist—have an obligation to share their wealth in order to help alleviate the suffering of the masses in Third

World nations. Suffice it to say that this is not the place to debate the relative willingness of modern, bourgeois societies over against contemporary socialist regimes in developing altruistic foreign policies to aid Third World countries. What does need to be underscored in this context, however, is that profound questions are currently blowing in the wind. The goals of liberation theology entail not only a redistribution of wealth and political power in Third World countries,[46] but they also entail a reorientation of cultural values which sets the collectivity above the individual, the people above the person, insofar as value priorities are concerned.[47] This overriding concern to transform economic, political, and value structures on a global scale prompts Cox[48] to suggest that the liberation theology movement constitutes nothing less than a new reformation which is implanting "the germ cells of the next era of our culture."

Conclusion: Religion and the Legitimazation of Violence

These six propositions pertaining to radical religion in general and radical religion in a totalitarian democratic mode in particular summarize the characteristics of a new form of religious presence in the modern world. The sheer size of radical religious movements, the rapidity of their growth, and the substantive nature of those social changes carried along in the agendas of these movements, all suggest that we are dealing here with a phenomenon of considerable social importance. In the very recent past probably few scholars would have believed that religious movements were capable of exercising such potent influence on such a wide scale.

In addition to developing the typology of radical religion of the totalitarian right, the liberal democratic center, and the totalitarian democratic left, one of the major concerns of this essay has been to place liberation theology, especially as it has developed in Latin America, in the category of totalitarian democracy insofar as its political stance is concerned. In the near future liberation theology stands out as one of the most potent among the radical religious movements. The success or failure of its leaders can have inestimable consequences for the future of religious and democratic freedoms in Third and First World nations. One cannot doubt the good intentions motivating liberation theologians, nor discount their legitimate concerns for the release of the peasant masses of Latin America from inundating poverty and political repression. One can question, however, the advisibility of their strategy for liberation when it entails an almost wholesale and uncritical religious legitimation of revolutionary violence. We may, then, be entering an era when we learn again one of the hard lessons of history, namely, that religion is not always benign; it also holds the potential for unleashing the most demonic of social forces.

Notes

1. Quoted in Francine Gray, *Divine Disobedience*. New York: Random House, 1971, 311–12.
2. J. L. Talmon, *The Origins of Totalitarian Democracy*. New York: Praeger, 1960.
3. See Roland Robertson, "Consideration from within the American context on the significance of church-state tension," *Sociological Analysis* 42, no. 3 (1981).
4. Talmon, *Origins*.
5. Ibid., 1–2.
6. Ibid., 6.
7. Leo Straus, *Natural Right and History*. Chicago: University of Chicago Press, 1953, 258.
8. Jean Jacques Rousseau, *The Social Contract*. Chicago: Henry Regnery, [1762] 1954, 44–47.
9. Ernst Cassirer, *The Philosophy of the Enlightenment*. Boston: Beacon, 1955, 272.
10. David McLellan, ed., *Karl Marx: Selected Writings*. New York: Oxford University Press, 1977, 156, 381, 356–57.
11. Daniel Bell, *The Cultural Contradictions of Capitalism*. New York: Basic Books, 1978, xl–xv, 38. See also, Karl Marx, *Surveys From Exile*, ed. David Fernbach. New York: Random House, 1974; and Karl Marx, *Early Writings*, ed. Quinton Hoare New York: Random House, 1975.
12. Rousseau.
13. Peter L. Berger, *Pyramids of Sacrifice*. Garden City, N.Y.: Doubleday, 1974.
14. Rousseau, 204–23.
15. See Dermot A. Lane, *Ireland, Liberation, and Theology*. Maryknoll, N.Y.: Orbis Books, 1978.
16. See Jeffrey K. Hadden and Charles E. Swann, *Prime Time Preachers*. Reading, MA.: Addison-Wesley, 1981.
17. Anson Shupe and William A. Stacy, *Born Again Politics and the Moral Majority*. New York: Edwin Mellen, 1982.

18. Max Weber, *From Max Weber*. New York: Oxford University Press, 1958, 323–59.
19. Max L. Stackhouse, *Creeds, Society, and Human Rights*. Grand Rapids, MI.: Eerdmans, 1984.
20. Harvey Cox, *Religion in the Secular City*. New York: Simon and Schuster, 1984, 123.
21. See Juan Luis Segundo, *The Liberation of Theology*. Maryknoll, N.Y.: Orbis Books, 1976; Gustavo Gutiérrez, *A Theology of Liberation*. Maryknoll, N.Y.: Orbis Books, 1973; Matthew L. Lamb, *Solidarity With Victims*. Maryknoll, N.Y.: Orbis Books, 1982; and Rosina Gibellini, ed., *Frontiers of Theology in Latin America*. Maryknoll, N.Y.: Orbis Books, 1979.
22. See Hugo Assman, *Theology for a Nomad Church*. Maryknoll, N.Y.: Orbis Books, 1976; Sergio Torres and John Eagleson, eds., *Theology in the Americas*. Maryknoll, N.Y.: Orbis Books, 1976; Camilo Torres, *Revolutionary Priest*. Middlesex, England: Pelican Books, 1973, 373–78, 422–25.
23. Kofi Appiah-Kubi and Sergio Torres, eds., *African Theology En Route*. Maryknoll, N.Y.: Orbis Books, 1979; John W. de Gruchy, *The Church Struggle in South Africa*. Grand Rapids, MI: Eerdmans, 1979.
24. Lane, *Ireland, Liberation, and Theology*.
25. Assman, 123–24.
26. Gutiérrez, 11.
27. Segundo, 76.
28. Peter L. Berger, "Continuing the discussion: 'a politicized Christ,'" *Christianity and Crisis* 39, no. 4 (1979): 52–54.
29. Marvin M. Ellison, *The Center Cannot Hold*. Washington, D.C.: University Press of America, 1983, 248–64.
30. See Andre Gunder Frank, *Latin America: Underdevelopment or Revolution*. New York: Monthly Review Press, 1969, 371–409.
31. René Laurentin, *Liberation, Development, and Salvation*. Maryknoll, N.Y.: Orbis Books, 1972, 150–66.
32. Jose Miguez Bonino, *Doing Theology in a Revolutionary Situation*. Philadelphia: Westminster, 1975, 106–30; Arthur F. McGovern, *Marxism: An American Christian Perspective*. Maryknoll, N.Y.: Orbis Books, 1980, 288–92.
33. Gustavo Guetiérrez and Richard Shaull, *Liberation and Change*. Atlanta: John Knox Press, 1977, 74–95.
34. Leonardo Boff, *Liberating Grace*. Maryknoll, N.Y.: Orbis Books, 1979, 154.

35. V. I. Lenin, *The Essential Works of Lenin*. New York: Bantam Books, 1966, 272–464.
36. See Stackhouse, *Creeds, Society, and Human Rights*.
37. Karl Mannheim, *Ideology and Utopia*. New York: Harcourt, Brace & World, 1936, 211–19.
38. See Cox, 136–37.
39. See Segundo, 81–95.
40. Gutiérrez, 15.
41. Ibid., 10.
42. See Segundo, 154–81.
43. Cox, 181.
44. Ibid., 197.
45. See Ellison, 230–38; and Dom Helder Camara, *Revolution Through Peace*. New York: Harper, 1971.
46. Segundo Galilea, "The church in Latin American and the struggle for human rights," 100–106 in Alois Müller and Norbert Greinacher, eds., *The Church and the Rights of Man*. New York: Seabury Press.
47. Leonardo Boff, *Jesus Christ Liberator*. Maryknoll, N.Y.: Orbis Books, 1978, 46; and Gutiérrez and Shaull, 103–104.
48. Cox, 266–67.

7

Indigenous Religions and the Transformation of Peripheral Societies

PAGET HENRY

THE study of the cultural systems of peripheral societies currently finds itself at a major theoretical impasse resulting largely from the decline of modernization theory and the rise of dependency theory. While the former has emphasized the cultural orientations of peripheral societies, the latter has emphasized political economy. One result of the rise of dependency theory has been a sharp decline in the systematic treatment of culture in the analysis of Third World development. Much of the literature on the cultural systems of peripheral societies, thus, has remained within the framework of modernization theory, while analysis of their political and economic systems is taking place within the newer paradigm. Consequently, the study of peripheral cultural systems remains separated by significant paradigmatic differences from the study of peripheral economic and political systems. The nature of this disjuncture is sufficiently serious as to constitute a crisis in the analysis and understanding of the development of peripheral societies.

This paper attempts to address this deficiency by developing a

---

The author gratefully acknowledges the helpful suggestions of Jeffrey K. Hadden in the revision of this paper.

123

theoretical perspective that brings the analysis of peripheral cultural systems squarely within the framework of dependency theory. This perspective rests on a theory of peripheral capitalism that extends much of the analysis of dependency theory to cultural systems. It is argued that the broad patterns of cultural change in peripheral countries have been different from those in the central countries. Whereas patterns of change in central societies have indeed been dominated by processes of formal and scientific rationalization, as suggested by modernization theory, in peripheral societies patterns of cultural change have been dominated by structural and symbolic processes of rationalization that have served to legitimate the external hegemony that accompanied the process of peripheralization.

As a means of partially illustrating the utility of this new theoretical perspective, this paper examines three cases of change in Third World relations: (1) the Rastafarians of Jamaica; (2) liberation theology in Latin America and; (3) Islamic revivalism. Examination of these cases focuses on similarities and differences, as well as continuities and shifts in patterns of symbolic interpretation and rationalization. Hopefully, this approach will help clarify persistent patterns of change that are characteristic of peripheral cultural systems. I begin by identifying several basic propositions about capitalism and cultural change in both center and peripheral societies.

Central Capitalism and Cultural Development

Prior to the emergence of the capitalist world system in the sixteenth century, the broad patterns of cultural development were basically similar in what are now identified as center and peripheral societies. Sociologically, these patterns of development were dominated by the legitimacy needs of religious elites and the identity maintaining needs of the population. As identity needs were met primarily by religious symbols, religion was the dominant subsector of the cultural systems. Under the leadership of religious elites, this subsector succeeded in subordinating the claims of the arts, philosophy, and instrumental knowledge to its own cognitive claims.

With the emergence of capitalism as a world system, this pattern of development was radically disrupted. Cultural development in the centers and peripheries of the system moved in different directions. As the capitalist mode of production was established in the central countries, religious elites found themselves in competition with the new economic, scientific, and political elites for control of the cultural system. Gradually the power of religious elites was eclipsed by the new economic elites who were taking control of the state, systematically linking science to production and establishing a global system of trade.

This conflict represented more than a mere struggle for resources between two competing groups of elites. Capitalism is characterized by a mode of production that has the power to negate traditional or pre-capitalist cultural formations. It does so by confronting the rationality of myths, rituals, religious, and metaphysical world-views with the rationality of the market, and the technical-instrumental rationality of scientific production. Culturally, capitalism required the ascendency of the latter types of rationality over the former. In other words, the introduction of the capitalist mode of production in the central countries radically altered the balance between areas of society that were organized on principles of formal-instrumental rationality, and those organized on principles of value oriented rationality.

As Habermas (1970, 96) has argued, capitalism altered this balance by making the expansion of subsystems of purposive-rational action independent of the legitimating and reality defining power of traditional belief systems. With the aid of science and spectacular increases in production, systems of purposive-rational action gradually developed the capacity to generate and institutionalize their own definitions of reality and, thus, tended to become self-legitimatizing. Consequently, as the productive forces expanded, more and more areas of these societies came to be interpreted and manipulated within the framework of this instrumental logic. It was the growth of this secular and instrumental orientation that surpassed the growth of religious rationalization to become the dominant pattern of cultural change in the central countries.

Peripheral Capitalism and Cultural Underdevelopment

Turning to the peripheries of these central societies, we find very different patterns of cultural change. As noted before, cultural development in what are now considered peripheral societies was similar to that in the centers prior to their integration into the capitalist world-system. With the peripheralization of some areas to the major centers of the capitalist world-system, long established patterns of social interaction ceased to provide the primary sociological context within which cultural change would take place. Their place was taken by the organizational demands and legitimation needs of the system of domination that mediated and institutionalized the peripheralization of the penetrated country. Cultural change came to be dominated by patterns of structural and symbolic rationalization that were required for the legitimation and delegitimation of peripheral domination. As this situation of domination was expressed primarily through the state, it was the particular set of relations with the state that became the primary set of relations affecting the pattern of cultural development.

To understand why these legitimacy relations with the state take precedence over relations with an expanding productive system, we need to take note of two structural characteristics of peripheral capitalism. First, peripheral capitalism rests on a foundation of external domination which significantly increases the importance of the political and military institutions. The state is usually a highly militarized and authoritarian institution. Second, peripheral capitalist economies tend to have narrow productive bases which stem from the specific roles these economies are allocated within the framework of the global system. Peripheral economies are essentially single crop economies in which growth is determined not by local demand and technological innovation, but by external demand. Consequently, their economies continue to produce the same commodities indefinately without significant diversification. The highly circumscribed and primary nature of the functions performed by these economies generates little demand for new scientific knowledge. Hence, there is only limited internalization and institutionalization of science which, in turn, limits the base for the growth of cultural patterns of formal and scientific rationalization.

The combination of external domination and narrow productive base, makes the primary expanding forces in peripheral capitalist societies the political institutions. As these imperial institutions expand, they generate patterns of cultural rationalization that delegitimate local authority and legitimate the extention or continuation of imperial rule. It is this conflict between the systems of external and local authority that constitutes the new sociological context for cultural change in the periphery.

In the course of this conflict, traditional authority, including religious authority, is overthrown in a manner very different from the way it experiences diminished authority and influence in the center. The first important difference is that in the periphery the overthrow is primarily a political act. The process is achieved by colonizing elites who are supported by an imperial military, as opposed to an indigenous class whose strength rests in part upon its scientization of the mode of production. In the absence of such a class, science is unable to pose the challenge to religion that it does in the center.

A second important difference in the nature of the conflict with traditional authority stems from the fact that capitalist production processes are never subject to the normative constraints of peripheral cultural systems. In center societies capitalist production processes must be liberated from the control of the pre-capitalist value systems. This is not the case in peripheral societies. The processes of production can be superimposed without establishing corresponding rationalization of the economic norms of peripheral cultural systems. However, the traditional orientations of these cultural systems, particularly the attitudes of the dominated working classes towards work, created problems for capitalist production.

A third factor which makes the conflict with traditional authority different is the fact that capitalist production is not dependent upon peripheral cultural systems for supplies of technical information. These supplies come from the center. Hence, there is no pressing need to scientize or liberate the knowledge producing sectors of peripheral cultural systems from the control of traditional authority. In short, this initial freedom of the capitalist production process, and its supply of technical information from the normative control of traditional authority in the periphery make the control and secularization of the cultural system unnecessary. Rather, only control of the state is necessary. This resolution of the conflict with traditional authority does not lead to processes of scientific rationalization but, rather, to processes of resistance, stagnation, assimilation, hybridization, and deculturalization. Hence, the perpetuation of the phenomenon of cultural underdevelopment.

In sum, the primary obstacles to the rise of capitalist production in the periphery is the system of local national authority. It is the restraints of this system that have to be broken and, hence, it is here that the major conflicts are located. The dislodging of traditional authority, including religious authority comes as part of the dislodging of local national authority. Local elites must be replaced by foreign elites. Local authority must be delegitimated and bourgeois authority legitimated. This competition gives rise to patterns of cultural rationalization that support both sides of the conflict.

Ironically, the institutionalization of this conflict creates the sociological conditions which result in the linking of cultural underdevelopment to the expansion and challenging of external political forces.

Thus, what is peculiar to peripheral cultural systems is that they have been changing under the imperatives of the conflict between external and local authority.

Religion and Cultural Development in the Post-Colonial Period

The above discussion of peripheral capitalism and cultural underdevelopment focused primarily on the colonial phase of the external domination that is basic to these types of societies. Analysis focused on the institutions and processes of legitimation that suppress local attempts to exercise national authority. This emphasis is necessary as there is no legitimate place for peripheral nationalism in the colonial phase. With the transition to the monopoly phase of capitalism in the center, however, this possibility emerges.

Throughout this period the hegemony of central capitalism has been able to accommodate and contain peripheral nationalism. Accommodation of peripheral nationalism is marked by policies of decolonization and controlled nation building that have been in operation since the turn of the century. The growth of peripheral nationalism has significantly altered the manner in which conflict between center and periphery manifests itself. There is a decided shift from a demand for nationality authority to demands for the removal of restrictions on the authority these countries are currently allowed to exercise.

This growth of peripheral nationalism is very important for patterns of cultural change in the post-colonial period. It has interrupted the patterns of deculturalization and assimilation that were characteristic of the late nineteenth and early twentieth centuries, a process which partially westernized the identities, belief systems and lifestyles of elites in peripheral countries. This westernization has generally been accompanied by the abandonment and devaluation of indigenous identities, belief systems and lifestyles. The growth of peripheral nationalism is producing a greater acceptance and even revalorizing of indigenous identities, belief systems, and lifestyles.

These tendencies toward cultural indigenization are evident in the arts, education, language, religion, and secular ideologies; in short, throughout the cultural systems of post-colonial societies. If we take the cases of African and Caribbean literature it is easy to mark the onset of this period between the 1930s and the 1950s. Running through this literature is a concern for the possibilities and prospects of nationhood in these regions. Some writers (Lamming and Achiebe) express and legitimate hope, while others (Patterson and Naipaul) express despair in the face of the "steep ascent" that is ahead for these countries. Whether these writers are hopeful or not, what is important is their creative use of symbols to interpret reality, rationalize and critique existing values, and to fashion alternative visions for reconstruction in the periphery.

Thus we arrive at the proposition that in the post-colonial period the legitimating and the delegitimating of conflict between external hegemony and local national authority still dominates the process of change in peripheral cultural systems. Throughout this period, the conflict has led to the production of dramas, arguments, songs, portraits, etc., that have either supported or denied the demand for more substance to, and fewer restrictions on the national power that has so far been won. The cultural demands that stem from this conflict, together with the identity maintaining needs of the population, constitute the sociological context in which peripheral cultural systems are currently developing or failing to develop.

As religions are integral parts of cultural systems, they are necessarily affected by the changing legitimacy demands generated by the hegemonic conflict. Patterns of change in religions are shaped both by their attempts to affect the outcome of social conflict, and by the outcomes themselves. To the extent that religions introduce creative symbols into the arena of social conflict, it is to that extent they will incorporate an explicitly political dimension. In the post-colonial period, critique of the political situation is likely to lead religious elites in the direction of interpreting traditional religion as a legitimizing foundation for resistance, autonomy, and indigenous authenticity.

Modernization theory suggests that the patterns of change are the same in both the center and the periphery. Thus, we should expect the progressive secularization of peripheral societies. This tendency towards secularization results from the diffusion of Western values and technology. I have not argued against the secularizing trends of modernization; rather, my position is that these tendencies are subordinate to other even stronger tendencies operating in peripheral cultural systems.

These tendencies toward secularization, to be sure, are present in central as well as peripheral societies. However, while the long term patterns of cultural change in center societies have been dominated by processes of rationalization that are related to the expansion of the productive forces, these patterns of change have not gone uninterrupted. They have been challenged by movements in art (romanticism, surrealism, etc.), in philosophy (existentialism) and, of course, in religion. The secularization thesis of modernization theory is probably overstated even for the cases of the central countries.

A central idea in a critique of the "over-secularized" view of man is the recognition of the fact that human identities are fragile structures that must be supported and maintained. Human identities, no less than social structures, are structures that need to be legitimated. The formation of the human self is a symbolically mediated process.

Central to the formation of the human self is the securing of the self against various types of anxiety. Symbols and rituals help to allay anxiety, and thus remove threats to our identity. These symbols and rituals may be artistic, philosophical, scientific, or religious in nature. For most of the people of the world they have been primarily religious.

Such a connection between anxiety and religious symbols was clearly recognized by Weber (1958, 109–12) in his analysis of the Protestant religions. In these religions the primary anxiety was a dread of being divinely judged and condemned to eternal punishment. This was the anxiety that threatened the everyday identities of the members, and which the ascetic work ethic was designed to allay. Thus in Weber's analysis, the production of a symbolically mediated and ritualized work ethic was directly related to the allaying of anxiety.

This correlation between anxiety and the production of interpretive symbolism has been further corroborated by a number of existentialist writers. For example, Tillich (1971, 32–36) has argued that the production and use of religious symbols is one response that can provide an individual with "the courage" to be him-or-herself in spite of threats of "non-being." Ricouer's (1969) analysis of the "symbolism of evil" and its roots in subjective states such as "stain," "guilt," and "sin" is also an excellent demonstration of this correlation.

A central concern of this inquiry is whether there has been any appreciable decline in the extent to which people of peripheral societies derive their identity maintaining legitimations from religion. Such a decline, of course, is a logical deduction from modernization theory. I would like to suggest that the available evidence on religions in the post-colonial period does support such an expectation.

First of all, pre-colonial religions in peripheral societies have general-ly survived the centuries of colonial domination essentially intact and with large followings. In the cases where the indigenous religions did not survive, their places were taken by Christianity. The people of these societies are thus deeply embedded in religious symbolism.

Second, the post-colonial period has seen a phenomenal growth of cults and new religions that have been either movements within major traditions or various types of syncretic innovations. Rastafarians in the Caribbean, Kimbanguism in Zaire, the Cross and the Star and the Aladura movements in Nigeria, Umbanda in Brazil, the Olive Tree and Unification church movements of Korea, and the Huniyan movement in Sri Lanka are just a few of the new religious movements originating in the periphery during the post-colonial period.

Some of these movements, such as Kimbanguism and Rastafarian-ism, are highly politicized religions whose symbolism explicitly delegiti-mate external authority. Others, such as the religions of the Aladura movement are oriented towards social mobility, while movements such as Transcendental Meditation are oriented towards spiritual liberation and the legitimation of individual identities. Another important charac-teristic of these religions is that they are largely urban phenomena. This suggests that the patterns of class formation, political exclusion, and unequal income distribution that currently characterize the process of urbanization in the periphery, do not encourage a turn away from the use of religious symbolism, but to different ones. The growth of these new religions as well as their social characteristics, do not support the decline in religious orientation that would be expected from moderni-zation theory. Rather, the evidence points to the continuing impor-tance of religion as a primary source of both individual and societal legitimation.

With this conceptual background, the focus of analysis shifts to the demonstration of the relation between the legitimacy needs of the conflict between external and national authority on the one hand, and patterns of symbol formation and value rationalization on the other. It is this process, I contend, that has been responsible for the dominant patterns of change in peripheral cultural systems.

Three very different patterns are observed: First, we will look at the Rastafarians, a *new religious movement* among the working and lower classes of Jamaica. Rastafarianism is important because its theology contains a comprehensive argument that delegitimates both racism and peripheral domination. The Rastafarians constitute only a small minori-ty of Jamaicans, but their theology is having a profound effect on Jamaicans' understanding of themselves and their history of external domination. And in a broader context, Rastafarianism is impacting the consciousness of most of the peoples of the Caribbean. In this case, a new religion renders illegitimate old values and cultural systems which heretofore had reinforced central domination of the periphery.

The second case is liberation theology in Latin America, a movement

to *transform* a religion which was imposed upon indigenous populations by the conquering colonialists. The leadership of the movement is
predominantly a new breed of intellectual elites. Their goal is to
transcend and transform a faith which was initially used to legitimize
colonial dominance and, later, domination by a social and military elite.
Their strategy is the mobilization of the masses into indigenous "base
communities."

The third case to be examined is the phenomenon of Islamic *revival*.
This case is differentiated from the others in that Islam represents an
indigenous religion which survived the colonial period. Islamic revival
is anything but monolithic, but underpinning the many faces of Islam is
a commitment to faith and cultural traditions as central components of
both individual identity and national response to modernization and
westernization.

In each of these instances we see how religion has served as a carrier
of cultural traditions and symbol systems. In each instance, religion
contributes a powerful antidote to the assault of westernization and
modernization on peripheral societies. And, in each instance, religion—
be it new, transformed or revived—serves simultaneously to delegitimate the order established by the colonialists while pointing the way to
a new order. It cannot be known, of course, how each of these three
cases will be worked out in history. The important conceptual argument made here is that dependency theory needs to incorporate a
deeper understanding of cultural systems as a central component in the
emergence of peripheral societies. Religion is a central, but certainly not
the only dimension of cultural systems which beg for systematic analysis
and understanding.

The Rastafarians

The Jamaican religious landscape is complex: In addition to the
Rastafarians, there are a number of major Christian denominations and
a vast array of Afro-Christian syncretic movements such as Pocomania,
Zion, and Revival Zion. A socio-historical analysis of these religions
would reveal that most have been primarily concerned with the
legitimation of individual identities. In the case of the Christian
churches, the dependence of dominated populations on these sources of
personal legitimacy has also been used to gain submission to the
colonial order as well. In short, the Christianization of Jamaican society
was one of the important changes in its cultural system that facilitated
the acceptance and routinizing of peripheral domination.

In addition to supplying the colonial state with legitimacy, the patterns of church-state relations that emerged in the colonial period also had important consequences for the post-colonial period. In Jamaica, and much of the English-speaking Caribbean, the colonizing elites succeeded in reproducing the hegemony of secular authority over religious authority that had been achieved in England. This displacement of both Christian and indigenous religious authority established the precedent of secular political elites or political parties as the primary instruments for the control of state power. Thus, in spite of being a major supplier of legitimacy, the extent to which the church as a distinct group would be able to make a bid for the control of state power in the post-colonial period was severely limited. As we will see, this overall position of religious elites in Caribbean systems of national power is quite different from that of religious elites in the Latin-American and Muslim countries.

In spite of the significant role of the church in the legitimating of colonial authority, it is possible, particularly in the post-colonial period, to observe trends in the opposite direction. For example, the Afro-Christian religions are dominated by rituals and processes of symbol formation that attempt to answer the existential questions that threaten individual identity. However, this concern has not completely eclipsed questions of political liberation. In the course of everyday life, these issues usually play themselves out in a quiet but socially unsanctioned commitment to African modes of religiosity. As the history of slave and post-slavery revolts suggests, there has been a strong connection between this commitment to African religiosity and political liberation. Thus, while there has been no explicit thematizing of the political implications of this commitment, it has manifested itself in concrete political actions.

Among the major Christian denominations, contemporary patterns of change can be directly linked to the conflict with external authority. Until the end of the colonial period, formal control of these churches was in the hands of external religious elites. With the growth of peripheral nationalism, these institutions also experienced processes of decolonization. This has occurred on two levels: the formal/organizational and the theological. As a result of changes on the first level, most of the major denominations have severed controlling ties with parent bodies in the center, and have established themselves as independent members of the World Council of Churches. At the theological level the pattern of change is more ambivalent. A rather clear division has emerged among the local religious elite in their response to developmental and political issues. This division has produced a conservative wing that wants to continue the colonial tradition, and a more radical wing which insists on change, but has not yet produced a liberation theology comparable to that of Latin America. This theology is still in very rudimentary states, as the works of Erskine (1981), Davis (1977), and Hamid (1977) suggest.

Among the various groups that make up the Jamaican religious landscape, the Rastafarians have devoted the most theological space to the delegitimating of imperial domination. To understand this particular characteristic of Rastafarianism, we must recognize the peculiar state of "non being" that its symbolic productions attempt to analyze, interpret, and overcome. The word most often used by Rastafarians to describe both their subjective and objective condition is "dread." Although closely related, this is not the dread of Kierkegaard (1944). Kierkegaard's concept of dread concerns the anxiety that paralyzes the human self as it senses its aloneness in the face of the cosmic dance of life. The dread of the Rastafarians does not derive immediately from such an anxious relation of the self to nature's continuous movement. That is, it is not immediately existential in its source. Rather, this dread springs from the dance of social life; from the unjust and impersonal conventions of Jamaican society that threaten the identity of many of its members with insignificance.

Rastafarianism is the creation of the Jamaican working and lower classes. In slightly varying degrees the members of these classes experience themselves as being marginal and expendable in relation to rules and activities that govern social life. Historically, this marginalization has been the result of the processes of class and racial domination that accompanied the introduction of African labor and the capitalist mode of production to the region. These processes of domination were not simply physical or external in nature; they also had their subjective aspects. These included the stereotypical redefinition of Africans as "Negroes" and the devaluation and disruption of their traditional cultural practices. As a result, Afro-Jamaicans were unable to project and legitimate their accustomed identities. Positive self-images were routinely contested by the stereotypical images and patterns of racist interaction. The major threat to the identity of many Jamaicans, thus, came from the grinding of the social machine, not from the natural dangers and chances of life. This, I believe, is a critical source of the extensive linking of political and religious symbols we find among the Rastafarians.

The existence of this peculiar pattern of symbol formation among colonized people has already been pointed out by Fanon. He suggested that "in the *Weltanschauung* of a colonized people there is an impurity, a flaw that outlaws any ontological explanation. . . . Ontology" he continues, "does not permit us to understand the being of the black man. For not only must he be black; he must be black in relation to the white man" (1967, 109–110). In other words, in colonial societies, anxiety in relation to rhythm of social life replaces, or eclipses, the anxiety experienced in relation to the rhythm of cosmic life. Hence the shift in the pattern of symbol formation that sustains the construction of worldviews. This, it seems to me, is the key to the particular characteristics of Rastafarianism.

Rastafarian theology is based upon a dialectical projection of a symbolically mediated presence that negates the specific subjective absences generated by the processes of marginalization and stereotypical redefinition. The salvific project of Rastafarian theology is not founded on a "courage to be" that maintains the self in spite of such natural phenomena as sickness, death, the hiddenness of God, and other obscure and paradoxical aspects of life. Rastafarians assimilate these matters quite readily as nature is for them a very positive and friendly force. Rather, the soteriological program of Rastafarian theology is oriented towards a courage that reconstitutes the self in spite of such social phenomena as class/race domination and stereotypical redefinition. That Rastafarian theology is based on such a dialectical projection can be shown from an analysis of some of its central symbols.

More than any other set of symbols, the interpretations that have developed around the symbolic use of Ethiopia gives us the clue to the salvific project of the Rastafarians. The Rastafarians were not the first to create a complex mythology around Ethiopia. This has been a persistent theme in the thought of Africans in the Western world. Along with Egypt, Ethiopia is one of the oldest and better known African nations, and it serves as a symbol for all Africa. References to Ethiopia appear in the Bible. Also, the symbolic importance of Ethiopia increased in the early decades of the twentieth century as it was the only nation in Africa that was not colonized. It continued to crown its own kings and to govern itself. In short, it was doing everything that the racist redefinition of Africans claimed that they were incapable of doing. This phenomenon of Ethiopianism has received its most detailed elaboration among the Rastafarians.

Sparked by the crowning of Haile Selassie as Emperor of Ethiopia in 1930, the Rastafarian religion started in Jamaica in the ashes of Garvey's movement. Garvey's many references to the crowning of

African kings and to African redeemers were seen by many as prophecies that had been fulfilled by this event. Leonard Howell, Archibald Dunkley, and Robert Hinds, among others, were convinced that Haile Selassie's coronation was a fulfillment of prophecy. Quite separately at first, they elevated Haile Selassie to divine status, proclaiming him the long awaited redeemer from Africa, and gave him the additional title of *Ras Tafari*. Armed with this new message, these early Rastafarian leaders set out to preach the good news.

This attempt to spread the news of the arrival of a redeemer soon brought these leaders into conflict with the colonial authorities. In January of 1934, Howell and Hinds were arrested and sent to prison on charges of sedition. The guilty verdict rested largely upon a public speech in which Howell advocated the following: (1) hatred of the white race; (2) the superiority of the black race; (3) revenge on whites; (4) the rejection and humiliation of the colonial government in Jamaica; (5) preparation for the return to Africa and; (6) the recognition of Haile Selassie as the Supreme Being, and sole ruler of African people (Barrett 1977, 85). This account of Howell's address is one of the earliest formulations that we have of Rastafarian doctrine. Very visible are its delegitimating stands on colonial domination that are inseparable from their religious framework.

After his release from prison, Howell formed a commune in the hills where he continued to develop and institutionalize the Rastafarian alternative. His community was attacked by the police in 1941 and again in 1953. These attacks came as Howell, among other things, advocated the paying of taxes to Haile Selassie and not to the Jamaican government. Thus, the period from 1934 to about 1960 was a violent one for the Rastafarians. It was in the latter phases of this period that members of the group began growing and wearing their hair in "locks," first calling themselves "Ethiopian warriors" and later, "locksmen." It was also the period in which the term "Babylon" became the primary symbol for the interpretation and assessment of the colonial establishment. The delegitimating power of this symbol clearly allowed the Rastafarians to extend to contemporary Jamaica the Biblical destruction of ancient Babylon.

This violent phase ended, and was followed by one in which faith was placed in the divine fulfillment of the prophesied destruction of European imperialism and the global redemption of Africans. This shift was accompanied by the more careful study of the Bible and its reinterpretation. This was a very fruitful period for the growth of

Rastafarian doctrine. In examining these beliefs our focus will be on the delegitimating aspects. However, it is important to stress that these are systematically linked to a larger whole that includes a doctrine of man, a well developed mysticism, rituals for living, a doctrine of divine judgment, and view of the future of the world.

The foundation of Rastafarian theology is the mystical knowledge of the divinity of Haile Selassie. Intuitive knowledge of this fact is the basic experience that defines the Rastafarians and is the source of their prolific interpretive activities. In one sense the development of Rastafarian theology is the result of simultaneously rejecting and reinterpreting their Christian heritage in the light of the intuitive knowledge of the divinity of Haile Selassie. This hermeneutic undertaking reveals both the extent to which Rastafarian thought has remained within and moved beyond the categorical framework of Christian thought.

The Rastafarians are very bold in their approach to the Bible: They do not take it literally, but feel it is a text that must be interpreted and will yield additional insights about their condition and fate. In this spirit the Rastafarians begin by making themselves the heroes of the biblical drama. They see themselves as the descendents of the ancient Israelites. Thus, it is through the Rastafarian experience that the biblical odyssey continues in the present period. Parallels and continuities are established between the suffering and enslavement of Africans in the Western world, and the suffering and enslavement of the Israelites by groups such as the Babylonians. In both cases the enslavement is seen as divine punishment for sins committed.

In the context of Jamaican society, the interpretation of the concepts of good and evil goes beyond personal disobedience of divine laws. They are reinterpreted to include the socio-historical forces that "downpress" the Rastafarians and threaten them with personal and social insignificance. The "Downpressors" are, of course, Babylonians, and Rastafarians often refer to themselves as "being in captivity in Babylon." Babylon refers to the central countries of the West. However, this reference also includes their local supporters and representatives, particularly within the police, the state leadership, and the church. In this biblical representation of the imperial West, Rastafarian theology reserves very specific places for Britain and the United States. The former is responsible for the relocation and enslavement of Africans in the Western hemisphere. However, the coronation of Haile Selassie was the sign that marked the end of British hegemony and the decline of Babylon. But, during this period of decline, a new power, the United

States, known to the prophets as Rahab, has attempted to set itself up in Britain's place. The United States, according to Rastafarian theology, "is the Northern country of which the prophets Jeremiah and Isaiah spoke. The brutal invader which seeks to blot out the life of God's chosen ones" (Owens 1976, 80). But in the Rastafarian reading of Isaiah, this imperial project of the United States is also doomed to failure.

Although both of these imperial projects are expected to collapse in the future, at present the British and the Americans along with their local supporters are the "downpressors." They are the evil ones that are keeping Rastafarians oppressed in Jamaica and away from Africa. In this context Jamaica becomes identified with hell and Ethiopia with heaven. Haile Selassie becomes not only the Supreme Being, but the returned Christ who is expected to judge the world and set it right. This setting right of the world should bring about the liberation of Africans and their return to the homeland (heaven).

What is truly remarkable about this salvific project is its use of Christian categories and symbols to make coherent a set of contents that are anti-Christian and largely this-worldly. In other words it uses the cosmic framework of the Christian drama of human creation, fall, and salvation to make coherent the socio-historical fall and future salvation of Africans. This shift in the pattern of symbol formation is suggestive of the particular type of non-being in spite of which the Rastafarians have been attempting to maintain a positive identity and a sense of significance.

Space does not permit an extended account of Rastafarian theology, but this discussion should suffice to give an idea of the forces that are motivating this reinterpretation of a transcendent drama into such an explicitly socio-historical one. Sociologically speaking, the significance of the Rastafarian movement is its theology, which strongly delegitimates a secular system of external authority that undermines both individual and collective identity. This tendency is an important factor in the shift from more metaphysical modes of thought to more socio-historical ones that have been characteristic of peripheral countries in the post-colonial period.

The importance of Rastafarianism is not in the size of its following— indeed, the number of members is small. Rather, the world-view and value system expounded has permeated not only Jamaica, but a good bit of the Caribbean as well. Rastafarianism is an unlikely candidate to become a major religion in the region, however, by delegitimizing old cultural and economic arrangements, it serves as a transition to something new.

Liberation Theology

As in the case of the Caribbean, the Latin American religious landscape is also complex. In spite of the long hegemony of the Catholic church, it is a landscape that is presently marked by a wide variety of trends and developments. Like the Christian churches in the Caribbean, the hegemony of the Catholic church was related to the legitimacy it provided the colonial state. Since the turn of the century this earlier relationship has been challenged by a number of developments. These include the extension of the Catholic church's social and political activities through such organizations as Catholic Action and Christian Democratic parties, the growth of Protestantism, fundamentalism, indigenous syncretic religions, and most recently, the emergence of liberation theology.

The latter represents the most revolutionary stand that segments of the Latin American religious establishment have taken in response to the political challenges of being a Christian in that part of the world. It is among this group, principally the Roman Catholic contingent, that the creating of symbols that delegitimate external authority is most visible.

The colonizing elites of Latin America did not establish as great a degree of institutional differentiation between church and state as their counterparts in the Caribbean. Consequently in the post-colonial period the political power and political involvement of the church in Latin America has been much greater than in the Caribbean.

These differences with the Caribbean case were not enough, however, to produce the hegemony of religious authority in the post-colonial period. On the contrary, they were only sufficient for the production of different patterns of conflict between religious and secular authority. These differences in the location of the church in various systems of national power, are important in our understanding of differences in the patterns of legitimation and delegitimation that exist between peripheral countries.

Just as Rastafarian theology was the result of a politically oriented reinterpretation of Christianity in the light of the oppression of Africans in the Caribbean, liberation theology is the result of a similar reinterpretation of Christianity in the light of the experiences of the oppressed classes of Latin America. In spite of the differences in the level of intellectual craftsmanship, the basic orientation of these hermeneutic undertakings is quite similar. This claim is substantiated by the parallels that can be observed between Latin American liberation theology and the liberation theology of African Americans. In spite of the class differences that separate these two from Rastafarian theology, all three are attempts at reinterpretation in response to similar conditions of domination. In the cases of the Rastafarians and African Americans, the key symbol in this reinterpretation is race and its connection to Africa. In the case of Latin America, the new symbol for the reinterpretation of Christianity is that of dependence and its connections to poverty and external domination.

It is of some importance to note that this new set of symbols was not developed by Latin American theologians, but by secular intellectuals who were attempting to replace modernization theory. Subsequent adoption by the theologians stems from the fact that the symbols mark an important step in the decolonization of Latin American thinking. All complex systems of thought such as mythology, philosophy, or theology rest upon important symbols which emerge out of the concrete experiences of a group. These symbols have a loosely integrated metaphorical structure, and are capable of several levels of elaboration and development. The emergence and elaboration of the symbolism of dependence represent an area in which Latin American thinking has returned to its own roots.

The connection between dependency theory and liberation theology is explicit in the works of its major exponents. However, it is probably most explicit in the work of Bonino (1979, 14):

> The fundamental element in the new Latin American consciousness is the awareness that our political emancipation from Spain was—however justified and necessary—a step in the Anglo-Saxon colonial and neo-colonial expansion. Our independence from Spain made us available as suppliers of raw materials first and of cheap labor and manageable markets later on . . . The much better known and often condemned political and military interventions particularly of the United States in Latin America, are only the necessary maneuvers for the protection of this economic relation. Latin America has discovered the basic fact of its dependence. This is the real meaning of the liberal-modernist project.

This statement describes clearly the new element in contemporary Latin American consciousness. This element is the discovery of Latin American dependence beneath the symbolism of capitalism as a progressive and modernizing force. This discovery has changed not only economic and political theory, but theology as well. This theological adoption of the symbolism of dependence is not simply the result of reading new secular texts. Rather, it stems from the light these new texts are able to throw on contacts with poverty that various members of the clergy experience in the course of their work.

Central to the task of reinterpreting Christianity is the work of Gustavo Gutiérrez, who not only affirms the symbolism of dependence, but reinforces it with a critique of some of the fundamental assumptions of classical theology. Included in this undertaking is Gutiérrez's critique of the doctrine of the distinction of planes, which contends that the work of the church should be confined to the spiritual plane, thus leaving work on the temporal plane to the secular authorities. Gutiérrez finds this separation unacceptable. History, Gutiérrez argues, is a unified and indivisible process in which human beings either achieve or fail to achieve self-realization. Because history is thus a unified process, spiritual salvation is impossible without liberation on the socio-economic and political levels. The whole concept of spiritual salvation, thus, is radically historicized, as it is rendered inseparable from conditions of social and political emancipation.

One important consequence of this reinterpretation is that the key Christian concept of sin is also historicized. As in the case of the Rastafarians, the concept is no longer restricted to the inability of men and women to abide by biblical laws. "Sin" says Gutiérrez, "occurs in the negation of man as a brother, in the oppressive structures created for the benefit of the few and for the exploitation of peoples, races and social classes. Sin is fundamental alienation which, because it is such, cannot be reached in itself; it occurs only in concrete, historical situations, in particular alienation" (1979, 66). This linking of the concept of sin to particular alienations allows Gutiérrez to extend the concept to include the exploitation of workers in Latin America by the system of international capitalism.

The delegitimating consequences of such an extension should be clear; but they are made even more explicit when Gutiérrez discusses the problem of deliverance from sin. Given this historicized interpretation of the notion of sin, it follows that deliverance must be equally historical. "Sin," Gutiérrez tells us, "requires a radical liberation, but this necessarily includes liberation of a political nature" (1977, 66). Consequently, deliverance must include not only the projection of a spiritual alternative but also a socio-historical one. This alternative social order must be one in which the social structures do not systematically sunder the friendship with God and with one's brothers and sisters. For Gutiérrez, and many other liberation theologians, this alternative is envisioned as a socialist project of liberation. Although influenced by Marxism, this alternative must be rooted in local symbols and experiences. Elaborating and putting into practice such an alternative has become an inseparable part of the Christian message of these theologians. By linking salvation to a socialist order, the existing capitalist order has very clearly been made illegitimate.

Not surprisingly, this reinterpretation has occasioned a lot of criticism from more traditional Christian theologians. For example, Richard Neuhaus criticizes Gutiérrez for taking Christianity away from the transcendent dimensions that it ought to represent and making it a captive of revolutionary culture (1979, 44). In responding to criticisms such as these, liberation theologians are forced to clarify a number of positions including their methodological foundations. This discussion of methodology has led to a very lively debate about hermeneutics and its role in theology. Important work in this area has been done by Segundo (1976) and Miranda (1974). For example, in his effort to liberate theology from the captivity of atemporal concerns, Segundo develops a model of the hermeneutic enterprise in which the actual process of theologizing is always the second step. The first step or the point of departure is not transcendent assumptions, but the concrete situation in which one is immersed (1976, 75–76). From this vantage point reality becomes the only text from which one can begin. Having gained this understanding of the existing situation, the theologian may then proceed to interpret the texts of the Bible. The similarity with the Rastafarian approach to the Bible is quite striking. Clearly, the task of interpreting texts is an ever changing one, as social situations are always changing.

Again, space prevents a more detailed discussion of liberation theology. The point to be stressed from this discussion is the existence of a process of symbol formation and value rationalization that is oriented towards the delegitimating of external authority. These processes are terribly important. They constitute one of the most dynamic and creative aspects of peripheral cultural system development in the present period.

In the cases of both Rastafarian and liberation theology, we observe a commitment to social change which is profoundly influenced by the processes of symbol formation and value rationalization. In spite of the secular orientation of these processes of delegitimation, the commitment remains firmly rooted in a religious framework. Commitment to the religious framework is indicative of the persistence of religion in peripheral countries, while the political content is indicative of the primary symbols that have been taking hold of the peripheral consciousness.

The Islamic Revival

The shift from the Christian and Afro-Christian worlds of the Caribbean and Latin America to the Muslim world of the Middle East, Africa, and Asia, brings us into contact with a very different religious experience. However, along with these differences there are a number of similarities that grow out of the fact that the Muslim countries have also experienced processes of peripheralization. Consequently, the usefulness of the theory will be significantly enhanced if it allows identification of similar processes of symbol formation and value rationalization, without doing injustice to the important differences.

A number of important differences are immediately obvious with respect to the manner in which Muslim countries are integrated into the capitalist world system. First, most Muslim countries came under European influence much later (late nineteenth century) than the countries of Latin America and the Caribbean. The period of colonial or semi-colonial rule, hence, was much shorter. Second, the patterns of political control were, for the most part, very different. In contrast to the patterns of direct colonial rule that prevailed throughout the Western hemisphere, forms of indirect rule that retained a place for the cooperative sectors of the local political elites were common throughout the Muslim world. Both of these differences were related to the degree of political centralization and military strength that several Muslim states attained, a development dating back to the imperial phase of these societies in the sixteenth and seventeenth centuries.

One important result of these differences is that Western reorganization of these societies was significantly less than was the case in the Caribbean and Latin America. With regard to the institution that concerns us most, these societies were not Christianized. The Muslim religion, like the Muslim state, attained a higher degree of institutionalization than the indigenous religions of the Caribbean and Latin America. Not only did its interpretive and explanatory systems attain a high degree of universalism, it was also able to preserve these in writing. This preservation was usually the work of an elite, the Ulama, who, in addition to being responsible for religious education, were close to the centers of power. Detaching such a large number of people from such a well established religion would have been too costly politically. Consequently, the Muslim world did not experience as radical a severing from its own primary interpretative symbols as did Latin America and the Caribbean.

Because the reorganization of Muslim societies produced by the colonizing process was significantly less than the reorganization of Latin American and Caribbean societies, changes in pre-colonial church-state relations were also less far-reaching. In these societies colonizing elites were less successful in reproducing the displacement of religious authority that had been achieved in a number of other European dominated colonies. Although religious elites were replaced by imperial ones, the basic institutional structures and norms of Islam persisted.

In spite of these political and religious differences, the Muslim societies were unable to resist *de facto* subjugation to secular European authority. Even though in a less extreme way, they shared this condition with other peripheral countries. Inasmuch as the authority of local religious elites was never completely displaced, there was an ever-changing balance of power between them and the external elites.

To further concretize the situation of the Islamic countries, it is useful to recall the patterns that governed the displacement of the authority of religious elites in central capitalist countries. In these countries religious elites were replaced by local economic elites who captured state power and married science both to their productive and ideological enterprises. As a result of the latter, they were able to declare their independence of traditional religious protection and legitimation.

In spite of the special characteristics of the Islamic countries outlined earlier, this was not the pattern by which the authority of the religious elites was displaced. Displacement occured through the agency of a colonial elite which was backed by the might of an imperial military. This political elite thus took the place of a local economic class whose power derived largely from its monopoly over a new mode of production that was largely self-legitimating. In contrast to the Caribbean and Latin America, this displacement was not only partial but it left intact the institutional foundations of the Islamic religion.

Under these conditions our theory would lead us to expect that initially there would be similar patterns of cultural reassertion and new symbol formation, but that subsequently there would also be different ones, given the strength, norms, and traditions of the religious elites. The initially similar patterns can be seen throughout the phase of nationalist mobilization that resulted in the gradual withdrawal of

European authority. Among the more well-known cases of this nationalism were the modernizing reforms in countries such as Turkey, Iran,
and Afghanistan, which had retained formal independence (Voll 1982).
At the other extreme were the more socialist and revolutionary
expressions of nationalism that occured in such countries as Tunisia,
Egypt, and Algeria. In whatever form this nationalist drive was
expressed, the reassertion of Islamic religion played a largely supportive
role in what was essentially an anti-imperialist political project. This
role was not very different from the role played by indigenous religious
and politicized sectors of the Christian church in the growth of
nationalism in the Caribbean. This supportive role which Islam played
throughout this phase did not reflect its real power *vis-à-vis* the secular
nationalist elites that were gaining control of the state. Rather, the
situation reflected the decolonizing policies of the central countries in
the more or less orderly transfer of power to secular elites who were
able to justify their claims to power in terms of Western liberalism or in
some cases, socialism. Thus, throughout this period, Western and
secular oriented political elites emerged throughout the Muslim world.
This hegemony was not because these elites were, in fact, stronger than
the religious elites or because they represented new local interests that
were capable of legitimizing their own rule in the eyes of the public. On
the contrary, their ascension to power rested upon legitimating arguments that appealed to Western traditions, and the support of a local
economic elite that itself was a junior partner of the central capitalist
classes. The overall position of these governing elites was therefore
quite vulnerable as the foundations of their support were largely
external.

Under fragile conditions such as these, only high standards of
governing, improved rates of production, significant changes in patterns of resource distribution, and meaningful compromises with
important opposition groups could come close to ensuring stability. As
the opposite occured in many cases, these secular, post-colonial regimes
fell into periods of crisis. These crises produced the rapid growth of
delegitimating arguments which together with the hidden strength of
the religious elites pushed the Muslim world in a different direction
from that of the Caribbean and Latin America.

Movement in this different direction was made possible by the real
strength of the religious elites. This became increasingly obvious as
fissures began to appear in the bases of the secular regimes. The onset of
these crisis periods, combined with the hostile policies of many of these
regimes toward the *Ulama,* created the basis upon which religious elites

have made their bid to reestablish the primacy of their authority. The crises in these regimes have destroyed confidence in national experiments with liberalism and socialism, thus paving the way for a return to Islamic authority.

Examples of this bid to reassert the hegemony of religious authority through the control of state power can be seen in varying degrees of strength throughout the Muslim world. From Iran to Malaysia the calls for a Muslim state have been echoing. The 1979 revolution in Iran resulted in the collapse of one of the major experiments in liberalism and the recreation of an Islamic state. In countries such as Saudi Arabia where Islamic traditionalists have succeeded in keeping secular elites under control, the power of religious elites have only increased. In countries such as Egypt, Pakistan, and Libya, major examples of Islamic socialism, the emphasis has shifted more and more to the Islamic side.

This is particularly clear in the case of Pakistan where the Bhutto regime, which came to power on a socialist platform, was forced by organized religious groups to adopt a program of Islamization. This trend has been greatly strengthened under the military regime of General Zia which overthrew Bhutto in 1977. Thus, although state power has been in the hands of the military, the Islamization of the society has continued to increase.

It is this bid to reestablish the hegemony of religious authority that has sustained the current production of new legitimating and value rationalizing arguments, and sets the case of the Muslim countries apart from those of the Caribbean and Latin America. These arguments have been quite perceptively described by Arjomand as traditionalistic justifications and defenses for the reassertion of Islam. By traditionalism, Arjomand is referring to "the type of social thought, action or movement which arises when a tradition becomes self-conscious either in missionary rivalry with competing traditions or in the face of a serious threat of erosion or extinction emanating from its socio-political or cultural environment" (Arjomand 1984).

These traditionalistic patterns of argument and symbol formation are restorative in intent. Their aim is to provide justifications for the restoration of Islamic authority and abandoned Islamic traditions. As such they are in contrast to the reinterpretive patterns that were examined in the cases of the Caribbean and Latin America. In these countries there were reinterpretive processes that legitimated a greater assertion of national authority and a revalorizing of indigenous religious activity. However, there was no similar bid for power as either class domination or church acceptance of secular control of the state limited the extent of such a move. Consequently, there was little need for traditionalistic justifications in the Caribbean and Latin America. These contrasts demonstrate the important differences in the political positions of these two sets of religious elites.

Along with the crises of the post-colonial regimes, the strength of the Muslim elites rested on the fact that they were still in control of the most important interpretive symbols of these societies. These elites had been able for centuries to contain the independent and secular tendencies of philosophy, art, and other cultural forms. Similarly, the brief post-war period of secular hegemony was not able to make science the dominant cognitive form and so lessen the power of the religious elites. As we have already seen, the very nature of peripheral capitalist societies is not very supportive of such an expanded internalization and institutionalization of science. Given this weak challenge from the scientific establishment, religion retained much of its importance, thus maintaining the power base of the religious elites.

The activation of this dormant power base was brought on by the crises of the secular regimes and their attempts to erode the power of the Ulama. This suppression was an integral part of the nationalist movements. The traditionalistic arguments that are so prevalent today are essentially the intellectual interpretation and rationalization of the responses of the religious elites to their position in the post-colonial order. In sum, it is this reversal of direction in the conflict between secular and religious authority that has been primarily responsible for the patterns of traditionalistic rationalization that are currently sweeping through the Islamic world.

Conclusion

This paper began by noting the intellectual crisis that presently confronts the study of peripheral cultural systems. It was suggested that the roots of this crisis are located in the decline of modernization theory and the rise of dependency theory. The latter approach, because of its economic and political orientation, has either deemphasized culture or pursued its analysis within the traditional modernization framework. This paper attempts to bring the study of peripheral cultural systems within the same paradigm that is currently used to study peripheral economic and political systems.

The central theoretical proposition of the paper is that the dominant patterns of change in peripheral cultural systems are being shaped by conflicts between external and local national authority which are characteristic of Third World countries. Internalizing the experience of peripheral domination is the primary source of cultural change in these societies. Once internalized, this experience has to be assimilated, interpreted, explained, and transcended. Threats to individual identity and to local authority are particularly important events to be explained or countered. These developments are productive of the cultural symbols that either legitimate or delegitimate the peripheral order. Usually these patterns of symbol formation and value rationalization contrast sharply with the dominant patterns of the central countries. There, the production of symbols in response to situations of domination (Marxism, for example) has been the subordinate to the production of symbols in response to the permanent expansion and scientization of the productive forces.

The theoretical perspective here outlined rests upon these two contrasting principles concerning patterns of cultural change in the center and periphery.

In the second section of the paper three case studies are presented in an attempt to demonstrate utility of the first. This utility is demonstrated in two ways. First, the existence of a relationship between the hegemony of the political forces and patterns of cultural change in peripheral societies is demonstrated through the cases of the Rastafarians, liberation theology, and Islamic revival. Second, in addition to demonstrating the existence of the purported relationship, I showed ways in which this generalization is modified by a variety of factors such as the degree of peripheralization, patterns of colonization, and the location of religion in national systems of power.

In the case of Rastafarians in the Caribbean, it was demonstrated that the production of delegitimating symbols is primarily a reinterpretive process. In the absence of indigenous religions to reestablish, delegitimation took the form of reinterpreting Christianity in the light of new indigenous symbols. This emphasis on resistance at the reinterpretive level is related to the power position of religious elites in the Caribbean. The Rastafarians are a small section of the Caribbean working and lower classes and, as such, have very little institutionalized power. Consequently, the ability to make the transition from reinterpretive critique to direct politico-religious action is not very great. Still, the indirect effects of Rastafarianism on the consciousness of the Caribbean is much greater than their numbers.

In Latin America, liberation theology is actively contributing to the production of delegitimating symbols. The political action that has accompanied this reinterpretive action has been significantly greater to date and the potential for widespread political action is abundantly evident. This difference is related to the stronger position of the church in Latin American national systems of power, and the more general acceptance of a role for the church in the control of state power.

In Islamic countries I demonstrated that the production of delegitimating religious symbols moved through two phases: The first was both reinterpretive and reevaluative. As the indigenous religions of these societies survived the colonial period, decolonization and independence resulted in their revalorization and the return of their status as the primary symbols for legitimating identities in these societies. This phase was also reinterpretive, in that the revitalized religions now share with secular ideologies the role of legitimating state power. Hence, we see various versions of Islamic liberalism, Islamic socialism and Pan-Islamism. In the second phase, which follows the crises of these secular regimes, symbol formation is primarily traditionalistic. Delegitimation takes the form of the self-conscious reasserting of religious authority over the state. This pattern of response is made possible by the crises that these weak Western oriented regimes have been experiencing in the presence of a stronger and more firmly established indigenous religious elite.

These differences in patterns of symbol formation point to the variety of cultural responses that we can expect from the current specification of the conflict between external and national authority in peripheral societies. They suggest that we should not expect a uniform response. In spite of the variety, the patterns observed in these cases do not suggest that the variety is likely to include the patterns of cultural change that have been dominant in the center. In other words, patterns of change that stem from the adjusting to and the resisting of limited national sovereignty are likely to dominate peripheral cultural systems for some time to come. These patterns in turn should strengthen existing indigenizing trends in these societies. Consequently, if the productive systems of these societies are eventually scientized, one outcome could be the internal rationalization rather than the westernization of peripheral cultural systems. The likelihood and conditions under which such a scientization might occur are open questions.

References

Arjomand, Said. 1984. Traditionalism in twentieth-century Iran. In *From Nationalism to Revolutionary Islam.* Ed. S. Arjomand. London: Macmillan Press.

Barrett, Leonard E. 1977. *The Rastafarians*. Boston: Beacon Press.

Bonino, Jose. 1979. *Doing Theology in a Revolutionary Situation*. Philadelphia: Fortress.

Cone, James. 1970. *A Black Theology of Liberation*. Philadelphia: J. B. Lippincott.

Davis, Kortright, ed. 1977. *Moving into Freedom*. Bridgetown, Barbados: Cedar Press.

Erskine, Noel, 1981. *Decolonizing Theology: A Caribbean Perspective*. Maryknoll, N.Y.: Orbis Books.

Fanon, Frantz. 1967. *Black Skin, White Masks*. New York: Grove Press.

Gutiérrez, Gustavo. 1979. The hope of liberation. In *Mission Trends No 3*. Ed. G. Anderson & T. Stransky. New York: Paulist Press.

——. 1979. *A Theology of Liberation*. Maryknoll, N.Y.: Orbis Books.

Habermas, Jurgen. 1970. *Towards a Rational Society*. Boston: Beacon Press.

Hamid, Idris, ed. 1972. *Troubling of the Waters*. San Fernando, Trinidad: Rahaman Press.

Kierkegaard, Sören. 1944. *The Concept of Dread*. Princeton: Princeton University Press.

Miranda, Jose. 1974. *Marx and The Bible*. Maryknoll, N.Y.: Orbis Books.

Owens, Joseph. 1976. *Dread*. Kingston, Jamaica: Sangsters.

Ricouer, Paul. 1969. *The Symbolism of Evil*. Boston: Beacon Press.

Segundo, Juan. 1976. *The Liberation of Theology*. Maryknoll, N.Y.: Orbis Books.

Tillich, Paul. 1971. *The Courage to Be*. New Haven: Yale University Press.

Voll, John. 1982. *Islam: Continuity and Change in the Modern World*. Boulder, CO.: Westview.

PART THREE
PROPHETIC RELIGION IN THE SERVICE OF NATION BUILDING

8

Modern Islamic Sociopolitical Thought

JOHN L. ESPOSITO

THE world of twentieth-century Islam has been one of rapid and dramatic change—colonialism, independence, and the emergence of separate Muslim nation states. Political, social, and economic changes have had to be absorbed within a compressed period of decades rather than the several centuries permitted the West.

Modern Islamic sociopolitical thought reflects many of the conflicts and tensions which have accompanied the establishment of modern states and societies in the Muslim world. This essay will trace the development of Islamic sociopolitical thought from 1945 to the contemporary Islamic revival, identifying some of the important currents and movements.[1]

Modern Muslim politics must be understood against the background of European imperialism and colonialism. By the nineteenth century European states (in particular the British, French, and Dutch) had penetrated and had increasingly dominated the Muslim world from North Africa to Southeast Asia. In the Islamic world, Western colonial rule precipitated a religious as well as a political crisis. For the first time since the birth of Islam in seventh-century Arabia, political and cultural sovereignty was lost to non-Islamic powers. No longer were the

The author would like to acknowledge the contribution of Laura Quinn to this chapter.

153

trappings of an Islamic state present: the ruler (caliph-sultan), Islamic law *(Shariah)*, *ulama* (religious scholar-leaders) who served as government advisors and administrators of the state's educational, legal and social welfare systems. Muslim subjugation by Christian Europe confirmed not only the decline of Muslim power, but also the apparent loss of divine favor and guidance. The Islamic concept of history views success and power as integral to the Muslims' universal mission to spread the rule of God and as dependent upon their obedience to God's will. Departure from the straight path of Islam meant loss of God's guidance and protection. Divine revelation (the *Quran*) proclaimed this truth. The early extraordinary expansion and conquests of Islam had provided historical validation. Within one hundred years of Muhammad's death, Muslim rule extended over an area which stretched from North Africa to India. During subsequent centuries Islam continued its political expansion and developed a rich and flourishing civilization and culture. Western colonial rule, unlike previous wars or invasions, terminated this long and glorious history of Muslim self-rule, raising the questions: What had gone wrong in Islam? How could Muslims realize God's will in a state governed by non-Muslims and non-Muslim law? How were Muslims to respond to this challenge to Muslim identity?

A variety of responses emerged from Muslim self-criticism and reflection upon the causes of Muslim decline. Secularists blamed an outmoded tradition. They advocated a separation of religion and politics and the establishment of modern nation states modeled on western political and socioeconomic practices. Conservative religious traditionists attributed Muslim decline to divergence from Islam and excessive innovation *(bida,* deviation from tradition). Islamic modernists blamed a blind acceptance and unquestioned following *(taqlid)* of the past; they proclaimed the need for Islamic reform. Many traditionists advocated a total rejection of the West. Muslims no longer lived under Islamic rule in an Islamic territory *(dar al-Islam)* and were thus in a land of warfare *(dar al-harb)*. Among the possible courses to follow in response to this situation were holy war *(jihad)*, emigration *(hijra)* to an Islamically-ruled land, or passive withdrawal and non-cooperation. On the other hand, Islamic reformers stressed the flexibility and adaptability which had characterized the early development of Islamic state and society and pressed for internal reform through a process of reinterpretation *(ijtihad)* and selective adaptation (Islamization) of Western ideas and technology. This early internal self-criticism and struggle to define Islam to make it relevant to contemporary society was the first stage in an ongoing process in which successive generations of Muslims have attempted to build twentieth-century religious, political, and social thought. It is important because it set the tone and direction of modern Muslim political thought.

Early Responses

An early and major catalyst of Islamic modernism was Sayyid Jamal Al-Din Al-Afghani (1838–1897), the Father of Muslim Nationalism.[2] Afghani advocated Islamic reform and reemphasized the role of Islam in society and politics at a time when many were ready to either reject or accept modernity wholesale. He traveled throughout the Muslim world to spread his message through an unceasing political activism. Afghani believed that Muslims could repel the West not by rejecting or ignoring the sources of Western strength, but rather by reclaiming and reappropriating reason, science, and technology which were part of Islamic history and civilization. Islam is more than just religion in the Western sense; it is, he contended, the root of civilization, the essence and basis for Muslim survival as individuals and as a community of believers *(ummah)*. The strength and survival of the *ummah* was dependent upon the reassertion of Islamic identity and the reestablishment of Islamic solidarity. Afghani exhorted Muslims to realize that Islam was a dynamic, creative force capable of responding to the demands of modernity. For Afghani, Islam was the religion of reason and science. Therefore Western ideas and science did not pose a threat to Islam; they could be studied and utilized. Muslims must reinterpret Islam, making it a relevant force in their lives intellectually and politically. In this way Islam would serve as the source of Islamic renewal through which colonial rule could be repulsed, and independence and the establishment of Muslim nations achieved. Once Islam was revitalized, it would mobilize Muslims, uniting them and providing the means to regain their lost glory and take their rightful place in the modern world. However, Afghani did not resolve the question of the relationship of modern nation states to the traditional notion of an Islamic *ummah,* i.e., a transnational community of believers. Rather he appealed to both Muslim nationalism and pan-Islam.

If Afghani was the catalyst, his disciples Muhammed Abduh (1849–1905) and Rashid Rida (1865–1935) were the synthesizers. Their Manar or Salafiyya Movement was to influence Islamic reform movements from North Africa to Southeast Asia. The Egyptian, Muhammad Abduh—the "Father of Islamic Modernism"—called for internal reform, viewing Islam as the framework for the intellectual, social, and political revival of the *ummah*. Abduh was a religious scholar *(alim,* pl. *ulama),* Rector of Al-Azhar and from 1898 Mufti of Egypt (Chief Judge of the Religious Courts).[3] Through his writings and legal opinions *(fatwas),* Abduh emphasized that there was no contradiction between religion and reason, Islamic belief and modernity. Advocating a reformulation of Islam, Abduh dismissed the unquestioned following *(taqlid)* of tradition or past authority as the reason for Muslim weakness and decline.[4] Unless a new path was forged through reinterpretation *(ijtihad)* and reform, Islam and Islamic culture would continue in a state of stagnation and decay. He argued that the process of reinterpretation was consonant with the nature of Islam. Abduh distinguished between Islam's inner core, composed of unchanging truths and its outer layers, which society's application of those truths and values to the needs of a particular age. Thus, Abduh stated that while those regulations of Islamic law (Shariah) which concerned prayer and worship *(ibadat)* were immutable, the vast majority of Islamic laws concerned with social relations *(muamalat)* i.e., international, penal, commercial, and family laws were open to change. As historical and social conditions warranted, the core of Islamic principles should be reapplied to new realities and, where necessary, the old layers of tradition discarded. The crisis of modern Islam was precipitated by Muslim failure to uphold this distinction between the immutable and mutable, the necessary and the contingent.

The attempt to reinterpret Islam, and thus enable Muslims to be both Muslim and modern without contradiction, marked a first stage in the search for a modern Islamic identity. With the achievement of independence, the vast majority of Muslim countries under the leadership of Western-oriented elites followed a more secular path based upon Western models of political, social, and economic development. Yet throughout the period from 1945 to the present, Muslims continued to grapple with the relationship of Islam to the modern state. This is reflected in both Muslim politics and Islamic sociopolitical thought. Its major themes have included the relationship of Islam to nationalism, socialism, and secularism. Moreover, as we shall see, the failure to address the problem of modern Islamic sociopolitical identity adequately is a major theme in the contemporary resurgence of Islam in politics.

Islam and the Modern State

The idea that nationalism could provide a legitimate basis for the state struck at the very heart of traditional Islamic political thought. The solidarity of the modern nation state is based upon common language, history, territory, or ethnic heritage, not religious faith. This stands in sharp contrast to the traditional definition of the Islamic state. In an Islamic state, the *ummah* is a community of believers, unified by their common religious faith; this religious bond supercedes all other loyalties or ties. Modern nation building spawned a variety of positions, ranging from total rejection of any "foreign" political influences or ideologies to complete adoption of Western, secular nationalism and the concept of the nation state. For some like Mawlana Abu'l Ala Mawdudi (1903–1979), Islam and any form of nationalism (Indian, Arab, Egyptian or Muslim) were antithetical since the Islamic community or state *(ummah)* transcends all ethnic, tribal, regional, and racial divisions. Islam's universal ideals and values are sustained by a divinely revealed law (Shariah) while those of nationalism emerge from a narrow particularism and opportunism. For Muslims, the universal, permanent laws of Islam do not alter with individual or national interests. Whereas, "nationalism makes man unprincipled. A nationalist has no principles in the world except that he wishes the good of his nation."[5]

For other Muslims like Taha Hussein (1889–1973) and Lutfi al-Sayyid (1872–1963) traditional Islamic political and social teachings were inappropriate in the modern world: "[the traditional Islamic] formula has no *raison d'être* because it fits neither the present state of affairs in Islamic nations nor their aspirations."[6] The path to be followed was a liberal nationalism rooted in patriotism, "love of fatherland." Love of country (Egypt) "must be free from all conflicting associations . . . self sacrifice in its service must take precedence over every other consideration."[7]

For Sati al-Husri (1880–1964) nationalism was primarily based upon common language and a shared history. Thus he advocated neither "love of country nor a pan-Islamism based on general shared religious sentiment of Muslim brotherhood; al-Husri stressed Arab nationalism. It was not Islam that defined Arab culture but, rather the

Arabs that gave meaning and brought glory to Islam. Moreover, political unity required mutual ideological goals and political consensus which necessitated a more concrete foundation than a shared faith or moral affinity. Religion had failed to provide the necessary political unity in the past when political and social life were simpler and when religion controlled behavior. Muslim life with its far more complex political and social realities and the diminished control of tradition and religious beliefs, made any such Muslim unity even more remote."[8] The answer then was Arab unity. Common language, history, and geography, not religion, are the only feasible basis for political union. Arab nationalism provided the ideology which could join Arab lands: "It is a social force drawing vitality from the life of the Arabic language, from the history of the Arab nation, and from the connectedness of the Arab countries."[9] Despite al-Husri's regard for Islam, such argumentation did not allay traditionists who, like Mustafa al-Maraghi, the Shaykh (Rector) of al-Azhar, had condemned Arab nationalism as contrary to Islamic solidarity. However, other Arab nationalists like Amir Shakib Arslan and the Iraqi Abd al-Rahman al-Bazzaz (1913–1978) argued the compatibility of Islam with Arab nationalism. For these Muslims, Islam is the religion of the Arab nation; Arab language and culture are integral to Islam. "Islam, although it is a universal religion . . . is undoubtedly a religion revealed first to the Arabs themselves. The Prophet is from them; the Koran is in their language; Islam retained many of their previous customs, adopting and polishing the best of them."[10] However, al-Bazzaz argued that the social cohesion generated by Islam does not extend beyond Arabism to a pan-Islamism: "Pan-Islamism . . . aims to form a comprehensive political organization which all the Muslims must obey. This organization, although it may be desired by all pious Muslims, is not possible in practice . . . under the present conditions . . . the call to unite the Arabs . . . is the practical step which must precede the call for Pan-Islamism."[11]

A third stage in Islamic sociopolitical thought occurred in the late 1950s and 1960s as Islam reemerged in Muslim politics in the newly independent North African states and the radical politics of Egypt, Syria, and Iraq. In Morocco Islam was used to legitimate and buttress the monarchy which became both the key political and religious institution of the state. In Algeria Houari Boumedienne, Islamically educated at Cairo's al-Azbar University, came to power in 1965, placing greater emphasis on Islam and Arabization. This linking of Islam to Algerian socialism was reflected in Algeria's *National Charter* of 1976.

In several Middle East countries liberal nationalist regimes were overthrown by more radical groups which tended to emphasize Arab unity and a more socialist orientation. Claiming that the old liberal nationalist governments had failed politically and especially socioeconomically, new regimes in Egypt, Syria, and Iraq distinguished themselves from their predecessors' reliance on borrowed or "foreign" ideologies by advocating an Arab socialist ideology rooted in their Arab/Islamic heritage. Disillusioned with the liberal West and attracted by socialism, this new generation viewed independence as positive neutrality, politically and ideologically. National unity required a national ideology more authentically rooted in Arab identity. Arab nationalism/socialism of the Baath party and of Nasserism represented this new "progressive" outlook and became the two major ideological forces in the Arab world. Both appealed to Islam for legitimacy and to win mass support.

The Baath party was founded in Syria in 1940 by Michel Aflaq (b. 1910) a Christian, and Salah al-Din Baytar (1911–1980), a Muslim. Aflaq was its principal ideological architect. Like Nasserism, Baathism was critical of the bankruptcy of Western liberal nationalism and the materialistic preoccupations of both Western capitalism and Marxism. As Aflaq wrote:

> The Arabs' connection with the West is commonly traced back to Bonaparte's campaign against Egypt and symbolized by his act of hanging up verses from the Quran beside a text of the "rights of man." Since that time the Arabs (or the leaders spuriously converted to Arabism) have been pushing their new renaissance in this distorted direction. They contort themselves and warp the texts of their history and the Quran to show that not only is there no difference between the principles of their civilization and creed and those of Western civilization, but they, in fact, preceded Westerners in their declaration and application of the same . . . they stand as accused before the West, affirming the soundness and superiority of Western values . . . Before long they pushed this logic to its conclusion by admitting that with European civilization they had no need of their own.[12]

Baathism was to provide a comprehensive ideological alternative informed by Arabism and socialism. It affirmed the existence of a single Arab nation and emphasized the Islamic origins of Arab nationalism in its revolutionary spirit and message. ". . . this religion represented the leap of Arabism to unity, power, and progress . . . The Arabs are singled out from the nations by this characteristic . . . their national consciousness is joined to a religious message; or more precisely this message is an eloquent expression of that national consciousness."[13] For Aflaq, Baath socialism, like its nationalism, was indebted not to a foreign source but to Islam's revolutionary ideology with its emphasis on equality, brotherhood, and social welfare.

While advocating constitutional democracy, the realities of Arab politics led the Baath to align themselves more closely with military regimes. Shared interests led to the union of Syria and Egypt and the formation of the United Arab Republic (1958–1961). Subsequently Baathism became more radical, secularist, and divisive, serving as the official party of competing military regimes in Syria and Iraq as well as influencing party politics in Lebanon and Jordan.

The second major form of radical Arab nationalism/socialism was that of Gamal Abd al-Nasser (1918–1970) in Egypt. Nasserism, like Baathism, was essentially a secular movement that employed Islamic symbolism to legitimate and mobilize mass support. Nasser increasingly used Islam to enhance not only his rule of Egypt but to establish himself as a pan-Arab/Islamic leader.[14] Thus, Islam was a factor in both his domestic and foreign policy. Government reforms (land reform, nationalization) were often justified by or, at least, portrayed as in harmony with Islam. A government sponsored journal *Minbar al-Islam* (*The Pulpit of Islam*) published articles by leading religious scholars and intellectuals supporting the Islamic character of the state's socialist policies. Nasser was able to get Shaykh Mahmud Shaltut (1892–1963) to assert that Islam and socialism were completely reconcilable because Islam was more than just a spiritual religion; it regulated "human relations and public affairs with the aim of ensuring the welfare of society."[15]

At the height of his popularity Nasser became the symbol of anti-imperialism in the Arab world, the chief spokesman for an "authentic" Arab nationalism and radical socialism which, by the mid 1960s, was the dominant ideology in the Arab world.

Islamic Fundamentalism

For many Muslims Nasserism and Baathism represented opportunistic uses of Islam by secular governments. Islamic organizations such as the Muslim Brotherhood in the Middle East and the Jamaat-i-Islami in South Asia found a truer answer in a comprehensive and integral vision of Islam as the complete ideology for Muslim society.

Their position is reflected in such statements as that of Hasan al-Banna: "Until recently, writers, intellectuals, scholars and governments glorified the principles of European civilization . . . adopted a Western style and manner . . . Today, on the contrary, the wind has

changed . . . Voices are raised . . . for a return to the principles, teachings and ways of Islam . . . for initiating the reconciliation of modern
life with these principles, as a prelude to a final Islamization."[16]

For the Muslim Brotherhood and the Jamaat-i-Islami, Islam was not
a component or factor in Muslim politics/ideology but rather *the
foundation* for Muslim state and society.

The Muslim Brotherhood was founded by Hasan al-Banna (1906–
1949) in Egypt.[17] The product of both a traditional religious and a
modern education, he was a teacher who became increasingly convinced that only through a return to Islam (the Quran and Sunnah of
the Prophet) could the Islamic world be awakened from its lethargy and
decline. Established in 1928, the Brotherhood drew popular support
for its educational and social welfare projects as much as its religious
ideology. However, it became progressively embroiled in militant
political action. In 1949 al-Banna was assassinated. Initially, the
Brotherhood supported the revolution of 1952 that brought Gamal
Abd al-Nasser and the Free Officers to power. However, disillusioned
by Nasser's unwillingness to establish an Islamic state, the Brotherhood
became an opposition movement. Several attempts on Nasser's life were
blamed on the Brotherhood, leading to the arrests, executions, and
suppression of the Brotherhood in 1965. Among those executed was
Sayyid Qutb, prolific and prominent ideologue, who is regarded by
contemporary Muslim revivalists as the martyr (al-Shahid) of Islamic
revivalism and among its most influential voices.[18] The Brotherhood
continued underground, inspired similar organizations in many Muslim countries, and resurfaced in Egypt under President Anwar al-Sadat.

Ideologically, the Brotherhood emphasized the union of religion and
society in Islam as rooted in the unity of God *(tawhid)* and embodied in
the comprehensive nature of the Shariah. Emphasizing the universality
of the *ummah* and its mission, it rejected nationalism and called for an
Islamic state governed by the Shariah. While open to modernization
and technology, the Brotherhood renounced Muslim intellectuals' and
governments' dependence upon the West. Instead of westernization and
secularization, the renewal of Muslim society must be rooted in Islamic
principles and values. Both Western ideologies and radical Arab
nationalism/socialism were eschewed. The social transformation of
Muslim society, according to Brothers like Sayyid Qutb and Mustapha
al-Sibai, should be based upon the social teachings of Islam or Islamic
socialism. While affirming the right to private property, socialism in
Islam recognizes the right of the state to limit landed property and to
nationalize where demanded by social justice. Such a socialism is

"totally different from the type of socialism that attaches no importance to religious values, relies on the class struggle in society, seizes private property without good reason, nationalizes industry and economic concerns that contribute to the national economic prosperity, paralyzes initiative and competition . . ."[19]

The death of the charismatic Arab leader Gamal Abd al-Nasser in 1970 created a void which his long-time admirer, Libya's Colonel Muammar al-Qaddafi tried to fill. Qaddafi combined radical Arab nationalism/socialism with his own brand of Islamic fundamentalism. He has taken up the banner of radical Arab nationalism/socialism and relied heavily upon an Islamic fundamentalist rationale both to legitimate his domestic reforms and to influence the politics of other Muslim states. Qaddafi's prescription for social revolution is contained in *The Green Book*. First published in 1973, there have been two subsequent volumes in 1976 and 1979 which set forth his "Third Way" or "Third International Theory," necessitated by the fact that: ". . . non-Islamic civilization brought war to the world of doubt . . . Islamic civilization is the only one that brought war to certainty and faith."[20] Indigenously rooted, the "Third Way" is an alternative to the extremes of capitalism and communism, both of which are exploitive and doomed to failure: "The world, East and West, is incapable of arriving at a true solution. . . . One sets wealth at liberty and allows all things to follow their inclinations arbitrarily . . . the other maintains there is no way except for us to interfere violently, uproot everything and then reshape it all even though it is contrary to the nature of man such as is done in communism."[21] Qaddafi appeals to the *Quran* as the focal point and source for his revolutionary theory: ". . . in it are solutions to the problems of man . . . from personal status . . . to international problems."[22] Democracy, the legacy of European colonialism and contemporary American neo-colonialism, he emphasizes as the Arabization and Islamization of society. Thus *Shariah* law was reintroduced and an ambitious, experimental "Islamic" socialist program undertaken: It is "a socialism emanating from the true religion of Islam and its Noble Book . . . not the socialism of Lenin and Marx."[23]

Qaddafi's brand of Islamic sociopolitical beliefs and programs have employed an "innovative," idiosyncratic and selective use of Islam. In recent years he has restricted the place of the *Quran* to religious affairs alone; *The Green Book* has displaced much of the traditional Shariah's governance of the political and social order. Qaddafi has ignored the guardians of tradition—the *Ulama* and instead has substituted his own interpretation of Islam.[24] Mixing ideological statements with a broad range of political, social, and economic experimentation, Qaddafi has attempted nothing less than a cultural revolution. Progressively, the centralized, bureaucratic socialist state headed by Qaddafi's Revolutionary Command Council has given way to a more decentralized, populist, participatory government of peoples' committees which control government offices, schools, the media, and many large corporations. This change was symbolized in 1977 when the General People's Congress renamed Libya, the Socialist People's Libyan Arab Jamahiriya. Similarly, a more egalitarian spirit has effected socioeconomic reforms. While private ownership is maintained, it has been restricted. Wages and rent have been abolished in favor of worker control of and participation in the means of production. Women's place in the revolution has been underscored by greater emphasis on their economic and social rights in society.

As in Libya's domestic policy, its foreign policy has also utilized an ideology which emphasizes Islamic unity, equality, and brotherhood. Qaddafi has attempted political unions with a number of Muslim states: Syria, Egypt, Tunisia, Sudan, and Chad. Libyan funds have supported revolutionary movements from Palestine to the Moro Islands. Qaddafi's interpretation of Islam come under heavy criticism from Libya's religious establishment (the *ulama*) and other Muslim governments and leaders. However, his brand of Islamic fundamentalism, fueled by oil revenues has had a significant impact on Libya and many other countries throughout the Muslim world.

The Islamic Resurgence

Political events in the Muslim world during the 1970s have in a dramatic way drawn attention to the political and social implications of Islam. Contrary to accepted norms of political development and the predictions of many analysts, religion reemerged in the Muslim politics of Iran, Pakistan, Afghanistan, Saudi Arabia, Syria, and Malaysia.[25] Islamic ideology, symbols, slogans, and actors have become prominent fixtures. Iran has established an "Islamic Republic" and Pakistan has committed itself to a more Islamic system of government *(Nizam-i-Islam)*. Islamic laws, dress, taxes, and punishments have been called for and/or introduced in many Muslim countries. Both incumbent governments and opposition movements often vie with one another in declaring their allegiance to Islam and to a more Islamic order. Thus, Islamic politics, economics, law, and education are hotly contested issues.

Amidst the diversity of Islamic revivalism there are common sociopolitical concerns and themes rooted in a general consensus that Muslims have failed to produce a viably authentic synthesis which is both modern and true to their own history and values. Among the chief concerns of contemporary Islamic sociopolitical thought are: (1) continued impotence of Muslim society, i.e., the ineffectiveness of Muslim governments and nationalist ideologies; (2) disillusionment with the West; and (3) the need to articulate a more authentic identity.

If Islam's glorious political and cultural past had been reversed by colonial rule, independence did not greatly improve the political and socioeconomic conditions of most Muslim countries. They continued to be subservient to the West both politically and culturally. Moreover, political elites had failed to establish a legitimate, effective public order and to adequately address the profound socioeconomic disparities in wealth and class in most Muslim countries.[26] Their sense of disillusionment and failure was reflected in Muslim literature in the late 1960s with its growing criticism of the West and its concern to reclaim historical and cultural identity.[27] For the religiously oriented, the problem had always been clear—departure from the straight path of Islam was doomed to failure. For Western-oriented intellectuals and elites, the disillusionment was more unsettling. They had embraced the West as both an ally and a model for economic development.

Despite significant differences from one Muslim context to another, the general outlook *(Weltanschauung)* of contemporary revivalists may be divided into three categories: conservative, fundamentalist, and modernist reformers. While all advocate a "return to Islam" their meanings and methods are different. For conservatives, who represent the majority of the religious establishment, the Islamic system is expressed quite adequately and completely in the classical formulation of Islam as embodied and preserved in Islamic law. This is the interpretation of Islam which governed the Muslim community down through the centuries and which remains valid for today. Therefore, conservatives emphasize following past authority *(taqlid)* and are wary of innovation *(bida,* deviation from tradition). While change does occur, it is very gradual and by way of exception. Thus, for example, when the Ayatollah Khomeini and the religious leaders who dominate Iran's Islamic Republican party and its Parliament implement Islamic laws, they turn to the medieval legal manuals. Similarly, the *mullahs* of Pakistan agitate for the repeal of modern family law reforms (marriage, divorce, and inheritance) as an unwarranted deviation from the *Shariah*.

Fundamentalists share many similarities with conservatives. Like conservatives, they advocate a return to the Quran and Sunnah of the Prophet. However, they differ in that fundamentalists, while respecting the classical formulations of Islam, claim the right to go back to the fundamental sources of Islam to reinterpret *(ijtihad)* and reapply them to contemporary needs. Thus, while in many matters fundamentalists and conservatives turn to classical Islam, fundamentalists are more flexible in their ability to adapt to change. Saudi Arabia and Libya provide two examples of fundamentalist flexibility—the Saudi a more traditional and Qaddafi a more radical fundamentalism. Both have had to contend with the more conservative bent of their *Ulama*. A similar flexibility may be seen in Islamic organizations like the Muslim Brotherhood and the Jamaat-i-Islami. The net result of the fundamentalist outlook is a variety of interpretations regarding the nature of Islamic government.[28] Moreover, over a period of time, changed leadership and/or circumstances can lead to differing Islamic positions on the same issue. While Muslim Brotherhood writers like Sayyid Qutb and Mustapha al-Sibaii advanced Islamic socialism as a means to social justice, the Muslim Brotherhood in Egypt today tends to emphasize private ownership as the Islamic norm to a far greater extent. In addition, while in the past, the Brotherhood spoke of Arab nationalism and unity as a necessary stage in the revival of Islam, the new Brotherhood emphasizes Islamic solidarity rather than Arab unity.[29]

Finally, the most adaptive are the Islamic modernists. Many are individuals who, after an early traditional religious education, have received a Western education. They neither opt for a Western secular orientation nor, in their view, are they as Western-oriented as earlier generations of Islamic reformers. Educated often at the best American, British or French universities, they remain Islamically oriented and emphasize a commitment to "Islamic modernization" i.e., a future in which political and social development are more firmly rooted in past history and values. They have learned from the West but do not wish to westernize Muslim society. The method modernists advocate for sociopolitical change is that of Islamization—a process utilized in the formation and development of classical Islam. It includes: (1) implementation of Quranic and Prophetic prescriptions; (2) the application of Islamic (revelation) principles and values to socio-historical conditions; and (3) adoption and adaptation of the best (thought, institutions, laws) that is to be found in other cultures, provided it is not contrary to revelations.

Islamic reformers distinguish between an immutable revelation and its mutable (historically and socially conditioned) laws and institutions.

They maintain that while classical Islamic law was formulated in light of, and therefore responded to, the needs of the past, modern life requires a reformulation of Islam by once more undertaking the process of Islamization. If Islamic law had had four sources: *Quran, Sunnah, ijtihad* (interpretation) and *ijma* (community acceptance or consensus), then Muslims today must once more vigorously reinterpret *(ijtihad)* in order to arrive at a new consensus *(ijma)*, i.e., Islamic models for modern Muslim states and societies. Unlike earlier reformers, contemporary revivalists believe they live at a time and in circumstances that provide more opportunities and better resources to develop and implement specific programs. While all modernists claim an Islamic basis and ideology, their ideological positions and degree of political activism range from moderate to revolutionary. For Hassan Turabi,[30] the Attorney General of the Sudan and leader of Sudan's Muslim Brotherhood, and for Anwar Ibrahim,[31] head of the Muslim Youth Movement of Malaysia (ABIM) and currently a deputy Prime Minister, Islamization of politics and law should be a gradual process. For others, like Egypt's Islamic socialist Hassan Hanafi or Iran's Mujahidin-i-Khalq, a more radical, revolutionary process is required. As with Iran's Ali Shariati, Islam provides a political ideology capable of mass mobilization for a much needed revolution.[32]

Although the leadership of both fundamentalist and modernist Islam is primarily lay, the modernists tend most often to clash with the conservative *ulama*. Unlike fundamentalists, Islamic modernists feel freer to bypass classical formulations of politics and law and to exercise a wide ranging *ijtihad* (reinterpretation). The *ulama* attack their "deviationism" and question their qualifications as *mujtahids* (reinterpreters) maintaining that the *ulama* alone are the guardians of Islam. Islamic modernists ignore or reject the *Ulama*, claiming that there is no clergy in Islam and any Muslim can qualify as a scholar. Moreover, due to their traditional education and outlook most *ulama* are viewed as ill equipped to respond to the modern world.

A vivid example of the clash of modernist and conservative religious world-views has occurred in Iran. During the revolution posters of Dr. Ali Shariati (the revolution's ideologue) and the Ayatollah Khomeini, the symbolic leaders of the opposition were often placed side by side. Shariati was a Sorbonne educated socialist and hero of Iranian youth while Khomeini, the traditional religious leader, trained at Qum, a leading center of Islamic education. Their followers stood united in their Islamic opposition to the Shah. However, during the post-revolutionary period the contrasts between Muslim modernists like

Shariati and Abul Hasan Banisadr, Iran's former President and the ruling *mullahs* (religious) have led to a rupture in their relations. For Khomeini and the *mullahs,* the Islamic government is governed by the legal specialists *(wilayat-ul-faqih)* according to medieval Islamic law, delineated by the *faqihs* (legal specialists) of the past.[33] Shariati's Islam is a revolutionary Islam, a religion of protest. He distinguishes between two Islams: Islam the ideology and Islam the culture. Islam the ideology, "responsibility, consciousness and leadership,"[34] is future oriented. Islam the culture is the creation of the *faqih* who "have suppressed true knowledge of religion . . ."[35] Shariati sees theirs as a stagnant, retrogressive Islam.

While contemporary Islamic sociopolitical thought is vibrant and diverse, it is seminal and tentative in its forms and expression. With few exceptions, developed Islamic models for political, social, and economic change await construction and implementation. The most visible experiments thus far have occurred in Saudi Arabia, Libya, Iran, and Pakistan.[36] With the exception of Saudi Arabia where Islam has for sometime legitimated the al-Saud monarchy, the others have been relatively recent experiments by regimes that have come to power through a revolution or coup d'état. Their Islamic character has been in large part determined by their military or religious regimes. On the other hand Islamic political writings and manifestoes appear somewhat general and abstract, lacking detailed development. Muslim revivalists respond that the necessary political and intellectual climate has been wanting but that a period of research and experimentation in Islamic political, legal, and economic reforms has begun.

This process has already raised many issues. Because of the *ad hoc* nature of Islamization, sharp differences in Islamic interpretation on political and social development have been evident in Muslim politics as well as Muslim political thought. The power exercised by the Ayatollah Khomeini, Colonel Qaddafi, General Zia ul-Haq, and the al-Saud family in the name of Islam has raised many questions about the nature of Islamic government and the role of political authority. The use of Islam not only by incumbent governments but often by opposition movements underscores the two primary questions which Muslim thinkers and governments face in policy making: "Whose Islam?" i.e., who is to interpret, formulate, and implement Islamic programs and policies; "What Islam?" i.e., how is the Islamic character of a government and its policies to be determined.[37] As previously noted, current Islamic governments include Saudi Arabia's monarchy, Iran's cleric dominated state, and Pakistan's martial law regime. All claim to be

Islamic states or republics and appeal to Islam to legitimate their rule and many of their policies. At the same time, they are criticized by others as using Islam to justify authoritarian rule, suppress political parties, limit the rights of women, and impose censorship. For many Muslim critics such measures constitute the manipulation of religion through the use of a "negative (restrictive) Islam." Thus, while establishing more authentically rooted Islamic societies is a desideratum for many, determining the shape and form of such states will be no easy task.

From the establishment of the first Islamic community/state at Medina in 622, Islam has played an important role in the development of Muslim politics and society. During the twentieth century, Muslims have faced the task of redefining their political and social identities. Muslim politics and thought demonstrate the extent to which Islam continues to be a significant factor in contemporary Muslim societies.

Notes

1. For a more extensive discussion of Islamic politics see John L. Esposito, *Islam and Politics* (Syracuse, N.Y.: Syracuse University Press, 1984).
2. For a summary of Afghani's contribution, see Albert Hourani, *Arabic Thought in the Liberal Age.* (London: Oxford University Press, 1970), chap. 5. See also, Nikki R. Keddie, *Sayyid Jamal al-Din al Afghani: A Political Biography* (Berkeley: University of California Press, 1972) and *An Islamic Response to Imperialism: Political and Religious Writings of Sayyid Jamal al-Din al Afghani,* trans. and ed. by Nikki R. Keddie (Berkeley: University of California Press, 1968).
3. Hourani, chap. 6 and Abduh's *The Theology of Unity,* trans. I. Musaad and K. Cragg (London: George Allen & Unwin, 1966).
4. In South Asia similar attempts to revitalize the Muslim community through Islamic reform were undertaken by Sir Sayyid Ahmad Khan (1817–1898) and Muhammad Iqbal (1875–1938). See for example Aziz Ahmad, *Islamic Modernism in India and Pakistan* (New York: Oxford University Press, 1967), chaps. 2 and 7. Christian W. Troll, *Sir Sayyid Ahmad Khan: A Reinterpretation of Muslim Theology* (New Delhi: Vikas Publishing House, 1978), Muhammad Iqbal, *The Reconstruction of Religious Thought in Islam* (rept. Lahore, 1968); and John L. Esposito, "Muhammad Iqbal

and the Islamic State" in *Voices of Resurgent Islam*, ed. by John L. Esposito (New York: Oxford University Press, 1983), chap. 8.

5. Abul Ala Mawdudi, "Nationalism and India" in *Islam in Transition: Muslim Perspectives*, ed. by John J. Donohue and John L. Esposito (New York: Oxford University Press, 1982), 96.

6. Ahmad Lutfi al-Sayyid *Ta'ammulat* in Donohue and Esposito, 70. For Taha Husayn, see *The Future of Culture in Egypt*, trans. by S. Glazer (Washington, D.C.: American Council of Learned Societies, 1954).

7. Ibid.

8. Hourani, 311–16.

9. Sati al-Husrim, "Muslim Unity and Arab Unity," in Donohue and Esposito, 69.

10. Abd al-Rahman al-Bazzaz "Islam and Arab Nationalism" in *Arab Nationalism*, ed. Sylvia Haim (Berkeley: University of California Press, 1962), 176.

11. Ibid.

12. Michel Aflaq, *Dhikra-l-Rasul al-Arab* "In Remembrance of the Arab Prophet" in Donohue and Esposito, 110.

13. Ibid., 109.

14. See Daniel Crecelius, "The Course of Secularization in Modern Egypt" in *Islam and Development: Religion and Sociopolitical Change*, ed. John L. Esposito (Syracuse, N.Y.: Syracuse University Press, 1980), 63 ff. and Geunter Levy "Nasserism and Islam: A Revolution in Search of Ideology," in *Religion and Political Modernization*, ed. Donald E. Smith (New Haven: Yale University Press, 1974), chap. 14.

15. Shaykh Mahmud Shaltut, "Socialism and Islam" in Donohue and Esposito, 99.

16. Hasan al-Banna, "The New Renaissance," in Donohue and Esposito, 78.

17. The best study of the Brotherhood is Richard P. Mitchell's *The Society of the Muslim Brothers* (London: Oxford University Press, 1969). Cf. also I.M. Husaini, *The Moslem Brothers* (Beirut, 1956) and C.P. Harris, *Nationalism and Revolution in Egypt* (The Hague: Mouton, 1964).

18. Yvonne Haddad, "Sayyid Qutb" in *Voices of Resurgent Islam*, chap. 4.

19. Mustapha al-Sibaii, "Islamic Socialism" in Donohue and Esposito, 122.

20. Muammar al-Qaddafi, *Fil-Nazariyyah al-Thalithah* (The Third Way), (n.p.: n-d) in Donohue and Esposito, 106.

21. Ibid., 105.

22. Ibid., 103.

23. "The Libyan Revolution in the Words of Its Leaders," *The Middle East Journal* 24 (1970): 208.

24. As Ann Mayer has observed: "Qadhdhafi has himself undertaken the role of supreme interpreter of Islamic law." Ann Mayer, "Islamic Resurgence or a New Prophethood: The Role of Islam in Qadhdhafi's Ideology" in *Islamic Resurgence in the Arab World,* ed. Ali E. Hillal Dessouki (New York: Praeger, 1982), 211. Cf. Lisa Anderson, "Qaddafi's Islam" in *Voices of Resurgent Islam,* chap. 6.

25. A number of volumes containing country case studies have appeared. Among the more useful are: Muhammad Ayoub, ed., *The Politics of Islamic Reassertion* (New York: St. Martin's Press, 1981). Dessouki's *Islamic Resurgence,* Esposito's *Islam and Development.*

26. R. Hrair Dekmejian, "The Anatomy of Islamic Revival: Legitimacy Crisis, Ethnic Conflict and the Search for Islamic Identity," *The Middle East Journal* 34 (1980): 3ff.

27. John J. Donohue, "Islam and the Quest for Identity in the Arab World," in *Voices of Resurgent Islam,* chap. 3 and Ali Merad, "The Ideologisation of Islam" in *Islam and Power in the Contemporary Muslim World,* ed. Alexander S. Cudsi and Ali E. Hillal Dessouki (Baltimore: Johns Hopkins University Press, 1981) 45 ff.

28. See, Charles E. Butterworth, "Prudence versus Legitimacy: The Persistent Theme in Islamic Political Thought" in Dessouki, *Islamic Resurgence,* chap. 5 and Esposito, *Voices of Resurgent Islam,* chaps. 4–7.

29. Abd al-Moneim Said Aly and Manfred W. Wenner, "Modern Islamic Reform: The Muslim Brotherhood in Contemporary Egypt" *The Middle East Journal* 36 (1982): 351–52.

30. Hassan Turabi "The Islamic State" in *Voices of Resurgent Islam,* chap. 11.

31. Fred R. von der Mehden, "Islamic Resurgence in Malaysia" in Esposito, *Islam and Development,* 174 ff.

32. Mangol Bayat, "Islam in Pahlavi and Post Pahlavi Iran" in *Islam and Development,* chap. 10. Abdul Aziz Sachedina, "Ali Shariati" in *Voices of Resurgent Islam,* chap. 9 and Ervand Abrahamian "Ali Shariati: Idealogue of the Iranian Revolution", *Merip Reports* 102 (1982): 24–28.

33. Bayat, 97–98.

34. Ali Shariati *Intizar* in Donohue and Esposito, 300.
35. Ibid., 301.
36. See Ayoub, Dessouki, *Islamic Resurgence* and Esposito, *Islam and Development* for case studies.
37. For a more extensive discussion of this problem see my *Tradition and Modernization in Islam,* 19 ff.

References

Ahmad, Al-e. 1982. *Gharbzadegi* (Weststruckness). Lexington, KY.: Mazda Publishers.

Ahmad, Aziz. 1967. *Islamic Modernism in India and Pakistan.* New York: Oxford University Press.

Ahmad, Khurshid. 1979. *Islamic Perspectives.* Leicester: The Islamic Foundation.

Ahmad, Khurshid, ed. 1975. *Islam: Its Meaning and Message.* London: Islamic Council of Europe.

Akhavi, Shahrough. 1980. *Religion and Politics in Contemporary Iran.* Albany, N.Y.: State University of New York.

Asad, Muhammad. 1961. *The Principles of State and Government in Islam.* Berkeley: University of California Press.

Ayoub, Muhammad, ed. 1981. *The Politics of Islamic Reassertion.* New York: St. Martin's Press.

Banisadr, Abolhassan. 1982. *The Fundamental Principles and Precepts of Islamic Government.* Lexington, KY.: Mazda Publishers.

Cudsi, Alexander E. and Dessouki, Ali E. Hillal, eds. 1981. *Islam and Power in the Contemporary Muslim World.* Baltimore: Johns Hopkins University Press.

Dessouki, Ali E. Hillal, ed. 1982. *Islamic Resurgence in the Arab World.* New York: Praeger.

Donohue, John J. and Esposito, John L., eds. 1982. *Islam in Transition: Muslim Perspectives.* New York: Oxford University Press.

Enayat, Hamid. 1982. *Modern Islamic Political Thought.* Austin: University of Texas Press.

Esposito, John L., ed. 1980. *Islam and Development.* Syracuse, N.Y.: Syracuse University Press.

Esposito, John L., ed. 1983. *Voices of Resurgent Islam.* New York: Oxford University Press.

Esposito, John L. 1984. *Islam and Politics.* Syracuse, N. Y.: Syracuse University Press.

Gauhar, Altaf, ed. 1978. *The Challenge of Islam.* London: Islamic

Council of Europe.

Haddad, Yvonne. 1982. *Contemporary Islam and the Challenge of History*. Albany, N.Y.: State University of New York Press.

Hanafi, Hassan. n.d. *Religious Dialogue and Revolution*. Cairo: The Anglo Egyptian Bookshop.

Harris, C.P. 1964. *Nationalism and Revolution in Egypt*. The Hague: Mouton.

Hourani, Albert. 1970. *Arabic Thought in the Liberal Age*. London: Oxford University Press.

Husaini, I.M. 1956. *The Moslem Brothers*. Beirut: n.p.

Iqbal, Muhammad. 1968. *The Reconstruction of Religious Thought in Islam*. Reprint. Lahore: n.p.

Keddie, Nikki R., trans. and ed. 1968. *An Islamic Response to Imperialism. Political and Religious Writings of Sayyid Jamil al-Din al-Afghani*. Berkeley: University of California Press.

Keddie, Nikki R. 1972. *Sayyid Jamal al-Din al-Afghani: A Political Biography*. Berkeley: University of California Press.

Khomeini, Ayatullah Ruhullah. 1979. *Islamic Government*. Arlington, VA.: National Technical Information Service.

Mawdudi, Mawlana Abul Ala. 1967. *Islamic Law and Constitution*. Lahore: Islamic Publications.

Mawdudi, Mawlana Abul Ala. 1955. *The Process of Islamic Revolution*. Lahore: n.p.

Mitchell, Richard P. 1969. *The Society of the Muslim Brothers*. London: Oxford University Press.

Mortimer, Edward. 1982. *Faith and Power: The Politics of Islam*. New York: Random House.

Qutb, Sayyid. 1970. *Social Justice in Islam*. Trans. John B. Hardie. Washington, D.C.: American Council of Learned Societies.

Shariati, Ali. 1980. *The Sociology of Islam*. Trans. by R. Campbell. Berkeley: Mezair Press.

Smith, W.C. 1957. *Islam in Modern History*. Princeton: Princeton University Press.

Troll, Christian W. 1978. *Sir Sayyid Ahmad Khan: A Reinterpretation of Muslim Theology*. New Delhi: Vikas Publishing House.

Voll, John O. 1982. *Islam: Continuity and Change in the Modern World*. Boulder, CO.: Westview Press.

Welch, Alfred T., ed. 1979. *Islam: Past Influence and Present Challenge*. Albany, N.Y.: State University of New York Press.

9

What Is Islamic Fundamentalism?

NADER SAIEDI

Introduction

THE Iranian revolution of 1979 and recent developments in the Middle East pose serious theoretical questions for students of sociology. The 1979 revolution, and particularly its socio-political consequent form, were largely surprises for specialists in comparative political development as well as students of the sociology of economic change. The surprise was common to both Marxist and modernization theorists. Even experts on Middle Eastern societies and Islamic studies found that recent events in Iran contradicted their expectations and theoretical formulations. The result was an abundance of *ex post facto* explanations and reconstructions to reconcile theory and reality.[1]

The alternative is to affirm the problematic character of Islamic fundamentalism and try to learn new theoretical lessons from it. This paper attempts a modest endeavor in that regard. In what follows I will first locate Islamic fundamentalism in a historical perspective; next, I will present an outline of the theoretical framework of Islamic liberalism, and finally, I will try to conceptualize the basic characteristics of Islamic fundamentalism as a cultural, political, economic, and religious movement. Although I will not discuss the causal configuration that gave rise to the contemporary resurgence of Islamic fundamentalism, my formal and phenomenological analysis may help us to avoid the pitfalls of abstract and stereotypical causal generalizations in dealing with Islamic fundamentalism.

Historical Perspective:
Islamic and Western Imperialism

In discussing Third World economic and political events it is a common practice to reduce them to either external (imperialism) or internal (backward culture) explanations. Dependency theorists and advocates of world-system theory usually overlook the significance of internal social, cultural, economic, and political factors in explaining the current state of Third World societies. From these perspectives it is the location of a country within the international structure of trade and the division of labor that determines its socio-economic destiny (Wallerstein 1974). Conversely the advocates of modernization theory overlook the international structure and the reality of economic and political domination of imperialism and emphasize the internal ideology, religious, cultural, and personality traits as the major explanatory variables (McClelland 1976).

The underlying assumption of this paper is that both the international structure of the capitalist world-system and the internal cultural, social, economic, and political configurations are real causal; factors whose dynamic interaction defines the basic variables of the Third World reality.

Neither the stages and forms of penetration of capitalism nor the stages and forms of Islamic response to the Western ascendency and domination were identical among different Middle Eastern societies. In spite of this social heterogeneity of the region, it is possible to make some general observations of the alternative historical reactions of Islamic societies to capitalism and modernization.

The sixteenth century, the century of the so-called gunpowder empires of Safavid, Ottoman, and Mongul India, was a century of centralized and strong states in the Middle East. The ascendency of the Occident in the seventeenth and eighteenth centuries, however, was accompanied by decentralization and disintegration of the Muslim empires in the eighteenth century (Voll 1982, 33–86). The relation of the Western capitalist economies to the Middle Eastern societies was at first based upon external trade of luxury goods that did not significantly affect the natural economy and the pre-capitalist mode of production of the Middle East. The extension of trade from luxury to necessary goods, however, produced an international division of labor in which many parts of the Middle East became specialized in production of primary agricultural products in response to the demands created by the industrial production in the West (Hodgson 1974, 3:214–19). The basic mechanism of imperialism in Middle Eastern societies was based upon exchange relations and trade, and the transfer of surplus products from the Middle East to the West was also effected through production relations. The bulk of direct Western influence in the production process was centered around foreign loans and production concessions to the foreign entrepreneurs.

Both mechanisms of loans and concessions became particularly significant during the nineteenth century. This was a century of military and administrative reform and modernization by many states in the area. As a buffer zone between British influence in India in the South and the Russian tsardom in the North, most of the Eastern parts of the Middle East did not endure a prolonged subjection to the direct Western colonial occupation. From the second half of the nineteenth century, British, French, and Italian forces occupied most of North Africa and the Southern and Eastern coasts of the Arabian peninsula. Middle Eastern colonialism was mainly due to the strategic significance of the area as the intermediate zone for access to India and Africa in the midst of colonial rivalry among the Western imperialist powers. Finally, the British and French mandates of the Fertile Crescent enacted after World War I were followed by significant political developments in the post-World War II period. Gradual formal political independence, neo-colonialism, resurgence of nationalism, the emergence of the State of Israel and the Palestinian question, the politics and economics of oil production, the increased significance and role of the United States in the area, and a heightened strategic importance of the Middle East in the conflicts between the United States and the Soviet Union are among the major recent political developments of the region.[2]

The response of the Islamic Middle East to the penetration of Western capitalism was defined through a limited range of alternatives determined by cultural, political, social, and religious heritage and ideology. The political formation was conceived in terms of three possibilities: independent nation states, pan-Arabism, and pan-Islamism. The religious reaction to the secular alternative took three major forms: Islamic liberalism, Islamic radicalism-socialism, and Islamic fundamentalism. Although there exists no necessary or one-to-one relationship between political alternatives and religious ideologies, there have been close relations between pan-Arabism, pan-Islamism, and Islamic liberalism-radicalism, and fundamentalism respectively.

While no abstract historical generalization can do justice to the complexity of the historical totality of the modern Middle East, it might be argued that the original reaction of the Islamic world to the Western penetration was a simple form of fundamentalism (eighteenth century). At the second phase of development, during the early and mid-nineteenth century, the pro-Western liberal response was the dominant Islamic ideology in the Middle East. The failure of Islamic liberalism in the late nineteenth century was followed by a conflict between the radical-socialist and fundamentalist interpretations of Islam during the twentieth century (Hodgson 1974, 3:176–409).

During the post-World War II period Islam has taken a more active and polarized role in political conflicts. The 1950s and 1960s represented the dominance of Islamic radicalism, Arab socialism, and pan-Arabism in most of the Middle Eastern societies with the leadership of Nasserist politics. The failure of Arab socialism and pan-Arabism in the 1970s paved the way for a significant resurgence of Islamic fundamentalism and pan-Islamism in the late 1970s and early 1980s.

It is not difficult to understand that the original response in the eighteenth century to the modern tendencies was mostly fundamentalist (e.g., the wahhabi movement in the Arabian Peninsula and Shah Waliullah's militant ideas in India). This was the first encounter of the Middle East with the "infidel" and "inferior" Western Christians. The simple fundamentalism of the eighteenth century is to be understood in the context of a disintegrating Middle East that still preserved its centuries-old ideology of superiority over the Christians. It was a rejection of the strange and the un-familiar.

The nineteenth-century pro-Western liberal response, however, takes a different stance. The Egyptians' observation of the military and administrative superiority of the French forces during Napoleon's occupation of Egypt in 1798 and the successive defeats of Ottoman forces in confrontations with the Western and Eastern European powers brought about a different situation. Now the good aspects of Europeans could be taken and imitated to realize the authentic superiority of the Islamic world that had been temporarily eclipsed due to an outmoded reading of Islam. The result was extensive attempts for military, administrative, and cultural reforms by the states (Mahmud's reforms after Greek independence in 1821 in the Ottoman empire, Muhammad Ali's French–style reforms in Egypt, Ahman Beig's attempts for modernization in Tunisia, and Abbas Mirza/Amirkabir's reform endeavors in Iran inspired by the defeat by Russia) and sophisticated liberal interpretations of Islam, e.g., Abduh in Egypt and Sir Ahman Khan Hindi in India (Voll 1982, 87–148).

But disillusionment with capitalist modernization and colonial domination encouraged a negative reaction toward westernization which took the form of Islamic radicalism-socialism and Islamic fundamentalism. While it is correct to say that at any point in the modern history of the Middle East all three alternative Islamic interpretations existed with different degrees of significance, the twentieth century conflict between the fundamentalist and radical-socialist alternatives has been particularly pronounced. Although in the 1950s and 1960s the rhetoric of Islamic socialism and pan-Arabism had been dominant, the failure of any pan-Arabist attempt, the emerging contradictions of Nasserism, and the humiliating defeat of 1967 in the war with Israel encouraged strong fundamentalist tendencies in the area. Although various fundamentalist movements (Muslim Brotherhood in Egypt and Syria, Jamaat-i-Islami in Pakistan and Fidaiyan-i Islam in Iran) had been active during most of the twentieth century, the most extreme and politically successful form of Islamic fundamentalism is to be found in the revolution of 1978 and its subsequent Shi'ite clergy in Iran.

Islamic Liberalism vs. Islamic Fundamentalism

As an ideal type, Islamic fundamentalism can best be characterized in terms of its relation, opposition, and affinities with Islamic liberalism.[3] On a more abstract and general level it may be claimed that the distinctions underlying Islamic fundamentalism and Islamic liberalism have been present from early periods of Islamic theology and philosophy.

After a brief period of charismatic revelation and authority, seventh and eighth centuries, Muslims tried to articulate revelation in the form of attitudes, concepts, interpretations, methods of legitimate deductions, legal schools, and regulations (eighth through eleventh centuries). In this process of definition, articulation, and regulation three distinct attitudes and interpretations emerged whose conflicts and clashes had significant theological and political implications. Each interpretation was based upon a specific assumption about the nature of truth and represented a unique approach to the Islamic revelation. The three interpretations may be designated as literalist, rationalist, and mystical approaches to the knowledge of reality and textual hermeneutics.

The literalist interpretation emphasized the significance of the Quran and Hadith, rejected the authority and significance of reason, and repudiated the use of reason for deducing hidden meanings of the divine texts. This approach was mainly institutionalized in the group of legally-oriented *Ulama* who advocated strict and literary obedience to the *Shariah,* or the law.

Contrary to the literalist interpretation, the rationalistic approach emphasized the legitimacy and authority of human reason for understanding the truth and deciphering the hidden meanings of the holy texts. According to their approach, the *Quran* possessed real, hidden, and metaphorical meanings whose understanding required penetration beyond the literal appearances of the text and the use of rational discourse and analysis. Philosophers represented the intellectual embodiment of the rationalistic interpretation and were constantly in conflict with the *Ulamas*.

Finally there was the mystical interpretation that again rejected the literalist reading of the texts and sought understanding of the higher realm of hidden essences and truths beyond the superficial realm of *Shariah's,* regulations, and appearances. The mystical approach was opposed to the rationalistic interpretation in its rejection of the authority of discursive reason and its reliance upon the emotions, intuitions, and personal feelings for understanding the truth and participating in the original source of the divine Word and revelation itself. The mystic interpretation was institutionalized in various sufi traditions.[4]

Islamic mysticism was a glorious historical achievement that reached its highest level of complexity during the period between the ninth and twelfth centuries. After that it mostly degenerated into a cult of personality, veneration of the dead, and irrational superstitions (Schimmel 1975). The battle between rationalist and literalist schools ended with the unfortunate triumph of the legalistic and dogmatic-oriented *Ulama* and their authoritarian reading of Islamic precepts. At a theological level a battle was waged between the Mu'tazila school (rationalist) and the Asha'ira school (literalist) with the ultimate victory of Asha'ira and the suppression of Mu'tazila in the eleventh century (Rahman 1968, 97–116, 139–52). Modern Islamic fundamentalism follows the dogmatic, legalistic, and anti-rationalistic premises of the literalist interpretation with strong theoretical, organizational, and structural tendencies for political activity and militancy.

Contemporary Muslim fundamentalism can best be understood in light of the failure of Islamic liberalism in the nineteenth and twentieth centuries. While this paper is not directly concerned with Islamic liberalism, a brief outline of its major theoretical principles can help us better understand its rival reaction, i.e., Islamic fundamentalism. An examination of the writings of the major advocates of Islamic liberalism from Abduh to Iqbal reveals at least six ideas common to the movement as a whole.

1. *Dialectical philosophy:* The fundamental philosophical premise of Islamic liberalism is dialectics.[5] Although the Western tradition of dialectical philosophy and logic is essentially influenced and inspired by Hegel's writings, Islamic liberalism found its dialectical system primarily in the writings of the seventeenth-century Iranian Muslim philosopher Mulla Sadra. Sadra's theoretical system offers rich and sophisticated philosophy with an explicit existentialist, vitalistic, and dialectical structure.

Three major ideas of Sadra present a very dynamic world view. The thesis of the primary of existence over essences and his conceptualization of essence and form as the moments of the unfolding of dynamic existence emphasized the reality of change and process within a dynamic logic. Similar to Hegel's dialectic, Sadra's notion of existence is based upon his theory of the grades of existence and the equivocal nature of being. Accordingly, existence is simultaneously one and many; consequently, not only identity is to be defined through change, process, and movement, but also the transition from quantitative to qualitative change is considered to be essential to the structure of reality. Finally, Sadra's historical thesis of substantive movement represents an epistemological break with the Aristotelian static philosophy that considered change as secondary and only applicable to accidents and attributes and not applicable to substances themselves.[6]

2. *Historicism:* While a dialectical world-view represents the general awareness of change and movement, a historical attitude reflects the liberal understanding of the changed social, economic, political, and cultural conditions of the Middle East in the new era. The Islamic liberal thesis of history emphasized the relative character of norms and values in relation to the changing historical conditions.

Ultimately it was believed that contrary to the Orthodox Muslim theology, Islamic sacred writings should be reinterpreted in order to meet the new requirements of the changed historical conditions. Since values are not absolute but relative to the specific situation, Islamic writings should not be considered dogmatic and orthodox commandments valid for all times and situations. On the contrary, each statement of the *Quran* should be understood in terms of its own historical situation and as a response to its own specific modality of revelation. Also, the holy writings should be considered as symbolic, metaphorical, and representing diverse meanings to be reinterpreted on the basis of the requirements of a new age (Malik 1971, 187–287).

3. *Reopening the gates of ijtihad:* The call for historical interpretation of texts and adapting Islam to the new requirements of the modern age needed an institution for its fulfillment. This institution was provided through "reopening the gates of Ijtihad." *Ijtihad* is the rational deduction of new decrees in accordance with the spirit of Islam and the precepts of reason. *Mujtahid* is the Muslim learned scholar who is supposed to be knowledgeable enough to engage in the act of ijtihad.

Ijtihad was extremely important for developing the five legal schools between the eighth and eleventh centuries. After the eleventh century the gates of ijtihad were closed. The idea of the end of ijtihad was based upon two ideas: first, it was assumed that the previous *Mujtahids* and their legal schools had explicitly answered all possible questions, consequently nothing unpredicted by previous regulations could emerge. Secondly, it was argued that it was impossible for anyone to attain the degree of knowledge and perfection necessary to become capable of genuine ijtihad (Hodgson 1974, 2:404–10). Although in practice *ijtihad* was never really suspended, the conservative and static implications of the theoretical consensus cannot be overstated. Confronted with the challenge of modernization, Islamic liberalism advocated the significance of ijtihad and "reopened its gates." This reopening of the ijtihad function was an attack against Islamic orthodoxy, representing a renewal of the significance of authority through reason (Hourani 1962, 130–60).

4. *Agreement of reason with faith:* The triumph of the Asha'ira over the Mutazila school in the eleventh century was a catastrophic defeat for the authority of reason in Islamic theory. Asha'ira rejected reason and rational understanding, denied the law of causation, believed in an extreme deterministic cosmology in which every event was

directly and immediately created by God, considered the *Quran* eternal and not created (hence a rejection of any form of historicism), believed in the literal meaning of scriptures including belief in the anthropomorphic attributes of God, attacked the validity of humanistic standards of reason and justice, and rejected any notion of free will (Rahman 1968, 97–116).

Islamic liberalism of the nineteenth and twentieth centuries, however, found the products of reason, science, and technology useful and necessary. Reinterpretation of Islam in order to create a theology suitable to the situation required a metaphorical and symbolic conception of the old texts and a strong defense of the validity of reason and rational sciences. The law of causation was assumed to have no contradiction with the will of God. In fact, it was argued that the purpose and will of God can be recognized through rational and scientific understanding of the laws and mechanisms of the universe. Islamic liberalism praised reason, humanism, and rationalism.

5. *Educational reform:* The thesis of the agreement of reason and faith was accompanied by a positive appreciation of Western technology and science. According to the advocates of Islamic liberalism, it was necessary for the Muslims to learn Western technology and science and to adopt the empirical and scientific method of discovery, analysis, and explanation. Consequently Muslim liberals asked for drastic reforms in educational institutions of Muslim societies. An important victory of the dogmatic and orthodox *Ulama* in the early centuries of Islamic civilization was that they gained a monopoly of control, administration, and teaching of colleges, called *madrasa*. The curriculum emphasized formal obsession, memorization of old texts, and a detailed legal discourse based upon the authority of the early *Mujtahids*. Islamic liberalism asked for modern and Western school systems, encouraged the teaching of natural and technical sciences, and emphasized history, interpretation, and philosophy in the realm of theological learning. Abduh's reforms in Al-Azhar University in Cairo were a pioneer example of this new development (Hourani 1962, 136–39).

6. *Sympathy with women's rights:* Finally, Islamic liberalism addressed the question of women's rights with a relatively sympathetic viewpoint. Contrary to the extremely patriarchal form of traditional Muslim discourse on gender and sex questions, the liberals tried to reinterpret Islamic theory and history in order to depict a more egalitarian picture of women's place in society. Although preserving

strong patriarchial tendencies, Islamic liberalism asked for more
education and active participation of women in social life (Hourani
1962, 238–40).

Characteristics and Forms of Islamic Fundamentalism

Modern Islamic fundamentalism is essentially a rejection of Islamic
liberalism and a reaction to the inherent contradictions and difficulties
of the attempt for reconciliation between Islamic precepts and the
challenge of modernization. In what follows I attempt to outline a
major set of defining characteristics of Islamic fundamentalism with
particular attention to its contemporary Iranian version.

1. *Repressive interpretation of the notion of God:* Religious symbols, like
   many other symbols, possess a certain level of generality and
   abstractness that make them capable of incorporation within
   contradictory ideological and political frameworks.[7] The notion
   of God exemplifies this capacity for diverse interpretation. The idea
   of God can be interpreted as a strong ideological justification of
   democracy, equality, liberty, and humanism, while the same idea of
   God can legitimize the most repressive anti-democratic, anti-
   humanist, and discriminating attitudes and practices. I call the first
   interpretation the democratic, and the second the repressive interpretation of the notion of God. The democratic interpretation
   holds that since everyone is created by the same God, all human
   beings are brothers and sisters and all reflect the divine attributes
   and divine unity. Consequently, all distinctions and discrimina-
   tions in terms of class, race, sex, religion, political belief, education,
   and the like should be considered as human made and contradictory to the will of God. The repressive interpretation, in contrast,
   emphasizes the absolute and divine nature of the word of God.
   Accordingly, humanity is divided into two groups: those who
   believe and behave according to the revealed word of God, and
   those who do not. Since the revealed word of God is absolutely
   true, there can be no room for beliefs that do not agree with God's
   word. Believers are the champions of light and truth, and the rest
   are the forces of evil and darkness whom believers must destroy.
   Suppression, discrimination, brutality, and violation of human
   rights are legitimized in the name of God and his absolute
   authority.

   Islamic fundamentalism clearly is an extreme example of the
   repressive interpretation of God. Before the triumph of the Iranian

revolution, the democratic interpretation was widespread, whereas after the revolution an extreme repressive interpretation became dominant. The reasons for such a transition are to be found not only in the changing role of the Muslim militants, from the challengers of the Pahlavi dictatorship to the incumbents of power positions, but also in the decline of the liberal and radical Islamic rhetoric of the late Dr. Shariati and its substitution with Khomeini's fundamentalist politics and ideology.[8]

2. *Unity of church and state:* An important characteristic of Islamic fundamentalism is its insistence upon an extreme theocratic form of state. Theocracy utterly contradicts democracy and humanism. Indeed, the most explicit form of intolerance, authoritarianism, and despotism is to be found in the undemocratic character of theocracy. Theocracy represents the ultimate victory of authority over reason, an explicit deprivation of the non-believer from various social and political rights, the suppression of freedom of speech and free discourse, the destruction of the principle of ethical autonomy, and the legitimization of savage violence in the name of divine mission and moral heroism.

According to advocates of Islamic fundamentalism, the ultimate cause of contemporary individual and social problems is the distortion of true Islam and deviation from the "real" Islam. Genuine Islam is the Islam of Muhammad and the early Caliphs wherein Islam was both a religion and a polity. Muhammad was not only a religious authority but the political head of the Muslim state as well. Islam represented concrete and specific commandments and teachings for all aspects of the daily individual and social life. It follows that Islam cannot remain an abstract religion parallel to a secular state. The goal of Islamic fundamentalism is to reestablish this idealized state. To achieve this goal, the secular state has to be destroyed so that the state becomes one with the church. Since the principles of legal deduction have concretely been laid out by Islam, there cannot be any genuine legislative function in a Muslim state. No human legislation can contradict the divine legislation. All fundamental legal issues have been specified by the *Shariah* and the legal expertise of the *Ulama*. Therefore, there is neither need nor the possibility for a democratic legislation to regulate according to the principle of popular sovereignty and representation (Enayat 1982, 83–110).

Post-revolutionary Iran established just such an extreme theocracy. Not only is Islam the state religion, and the constitution based upon the *Shari'ah,* the actual occupants of high positions of the state machinery are from the ranks of the *Ulama*. The initial power struggle between the secular-oriented wing of the revolution and the fundamentalist clergy ended in a decisive victory of the latter who moved swiftly to unify state and church (Mortimer 1982, 296–375). The most significant political institution of the Islamic Republic of Iran is *Wilayat-i-faqih*, the guardianship and rule of the jurist. According to this principle the ultimate political authority belongs to the most learned and respected *Mujtahid* who has an absolute veto power on any issue, including the power to dismiss the president. At present Khomeini is the ruling faith. Khomeini's theory of *Wilayat-i-faqih*—the blueprint of the Islamic Republic—represents a theocracy in an extreme and unprecedented form (Khomeini 1979, 43–72).

3. *Rejectionism and predominance of evil symbols:* Islamic fundamentalism is not a resolution of the contradictions and dilemmas presented by nineteenth-century liberalism but, rather, a rejection of the effort to accommodate Islam to the modern world. Still, it is possible to return to some idealistic state. Only selective attributes of the past can be restored.

Since fundamentalism cannot reconcile Islam to modern challenges nor fully restore the past, it is a natural sociological phenomenon that they should choose to attack everything associated with modernity and the Western world.

Another characteristic of Islamic fundamentalism, thus, is its characterization of everything modern and Western in terms of sin and evil. Islamic fundamentalism's discourse, politics, and ideas of the past are preoccupied with a mythology of evil dominance over positive symbols. The mission of Islam is defined primarily in terms of destruction of a vast multitude of evils rather than the development of positive programs of reconstruction.

Post-revolutionary Iran illustrates well these tendencies. Iranian media, controlled exclusively by the ruling *Ulama,* are obsessed with the mythology of martyrdom, blood, destruction, and intolerance. Their view of the predominance of evil over utopian symbols is accompanied by a paranoid conspiratorial consciousness wherein the hand of satanic forces, Eastern and Western, are seen engineering all the internal problems of the country. Their rhetoric serves not only to account for failures of the new regime, but it provides a rationale for legitimization of suppressive measures against any group perceived to be a threat to the Ulama (Algar 1969, 1–25).

4. *Scriptural literalism and rejection of historicism and rationalism:*

Islamic fundamentalism insists upon a literalist reading of Muslim holy scriptures without reinterpreting them in light of the modern situation. It condemns all new interpretation of Islamic texts that may deviate from the original perceptions and interpretations. The solution of social problems lies in a return to the early genuine Islam.

Khomeini's fundamentalism, in this regard, must be understood in historical context. As noted above, the controversy over the role of reason versus authority and tradition dates back to the eleventh century and a debate between Mu'tazila and Asha'ira. Mu'tazila emphasized the validity of reason and rationalism whereas Asha'ira insisted upon the authority of the literal texts and tradition.

In some respects this dispute was reproduced during the late eighteenth and nineteenth centuries in a debate between the Usuli and Akhbari schools within Shi'ite theology. But the dynamics of the differences and similarities of the two historical disputes are significant for understanding Islamic fundamentalism. The Usuli school articulated explicitly by Behbahani and Murtaza Ansari emphasized three major theological ideas. First, it emphasized the significance of reason and the validity of rational analysis for scriptural hermeneutics. Second, it affirmed the importance of the *ijtihad* function and the authority of *Mujtahids*. Third, it insisted upon the thesis of emulation according to which each Shi'ite believer had to imitate, counsel, and obey a *Mujtahid* during his lifetime. A hierarchy of the Mujtahids and a flexible structure of authority that could be either centralized or decentralized was presumed to exist (Cole 1983, 33–46).

There is no doubt that the victory of the Usuli school in Iran prepared the way for increasing the power of the *Ulama* and their eventual organizational resources. This does not mean, however, that the influence of the Usuli tradition makes Islamic fundamentalism to a reformist Islam. In fact there is a significant difference between the Mu'tazila and Usuli traditions. Although both emphasized the authority of reason, for Usuli theology reason was the reason of the *Mujtahids* and the center of emulation rather than the reason of the individual believer. Usuli theology utterly rejected individualism, rationalism, and humanism. According to Usuli theory the masses of believers are incapable of correct and rational independent judgment. That is why it is a religious obligation of each Muslim believer to obey and imitate the decrees of his *Mujtahid*. It is hardly necessary to emphasize the sociological importance of such a theology. Usuli tradition's thesis of reason and emulation simultaneously strengthens the power of *Ulama* and undermines the democratic and liberal institutions. It advocates more authority for Ulama and less power for individual believers.

It is also clear from the above analysis that Islamic fundamentalism cannot be likened to the Protestant Reformation against the papal authority of the Roman Catholic church. The Reformation emphasized the reason of individuals and undermined the authority of the priesthood. Islamic fundamentalism performs the opposite function. Such a tension between the significance of ijtihad and the validity of reason is also present in lesser degrees in Islamic liberalism.

Khomeini's fundamentalism goes even one step further than the traditional Usuli theology. While Khomeini emphasized the principle of *Wilayat-i-faqih* and the necessity of emulation, he defines the ijtihad function in very conservative terms. The function of *ijtihad* is not to create new decrees but to decipher the real decree in the all-encompassing scriptures of early Islam (Gregory 1983, 163–88).

5. *Obsession with superstructure:* A major characteristic of Islamic fundamentalism is its preoccupation, even obsession, with superstructural issues. Social evils, the problematic issues, and social problems are defined by the fundamentalists merely in terms of superficial, visible symbols of religiosity in the history and tradition of Islamic legality. For Khomeini the major problems of society are drinking alcohol, adultery, homosexuality, pornography, breaking the fast, and freedom of speech, practice, and assembly of religious minorities. It is not surprising then to see that the vision of the ideal society among Muslim fundamentalists is one of strict sexual control, suppression, and regulation, banning of alcohol consumption, and elimination of the religious minorities.

In contrast to extensive attention given to these superstructural matters, one finds a virtual preservation of the *status quo* with regard to matters of ownership and economic relations. In fact, a few initial post-revolutionary state policies that called for minor changes in production and ownership relations were soon renounced as contradictory to Islam and were effectively reversed.[9]

An important sociological implication of such a standpoint of Islamic fundamentalism is its attempt to dilute class consciousness and replace it with a popular religious identity. Islamic fundamentalism attempts, consciously or structurally, to create subjectivities that are defined primarily in terms of Muslim, non-Muslim, believer, non-believer, and godly-satanic categories. The rhetoric of Islamic fundamentalism rejects the significance of class categories, class interests, class formation, and class organizations. The legitimizing function of such an ideological practice is clear: to justify the preservation of the status quo in structural issues and to emphasize strict obsession with symbols of the rule of Islamic culture.

6. *Pan-Islamism:* Another manifestation of the urge to return to a selective past in Islamic fundamentalism is the theory of pan-Islamic state. In the early Islamic civilization the fundamental political category was defined as *ummah,* or the community of believers. The institution of caliphate also was presumed to reflect a state defined not in territorial but in ideological terms. The theory of pan-Islamism calls for the establishment of one nation, the Muslim nation, comprised of the *ummah,* defined in terms of ideological belief in Islam. Pan-Islamism is assumed to transcend both the diversity of present national institutions and the idea of pan-Arabism—the latter defined in ethnic and linguistic terms. In the late nineteenth century the Ottoman Sultan Abdulhamid, who called for pan-Islamism by calling himself Caliph, the leader of all Muslims, asked for allegiance and support from various Muslim nations. Abdulhamid's attempt was a response to both external and internal threats to his rule over the shattering Ottoman empire. Pan-Islamism was a strategy to mobilize support for defense against Western military expansion and to suppress national, local, and ethnic movements for autonomy, equality, and independence. Al-Afghani was the famous theoretician of Pan-Islamism who supported Abdulhamid and asked for Muslim unity against the Western intrusion, particularly British imperialism (Keddie 1972).

The theory of pan-Islamism had been emphasized by the Muslim Brotherhood in Egypt and is now advocated by Khomeini's fundamentalism. In both cases a deemphasis of national identity and an overemphasis of religious identity has been the agenda of ideological and political practice (Menashri 1980, 119–46).

The unity of political and ideological institutions implies an immediate political segregation and discrimination mediated through a social system of stratification in terms of ideological and religious beliefs. The non-believers are, at most, second-class citizens and are explicitly deprived of various social, political, economic, and cultural rights and privileges. The Islamic Republic of Iran exemplifies such a discriminatory tendency in its most clear form: harrassment, insult, confiscation of property, imprisonment, torture, and even execution have been carried out against individuals simply on the grounds of personal beliefs. The systematic brutality of Khomeini's regime against members of the Baha'i faith is a tragic expression of the anti-democratic consequence of the unity of polity and Islam *(Baha'is in Iran* 1981).

7. *Patriarchy:* Islamic fundamentalism systematically and explictly encourages and enforces suppression of women. In fact, after the triumph of the revolution, the first protest demonstration against Khomeini's ideology and practice was organized by women who were confronted with brutal attacks by the Muslim male militia. The purpose of the protests was to reject Khomeini's systematic undoing of family protection laws initiated during the Shah's rule and to ask for further elimination of patriarchal institutions and practices.

The fundamentalists condemned the Shah because he approved of some liberal measures for the liberation of Iranian women from the historical bondage of patriarchal institutions and laws. The Shah rejected the veiling of women, encouraged formal equality of men and women before the law, disapproved of the male right to marry four women, rejected the eligibility of a nine-year-old girl for marriage, discouraged the institution of temporary marriage or *Muta,* denied a husband's exclusive right of divorce, and encouraged formal education and social participation of women.

Khomeini did not criticize the nominal and formal character of many of the Shah's reforms. Instead he asked for the elimination of all liberal legislation and called for a return to the old patriarchal institutions of a thousand years ago. The Islamic Republic of Iran permits a husband to have four wives and to marry a girl as soon as her body permits her to reproduce; utilizes coercion, threat, and severe punishment for enforcing universal veiling of all the women, even for little girls; encourages the sexist practice of temporary marriage; asks for a total segregation of men and women from one another; and offers a different school curriculum for girls to fit their proper sex role images and training.[10]

8. *Neither Eastern nor Western:* A frequently mentioned slogan of Islamic fundamentalists is "neither Eastern nor Western." The phrase is taken from a beautiful statement in the Quran:

Allah is the light of the heavens and earth;
His light is like a niche in which is a lamp, the lamp in glass and
the glass like a brilliant star, lit from a blessed tree, an olive
neither of the East nor of the West whose oil would almost give
light even though no fire did touch it (24:35).

Although there are different interpretations of this allegorical statement, it might be suggested that by East and West Muhammad could refer to the Zoroastrian Sasanid empire of Iran and the Christian Byzantine empire located to the East and West of the Arabian Peninsula, respectively. In the present political discourse, however, East and West are assumed to be equivalent to the capitalist and the communist blocs.

To claim that Islam is a religion, a polity, and a culture is to claim that it is neither Eastern nor Western. More specifically, the thesis and slogan of neither Eastern nor Western implies two related but distinct ideas. First, it implies national sovereignty and independence from economic, political, social, and cultural domination of any country, including the United States and the Soviet Union. In this sense the theory implies a rejection of imperialism and calls for national liberation (Khomeini 1979, 5–17). The second implication of the thesis is a rejection of both capitalist and socialist models of development and a call for basing political decision-making upon Islam and Islamic cultural traditions. An intellectual rationalization of the second implication rejects the "external" and "foreign" models of development and emphasizes the necessity of the definition of ideas, values, and development in accord with the indigenous cultural traditions and religious heritage of the nation. The anti-imperialist slogan of Islamic fundamentalism is not without progressive implications. But the general structure and mentality of Islamic fundamentalism turns even this potentially progressive slogan into mostly reactionary and suppressive measures.

9. *Authoritarianism and intolerant structure of consciousness and speech act:* Another and perhaps the most important characteristic of Islamic fundamentalism is its authoritarian form of discourse, speech act, and consciousness. A detailed explication of the elements of this authoritarian culture and discourse would require a separate paper. However, because of the importance of this characteristic of Islamic fundamentalism to my general thesis, it is important that I develop my argument in some detail here. I shall limit my presentation to an outline of some of the major issues:

(a) *The primacy of normative statements:* One of the most important elements of the authoritarian code in Islamic fundamentalism is the primacy of normative over descriptive-factual statements. The predominant form of discourse is value-oriented. Fundamentalist mentality is obsessed with the question of virtue and vice and constantly feels a mission to fight evil. At a theoretical level, an Islamic fundamentalist rejects objectivity as a myth and advocates the unity of fact and values. A fundamentalist discourse is dissociated from the humble realm of facts, is immersed in normative and authoritative claims and judgments, and is impatient with the ideas of the "evil forces."

(b) *The primacy of holistic assertions:* A closely related but distinct characteristic of the fundamentalist form of discourse is the primacy of the holistic and totality-oriented over the piecemeal and specific. Islamic fundamentalism makes claims and assertions about the entire universe, the entire history, all societies, all institutions, and the totality of social, economic, political, and ideological structures. It is clear that such a holistic discourse is bound to be normative and to lie beyond the scope of rational frontiers. Hence, an authoritarian and intolerant rather than a humble and democratic mentality.

(c) *Significance of institutionalized rhetoric:* The art of rhetoric is one of the special trainings of the *ulama.* The primary function of the Ulama's sermons and religious lectures is to play with people's emotions and mobilize alternative resources through influencing the audience. Frequent reference to the story of Imam Husain's martyrdom is a common norm of such lectures.

(d) *Infrequent use of subjunctives:* One of the most visible features of Muslim Middle Eastern discourse, particularly that of fundamentalist is the general imperative form of assertions and little use of subjunctives. Speakers are dogmatic about ideas and ignore the complexity of reality and the viewpoints of other speakers. Authoritarianism and intolerance are built into sentence structures.

(e) *The myth of absolute knowledge:* Corresponding to the imperative form of speech acts is the fundamentalists' belief in their monopolistic access to the absolute knowledge of reality. It is the case that any belief in possession of a total, exact, and absolute "science" or knowledge of society, history, and truth feeds the germs of intolerance, fascism, and savage brutality. Stalin's version of the science of the iron laws of history and Hitler's "scientific" demonstration of racism are familiar examples. Fundamentalism in general, and Islamic fundamentalism in particular, claims a monopoly on truth, absolute, divine in nature and all-encompassing. For a Muslim fundamentalist every issue has a clear categorical answer. Alternative answers are just illusions and evil-thinking that must be eliminated.

(f) *The myth of absolute values:* Similar to the belief in absolute truth is the fundamentalists' belief in an absolute and objective system of values. For fundamentalists, values can be neither relative nor relational. Every issue has a clear-cut moral answer. Every problem is black or white with no possible gradations in between. Again, the objectivity of these absolute values is justified through divine origin. Intolerance and repression are the predictable outcomes of such a mental structure.

(g) *The myth of the end of history:* The culmination of the epistemological structure of Islamic fundamentalism is reflected in its belief in the end of history. By the myth of the end of history, I mean the belief in an ultimate, final, and total resolution of all human problems and sufferings through the application of a specific absolute ideology. Such a simplistic perspective reduces all the complex problems of individual and social existence to a deviation from the premises of a specific ideology whose application would solve all the difficulties, and would return humanity to the pre-fall paradise. Islamic fundamentalism exemplifies such a mythology. It is the rule of true Islam that ultimately would solve every problem in the world. The viewpoint is both archaic and utopian with a strong tendency to encourage extremism, fanaticism, and intolerance.

(h) *Authority-reference rather than rationalistic reasoning:* The final element of the speech and dialogue structure of Islamic fundamentalism is the authoritative and traditional mode of reasoning. By authoritative reasoning I mean the ultimate justification of a proposition through a recourse to the authority of past texts that are claimed to be divine in origin. In a situation of dispute and disagreement, the final word is the word of experts, the emulated *Ulama,* and the absolute revelation of the *Quran.* It is interesting that for Islamic fundamentalism, the validity of the authority of Islam and the *Quran* ultimately transcends the norms of rational discourse, free choice, and personal belief. Reason is accepted if and only if it leads the person to belief in Islam.[11]

10. *Return to a mechanical solidarity:* The final characteristic of Islamic fundamentalism is its emphasis on an extended, rigid, and intense "collective conscience." Islamic fundamentalism finds in Islam a

way of life that should regulate the detailed social and personal affairs of individuals. This emphasis on "we-consciousness" is accompanied with a strong concern with conflict between "we" and "they." The world is divided into two camps of God and satan, with no gradation in between. A group-narcissism is accompanied by an intense hatred of "others."[12] Legitimization of violence and coercion against non-believers is a natural consequence of such a mental structure. In the present cult of the Iranian Islamic Republic, brutal and ruthless violence is praised and the smell of blood glorified. Likewise, severe punishment is assumed to be the effective means for solving the problem of "crime" in society. The translation of fundamental group-narcissism into the legitimization of violence is facilitated by the presence of violence as a means of conflict resolution in the early history of Islam.[13]

Sociologically speaking, Islamic fundamentalism attempts to return to a situation of mechanical solidarity. The significant point is that such a strategy is a conservative reaction to the anomic situation of contemporary Middle Eastern societies. In fact, an extended and inflexible scope of collective norms and values contradicts the structural trend and reality of the Middle East in the twentieth century. Durkheim's analysis of the individualistic implications of the division of labor (1933, 111–232), and Simmel's phenomenology of the emergence of self-consciousness and distinct identities due to the modern reality of overlapping group memberships and role structures (1955, 138–55) are particularly relevant to the transitory situation of the Middle Eastern societies. The structure and dynamics of modernization under a situation of imperialistic domination have created a serious state of anomie in the urban areas of the Middle East. Islamic fundamentalism appears, thus, as a paranoid reaction to the present social contradictions that seeks a solution by imposing a mechanical form of collective conscience upon society. Basil Bernstein's suggestion of an association between mechanical solidarity, inflexible role definitions, and restricted code is clearly manifest in the contemporary phenomenon of Islamic fundamentalism (Bernstein 1971).

Conclusion

This paper examined the general structural and formal characteristics of Islamic fundamentalism without discussing the sociological causes that led to its triumph in the course of the Iranian revolution and its present revival in the Muslim Middle East. Islamic fundamentalism represents an extremist, militant, intolerant, and repressive alternative to Islamic liberalism. The historical failure of Islamic liberalism should be explained in at least three terms: the unfortunate coincidence and association between imperialistic Western domination and Islamic liberal theory; the contradiction between Islamic liberal thought with concrete, specific, and extended scope of Islamic teachings and obligations; and a conflict between the urge for historical interpretations and an ultimate conformity to the explicit statements of the *Quran*.

The ascendency and triumph of Islamic fundamentalism represents a situation of sociological anomie in which, due to the inaccessibility of institutionally relevant means, religion undertakes to perform alternative political, social, economic, and ideological functions. Islamic fundamentalism combines a real question, the reality of imperialist domination and capitalist socio-economic contradictions, with a reactionary, intolerant, obsessive, and brutal response. The consequence is the presence of occasional progressive slogans within a predominant structure of intolerant and repressive theory and practice.

Notes

1. As an example of ex post facto explanation of the Iranian revolution of 1978, see: Algar, Hamid, *Religion and State in Iran,* Berkeley, CA: University of California Press, 1969; and Algar, Hamid, *The Islamic Revolution in Iran,* London: Open Press, 1980.
2. For a short periodization of capitalist penetration in the Middle East see: Halliday, Fred, *Arabia without Sultans,* New York: Vintage Books, 1975, pp. 17–58.
3. The use of the concept of Islamic fundamentalism is already prevalent in the literature. See, e.g.: Enayat, Hamid, *Modern Islamic Political Thought,* Austin, TX: University of Texas Press, 1982, pp. 83–110.
4. For a historical and sociological analysis of the intellectual tradition of Muslim communities, see: Keddie, Nikki R., ed., *Scholars, Saints, and Sufis,* Berkeley, CA: University of California Press, 1972.
5. For a good historical discussion of Islamic liberalism, see: Hourani, Albert, *Arabic Thought in the Liberal Age, 1798–1939,* London: Oxford University Press, 1962.
6. For an excellent description of Sadra's philosophy, see: Rahman Fazlur, *The Philosophy of Mulla Sadra,* Albany, NY: State University of New York Press, 1975.

7. Lewis Feuer calls the capacity of abstract symbols for contradictory interpretations "the Law of Wings." See: Feuer, Lewis S., *Ideology and the Ideologists,* Oxford, Basil Blackwell, 1975, pp. 20–55.

8. For a presentation of Shariati's liberal approach to Islam, see: Shariati, Ali, *On the Sociology of Islam,* Berkeley, CA: Mizan Press, 1979.

9. In June 1979, major industries were nationalized and subsequently foreign trade became a state monopoly. In August 1984, Khomeini denounced nationalization of industry and foreign trade as against the Islamic laws.

10. Insightful documentation of the oppression of women in post-revolutionary Iran can be found in Azar Tabari and Nahid Yeganeh, eds., *The Shadow of Islam: Women's Movement in Iran,* Zed: 1982, pp. 191–98.

11. My explication of the general structure of the fundamentalist-Middle Eastern speech acts is solely based upon my own phenomenological analysis using both field research and content analysis methods of observation.

12. For a good analysis of the concept of group narcissism, see: Fromm, Eric, *The Heart of Man: It's Genius for Good and Evil,* New York: Harper and Row, 1968, pp. 62–94.

13. An example is the treatment of Beni-Quaraiza by the Muslims during the time of Muhammad himself. See: Bernard, Lewis, *The Arabs in History,* New York: Harper and Row, 1966, pp. 40–45.

References

Algar, Hamid. 1969. *Religion and State in Iran.* Berkeley, Calif.: University of California Press.

Algar, Hamid. 1980. *The Islamic Revolution in Iran.* London: Open Press.

Baha'i International Community. 1981. *The Baha'is in Iran.* New York: Baha'i International Community.

Bernard, Lewis. 1966. *The Arabs in History.* New York: Harper & Row.

Bernstein, Basil. 1971. *Class, Codes and Control,* vol. 1: *Theoretical Studies Toward the Sociology of Language.* London: Routledge and Kegan Paul.

Cole, Juan R. 1983. Imami jurisprudence and the role of the Ulama. In *Religion and Politics in Iran,* ed. Nikki R. Keddi, 33–46. New Haven: Yale University Press.

Durkheim, Emile. 1933. *The Division of Labor in Society.* New York: Free Press.

Enayat, Hamid. 1982. *Modern Islamic Political Thought*. Austin: University of Texas Press.

Feuer, Lewis S. 1975. *Ideology and the Ideologists*. Oxford: Basil Blackwell.

Fromm, Eric. 1966. *The Heart of Man: It's Genius for Good and Evil*. New York: Harper & Row.

Gregory, Rose. 1983. Velayat-e-faqih and the recovery of Islamic identity in the thought of Ayatollah Khomeini. In *Religion and Politics in Iran*, ed. Nikki R. Keddi, 163–88. New Haven: Yale University Press.

Halliday, Fred. 1975. *Arabia Without Sultans*. New York: Vintage Books.

Hodgson, Marshall G. S. 1974. *The Venture of Islam*. 3 vols. Chicago: University of Chicago Press.

Hourani, Albert. 1962. *Arabic Thought in the Liberal Age, 1798–1939*. London: Oxford University Press.

Keddie, Nikki R., ed. 1972. *Scholars, Saints, and Sufis*. Berkeley: University of California Press.

Keddi, Nikki R. 1972. *Sayyid Jamal Ad-Din Al-Afghani*. Berkeley: University of California Press.

Khomeini, Ruhollah. 1979. *Islamic Government*. New York: Manor Books.

Malik, Hafeez, ed. 1971. *Iqbal*. New York: Columbia University Press.

Menashri, David. 1980. Shi'ite leadership: In the shadow of conflicting ideologies. *Iranian Studies* 13: 119–46.

Mortimer, Edward. 1982. *Faith and Power*. New York: Vintage Books.

McClelland, David C. 1976. *The Achieving Society*. New York: Irvington.

Rahman, Fazlur. 1968. *Islam*. New York: Anchor Books.

Rahman, Fazlur. 1975. *The Philosophy of Mulla Sadra*. Albany: State University of New York Press.

Schimmel, Anne Marie. 1975. *Mystical Dimensions of Islam*. Chapel Hill: University of North Carolina Press.

Shariati, Ali. 1979. *On the Sociology of Islam*. Berkeley: Mizan Press.

Simmel, Georg. 1955. *Conflict and the Web of Group-Affiliation*. New York: Free Press.

Tabari, Azar and Nahid Yeganeh, eds. 1982. *The Shadow of Islam: Women's Movement in Iran*. London: Zed.

Voll, John O. 1982. *Islam: Continuity and Change in the Modern World*. Boulder, Colo.: Westview Press.

Wallerstein, Immanuel. 1974. *The Modern World System*. New York: Academic Press.

10

Dakwah Islamiah Islamic Revivalism in the Politics of Race and Religion in Malaysia

ZULKARNAINA M. MESS AND W. BARNETT PEARCE

MALAYSIA is currently experiencing a conflict between progressive and revivalist Islamic groups. The relationship between religion and politics is at issue, and is troublesome for two reasons: Pakistan and Iran, where prophetic religion has replaced conventional politics, and Lebanon and Libya, where it has entered politics as a potent partisan force, provide models for those who seek as well as for those who oppose the "Islamization of society." And the conflict concerning Islam in Malaysia threatens to divide the majority Malays and make them vulnerable in Malaysia's racially-charged political struggles.

In Malaysia the social movement promoting "Islamization" is called *dakwah.* From outside the movement *dakwah* seems regressive, divisive, and impractical. From within the movement "Islamization" seems benign in effect and divine in origin. It is presented as a means of preserving the faith, traditional morality, and personal pride against the social ills brought by westernization. On a personal level *dakwah* spokespersons call for strict observance of Muslim moral prescriptions. At a national level they call for legislation to enforce Islamic morality and to institutionalize Islamic practices.

The political and racial history of Malaysia makes the government particularly vulnerable to these appeals and places it in a dilemma. If the government defends itself against the charge of being "insufficiently Islamic" by protesting its Islamic credentials—in effect co-opting *dakwah* on the political right—it risks alienating the large Chinese and Indian racial minorities which are part of the ruling National Front. On the other hand if it yields the right to *dakwah,* it risks dividing the Malays who comprise a slim majority and opens itself to the passions of Islamic revolutionaries.

This paper has three purposes: 1) to situate the conflict between *dakwah* and the government in its historical context; 2) to describe the current status of the *dakwah* challenge and the government's response to it; 3) to attempt to illumine the conflict between *dakwah* and the government with reference to concepts which originated in the West, including "secularization theory" and "civil religion."

Islamic Fundamentalism[1]

Islam presents itself as a "complete way of life," inimical to any other religion or political system. Its scriptures, traditions, and *Shariah* (courts) depict themselves as providing sufficient and authoritative guidance for all aspects of life, from the ways of administering a nation to the manner of conducting oneself correctly in society. This aspect of the Islamic tradition lends itself to political activism, legitimating opposition to non-Islamic (or impurely Islamic) social practices or political structure.

Throughout this century, the Muslim countries have felt a tension between their religious traditions and their desire to participate in what seemed to be superior political and economic institutions of the West. The difference between revivalists and progressives lies in the extent to which they believe the traditions are appropriately interpreted to fit contemporary circumstances. Progressives believe that any area of life which does not conflict with matters of worship and the injunctions of the scriptures are open to interpretation; proponents of *dakwah* restrict adaptation of tradition and insist on reconstructing traditional forms of life.

Malaysia as a Democratic State

Malaysia has been independent for about twenty-five years, emerging from British colonial rule as the eventual outcome of Japanese conquests and the break up of the British Empire in the post-World War II period. A few decades ago scholars had great confidence that newly independent countries like Malaysia could—and should—establish Western-style democracies. However, there are unanticipated difficulties in implementing Western style democracy in Asian and African states. These states lack an important but previously unacknowledged characteristic of the Western democracies: an implicit moral consensus which underlies a much celebrated but tacitly limited religious and political pluralism. In the United States, for example, this moral consensus takes the form of a "civil religion" which comprises a "higher standard" to which the government is held to account (Bellah 1967). As Von Vorys (1975, 6) notes, however, in Non-Western states

> there is no predisposition . . . for limiting the range of issues to be submitted for settlement by the political process. . . . Indeed, not even the procedures are above political contests. Rules, laws, the constitution, are always fair game. Rarely are they perceived as symmetrical norms to be observed voluntarily by all parties; more often they are considered tools to be used or obstacles to be removed in the service of group interest. Not surprisingly, few constitutions outlast a decade.

Malaysia is a state (an autonomous political entity with recognized borders and institutions) which includes a number of nations (distinct racial/religious groups each with their own cultural heritage and language). Therefore one of the major tasks of government in Malaysia has been to achieve democracy without consensus. *Dakwah* is controversial because its proponents argue that it provides the best way to achieve unity and modernity without the undesirable aspects of westernization while its opponents argue that it is itself the primary threat to unity and progressive policies.

The Development of a Racially-Mixed Society

Islam first came to the northern peninsula, brought by Arab and Indian traders, prior to the fifteenth century. However, Islam did not spread or develop until it was institutionalized by the Malaccan Sultanate in the fifteenth century.

The inhabitants of Southern Malaysia were mostly Hindu or practitioners of animistic folk religion. Their social and political structures were based on those of the Hindu Sri Vijaya and Majapahit empires centered in Sumatra and Java. What are now known as "Malay Customs" or *adats* are the remnants of the legal and political codes of these empires. In contemporary Malaysia these customs are expressed in folkways and maxims, and are treated with great respect, particularly by rural Malays (Din bin Ali 1963, 16).

The Majapahit prince Parameswara established the state of Malacca in 1402. Muslim traders from the Middle East and India were attracted to the trading center of Malacca, and Parameswara converted to Islam, taking the name of Sultan Iskandar Shah. The people of Malacca—Malays—followed suit and became Muslims.

To avoid domination by the king of Siam, Sultan Iskandar Shah submitted Malacca to the suzerainty of China and accepted the military presence of admiral Cheng Ho (himself a Muslim). Iskandar's son, Sultan Mansor Shah, married Princess Hang Li Poh of China. An unintended consequence of this marriage was to establish a multi-racial population. The princess brought with her a party of five hundred people, and settled at Bukit China, Malacca. Thus in contemporary Malaysia the "Straits-Born Chinese" claim that they are legitimate, hereditary citizens and not, as is frequently charged in racial political rhetoric, "immigrants."

Most Malaccan Muslims did not practice a "pure" form of Islam. The Malays have historically been socially syncretic, willing to incorporate new ways of life into existing patterns but reluctant to abandon traditions for the sake of consistency. "Malay Customs" themselves contain inconsistencies—e.g., some are matriarchal, others patriarchal—and include a mixture of Hindu and animistic practices. Many Malays find little difficulty in accepting the teachings and identity of Islam while continuing their traditional practices (Ahmad Ibrahim 1963, 48).

European colonization began in 1511, but had little effect on the religion of the Malays. The first colonialists, the Portuguese, made a systematic effort to introduce Christianity, but with little success. The Dutch and British who arrived later did not proselytize. The British intervention took the form of treaties with Malay sultans which allowed them to rule indirectly. In all secular matters the British "advised" the sultans; in matters of religion, the sultans were free to practice Islam as they wished.

Since Islam presents itself as a "complete way of life," it is used as a guide for everything ranging from personal morality to affairs of state. The terms of the British "advisory" role with the Sultans insured that Islam became the context and means of national identity and a limited amount of self-rule by Malays. A number of Islamic institutions lent themselves to the creation of a realm of autonomy within British rule. For example, Malays are born Muslim: there is no assumption of freedom of choice and no provision for the conversion of a Muslim to another religion or the renunciation of Islam by a Muslim. The *Shariah* is a court system which is empowered to enforce law on Muslims. Thus in modern Malaysia Malays—but not other races—are governed by two sets of laws: Civil law, based primarily on British models which govern "public" matters and Islamic law which governs personal matters such as matrimony, sexual conduct, gambling, and eating during the fasting month of Ramadan.

During the Chinese suzerainty and the European colonial period members of many races came to the peninsula. The Malays regard the other races—primarily Chinese and Indians—as "immigrants" who came (or were brought) to the country for economic reasons and who decided to stay only when returning "home" was inconvenient. On the other hand, the Malays portray themselves as the original and legitimate inhabitants of the country, linked to the sultans as the traditional authority and to Islam as the official religion. Their loyalty to the country is unquestioned, while that of other races is specifically suspect. Malays say that Malaysia is the only country they have, but that other races can "go home" if they choose.

Malays are the majority race in Malaysia by a small percentage (52.7 percent in 1980). This racial composition was constructed by separating (predominantly Malay) peninsular Malaysia and (predominantly Chinese) Singapore in 1965, and including in Malaysia the (predominantly Malay) states of Sabah and Sarawak on the Northwest part of the island of Borneo. Further, a special category for a people of non-Malay ethnicity was created: the *bumiputras* (literally, "sons of the soil"). These persons are counted as and receive the same privileges as the Malays. Even with these attempts to structure the racial balance, the Malays' plurality is small and they note ominously that Malaysians of Chinese descent control a disproportionate share of the country's economic resources, that (until recently) they outnumbered Malays in urban areas, and that both Chinese and Indians have a higher birth rate than Malays. Moreover, race and politics are closely linked. The religious composition of the country is virtually identical with the racial distribution.

Political Structure and the May 13 Incident

Were Malaysia deliberately designed to produce lingering political tensions, it might well look just as it does. By fact and by history, Malaysia is a multi-racial, multi-religious society. Yet by constitutional edicts Malaysia is a secular state, Islam is its official religion, all Malays are Muslim, and there is to be no discrimination solely on the basis of race or religion.

Since 1957, Malaysia has been a federation of autonomous states with a constitutional monarchy and an elected parliament. Nine of the eleven states each has a sultan (or equivalent), one of whom is elected by his peers to serve a five year term as king of Malaysia. Echoing the structure of British colonial rule, each sultan has jurisdiction over "Malay Religion and Custom" in his state. Most sultans have a Council of Religious Affairs which interprets and enforces Islamic law for Muslims through the *Shariah*. Since Islam is "a complete way of life" and the *Shariah* "infallible" (Abu Bakar 1981, 1044), the power of the sultan is in principle limitless so long as he remains true to Islamic teachings and deals only with Muslims. The federal government is secular and exerts its authority in terms of the economy, the military, and civil law.

A semblance of consensus was provided by the Alliance Party which governed from the formation of the current nation in 1963 until 1969. This party included the United Malays National Organization (UMNO), the Malayan Chinese Association (MCA), and the Malaysian Indian Congress (MIC), and portrayed itself as representing the interests and traditions of all races.

The claim was undermined by the 1969 elections. An unprecedented long period of time was allocated for the campaign, perhaps because the existing government was confident that their greater resources would constitute an advantage during a lengthy campaign. However, bitter racial resentments were exacerbated during the protracted politics: a UMNO publicity official was beaten to death in Penang, a Labour party member was shot, and the various opposition parties based their campaigns on appeals to their own racial/religious groups (Mahathir 1970, 14). In the urban states of Perak and Selangor the Alliance party did not win a majority and could not form a government without a coalition with some opposition parties—all organized around racial/religious lines. The strongest of these, the Chinese party *Gerakan* not only spurned the offer of coalition but taunted the Malays about their defeat. A government-sanctioned victory celebration in Selangor by the opposition parties inflamed already bruised sensibilities. Statements attributed to non-Malays included taunts such as "The Malays have lost. Why don't you just pack and go back to the village," and the popular doggerel:

> The sailing boat is leaking.
> The Malays have fallen,
> Malays now no longer have power,
> K.L. now belongs to the Chinese

A race riot broke out, lasting for three days. Although reliable information about the riot is difficult to obtain, it is obvious that it was a traumatic shock to those attempting to maintain the syncretic government position. To progressive Malays, the riots disclosed the absence of consensus. Concerning this Mahathir (1970, 4–5) states:

> What went wrong in a multiracial, multilingual and multireligious country which for twelve years had enjoyed racial harmony and coopera-tion, that tolerance and understanding could be so abruptly terminated and the various races should sullenly glare at each other and reject a way of life that apparently began long before Independence? Looking back through the years, one of the startling facts which must be admitted is that there never was true racial harmony. There was accommodation . . . What was taken for harmony was absence of open interracial strife. And absence of strife . . . [was] due to a lack of capacity to bring about open conflict.

Democracy was suspended after the May 13 riot, with the govern-ment being conducted by the National Operations Council (NOC). Meanwhile, there was considerable disagreement within UMNO (the largest and Malay political party within the ruling Alliance) about the causes of the riots and the shape of a solution. The opponents included then-Prime Minister Tunku Abdul Rahman and the current Prime Minister Mahathir. Rahman blamed the riots on "racial politics" instigated by Chinese communists. Mahathir, in a letter to the prime minister which was widely circulated, blamed the policies of the government. Rahman and UMNO, he charged, were catering to the Chinese, had encouraged Chinese and Indians to behave "outrageous-ly," and had lost the confidence of Malays. Mahathir called for Rahman's resignation. For this, Mahathir was expelled from UMNO (von Vorys 1975, 345–85).

Three "preconditions" were established by the NOC for the return to democracy: integrity in government, depolitization of the constitution, and decommunalization of politics. The second and third of these may be seen as an attempt to provide a political consensus which transcends racial groupings, or at least deemphasize racial issues.

A National Consultation Council was established which declared itself as representing a national consensus committed to the task of creating a united, socially just, economically equitable, and progressive Malaysian nation. On 31 August 1970, it proclaimed the principles of *Rukunegara,* or "National Ideology":

> Our nation, Malaysia, being dedicated to achieving a greater unity of her peoples; to maintaining a democratic way of life; to creating a just society in which the wealth of the nation shall be equitably shared; to ensuring a liberal approach to her rich and diverse cultural traditions; to building a progressive society which shall be oriented to modern science and technology.
>
> We, her peoples, pledge our united efforts to attain these ends guided by these principles:
>
> Belief in God
> Loyalty to King and Country
>
> Upholding the Constitution
> Rule of Law
> Good Behavior and Morality.

Part of the official commentary on these principles spoke to the concerns of various racial groups. Freedom of religion was guaranteed, as was protection of "immigrants" (i.e., non-Malays) against banishment. In addition, "good behavior" was interpreted as avoiding "any conduct or behavior which is arrogant or offensive to any group" (van Vorys 1975, 395–96).

With democracy restored, the Alliance changed its name to the National Front and included "all those parties which subscribe to its principles." However, UMNO continues to be dominant: for example, its top executive is the prime minister. The "principles" which guide the National Front are articulated in the *Rukunegara* and in the Second Malaysia Plan initiated in 1971.

The Second Malaysia Plan includes a two-pronged economic program, but its explicit goal is to promote national unity. The means of accomplishing unity are, first, to reduce and eventually eradicate poverty by raising income levels and increasing employment opportunities for all Malaysians irrespective of race, and second, to accelerate the process of restructuring Malaysian society to correct economic imbalance, so as to reduce and eventually eliminate the identification of race with economic factors. Since Malays are the most economically disadvantaged, this plan was implemented in the form of "special privileges" for Malays.

The National Front seems to have a firm control of politics. In 1982, Dr. Mahathir held elections only nine months after succeeding Hussein as prime minister and more than a year earlier than legally required. The National Front was never expected to lose, but surprised political *savants* by the strength of its showing. However, the real implication of the election lies within the coalition: More incumbents were replaced than in any other election. Bass (1983, 192) interpreted these results as leaving the National Front structure intact but providing a cadre of younger, better educated, more professional members of parliament who reflect and respond to the style of Dr. Mahathir's government.

There are two major domestic opponents to the government, the combination of which poses a particularly vexing political problem: The Democratic Action Party (DAP) is mainly Chinese and is committed to progressive, liberal government. The *parti Islam Sa-Malaysia* (PAS) is a Malay group critical of un-Islamic policies, such as secularism, cooperation with Chinese and Indian Malaysians, and the practices of contemporary national statecraft.

The National Front successfully defused DAP in the 1982 elections by co-opting their concerns with "efficiency" and "professionalism." Dr. Mahathir's government introduced programs (and slogans) to make government "clean, efficient and trustworthy"; required civil servants to declare their assets and reestablished the Anti-Corruption Agency; initiated a motivational campaign designed to stimulate leadership by example; and increased business contacts with Japan and Korea as part of a comprehensive "Look East" program, giving specific attention to the work ethic, harmonious industrial relations, and social discipline to be found in these examples. The "Look East" policy represents a deliberate turning away from both the easygoing lifestyle Malays inherited from village life and from the post-industrial West as a role-model. The West—particularly Britain—is characterized as manifesting worker-employer strife, decreasing productivity, and fostering general decadence. Perhaps as a result of these policies, DAP was the major loser in the 1982 elections, dropping from sixteen to nine seats in parliament; including that of the secretary-general of the party (Bass 1983).

PAS is the political voice of *dakwah,* and poses the more serious threat to the government's attempt to achieve consensus and democracy. We now turn to a separate analysis of this movement.

Dakwah

The *dakwah* movement is an indirect consequence of the May 13 riot, but the link between them is geographically circuitous. The New Economic Policy was designed, in part, to reduce the economic disparity among races. This was achieved by giving Malays "special privileges" which would enable them to achieve parity with the Chinese. One of these "privileges" was a large program of scholarships for Malays to study in universities in the United States, England, and Australia. While studying abroad they came into contact with both the conspicuous social permissiveness of the secular, Western societies, and the well-organized, well-financed international groups of charismatic fundamentalist Islamic persuaders.

Many Malay students are shocked and repelled by the secularity of the societies in which they sojourned. An Iraqi student told a New York *Times* reporter that "disorientation" led to either of two responses: "Some become more American than the Americans—for example, the obsession with going to discos and drinking huge amounts of alcohol." For others, "Islam becomes a way of putting their feet back on the ground" (Campbell 1984, 44). Islamic fundamentalist groups provide well-organized social networks for Islamic students who, for one reason or another, do not become enmeshed in the—to them astonishingly secular—host society. Some are excluded from social activities and must cope with loneliness; others are repelled by what they perceive as materialistic, sensual values, or the excessive celebration of Western traditions. Fundamentalist groups anticipate their needs and greet new arrivals with activities which might uncharitably be described as indoctrination or emotionally exploitative.

Many sojourning Malay students learn of previously unknown dimensions of their religious heritage under the guidance of dynamic leaders and in the context of a multinational Islamic fraternity:

> For many, their first exposure to a concerned Islamic community and way of life and to active religious *ulama* and proselytisation occurred abroad, in such infidel outposts as Australia, the United Kingdom and North America, or else the Middle East. Their mentors and mediators are colleagues and fellow students from other Muslim countries, particularly Pakistan, Saudi Arabia and Libya. Through these contacts, a form of

non-traditional 'peer learning', young Malays are suddenly made aware of their religious deficiencies. They become intent on improving their religious knowledge, and in consolidating an identity as 'Muslim,' a status with more impact and universalistic significance than that of 'Malay' alone. This they do through attendance at *dakwah* lectures and conferences, and through the study of Arabic as well as of the voluminous Islamic literature, much of it in English, now in wide circulation. These youths are deeply preoccupied with theological issues, particularly of a fundamentalist cast, which tend to take priority in their relationship with fellow Muslims and in evaluating behaviors. They also make a general attempt to re-orient their personal lives along more devout lines, some very privately, others by a conspicuous attention to ritualized behavior and observances (Nagata 1980, 48–49).

Many others experience a form of reverse culture-shock when they return to Malaysia. They find a secular, westernized government which uses Islamic symbols "loosely," rural Malays practicing "impure" forms of Islam mixed with "Malay customs," and strong contingents of non-Malays whose cultural heritage is often offensive to Muslims. Having rejected the dominant values of the Western society in which they studied, they are prepared to reject the impure Islamic institutions and practices of their native society. Many adopt the *dakwah* way of life, and some also join *dakwah* organizations and actively seek to lead other people to a pure form of Islam. Among the most important of these organizations are PERKIM, ABIM, Jamaat Tabigh, and Darul Arqam.

PERKIM, the Pertubuhan Kebanjikan Islam Malaysia or Muslim Welfare League, was the first *dakwah* organization. Relatively affluent, it is supported by the government and receives funds from Saudi Arabia. Its leadership has always been made up of retired government officials. Established to promote Islam among non-Muslims, PERKIM is deliberately non-political. Its activities are careful to be non-offensive and non-militant. PERKIM's philosophy and practices were not universally popular among Muslims, particularly those inclined toward a more active and powerful *dakwah* movement.

ABIM, The Angkatan Belia Islam Malaysia or Islamic Youth Movement of Malaysia, originated at least in part from frustration with PERKIM, and took as its mission the task of addressing all Muslims and the country as a whole with the message of *dakwah*. During the 1970s ABIM was much better organized and well run than its closest ideological counterpart, PAS (the Malaysian Islamic Party). As a result ABIM became, for a time, the most visible, the largest, and the most politically potent of the *dakwah* organizations.

It had been founded by Anwar Ibrahim who had been head of the Islamic Association at the University of Malaya soon after he graduated.

He, along with other leaders in the movement, maintain close ties with counterparts in Libya, Saudi Arabia, Egypt, Pakistan, and other countries.

In the 1970s, Ibrahim traveled widely, speaking to Malay students at universities around the world. He told them about ABIM, exhorted them to maintain Islamic virtues, and stressed their ethnic identity in modern Malaysia. He asked their support for those issues which the government had neglected. For example, in 1974 he was arrested for inciting a student demonstration in support of impoverished farmers in Kedah who criticized the government economic policies. ABIM also opposed the government in support of the "squatters" who were evicted from their homes in Tasik Utara.

In addition to its political activities, ABIM operates a chain of secondary schools which combine "a secular, examination-oriented curriculum within a solid Islamic framework." ABIM is the most academic of the *dakwah* organizations, and takes a didactic mode of advocacy. It is the most severe critic of syncretic (rural) Islam, and calls for a return to the original teachings of the Quran undiluted by the Hindu and animistic elements of Malay Customs.

The Jamaat Tabligh *dakwah* movement was brought to Malaysia from India by followers of Mowlana Mohamed Alias. It is seen by the government and by non-Malays as the least threatening form of *dakwah*. It stresses equalitarianism, private virtues, devotionalism, and evangelism rather than political or economic activism. It is intended to purify the religion of Muslims more than the institutions of secular society, and proceeds by personal evangelism in the mosques. Unlike ABIM, it has some success in rural as well as urban areas. Unlike all other *dakwah* organizations, it excludes women.

Groups of young men seclude themselves overnight or longer in the mosque, for religious retreats, during which they share food and discuss personal religious problems and experiences. Coupled with a rejection of much of contemporary culture, Jamaat Tabligh creates a form of an alternative youth culture for unmarried men, in which religious fraternity and Arabic customs and dress replace the urban-coffee shop and blue jeans secular lifestyle.

All *dakwah* call for a society based on revealed religion, and criticize contemporary society to the extent that it deviates from the ideal of Islam. Darul Arqam is not content to criticize or wait for an eventual Islamization: It has created what it portrays as an Islamic society in the commune of Sungai Penchala, about seventeen miles from Kuala Lumpur.

Dural Arqam was started by Ustaz Ashaari, a government religious teacher who became disgusted with the moral values the secular government inculcated among young people. He established Sungai Penchala as an economically self-sufficient community based as far as possible on scriptural principles. The economy includes small manufacturing enterprises, agricultural products, and a network of small Malay traders. By being independent the people are able to practice a "true Islamic system, free of both secular and non-Muslim influence" (Nagata 1980, 50).

Darul Arqam presents itself as an indigenous, Malay movement celebrating pastoral virtues. Ironically, the commune is the product of the urban, often foreign-educated Malay intelligentsia of the universities. The community deliberately isolates itself by its practices. It teaches that food prepared by non-Muslims is tainted, and thus they produce their own. Following this precept, many *dakwah* students at the university refuse to eat in public restaurants, and protest university activities in which food is prepared by non-Muslims or for mixed clienteles. The food, they explain, might have been cooked in the same container used for preparing pork. The Darul Arqam emphasize the importance of distinctive forms of dress. They emulate Arab customs in their lifestyle. Males wear white turbans and green robes; women wear a complete veil and cover their heads, hands, and feet. Arabic is the language for conversation; men and women are segregated; and meals are eaten with hands from a common dish. They run their own school system (some parts of which are open to children who do not belong to the commune) and their own public restaurants.

They present themselves as gentle, peace-loving, and withdrawn persons, contrasting sharply with the vocal, aggressive ABIM. They make contact with outsiders by being willing to perform religious ceremonies outside their community.

The Attractions of *Dakwah*

In contemporary Malaysia, an increasing number of urban, educated, young men and women are becoming members of *dakwah* organizations or adopting the conventions of *dakwah* in their style of dress and manner of life. They submit to the judgment of the *Shariah*, limit their education to Islamic studies, and observe Islamic dietary restrictions. Women often quit school or abandon careers in order to fulfill the role of traditional Muslim wives. Some criticize "Malay Customs" or the government even though they may suffer painful consequences. To the devout, it is surely sufficient to say that *dakwah* is the pure form of Islam, and that Islam is right.

A more critical analysis may suggest other, more prosaic attractions of *dakwah* which do not necessarily contradict the faith of the devout. Some young Malay men find participation in ABIM an otherwise hard to find opportunity for political involvement. ABIM not only offers a comprehensive political program, much clearer than those taken by the Malay parties affiliated with the ruling National Front, but also provides greater opportunities for gaining power and responsibility. More well-established parties follow the Malay tradition of deference to elders, expressed in maxims such as "seniority takes precedence" and "we have tasted salt before you youngbloods." By contrast, the leadership of ABIM is young, mostly under forty.

The attractiveness of *dakwah* for Malay women may be somewhat different. In general, *dakwah* is considered to be unsympathetic to professional careers for women and of equality between the sexes. The modern secular state offers career opportunities to Malay women, but these often turn out to be less satisfying than expected because the egalitarianism of the workplace is not often reproduced in the patterns of social relationships within families. As a result, female professionals are required to have careers *and* be traditional wives, mothers, and housekeepers. A progressive Malay woman asks her husband to share domestic responsibilities, but in Islamic society such a request is a sufficient justification for his taking a second wife. Particularly for westernized, educated career women, being a part of a polygamous relationship is felt to be degrading. Confronted by this dilemma, at least some women have changed their world-view and conformed to traditional Islamic roles for women. Becoming a follower of *dakwah* is a legitimate way of explaining to themselves and their secular friends their new practices and roles.

Another explanation for the appeal of *dakwah* is that it offers a way of thinking which is an antidote for the loss of meaning and social dislocations brought about by rapid economic change. Naipaul (1982, 226–29) attributes the appeal of *dakwah* in Malaysia to "an angry nostalgia for a more simple and pure lifestyle which they left behind in their geographic and social mobility. For many Malays, modernization and prosperity mean a move to the city, a break with traditional values, and an awareness of cultural diversity." Rapidly changing times, Bass (1983, 199) said, make people lose a sense of meaning in their lives, and some have turned to *dakwah* as a means of "retreat from the traumas of rapid change."

Some are attracted to *dakwah* because it offers a program for personal and public reform. The evils attending westernization are all too obvious, and *dakwah* exposes these evils and prescribes an alternative.

This moralizing function of *dakwah* is part of its appeal, and the reason it is seen as a threat by less devout Muslims and particularly by non-Malays. Non-Malays are deeply disturbed and intimidated by the fact that the *dakwah* and the government share a commitment to Islam. They hear the call for Islamization of all of Malaysian society as a program for using the *Shariah* to enforce a strict reading of Islamic laws on all citizens, regardless of religion. A number of changes have occurred slowly, but—to the non-Malays—ominously: Pork is considered "unclean" by Muslims but not by Chinese. It has disappeared from the menus of restaurants in the colleges, government buildings, hospitals, and the airline. Customers at the casinos in Genting Highlands must show proof that they are not Muslims before they can be admitted. "Codes of Dressing" for women have been imposed in government offices. There have been calls for non-Muslims to be tried in Muslim courts if they are caught committing *khalwat* (being in close physical proximity with a member of the opposite sex in a suspicious circumstance) with a Muslim. This demand raises fear that the *Shariah* officials will be given permission to break into a non-Muslim's house or hotel room if they suspect that a Muslim is involved in *khalwat*. To counter such fears, *dakwah* apologists sometimes offer themselves as the embodiment of a tradition known for religious tolerance. For example, a part of the "sacred history" reconstructed by Islamic fundamentalists shows that Islam has a much better record of tolerance than does Christianity (see Akhtar and Sakr 1982).

The Dialectic Between the Government and *Dakwah*

Dakwah poses a problem and an opportunity for the government. On the one hand, the *Rukunegara* specifically permits the exercise of religious freedom, such as *dakwah*. On the other, the content of what *dakwah* teaches is at least perceived by some as inimical to the National Ideology. At its worst, *dakwah* can be seen as arrogant and offensive to non-Muslims, and subversive to the government.

In the best of all worlds Islam would provide a common bond between the government and the people, serving as the basis for a national consensus. But the racial/religious composition of the country precludes this happy eventuality for the country as a whole. Further, the dialectic between *dakwah* and the government makes religion a divisive force even among Malays. It is popularly believed that *dakwah* activities are detrimental to national unity. For example, some teachers alleged to be involved in PAS are reported to urge their students to refuse to sing the national anthem, withdraw from participating in sports, and to "focus on the Iranian revolution" (*New Straits Times* 9 August, 1984).

The government cannot be oblivious to the possibility of an Iranian-style Islamic revolution. Since the 1982 elections, PAS has become much more outspokenly partisan in its criticisms of the government. It has initiated a program of *ceramah* (political rallies) and *ijtimak* (symposiums) in which it calls for an Islamic state, and has started distributing cassette recordings of its leaders giving stirring speeches against the government. The *ceramah* have been declared illegal in four states by the government, but PAS spokespersons promise to continue. One said, "We'll continue as before and if they want to arrest us, let them. We'll see if their prisons can take in all 200,000 of us" (*New Straits Times* 9 August, 1984). Deputy Home Minister Radzi Sheikh Ahmad explained the restrictions on meetings and on the distribution of cassettes as an attempt to preserve "peace and tranquility in the country." The cassettes are objectionable, he said, because they contain misinterpretations of the *Quran*. Proposed legislation would direct the Home Affairs Ministry to study the contents of such tapes before they could be used. "We want to ensure that all the *Quranic* verses cited in the tapes are correctly used to avoid any misinterpretation" (*New Straits Times* 12 August, 1984).

Some Indian *mullahs* who teach a particularly militant brand of fundamentalist Islam are paid by Libya, and some Malay *dakwah* have been trained in and are paid by Libya to teach Islam in Malaysia. The government restricts the entry of some foreign Islamic teachers, and seeks to discredit Malaysians who are sponsored by the governments of other countries. The government recently outlawed possession of *parangs* (swords), a move popularly interpreted as intended to discourage any thought of *jihad*. One teacher urged his audience not to throw away their old *parangs, cangkuls,* and other old farming implements which could be turned into bullets "when the time comes." Members of ultra-militant groups are reputed to have this as their creed: "Mohammad is our Prophet, he is our Leader, the *Quran* is our constitution, *jihad* is our objective and *syahid* (martyrdom) is our wish" (*New Straits Times* 9 August, 1984).

A more likely scenario is that *dakwah* will create both the fact and appearance of political disunity among Malays, giving the non-Malays the chance to seize control of the government. This fear is directed primarily toward the activities of ABIM and PAS, but also draws from the conflict between *dakwah* leaders and rural Malays. To prevent the fact or appearance of disunity among Malays arguing about religion, recent legislation forbids anyone from calling anyone *kafir,* the Islamic term for "heathen."

A very real concern is that *dakwah* draws off many of the best educated young people into activities which do not further the cause of good government or national development. Anti-westernism is a recurrent theme among *dakwah.* Some *dakwah* groups have urged Muslims to throw their television sets into a river, to refuse to use chairs, and to study Islam to the exclusion of Western science, engineering, or business. To counter this trend, the government itself has set itself up as the judge of "correct" Islam, arguing against "false" *dakwah.* Prime Minister Hussein was very frank in his critique of what he perceived as:

> . . . cranks, dangerous cranks the problem is the extremists. You get a lot of them coming from Pakistan teaching these very orthodox views, they insist on women going around with a lot of curtains around them. We don't practice that here. They want us to do what the Prophet did. The Prophet did not ride in cars. He rode a camel. But these people will not use a camel (Tasker 1979, 23).

Dakwah spokespersons counter with sharp criticisms of the government. They regard the majority of government officials—including "official" religious officers and scholars—as "mere mercenaries of a secular system" who perhaps unconsciously "continue to proclaim Western values in public life" (Abu Bakar 1981, 1055). *Dakwah* speakers cite the shortcomings of society as proof that the current regime should be replaced by an Islamic state, citing immorality and decadence among the population, increasing drug use by the youth, persisting racial problems, and the failure to achieve national economic objectives.

The activities of *dakwah* puts the government in a three-pronged dilemma. To the extent that it opposes *dakwah,* it becomes itself an agent of what it fears—Malay disunity; but if it does not oppose *dakwah,* the *dakwah* attacks on the government and on the practices of rural Malays create Malay disunity anyway. If the government embraces *dakwah,* it defeats its own goals of modernization and interracial tolerance, while simultaneously jeopardizing the coalition comprising the National Front.

Since the 1982 elections the shape of the government response has become more clear. It has chosen to oppose *dakwah* but from within the universe of discourse of Islam. While presenting itself as Islamic, it attacks *dakwah* as extremist and based on misunderstandings of Islam. This strategy seems reconciled to splitting the Malays but seeks to portray *dakwah* as a small and politically impotent segment of the majority ethnic group. At the same time, it allows the government to use Islamic institutions and symbols to appeal to the Malays while presenting itself to non-Malays as the sane, progressive protector of their liberties.

The government's attempt to displace *dakwah* as the "true Islamic" force in society is very obvious. The most surprising event was the induction of ABIM leader Anwar Ibrahim into the government. Anwar was expected to assume leadership of PAS and pose a Malay opposition to the government on the grounds of Islamic traditions. Instead, he ran for parliament on the UMNO ticket (winning by the largest margin of any UMNO candidate), and then was appointed as Minister of Youth, Culture, and Sports in the Mahathir cabinet. Recently he was reassigned as Minister of Agriculture. With Anwar's defection, ABIM has declined. Others of its leadership have left the country to continue their education, while some have devoted their energies to businesses in the private sector.

Meanwhile the prime minister made well publicized trips to Egypt and Jordan, during which he emphasized his unity with other Muslim countries. Under former Prime Minister Hussein, the government involved itself in *dakwah* activities in order to control them and to establish its Islamic credentials. Recently the government passed legislation prohibiting Muslims from working at or entering gambling casinos, in effect making violations of Islamic law subject to civil courts in addition to the *Shariah*. In 1983 the government established the Islamic Bank and the Islamic University, at which Islamic traditions are practiced. Finally, the government has formally committed itself to "Islamization" by charging the Religious Affairs Department to make itself more effective in assimilating Islamic values in the National Administration.

Thus, although the government uses the term "Islamization" in a manner considerably different from *dakwah* spokespersons, the most far-reaching effect of *dakwah* may well be that the government has adopted the universe of discourse of Islam as a way of legitimating its actions. The implications of adopting this universe of discourse in promoting governmental policies are likely to be subtle. For example, there is now some government pressure on women to resign their jobs and to marry earlier than before. This policy is consistent with Islamic traditions about gender roles. There is also now a campaign to shift the "weekend" to Thursday and Friday to fit the Islamic calendar rather than that of Christians; for civil prohibitions against serving liquor to Muslims in public; for *suraus* (places for prayer) to be built in government and private sector offices; and so forth. If the government deliberates about these issues, it is much more likely to adopt them in an Islamic universe of discourse than in a secular one.

On the other hand, the government has openly opposed specific *dakwah* activities. PAS *ceramahs* have been banned in four states. When the bans were defied, the use of loudspeakers was banned. When even this did not discourage attendance, roadblocks were set up to prevent crowds from attending. Deputy Health Minister Pathmanaban warned of groups which think they have a "safe haven" in society from which to "trample on others' sensitivities." In a well publicized statement, he commented that a "tender, young, multi-faceted nation" such as Malaysia could not afford to wait for the damage to be done before acting. "We have too much to lose if we do so. We have to curb such forces in their tracks" (*New Straits Times* 9 August, 1984).

In this way the government has reserved for itself a legal means of doing otherwise illegal acts. The constitution provides that the government may pass legislation which is "inconsistent with certain provisions of the constitution," specifically the guarantees of liberty, speech, and assembly and the prohibition against banishment, or which is "outside the legislative power of Parliament." These powers of parliament may be used if "any substantial body of persons" should cause a substantial number of citizens to fear organized violence, excite disaffection against the government, or promote hostility between races or other classes of the population. The Internal Security Act was implemented on 1 August, 1980, under the provisions of this article. This act provides the means of restricting public meetings and arresting opponents of the government. At the time of this writing, three PAS leaders have been arrested under the Internal Security Act.

The headline story in the *New Straits Times* on 18 August, 1984, concerned "the use of religion for political ends." Home Affairs Minister Datuk Musa Hitam said, "The Government will not compromise with groups which use verses from the Quran for their political ends." He stated that the emphasis on religion in the constitution "was based on the belief that an individual with deep understanding of religious teachings was tolerant and responsible in his everyday life and in championing a cause." Unnamed groups, however, are using "slanderous campaigns and deviationist teachings" which threaten national security because the different religions in the country are closely related to race. He ended with an appeal for all citizens to take responsibility for issues related to national security.

Dakwah, Secularization, and Civil Religion

Dakwah is analogous to other forms of religio-political activism, such as the New Christian Right in the United States, liberation theology in Latin America, and Islamic fundamentalism in Northern Africa and West Asia. But can *dakwah* be understood with concepts devised to explain other politically-involved religious movements, such as secularization theory and civil religion?

Secularization theory states that "as a society becomes increasingly modernized, it inevitably becomes less religious" (Berger 1982, 14). There are, as this volume illustrates, so many exceptions as to render the rule obsolete. But whether secularization theory is correct or not is less important than whether its central concepts—modernity, religion, and secularization—provide a useful scheme for thinking about the issue. Do these concepts perhaps express an unacknowledged set of assumptions grounded in Western culture?

Many non-Western analysts believe that Westerners do not distinguish among particular aspects of the Western heritage and that which is essentially modern. Many even agree about what counts as unnecessary and undesirable "Western" accretions to modernity: pornography, individualism, materialism—and secularization. The international Islamic fundamentalists have developed an explicit critique of Western-style modernity in which undesirable aspects of the most developed countries are linked to the Judeo-Christian tradition, and distinguished from modernity *per se*. For example, as early as 1966 (447), Abu-Lughod claimed that secularization theory was ethnocentric:

> It has been widely assumed that the future of all political systems the world over will be secularized as much as possible and that religion, as a normative system or as a set of institutional arrangements, will have only tangential influence in the determination of public policies and the shaping of future societies. Such an assumption is obviously derived quite narrowly from the Western Protestant experience.

Alternately, contemporary Islamic teachers have written a "sacred history" which shows Islamic society as having been progressive, tolerant, and peaceful in comparison to the societies based on Judeo-

Christian traditions. Muslim reformers were concerned to ignore those aspects of their own tradition which apparently tied them to a medieval state, and to isolate those aspects of modernity which were unessential accretions from Western culture. They use this history to legitimate a distinction between modernity and westernization and to guide the development of a non-secular, modern Islamic society.

The "backwardness" of the Islamic states is explained as the result of Western exploitation, including a creation of a particular, undesirable "social reality." Western cultures perceived Islamic and other nations as "backward," and "taught" other nations to see themselves as culturally —as well as technically and economically—inferior. Some Islamic leaders who wanted to improve the lot of their people mistakenly accepted the West's view of themselves, and imported Western culture as well as economic and technical procedures. This westernization is criticized both by Islamic Progressives and *dakwah*. Both groups celebrate the moral superiority of the Islamic tradition.

Given the centrality of Islam to the Malays, the question is whether they can create a civil religion of sufficient legitimacy to provide national—that is, interracial—consensus. Regan (1976, 105) suggested that after the May 13 incident the government deliberately turned to civil religion as a "functional alternative to consociational politics of accommodation," emphasizing defense of the constitution, and loyalty to it, the overarching duty of the citizenry. Thus the civil religion offered by the government has drawn upon the symbols of Islam, but seeks to promote a multi-racial, pluralistic society.

It has not worked. The Malay intellectual elites support religion, but they do not necessarily endorse civil religion. "They view Islam somewhat paradoxically, as the official 'state' religion (though without a clergy) of divided Malaysia, but not as a national *civil* religion. Their commitment is not primarily to Islam as a Malaysian civil religion, but rather as a universal religion which represents a religious and also a cultural alternative to the Judeo-Christian West" (Regan 1976, 108).

The concept of civil religion has been applied almost exclusively to Christianity and the United States (Hammond 1976). But Islam is not so easily reconciled to the institutions and fate of any particular nation. As a complete way of life, it is not nationalistic. Likewise, Malaysia as a state does not figure largely within the sacred history of *dakwah*. The lines of affinity are to Muslims *wherever* they are found, and their allegiance is to the Islamic way of life at any point where it conflicts with the state, as to *any* Muslims in *any* state. The second, third, and fourth principles of *Rukunegara* (Obedience to the Sultans; Upholding the Constitution; and the Sovereignty of the Laws and Legislation of the Government) are in unresolved tension with the Islamization of all of Malaysian society.

Nevertheless, the government has sought to practice the politics of accommodation, which necessarily dull the horns of this dilemma. Islam both is and is not a civil religion. *Dakwah,* on the other hand, seeks purity in religion and clarity in politics. As such, it is a direct threat to the tenuous but determined effort by the government for multi-racial national unity.

The quests for certainty and clarity may be the crucial clues to understanding *dakwah. Dakwah* is a response to the perception of radical disorder, and an attempt to achieve collective coherence and coordination[2] without consensus.

In Malaysia coherence and coordination are not solely abstract concerns of academicians. The race riots in 1969, and their aftermath, exposed fundamental differences among racial and religious groups in their interpretation of the world and their "scripts" for acting with each other. Further, modernization itself has brought wider horizons, upward economic mobility, and urbanization. These factors place traditional faith, mores, and identities at risk. The result has been a society in which some have become extremely secular and others extremely devout. Some Malays are "happy modernists." They interpret uncertainty and change as opportunities rather than problems. Others are more distressed by the recurrent deconstructions of modernity, and raise what Hunter (1981, 7) called "the anthropological protest against modernity."

There are (at least) three recipes for achieving coherence and coordination. One is a commitment to tolerance or civility (Hunter 1984), in which no one would impose a value which they cannot persuade others to accept. This seems to have been the dominating image of the government of Malaysia prior to the May 13 incident in 1969. For this recipe to work, there must be a substantial moral consensus which itself is not at risk. The May 13 incident demonstrated how fragile are the doctrines of tolerance and mutual respect in the crucible of ethnic conflict.

A second recipe is to locate—and enforce—a deep enmeshing in a shared tradition. This is the strategy followed by the government after the May 13 incident. The *Rukunegara* is a deliberate attempt to create a civil religion which is inextricable from Islam (although perceived by *dakwah* as unIslamic). Other efforts include the adoption of Bahasa Malaysia as the national language in 1970; an emphasis on a national culture embracing all the racial heritages; a strong national govern-ment; and continued reference to the threat posed by the Malaysian Communist party—a common enemy.

The third recipe is the subordination of individuals to a common authority. For *dakwah,* various practices or doctrines are right because they are derived from a Divine authority, not on the basis of their (anticipated) effect or as the product of reasoned choice among options. In this sense, *dakwah* is a counterpractice of modernity, a way of achieving coherence and coordination in a society in which they are threatened. Hunter (1981, 9) argued that "the new religions are concrete attempts to resolve the perplexities experienced by modern man." The revitalization of the "old" religions serves the same functions for those less disillusioned with the traditional symbolic systems.[3]

Notes

1. The term "fundamentalist," of course, derives from Christian history in the United States in this century. However, it has come to be used in a more general sense for any group which seeks to preserve tradition by returning to basic aspects of their collective commit-ment. In using this term here, we are following Akhtar and Sakr, 1982. Their self description as Fundamentalists indexes a perception which we share: that there are some important commonalities among the New Christian Right in the United States and the *dakwah* movements in Islamic countries. This commonality is hinted at in a later section of this paper.

2. These terms are taken from the theory of the coordinated manage-ment of meaning as developed in Pearce and Cronen (1980). "Coherence" refers to the array of stories with which persons explain themselves, others and their environment to themselves. "Coordina-tion" refers to the ability to interact with others to produce coherent patterns of social acts.

3. After completing this paper, we discovered Judith Nagata's *The Reflowering of Malaysian Islam: Modern Religious Radicals and their Roots* (Vancouver: University of British Columbia Press, 1984). Nagata describes various *dakwah* groups in Malaysia in much greater detail than we were able to do here. In addition, she makes an impressive argument that *dakwah* in Malaysia must be seen in the context of the specific history of the region, not as "a mere fashion or fad imported as if by whim from other parts of the Muslim world." She bases her analysis on the struggle of Malays to establish their

ethnic identity as well as their political structure. Islam is an important part of the emergence of Malay self-consciousness, but has always been held in some tension with the "adats" or "Malay Customs." "In the cultural domain," she writes (18), "the questions raised by the *dakwah* revivalists are substantially of the same tone as those asked half a century, one and a half centuries, and several centuries ago, namely, the status of Islamic culture in relation to Malay custom (adat). . . . the *dakwah* revival reflects issues and interests, cleavages and conflicts long present in Malay society, regardless of the personal religious commitment for the individuals involved."

References

Ahmad Ibrahim. 1963. *Islamic customary law*. Kuala Lumpur: Intisari.

Bass, Jerry. 1983. Malaysia in 1982: A new frontier? *Asian Survey* 23: 191–200.

Bellah, Robert. 1967. Civil religion in America. *Daedalus* 96: 1–21.

Berger, Peter L. 1982. From the crisis of religion to the crisis of secularity. In *Religion and America*, ed. Mary Douglas and Steven M. Tipton, 14–24. Boston: Beacon Press.

Berman, Marshall. 1982. *All That is Solid Melts Into Air: The Experience of Modernity*. New York: Simon and Schuster.

Campbell. 1984. Muslim students in America. *New York Times* 22 April.

Douglas, Mary. 1982. The effects of modernization on religious change. *Daedalus* 3: 1–19.

Gallup, George, Jr. 1981. Divining the devout: The polls and religious belief. *Public Opinion* 4: 20–21.

Hammond, Phillip E. 1976. The sociology of America civil religion: A bibliographic essay. *Sociological Analysis* 37: 169–82.

Hj. Mohd. Din bin Ali. 1963. *Two Forces in Malay Society*. Kuala Lumpur: Intisari.

Hunter, James Davidson. 1981. The new religions: Demodernization and the protest against modernity. In *The Social Impact of New Religious Movements*, ed. Bryan Wilson. Barrytown, N.Y.: Unification Theological Seminary.

Hunter, James Davidson. 1984. Religion and political civility: The coming generation of American evangelicals. *Journal for the Scientific Study of Religion* 23: 364–80.

Ibrahim Abu-Lughod. 1966. Retreat from the secular path? Islamic dilemmas of Arab politics. *Review of Politics* 28: 447–76.

Karm B. Akhtar and Ahmad H. Sakr. 1982. *Islamic Fundamentalism.* Cedar Rapids, IO.: Igram Press.

Mahathir Mohamad. 1970. *The Malay Dilemma.* Kuala Lumpur: Federal Publications.

Mohamad Abu Bakar. 1981. Islamic revivalism and the political process in Malaysia. *Asian Survey* 21: 1040–59.

Nagata, Judith. 1980. Religious ideology and social change: The Islamic revival in Malaysia. *Pacific Affairs* 20: 42–57.

Naipaul, V. S. 1982. *Among the Believers: An Islamic Journey.* New York: Random House.

Pearce, W. Barnett and Vernon E. Cronen. 1980. *Communication, Action and Meaning: The Creation of Social Realities.* New York: Praeger.

Regan, Daniel. 1976. Islam, intellectuals and civil religion in Malaysia. *Sociological Analysis* 37:95–110.

Tasker, Rodney. 1979. The explosive mix of Muhammad and modernity. *Far Eastern Economic Review* (February 9): 22–27.

von Vorys, Karl. 1975. *Democracy Without Consensus.* Princeton, N.J.: Princeton University Press.

Wallace, Anthony F.C. n.d. Revitalization movements. *American Anthropologist* 58: 264–81.

11

Religion and Politics in Post-World War II Poland

KAROL H. BOROWSKI

THE complexity of church-state relations in countries dominated by Marxist-Leninist ideology and political systems has been the recent focus of a number of studies (see, e.g., Pankhurst in this volume). Particular attention has been given to Poland due to developments occurring during the social and economic unrest of the "Solidarity phenomenon" (Borowski 1983; Pomian-Srzednicki 1982). In addition, the publicity generated by the first Polish pope, and his continuing commitment to strengthening the Roman Catholic church in that country, have helped create a unique situation with respect to the interface of religion and communist politics.

Post-World War II Poland represents a case of conflict between a well-entrenched priestly church establishment and an officially atheistic regime which is, by comparison, only recently installed. Whereas the church has had centuries to develop strong nationalistic identifications and emotional roots in the folk cultural tradition, the regime is only decades old and its political legitimacy is supported from outside the cultural tradition, as it were, by the Soviet Union. As a result, the Roman Catholic church, for all its priestly hierarchy and theological complexity, has found itself thrust into a prophetic role in promoting societal change in Poland.

The question to be answered here deals with this distinctly prophetic

221

role of modern Polish Catholicism: What are the circumstances that have allowed the church's struggle for its own survival in a hostile communist state to dovetail with the popular struggle for civil liberties and economic determination? Examining the Polish situation will provide some clues as to the conditions under which religion can shift from priestly to prophetic, and therefore from a conservative to a progressive or even radical force for social change. Given what appears to be a resurgence of prophetic religion worldwide, and the failure of secularization to reduce religion's importance in industrialized societies, there are good reasons to believe that Poland's experience is only a harbinger of other such church-state conflicts.

Major Post-World War II Developments: An Overview

Jerzy Wiatr, a leading Polish Marxist and former president of the Communist Central party's school in Warsaw, has recently made a number of optimistic statements concerning church-state relations in modern Poland. Such relations, he claimed, have improved considerably, especially since the last visit by Pope John Paul II. Moreover, Wiatr contended, there is a growing cooperation between the Roman Catholic church and the Jaruzelski government in matters pertaining to national survival. The state welcomes the church's contributions toward political stabilization and economic improvement, such as through its Agricultural Fund. Wiatr acknowledged that there still remain differences and conflicts of interest, but that they are being pragmatically resolved. He portrayed the Roman Catholic church and church-related intellectual circles in Poland as an "orderly opposition" to the government.[1]

This portrait of relative calm and "loyal opposition" ignores a fundamental, ongoing conflict in Polish church-state relations. In this writer's view, there has been little, if any, meaningful dialogue between Marxists and Christians in post-World War II Poland. Despite the government's wishes, the "opiate of the masses" stubbornly refuses to fade away under the "dictatorship of the proletariat." Direct and indirect confrontations and conflicts have dominated church-state relations during the past forty years. Much to the government's chagrin, the Roman Catholic church, through its activist clergy, has become a major force spearheading dissent from political policies as well as a rallying point for popular dissatisfactions.

The purpose of this paper is two-fold. First, it seeks to trace the post-World War II history of tensions between the Roman Catholic church and the state. Second, out of this history emerges an understanding of how a well entrenched priestly institution can assume a prophetic role.

A Historical Overview of Church-State Relations in Poland

After World War II Poland was forced into political, social, cultural, and economic changes induced by the Soviet-supported resistance group, later known as the Polish Committee of National Liberation, which eventually became the base of the Polish government. Since then, the Polish society, while guided by its over one-thousand year-old Judeo-Christian tradition, has simultaneously been under systematic pressures to implement Marxist-Leninist ideals and models.

The tension between religion and the political regime in Poland can conveniently be organized into six distinct chronological periods.

1. *The 1944–48 period:* During the early years of Marxist initiation a relatively peaceful and friendly coexistence marked the relations between organized religion and the new political system. The Roman Catholic church—representing over ninety percent of the Polish society—continued its activities, although its economic base and social outreach programs became gradually restricted. No major systematic attacks on religion and church were openly made during this period.

   Opposition to the church occurred following the merger of the Polish Socialist party and the Polish Workers' party in December, 1948 which resulted in the formation of the Polish United Workers' party. This party, a genuine Marxist-Leninist Communist party, has since attempted to dominate the Polish society by trying to implement Marxist-Leninist principles in all spheres of social and individual lives. The party declared its leadership as exclusive in the alleged growing class struggle; it promised successful liberation and creation of a society free of exploitation, oppression and social conflict. The regime's attempts to achieve these goals, however, have severely limited basic civil and religious liberties of the Polish society, thus resulting in lasting tensions and growing conflicts.

2. *The 1949–56 period:* The state-party efforts to create a socio-cultural,

economic, and political system based on Marxism-Leninism resulted in conflicts between church and state, and consequently, between the Polish society and the regime. Repressions against religion such as dissolving of religious associations, ceasing of non-liturgical activities, imprisonment of religious leaders, and discrimination against church members were perceived by the Polish society as direct attacks on its fundamental liberties and Christian tradition.

With the worsening of economic conditions and indirect limitations of basic human rights, the growing discontent of the working class resulted in riots during the International Trade Fair in Pozan in June 1956. The rebelling proletarians, by demanding "Bread and God," openly expressed their dissatisfaction with the Marxist-Leninist system for the first time in modern Poland. This uprising revealed discrepancies between Marxist-Leninist theory and practice. The state-party power elite inflicted material and spiritual oppressions upon the people, whom, they claimed, they have represented as "the workers' and peasants' government." Church-state relations seemingly improved following the uprising.

3. *The 1957–70 period:* After a short-lived cessation of governmental abuses and moderate improvements in civil and religious liberties during the early years of Gomulka's regime, conditions of Polish society, both material and spiritual, once again began to deteriorate. New anti-religious campaigns were launched. The church resisted openly the state-party's attempts at limiting its function in society. It also defended the society's rights to practice religion without discrimination, as guaranteed by the Constitution.

The church's contributions to the nation's awareness of the Marxist-Leninist policy, strategy, and contradictions soon became evident in the workers' uprisings at the shipyards of Gdansk and Szczecin in 1970 (Raina 1978). The party-government block first responded to these events with violence, then made a tactical change in leadership, promising improvements in Poland's quality of life.

4. *The 1971–79 period:* Under the leadership of the new First Secretary Edward Gierek, the regime initially promised to restore "socialism with a human face" and to provide necessary conditions for a decent and dignified life accessible to all Poles regardless of their ideological convictions.

International *détente* and accompanying economic and cultural exchanges during the early years of Gierek's hegemony provided favorable conditions for improvements. During the early 1970s Poland's contacts with the Western hemisphere significantly increased. Thus, an impression of substantial changes in the nation's cultural, social, political, and economic conditions was fostered. However, in reality, the quality of life further deteriorated. By 1976 abuses of power, increasing corruption, and economic hardships led to a wave of strikes in Poland's major industrial cities. Once again the government-party elite implemented force against striking workers "to restore peace and order."

The government's increasing oppression did not stop the growing wave of dissent. Rather, it embraced all Poland's social strata. A committee for the defense of persecuted workers (KOR) was established by leading dissidents. "Flying" universities, underground publications and political cabarets were among the many factors that further inspired and promoted opposition. In factories, on farms, and in universities agitation for free autonomous unions and associations were initiated by KOR members, dissatisfied workers, and intelligentsia.

The Roman Catholic church played a particularly important role during this time by providing inspiration and guidance for the people. Cardinal Wyszynski was personally involved in fostering campaigns for human rights and dignity, especially when governmental abuses and various kinds of oppression were evident. The church's organization and communication network amply helped to raise the people's awareness of their violated human rights. It published several pastoral letters criticizing unjust governmental policies concerning such issues as a proposed constitutional amendment subordinating Poland to the Soviet Union, abortion, family policy, working conditions in mines and in factories, education, etc.

Meanwhile, Poland's new postwar generation, raised and educated under Marxist-Leninist supremacy, began seriously questioning the *status quo* and scrutinizing the government's policy of fulfilling constitutional rights and other promises. Discovery of the discrepancy between the nation's and the state-party elite's standards of life was shocking, and this led to a lasting discreditation of the Marxist-Leninist system, particularly among the youth (Borowski 1972).

5. *The 1980–81 period:* On July 1, 1980, the Polish party-state announced an increase in food prices, and, consequently found itself on the road to the largest eruption of protest in postwar Poland. In the summer of 1980, the Solidarity phenomenon became manifest (Weschler 1982). Beginning with a strike by the Lublin Railroad and Ursus Tractor Company workers, the ranks of the strikers grew

to virtually include the entire nation. At first, the government-party elite stood by its price rises, but later it retreated under multiplying demands for compensatory wage increases and improvements in working conditions. Throughout this tumultuous period, the workers themselves showed self-discipline by keeping their growing number of strikes nonviolent. Meanwhile, the police undertook repressive measures mainly directed against KOR activists.

In the course of the summer the diverse strikers' demands, with KOR and the church serving as the contact centers for various strike committees, escalated from wage issues to labor reform and, finally, to political, social, cultural, and religious demands. By mid-August the Gdansk Inter-Factory Committee, headed by Lech Walesa, was created to coordinate nationwide strike activities and to represent all strikers in negotiations with the government.

The party-state, faced with spiraling labor unrest which it had no further hopes of controlling, was left with no option but to negotiate labor peace with the "proletarians." On 31 August, 1980, the government capitulated to the workers' major demands by signing the Gdansk Agreement, a document consisting of major concessions towards democratization of Poland. Simultaneously, meetings of Joint Government-Episcopate Commission took place in order to discuss religious freedom, tolerance, and the return of church properties confiscated by the government in previous years. The Commission also addressed the multifarious dangers facing the country. The Episcopate appealed for respect for truth, justice, and dignity, emphasizing that the Polish nation has the right to create its own history. It thereby urged both the government and the people to arrive at a peaceful solution.

All these events further awakened a genuine national consciousness that initiated and fostered a trend for a complete renewal of Poland's conditions. Thus, a variety of social and political ideas came to life offering opportunities of open critique and confrontation with Marxist-Leninist ideology and practice.

Further negotiations and struggles with the government led to the official registration of Solidarity as an independent trade union; it claimed ten million members by 10 November, 1980. Under Solidarity's leadership, and through the experience of the Roman Catholic church, Poles obtained many democratic concessions, including the right to criticize public officials openly, a shorter work week, less restricted traveling abroad, and promised participation in decision-making.

During its early months, the Solidarity movement was a success. By the summer of 1981 Solidarity began to lose control of its destiny. Overwhelmed by the rapid growth of its organization, internal leadership factions arose and outside infiltrations by the government contributed to a gradual weakening of the movement. In addition, deterioration of the Polish economy, demands for loan repayment from Western banks, rapid decline of the average standard of living, and increasing Soviet pressure led to the imposition of martial law on 13 December, 1981. The promise initiated by Solidarity for Poland's genuine renewal was shattered. Again, the church remained the people's only hope.

6. *The 1982–present period:* The democratic concessions obtained through the efforts of Solidarity were suspended and eventually revoked. The split between the nation and the regime deepened. The Solidarity movement went underground, claiming it would continue to act until all basic needs of the Polish society were satisfied and the discrepancy between Marxist-Leninist theory and state-party policies were eliminated.

The church's material and spiritual support of the Polish people has been of great importance, especially after the imposition of martial law and the delegalization of Solidarity. At the same time the government-party attitudes and policies have made the church's attempts at bridging the nation's split even more difficult by creating new tensions and conflicts. It is a fair generalization to say that Polish society, especially the youth (over sixty percent of Poland's population is under age thirty), has lost its trust and confidence in the Marxist-Leninist regime. Despite governmental vigilance, popular opinion supports restoration of Solidarity's ideals, democratic political principles, Socialist socio-economic principles, Judeo-Christian ethical principles, and Poland's historical traditions.

The June 1983 visit of John Paul II to his native country provided renewed evidence of the church's commitment to assist the Polish people in their struggle against the oppression of the Marxist-Leninist government-party elite. Church-state relations following the Pope's visit became less tense, thus allowing for a dialogue which seemingly has benefited the nation (Bird 1982; Borowski 1983). The lifting of martial law on 22 July, 1983, after nineteen months, provided some easement in the mutual hostility shared by different segments of the Polish nation.

Still, it is not clear that the situation in Poland has significantly improved. In some instances at least, opposition appears to have been brought under even tighter control and tensions remain high. Sympathizers and supporters of Solidarity ideals, including clergy, have been harrassed and even murdered. The most visible case to the Western World is that of Father Jerzy Popieluszko, a charismatic supporter of Solidarity, who was abducted and murdered in late 1984 by Polish security police officers.

Cardinal Glemp has been given a list of clergy, including bishops, charged with "activities detrimental to the renewal process and improving church-state relations." Furthermore, the regime threatened to charge them with anti-state crimes if Cardinal Glemp continued to tolerate them. As a result of this pressure, those directly under Glemp's jurisdiction were reprimanded or transferred to other assignments. Still others were "fraternally reminded" by Cardinal Glemp to cease their political involvement.

In short, the history of church-state relations in Poland is one of cylical tension. Conflict mounts until it reaches critical proportions and is then followed by the government assurging its repressive tendencies. Tensions ease only to have the cycle repeat itself.

The Roman Catholic Church as Prophetic Agent

In an allegedly secular age when well-entrenched priestly religions have been assumed to be merely trustees of archaic traditions and a once-great, declining influence on worldly affairs, the Roman Catholic church in Poland has shown that such organizations are capable of becoming significant prophetic forces for societal change. They can appeal to ideals and exhort the powers that be for reform and even repentance. They can, by their example, deny legitimacy to regimes and serve as catalysts for popular discontent. How this is possible is better understood in the context of the history of the Roman Catholic church in Poland. Polish sociologists (e.g., Majka 1981; Piwowarski 1971) have emphasized the following elements in the structure and functioning of Roman Catholicism in Poland:

First, *Polish Catholicism never became a state religion*. The church throughout Poland's history has been emancipated and organizationally independent. It has played the role of moral opposition and defender of the oppressed. In the time of Poland's partitions and foreign occupations, the church provided identity and refuge for the people.

Second, *Polish Catholicism is the nation's faith and not a political ideology*. Because of its remaining in moral opposition against the oppressive state, Polish Catholicism is the people's religion. Poles comprehend Christianity as "a teaching which is liberating, heartlifting, fortifying, and providing perspectives." Therefore, it has not and cannot be a basis for oppression. Rather, it has been and continues to be a basis for encouragement and creative efforts. Christianity experienced in this way cannot provide social oppression and political conquest with legitimacy. Catholicism, as the faith of the majority, plays an important role in defending national and moral values that are very closely interconnected. Betraying one set of values amounts to betraying both. The intertwining of nationism and religious value, thus, is an important source of Polish religious patriotism as well as the foundation of a civil religion.

Third, *Polish Catholicism is not merely a set of beliefs but also a way of life.* Polish Catholicism provides a link between the nation's life and culture and the individual's life in all dimensions. It provides the individual with a source for retaining psychological balance in evaluating actions as well as in motivating personal and social growth. As a result, Polish Catholicism is not only a system of beliefs but an important educational factor throughout recent Polish history.

Fourth, *important contributions have been made by the leadership of the Roman Catholic church to the Polish nation.* The role of many Polish churchmen through history has been of great importance to the nation's developments. At times, when governments failed, capable church leadership helped guide the nation. In recent times Cardinal Wyszynski and Cardinal Wojtyla have challenged Marxism on its own ideological grounds and enabled the church to maintain its institutional autonomy without ultimately subordinating its leadership, hierarchy, or values to the totalitarian Marxist-Leninist state.

Post-World War II changes and the methodical attacks on religion and church have forced both the hierarchy and the believers to revise their commitment to Christianity. The link between the clergy and lay people has become close and strong. Genuine pastoral work has enabled the church to penetrate the nation's values and behavior in spite of state-supported counteractions.

For example, the church has given special attention to the youth. After religious instructions were removed from schools, the parish center became a vital component of socialization. Priests, assisted by nuns and some lay persons, mostly retired teachers, have provided all age groups with high-leveled instructions in nearly twenty-five thousand parish centers throughout Poland. The participation is very high and intense. In rural areas attendance reaches approximately ninety-five percent, and in urban areas it is approximately eighty percent. Great emphasis is placed on cooperation between parents and teachers. For college and university students there are special programs combining campus ministry with religious studies. Specially-trained priests have been engaged in this type of service with the assistance of lay experts. In addition, a network of centers for intellectuals has developed in major Polish cities.

In addition to the parish centers, several regional and national shrines (e.g. Czestochowa, Kalwaria Zebrzydowska, Gora Swiety Anny, Piekary) are important factors in strengthening the link between church and nation. They constitute alternative educational and communicational networks often used by the church leadership for reinforcing the people's religious commitment and providing necessary information on issues related to church-state conflicts. Frequent pastoral visits to families, legitimated by an old Polish tradition, further strengthen the close relationship between the church and the family as the basic unit of Polish society.

The church's concern for the entire Polish society, especially the oppressed, has gained for it trust and respect, a fact acknowledged even by adversaries. The persistent strength of the Roman Catholic church in Poland has compelled many students of religion to revise their views of the function of religion in a Marxist-Leninist society (Kolakowski 1979; Michnik 1981). They now reject the traditional Marxist theory that religion, under the conditions of a Marxist-Leninist state, will undoubtedly cease to exist. On the contrary, they argue that organized religion, after being deprived of political influence and material assets, has increased its ideological influence by creating a more genuine religious system able to inspire and motivate people in their search for social betterment.

Analytic Implications

The case of Polish Catholicism demonstrates that organized religion of a mainstream—(as opposed to a sectarian)—tradition can provide inspiration, motivation, and a structural network to resist authoritarian regime control. This paper has outlined a number of historical and cultural circumstances that have allowed the Roman Catholic church's struggle for survival in a hostile Marxist-Leninist state to dovetail with a popular struggle for civil liberties and economic determination. Polish church-state tension also suggests some generic circumstances hypothetically necessary for a change of political regime to thrust an entrenched, priestly religion into a prophetic social role.

Stated as a value-added hypothesis, we may say that prophetic tension in church-state relations will occur when a religious tradition:

(1) has become thoroughly indigenousized by centuries of interaction with the mass of citizens;
(2) has occupied a church-like (i.e., near-monopolistic) status during that time with its own bureaucratic and hierarchical apparatus parallel to and independent of the state's; and the new regime. . . .
(3) promotes an official ideology that is atheistic and utopian;
(4) comes to be popularly defined as in part implanted and maintained by forces outside the nation and culture; and
(5) claims ultimate allegiance and legitimacy over all other competing symbol systems and interest groups in the society.

In other words, the presence of a religion such as described above is anathema to a totalitarian political philosophy such as Marxist-Leninism. While the state may be successful in achieving a near monopoly over symbols of authority in secular spheres, including the polity and the economy, its staunch irreligious philosophy actually works against its goals of consolidating all political loyalty for the regime. The religious entity, as in communist Poland, comes to be one of the few viable nationalistic symbols around which discontent over the economic and social failures of utopia can rally. This conclusion still remains hypothetical, of course, and more comparative research on nations where religion and state resemble these conditions will be needed before the strength of the hypothesis can be assessed.

Notes

1. Wiatr's comments were made at a roundtable discussion at Harvard University 23 March, 1984, attended by the author.

References

Bird, Thomas E. 1982. The new turn in church-state relations in Poland. *Journal of Church and State* 24: 1–6.

Borowski, Karol H. 1975. Secular and religious education in Poland. *Journal of Religious Education* 70, no. 1: 71–6.

———. 1972. *Kontestacja w Swiecie i Jej Ekwiwalent w Polsce (Youth Protest in the Western Societies and its Equivalent in Poland)*. Lublin: CUL.

———. 1983. Christians and Marxists in Poland: Conflict or dialogue?

Paper presented at the joint meetings of the Society for the Scientific Study of Religion, the Association for the Sociology of Religion, and the Religious Research Association, Knoxville, TN.

――――. 1985. Sociology of religion in Poland: A critical review. *Sociological Analysis*. Forthcoming.

Kloczowski, Jerzy. 1980. *Chrzescijanstwo w Polsce (Christianity in Poland)*. Lublin: CUL.

Korbonski, Andrzej. 1979. Poland. In *Communism in Eastern Europe*, ed. Andrew Gyorgy. Bloomington, IN.: Indiana University Press.

Majka, Jozef. 1981. Historical and cultural conditions of Polish Catholicism. *The Christian in the World* 14: 24–38.

Michnik, Adam. 1980. *Polski Dialog*. London: Overseas Publications.

Piwowarski, Wladyslaw. 1976. *Religijnosc Wiejska w Warunkach Urbanizacji (Rural Religion in Urbanization)*. Warsaw: Wiez.

Pomian-Srzednicki, Maciej. 1982. *Religious Change in Contemporary Poland*. London: Paul.

Raina, Peter. 1978. *Political Opposition in Poland, 1954–1977*. London: Poets and Painters Press.

Weschler, Lawrence. 1982. *Poland in the Season of Its Passion*. New York: Simon and Schuster.

PART FOUR
PROPHETIC RELIGION
AND THE
POLITICS OF
ACCOMMODATION

12

Militancy and Accommodation in the Third Civilization: The Case of Japan's Soka Gakkai Movement

ANSON SHUPE

THE interface of prophetic religion and socio-political infrastructures is frequently one of controversy, conflict, and, sometimes, violence and revolution. However, as students of Max Weber know, prophetic religion is only part of the cycle. There is also a subsequent priestly phase, a time of accommodation during which much of the controversy and conflict fades along with the prophetic emphasis. This study examines this latter process of accommodation, using the case of Japan's Soka Gakkai movement. Soka Gakkai is a lay Buddhist group, officially established in 1951 and closely affiliated with the Nichiren Shoshu sect of Mahayana Buddhism.[1] Both groups are notorious among Japanese forms of Buddhism for their vigorous recruitment efforts and intolerance of all other religions, including other Buddhist groups (even other Nichiren branches). Soka Gakkai also proclaims the militant goal of eventually creating a "Buddhist democracy" in Japan and through evangelizing eventually building *Daisan Bunmei*—The Third Civilization—

worldwide. How Soka Gakkai's recent rhetoric and activities in Japan have begun to mellow in recent years, and to what effect, is worth examining in order to work towards the eventual goal of comparative conceptualization of all such movements and processes.

The Place of Soka Gakkai in Japanese Religion

In order to understand the activities and developments of the Soka Gakkai movement, it is necessary first to review briefly the origins of the Nichiren Shoshu sect with which Soka Gakkai is affiliated.[2]

The great Buddhist prophet/saint/messiah/patriot called Nichiren (1222–1282 A.D.) founded a unique strand of Japanese Buddhism in the thirteenth century, an age of significant change and reform. The old Heian period, with its cultural and political machinery centered in the imperial city of Kyoto, was dying as a new military-political capital emerged at Kamakura. The thirteenth century also witnesses a number of far-reaching religious innovations. For example, the ascetic monk known as Dogen imported the Zen tradition from China. Zen's contemplative style of Buddhism was quickly adopted by the emerging samurai estate. Meanwhile, the monk Honen, seeking an easier, more practical way for the masses to achieve *nirvana*, or salvation, without resorting to the arduous, elitist route of monasticism, founded the "Pure Land" approach of worshipping the Amida representation of Buddha. The "Pure Land" school of Buddhism maintained that invoking Amida's name was sufficient to bring a devoted believer into nirvana after death. Shinran, Honen's disciple, went further in emphasizing the *tariki* path to nirvana (i.e., salvation by another's aid rather than self-reliance) and elevating faith in Amida over any works, eventually founding Jodo-Shinshu Buddhism.

Most importantly, Honen and Shinran, like their contemporary Nichiren, believed in the Buddhist doctrine of *mappo*. Analogous to the millennial expectations of fundamentalist and dispensationalist Christians, the doctrine of *mappo* dictated that the world is thrust into a last days apocalyptic situation, the literal "End of the Dharma." It has become so corrupt that the way to nirvana as originally preached by the historical Siddhartha Gautama in sixth century B.C. India is no longer possible for most persons. Therefore the altruistic help of Bodhisattvas (advanced beings, once humans, who seek enlightenment not only for themselves but for others) or some other superhuman agency is required. As Robert Ellwood (1974, 84) describes *mappo*: "If one were to be saved at all in such a time, people said it could be only by faith. The *mappo* idea was originally connected with an idea that times were getting worse and true faith was about to vanish from the earth until the coming of the next Buddha in the far-off future."

Nichiren, who studied various forms of traditional Buddhism, became convinced while a student in a monastary of the Tendai denomination that the Lotus Sutra contained the most advanced and quintessential form of the Buddha's message. All other Buddhist schools and persuasions and even other sutras were either perversions of the ultimate truth or insignificant. Indeed, Nichiren began to preach that merely chanting (i.e., invoking) the name of the Lotus Sutra (*Namu Myoho Renge Kyo*—"Hail to the Wonderful Truth of the Lotus Sutra") could produce salvation for the believer in the next life and bestow temporal benefits, such as good health and worldly success, in this one.

However, Nichiren infused his interpretation of Buddhism's essence with other prophetic elements. One was elitism: Nichiren declared flatly that other sects and denominations of Buddhism were wrong, inappropriate, and misleading in the age of *mappo*. Moreover, the original ascetic message of Gautama Buddha, who had enjoined followers to "work out their salvations diligently," i.e., ascetically and individually, was declared *passé*. Intensely patriotic, Nichiren blamed a succession of natural and political calamities on his claim that the Japanese people and their leaders had been lured into worshipping false faiths and incorrect versions of Buddhism. As alleged punishment, therefore, the country endured a number of earthquakes, hurricanes, famines, and epidemics of disease throughout the thirteenth century. In 1261 Nichiren predicted that Japan would be invaded by a mighty foreign power as retribution for its religious waywardness, and indeed in 1268 the Mongol armada of China's emperor Kublai Khan landed off the shores of Japan, overrunning coastal garrisons and threatening the entire country. (The fleet, however, was "miraculously" sunk by a ferocious typhoon, nicknamed the "wind of the gods" or *kamikaze,* for which Nichiren's reform movement could opportunely claim credit.)

Nichiren was a persistent critic of the Kamakura warlords. As an annoying dissident he was twice exiled (once almost executed) and finally forced into permanent retirement when, late in life, he organized what became the rudiments of a new Buddhist tradition. Brannen (1968, 60–1) regards Nichiren as the Japanese counterpart of the ancient Hebrew prophet Amos:

> . . . Amos and Nichiren alike were prophets in the original Hebrew meaning of the term—men who read the signs of the times in terms of their religious faith. And both were men of unswerving dedication to a

single, unyielding ideal. Amos' message is summed up by a single metaphor which he used—the plumbline, which stood for the righteousness of God who judges and punishes man's unrighteousness. Nichiren summed up his own message with the invocation-prayer, *Namu Myohorengekyo,* which stood for the central truth of the *Lotus Sutra,* giving man the only means of escape from the calamities of the period of the End of the Dharma.

Following Nichiren's death there were internal disputes among his followers, and the inevitable factions arose to champion alternative interpretations of his revelations. Before World War II (in part because of government demands for consolidation of all non-Shinto religions) there were nine separate offshoots claiming to belong in the Nichiren tradition. By the late 1960s there were over forty. Nichiren Shoshu is the most strident of the competing versions, proclaiming itself the only authentic form of Nichiren Buddhism. (*Nichiren Sho* means "True Nichiren.") In classic sectarian fashion it does not hesitate to condemn its cousin Nichiren derivatives as false. While these others are more pluralistically oriented, they nevertheless are not loath to return the animosity, some publishing books denouncing Nichiren Shoshu (Brannen 1968, 79–80). Most other Nichiren groups reject Nichiren Shoshu's elitist precepts, and most do not accord Nichiren the ultimate status of Buddha as does Nichiren Shoshu. Nichiren Shoshu refers to Nichiren as *Nichiren Dai Shonin*—"The Great Holy One," the Buddha for the "latter age" or "last days *[mappo]* " who displaced and superceded the earlier historical Buddha. Even more so than in other Mahayana Buddhist denominations where Bodhisattvas are worshipped as representations of the Buddha principle, the historical Nichiren is regarded as nothing less than a Christ-like, messianic figure.

The Origin of Soka Gakkai

Soka Gakkai (Society for the Creation of Value) is a lay Buddhist organization affiliated with Nichiren Shoshu. It began in 1937 as Soka Kyoiku Gakkai (Society for Education in the Creation of Values), a group created by a Tokyo elementary school principal named Tsunesaburo Makiguchi. Makiguchi was vitally interested in geography, ecology, a crude existential philosophy (though such thinking was of course yet unnamed in the 1930s), and what (in sociological theory) might be termed the "materialist" approach to social change.[3] Makiguchi teamed up with another public school teacher, Toda Josei, who became the organizational/managerial force behind the Soka Kyoiku Gakkai movement to complement Makiguchi's intellectual/

philosophical role. While the movement was yet young and still sorting out the precepts of its evolving philosophy, having recently affiliated with the uncompromising Nichiren Shoshu sect, Makiguchi and Toda were imprisoned (in 1942) for not agreeing to unite with other Nichiren sects and for refusing to participate in state Shinto worship rites. In 1943 the movement had its critical martyr: Makiguchi died in prison. With Allied Occupation beginning in 1945, Toda, who took charge of the movement in Makiguchi's name, changed the official organizational title to Soka Gakkai and infused a less educational, more evangelistic Buddhist spirit into the group, transforming it into a proselytizing/mobilizing arm of Nichiren Shoshu.

Absolute numbers of Soka Gakkai membership are not reliably recorded or obtained. It is an old joke among scholars and officials who monitor the purported "official" memberships of Japanese "new" religions that their annual total exceeds the size of Japan's entire population. Groups like Soka Gakkai contribute to the statistical problem of estimating membership sizes by their undoubted exaggeration. Soka Gakkai counts families, not individuals, as its member units. While there are entire families who join *en masse* when one or both adult heads convert, there are also many cases of single young adults still living with their parents, the latter *not* converting. Ellwood (1974, 91) cites a figure of approximately 7,500,000 families belonging to Soka Gakkai in 1974 which seems consistent with the range of ten-to-fifteen million individual members cited by others, such as Brett (1979, 366). In 1963 Soka Gakkai's president claimed that the group was making converts regularly at the rate of twenty thousand per month, and in 1968 Soka Gakkai's Student Department boasted that one out of every seven Japanese university or college students belonged (Brannen 1968, 15, 81). While such estimates seem grandiose and quite in keeping with the tendency of many non-mainstream religions to inflate membership for public relations or morale reasons, there is no question that Soka Gakkai (and indirectly its affiliate sect, Nichiren Shoshu) is the fastest growing religious movement in Japan, perhaps in the Far East. It has also had the most impact of any Japanese "new" religion in recent years in terms of winning Occidental members, according to Ellwood (1974, 75).

The Soka Gakkai's Militancy-Accommodationist Shift

The Japanese have a well-known, culturally reinforced predilection for avoiding unpleasant, open conflict. This pattern is as fundamental linguistically as it is in situations of diplomacy and negotiation. It also carries over to religion where Japanese generally dislike *rikutsu,* or arguing, especially over matters of religion and ultimate truth which are regarded as separate from everyday pragmatic reason. Moreover, despite the widespread influence of culturally rich Buddhist and Shinto traditions, devotional religion on a regular basis has little personal relevance for many Japanese. As Roggendorf (1951, 22) observes: "That religion means nothing but an occasional service during one's lifetime can be said of wide cross-sections of Europeans but by no means all, while it does apply to the overwhelming mass of modern Japanese. . . . The lack of interest is almost total."

For these reasons Soka Gakkai runs against the grain of tolerance and the relativist position on matters of absolute truth shown by most Japanese. Whereas the latter are typically apathetic or otherwise content with a pluralism of religious styles and alternatives, Soka Gakkai members are zealous, aggressive proselytizers and confident in the superiority of their narrow interpretation of Nichiren Buddhism. During the early post-World War II era in particular, Soka Gakkai developed a negative image on account of its members' belligerence and sometimes uncouth activities that offended much of the public. Members were often encouraged to destroy the *kamidana* (miniature Shinto shrines) and the ancestral tablets of *butsudan* (Buddhist) altars in their homes and in relatives' homes (actions appalling to most Japanese who, regardless of secularization, still feel a traditional Confucianist obligation to honor immediate ancestors). Soka Gakkai followers were known for making obscene gestures and spitting as they passed by Shinto shrines and Buddhist temples of other denominations or yelling *"Jashu!"* ["False Religion!"] (Brannen 1968, 103). Home meetings of local Soka Gakkai groups sometimes sit up late into the evening loudly chanting *"Namu Myoho Renge Kyo!",* singing, and otherwise disturbing neighbors in dense apartment complexes and urban neighborhoods.

Perhaps the best known (from the standpoint of media coverage and public offensiveness) of Soka Gakkai's unconventional practices is *shakubuku.* Nichiren originally preached that some persons could not be converted by calm debate or unhurried reason alone; rather, they would require pressure or even coercion to help them "see the light." The literal meaning of *shakubuku* is "to destroy and conquer" or "to break and subdue." The outcome of such a determined philosophy is a persistence that worked its way out in various ethically questionable strategies. For example, at one time enthusiastic young Soka Gakkai women took jobs as bar hostesses in the Tokyo Metroplex area and flirted with American military personnel or even slept with them in attempts to get them to visit Nichiren Shoshu temples (Dator 1969, 50–8).[4] Likewise, because they received spiritual merit as well as intro-group status for making conversions, Soka Gakkai members made their neighbors, fellow employees, and even complete strangers riding public transportation the targets of persistent, annoying witnessing efforts. The uglier aspects of *shakubuku* included the physical coercion of "backsliders" or those who had second thoughts about conversion; overzealous adult children smashing *kamidana* and *butsudan* altars in the homes of their parents and any other relatives whom they thought needed Nichiren salvation; and the dogged pursuit of persons thought to be "good prospects."[5] Thus it came as no surprise in 1964 when the NTV television network conducted a telepoll of 1,500 persons and found that forty-two percent of the respondents used the word "fanatical" to describe the Soka Gakkai movement (Dator 1969, 80). Even the understandably tolerant Nihon Shinshukyo Dantai Rengokai (the League of Japanese New Religious Movements) condemned the Soka Gakkai. In 1965 representatives of the League's various member groups met to announce their intention to work together against Soka Gakkai.

One of the most frustrating facts for would-be "world-transforming" social movements is their overall negative public image, whether justified or undeserved. Widespread rejection of a group's goals and ideology therefore motivates many groups to seek to upgrade their reputations, both by engaging in positive public relations efforts and by attempting internal reforms that will eventually contradict and undo outsiders' unpleasant stereotypes (e.g., Bromley and Shupe 1979, 235–8). Soka Gakkai leaders have done this in the interest of mellowing public distaste for their recruitment methods and elitist ideology. Soka Gakkai President Daisaku Ikeda, who assumed office in 1960, explicitly directed members to cease their open contempt of other religions and even permitted members to retain *kamidana* and ancestral tablets in their homes. (They were told they could honor and respect ancestors but not worship them.) He discouraged the excessive *shakubuku* practices that were so offensive to many Japanese and began to promote more humanistically sensitive *shoju* (tolerant conversion by gradual persuasion)—see Dumoulin (1976, 265). Dator (1969, 55–6) reports that the bar hostesses' conventional seduction tactics used to lure American servicemen to Nichiren Shoshu temples were stamped out in 1965 by Japanese Soka Gakkai leaders after *Time* magazine published an exposé about the controversy and horrified American members complained. By 1969 Dator saw indications of such internal reforms:

There are some signs that the Soka Gakkai is domesticating. Since 1964, for example, the Soka Gakkai media have been urging members to be more "socially responsible people" *(shakai-teki ningen)*. It has specifically enjoined the members not to disturb others by chanting the Daimoku at inconvenient hours or in inconvenient places. It also has encouraged the use of *shoju*, a milder method of conversion than *shakubuku*.

Dater cites a 13 August, 1964, issue of *Seikyo Graphic* (a glossy Soka Gakkai magazine) which displayed cartoons depicting "obnoxious" recruitment behavior that the movement leaders wanted to discourage (1969, 83).[6]

But the most dramatic example of Soka Gakkai's accommodation, and the one most pertinent to this conference's theme, is the "about-face" transformation of Soka Gakkai's political party, the Komeito (Clean Government party), from a much ballyhooed distinct "alternative" to otherwise corrupt status quo politics, into a status quo-seeking party of mainstream Japanese politics. The Komeito was founded in 1964 (in fact it was an incarnation of the earlier Komeikai, or Clean Government Association, first registered with the government in 1962), but Soka Gakkai actually entered politics in 1955 when a member of its Board of Directors won election to Tokyo's Prefectual Assembly and thirty-three other Soka Gakkai candidates were elected to their ward (neighborhood) assemblies. Since then it has vigorously participated in local, prefectual, and national politics. In 1956, for example, three of four Soka Gakkai candidates won seats in the House of Councilors (the National Diet's Upper House). In 1959 six Soka Gakkai candidates won Upper House seats, each obtaining nearly three million votes. By the late 1960s the Komeito had become the third largest political power in the National Diet (considering both the Upper and Lower Houses), behind the conservative Liberal-Democrats and the Japan Socialist party in number of seats, but ahead of the older Democrat Socialist party and the Japan Communist party. Although the Komeito formally separated from Soka Gakkai in 1970, virtually all of Komeito's candidates and supporters are Soka Gakkai members. Noted observer Chalmers Johnson (1975, 39) estimates the Soka Gakkai share of backing and participation in Komeito activities at "close to 100 percent"; more recently, Brett (1979, 370) found that as many as approximately ten percent of the vote for Komeito candidates may be non-Soka Gakkai. Nevertheless, the Clean Government party may be still legitimately regarded as an appendage, however nominally independent, of the Soka Gakkai's perspective and political mission.

What is this political mission? Soka Gakkai is a dispensationalist, millennial form of Buddhism that has articulated plans for *kosen rufu,* "the propogation of True Buddhism," through a time-table to rebuild and convert Asia by the year 2200 A.D. The goal is what is sometimes called by the movement "Buddhist Democracy." It was first articulated by Toda Josei, the co-founder of Soka Gakkai and its leader throughout the post-war 1940s and 1950s, in his book *Obutsu Myogoron. Obutsu Myogoron* means the "unity of the law of the king and the Buddhist *Dharma*" and outlines a theory of the unity of church and state. As Brannen (1968, 126), an outsider, describes it:

> According to the *Obutsu Myogoron,* as long as there is confusion in the religion of a country there will be confusion in the government. Government is a technique. The function of government is to achieve a condition which fosters happiness for the citizen. The means by which government achieves this is through order and regulations. Religion, on the other hand, if it is true religion, removes the barriers to happiness. The *true religion,* as taught by or discovered by Nichiren, removes unhappiness and achieves a union of government and religion both working toward the complete happiness (or fortune) of the individual.

Brannen's description is consonant with one Soka Gakkai director's more specific statement of political intentions *circa* 1967: "Our purpose is to purify the world through the propagation of the teaching of the Nichiren Sho Denomination. Twenty years from now we will occupy the majority of seats in the National Diet and establish the Nichiren Sho Denomination as the national religion of Japan and construct a national altar at Mt. Fuji" (quoted in Brannen 1968, 127).

Initially Komeito and Soka Gakkai leaders issued bold statements of their reformist intentions for the party. They decried the amorality of the entire electoral system. Their elected officials would be, the nation was told, immune to the bribery and corruption so rife in Japanese electoral politics. (The party's name literally means "the Way of Clean Government.") Their Buddhist commitment to world peace would presumably lead them to resist all military involvement (such as allowing United States military bases in Japan), and their steadfast Buddhist beliefs would help stem the growing tide of atheistic communism in Japan. Their grounding in the nationalist zeal of Nichiren would restore pride among Japanese in their country and return the nation to its destined, preeminent place in the world.

The Komeito is not the only example of a Japanese "new religion" becoming involved in that country's political system. Curtis (1971, 198) notes that "direct political activity, in the sense of putting forth or recommending candidates for office, is a practice engaged in by many religious groups in Japan." (In one campaign for a seat in Japan's House of Representatives that Curtis followed in detail, the candidate made "the rounds" in his district to meetings of many "new" religions, including PL Kyodan, Rissho Koseikai, Tenrikyo, Shingonshu, Kokok-yo, Seicho No Ie, and Soka Gakkai seeking their official endorsements and memberships' support.) Likewise, Davis (1980, 257), in his study of the Sukyo Mahikari cult, mentions that the group's leaders would frequently invite Japanese political candidates and politicians to speak to members. Passin (1976, 30–2) and Blaker (1976, 100) also concur that it is a common practice for Japanese "new religions" to endorse and support openly certain political candidates.

But most of these groups do not have either the local constituencies that can field local candidates or sufficiently large national memberships to elect their own people. Here Soka Gakkai alone has made impressive and unique inroads to both national and local levels in electing its own candidates. In large cities it has successfully recruited and then mobilized as voters "socially unstable sectors of the urban population," i.e., migrants and semi-skilled laborers not tied to big corporations or unions. In a number of Tokyo wards, for instance, the Komeito has been able to rely on many young workers and apprentices who are not otherwise tapped by either the dominant conservative Liberal-Democratic party or by either of the major labor union parties (the Japan Communist party and the Japan Socialist party—see Ikado (1968, 106–8).[7] A number of studies converge on a portrait of the typical Soka Gakkai member: lower class, less educated, lower income (Dator 1969, 59–105). These are the characteristics of many persons not integrated into the formally, tightly structured system of bailiwicks whose votes could once be "delivered" by landlords, village headmen, union officials, office managers, or local politicians. Such persons represent what have come to be called uncommitted "floating votes," and Soka Gakkai has become adept at capturing them for Komeito.

Unfortunately for plans to "take the high road" in politics, however, compromise often becomes an unavoidable necessity. Radical rhetoric becomes an impediment to gaining access to real corridors of influence in a parliamentary democracy. The Komeito has had to face this fact. For example, any number of persons may register as candidates to represent a given district. However, in Japan political races are much like American primaries. Thus ten candidates of "Party X" may run for three seats, but few will receive enough votes to win, and many will simply be stealing votes away from one another. Thus the number of same-party candidates in any race is a delicately arrived-at decision by potential candidates and party officials. Likewise, if candidates from separate parties are sufficiently similar so that they will be appealing to the same type of voters, it may be a matter of negotiation between separate parties' officials (however tacit or informal) as to how not to run "redundant" candidates against each other, splitting a finite number of votes, and possibly allowing some third party (perhaps mutually disliked) candidate to win.

In recent years the Komeito has cooperated in various elections with the moderate Democratic Socialist party so as to maximize the chances of its own candidates winning office (Baerwald 1980, 264). It has also done such maneuvering with the majority conservative Liberal-Democratic party which has seen its own support base eroding in recent years. (For example, the Komeito supported the same candidate as the Liberal-Democrats in eight prefectures in 1979 and opposed *no* Liberal-Democrats)—see Samuels (1982, 633). This is ironic since the Liberal-Democratic party once was a prime target of Komeito denunci-ations about corruption and big money. However, the LDP is more often in need of allies than it once was, and with the Komeito now the third largest party represented in the Japanese National Diet it is in more of a position to seek concessions in exchange for participating in coalitions. Now the two parties' overlapping stances on conservative issues, such as pro-nationalism, are more often stressed than the talk of reform and corruption. Such cooperation between the LDP and the politicians of the Komeito also lend the latter respectability. Writes Samuels (1982, 633): "As the LDP became weaker, the centrist parties [Komeito] and the Democratic Socialist Party began to recognize the possibility for coalition at the national level. They grew increasingly eager to join hands with the LDP in order to demonstrate their 'respectability.'"

Many observers see a "centrist" trend currently underway in Japanese elections. Voters are allegedly tired of the unkept promises and radical rhetoric of leftist parties (both the Japan Socialist and Japan Commu-nist parties) as well as the "business-as-usual," ethically gray tactics of the reigning Liberal-Democrats with their bribery scandals of the 1970s (e.g., Uchida and Baerwald 1978; Samuels 1982). Blaker (1978) sees an "emerging consensus" along moderate lines on many issues and on which the Komeito (with its claims to be following a non-aligned "middle way" in politics) has been able to capitalize. What this suggests is that the Komeito has surrendered the reality of its claims to be a genuine alternative to the partisan denizens of the murky world of

Japanese political coalitions in exchange for political acceptance and respectability. In the process it has made itself a valuable bargaining ally to the *status quo* party, the Liberal-Democrats.

On the other hand, Komeito and Soka Gakkai can be accused of opportunism and violation of their own principles in another direction. In October 1977 Komeito and Democrat Socialist party leaders announced an agreement never again during any political race to enter into a local coalition in which communists also participated. In doing so Komeito stressed its standard objection to Marxism's atheistic elements. Yet despite this agreement there was actually an *increase* in the number of coalitions across the nation in which the three parties participated (Samuels 1982, 634). Even more telling of Komeito/Soka Gakkai willingness to accommodate can be seen in their *sub rosa* dealings with atheistic communists. It is now no secret that the secretary general of the Japanese Communist party once sought an alliance with Komeito through the Soka Gakkai despite the fact that to reconcile with any religious group was considered by JCP idealogues as a "Marxist heresy." Johnson (1976, 39) reports that in July 1975: ". . . the political world was astounded when . . . it was revealed that some seven months earlier, in December 1974, the JCP and Sokagakkai had entered into a secret ten-year accord of rapprochement. . . . Even more sensationally, Miyamoto Kenji of the JCP and Ikeda Daisaku, president of the Sokagakkai, had been holding meetings with each other since the start of the year . . ." A well-known Japan Communist party councillor and the head of Soka Gakkai's Men's Division had signed the agreement without any apparent knowledge or approval by the Komeito's chairman or by its secretary-general. Indeed, they publicly renounced the agreement. Soka Gakkai leaders quickly tried to "back-peddle," claiming that they only had meant "coexistence" with the JCP, but the JCP insisted that the understanding of the agreement was "joint struggle" and cooperation. (A number of persons in both camps, needless to say, felt betrayed.) The issue was never resolved and proved an embarrassment for Soka Gakkai.

There are other examples, such as the Komeito's support for ratifying United States—Japan security treaties (pragmatic, perhaps, but a violation nevertheless of the Komeito's lofty rhetoric about anti-militarism). However, it is in the real maneuvering of Soka Gakkai's political arm, the Komeito, that accommodation can most clearly be recognized. The Komeito has negotiated, compromised, moderated, and adapted to parliamentary democracy, succeeding in establishing itself as a respectable and important force. But in doing so it has become part of the very political establishment it denounced when it was an insignificant minority force, and its formally bold reformist intentions have been casualties of the transformation.

The Soka Gakkai/Komeito Accommodation in Cultural Context

The accommodation of Soka Gakkai and its offspring, the Komeito, to mainstream Japanese society is a process now underway and by no means complete (if it ever will be). We need to consider its importance in two contexts: the more limited one of Japan; and the more generic or analytic one of prophetic religion interacting with other social institutions.

The Japanese context: Brannen (1968, 51) has linked Buddhism closely to national consciousness among the Japanese: "Most Japanese claim Buddhism as their religion, at least when a census is taken. Consequently, a revival in Buddhism in Japan is tantamount to a recovery of the national identity."

Brannen's emphasis on nationalistic identity is, I believe, correct. I propose that Soka Gakkai be primarily interpreted as a revitalization movement along the lines intended by anthropologist Anthony F. C. Wallace (1966). It is an attempt to rekindle nationalistic sentiments and construct a new moral orthodoxy to serve as civil religion to fill the gap left by the declining, discredited State Shinto outlawed after World War II. Soka Gakkai elevates a new set of sacred persons and symbols (e.g., the saint Nichiren and a succession of Nichiren Shoshu abbots, the *Daimoku* chant of *Namu Myoho Renge Kyo,* and so forth) with a recognized venerable tradition, sacralizes Japanese history with a new perspective that attempts nevertheless to be meaningful to modern Japanese, and provides a new justifying principle (albeit Buddhist instead of Shinto) for the current policy. It is future-oriented even as it is busily engaged in the here-and-now. It appeals to those persons logically least integrated into networks of stable interpersonal relations and provides them primary group support.

This "urban anomie" explanation, described aptly in Rajana (1975), admittedly is based not on a study of converts' motives but rather on examination of the functions deduced from movement claims, activities, and member characteristics. Scholars of Japanese "new" religion, such as Davis (1980, 1977), see such movements providing adherents with a return to the traditional particularistic values of rural Japan that industrialization and urbanization have shattered. Like eighteenth-century feudal villagers who had their own local dieties *(ujigami)* and who believed themselves its "children" *(ujiko)*, adherents of new religions like Soka Gakkai consider themselves part of the same type of insular subsocieties that clearly demarcate members from non-members yet (with a modern universalistic twist) provide much easier avenues for outsiders to join.

The result, in many groups including Soka Gakkai, is a realistic appraisal of the religious pluralism scene but not an acceptance of it as desirable or inevitable. Says Davis (1977, 90): "While there are hundreds of such religious groups to choose from, the particularistic loyalties they generate result merely in a pluralism of memberships and external doctrines. The growth of any deeply rooted pluralism in thought, feeling or values is quickly stifled by a dominant internal ethos redolent of the gross national custom of Japan before 1945."

The analytic context: The pressures on any unconventional religion to modify its doctrines and activities toward less radical forms are obvious. Respectability and legitimacy ease persecution and rejection which in turn affect recruitment and membership retention. Fewer resources must then be expended to repel attacks by competitors and opponents, freeing time and energies as well as other resources for more productive pursuits.

The pressures within such a group to achieve *proximate* as opposed to *ultimate* goals are equally strong. Achieving proximate goals lends a sense of successive approximation toward ultimate goals. The former act as immediate rewards, or reinforcers, that help morale and develop a sense of validity about the latter. Each rung on the latter achieved, believers reason, confirms the validity and practicality of seeking larger ultimate ends.

But there is a probable fate awaiting prophetic religions when they wish to achieve political structural change and decide to use non-violent or conventional means to do so. Proximate goals such as increased public respectability, election of certain candidates to give leverage (not control) in legislatures, better relations with the mass media, and cooperation of other power groups, which are what the Soka Gakkai/ Komeito have achieved in Japan, become consuming. They involve the very moderation and compromise that divert the movement from ultimate goals. Cooperation with other political parties to insure election of Komeito candidates or the sort of diplomatic bridge-building that brought out the Liberal-Democrat Prime Minister in 1964 to attend ceremonies dedicating a new Soka Gakkai building (Norbeck 1970, 20) help the movement in terms of easing tensions in its immediate circumstances. Yet such factors deter the movement from ultimate reformist goals and, rationalizations aside, do little to promote the Third Civilization.

Prophetic religion deals with ultimate goals as do prophetic/ revolutionary politics. Together they can upset regimes and create new large-scale possibilities, as Iran has shown the world in the past half-decade. Neither set of values and goals has much stake in the status quo. However, prophetic religion and proximate politics (e.g., "the politics of moderation") are a poor mix from the religion's standpoint. Prophetic religion is inevitably the loser in such instances, for it makes the biggest compromises of its principles. For all its rhetoric about meaningful reform, the Soka Gakkai's Clean Government party has had to wade into the swamp of Japanese electoral politics and come away muddied. Those politics, on the other hand, go on relatively unchanged from contact with the Komeito. It is Soka Gakkai and Komeito that have adapted to a new set of rules.

In short, the lesson of Soka Gakkai's experience is that unless a prophetic religious group is willing to adopt a political style as equally radical as its own prophecy and forego the short-run successes (and benefits) of acceptance in the conventional political system, then its prophetic potential has few prospects. Instead, it increasingly comes to settle for proximate rather than ultimate goals and soon develops too many interests in upholding the status quo to reform or significantly change it. The fact that so many prophetic religions have failed in their anticipated societal changes can in part be attributed to their choice of strategies when entering the political arena.

British sociologist Bryan Wilson (1981, 229) has succinctly discussed this naïveté of the vast majority of sectarian movements when pursuing their ambitious goals: "That new movements should address contemporary issues is, of course, expectable, but that they should so readily adopt strategies that imitate secular modern methods of operation indicates the measure to which they are hostages to the cultures in which they work."

Wilson makes a point which seems as applicable to the Soka Gakkai, racing as it is to gain a share of respectability and influence in the Japanese socio-political status quo, as it is to other religious movements in Asia and the United States. I conclude with a summary statement by Wilson (1981, 223) that must, from a given movement enthusiast's viewpoint, seem indeed cynical but which is simply a statement of probability, or "sociological fatalism," that we can be confident in accepting: "The impact of a new movement on the world may be, at times, considerable: but the impact on any new movement of the need to survive in the world must, in the long run, be somewhat greater."

Notes

1. In this paper I purposefully omit accent marks in Japanese words that would otherwise signify long vowels (e.g., *Soka Gakkai* or *Nichiren Shoshu*) for the sake of simplicity in preparation. For speakers of Japanese the pronunciations are already known; for non-speakers it will not matter.

2. Some scholars refer to all the varieties of Japanese Buddhism as sects. Others call them denominations, following the pluralistic model of American religion. I use the term "sect" to refer to *Soka Gakkai* much as I would in reference to Pentecostals or Jehovah's Witnesses in Protestant Christianity. I reserve the term "denomination" for larger, mainline Buddhist traditions such as the "Pure Land" schools (e.g., *Jodo-Shinshu*) or *Shingon* and Zen groups, much as I would use the term to refer to Presbyterianism or Methodism in Protestant Christianity.

3. For a discussion of the basic precepts of *Soka Gakkai* philosophy, which often ranges far afield from Nichiren Buddhism *per se* and the Lotus Sutra, see (among Western interpretations); (Offner and Van Straelen 1963, 98–109; Dumoulin 1976, 251–76; McFarland 1967, 194, 220; and Brannen 1968, 133–54.)

4. This "spiritual ends-justify-the-sexual means" technique is similar to the practice of "flirty fishing" that caused a good deal of bad publicity for the Children of God sect (now called the Family of Love) in Great Britain some two decades later (see Wallis 1978, 1978a).

5. As a college student in Tokyo in the late 1960s I was approached more than once on subways cars by *Soka Gakkai* missionaries who abruptly thrust movement literature into my hands and stood attentively at my side until I had looked through it. One American student friend was literally trailed by a carload of *Soka Gakkai* members until he agreed to ride with them and listen to a specially prepared lecture on the virtues of Nichiren.

6. The *Soka Gakkai's* attitude toward other "competitors" in the United States reflects this new tolerant posture. Ellwood (1974, 103) reports: "The attitude toward Nichiren Shoshu's Judeo-Christian environment had also gone great lengths toward openness [since its early days in the USA]. In the early 1950's, Sokagakkai in Japan

published a *shakubuku* manual presenting extremely harsh arguments against Christianity and other religions, and saying that to join Nichiren Shoshu one must destroy all shrines and traces of other faiths in home and heart . . . But it is now said that Nichiren Shoshu is a 'philosophy' and one can practice it and still be a good Protestant, Catholic, or Jew. It is said that in a non-Buddhist country such as America, Nichiren Shoshu comes only to embellish other faiths, not to replace them."

7. Much of the credit for the *Komeito's* ability to mobilize *Soka Gakkai* members at the polls must go the latter group's paramilitary structures and to the primary group relations that enmesh every member in group activities. Families are typically organized into blocks which are successively grouped in more inclusive levels: squads, districts, areas, general areas, headquarters, and general headquarters. As Ellwood (1974, 92) observes: "The real sociological strength of Sokagakkai lies in the tightness of its neighborhood groups, in which there is continual contact, jobs to be done, and mutual help."

References

Asahi Nenkan. 1968. *Asahi Nenkan [Asahi Yearbook]*. Tokyo: Asahi Newspaper Company.

Baerwald, Hans H. 1980. Japan's 35th house of representatives election: The LDP toys with a return to 1954. *Asian Survey* 20 (March): 257–68.

———. 1980a. Japan's "Double" election. *Asian Survey* 20 (December): 1169–84.

Blacker, Carmen. 1962. New religious cults in Japan. *The Hibbert Journal* 60 (July): 303–13.

Blaker, Michael. 1978. Japan in 1977: An emerging consensus. *Asian Survey* 18 (January): 90–102.

———. 1976. The outcome of the 1974 election: Patterns and perspectives. *Japan At the Polls*. Washington, D.C.: American Enterprise Institute for Public Policy Research, 81–127.

Brannen, Noah S. 1968. *Soka Gakkai*. Richmond, Va: John Knox Press.

Brett, Cecil C. 1979. The Komeito and local Japanese politics. *Asian Survey*. 19 (April): 366–78.

Bromley, David G. and Anson D. Shupe, Jr. 1979. *"Moonies" in America: Cult, Church, and Crusade*. Beverly Hills, CA.: Sage Publications.

Curtis, Gerald L. 1971. *Election Campaigning Japanese style*. New York: Columbia University Press.

Dator, James Allen. 1969. *Soka Gakkai, builders of the Third Civilization*. Seattle, WA.: University of Washington Press.

Davis, Winston. 1980. *Dojo: Magic and Exorcism in Modern Japan*. Stanford, CA.: Stanford University Press.

————. 1977. *Toward Modernity: A Developmental Typology of Popular Religious Affiliations in Japan*. East Asia Papers #12. Ithaca, N.Y.: Cornell University.

Dumoulin, Henrich and John C. Maraldo, eds. 1976. Buddhism in Modern Japan. *Buddhism in the Modern World*, 215–76. New York: Macmillan.

Ellwood, Jr., Robert S. 1974. *The Eagle and the Rising Sun*. Philadelphia: The Westminster Press.

Johnson, Chalmers. 1976. Japan 1975: Mr. Clean muddles through. *Asian Survey* 16 (January): 31–41.

Ikado, Fujo. 1968. Trend and problems of new religions: Religion in urban society. *The Sociology of Japanese Religion*. Eds. Kiyomi Morioka and William H. Newell, 101–17. Leiden, Neth.: E. J. Brill.

Norbeck, Edward. 1970. *Religion and Society in Modern Japan: Continuity and Change*. Houston: Tourmaline Press.

Passin, Herbert. 1976. The House of Councillors: Promise and achievement. *Japan at the Polls*. Ed. Michael K. Blaker, 1–43. Washington, D.C.: American Enterprise Institute for Public Policy Research.

Rajana, Eini Watavabe. 1975. New religions in Japan: An appraisel of two theories. *Modern Japan: Aspects of History Literature and Society*. Ed. W. G. Beasely, 187–97. Berkeley: University of California Press.

Roggendorf, Joseph. 1951. The place of religion in modern Japan. *Japan Quarterly* 5:21–9.

Samuels, Richard J. 1982. Local politics in Japan: The changing of the guard. *Asian Survey* 22 (July): 630–7.

Saniel, Josefa M. 1965. The mobilization of traditional values in the modernization of Japan. *Religion and Progress in Modern Asia*. Ed. Robert N. Bellah, 124–49. New York: The Free Press.

Shupe, Anson D. 1977. Conventional religion and political participation in postwar rural Japan. *Social Forces* 55 (March): 613–20.

————. 1979. The urbanization dimension in Japanese religion and politics. *Proceedings of the First International Symposium on Asian Studies*. Hong Kong.

Uchida, Mitsuru and Hans. H. Baerwald. 1978. The House of

Councillors election in Japan: The LDP hangs in there. *Asian Survey* 18 (March): 301–8.

Wallace, Anthony F. C. 1966. *Religion: An Anthropological View*. New York: Random House.

Wallis, Roy. 1978. Fishing for men. *The Humanist* 38 (January/February): 14–16.

———. 1978a. Recruiting Christian manpower. *Society* 15 (May/June): 72–4.

Wilson, Bryan., ed. 1981. Time, generations, and sectarianism. *The Social Impact of New Religious Movements*. 217–34. Barrytown, N.Y.: Unification Theological Seminary.

13

Historical Perspectives on Religion and Regime: Some Sociological Comparisons of Buddhism and Christianity

RANDALL COLLINS

WHEN we think of contemporary religion and politics, we tend to think of religious movements which are politically activist. Examples spring to mind, such as fundamentalist Islam in the Iranian revolution, Catholicism and the Polish Solidarity movement, or the fundamentalist New Right in the United States. More generally, however, there are several possible relationships between religion and politics.

First, religion could be used for political ends. This might be done rather deliberately, perhaps even cynically, such as appears to be the case with Catholicism in Poland today, or Islamic fundamentalism in the guerilla movement in Afghanistan. But another variant is that the religious activists do not so much aim at political ends under a religious guise as unleash a powerful religious surge which simply washes over the political arena like an obstacle in its path. Full-scale millennial movements are often of this sort. Examples might include some of the Future Buddha (Maitreya) movements in the history of China, which I will discuss below. Between the cynical use of religious politics and the purely transcendental fervor there is a continuum, and it is not always possible to assign a particular case clearly to one end or the other. What they all have in common is religion affecting the political arena. Thus, in this first model relationship we are looking at the political consequences of religion.

But there is a second sociological relationship which is the reverse of the first one. Political factors can have religious results. This is implied in a variant of the old "societal strain" theory of religious movements, which sees millennial outbursts as responses to some crisis such as war or political breakdown. I would not subscribe to quite this mode of explanation. It has been asserted, for example, that the original rise of Buddhism in India of the fifth century B.C. was due to the downfall of the independent republics of the Himalayan foothills in the face of the expanding empire of Magadha from the lower Ganges. Since Gautama Buddha and his followers were largely from the aristocratic caste of these declining republics, the thesis has been advanced that Buddhism was a mystical flight from the world due to political failure and disillusionment of a group that was losing power. In my opinion, the thesis does not stand up under comparative evidence. There are numerous instances throughout world history of states losing their political independence without giving rise to religions of mystical mediators. Mystical religions, including Buddhism itself,[1] have been prominent in strong and growing states, such as periods of medieval China, Tibet, and Japan.

I do not think that religion can be regarded as merely a compensation for worldly failure, including political failure. Nevertheless, there is a way in which political events have had powerful effects upon religions. Let me mention two famous heresies in the history of early Christianity, Donatism and Pelagianism. The Donatist heresy, centered in Carthage, was a split between the ultra-righteous who had refused to recant during the persecutions ordered by the Emperor Decius in 250 A.D., and the backsliders who had given way under pressure (Chadwick 1967, 119–22). Once the persecution had ended ten years later, the issue was whether the surviving martyrs, tested by fire, should allow the backsliders back into the church, and especially into control of the bishoprics of North Africa. It has been asserted by some social historians that the religious split was merely a cover for ethnic and social class struggle between the indigenous Punic and Berber population and the wealthier Latin colonists. In response to this thesis, some church historians have pointed out that ethnic lines were crossed in the doctrinal struggle, and that both social factions could be found among the martyrs as well as the trimmers (Jones 1959). Nevertheless, the Donatist conflict may be regarded as an example of the effect of politics upon religion. The partisans were struggling over religious ends, not political ones. But it was politics in the first place (i.e., Decius' persecution) which set off the struggle within the church. It was preceded by a succession of emperors since around 230 A.D. who were alternatively sympathetic and hostile to Christianity, and which was to culminate in its establishment as the state church under Constantine in the next century. When the persecutions ended, the religious fervor of the Donatists and their opponents was affected by a political situation within the administration of the church itself: namely the question of how much centralized control was to be exerted over the internal affairs of the African church by the see of Rome.

In this case, the Roman church asserted its power over the provincial church; and the Donatists, upholders of local autonomy, were branded heretics. In the case of the Pelagian controversy two centuries later, the political circumstances are even more apparent. The doctrine of Pelagius is of course famous as the extreme position that salvation is won by free will alone. Pelagius was a Briton, and various interpretations have been advanced as to the culture of individualistic activism which he represented for the future of this historic part of the world. Such interpretations are unrealistically teleological. What is more striking is the lack of controversy over Pelagius's views during the early years of the fifth century A.D. when he visited Rome and carried out theological discussions. "Pelagianism" became a movement, and hence raised the issue of full-scale heresy, only after he returned home in 411 (Chadwick 1967, 225–34). What is significant about this date? Only that the full-scale German invasion of the Roman empire began in 407; that the Roman legions were pulled out of Britain in 411, making the province the first long-standing and Christianized part of the Empire to be irremediably lost. The British church was suddenly free of effective Roman control due to an extraneous political event. Pelagianism became notable in Britain at precisely this time. One might say it was a religious doctrine elevated by the tides of political history into an emblem of church independence as well as a doctrine which attacked the alleged moral corruption of the

Roman church as a reason for the disasters that were befalling the Empire.

In this second set of cases religion is the dependent variable of politics, not vice versa. There is no effort of religious activists to take political power. Their aims are religious, although political circumstances make it possible for them to mobilize to pursue particular religious aims. Let me add a Buddhist example in which the non-political aim of the religious movement is particularly clear: the rise of Ch'an Buddhism in China, better known by its Japanese name, Zen (Domoulin 1963; Ch'en 1964). Ch'an originally meant meditation, from the Sanskrit term, *dhyana*. Ch'an Buddhism was simply the school which specialized in meditation practice (the original and basic form of Buddhism, but one that had become overshadowed by ritualistic and magical practices in the popular Buddhism introduced into China from the fourth century A.D. onwards). What was distinctive about the Ch'an school was its hostility to the other sects and its insistence on meditation alone as the path to enlightenment. But what we associate with the image of Zen did not come until later, in the eighth and ninth centuries—its paradoxical sayings, emphasis on sudden enlightenment provoked by such practices as an unexpected blow of the master's staff, or its witty repartee among rival masters, such as:

"Where are you going?"
"I'm going to a changeless place."
"If there's a changeless place you won't be going there."
"Going is also changeless."

Beneath the wordplay one can discern an organizational change. The debate over sudden versus gradual enlightenment, which the Ch'an innovators carried out against their more orthodox forbears, had a structural significance for the monastic hierarchy. An enlightened monk was entitled to become an independent master with his own disciples. Gradual enlightenment meant working one's way up slowly through a long set of ranks. Sudden enlightenment skipped ranks or broke them down entirely, and allowed masters to promote their favorites to independent power. The impression that this implies an organizational decentralization of the church is strengthened when we connect it to another Ch'an innovation: requiring monks to engage in manual labor. This was a sharp break with the traditional method of economic support by begging for alms. In medieval China, the alms usually took the form of patronage by emperor and nobility, often in grants of land with serfs and slaves. The Ch'an rejection of alms was a move to cut the ties of dependence to the state. Instead of lavish establishment located in the capital cities, the Ch'an masters moved to remote mountains where they developed economically self-sufficient monasteries.[2]

If we examine the political situation, we see some structural forces motivating this break with Buddhist tradition. Somewhat like Christianity in the third century in Rome, Buddhism in China of the late seventh and early eighth centuries was becoming one of the major contenders for official recognition as the state church. Two empresses, during the years 690 to 701, and again during 705 to 712, had been deposed after reigns during which Buddhism had been elevated into a kind of Caesaro-Papist rule. The reaction from Confucians and Taoists had been vehement. Buddhism was yet too strong to suffer the kinds of persecutions and confiscations of monastery wealth that occured in the next century, and there was to be yet another period of very strongly pro-Buddhist government during 780 to 820. But the political writing was on the wall, particularly in conjunction with governmental crises and barbarian attacks that left any political support shaky at best. What I have called the "Ch'an revolution" was, sociologically speaking, a movement within the church to restructure the religion in a radically decentralized direction to make it safe from the vicissitudes of politics. The Ch'an masters were correct in their assessment. All the other sects of Buddhism, which had depended upon court patronage, disappeared during the persecutions of the next centuries, leaving only Ch'an in its mountain strongholds, together with salvation-oriented Amidaism based upon the support of the lower classes. Here, then, is a case of religion responding to politics, but in an anti-political direction.

We have now two main patterns of relationship between religion and politics. The direction of causality can go in either direction. It is also possible, of course, that the two processes can be combined in a chain: political causes could provoke religious movements, which in turn could have political effects, and so on. (Or the chain might begin at the opposite end.) Religion does not simply reduce to politics, even when it is affected by it or affects it. Nevertheless, I propose that these interconnections are historically very common, and that religion has rarely existed when it did not either cause or respond to political conditions.

As I remarked at the outset, our interest here is primarily in modern politically activist religion. The various examples I have given, chosen from widely dispersed periods of history, have been intended to set this in a larger context of possibilities. Some questions now arise: Under what conditions does one find one form or another? When does religion spill over into the struggle for political power, and when, on the contrary, does purely religious movement occur in response to political conditions? When does religious reaction to politics take the form of the effort to escape from politics to foster pure, independent religiosity, and when does it close the circle and bring a counterattack of religion back into politics?

To begin to answer these questions from the comparative-historical perspective, it is necessary to make some distinctions. The relationships between religion and regime have taken quite different structural forms throughout history, and only in certain eras could these questions even arise. Schematically (1) there are cases where religion is identical with political structure and activity; (2) cases where religion is independent of the state but is used by it as the major basis of political legitimation and sometimes even of organization; (3) cases where the state is fully secular in legitimation and organization, and hence religion can confront politics with the full range of options outlined above. Let us examine each of these in a little more detail.[3]

(1) *Religious/political identity:* This ideal type is approached in many tribal societies. There is neither state nor church with independent and permanent organizational resources, its own property, nor perhaps even full-time roles. Religious ritual and legitimation permeates most social activities, especially those which involve collective negotiation and alliance. The war leader, the tribal elder, the "big-man" are simultaneously ritual figure and politician, and their political charisma is described as magical/religious *mana* or its equivalent. There are many variants on this pattern: the god-king of the central African societies, the temporary war-coalition leader invoking the wrath of the gods familiar to us from Homeric Greece, or the household cult in which the patriarch is simultaneously priest and domestic dictator. This last form is particularly important in many of the historical civilizations, since the household structure is the fundamental unit out of which were built wider networks of alliance which constituted the state.

Here of course we approach the borderline of the ideal type, as a state structure begins to emerge with its own contours, different from the organizational forms which constitute religion. When this happens, the variety of relationships between religion and politics become possible. As long as religious and political action are virtually identical, it is not meaningful to ask for conditions by which one affects the other. It is no doubt for this reason that tribal religions strike one as both "magical" and "worldly." There is no independent transcendental focus, and religion seems to be merely part of the social mobilization of dealing with the ongoing social issues of power and collective organization. This also means, incidentally, that religious mobilization cannot proceed very far in tribal politics; it is localistic, and reinforces group loyalties and the boundaries among them. It lacks the potential for generating a mass movement, otherwise so characteristic of the politics of the universalistic world religions, such as Christianity, Buddhism, and Islam. But these religions have that power precisely because they break organizationally with a merely familistic or tribal organizational basis. They become special-purpose organizations, generating their own structures and capable of recruiting across the boundary lines of localistic groups. Their philosophical universalism, in the form of their unitary transcendent spiritual focus, and their moral injunctions depend upon this structural transformation in their organizational bases. It is because they have their own organizations and their own properties that the universalistic churches can play an independent role, both spiritually and politically.

(2) *The religiously-legitimated state:* It makes no sense to speak of the state as being religiously legitimated unless there is such a thing as the state as an organization in its own right. The rise of the state is also a fundamental requirement for the development of the transcendental "world religions" by breaking the identity between religious and political activities. It makes possible the rise of religious politics in the modern sense. It also makes possible, as I have pointed out above, the rise of anti-political religious movements, of which there are many examples especially in the history of Buddhism but also in Christianity as well. Here we approach the grounds on which our question can legitimately be asked, as to the conditions for politically active religion as well as the other alternatives. But there is a "joker in the deck." As compared to the modern situation, religion in this case is usually not free to choose whether to abstain or participate in politics, for the religiously-legitimated state is concerned precisely to use the independent church organization for its own ends, i.e., to bolster its own power.

There are actually two aspects of this, ideological and organizational. The Christian kingdoms of medieval Europe did not merely rely on priests to provide religious consecration for rulers, to invoke the blessings of God upon his wars and to ensure the majesty and rectitude of his rule. It is no accident that many of the Northern European kingdoms emerged at the time that they converted to Christianity. The church provided not only legitimation but also a literate administrative staff; monasteries colonized unsettled terrain and expanded royal power. Similarly in the Orient, the "barbarian" tribal coalitions which conquered Northern China in the early medieval period generally adopted Buddhism. In Tibet rival families of nobility supported their own monasteries, which served as sources of legitimation and emotional impressiveness, as well as economic centers and military fortresses. Often the monks themselves were armed, or else a monastery would employ numerous armed guards, usually peasants in lower religous orders. The pattern is similar to the crusading-monastics orders of Christian Europe such as the Cistercians, the Templars active in the Levant, and the Knights of the Sword who colonized the pagan Baltic. Again, armies of the Buddhist monasteries held a good deal of local power in the period of feudal wars in medieval Japan. These religious armies may seem contrary to the purer spirit of religion, especially in the case of a non-violent creed such as Buddhism. Nevertheless, the surrounding social/political conditions help explain why militarized religion emerges at precisely these times. They are all cases in which an essentially tribal or at most family/household organizational structure was the basis of political organization. Larger political coalitions among tribes or families (i.e. feudalism) were fragile, and hence the introduction by missionaries of a universalistic, quasi-bureaucratic organization in the form of the church provided a potent political weapon for whoever could mold it to military and administrative purposes.

Once the state itself became firmly enough organized in its own right, however, the need to rely on religious administrators and especially on religious troops declined. The crusading orders in Europe were eventually curtailed or even surpressed, such as in the confiscations of the wealth of the Templars by secular kings in the early 1300s. Similarly in China, Buddhism eventually was pushed out of the corridors of power as the barbarian states increasingly acquired the traditional Chinese structure of secular bureaucracy. The military monks lasted longest in Tibet because of relatively primitive economic and administrative conditions there, and in Japan, where centralized government was eclipsed for several centuries of the late Middle Ages. It is noteworthy that as soon as the Japanese feudal lords managed to consolidate military power in the late 1500s, one of their first acts was to destroy the military power of the monasteries (Sansom 1961, 283–90, 295–7, 343).

It is not merely the case that secular government struggles to free itself from dependence upon religious organization when it is strong enough to stand on its own resources. The drive for independence can also come from the religious side. For participation in political power tends to corrupt the church, from the point of view of its own ideals. The most extreme instance of this is of course the participation of Buddhism in warfare, which goes against a fundamental principle of not harming living beings. Christianity, with its background in the tribal war-coalition of Judaism, has not had this particular inhibition (Weber [1917–19] 1952). Nevertheless, religious ethics and transcendental aims are always compromised by the realities of maneuver over power that always constitute politics. Thus one of the themes of the state-church is precisely this conflict between pure religious interests and the pressure for religious support of secular political aims.

The struggles may continue for a long time after the period during which the nascent state is relying upon the church for its own organizational structure. After a relatively short period, crusading orders and monastic armies are not needed, nor are feudal relationships with religious fiefs so central a support of the state control over its territory. But even after a secular administration emerges there tends to be a long period during which high church officials are drawn upon as administrators of the state. This was particularly prominent in medieval and even early modern Europe. Cardinal Richelieu and Cardinal Mazarin were chief administrators of the absolutist French monarchy as late as the mid-1600s. Partly this was a matter of religious legitimation, of the state draping itself in holiness, which is a characteristic of the state on up until the secularizing revolutions of the modern period. But one might also argue that religion itself tended to lose its legitimating power to some extent precisely because of the cynicism that was evoked by the all-too-worldly maneuvers of such political prelates. Figures like Richelieu paid for this power in the long run with a declining respect for the spirituality of the church which characterized the liberal Enlightenment of the 1700s.

A better explanation of why the church remained prominent in political office would be that the church itself was still the cutting edge of literate, bureaucratic organization. It constituted the educational system (this would be true until the secularization of education in the 1800s), and hence administrative paperwork and legal maneuvers of the secular state itself often tended to gravitate into the hands of experienced church officials, much in the way that today in the United States corporate executives become cabinet officials. Another important factor was that the church remained a large, centralized propertied organization, and hence had its own internal structure of power in its own right. High church offices were political plums to be won by patronage or nepotism and were usually reserved for younger sons of noble families. This too introduced an element of secularism within the church itself and provided another strand in the crossing webs of politics in the era of the established church.

There are of course numerous structural variants among these ideal types. It is not necessarily the case that an imperial state must rely on legitimation (and organizational support) from a universalistic church. The Roman Republic began as a coalition among kinship (tribal) and household units, originally by establishing a joint worship of civic gods. The state soon outgrew the structural base because of its far-flung conquests. For a period of several hundred years, one might well describe the Roman state as essentially secular politics, with an anachronistic veneer of maintaining the old civic cults, in which hardly anyone believed any longer. Christianity emerged within this context, initially on the local basis of a reform movement within Jewish religious politics (Harris 1974, 133–177), though as it became ethnically universalistic it operated for several centuries as an essentially private cult, reacting more against politics than as an actor in the struggle for political power. It is only when the military and economic structure of the Roman Empire began to totter that Christianity began to be drawn upon as a political resource. The downfall of the Roman Empire was an essential precondition for its ascendance as a state religion.

Does the downfall of Rome prove that the state could not survive without religious legitimation? In my opinion that would not be an apt way to put it. The Republic and Empire lasted for over 500 years in a form that I would describe as essentially secular, perhaps even non-legitimated in any strong ideological sense. I am aware that the standard interpretation of Weberian theory is that a state cannot survive without legitimation. But in fact, the degree of survival is always a relative matter. Even the best-legitimated state is subject to its struggles and crises, most of them produced, so to speak, from "outside," from military and economic sources. The half-millennium of Roman survival without strong ideological legitimation is certainly a long enough period by anyone's standards. And if one looks more closely at Weber's own formulations, one discovers that for Weber, the more democratic or republican the structure of the state (as opposed to a highly authoritarian rule), the less it depends upon cultural legitimation and the more it survives merely by satisfying particular interests.

Interestingly enough, one might say the same thing about the political context within which Buddhism arose in India. In general I would characterize Buddhism as an anti-political religion, although of course we have already seen instances of its explicit political use in China, Central Asia, and Japan. And in India as well, it was promoted as something approaching a state religion by the Emperor Asoka, ca. 270–232 B.C., who for a relatively brief period established the only large-scale state to hold most of the territory of the Indian peninsula before the British conquest in modern times. But it is clear that the original precepts of Buddhism were strongly anti-political. There is not only its strong emphasis on non-violence, but also the renunciation of all worldly activities and attachments in favor of achieving enlightenment through meditation. Of course, in order for Buddhism in China or Tibet to adapt to political patronage these doctrinal elements had to be suppressed in favor of liturgical ritualism and the display of magical powers, all of which were aimed essentially at lay audiences. We have already seen how Ch'an Buddhism, in order to make the religion independent of politics, took a strong stance against ritualism. One may also see its paradoxical *koans* as the effort of religious "insiders" to develop an esoteric touchstone which excluded laypersons. Certain aspects of this certainly went beyond the techniques and stance of original Buddhism, but in general, its claim to recover the original religious impulse seems accurate.

How did such a non-political religion fit into the context of an emerging imperial state in the Ganges valley? One might suppose that as one moves beyond tribal and familistic organization there would be an automatic claim on universalistic religion to provide the legitimation and the administrative resources for the new state. But India, like Rome, proves that this is not necessarily so. Universalistic religions did indeed emerge in this context (Jainism as well as Buddhism grew up at precisely this time and in this area), but their stance, as we have seen, was anti-political. Though the state did patronize various sects, it did not use them for political administration nor rely on them for legitimacy. Instead, the Magadha kingdom which was the center of all this activity was famous for the secular, even cynical tone of its politics. It is here that the high official Kautilya wrote his famous Machiavellian treatise on power, the *Arthashastra*, and the Magadhan kings were known for their cut-throat tactics. Yet the state did not seem to need religious legitimation. One reason, as in the case of Rome, might be that nothing succeeds like success. The continued military expansion of the empire over several hundred years provided its own legitimation. Of course the expansion did not go on forever. The Empire fell not long after Asoka's death (ironically, the one emperor who is known for having sought to build a state church.) Thereafter the pattern of Indian politics and religion took a course that seems curious from the point of view of the rest of the world. The state-church was never characteristic of India, at least not before the Moslem conquests. Indian religion, including of course Hinduism, was unusually anti-political throughout most of its history, and the numerous Indian states were for the most part particularly Machiavellian and secularistic in their approach to politics. My own suspicion is that the answer to this puzzle has something to do with the caste system. But that topic leads us too far afield into what is already a rather dense jungle of historical sociology.[4]

(3) *The secularly legitimated state:* This is really the main focus of our attention in this volume. For the most part we are asking about the conditions under which religion, as a fully institutionalized, private organization, becomes involved in politics of the essentially non-religious state. The emergence of this state is of course the familiar story of the eighteenth century Enlightenment, the French Revolution, the disestablishment of the various state churches, and the spread of the model of secular politics and of private religion throughout the world. The materials here are rather more modern than those with which I am comfortable dealing. What I would like to ask, instead, is whether medieval Christianity and Buddhism give us any analytical clues as to the conditions that produce religious/political movements of this sort. The reason that it is possible to ask such a question of this medieval material is, again, the fact that the ideal types do not neatly line up with any alleged "stages" of historical development. Pulling apart the various strands analytically and giving relative weight to each type, we have just seen that something like the secular state may have existed in ancient Rome and the still more ancient Ganges. Moreover, in both China and medieval Europe, where the pattern is closer to that of the state church, nevertheless there are variants.

Let me concentrate for the most part on China. Certainly there is an aspect in which the Chinese empire was usually a religiously-legitimated state. The emperor himself was elevated to an object of worship, though this might be better described as a kind of carry-over of the primitive fusion of religion with politics in the same way that Confucianism extolled the remnants of the old familistic cult in an era in which the structure of the state had far outgrown family networks. In some sense China was structurally analogous to Rome. It developed a secular administrative organization and relied more on its sheer power and military success for a kind of ad-hoc legitimation than on the blessings of state-supported priests. Yet Chinese governments "covered

almost all the angles" in the sense of fostering religious pluralism.
Temples to the older nature gods were maintained, as were newer cults
which made offerings to a deified Confucius himself. Both Taoism
(transformed from a mystical philosophy into a worship of a pantheon
of "Immortals") and Buddhism at various times received imperial
patronage. The end result of all this variety of religious legitimation,
however, was more like a "party politics" of different religious factions,
something like that which prevailed in the declining period of the
Roman Empire. The competition among religions kept any from
acquiring a monopoly upon legitimation, and by reflex this situation
kept the Chinese state relatively secular.

If this description gives the impression that I am presenting the
medieval Chinese state as a relatively "modern" type, that is deliberate.
In general as I have argued elsewhere (Collins 1985), medieval China
pioneered in quasi-capitalist economic structures as well as in secular
political forms. Thus there is an aspect in which China is an appropriate
place to look for the dynamics of political religious movements of a
comparatively modern form. In particular China shows early instances
of millennial movements which took on an explicitly political goal of
taking state power en route to the arrival of a worldly paradise. These
movements frequently involved the form of popular Buddhism which
invoked the coming of one of the future Buddhas (although not
infrequently with an admixture of another religion, such as Taoism,
Islam, or even Christianity.) The doctrinal basis took off from the
orthodox Buddhist belief in reincarnation. Applied to the Buddha
himself, this implied that the Buddha had appeared many times before
and would come again many times in the future. Popular future
Buddhas included Maitreya, something of a power figure, and Amita-
bha (Amida); the latter became the focus of the most successful of all
popular Buddhist cults since it simplified the process of salvation down
to the faithful calling upon the name of Amida Buddha himself to grant
mercy and rebirth in his heaven.

The Future Buddha movements were not necessarily political. Buddhism early became known in China in the third century A.D. by a mass
movement of persons taking vows to become reborn in the Buddhist
heaven, but this movement was entirely apolitical. And again, in the late
sixth and early seventh centuries, wandering prosetlytizers spread
Amidaist Buddhism widely throughout China, appealing to the lower
classes and penetrating the rural areas, which had never been exposed to
the sophisticated religions of the upper class. Yet although this was a
period of dynastic upheaval—the end of the period of divided states by

the conquests of the pro-Buddhist Sui Dynasty during 581 to 589, then a civil war ushering in the more secularist T'ang dynasty in 618 to 624—most of these were strictly religious movements, not political mobilization to take over the state (Ch'en 1964; Wright 1959). (Some millennial sects of this period, though, such as the "sect of the Three Stages" which flourished during the fighting of the 580s, preached a doctrine that the earthly dissolution had arrived, and was hostile to all government.) Why did these movements lack political ambition? The structural reason is that Chinese politics was not organized on a level at which a movement of peasants and the provincial lower classes could have had any political effect. The property structure of China was beginning to shift from a kind of state-socialism of officials and nobility owning serfs and slaves into the beginnings of a monetary economy that eventually would become a kind of private agrarian capitalism (Elvin 1973). It is only after this process was completed, by the 1300s, that we begin to see the series of religiously-based revolts that were a constant threat in the later dynasties.

Thus in the early 1300s, the White Lotus society (a Future Buddha secret society) was banned as politically subversive. From 1351 to 1358 a related group, the Red Turbans, carried out a full-scale revolt that brought the Yuan dynasty to an end. From 1795 to 1804, a White Lotus rebellion started the Ch'ing Dynasty on its downward course. From 1850 to 1873, the T'ai-ping rebellion, a syncretism of Buddhism and Christianity, nearly conquered all of China. And from 1900 to 1901, the Boxer rebellion, another syncretism, foreshadowed the end of the dynasty in 1911. What was notable about these rebellions was their degree of success. Peasant revolts are relatively frequent occurrances, especially in European and Russian history, but none of them ever succeeded in overthrowing a government. In China several dynasties fell in that fashion: the Yuan, as noted; the Ch'ing (although more as an aftershock of a century of such revolts); in between, the Ming dynasty fell in 1644 through another peasant revolt, although in this case it was organized by dissident officials rather than under leadership of a religious secret society. Not all peasant revolts in China took place under religious auspices but in general, those which were organized in that way had a much better record of success. How are we to explain this? In comparative perspective, two facts stand out.

One is that religiously organized mass movements of peasants did not come on the scene at all until the medieval period. This is true both for China and for Europe; interestingly enough, it is true both for political and non-political movements. It would appear that the conditions for activist mass movements in the countryside did not exist until some structural change had taken place which allowed this kind of mobilization. What structural conditions could be involved? One might well be that the agricultural communities had become organized by elementary market relations which broke down the familistic or feudal isolation of local production units. Although these peasant movements occurred long before the development of full-fledged capitalism, nevertheless there seems to be a correlation between the first peasant movements and the rise of rural market networks. A second factor is the full-scale development of the universalistic church itself. Thus in China, the first peasant movements were not political, but rather the result of the spread of the Amidaist salvation religion in the 500s and 600s A.D. In medieval Europe the peasant rebellions of the 1300s were preceded by the popular religious movements of the new monastic orders in the preceding two centuries, which transformed the early medieval church of localistic, rather magically-inclined ritual centers into an organization of genuinely national, and international, scope (Southern 1970).

Moreover, the economic explanation and the religious explanation of why peasant movements become possible may be related. In both early medieval China and Europe, it was the monasteries themselves that were on the cutting edge of the initial economic development, acting as a kind of corporate form for rural capitalism (Collins 1985). They helped create the market structure and transform the isolated rural units into an economic network, at the same time that they provided the long-distance organizational links that could mobilize mass movements. Such movements at first were likely to be purely religious rather than political. Later, once the structural forms were established, they could be used for other purposes: either merging political and religious movements, or going on to become purely political ones.

A second interesting fact is that peasant rebellions in China, including religiously-organized ones, were generally more successful than those in Europe. Why should this be so? I suspect that the reason may be that the Chinese state was actually more secular than those in the West, and that mass religion—primarily Buddhism—was structurally more independent. Thus Chinese popular religion had more leverage to mount an independent political assault on the state. In Europe, by contrast, the state was in some sense more "medieval," more closely fitting the ideal type of the religiously legitimated state. That is to say, European Christianity tended to be too tightly allied with the state, or at least with the elite social classes, to provide much organizational resources for a movement of rural protest. This is of course only a matter of degree, since peasant movements were mounted in Europe, sometimes under religious auspices; but they tended to remain localized and hence easy for the military aristocracy to put down, in contrast to China, where they were often organized on a nation-wide level (such as the White Lotus and Red Turban movements).

A modern lesson may lurk in this comparison. The greatest potential for political power on the part of religion is when it is most extensively organized independently of the state. Thus when a religious organization is a large-scale, national structure, it has the greatest possibility to challenge the state from outside. For this reason, the evolutionary theory that was once popular, according to which there is a long-run trend towards secularism in politics, is probably not tenable. It may be true that the modern state does not need religious legitimation, and as Parsons would have said, that religious and political organization become increasingly differentiated from each other. But this very separation of organizational resources is what gives religion the possibility of mobilizing rebellions against an existing regime. The use of the Catholic church to anchor rebellion in Poland, or of Islam to overthrow a secularizing shah in Iran, are not anachronistic phenomena. These kinds of mass movements would not have been characteristic of medieval societies with a strongly established church. They are not transitional phenomena on the road to "modernity." On the contrary, they may well be permanent structural features of modern politics.

Notes

1. The term "mystical" is decidedly not used here in its popular pejorative sense, but to refer to the practice of non-worldly meditation as the central religious phenomenon. The core of Buddhism, above all ancient Buddhism, (though not all subsequent Buddhisms) is "mystical" in precisely the latter sense.
2. It is often believed that Chinese monasteries were always located in the countryside, because of the allegedly eternal Chinese propensity to be close to nature. This is an anachronism. The original Buddhist monasteries, which gained in prominence from the 300s A.D. onwards, were heavily dependent on court patronage, and for the most part were located in or near the major cities. This was true initially of the Ch'an school as well, before what I have called the "Zen revolution". The only other exception was the Amidaist movement, which proselytized heavily among the lower social orders; but for that reason its monasteries, although decentralized,

were nevertheless located in populated places, not in the remote areas favored by the aristocratic Ch'an monks. See Ch'en (1964).

3. My classification cuts up the field differently than Weber's three types of religion-state relationship (theocracy, hierocracy, and caesaro-papism). Weber's types generally are subtypes within my type (2), the religiously legitimated state. The nearer these types approach to the fusion of religion with the state, however, the more they approach my type (1), religious/political identity. The crucial point to bear in mind in all cases is whether the religious gives autonomous organizational resources that can enter into, or take a stance on, state politics.

4. An argument put forward by the anthropologist Louis Dumont (1970), among others, denies that this type of analysis of the religion-politics relationship is appropriate for India. It is claimed that the fundamental cosmological outlook is itself religious, and that this outlook ordains that religion be separate from politics. Hence politics is the religiously legitimated duty of the kshatriya caste (or of kings in particular), while the brahman caste (or in Buddhism or Jainism, the monks) are explicitly a non-political part of the social order. Dumont rather contentiously claims that it is a peculiar ideological failing of the West that it cannot see hierarchy in other than secularly-based, coercive terms. But this argument rests on the assumption that symbolic or cultural patterns are primal and determinative, rather than themselves explainable in terms of social organization. The culturological position also tends to be ahistorical, assuming an unchanging cultural pattern for at least 3000 years of Indian history. This presentist bias is already severe enough in traditional Indian historiography, which has for ideological reasons projected later developments back into the Vedic past. It is easy to multiply examples of how the caste rules were violated (as well as molded) by circumstances: for example, there were numerous brahman kings, as well as kshatriya monks (like Gautama Buddha himself). My point is that rather than reifying a mythologized Hindu culture, one should see it as an historical product of particular organizational developments in the realm of both state and religious structure.

References

Chadwick, Henry. 1967. *The Early Church*. Baltimore: Penguin.
Ch'en, Kenneth. 1964. *Buddhism in China*. Princeton: Princeton University Press.

Collins, Randall. 1985. The weberian revolution of the high middle ages. *Weberian Sociological Theory*. New York: Cambridge University Press.

Dumont, Louis. 1970. *Homo Hierarchicus. The Caste System and its Implications*. Chicago: University of Chicago Press.

Dumoulin, Heinrich. 1963. *A History of Zen Buddhism*. Boston: Beacon Press.

Elvin, Mark. 1973. *The Pattern of the Chinese Past*. London: Methuen.

Harris, Marvin. 1974. *Cows, Pigs, Wars, and Witches. The Riddles of Culture*. New York: Random House.

Jones, A.H.M. 1959. Were ancient heresies national or social movements in disguise? *The Journal of Theological Studies*. New Series, 10, pt. 2:280–97.

Parsons, Talcott. 1966. *Societies: Comparative and Evolutionary Perspective*. Englewood Cliffs, N.J.: Prentice-Hall.

———. 1971. *The System of Modern Societies*. Englewood Cliffs, N.J.: Prentice-Hall.

Sansom, George. 1958. *A History of Japan to 1334*. Stanford: Stanford University Press.

———. 1961. *A History of Japan 1334–1615*. Stanford: Stanford University Press.

Southern, R.W. 1953. *The Making of the Middle Ages*. New Haven: Yale University Press.

———. 1970. *Western Society and the Church in the Middle Ages*. Baltimore: Penguin.

Weber, Max. 1951. *The religion of China*. Glencoe, IL.: Free Press. Originally published in *Archiv Fuer Sozialwissenschaft Und Sozialforschung*. 1916.

———. 1958. *The Religion of India*. Glencoe, IL.: Free Press. Originally published in *Archiv Fuer Sozialwissenschaft Und Sozialforschung*. 1916–17.

———. 1952. *Ancient Judaism*. New York: Free Press. Originally published in *Archiv Fuer Sozialwissenschaft Und Sozialforschung*. 1917–19.

———. 1963. *The Sociology of Religion*. Boston: Beacon Press.

Wright, Arthur F. 1959. *Buddhism in Chinese History*. Stanford: Stanford University Press.

14

A Comparative Perspective on Religion and Regime in Eastern Europe and the Soviet Union

JERRY G. PANKHURST

EASTERN Europe as we usually conceive of it today, is a geopolitical entity defined by communist party dominance and Soviet influence (Aspaturian 1979; Shoup 1974; Rakowska-Harmstone 1979). Even though these factors are relatively recent additions to the scene, their influence over life in the region is great, and they have implications that will undoubtedly affect the future of the region for some time to come. One of the major areas being affected is that of religious life.

In fact, the antireligious policies practiced by the regimes of Eastern Europe (including the Soviet Union) are one variety of the kinds of common experiences that unite the diverse national populations of the region. For the citizens of all of the nine nations behind the Iron Curtain, atheism and antireligion are realities that are felt every day, and they have a significance without parallel in non-communist countries.

At the same time, just as we should not facilely lump the East European nations together as if they were all alike, we must not make the mistake of thinking that atheism or antireligion means the same

272

thing in all the countries of the region. Each regime has developed its own variation on the Marxist model of atheism, and the diversity of East European religions and cultures leads, in turn, to a diversity of response to the Marxist programs. While each society has its peculiarities in the religious sphere, we can divide the nations up between those with very severe antireligious programs and those with more benign ones (Beeson 1982).

The Variation In Severity of Antireligious Programs

Though not without some problems in the religious sphere, the most tolerant regime in Eastern Europe is that of Yugoslavia (Alexander 1979; Ramet 1982; Remington 1979). Having successfully separated itself from the Warsaw Pact and from Soviet dominance, Yugoslavia is a marginal member of the East European community, but its communist policies provide a clear alternative to the militant Marxist atheism that is found elsewhere. The followers of its three main faiths, Catholicism, Orthodoxy, and Islam, enjoy a freedom which is the envy of the faithful in other communist countries.

On the other end of the spectrum of religious tolerance is the other marginal member of the East European community, Albania (Pano 1979; Prifti 1975; Tonnies 1982). For many years a Chinese client and geographically shielded from direct Soviet military intervention by the stubborn Yugoslavs, Albania now finds itself almost completely on its own in the world. Its long isolation had preserved the dictatorial system of Enver Hoxha (d. 1985) and allowed it to prosecute the most cruel campaign against religion. In 1967 the Hoxha regime declared Albania to be thoroughly atheist and outlawed all religious forms of behavior and association. Although the specifics of religious life in this least-developed country of Europe are little known, it is clear that the Orthodox, Catholic, and Muslim believers there are forced to carry on their religious life in the deepest secrecy or face severe sanctions, including death.

Between the extremes of Yugoslavia and Albania lie the other nations of Eastern Europe (Walters 1983). Nowhere in the region are the religious groups without their share of problems with the regimes. If we allow ourselves the luxury of simplification, we can put the German Democratic Republic (GDR) as the second most tolerant regime in the region, followed in no particular order by Bulgaria, Hungary, and Poland. The circumstances of tolerance and intolerance in these nations vary greatly. The East German situation is unique, with the regime avoiding major interference with the dominant Protestant church and permitting it to carry on its organizational life relatively freely within the framework of close contact with co-religionists in West Germany (Hall forthcoming; Hanhardt 1979; Oestreicher 1978; Ward 1978). Poland's level of tolerance (or, conversely, intolerance) grows from the regime's accommodation with a powerful nationalistic church (Heneghan 1977; Korbonski 1979); Bulgaria's from the regime's pragmatic recognition of the Orthodox church's central role in the preservation of national identity under Turkish domination and its general political pliancy (King 1979a). Hungary is a more complex case, but it has developed a liberal civility in religious affairs generally, whether viewed from the side of the churches or from the side of the regime, which mitigates against extensive persecution (Aczel 1977; Cserhati 1977; Kovats 1977; Kovrig 1979). In our ranking, Romania occupies a transitional position (Hitchins 1975; King 1979b, 145-67). Although the indigenous Orthodox church has gained considerable prerogatives for itself and is closely tied to the development of national identity, it is not without its dissenters. Other denominations have had a rougher time securing their rights.

On the strongly intolerant end of the spectrum, though not as severe as Albania, are Czechoslovakia (Hall forthcoming; Ulc 1979) and the Soviet Union (Lane 1978; 1981; Powell 1975; Rothenberg 1971). The Soviet position has had longer to evolve than any other, and has wavered between Stalinist terror and the current condition of clearly delimited tolerance (Pankhurst 1980). Religious dissenters have been subjected to harsh punishments at the same time that some concessions have been given to the officially recognized churches. A fairly broad underground religious life has evolved among all major religious faiths, including the Orthodox, the Baptists and other Protestants, the Catholics, and the Muslims, but the official churches and mosques provide a semblance of normalcy to which most of the faithful have reconciled themselves.

Czechoslovakia has retained a very conservative antireligious policy through most of the years of communist rule, but it became significantly more severe after the experiments with freedom during the "Czech Spring" of 1968 that led to the Soviet invasion. An active human rights movement in which Catholics have played a leading role has plagued the authorities and led to many cases of imprisonment and harassment.

In evaluating the level of tolerance evident in church-state relations in the various nations, it would be wise to keep in mind the fact that such a ranking is only relative, and that "tolerance" does not mean in any case the *absence* of antireligious pressure. With the regimes all accepting the tenets of ideological Marxist atheism, there is always some amount of pressure.

Though this thumbnail sketch of the religious situations of Eastern Europe requires considerable refinement, it indicates both some of the similarities and some of the peculiarities which characterize the religious spheres there. The task of this paper is to provide some conceptual order to the information we have about these societies and to provide some indications of the processes and mechanisms at work that provide either similarity or diversity of condition in the religious spheres.

There are two major ways to approach the situation of religious groups in communist nations. One is to consider the options and constraints influencing the regimes as they develop their policies regarding religion, the other is to look at the options and constraints affecting the churches as they try to find their places in the nations. In other words, one could start with the question of the religious policies of the regimes, or one could start with the political activities and roles of the churches. The following discussion begins with the former question and then shifts its focus to the latter one.

Religion And Atheism In Eastern Europe

Religious groups in the communist nations of Eastern Europe are engaged in an interest group competition with the state/parties or regimes for adherents and supporters. Such a competition is mandated in a minimal sense by the antireligious ideology of Marxism which guides the regimes. Official militant atheism has split the populations of these nations into supporters of the churches and supporters of the regimes. In each specific nation, we should count both the various religious groups present and the regime as interest groups, and we can stress the complex but interrelated party and state or governing interests of the communist regime by designating it a state/party. Conceptually, this view of the competition is closely in line with the notions of interest group competition presented by Ralf Dahrendorf (1959) who saw the conflict between such corporate groups as the religious groups or the state/parties as essentially competition over the locus of authority in the social system.

Because the regimes promote atheism as an acknowledged and recognized part of official policy, the nations may be called "state atheist nations." Such a designation indicates two important characteristics of the situation which require comment. First, the state/party has at its disposal a much greater number of political power resources such that it can overcome much of the resistance of other groups and dominate the state apparatus. Other groups, including religious groups, have important resources, but in the realm of political power, the state/parties have an overwhelming edge. Unlike the religious groups, the wielding of political power is the ultimate *raison d'être* of the state/party. Second, and conversely, as the group occupying the role of the state, the state/party possesses, virtually by definition, resources not available to the other groups resident in the society.

Being institutionalized as the state, the state/party has a range of prerogatives associated with government, including the control of the military and police forces, the management of the economy, and the ability to develop foreign ties and supportive relationships. It holds a very special place among competing groups. Nevertheless, for conceptual purposes it is still possible to refer to the state/party as an interest group in competition with other such groups as long as the special characteristics of its role as the state are acknowledged. These characteristics may, in fact, be seen as another variety of resources that the state/party brings to the interest group competition. (The issue of resources is briefly addressed again after further material is presented.)

Besides the strictly ideological source of the interest group competition between the churches and the state/parties, the competition has developed further on the basis of various other historical antagonisms which have been built up during the course of the struggle for power by the state/parties. Usually, the churches have initially sided with the status quo ante in diverse ways, and have therefore come into counter-revolutionary conflict with the eventually victorious communist movements.

Furthermore, communist state/parties all share a characteristic which makes the interest group competition between them and other groups especially problematic. That characteristic is their monopolistic practices. The Marxist-Leninist model followed by all the communist movements in Eastern Europe requires that the ruling communist party be unchallenged by other parties, movements or interest groups in the political, social and economic spheres. Vis à vis the churches, the state atheist regimes are "secular monopolies of the left" in which "the left wing state endeavours to replace religion by politics" (Martin 1978, 47). Insofar as religious groups offer another ideological model for their societies, they threaten this monopoly. In fact, the churches of Eastern Europe represent the only major legal institutions which directly countermand a central tenet of the Marxian ideology.

It should be noted that the former religious establishments have some historically based monopolistic tendencies of their own. Such former establishments include the Orthodox churches of Russia, Bulgaria, and Romania, the Roman Catholic church of Poland and, to a lesser extent, the German Protestant church (Martin). This historical orientation alone indicates additional sources for the clash of interests between many religious groups and the regimes during the initial struggle for power of the revolutionary era. On the other hand, whatever monopolistic impulse the religious groups may have had has, during the last thirty years or so, been largely restricted to the desire to control the religious sphere rather than the whole of society, as is the case for the state/parties.

Taking hints from Georg Simmel and Lewis Coser (Coser 1956), let us examine this conflict relationship further, for it is basic to an understanding of the religious situations in the East European countries. My approach to this question is essentially utilitarian, seeing the motives on both sides of the competition as based in the desire to increase some kind of utility in the service of their own interests.

Before proceeding, some definitional clarification may be useful. As with the approach to resources that was indicated above, the focus on utility should not preclude an understanding of the broader contextual phenomena out of which utility arises. In the interest group competition between the state/parties and the religious groups, utility is gained partly by garnering the support of portions of the population because they perceive shared values with one of the competing groups. One must stress the *perception* of sharing values, for it is possible that the popular choice of which group to support and how strongly is based not on the distinctiveness of the values of the groups *per se* as on the perception of the genuineness of the implementation of the values in the behaviors of the competing groups. (In fact, as will be argued, the population adheres to values which are represented by both religious groups and the state/parties.) On the one hand, values underlie the "popular preferences" for change which motivate choice in the population, and, on the other hand, interest groups pursue interests which embody, in part, the group's values. More specifically, however, interests represent the self-preservation needs and goals for growth of a corporate group, and are analytically distinguishable from its values. Furthermore, though values may be sponsored by one or another group, they are essentially emotional and attitudinal qualities in the population; interests are particular to corporate groups and refer to the groups' organizational viability.

The Dynamics Of Legitimacy And Efficacy

First, we must ask what the regimes want. On a fundamental level, the regimes struggle for authority so as to gain efficacy. Efficacy is the ability to get done the job that they deem needs to be done. That job, by and large, is the job of socio-economic development, particularly as that development raises the relative prestige of their nations in the international status hierarchy. Not only is this the common quest of nations for greater honor among other nations, but in the East European communist cases it is also a quest to prove an ideological point about the superiority of socialism, in the communist mold, over other forms of government and economic organization. It should be noted that raising the standard of living through development and gaining international prestige for one's homeland are goals not without significant appeal for members of a national population. In this sense, we can assert that the state/parties are pursuing some goals consistent with a considerable body of "popular preference for change," to use the term of McCarthy and Zald (1977, 1212–41) for describing the basis for social movements upon which social movement organizations (or SMOs) are built. A state/party may be considered a social movement organization in this sense.

By introducing the terminology of utilitarian social movement theory, the dynamic nature of the situation is stressed. The periodic political upheavals in Eastern Europe indicate that the region is still not politically stabilized, and the competition between the state/parties and the religious groups plays a central role in this instability. Such instability reflects the inadequate institutionalization of the regimes and, consequently, their inability over time to pursue consistently a long-term development strategy. That is, they have not achieved the efficacy that they desire. Underlying this problem of the regimes is the problem of legitimacy.

The connection between efficacy and legitimacy can be seen by asking the question, how do the regimes of Eastern Europe get efficacy? After acknowledging that each country has its own special set of natural and other resources with which to work, there are only two options for achieving degrees of efficacy in prosecuting national development. Both options involve putting together a set of inducements for the population, or significant portions of the population, to join with the regime in its program. The first option is to induce the population to work together on the job of development through the use of coercion, force, or violence. The second option is to provide inducements based on the legitimacy of the regime. Most fundamentally, gaining legitimacy requires that the regime garner the trust and confidence of the people to a sufficient degree so that the government is seen as appropriate to govern and not appropriate to overthrow. In large part such trust and confidence depends upon the popular perception of shared values with the state/party.

The coercive option can be effective, at least for a time. The example of the forced mobilization of the Soviet Union under Stalin during the 1930s, in particular, indicates that coercion may play an important role in securing rapid and extensive development. However, it must be acknowledged that coercion was not the only inducement for popular assistance in attaining regime goals. A recognizable amount of legitimacy was developed by the Stalinist regime to encourage popular exertions for national development. To note that a considerable portion of the Stalinist legitimacy was built upon skillful use of propaganda and agitation does not negate the fact that people worked for development, often with great personal sacrifice, in part because they viewed it as a patriotic duty and an appropriate service to the homeland. The *perception* of shared values is again highlighted. Although the "homeland" may have been epitomized by the dictator, Stalin, so that devotion to him symbolically equalled devotion to the homeland, the result was some sort of ersatz legitimacy, but legitimacy nonetheless.

One could argue that such legitimacy was so ersatz as to negate the usefulness of the term legitimacy because it was also built upon a significant component of fear. Without denying the fact of widespread fear under Stalin, one also has to recall that, as shown in the Harvard Project Studies of displaced persons following World War II (Inkeles and Bauer 1968), members of the older generations who felt the fear most directly often hid that fear component from their children, and brought them up with a tolerance of the regime's developmental activities. Furthermore, however ersatz the legitimacy so gained, the personal loss felt by many when Stalin died in 1953 indicates the strength of commitment he inspired. A useful portrayal of this feeling is found in the profile of the dissenter Mikhail Meerson-Aksyonov (Kirk, 1975).

In the long run it is apparent that efficacy can only be achieved when there grows up a considerable measure of real legitimacy that ascribes to the present regime the right to govern and to lead the process of development. Stalinism has been recurrent but short-lived all over Eastern Europe, with the exception of Albania—an exception that proves the rule. (Albania is the least developed and most insular country of Europe.) It is in the evolution of regime legitimacy that the religious groups play an especially important role. If the regime is to gain legitimacy from a religious population, it must not be seen as in total conflict with religion.

What, then, do the religious groups want? They certainly are built upon a popular preference for enlarging the influence of religion, and each individual religious group builds up its own social movement organizations (SMOs) ranging from the national church organizations to the various associations of believers for special purposes. Like the state/parties, the churches and associations of the religious groups have goals that somehow serve the popular preference for religion in the specific forms taken by the particular religion. In general, the religious groups seek, first, to preserve their own privileges and prerogatives vis à vis religion per se. On a minimal level, this takes the form of preserving religious civil rights as perceived by each religious group. In a broader perspective, however, the religious groups are also striving to keep or gain a share of participation in determining the direction their nations take in development. While pursuit of this objective represents an interest of the religious groups, it also ties the groups' interests in with the values of portions of the population.

No religion is without some image of the kind of society within which it wants to exist, and, though this image may be more or less latent in the formal pronouncements of the spokespersons for the religious group, it necessarily implies some attitude of the religious public toward the secular order with which the religion seeks to come to terms. Insofar as the religious groups are perceived by religious people as implementing such a value orientation, they will gain popular support and adherence.

If this description of the goals of the regimes and the religious groups is basically correct, the conflict between them boils down, in each of the diverse national settings, to the fact that in various specific ways, the religious groups inhibit the quest for efficacy of the regimes, and, conversely, the regimes inhibit the efforts of religious groups to secure putative rights and participate in national development.

Coercion And Legitimacy

It may be obvious why religious groups in state atheist nations do support regime legitimacy in every way: (1) The antireligious parts of the Marxist ideology certainly do not encourage religious group support; (2) the loss of privilege, prerogatives, and rights in the revolutionary struggles that put communists in power do not lead to support; and (3) many religious groups will themselves have an ideology of development different from the regime, perhaps one more consistent with capitalism.

On the other hand, we must also recognize that there are reasons why religious groups might support the legitimization of the communist regimes. First, if the religious group is led to acknowledge the security of the regime in power, for whatever reason—for example, because they see the regime as backed up by the military might of the Soviet army—then it might support regime legitimization out of a desire for self-preservation. If the coercive strength of the regime is seen as so great, then a religious group may well strive to find a means to come to terms with the regime by granting it at least partial legitimacy in order to insure its own survival, even if the costs from its perspective are considerable. The resulting legitimacy may be another version of the ersatz legitimacy discussed above, but as such a pattern persists over time, it gains a validity of its own, and succeeding generations come to accept this legitimacy as natural and appropriate. The Polish situation suggests another way in which ersatz legitimacy can be manifested. The uneven stance of the Polish church and population towards its state/ party, especially the uneven stance of notable figures like Lech Walesa and Cardinal Glemp, since the "Solidarity crisis" represents a wavering over the ascription of legitimacy to the state/party when the ersatz nature of such legitimacy is so apparent.

A second reason for the support by a religious group for the legitimization of a communist regime may be a sense of shared destiny. Some religious groups in Eastern Europe seem to see themselves and the state/party of their nations bound together with the people in the greater task of nation-building. The clearest example of this is Bulgaria, where the Orthodox Church and the regime have maintained relatively amicable relations since shortly after the communist takeover. A similar, though less complete, consensus of this type may be emerging in Hungary and, to a lesser extent, in East Germany. In these latter two cases, the presence of greater religious diversity in the population mediates against such a full accommodation as has taken place in Bulgaria.

With these two ways in which the religious groups might come to support the legitimization of communist regimes, we can see as the other side of the coin two ways in which the regimes might try to move religious groups toward support of legitimization. The first option is to institutionalize coercion to a degree that keeps the religious groups always in fear for their survival. To some degree, all East European regimes have done so. Again, however, it is clear that such an approach has diminishing returns over time. Furthermore, too much coercive pressure against the religious groups leads them more into direct opposition, perhaps motivated by a sense of martyrdom, than into cooperative support. Finally, the regimes have had to moderate their coercive actions against the churches in many cases simply because they have found the churches too strong themselves, and able to mobilize considerable support from the population which could not be neatly or easily crushed by force alone.

The regimes, insofar as they have come to view the religious groups as an ongoing part of the scene in their countries, naturally desire the cooperation of the religious groups in gaining the legitimacy they need. Thus, their second option is to coopt them into the nation-building process itself, or at least to protect major church privileges so that the church does not have cause to oppose the regime on major initiatives. In this way the churches see good cause to support the legitimization of the regimes through non-interference, if nothing else. After the initial period of opposition, this pattern was characteristic of the Polish situation until the mid-1970s, with Cardinal Wyszynski leading the church (not compliantly) in its *modus vivendi* with the state/party.

The paradox of the relationship between antireligious communist regimes and religious groups is striking. Each is involved in a sort of approach-avoidance syndrome. But before examining this syndrome more closely, it will be instructive to look more closely at the constraints on regime coercion against religious groups. Other things being equal, the bearers of a militant atheist ideology might be expected to resort to stronger measures of coercion against religious groups. Why has this not been so?

The first constraint against the application of more massive coercion is the internal constraint: There simply is too great a popular attachment to religion in most nations of the region to allow for a more massive onslaught against religion. To carry out too great an antirelig-ious program may threaten to bring on national disintegration in many countries. Since the communist leaderships presumably do not want to fight their revolutions repeatedly, having won power once, they seek some degree of non-coercive relationship for their own self-preservation. To some degree, then, there is a "terror" available for the use of the religious groups against the regimes. This basic fact cannot be ignored in our considerations. It might be argued that this "resource" for the religious groups is unimportant, since, no matter how popular, any upheaval against a communist regime will be met with the forces of the Soviet and Warsaw Pact armies. At the same time, however, for the particular national leaders, such an upheaval almost inevitably brings their ouster and the installation of new leaders. This pattern has been evident in the communist-era national crises of East Germany, Poland, Hungary, and Czechoslovakia. Hence, it behooves regime leaders to keep coercion at some manageable level lest their heads roll too.

Another major constraint on the exercise of coercion against religious groups is the potential for international criticism and sanctioning. The communist regimes are particularly sensitive to international sanctions because they are so intent on gaining international prestige for their nations and their system of government and economics. Economic sanctions have become especially important over the last decade, and promise to become even more important as the economies of the East European nations are further integrated into the international market. Although the general effectiveness of formal economic sanctioning, like the withdrawal of most favored nation status from Poland during the Solidarity crisis or the grain embargo against the Soviet Union following the invasion of Afghanistan, is open to debate; there seems to be consequential damage to trade with non-communist countries because a regime carries on a stringent antireligious policy. This has clearly affected Soviet trade with the United States in connection with the problem of Jewish emigration, and it could potentially be a problem in other circumstances. Formal international sanctions aside, one can speculate that, even in the interpersonal relations between trade representatives from the religious West and those from atheist Eastern Europe, strong religious persecution could become a source of uneasi-ness, at least. In any event, the unseemly situation created by the threat of trade disruption because of religious concerns is something that the regimes of Eastern Europe would like to avoid.

This constraint on coercion against religious groups is, of course, less effective if the societies and economies of the region are less integrated into international networks. If greatly isolated anyway, the given country might simply rely on aid from fellow members of the Council for Mutual Economic Assistance (CMEA, an economic organization of socialist countries) or go into deep isolation, rather than change its religious policies. The latter situation is clearly the case in Albania. (This suggests that, if other nations are interested in having any impact on the religious situations of the communist regimes, driving them out of the world community altogether is probably not the appropriate tactic.)

In the end, of course, communist religious policy is not the core concern of non-communist foreign policy nor of trade agreements. The effect of these influences on the religious situations of the nations of Eastern Europe can be, therefore, only indirect. On the other hand, communist religious policy is bound up with policy in many other spheres as well, and when concern for human rights or for other questions arises, religion is likely to be involved and to be affected by whatever policy steps are taken vis á vis a more general concern. Thus, the conditions of coercion and persecution may play a role along with other factors in policy determination.

What Is The Major Thrust In Regime Policy Regarding Religion Today?

The above considerations lead logically to the question of what is the major thrust in the religious policies of the regimes today. It seems clear that, specific cases of significant coercion notwithstanding, the general thrust of East European religious policy is in the direction of co-optation. While maintaining a modicum of antireligious pressure and restrictions on the range of options, the regimes seek to involve—and to some degree entangle—the churches in the national goals that the state/parties pursue. This may be seen as a more or less temporary tactical maneuver in the long-run struggle to eradicate the influence of religion through overwhelming religion with the ultimate success of the secular regimes. This would certainly be consistent with the Marxist-Leninist ideology. On the other hand, it may also represent a growing pragmatic accommodation to the persistence of religious attachments and religious group survivability. Such an accommodation may come to be assimilated into a revised ideological vision. Whichever the case may be, a strong tendency toward co-optation prevails at the present. Acknowledging considerable variation in the form a predominantly co-optative strategy takes in each country of the region, the only current exceptions to this pattern are Albania—the persistently Stalinist case—and Czechoslovakia. For reasons that will become apparent, one can view the Czechoslovak situation as essentially a temporary adaptation that will likely move progressively closer to the co-optative pattern over time.

The co-optative approach to religion is mandated by several factors influencing the East European regimes. First is the greater communication and interaction with non-communist nations. As noted, there are subtle and direct sanctions which can affect domestic policy decisions, and these become ever more important as these nations look increasingly outward for economic and political ties.

More importantly, having discovered that religion will not simply go away under socialism, the monopolistic aspirations of the regimes mandate that religious initiatives, like all public initiatives, be guided by the party and oriented to serve party goals. Just as, for example, a variety of native peasant and labor parties have been co-opted into the political structures of these nations under communist leadership, the state/parties strive to bring the churches under their umbrellas of guidance. For the regimes, the churches serve particularly important roles in international affairs. More concretely, the churches are expected to serve party interests in foreign policy through carrying on peace campaigns and representing the interests of socialism in such international forums as the World Council of Churches or the various international religious organizations. Domestically, the political roles of the churches are much more limited; these international functions seem to provide enough rationale for the state/parties to justify some accommodation. Nevertheless, there are some important domestic functions served by some of the East European churches. They can, for example, channel popular energy into the building of national identity where that may be somewhat weak, as in Bulgaria, or they may serve a more broadly regulative role, as in Poland or East Germany, where the church discipline seems to serve, in part, to contain or refocus anti-regime energies.

Ironically, the partial accommodation with the churches not only reshapes the churches themselves, but it also alters the regimes in some ways. By giving the churches some spheres of activity, the regimes have entered, perhaps, into an interactive relationship with the churches that will not leave the state/parties themselves untouched. They have acknowledged the only legally tolerated non-party interest group, and that already indicates some new conditions of state/party representation of special interests. Maintaining regularized relations with churches also establishes new offices of government and party which then can be bases for power and careerism within the official system. Eventually, if the relationship lasts long enough, the incursion of the church into the party and state structure may influence the state/party more adequately to develop popular representativeness. And on the functional level, the inclusion of the churches, even merely symbolically at first, in the purview of state/party activities adds a degree of creative and healthy diversification to a typically bureaucratized and rigidified regime structure.

These last notions become more plausible when the developmental stage of these nations is considered. They are becoming ever more complex social, political, and economic systems, and major sociological thinking suggests that the fully modern system requires a labor force that is more or less freely giving its labor. Stalinism may serve mass mobilization goals for a while, but it does not seem to fit with the needs of truly modern systems. It is too crude a stick with which to beat the population. Under the conditions of modern society, subtle sticks are needed, and even a carrot or two. Persecution does not sit well with a highly trained and expansive citizenry.

But What Of Coercion Today?

None of these considerations negate the fact that there is real and violent coercion present in some degree in virtually all of the East European state atheist nations. General patterns aside, there are Many religious prisoners of conscience in Eastern Europe, pastors are denied the right to preach, people are denied the right to worship where and as they please, and so on. One cannot gainsay the suffering that exists.

As we look at the cases of overt coercion or force against religion in Eastern Europe, three major targets of the state/parties seem to predominate. Each type of target represents a violation of the co-optative accommodation which the regimes perceive as the basis for current religious policy.

The first target for overt coercion are minor "radical" groups who preserve an old-fashioned, anti-socialist antagonism. Examples of this type are found primarily in the Soviet Union and include some Seventh-Day Adventists, secret Orthodox groups like the True Orthodox Christians or the True Orthodox Church, sectarian Uniates from the Ukraine (namely, the "Pokutnyky") and Jehovah's Witnesses.

Activists in such groups have faced imprisonment and direct police harassment.

Direct coercion is also aimed at those who resist co-optative pressures in favor of greater independence or autonomy for religious groups as political actors. Embracing the role of the prophet, these persons step beyond the limits of tolerance of the regimes. Perhaps the best example of this type of target is Aleksandr Solzhenitsyn, who was eventually expelled from the Soviet Union. Many other cases could be cited from the 1940s, 1950s, and early 1960s, perhaps the most notable being the Hungarian Cardinal Mindszenty who took refuge in the United States embassy in Budapest from 1956 until 1971. The fact that there are fewer such cases at present indicates the normalization of the status of religion that has generally taken place during the last two decades.

With regard to this second type of target for persecution, a note should be added on the Polish church, since it, more than any other religious group in Eastern Europe, has adopted a political role since the late 1970s. Under other circumstances, activists in the church may well have been persecuted much more severely for their occasionally outspoken statements and organizational activities. However, the general social upheaval of the Solidarity era, and the delicate position in which it placed the regime have given church spokespersons a bit more latitude for themselves. To be sure, they have faced considerable pressure from the government to moderate their stands, and many have done so in order to avoid a social chaos that might inspire the Soviet army to intervene. In essence, the Polish religious leaders have found themselves caught between the Scylla of societal disorganization which might ensue if they fought too hard for their own and their society's interests and the Charybdis of probable Soviet intervention which would occur if their followers actually heeded their more strenuous calls for justice. The result is highly modulated overt political aspirations for the church, a position that does not encourage the emergence of clear and consistent prophetic voices. As an institution, while sometimes very outspoken, at other times the church has kept quiet and maneuvered very cautiously through the political thicket. At the same time, more than any other religious group in the region, the Polish church can claim a political centrality which the regime must take into account in its own policy making. It has clearly taken on certain political functions, most notably the general management of the dissent and the oversight of an agricultural development fund.

Returning to the question of the major targets of overt regime persecution, by far the major type of target during the last two decades has been those religious activists who energetically seek putative civil rights of religion currently denied or restricted. These activists have pursued the religious life as if they were in free societies, not in state atheist ones. Baptists and Pentecostals in the Soviet Union, Romania, and Bulgaria and Catholics in Lithuania have been the object of police interest because they have insisted, for example, that children should be allowed to have formal religious training and should participate in all aspects of religious life. Members of these groups have chafed under the requirement that pastors must be officially certified by the authorities, that local congregations must be registered with the government, and that notification of services must be given to the authorities. They have also resisted limitations on the publication of religious literature, sometimes resorting to underground printing or smuggling of Bibles and spiritual books and pamphlets. In the Soviet Baptist case, the anger against those of their co-believers who accepted regime intervention in church affairs, such as the meddling in the appointments of senior presbyters, led a large contingent of the church to separate themselves into an autonomous body which, perforce, has operated underground. Often referred to as the Reform Baptists, this SMO of the Baptist group has persisted for two decades, although it appears now to be losing some of its appeal for Soviet Baptists as the status of the official church has become somewhat more bearable and as the life under-ground has become more onerous. All Reform Baptist leaders have repeatedly experienced arrest and imprisonment, and its nominal head, Georgi Vins was deported to the United States in 1979 as part of a prisoner exchange with the Soviet Union.

Often allied with or participating in broader human rights move-ments in Eastern Europe, the problems of this third type of religious group activist have risen and fallen with the broader human rights experience (Walters 1983). In Czechoslovakia the widespread involve-ment of Catholics in the Charter 77 movement, one of the three major spokesmen of which has been the Catholic philosopher Vaclav Benda, has led to numerous forms of harassment and imprisonment. Orthodox activists in the Soviet Union created a Christian Committee for the Defense of Believers Rights which was linked with the Democratic Movement in surveillance of human rights problems, and the leaders of both movements are now all in prison or in exile. The Catholic Committee for the Defense of Believers Rights in Lithuania has found itself the object of great official restriction, but it has steadfastly persisted and stubbornly defended its leaders, including several important clergymen. A similar committee in Romania that is spearheaded by Baptists has come under stringent police restraints, and the Orthodox priest Gheorghe Calciu, who has been an outspoken proponent of human rights, is imprisoned.

Numerous other examples of this type could be cited. Though the problem is less acute elsewhere, in the Soviet Union alone, the 300 to 400 known Christian prisoners are primarily of this type. There and elsewhere, however, the nature of state/party treatment should be explained. In almost all cases, the object of overt coercion is said by the regime to be engaged in anti-regime activities. This reasoning is apparently meant to appeal to the modicum of legitimacy that these regimes have gained and to build upon it the basis for further co-optation of religious actors. Presumably, such actors are expected to see that if they adopt a stance of prudent religiosity, they may continue to pursue their message of salvation to a reasonable degree; if they overstep fairly well-understood boundaries, however, they risk reducing their range of activity to zero because of official sanctions. As some are persecuted, those who adopt the "prudent" stance are allowed to continue preaching, worshiping, and otherwise carrying out the essential core of religious life.

In effect, the regimes' persecutions seem to be aimed at excluding religious activism from the range of behaviors appropriate for citizens. By converting religious activists into violators of the laws of the lands, the regimes hope to encourage most people who persist in their religious concerns to circumscribe those concerns within the co-optative framework of the legally recognized churches where they are ideologically less dangerous and more manageable. At the same time, the officially recognized churches must strive to balance their pursuit of religious interests with the need to keep a legitimate public face. While they may try to expand the range of options for themselves, they also must try to convince their adherents that what they have now is better than the activist option in that it preserves the essential core in the face of an antagonistic ideology and allows the churches some input into the life of civil society. This latter thrust is important, for it indicates that the churches play some role in the national development, which is a popular interest, and have a means to fulfill their own expectations that they participate in the building of a better society.

The religious groups and the regimes are caught in an approach-avoidance syndrome. Each interest group, mustering the resources available to it, tries both to win the population over to its side and, on the other hand, to join with its competitor in the common cause of national development. Because it is an approach-avoidance syndrome, there is a continuing uncertainty as to the attitude of the competitor toward any specific initiative that one interest group takes. Thus, the religious situations in Eastern Europe are relatively unstable and changeable within certain broad limits specific to each country. But that very changeableness represents the quandary each side faces in relating to the other.

The relationship between state/parties and religious groups in the state atheist nations of Eastern Europe is not a balanced one, since each side has differential resources which it brings to the interest group competition. The balance of resources varies a great deal from country to country, but one stable resource category for all the state/parties is their monopoly of the means of coercion and, more generally, of political power resources. This gives the state/parties a greater influence in determining the level of activity permitted to the religious groups under a condition of normalization. Nevertheless, the religious groups bring to the competition with the state/parties considerable resources of other types. The exact form and potency varies from religious group to religious group, but one could count the traditional popular attachments to religion as a type of resource (which varies from setting to setting). Such attachments are often based in the historical roles of the churches and tied up with national identity or the local nationalism of particular sub-populations. Other kinds of resources possessed in no mean portion by the religious groups include their contributions to the aesthetic styles of their societies, their own organizational abilities and characteristics, their significant contacts with foreign influences which may facilitate certain aspects of state relations abroad, and the like (Pankhurst 1984).

Options And Constraints For Religious Groups

Numerous examples of religious group activities have already been given, and space limitations do not permit development of a complete picture of church-state relations for every society and each religious group within the society. Instead, this section will focus on the options and constraints for religious interest groups as they seek to find roles of influence within their societies. It begins by presenting a list of group-centered variables that condition the social activism of a religious group. A discussion of these variables as they fit into the matrix of influences in Eastern Europe will conclude the paper.

The variables below, which involve the strength of religious groups in the interest group competition they experience in their national settings, are implied in the preceding discussion of the role of state/ parties in Eastern Europe. The list is probably not exhaustive, but it is hoped that the most important bases for variation among religious groups are included. On the basis of this list and subsequent discussion, we can suggest some hypotheses as to why there is so much effective religious activism in some countries while in others there is so little.

It should be noted that the list as a whole takes into consideration the interactive patterns between the regimes, the national populations and the religious groups. The context of action is accounted for. In turn, some of the variables refer specifically to the resources centered in the religious group itself, some relate to the population's popular preferences, and others stress more strongly the interaction between the state/party and the religious group. Thus, "group structure variables" describe potential internal or structural resources that religious groups may possess; "popular preference variables" account for the popular preferences in the society as they may relate to the religious group; and "political context variables" refer to possible advantages a religious group may have because of its relationship with the regime.

Note that the outcome of an interest group competition depends upon the balance of resources among all competing groups. The state/party's possible resources are not indicated here, though they have been mentioned in the prior discussion, and they must be kept in mind in what follows. In addition, religious groups compete with each other in significant ways. Therefore, the balance of resources between religious groups in the same society is an issue in some cases.

Religious Interest Group Variables

1. Number of Adherents of Religious Group.
2. Proportion of Nation's Population that Are Adherents to Religious Group.
3. Strength of Tie Between Ethnic or National Identity and the Religious Group.
4. Organizational Structure of Religious Group, in Particular, Level of Hierarchization or Bureaucratization.
5. Type of Historical Relationship Between the Pre-Communist Government and the Religious Group. That is, was the church the prior establishment; was it legal or illegal; was it active in politics under the old regime; etc.?
6. Strength of Ties with Groups Outside the Communist Bloc That Have Policy Relevance for the State/Party. Specifically, does the

TABLE 1 Factors Influencing the Ability of Major Religious
Groups in East European Nations to Develop a Role of
Social Influence[a].

	1. Number of Adherents	2. % of Pop.	3. Ethnic or Nat. Tie?	4. Hier- archi- zation	5. Pre- Comm. Tie?	6. Ex Tie
ALBANIA	population = 2,831,000					
Muslims	580,000	20.5	NN	weak	no	no
BULGARIA	population = 9,075,000					
Orthodox	5,737,570	63.2	CNS	strong	yes	we
Muslims	962,000	10.6	NN	weak	no	we
CZECHOSLOVAKIA	population = 15,189,000					
Roman Catholics	10,041,400	66.1	CNS	strong	no	str
Protestants	1,139,200	7.5	MN	weak	no	no

[Major denominations: Czechoslovak Hussite Church (650,000
members), Slovak Evangelical Church of the Augsburg
Confession (510,000), Evangelical Church of Czech Brethren
(295,354) and the Reformed Christian Church in Slovakia
(165,000).[c]]

GERMAN DEM. REP.	population = 17,358,000					
Protestants	9,535,300	54.9	CNS	weak	yes	str

[Major denominations: the Federation of Evangelical Churches
vastly outnumbers all other denominations with its
membership at more than ten million.[c]]

Roman Catholics	1,267,100	7.3	NN	strong	no	str
HUNGARY	population = 10,721,000					
Roman Catholics	6,284,480	58.6	CNW	strong	yes	str
Protestants	2,562,300	23.9	CNW	weak	no	we

[Major denominations: Reformed Church of Hungary
(1,950,000 members) and Evangelical Lutheran Church
(450,000).[c]]

POLAND	population = 35,316,000					
Roman Catholics	31,148,700	88.2	CNS	strong	yes	strong

ROMANIA	population = 22,057,000					
Orthodox	17,398,340	78.9	CNS	strong	yes	weak
Protestants	1,690,000	7.7	MN	weak	no	weak

[Major denomination: Reformed Church of Romania (693,511 members), Baptist Union of Romania (250,000), Pentecostal Churches (200,000), Evangelical Church of the Augsburg Confession (184,000) and Christian Brethren (120,000).[c]]

Roman Catholics	1,360,000	6.2	MN	strong	no	strong

USSR	population = 268,115,000					
Orthodox	84,188,000	31.4	CNS	strong	yes	weak
Muslims	30,297,000	11.3	MN	weak	no	weak

YUGOSLAVIA	population = 22,299,000					
Orthodox	8,607,000	38.6	CNS[d]	strong	yes	weak
Roman Catholics	7,403,000	33.2	CNS[d]	strong	no	strong
Muslims	2,319,000	10.4	MN	weak	no	weak

KEY
1. Number of Adherents of Church or Religion[b].
2. Percent of Population That Is Affiliated with Church or Religion[b].
3. Ethnic or National Tie with Church?
   CNS = Central Nationality, Strong Tie
   CNW = Central Nationality, Weak Tie
   MN = Minority Nationality Tie
   NN = No Significant Nationality Tie or Diverse Ethnic Ties
4. Strength of Hierarchization of Church Organization. (strong, weak)
5. Church Tied with Pre-Communist Government? (yes, no)
6. Strength of External Ties of Church. (strong, weak, none significant)

NOTES:

[a]All numerical data are for mid-1980 and are taken from the *World Christian Encyclopedia*, ed. David B. Barrett (New York: Oxford University Press, 1982). Information is provided only for those religious groups that comprise five percent or more of the population of a nation.

religious group have international support that makes a difference
to the state/party?

For easy reference, the status of each major religious group on each of
the preceding variables is summarized in Table 1. The table lists all
religious groups in Eastern Europe that comprise five percent or more
of their home nation's population.

Other variables, though not amenable to presentation in this tabular
format, may also have some significance for the interest group conflict
in the religious sphere of East European nations.

7. Segmentation of the Religious Sphere of the Society. That is, how
   many significant religious groups exist in the society? (This is
   partially indicated in Table 1 by the number of groups that are
   listed for each country.)

8. Type of Traditional or Dominant Theological Perspective on
   Government and Politics. Though there may be significant variation from group to group, it is most relevant for present purposes
   to note that Orthodox churches have seldom developed a political
   stance autonomous from that of the state within which they have
   existed. This is probably related to their constitution as separate
   national churches tutored in the Byzantine tradition of "symphonia" or harmonious relations with the political authorities.
   Such a doctrine is not found in Roman Catholicism, nor in most
   Protestant churches, though they all possess relevant theologies of
   politics and church-state relations. (The complexities of this variable will have to be treated elsewhere.)

9. Nature of Popular Piety in a Given Nation. In particular, is the
   population well informed in theology; is it saturated with strong
   and clear religious symbolism; is faith personally held or is it
   largely ritualistic; etc.?

10. Relationship Between a Religious Group and Other Important
    Interest Groups in the Society. In particular, has the religious
    group established a positive relationship with organized labor or
    the agricultural population or the intelligentsia? More concretely,
    what other groups provide organized support for the religious
    group?

To summarize this list, the three types of variables defined above may
now be specified:

Group Structure Variables include number of adherents (var. 1),
proportion of population (var. 2), and hierarchization (var. 4).

ᵇData for columns 1. and 2. are taken from Table 1. of each of the country summaries in the *World Christian Encyclopedia*. Both columns refer to the category "affiliated" in the *Encyclopedia*. Specific page citations by country are as follows: Albania, p. 134; Bulgaria, p. 199; Czechoslovakia, p. 258; German Democratic Republic, p. 310; Hungary, p. 364; Poland, p. 569; Romania, p. 584; USSR, p. 689; Yugoslavia, p. 753.

ᶜMembership corresponds with the "Affiliated" category on Table 2 for each country in the *World Christian Encyclopedia*. Specific page citations by country are as follows: Czechoslovakia, p. 262; GDR, p. 313; Hungary, p. 367; Romania, p. 588. The reason for the discrepancy between the total number of East German adherents and the membership of the Federation of Evangelical churches is not known. Though linked together in a federation, this group encompasses a great deal of diversity in liturgy and tradition within its eight regional member churches.

ᵈThe two largest and strongest nationalities in Yugoslavia are the Serbs and the Croats. The Orthodox Church tends to represent the Serbian nationality and the Roman Catholic church gains support from Croatian nationalism. Since both are very important, both the Orthodox and Roman Catholic churches are given a high score for central nationality tie.

Popular Preference Variables include ethnic or national ties (var. 3), segmentation of religious sphere (var. 7), popular piety (var. 9), and ties with other interest groups (var. 10).

Political Context Variables include pre-communist tie (var. 5), external ties (var. 6), and theological perspective on government (var. 8).

The Comparative Strengths of Religious Groups in Eastern Europe

It is now possible to contemplate a kind of balance sheet that weighs the relative strengths and weaknesses of the various religious groups in the various societies of Eastern Europe. In principle, this will allow us to hypothesize as to why, for example, the social and political role of the Polish Catholic church—and the associated activism of its adherents and leaders—is so much greater than, say, the similar role of the Bulgarian or the Soviet Orthodox church. What are the comparative strengths of the Polish church?

First, these three cases have several notable similarities. They were all pre-communist establishments which were deeply involved in the political sphere of the status quo ante (var. 5), they are all very large in number of adherents (var. 1), and they are all hierarchically and bureaucratically organized (var. 4), the latter possibly giving greater ability for disciplined coordination of actions than in a decentralized church. In addition, all three have deep ties to national identities (var. 3). However, this last potential asset is undermined for the Russian Orthodox by the fact that the Soviet Union is a multi-ethnic and multi-religious nation, with several other ethnic and religious groups able to exert some influence upon the regime for their own interests in at least partial competition with the Orthodox group (vars. 7 and 10). Although ecumenism would bolster the combined strength of two or more interest groups in Soviet society, any substantial efforts along this line are suppressed by the regime. Even though the Russian Orthodox church is tied to the dominant ethnic identity and receives favored treatment in certain largely symbolic ways, it has not been able to muster this resource in sufficient quantity to support significant expansion of its national role.

The Bulgarian and Russian Orthodox churches (and the Romanian could be added to the list) also share a distinct weakness as compared to the Polish Catholics on variables 8 and 9. Caesaro-Papism (or "right-wing religious monopoly," to use David Martin's term) was institutionalized in the Eastern Orthodox churches from ancient times, and the loss of the Bulgarian and Russian tsars (Slavic for Caesar) was extremely disorienting for these churches (a problem with var. 5). Led by a theology of "symphonia," these churches were hard pressed to establish a clear position in a state which directly rejected their legitimacy. The Russian church, in particular, had been so entangled with the distasteful politics of the last tsars that its call for a legitimate position in a new society rang hollow. Furthermore, it could not rely upon a deeply institutionalized spirituality of the people (var. 9), a quality which it had tended to neglect for the two centuries before the Revolution of 1917. While the popular tie with the church was strongly ritualized, it did not have great depth of content. The Bulgarians had some compensation in the unity of national identity which they had steadfastly championed (var. 3), and they had the luxury of being relatively unchallenged by other religious groups for the allegiance of the people.

On all these accounts, however, the Polish church comes out as comparatively strong. It has preserved national identity through a long history of endangerment and subjugation. It began the communist era as the champion of a free Poland following the disastrous experience of World War II, and it had the recent experience of massive threat to survival to draw upon. It also treasured the deeply felt allegiance of the vast majority of the Polish population, a proportionality enhanced by the way the borders were drawn after the war. Furthermore, it found itself in a position to mediate between a comparatively weaker regime (than the Bulgarian one) and a populus frequently hostile to that regime. In this role, the church forged strong links with other interest groups in Polish society, notably the workers, peasants, and intelligentsia (var. 10). Thus, the church gained a unique role *vis à vis* the regime.

Finally, it should be noted that at various times, the church has been aided by implied or direct aid from abroad (var. 6), primarily from the large Polish diaspora in the United States—a "significant other" for the regime—and from the international Catholic church itself.

No other church in Eastern Europe has a level of national prestige and honor comparable with that of the Polish church, and to the degree that the other churches have less, they have been less able to support social activism and to influence regime policies. Even though the German Democratic Republic and Yugoslavia have less severe religious situations in general, the churches there have not developed their political roles to a comparable extent. One reason is that in neither of these countries does a single church hold the allegiance of so large a proportion of the population. In Yugoslavia religion and ethnicity are strongly related, but each religion and each ethnicity is engaged in considerable competition for rights and privileges with other major groups (var. 7). The positive conditions for religion in Yugoslavia probably reflect not so much the strengths of the three major religions as the strengths of the inter-ethnic antagonisms which the regime has had to overcome. In addition, the Yugoslav regime has chosen a generally less Leninist approach to Marxism, and this choice has not been consistent with a strong antireligious stance. Finally, Yugoslavia has had to relate to a broader international arena than the other Soviet-tied regimes, and this has mediated against a strong antireligious campaign.

In East Germany, the inter-religious antagonisms have not been so strong, but the regime and the churches have had to join together in the quest to overcome the legacy of Nazism and to promote German national identity (var. 3). Furthermore, the Protestant church has served important functions in its intimate relations with co-religionists in West Germany (var. 6). These factors have lightened the burden of militant atheism for East German believers. Though it is probably appropriate to note that the theological stance of the East German church is rooted in state church Protestantism—a pattern which seldom encouraged strong social or political activism on its own—the experience of Nazi co-optation of the church has seemed to make the Germans especially sensitive to the political distortion of church prerogatives (var. 5). Currently, peace movement activism in the German Democratic Republic is centered around the church (Hall 1984). The Protestants, who have condemned Soviet as well as American militarization of Europe, have clearly been influenced in their activism by the West German peace movement. The Catholic hierarchy has also made strong statements on peace, apparently partly under the influence of the success of the Protestants, as well as its ties to West German Catholics and to the Vatican (var. 6).

Four cases remain to be considered directly in this section, and, although little justice can be done to each, the kind of reasoning pursued thus far provides a model for further treatment as that might become possible. First, Romania: This nation shares the problem of Orthodoxy as outlined for Russia and Bulgaria *vis à vis* the political role (vars. 8 and 9). This, along with the power of the central regime, are probably the main reasons for the lack of strong political activism from the church. The Romanian Orthodox church has retained a central position in the protection of national identity (var. 3) and has been granted considerable privilege by the regime. The personality of President Nicolae Ceausescu is implicated in all things political in this land, and his personal feelings about the church are certainly germane to this discussion.

Even more dominant than Ceausescu in his own country was Enver Hoxha of Albania, and his rigidly Stalinist approach in his isolated, underdeveloped land determined the religious silence there. Table 1 may be somewhat misleading regarding the religious group composition of Albania because it excludes groups comprising less than five percent of the population as of mid-1980. However, it is estimated that as late as 1953 the population included some 66.3 percent Muslims, 22.4 percent Orthodox and 11.2 percent Roman Catholics (World Christian Encyclopedia 1982). The mid-1980 figures—Muslims at 20.5 percent, Orthodox at 3.3 percent and Roman Catholics at 2.1

percent—represent the fruits of the great repression of religion, especially since 1967. In fact, national culture traditionally grew out of Muslim, Orthodox, and Catholic sources, although the Catholics had been given an aura of outsiders for historical reasons (vars. 2, 3, 5, 6, and 7). Islamic numerical strength in the country grew out of a series of mass conversions in the seventeenth and eighteenth centuries, and this suggests the possibility that popular piety may have relatively shallow roots (var. 9). Furthermore, the Muslim population is split between Sunni and Bektashi adherents (var. 7). Finally, it is also possible that Islamic faith is able to maintain a considerable hold on the people even if underground, and this may serve as an adequate adaptation (the alternative being political activism) to circumstances of extreme persecution.

The final cases are those of Hungary and Czechoslavakia. Both are religiously diverse (var. 7), though Catholics make up a considerable majority in each (var. 2). However, their religious situations are strongly contrasting. There seems to be greater religious social activism in Czechoslovakia, perhaps because the regime has been one of the most persistent in meddling in church affairs and trying to use the church to manipulate the difficult ethnic tensions between the Czechs and Slovaks (var. 3). Catholic support and leadership was central to the Charter 77 human rights movement, and the church has significant ties with other corporate groups (var. 10). Criticism of the regime has risen recently under the influence of the pronouncements of Pope John Paul II (6.), and the Czechoslovaks seem to be less secular in general than the Hungarians (var. 9).

As in economic policy, the Hungarians have taken a notably more liberal path than the Czechoslovaks, and, since the settlement of the Mindszenty affair in the early 1970s (related to the pre-communist dominance of the church, var. 5) the regime has normalized relations with the Catholic church. It has apparently enlisted the church in the general program of development to a considerable degree, though permitting it no special sphere of influence comparable to that of the Polish church. Politically critical activism among participants in "basis communities" has been criticized by the Catholic hierarchy; this movement represents not only an unviable stance for the church, but also a breach of church discipline. More generally, perhaps there is enough co-optative participation on the part of the church to satisfy the Catholic tendency to activism. Hungarian Reformed and Lutheran adherents and clergy, still perhaps hindered in relations with Catholics by the memory of Catholic Hapsburg rule (var. 7), maintain at present a generally co-operative stance toward the regime. Lutheran Bishop Karoly Toth serves in the government as Minister of Culture.

Hypotheses Regarding The Level Of Social Influence A Religious Group Can Exercise In An East European Society

Although there is a great deal more that could be said about each of the cases under discussion, it is now possible to formally state a series of hypotheses regarding the sources of a role of social influence for the religious groups of Eastern Europe. Each hypothesis that follows corresponds to one of the religious interest group variables identified above, and the numbers correspond to the variable numbers. As a hypothesis, each statement is problematic and subject to further, more detailed, empirical examination. Finally, it must also be remembered that the variables being treated here are intended to be seen in a network of interaction in which positive tendencies of one may be reduced or cancelled out by negative tendencies of another. In other words, a multivariate model is being proposed in which no single hypothesis can be seen as exclusively determinative.

1. *The greater the number of adherents a church possesses, the greater the potential for the church to wield social influence in its home society.* Little has been said in this paper in support of this hypothesis, though it underlies the discussion. The fact that certain smaller groups—the Soviet Baptists and the Czech Brethren come to mind—seem to have undue importance in their countries suggests that the hypothesis does not have universal applicability. On the other hand, the fact that these groups' position seems "undue" in itself supports the hypothesis as a general notion. Nevertheless, by focusing on dominant groups here, this issue has been sidestepped.

2. *The greater the proportion of the society's population which is made up of adherents of a religious group, the greater the social influence that given group may wield in the society.*

3. *The stronger the identification of a religious group with the central ethnic or national identity of a nation, the stronger will be its role of social influence in that nation.*

4. *Assuming autonomy from state pressure, the stronger the hierarchical organization of a church, the greater the potential for the leadership to mount activities of social influence. The less the level of autonomy, the greater the likelihood that the hierarchy will be co-opted by the regime.*

Co-optation, in turn, means that the church will be less able to engage in independent (i.e., unsponsored by the regime) social activism. Note that this conceptualization permits a religious hierarchy to lose autonomy but not be co-opted, as is the case in Albania, or it may lose autonomy and be co-opted, as in the Soviet Union. The likelihood of hierarchy cooptation by the regime depends upon other factors, most notably the orientation of the regime and of the religious group toward the use of power.

5. *The greater the involvement of the church with the state structure before the communist revolution or takeover, the greater will be the likelihood of the communist regime to impose structures on the social role of the churches in the name of preventing anti-state or counter-revolutionary activities.*

This hypothesis should hold most strongly for the period immediately following the communist takeover, less so as time passes after the takeover. Similarly, the churches that experienced discrimination or persecution at the hands of the prior regime will be more likely to engage in social activism under the communist regime, and the regime is more likely to allow such churches greater privileges, at least temporarily or from time to time, in exercising religious prerogatives.

6. *Churches in communist nations will be more likely to engage in social activism if they are part of, or are directly tied to, foreign or international organizations or groups that have policy relevance for the state/party and that can provide some form of support, direct or indirect, to the churches.*

Furthermore, the greater the policy relevance of the external organization or group for the state/party, the greater the potential for role enlargement for the churches associated with it.

7. *The greater the segmentation of the religious sphere in a society (that is, the greater the number of significant religious groups in the society), the less potential any single religious group will have for wielding social influence in the society.*

Note that coalitions of religious groups could potentially wield significant social influence, but insofar as such coalitions are inhibited in communist societies they are not central to present concerns. However, the Federation of Evangelical churches in the German Democratic Republic represents such a coalition which has itself become a denomination.

8. *Religious groups that possess an historical theology of "symphonia," namely, Orthodox groups, will be less likely to develop an active role of*

social influence than will groups not possessing—or possessing in lesser degrees—such a theological position.

"Symphonia" supports a harmonious relationship between the two institutions of church and state, not the absorption of one into the other. However, when faced with an ideologically hostile regime, the quest for such harmony may make adaptation particularly difficult. Such a theology was developed explicitly in Eastern Orthodoxy (Meyendorff 1962; 1978; Ware 1964), and this hypothesis, therefore, relates principally to the tendency against social activism among the Orthodox.

9. *The stronger and deeper the popular piety of a population, the greater the potential of the churches to exercise social influence in the society.*

It is very difficult to measure popular piety since, as intended here, it is not simply expressed in observance of religious rituals. The hypothesis suggests that ritualism itself, which may be retained in a formal sense even without broader expression of faith, may not foster social activism, but that intellectual and theological dimensions of faith may foster such activism.

10. *The stronger its bonds with other social interest groups (for example, organized labor, organized agriculture and the intelligentsia) in the society, the greater the likelihood that a religious group in a communist nation will enter into social activism.*

Concluding Remarks

As so frequently occurs in any comparative treatment of an important question, vast quantities of information are compressed into such a small format that one cannot use such a treatment alone to provide authoritative insight into any specific case. Single case studies, such as the ones upon which much of this paper is based, must be relied upon for greater detail and subtlety of analysis. Particularly lost in the system of this presentation has been a sense of the relationship minority religious groups have to the conditions of their homelands. One should not get the impression that there are only one or two churches in each East European country, nor that the condition of those churches fully represents the condition of all religious groups of significance. Also sacrificed here is the immediate feeling of the texture of everyday life that descriptive case studies provide.

The goal of this paper has been to find the general patterns which also have real effects upon religious life, and particularly social or political activism by the believers, in Eastern Europe. In the end, I have not developed a definitive analysis, but rather a conceptual approach and a series of interrelated hypotheses that can be explored in further research.

In conclusion, one central idea of my comparative approach seems worth stressing. It is that, in the relations between religion and regime in Eastern Europe, there is always a point of dynamic tension that is moving away from the location at which it was just found. Thus, to describe the religious situation in Eastern Europe is always to describe some bit of history now past.

Certainly, there are aspects of relative stability, but in the long run there is more change than stasis evident. Political and social crises come and go, and each, in turn, alters the balance between the religious and regime interests of the country. More fundamentally, beneath the surface of each crisis there is a build-up of tensions that reflects the underlying conflicts and competitions that I have tried to identify in this paper. If we understand these underlying factors clearly, the potentialities for the future are more within our grasp, and the conditions that might influence one or another outcome for the religious groups in the region can be more adequately predicted.

References

Aczel, Gyorgy. 1977. The socialist state and the churches in Hungary. *New Hungarian Quarterly* 18, no. 66: 49–62.

Alexander, Stella. 1979. *Church and State in Yugoslavia Since 1945*. Cambridge: Cambridge University Press.

Aspaturian, Vernon V. 1979. Eastern Europe in world perspective. *Communism in Eastern Europe*. Ed. Teresa Rakowska-Harmstone and Andrew Gyorgy, 1–36. Bloomington: Indiana University Press.

Beeson, Trevor. 1982. *Discretion and Valor: Religious Conditions in Russia and Eastern Europe*. Rev. Ed. London: Collins/Fount.

Cserhati, Jozsef. 1977. The open gates. *New Hungarian Quarterly* 19, no. 67: 48–62.

Coser, Lewis A. 1956. *The Functions of Social Conflict*. Glencoe, Ill.: Free Press.

Dahrendorf, Ralf. 1959. *Class and Class Conflict in Industrial Society*. Stanford: Stanford University Press.

Hall, B. Welling. Forthcoming. The Church and the independent peace movement in Eastern Europe. *Journal of Peace Research*.

Hanhardt, Arthur M., Jr. 1979. German Democratic Republic. *Communism in Eastern Europe*. Ed. Teresa Rakowska-Harmstone and Andrew Gyorgy, 121–44. Bloomington: Indiana University Press.

Heneghan, Thomas E. 1977. The loyal opposition: Party programs and church response in Poland. *Eastern Europe's Uncertain Future*. Ed. R. B. King and J. F. Brown, 286–300. New York: Praeger.

Hitchins, Keith. 1975. The Romanian Orthodox Church and the state. *Religion and Atheism in the USSR and Eastern Europe*. Ed. B. R. Bociurkiw and J. W. Strong, 314–27. Toronto: University of Toronto Press.

Inkeles, Alex, and Raymond Bauer. [1959] 1968. *The Soviet Citizen: Daily Life in a Totalitarian Society*. New York: Atheneum, 1968.

King, Robert R. 1979a. Bulgaria. *Communism in Eastern Europe*. Ed. Teresa Rakowska-Harmstone and Andrew Gyorgy, 168–88. Bloomington: Indiana University Press.

———. 1979b. Romania. *Communism in Eastern Europe*. Ed. Teresa Rakowska-Harmstone and Andrew Gyorgy, 145–67. Bloomington: Indiana University Press.

Kirk, Irina. 1975. *Profiles in Russian Resistance*. New York: Quadrangle.

Korbonski, Andrzej. 1979. Poland. *Communism in Eastern Europe*. Ed. Teresa Rakowska-Harmstone and Andrew Gyorgy, 37–70. Bloomington: Indiana University Press.

Kovats, Charles E. 1977. The path of church-state reconciliation in Hungary. *Eastern Europe's Uncertain Future*. Ed. R. R. King and J. F. Brown, 301–311. New York: Praeger.

Kovrig, Bennett. 1979. Hungary. *Communism in Eastern Europe*. Ed. Teresa Rakowska-Harmstone and Andrew Gyorgy, 71–99. Bloomington: Indiana University Press.

Lane, Christel. 1978. *Christian Religion in the Soviet Union: A Sociological Study*. Albany: State University of New York Press.

———. 1981. *The Rites of Rulers: Ritual in Industrial Society—The Soviet Case*. Cambridge: Cambridge University Press.

Martin, David. 1978. *A General Theory of Secularization*. Oxford: Blackwell.

McCarthy, John D., and Mayer N. Zald. 1977. Resource mobilization and social movements: A partial theory. *American Journal of Sociology* 82, no. 6: 1212–41.

Meyendorff, John. 1962. *The Orthodox Church: Its Past and its Role in the World Today*. New York: Pantheon Books.

———. 1978. Russian bishops and church reform in 1905. *Russian*

Orthodoxy Under the Old Regime. Ed. R. L. Nichols and T. G. Stavrou, 170–82. Minneapolis: University of Minnesota Press.

Oestreicher, Paul. 1978. Postscript, *Religion in Communist Lands* 6, no. 2: 95–96.

Pankhurst, Jerry G. 1980. Religion and atheism in the USSR. *Contemporary Soviet Society: Sociological Perspectives.* Ed. J. G. Pankhurst and M. P. Sacks, 182–207. New York: Praeger, 1980.

———. 1984. The strengths of weak parties in church-state confrontations: The Soviet religious situation. *Journal of Church and State* 26, no. 2: 273–91.

Pano, Nicholas C. 1979. Albania. *Communism in Eastern Europe.* Ed. Teresa Rakowska-Harmstone and Andrew Gyorgy, 189–211. Bloomington: Indiana University Press.

Powell, David. 1975. *Antireligious Propaganda in the Soviet Union: A Study of Mass Persuasion.* Cambridge: Massachusetts Institute of Technology Press.

Prifti, Peter. 1975. Albania—towards an atheist society. *Religion and Atheism in the USSR and Eastern Europe.* Ed. B. R. Bociurkiw and J. W. Strong, 388–404. Toronto: University of Toronto Press.

Rakowska-Harmstone, Teresa. 1979. Nationalism and integration in Eastern Europe: The dynamics of change. *Communism in Eastern Europe.* Ed. Teresa Rakowska-Harmstone and Andrew Gyorgy, 308–27. Bloomington: Indiana University Press.

Ramet, Pedro. 1982. Catholicism and politics in socialist Yugoslavia. *Religion in Communist Lands* 10, no. 3: 256–74.

Remington, Robin Alison. 1979. Yugoslavia. *Communism in Eastern Europe.* Ed. Teresa Rakowska-Harmstone and Andrew Gyorgy, 213–43. Bloomington: Indiana University Press.

Rothenberg, Joshua. 1971. The legal status of religion in the Soviet Union. *Aspects of Religion in the Soviet Union, 1917–1967.* Ed. R. H. Marshall, Jr., 67–103. Chicago: University of Chicago Press.

Shoup, Paul. 1974. Eastern Europe and the Soviet Union: Convergence and divergence in historical perspective. *Soviet Politics and Society in the 1970's.* Ed. H. W. Morton and R. L. Tokes, 340–68. New York: The Free Press.

Tonnies, Bernhard. 1982. Religious persecution in Albania. *Religion in Communist Lands* 10, no. 3: 242–55.

Ulc, Otto. 1979. Czechoslovakia. *Communism in Eastern Europe.* Ed. Teresa Rakowska-Harmstone and Andrew Gyorgy, 100–120. Bloomington: Indiana University Press.

Walters, Philip. 1983. Christians in Eastern Europe: A decade of aspirations and frustrations. *Religion in Communist Lands* 11, no. 1: 6–24.

Ward, Caroline. 1978. Church and state in East Germany. *Religion in Communist Lands* 6, no. 2: 89–95.

Ware, Timothy. 1964. *The Orthodox Church*. Baltimore Md.: Penguin Books.

World Christian Encyclopedia: A Comparative Study of Churches and Religions in the Modern World. A.D. 1900–2000. 1982. Ed. David B. Barrett. New York: Oxford University Press.

15

Prophetic Christianity and The Future Of China

FRANK K. FLINN

N the late summer of 1976, when China was hovering between the old creation of the 1949 revolution— symbolized by the Gang of Four—and the new creation of Ding Xiaoping's pragmatic socialism, Roger Garside, First Secretary of the British Embassy, attended the Protestant church in Beijing. He noticed that the Chinese order of service differed from the printed English version. In place of the assigned New Testament reading, the Chinese minister read from Romans 3: "None is righteous, no not one; no one understands, no one seeks for God. All have turned aside, together they have gone wrong; no one does good, not even one . . ." Experienced China watchers (e.g., Hinton 1983, 727) have come to see in such seemingly minute changes signs of far-reaching national trends. Garside took this last-minute alteration of a normally meticulously planned service to signal not only a criticism of the Gang of Four and the chaotic legacy of the Cultural Revolution of the 1960s but also a change in leadership and direction for the future China (Garside 1981, 151–52). Events have borne out this interpretation of the tiny prophetic candle that little change in a religious ceremony gave light to. And no text from the Scriptures, with the exception of the prophet Amos, could vent more sharply prophetic dissatisfaction with current political and social arrangements than Paul's universal indictment of all nations, Jew and Gentile alike.

307

Yet the first question to be asked is: What is prophetic religion? In his sociologically informed treatise *Models of the Church,* Avery Dulles (1974) proposed five paradigms which have shaped Christianity's self-conception. The Christian church has seen itself as institution, as mystical communion, as sacrament, as herald, and as servant. The church as herald has its roots in the prophetic tradition of the Old Testament which stresses the encounter between a sovereign God and a pilgrim church in a theology of the word. Karl Barth epitomizes this kerygmatic theology of the word in his "No!" to the "old Adam" and "Yes!" to the "new Adam" in Christ (1962). In the dialectical theology of the word, all institutions, including ecclesiastical institutions ("religion"), come under potential indictment because they can act "like a drug which has been extremely skillfully administered" (Barth 1933, 236). Thus prophetic religion reserves a perpetual space for discontent with the way things are.

It remains to be seen whether any of these models of the Christian church apply to the Chinese situation. First, the Christian church in China until the "Liberation" in 1949 remained a missionary church, sustained and dominated by foreigners. Even as late as 1946, only twenty-nine of the 137 Catholic dioceses in China had native bishops (Tu 1984, 69). In 1907 Protestant missionaries celebrated the centennial of the coming of Robert Morrision of the London Mission with no Chinese present. Many of the "unequal treaties" and suppressions of nativist uprisings, including the T'ai P'ing Rebellion (1850–65) and Boxer Uprising or Yi He Tuan (1900), were facilitated by Christian missionaries. Ironically both uprisings contained strong elements of prophetic Christianity. Hence, Christianity in China, despite the noble attempts at indigenization by Matteo Ricci (1552–1610), has had enormous difficulty overcoming its public image of serving as adjunct to foreign commercial and political powers.

Secondly, in missionary situations, Christianity's prophetic message has often been blunted by the exigencies placed on missionaries by the sponsoring country. The indigenization of the message depends on the indigenization of the leadership, and that did not take place in China. Today Christians represent only .007 percent of the population of China, whereas the Christian population of Korea may be as high as twenty-three percent. An important reason is that the Korean mission field accepted in 1890 the missionizing program of John Nevius,

Chinese missionary extraordinaire and Protestantism's answer to Matteo Ricci. The Nevius Method, which never met with support in China itself, stressed (1) personal evangelism and wide itineration; (2) the centrality of the Bible; (3) self-propagation (every convert an evangelist); (4) self-government; (5) self-support; (6) systematic Bible study; (7) strict discipline with biblical penalities; (8) cooperation and union with other religious bodies (Methodists and Presbyterians crusaded jointly); (9) non-interference in lawsuits; and (10) general helpfulness in economic problems (Clark 1937; Palmer 1967, 27–8). Where the Chinese missionaries suppressed tendencies toward national democracy, the Korean missionaries were overt in their support, no doubt owing to the strong native leadership that rose up as a result of the self-reliance program. In contrast with China, the adoption of the Nevius Method resulted in an explosion of prophetic religious movements, some spurred by Maitreya Buddhism and others by messianic Christianity, most of which embodied nationalistic sentiments (Palmer 1980, 1–10). In China, Christianity was not able to overcome its foreign body status.

Cycles of Christianity in China

The future of prophetic Christianity in China cannot be interpreted apart from the cycles of missionary incursions followed by suppression. Chinese Christian history falls into five main periods.

The first period was the Nestorian Era (A.D. 635–843). Although Syrian Nestorian Christians were the first to bring Christianity to China in 635, there were also Armenian, Jacobite, Byzantine, Jewish, Zoroastrian, and Manichaean proselytizing efforts during this same time (Bundy 1985). In the words of Kenneth Scott Latourette, the first phase of Christian missionizing was almost too "irenic." There was no denigration of "false idolaters," nor was there the protectionism and nationalism that accompanied eighteenth through twentieth century mission crusades (Latourette 1929, 59). One might even say they became too indigenized. In 843 the Emperor Wuzong issued a dissolution-expulsion edict, suppressing the missionizing efforts of import religions.

The second period came under the auspices of the Mongolian Era (ca. A.D. 1245–1368). In his effort to gain cooperation for the spread of the Mongolian Empire in the Holy Land, Genghis Khan allowed the Franciscan Giovanni de Plano Carpini and the Dominican André de

Longimel to open missions in the royal capital Cambaluc (Beijing). There is also evidence that Nestorianism revived again (Jiang Wenhan 1984a, 23). In 1289 the Franciscan Giovanni de Monte Corvino became the first Archbishop of Beijing. But Christianity was attached to the hegemony of the Mongols, and when they were overthrown missionary activity once again was suppressed during the Ming dynasty.

The third period is the Jesuit Era (A.D. 1555–1724). Under the tutorship of Alessandro Valignano, appointed Vistator of the East missions for the Jesuit order in 1573, Christianity underwent the first systematic attempt at indigenization and inculturation in a missionary situation (de Graeve 1985). This bold attempt infused the missionary activity of Roberto de Nobili in India and Michele Ruggieri and Matteo Ricci in China. This attempt, however, needs to be qualified, for it was inculturation "at the top." In particular, the Jesuit missionaries, who universally combined "profane" scientific and astronomical with "sacred" teaching, sought to identify with the ruling classes, brahmins, mandarins, or samurai, as the case might be. There could be no doubt about the success of the Jesuit indigenization of ritual. By 1700 the number of Catholics rose to approximately 300,000. This success did not impede the Franciscans and Dominicans from making the Far Eastern "Jesuit usages" suspect to the papacy. This became known as the "Rites and Terms Controversy" (Rouleau 1967, 611–17). The Jesuits sought the approval of wearing local mandarin garb for the Mass, acceptance of reverence for ancestors, use of the vernacular in the liturgy and the use of the classical Chinese terms Shang Ti ("Lord of the Sky") and T'ien ("Heaven"). At first Popes Paul V (A.D. 1605–21) and Alexander VII (1655–67) gave tentative approval to the Chinese rites, but in 1715 Pope Clement XI condemned sixteen of the Jesuit practices in the bulla Ex illa die. In 1742 the Dominican evangelical purists won the day; Pope Benedict forbade the Chinese rites outright in the bulla Ex quo singulari and mandated an oath by missionaries to uphold Western rites in the Far East. Upset by outside interference, Emperor Kangxi issued an edict in 1742 expelling foreign missionaries, although Jesuits were retained at court as official astronomers. Again Christianity came close to extinction in China. (Perhaps as a symbol of the cyclic nature of Christianity in China, the Peoples Republic announced in 1984 that Matteo Ricci's tomb in Beijing had been renovated after desecration during the Cultural Revolution and was now open to foreign visitors.)

The fourth period is the Protestant Era (1807–1949), although

Catholicism was permitted again to flourish after the Wangxia Treaty of 1844. It might also be called the era of the mission compound. As noted above, Protestant Christianity, one of the principle sources for the drive to democracy in the West, was severely fettered by its attachment to commercial and imperial interests in China and thus tended to side with current regimes against democratizing revitalization movements. Contemporary post-Liberation Christians are fond of pointing up the opprobrious connection between Protestant missionaries and the unequal treaties of Wangxia (1844) and Tianjin (1858), as well as the Protocol of 1901, giving foreign missionaries extraterritorial status. Those same missionaries are remembered for their opposition to the T'ai P'ing Movement, the Boxer Rebellion, and Sun Yat Sen's "bourgeois" democratic Revolution of 1911 (Ting 1984, 135–36).

The T'ai P'ing rebellion was and is an event of special symbolic importance in the history of Christianity in China. In *China Shakes the World* Jack Belden claimed that the T'ai P'ing crusade was the first harbinger of the Communist Revolution in that it sought to overthrow the old Confucian order (1970, 470). Mao Zedong himself interpreted the rebellion as belonging to a century long series of "struggles waged by the Chinese people, on different occasions and in varying degrees, against imperialism and the feudal forces in order to build up an independent, democratic society and complete the first revolution" (Mao 1968a, 73). Contemporary Chinese Christians see in it the example of Christianity being on the side of revolution (Zhao 1984, 30). The movement was begun by Hung Hsiu-ch'uan, a rural Sichuan noble who thrice-failed the state examinations for literati and hence was disqualified from entry into the bureaucratic administrative structure. After one failure he fell into a fever and saw visions. Six years later he read a Christian missionary tract "Good Words Exhorting the Age" which revealed the meaning of his visions and set him upon the crusade of restoring the *T'ien Wang* or "Heavenly King." The T'ai P'ing movement was both protological and eschatological. Its full name *t'ai p'ing t'ien kuo* ("heavenly kingdom of great peace") harkens back to hierocratic Daoist "rebellion of the yellow kerchiefs" against Confucian bureaucratism during the Han dynasty (202 B.C. to A.D. 220). Like its forerunner the T'ai P'ing rebellion marshalled the mystical, ecstatic, and magical elements of traditional Daoism which served as the matrix for the infusion of Christian elements. On the Christian side, it had a water purification ceremony like baptism, a tea-eucharist (alcohol was prohibited), a modified Lord's Prayer and an adapted Decalogue, ceremonial (indissoluble) wedlock (Hung had a vision that Jesus was married like

T'ien Wang), the prohibition of prostitution, drugs, foot-binding, and propitiatory rites at ancestral tombs, and the segregation of the sexes before marriage. Max Weber wrote that Hung's ethic was "half mystic-ecstatic and half ascetic" and compared the T'ai P'ing armies with Oliver Cromwell's Puritan "regiment of Saints" (1964, 219–21). To Weber the T'ai P'ing rebellion symbolized the revolt of biblical moral rectitude against Confucian ceremonial correctitude.

Though the movement may have fallen back into the Confucian principle of institutional grace, Weber concluded (1964, 222–23):

> Nevertheless, the movement signified a break with orthodoxy in important points and it allowed an indigenous religion to arise which inwardly was relatively close to Christianity. This opportunity was incomparably greater than that offered by the hopeless missionary experiments of the occidental denominations. And it may have been the last opportunity for such a religion in China.

Likewise Shupe (1985) sees in the T'ai P'ing rebellion not an illegitimate or atavistic "revitalization movement" but rather a prime example of Western Christianity as a vehicle for Eastern sentiments, including revolutionary ones. Yet the Western powers in China habitually forfeited the inward affinity of movements like the T'ai P'ing for mercantile interests. Political democracy kowtowed before commercial democracy. Lord Palmerston called in Charles G. "Chinese" Gordon to destroy the T'ai P'ing capital at Nanjing. In the cunning of history, Gordon later lost his life while trying to suppress another eschatological movement, this one led by the "Mahdi" Muhammad Ahmad at the Battle of Khartoum in 1885.

The twentieth century brought its own ironies. Just as missionaries like Gilbert Reid (1857–1927) were trying to indigenize backward by appealing to the ancient Confucian authors, thinkers of the indigenous New Thought Movement, whose slogans were "Democracy" and "Science," were repudiating Confucianism for its "passive ethics" (Lee 1983, 75–76). The heyday of Protestant missions in 1922 (375,000 members) witnessed the rise of the Anti-Christian Movement during which Christianity was labelled the "running dog of imperialism." The subsequent acquiescence of missionaries to puppet functionaries of the Japanese occupiers before and during World War II, as well as active recruitment for Chiang Kai-Shek's Koumintang immediately after the Japanese defeat, did not put either Catholic or Protestant Christians in a strong position once the Long March of Mao Zedong terminated at the Gate of Heavenly Peace in 1949. Following the victory of the communist forces, there occurred a mass exodus of native Christians from China and the expulsion of almost all foreign missionaries. The Christianity that remained can be said to have entered a cocoon phase. Unbeknownst to Western Christians, however, the larva remained surprisingly active.

The title Three-Self Era (1949–present) best characterizes the present period. As noted above, the ideas of self-government, self-support, and self-propagation formed the nucleus of John Nevius missionary method. The Three-Self method resonates well with the Chinese tradition of "self-cultivation," first introduced into China by Ch'an (Zen) Buddhism (Selover 1985). The Three-Self doctrine, which served the interests of both nationalism and indigenization, was revived by the Chinese Church of Christ in 1927 (Lee 1983, 83). In 1950 it was again resurrected by Chinese Christian leader Wu Yaozong and affirmed by the Marxist regime in accord with the United Front policy during the years of struggle against Japan and the Koumintang. Premier Zhou Enlai convened a conference of 151 Christian leaders which issued a "United Declaration" (contained in the *Documents of the Three-Self Movement,* 1963, 42, cited as DTSM) calling all Christians, ". . . to thoroughly, permanently and completely sever all relations with American missions and all other nations, thus realizing self-government, self-support, and self-propagation in the Chinese Church." The fate of the Christian Three-Self Patriotic movement runs like a zigzag subject to the successive mass movements which have swept communist China since 1949. It merits a separate discussion.

Three-Self Christianity: Between Collaboration And Cooperation

In 1922 Protestant missionaries published a report on the conditions of the Christian church in China. The report stated that there were 130 missionary societies, 6,250 missionaries, 375,000 (Protestant) Christians, 7,000 mission schools, and 210,000 students in the schools (Stauffer, 1922). For the Protestant missionaries the report manifested a real turning point for Christianity in China. But for those who espoused the Three-Self principle, the report represented missionizing on the coattails of imperialism. As contemporary Chinese Christians have remarked, the Chinese title of the report was *China for Christ,* but the title in English was *The Chinese* Occupation *of China* [emphasis added] (Jiang Wenhan 1984a, 26). Zhao Fusan, current Vice-

Chairman of the Three-Self Patriotic committee, has written: "In *The Christian Occupation of China,* published in 1922, it was stated that three-fourths of China was 'occupied' by Christianity, and that all but 18 Chinese cities with populations of more than 50,000 were 'under occupation'" (Zhao 1984, 30). Insensitivity to Chinese national sentiments both pre-dated and bolstered the push toward the Three-Self movement under communist rule. That rule, however, was subject to succeeding waves in different directions.

Chinese communist rule can be divided into four phases: Land Reform and Reconstruction (1943–1957), the Great Leap Forward (1958–1960), the Cultural Revolution (1966–1976) which was anticipated by the Socialist Education Movement (1963), and, finally, the current phase of Pragmatic Communism (1976–present) under the leadership of Deng Xiaoping whose motto is "seek truth from facts" and whose favorite proverb is "it doesn't matter whether the cat is black or white, so long as it catches the mouse."

After the 1949 Liberation, the key to understanding internal policy in China was not "revolution" *per se* but the "two contradictions" and "struggle." In "On the Correct Handling of Contradictions Among the People" (1957), Mao Zedong distinguished two types of social contradiction—"those between ourselves and the enemy and those among the people themselves" (Mao 1968b, 80). The two contradictions were between the "people" and the "class enemy," on the one hand, and "among the people," on the other. The real questions boiled down to "Who are the people?" and "Who is the enemy?" The answers depended upon the dialectics of the historical situation. The Koumintang, in so far as it partook in the Anti-Japanese campaign, was "among the people." But after the war it fell in the class of "enemy" because it represented the feudal and capitalist classes. So, too, went the fate of the Christian churches.

During the period of revolutionary struggle, Christian churches found themselves in the category of "enemy" by definition. In *Fanshen: A Documentary History of Revolution in a Chinese Village,* William Hinton, an obvious sympathizer of Mao Zedong's land reform policy, recounts how the Catholic church in Long Bow, Shanxi Province, had become the single largest landholder in the village and controlled the Catholic Carry-On Society, a benevolent as well as lending institution (Hinton 1966, 58–72). Liberation resulted in the expropriation of church property, which was first distributed to Catholic contributors and then to the people at large. The financial holdings of the churches throughout China, plus their extra-territorial status which exempted them from Chinese legal authority, placed them in an anti-national and hence "enemy" position. On the other hand, a few Chinese Christians sought to join Mao Zedong's "United Front" during the war years (Jiang Wenhan 1984b, 111). During the 1950s the Western world heard mostly about the fate of ex-missionaries through vehemently anti-communist tracts, most notably Raymond J. de Jaegher's *The Enemy Within* (1952). There was no doubt that post-Liberation China undertook a de-missionarizing campaign remarkably like the expulsion after 1742. In 1947 there were 5,496 Catholic foreign missionaries in China; by 1957 that number had been reduced to twenty-three. Meanwhile the Chinese Christians were forced to walk the razor's edge between cooperation and collaboration with the communist powers. Uncounted numbers retreated into a "home church" stance not unlike that taken by Japanese Christians during the Tokagawa persecutions. Many openly resisted and wound up in prison. A significant minority of Protestant clergy and Catholic laymen, later followed by the hierarchy, chose the Three-Self route.

The Three-Self Patriotic movement was established by Wu Yaozong with the active cooperation of Zhou Enlai in 1950. The Catholic side was led by Father Wang Lianzuo and five hundred laymen (Ting 1984, 136). The explicit aim was to establish a church apart from foreign control, financial assistance, and missionizing. The Constitution of the People's Republic assured "freedom of religion" but that freedom depended upon "oppose-America help-Korea" propaganda as well as support for "the Government land reform policy" and "repression of anti-revolutionaries" (DTSM, 42–43). During the first two phases of the communist period, the Christian churches were under severe duress but they survived. The Chinese Catholic Patriotic Association was founded in 1957, and in 1958 new bishops were elected in vacant dioceses. Pius XII condemned the Catholic Three-Self Movement in the encyclicals *Ad Evangelii praecones* (1951) and *Ad Sinarium gentes* (1954) and declared the election of native Chinese bishops invalid and their consecration illicit in 1958. The second Chinese National Christian Conference was held in 1960, to be followed by the Second Synod of the Chinese Catholic Patriotic Association in 1962. Then came the Socialist Education Movement (1963) and the Cultural Revolution (1966–1976).

The Land Reform phase of the communist revolution focused on the redistribution of land from large landholders to middle and poor peasants, central state purchasing, plus the establishment of cooperatives. The Great Leap Forward was centered on the collectivization of farms and other means of production, although the masses retained ownership of the instruments of production. These struggles produced counter-movements mostly because of economic setbacks. The Great Proletarian Cultural Revolution and its forerunner, the Socialist Education Movement, was Mao's last attempt to take the egalitarian principle to its logical conclusion through mass communalization of all relations and means of production. William Hinton (1983, 364), sympathetic to Mao's side of the cause, defines it as a struggle between the masses, championed by Mao (who wanted a mass mobilization of peasants), and the bureaucratized Party leadership, represented by Liu Shaoqi (who wanted top-down rectification of the errors of local leaders.

Others have described this difference in Mao's and Liu's positions as differing views of human nature (Hsia 1972, 137–42). Liu gravitated toward the classical Chinese position of harmony and felt that class struggle and the conflict between the individual and the collective was over in principle (Liu 1981, 18–38). Mao felt that the struggle to eradicate the contradictions between the classes, the individual and the collective, and centralism and democracy would take ten thousand years. In other words, it approximated eternity. Mao leapt over the heads of the Party leaders in Beijing and brought the struggle back to the rural peasants in a socialist "last hurrah." Within Marxist ideology, Liu and his "line" thought that the new social relations of production were ahead of the feudal forces of production. The solution was technological progress and the use of capitalist means of production. For Mao and his "line" pretty much the opposite was the case. Old relations (what Mao called the "Four Olds"—old ideas, old customs, old culture, old habits) held back the sudden release of China's productive forces (Hinton 1983, 493). The Great Proletarian Cultural Revolution was a massive re-education struggle toward the communalization of consciousness in anticipation of a productive utopia. Mao, it seems, leapt backwards over Marx to Hegel in maintaining that the revolution in the idea has to precede the revolution in the material conditions of existence.

For the Christian churches, as well as Buddhism, Daoism, and Islam, the Cultural Revolution spelled disaster. If no obvious "objects of struggle" in the shape of landlords were walking around, then the "objects" still existed in the hearts and minds of the masses, particularly descendants of landlords, those who adhered to religious "superstition," bureaucrats who enjoyed eating from "iron rice bowls," professors who seemed to constitute a new mandarin class, and so forth. But religion, of all the potential targets, most qualified as a category falling under the Four Olds. As a consequence, there were massive closings of churches, temples, and shrines, along with the suppression of geomancers and shamans. There are indications that the attacks against "superstitious" Daoism was even more virulent than against the historic religions (Butterfield 1982, 255; Garside 1981, 410). Daoists had a penchant for attributing good harvests to heaven and bad harvests to Mao and the Party. In the heat of the Cultural Revolution, it seems that religion, even in the form of the nationalist Three-Self movement, could no longer be classified as a contradiction "among the people" and subject to the "democratic method of education," but as a "class enemy" and therefore subject to the "method of dictatorship."

The ultra-leftists, however, seemed unconsciously to recognize the need for some kind of ultimate. Spurred on by Lin Biao, compiler of the handbook of the Cultural Revolution better known as the *Little Red Book*, the Red Guards were egged on to fashion a "cult of Mao," even to the extent of labeling the class enemies' path (feudalism, bureaucratic capitalism, imperialism) in Buddhist eschatological terms as "cow-ghosts" and "snake-gods" and Mao's path as the true Dao leading to salvation (Hsia 1972, 230–34). In this sacralization of the secular ideal we can perhaps detect a twinge of what Hegel called the "cunning of history," for after the Cultural Revolution disintegrated into a miasma of factionalism, the turn toward a more transcendental spirituality surged upwards (Matthews 1983, 328–30). The demythologization of the cult of Mao after the overthrow of the Gang of Four in 1978 entailed the resanctification of traditional religion.

Although the anti-religious ultra-left could argue that the resurgence of religion was the result of Koumintang and other outside agents, once the left extremism of Lin Biao and the Gang of Four spent itself, it became obvious to everyone, including the members of the Central Committee, that the survival and continued growth of religion was now a home-grown phenomenon. The Episcopal bishop of Fouzhou, Moses P. Xie summed it up succinctly: "People are thirsting for something spiritual" (Matthews 1983, 329). Recent foreign visitors and Chinese ministers and priests report that Christian services are now jammed with upwards to two thousand worshippers every Sunday, while home churches continue to outlast the days of persecution during the Cultural Revolution (Butterfield 1982, 422–23; Ting 1984, 57).

The fourth phase of the communist era goes by the title Pragmatic Communism. On the one hand, the policy of Deng Xiaoping and the new leadership in Beijing is a return to programs first enunciated by Liu Shaoqi and Deng in 1956 (Liu 1981; Deng 1981). In terms of

318   FRANK K. FLINN

religion, Liu had taken the United Front policy during the resistance years not as a temporary political ploy but as a long-term program (1981, 80):

> In regard to religious beliefs in the areas of national minorities, we must continuously and persistently adhere to the policy of freedom of religious belief and must never interfere in that connection during social reform. We should help those who live by religion as a profession to find a proper solution of any difficulties of livelihood with which they are faced.

On the other hand, Deng's Four Modernizations program (agriculture, industry, science, and army) is a struggle to make up for the ten lost years of the Cultural Revolution. It has entailed the loosening up for free market forces such that farmers can now sell their quotas to the central government purchasing agency (at a twenty-three percent rate increase) and peddle their surplus at local markets at an even higher rate. Perhaps more importantly, the National People's Congress has been so expanded that non-communist party membership constitutes thirty-seven percent and that religious believers are among the deputies (Ting 1984, 53; White 1983, 42). The freeing of the market forces, within limits, in the economic sphere has gone hand-in-hand with the free exchange of religious ideas, including Christian religious ideas. Apparently, post-Mao China has come to the conviction that freedom of religion within the limits of national purpose is conducive to modernization and that Christianity has a decided role to play in this process.

China And Christianity: The Virgin And Mao

When he wrote his classic book *Fanshen,* William Hinton came to what seemed like a final judgment on the future of Catholicism, which had comprised one-fifth of the population at the time of Liberation: "All the power of the Church and all its efforts to convert Long Bow to Catholicism failed in the end" (Hinton 1966, 67). When Hinton returned in 1970, he learned that not only did the Catholic population survive at the same percentage but that there had even been a massive Catholic pilgrimage numbering tens of thousands to the shrine of the Virgin of Taiyun in 1966 (Hinton 1983, 282–83). Again in 1980 he returned to Long Bow to aid the villagers with farm mechanization. This time he found Catholic homes adorned with pictures of the Virgin and Mao and open celebrations of the Mass in the loft of the house of a carpenter. Somewhat incredulously Hinton commented to journalist Fox Butterfield: "There are so many people the crowd spills out into his courtyard" (Butterfield 1982, 423).

Long Bow does not seem to be alone in this revival. Catholic layman Lu Weidu reported a Catholic pilgrimage of twenty thousand from the diocese of Shanghai to the shrine of the Virgin in Seshan in 1981 (Lu 1984, 132). The affection of Chinese Catholics for the Virgin is nothing new. In his masterful treatise *The Memory Palace of Matteo Ricci,* Jonathan Spence records that many converts of Ricci's time thought that God was a female in the form of the Virgin, whom they had assimilated with Guanyin, the Buddhist goddess of mercy (Spence 1984, 232–68). In the phase of Pragmatic Communism, it seems that images of the Virgin and Mao can coexist in the hearts and minds of Chinese Christians as grace and nature coexisted in the theology of the Middle Ages.

Almost daily newspapers relate bits of information which confirm a changed attitude toward religion in China under Deng Xiaoping. Western journalists have reported similar revivals among Buddhists and Daoists, the refurbishing of ancestral tombs, the restoration of the tombs of Confucius and Matteo Ricci, and renewed Islamic worship among the Western peoples of China. For some, this changed attitude is mere window dressing. Others claim that it is genuine and coincides with the radical policy changes that have built up step by step since Deng resumed power (Wren 1984a, b). Those policy changes include dramatic ideological modifications such as the comment in the *People's Daily* that the works of Marx and Lenin could not "solve all of today's problems", and the ritual listing of Mao's "many mistakes" (Wren 1984b, 10 Y). The leadership in China now makes a distinction between Mao Zedong Thought and the (individual) thoughts of Mao. (One Western diplomat has commented, "Chinese communism is becoming more like Zen.") It also makes careful distinctions between mistakes, errors, and crimes. Mao Zedong Thought, it seems, includes the moderate policies of the earlier days of the United Front. The later individual thoughts of Mao were subject to "mistakes," while the Lin Biao-Jang Quing clique and the Gang of Four were guilty of serious ideological "errors" and actual legal "crimes." As the programs of Pragmatic Communism have gained success, Mao's "mistakes" have grown from being "some" to "several" and even "many." Among those "mistakes" was the abandonment of the religious policy worked out during the early 1950s.

The religious revival came out in the open in 1978. In 1980 the

Catholic Patriotic Association held its third synod, the first since 1962. Both Protestant and Catholic emissaries have been allowed to travel the world and address assemblies on the state of the church in China (Ting 1982, 1). Then in 1982 the Central Committee of the Communist party of China issued a definitive policy statement entitled *The Basic Viewpoint and Policy on the Religious Question During Our Country's Socialist Period* (cited as BVP). The document purports to be "the summing up of [the communist party's] own historical experience" since Liberation in 1949 (BVP, 1). After repudiating the repressive excesses of the Gang of Four against religion during the Cultural Revolution, the document classifies religion as a contradiction "among the people" and not a contradiction "between the people and the class enemy": "The contradictions concerning religious questions now belong primarily to the category of contradictions among the people" (BVP, 4).

Three factors underlie the restoration of the pre-Great Leap Forward policy on religion. First is the desire for "national stability and ethnic unity" (BVP, 4). This coincides with the old United Front policy of revolutionary days. Secondly, religion, although reportedly on the decline in relation to population growth, is on the "increase in absolute numbers." *The Basic Viewpoint* document itself gives the following figures for Islam, Protestantism, and Catholicism (BVP, 3–4):

	Catholics	Protestants	Muslims
1949	2,700,000	700,000	8,000,000
1982	3,000,000+	3,000,000	10,000,000

The document does not state how many are members of Buddhism-Daoism, but Zhao Puchu, acting president of the Buddhist Association of China, claims a figure of 100,000,000 or more (Garside 1981, 410). The last Catholic census in 1949 gave a figure of 3,275,000 Catholics (Rouleau 1967, 599). The figures are telling. They are no doubt considerably underestimated in the official document, particularly in regard to the figures for Muslims and Catholics, not because the communists are embarrassed by the numbers—they are unusually forthright on all kinds of figures—but because so many Christians kept their faith secret during the days of persecution. The 1982 Catholic population could be as high as 5,000,000, and the Protestant population probably is 3,500,000 or more. In 1949 the total Chinese population was estimated at 461,000,000. In 1982 the estimates vary between 800,000,000 and 1,100,000,000,000. In rough figures the population has doubled in the last thirty years, and the best guess is that the Christian population may have also doubled despite heavy persecution, flight to Hong Kong and Taiwan, and the elimination of landlord class Christians. The document also gives figures for religious professionals (priests, nuns, imams, etc.): Buddhist: 27,000; Daoist: 2600; Muslim: 20,000; Catholic: 3,400; and Protestant: 5,900 (BVP, 8). The role of religious clergy is specifically recognized as beneficial: "Many of these professional religious not only maintain intimate spiritual ties with the mass of religious believers, but have an important influence over the spiritual life of the masses which should not be ignored" (BVP, 8).

The obvious growth of religion under socialist rule, even against heavy odds, is behind the third factor in the new policy: a realization of "the protracted nature of the religious question under socialist conditions" (BVP, 3). The communist party claims atheism for itself, forbids religious affiliation to any Party member, but warns against those who think that religion will die out in a short period under socialism and against those who think they can help the process along with "administrative decrees or other coercive measures": "Religion will eventually disappear from human history. But it will disappear naturally, only through the long term development of socialism and communism, when all objective conditions are met" (BVP, 3). In particular, the document states that the "anti-revolutionary Lin Biao-Jiang Qing clique out of its ulterior motives made use of these leftist errors, and wantonly trampled upon the scientific theory of Marxism-Leninism and Mao Zedong Thought concerning the religious question" by forbidding "normal religious activities," treating religious persons as "objects for dictatorship," misinterpreting "customs and practices of the ethnic minorities as religious superstition," and destroying religious shrines (BVP, 5–6).

In response to the excesses of the Cultural Revolution, the document reaffirms "respect for and protection of the freedom of religious belief" (BVP, 6), makes clear "that the crux of the policy of freedom of religious belief is to make the question of religious belief a private matter, one of individual free choice for citizens" (BVP, 7). In line with

322

this classic Jeffersonian understanding of religious freedom, the *Basic Viewpoint* document states a qualified principle of separation of church and state (BVP, 8):

> The political power in a socialist state can in no way be used to promote any one religion, nor can it be used in any way to forbid any one religion, as long as it is only a question of normal religious beliefs and practices. At the same time, religion will not at all be permitted to meddle in the administrative or juridical affairs of state, nor to intervene in the schools or public education. It will be absolutely forbidden to force anyone, particularly young people under 18 years of age, to become a member of a church, to become a Buddhist monk or nun, or to go to temples or monasteries to study Buddhist scripture.

In an address given in Hong Kong, Protestant Bishop K. H. Ting outlined the administrative organizations to handle church-state affairs (Ting 1984, 53–56):

NATIONAL PEOPLE'S
CONGRESS
elected body, including
religious people

RELIGIOUS AFFAIRS
BUREAU
implements policy of State
Council

CHINESE PEOPLE'S
CONSULTIVE
CONFERENCE
appointed members from all
sectors of society

THREE-SELF PATRIOTIC
MOVEMENT
a non-government organization
with Protestant and Catholic
branches

STATE COUNCIL
central government

CHINA CHRISTIAN
COUNCIL
a church affairs organization

The *Basic Viewpoint* document recognizes that there has been a great attrition in the number of religious personnel since Liberation. Since the present government recognizes that clergy "have an important influence over the spiritual life of the masses" the Central Committee proposes the restoration of churches and shrines, provisions for the livelihood of professional religious [people], including redress of wrongs committed against them, freedom to receive contributions and to sell a quantity of religious reading matter, freedom from harassment by those propagating atheism, the reopening of seminaries and training centers, ecumenical contacts, etc." (BVP, 9–13). This is a distinct reversal of earlier policy, K.H. Ting (1984, 36) recalled the gruesome experience of theological educators during the Cultural Revolution:

> During the years of the "cultural revolution," the [Nanjing] seminary was closed down by a group of Red Guards, who came to the seminary to search out what was called the "Four Olds," and many of the books in our library were burned or taken away. We stopped working. Most of our faculty members went to work on a farm near Nanjing while others were allowed to stay in our homes awaiting to be assigned to new work, although these assignments never came at all. Since the downfall of the Gang of Four, we have reestablished the Nanjing Union Theological Seminary.

The condition of places of worship is not nearly as heartening. At the time of Liberation, the document states, there were about 100,000 places of worship for believers of all faiths, but by 1982 the number had decreased to 30,000, most being damaged or destroyed during the Cultural Revolution (BVP, 10). By 1982 only eighty churches had been reopened, so it seems that the new policy is being implemented cautiously (Ting 1984, 57). The document explicitly discourages underground "home church" gatherings—an implicit recognition of their steady growth during the days of persecution in the Cultural Revolution period. Yet K. H. Ting (1984, 38) acknowledges that "the number of Christians worshipping in churches is still smaller than those who worship in homes."

The theological response to the *Basic Viewpoint* provisions within the Chinese Christian community is guarded but optimistic. Chen Zemin, professor of systematic theology at Nanjing Union Theological Seminary, summarizes the current theological climate of Christians in China in an essay entitled "Theological Reflections" (Chen 1984). First, the point of theological departure is "to opt for the people" (Chen 1984, 44). This sounds like the "preferential option for the poor" among Latin American theologians, but Chinese Christians now feel that they are in a post-liberation situation: "Our theological task is not liberation in the Latin American sense, but reconciliation—reconciliation to and identification with the Chinese people as a whole, from whom we had long been alienated" (Chen 1984, 50). Reconciliation for the Chinese Christians, however, does not mean 100 percent approval. K. H. Ting (1984, 52) says, "Of course, our patriotism is not without a prophetic and critical character. It does not mean blind praise for everything in our motherland."

Another interesting aspect of Chinese theological thinking is its
socialist appropriation of Thomas Aquinas' theory of nature and grace.
Chen writes, "To retain the classical terminology I endorse the Thomist
declaration that 'grace does not remove nature but fulfills it'" (Chen
1984, 45). The community of grace is the *donum superadditum* to the
natural community. For K. H. Ting (1984, 86), the redistribution of
material wealth under socialist rule represents a "Sacrament in the
rudimentary sense of the word, for these material things now represent
and convey something of God's love and care to people."

Finally, the option for the people and the theory of grace fulfilling
(socialist) nature is leading current Chinese theologians to a theology of
the social community that can harmonize with the socialist aims of the
People's Republic (Chen 1984, 47–48; Ting 1984, 86–87; Jiang Peifen
1984, 120–21). This retrieval and adaptation of Thomas Aquinas'
theology of the common good in terms of grace adding to nature and
the sacramentalization of the material world for the common good
bears close attention. Western interpretations of Aquinas have tended to
accommodate his teaching on law and the common good (Aquinas
1948, 609–50) to the modern liberal theories of "individual rights" in
Hobbes and Locke. In the liberal tradition there are perfect (personal
and individual) rights but no perfect (social and communal) duties.
Protestant and Catholic theologians in China are now attempting to
release the social utopian content of a tradition long held captive to
individualistic and capitalistic interpretation. This represents a remarkable theological development.

The Chinese Church as Prophetic

At present Chinese Christianity seems to be hovering between a
harmonious sacramentalization of the socialist order and a quiet
prophecy of discontent with the way things have been in the last twenty
years. The continued growth of Christianity in "home churches" during
the Cultural Revolution signifies that it is something like a prophetic
movement without a prophet. Clearly the remarkable pilgrimages to
Taiyun in 1966 and to Seshan in 1981 can be interpreted as rituals of
rebellion and remind us of the millennial pilgrimages and crusades of
the poor in medieval Europe (Cohn 1961, 87–98). To the outsider,
such events may appear miniscule against the landscape of a billion
people, but William Hinton reminds us that in China small seeds
quickly become massive trees. The Great Proletarian Cultural Revolution itself began with a review of a play "Huai Jui Dismissed from

Office" by Wu Han, vice-mayor of Beijing, and was announced with remarkable speed throughout the nation with use of a single big character poster done by a student (Hinton 1983, 494 ff.). Coupled with the downfall of the Gang of Four, the endurance of the Christians under pressure has given them almost the mark of revolutionary legitimacy. "We deem it an honor that Christianity was not tolerated by the Gang of Four" (Ting 1984, 10). Christians retain the option for the prophecy of protest.

On the other hand, the development of a social sacramental theology among Chinese Christian theologians and the resurgence of ritual in general would seem to confirm a blessing on the status quo. In this regard, two things may be said. First, the *status quo* in China is in considerable flux. Many westerners like to think that Deng Xiaoping has opened the road to unrestrained capitalism. The more accurate picture, however, is that China will retain a socialist base, with emphasis on the production teams and brigades of the large communes, and allow for a free market exchange on the top, with emphasis on households and individuals. Under the new "responsibility system" *(zeren zhi)*, inaugurated in 1980, as much as fifteen percent of the agricultural land can be put under household or private production (Chance 1984, 156). This looks remarkably like an economic equivalent of the nature/grace theology developed by the theologians. There seems to be a symbiosis between changing economic policy and developing theology. Secondly, social science tends to see ritual as a means of maintaining the status quo. A distinction is in order in this regard. Anthropologist Victor Turner (1970, 95) differentiates "ceremonies," which do confirm the status quo, from "rituals" proper, which transform individuals and groups from one status to another. Rituals can often be occasions for hurling "insults at the king" (Gluckmann 1965, 288). Thus, to return to Avery Dulles's models of the Christian church, there is no absolute distinction between a sacramental, ritual model of the church and a prophetic, eschatological model. The Christian church in China seeks to be both a focus of sacramental reconciliation and a repository of prophetic hope.

References

Aquinas, Thomas. 1948. *Introduction to St. Thomas Aquinas*. Ed. Anton C. Pegis. New York: Modern Library.

Barth, Karl. 1933. *The Epistle to the Romans*. London: Oxford University Press.

————.1962. *Christ and Adam: Man and Humanity in Romans 5.* New York: Collier.

Basic Viewpoint and Policy (BVP) *The Basic Viewpoint and Policy on the Religious Question During Our Country's Socialist Period.* Beijing: Central Committee of the Communist Party, Document #19, 1982. Translated by J. Wickeri, Tau Fong Shan Ecumenical Centre, Hong Kong, 1982, 18 pp.

Belden, Jack. [1949] 1970. *China Shakes the World.* New York: Monthly Review.

Bundy, David. 1985. Missiological reflections on Nestorian Christianity in China. *Religion in the Pacific Era.* Ed., Frank Flinn and Tyler Hendricks. New York: Paragon House. Forthcoming.

Butterfield, Fox. 1982. *China: Alive in a Bitter Sea.* New York: Times Books.

Chance, Norman A. 1984. *China's Urban Villages: Life in a Beijing Commune.* New York: Holt, Rinehart and Winston.

Chen, Zemin. 1984. Theological reflections. *Chinese Christians Speak Out,* Ed. K.H. Ting, 43–50. Beijing: New World Press.

Clark, Charles Allen. 1937. *The Nevius Plan for Mission Work.* Seoul: Christian Literature Society.

Cohn, Norman. 1961. *The Pursuit of the Millennium.* New York: Harper and Row.

deGrave, Frank. 1985. Roberto de Nobili: A bold attempt at inculturation? *Religion in the Pacific Era.* Ed., Frank Flinn and Tyler Hendricks. New York: Paragon House.

de Jaegher, Raymond J. 1952. *The Enemy Within: An Eyewitness Account of the Communist Conquest of China.* New York: Doubleday.

Deng Xiaoping. 1981. Report on the revision of the constitution of the communist party of China, September 16, 1956. Documents of the Eighth National Congress of the Communist Party. Beijing: Foreign Language Press.

Dulles, Avery. 1974. *Models of the Church.* New York: Doubleday.

Flinn, Frank K. and Tyler Hendricks, eds. 1985. *Religion in the Pacific Era.* New York: Paragon House.

Garside, Roger. 1981. *Coming Alive: China after Mao.* New York: McGraw-Hill.

Gluckmann, Max. 1965. *Politics, Law and Ritual in Tribal Society.* New York: Mentor.

Hinton, William. 1966. *Fanshen: A Documentary History of Revolution in a Chinese Village.* New York: Vintage.

———.1983. *Shenfan: The Continuing Revolution in a Chinese Village.* New York: Random House.

Hsia, Adrian. 1972. *The Chinese Cultural Revolution.* New York: McGraw-Hill.

Jiang Peifen. 1984. An evangelical perspective. *Chinese Christians Speak Out.* Ed. K.H. Ting, 118–24. Beijing: New World Press.

Jiang Wenhan. 1984a. How 'foreign' was Christianity in China? *Chinese Christians Speak Out.* Ed. K.H. Ting, 22–28. Beijing: New World Press.

———.1984b. What China means to Me. *Chinese Christians Speak Out.* Ed. K.H. Ting, 110–17. Beijing: New World Press.

Latourette, Kenneth Scott. 1929. *A History of Christian Missions in China.* New York: Macmillan.

Lee Meng Ng. 1983. Christianity and nationalism in China. *East Asia Journal of Theology* 1, no.1: 71–8.

Liu Shaoqi. 1981.

———.The political report of the Central Committee of the Communist Party to the Eighth National Congress of the Party, September 15, 1956. Documents of the Eighth National Congress of the Communist Party. Beijing: Foreign Language Press.

Lu Weidu. 1984.

———.Reflections of a Chinese Catholic Layman. *Chinese Christians Speak Out.* Ed. K.H. Ting, 125–33. Beijing: New World Press.

Mao Zedong (Tse-Tung). 1968a. *The Wisdom of Mao Tse-Tung.* New York: Philosophical Library.

———.1968b. *Four Essays on Philosophy.* Beijing: Foreign Language Press.

Matthews, Jay and Linda Matthews. 1983. *One billion: A China Chronicle.* New York: Random House.

National Council of Churches of Christ in the USA. 1963. *Documents of the Three-self Movement.*

Palmer, Spencer J. 1967. *Korea and Christianity.* Seoul: Hollym.

———, ed. 1980. *The New Religions of Korea.* Seoul: Transactions of the Korea Branch of the Royal Asiatic Society. 43: 1–10.

Rouleau, F. A. 1967. Chinese rites controversy. *New Catholic Encyclopedia III,* 611–17. New York: McGraw Hill.

Selover, Thomas. 1985. San Chiao: Religious dimensions of pacific culture. *Religion in the Pacific Era.* Ed., Frank Flinn and Tyler Hendricks. New York: Paragon House.

Shupe, Anson. 1985. Western Christianity as a vehicle for eastern sentiments. *Religion in the Pacific Era.* Ed., Frank Flinn and Tyler Hendricks. New York: Paragon House.

Spence, Jonathan D. 1984. *The Memory Palace of Matteo Ricci.* New York: Viking.

Stauffer, Milton T. 1922. *The Christian Occupation of China.* Shanghai: China Continuation Committee.

Ting, K. H. 1982. *The Church in China.* London: The British Council of Churches.

Ting, K. H., ed. 1984. *Chinese Christians Speak Out.* Beijing: New World Press.

Tu Shihua. 1984. An independent, self-ruled and self-managed church is our sacred right. *Chinese Christians Speak Out.* Ed. K.H. Ting, 66–72. Beijing: New World Press.

Turner, Victor. 1970. *The Forest of Symbols: Aspects of Ndembu Ritual.* New York: Cornell University Press.

Weber, Max. 1964. *The religion of China: Confucianism and Daoism.* Trans. Hans H. Gerth. New York: Macmillan.

White, Theodore H. 1983. China: Burnout of a revolution. *Time Magazine* (September 26): 30–49.

Wren, Christopher S. 1984a. Improving quality of life is first priority in Peking. *New York Times* (16 Dec.) 1yff.

———. 1984b. Peking reshaping ideology to fit new economic policy. *New York Times* (17 Dec.) 1yff.

Zhao, Fusan. 1984. Christianity in China in the 19th and first half of the 20th centuries—notes on colonialism and missionary activity. *Chinese Christians Speak Out.* Ed., K.H. Ting, 29–35. Beijing: New World Press.

16

Pentecostals and Politics in North and Central America

MARGARET M. POLOMA

W ITHIN the past decade sociologists of religion have witnessed the development of anomalies that have questioned aspects of secularization and modernization theories. Two anomalies of particular significance for this paper have been the worldwide growth of the Pentecostal-charismatic movement and the alleged impact of religious fundamentalism on political behavior. Given the fundamental bent of Pentecostals and charismatics, there is a tendency to view this growing movement as a component in the politico-religious mosaic.

I believe this is an erroneous position that fails in its understanding of the supernatural orientation of charismatic ideology that leaves most believers apolitical. Those few who are in the forefront of political action often represent antithetical positions that threaten to divide the

I wish to thank Alberto Arroyo who served more as a colleague than a graduate research assistant in preparing this paper. I also wish to acknowledge Jim Wallis, Peter Wagner, and Orlando Costas for their suggestions and references. Although I was unable to address all of the issues raised by Stephen D. Glazier, Jeffrey K. Hadden, and Roland Robertson in their respective critiques of an earlier draft, the helpful comments and suggestions each offered undoubtedly strengthened this article.

329

movement. Should Pentecostals and charismatic leaders become politically active there is evidence that such involvement would tend to fragment the charismatic movement as it has the Catholic church in Central America, and even hamper the movement's worldwide appeal.

Before this thesis can be developed, it is necessary to make certain conceptual distinctions. One is the distinction and overlap between *fundamentalist* and *evangelical, evangelical* and *Pentecostal,* and *Pentecostal* and *charismatic.* The second distinction is a perhaps futile attempt to delineate the essence of *political action* from *moral* and *social action.* It is only as some working definition of these key concepts can be agreed upon that any meaningful discussion can proceed.

What is Charismatic?

There has been a trend in both popular and social scientific literature to view charismatics and Pentecostals as two distinct species. Charismatics are seen as the tongues-speakers in mainstream and new independent churches, while Pentecostals are those belonging to the established denominations who first preached the "baptism of the Spirit" earlier this century. As I have attempted to demonstrate elsewhere (Poloma 1982), the Pentecostals and neo-Pentecostals can best be viewed as two tributaries of the charismatic stream that includes Pentecostals, neo-Pentecostal Catholics, Protestants, and Orthodox, as well as independent and parachurch ministries.

A charismatic is then defined as a born-again Christian who accepts the Bible as the inspired Word of God and who emphasizes a part of Christian tenet that is often downplayed by other Bible believers, namely the power, the baptism, and the gifts of the Holy Spirit. Not only glossolalia, but prophecy healing, miracles, and an acceptance of other biblical paranormal phenomena are accepted as valid contemporary religious experiences.

Charismatic believers are found in all Christian denominations. In addition to the nearly ten million adherents to Pentecostalism in the United States (Poloma 1982, 130–31), it is estimated that eight million Catholics and some six million Protestants call themselves charismatic (Barrett 1982, 712). Quebedeaux (1983, 222) has given a very tentative worldwide estimate of at least five percent of Christianity being charismatic or Pentecostal. Although the exact numbers and degree of participation may be questioned, there is no doubt that charismatics are a major force in Christendom, both in the United States and abroad.

Whether Pentecostal or neo-Pentecostal, charismatics consider themselves evangelical and readily ally with most evangelicals—but not extreme fundamentalists. Fundamentalism basically continues to view the charismatic movement as the "work of Satan," whereas most evangelicals have been open to fellowship first with Pentecostals and later with neo-Pentecostals (Poloma 1982, 6–7). Although some conservative evangelicals have a view of the charismatic movement akin to fundamentalists, asserting that the gifts of the Holy Spirit are not intended for modern times, even members of such groups appear accepting of aspects of the charismatic movement.

As Hunter (1983), Quebedeaux (1978) and Reese (1983) have demonstrated, the term evangelical covers diverse believers, with charismatics representing one facet of the larger movement. It is accurate to say that while charismatics are evangelical believers, only some evangelicals are charismatics.

Politics, Morality and Social Action

Although many of the forerunners of evangelicalism took liberal and even radical stands on some social issues (noteworthy are abolition and nineteenth century feminism), a shift away from direct involvement began as early as the 1870s (Dayton 1976). Whatever the disputed socio-historical cause of the retreat, the post-Civil War evangelicals became more concerned with "personal purity" than social reform. This emphasis on personal piety continues to dominate the charismatic movement, disregarding its diverse denominational roots.

The apolitical stance of most Pentecostals may be traced to the shunning by political-active fundamentalists of the early twentieth century. Pentecostals were spared fundamentalism's humiliating defeat, particularly in the Scopes Trial, because they were not welcome in the fundamentalist camp. This original exclusion by fundamentalists and Pentecostalism's lower class origins led Shriver (1981, 36) to correctly observe, "Pentecostals emphasize the importance of spiritual empowerment and conversion and tend to resist political involvement or identification with social causes."

Nevertheless, some charismatics have recently become involved in political action, primarily in issues related to the private sphere or morality. The family, in particular, is viewed as an embattled institution and limited political activities are regarded as necessary to guarantee its future. It is around privatized moral concerns such as abortion, pornography, and homosexuality that a strong voice has developed to "protect the family."

As I will attempt to demonstrate in this article, the private "moral" issues may provide some political unity for many charismatics, but stepping into the arena of the public sphere appears to cause division. Public issues, including economic problems, social welfare legislation, and international affairs, are generally regarded by charismatics as outside the concerns of religion. When "political" positions are taken by charismatics they are usually regarded as involving "moral issues" that touch upon "personal purity." When charismatic leaders have been perceived to step out of the realm of private moral concerns and into the public sphere, controversy has errupted.

Charismatic Politics: A Study in Ambivalence

It is only with the 1984 election in the United States that any noteworthy direct political action by charismatics has become evident. And when it has occurred, such action has been divisive. The tension within the charismatic community over the decision to become or to remain uninvolved in political action was most apparent in its leading American nondenominational publication *Charisma*.

Charisma openly endorsed Ronald Reagan for president stating: "The basic choice is plain—if for no other reason than opposition to the murder of infants." In his editorial for this issue Stephen Strang, editor and publisher of *Charisma* (October, 1984, 6) noted that readers may be surprised by the magazine's action. "As far as we know, *Charisma* is the first major Christian magazine to endorse a political candidate for president." Defensiveness and a need to justify this action was present within most of the articles of that issue. There was a sounding of a tentative note in many articles, as if the politicized editors were testing the charismatic waters. Columnist Jamie Buckingham (1984, 182), although endorsing the position of his employer, did quip: "Now, having said that, I only hope Reagan and Mondale don't both show up in my church next Sunday."

The apprehension of the editors was well founded, if the following two issues' (December, 1984 and January, 1985) letters to the editor may be used as a barometer. Assuming the ten reprinted letters were in fact "a sampling of the mail we received" as claimed, the reaction from readers was from mildly to strongly negative. One cancelled his subscription and nine of the ten letters reported negative reactions to *Charisma's* "preaching the gospel of Saint Reagan." These attacks led the editor to respond:

> We wrote in our editorial that we do not favor Republicans over Democrats, nor do we think one candidate was more Christian than the other. This statement was apparently overlooked by many of our readers who blasted our endorsement of Reagan which was based on his strong stand against abortions *(Charisma,* December 1984:14).

The bottom line appears that the editors of *Charisma* viewed such an endorsement as the prerogative of religion given its obligation to uphold morals. Readers expressed little, if any, disagreement with the anti-abortion position taken by *Charisma* authors in earlier issues. The outright political endorsement was received as "meddling in politics," with criticisms of the magazine's being "used" by Republicans and attendant dangers of mixing the gospel with politics. The subscribers protested the political endorsement. "Your function to your readers," wrote one couple, "is to inform them of the issues and problems. For you to go beyond this responsibility, especially as a Christian publication, does an injustice to your readers."

The case of *Charisma* illustrates a wariness among many charismatics about becoming political that may be further illustrated by other evangelical-charismatic writers. Those more versed in political history (see for example, Colson 1984; Lovelace 1984; Noll 1984) are cautioning those who would venture into political waters. Not only do politically active Christian leaders run the risk of misjudging candidates (Noll 1984) and taking extremist positions (Lovelace 1984), they might become naïve pawns in the sophisticated game of politics (Colson 1984). The cautionary notes are addressed to those who would become involved in partisan politics and/or in public issues calling for certain structural solutions.

The dividing lines between private morality and public political issues are blurred. This blurring may account for the apparent ambiguity and inconsistency found in a recent survey I conducted among members of two Assemblies of God congregations, the largest of Pentecostal dominations.

The apolitical character of many Assemblies of God members is demonstrated by the fact that approximately one-quarter of them had no opinion on any of four questions I asked about the relationship between religion and politics. I was initially surprised to learn that fifty-seven percent agreed with the statement "Churches have a responsibility to inform their congregations about relevant political matters." And, sixty-one percent disagreed with the proposition that "Pastors should never include political issues in their sermons."

On first glance, these responses do not appear to conform to my thesis that, on balance, charismatics are apolitical. The other two items, however, provide clues as to the conditional character of these responses. Sixty-two percent reject the idea that "Churches must be willing to promote political candidates who reflect sound biblical teachings." Only seventeen percent agreed with this statement. Thus, the large majority do not support the actual endorsement of candidates, a norm broken by *Charisma's* support of President Reagan. The fourth item about politics in my survey read "It is best not to mix politics and religion." Again, somewhat surprising to me, only twenty-five percent agreed and forty-nine percent disagreed.

Taken together, these responses in my survey reveal a great deal of ambivalence and ambiguity. Those who advocate, or at least do not oppose, involvement in politics seem to be saying: "We would rather not be politically involved, but given the immorality of our nation, we are given little choice."

After further analyzing the data, I reached three conclusions. First, if the majority of my respondents are unwilling to rule out the possibility of "going political," they seem clearly to impose rather serious limitations on the nature of involvement. In other contexts and other religious groups, endorsing a candidate is not a very bold political move. With only seventeen percent willing to promote this move, it seems unlikely that Assemblies of God members are likely to become caught up in a social movement. Second, those most displeased with the prospect of religion getting involved in politics are less educated and likely have less say in running the congregation. Engagement in politics would likely create in them feelings of alienation. Third, it seems clear that any effort to move a congregation into the political arena in a serious way would be disruptive to congregational life.

Still, charismatics have discovered politics and it is likely to remain a concern. But concern with matters political is not the same as being at home in this arena. Many would readily concur with the French Christian social philosopher, Jacques Ellul (1972, 13): "The Bible shows us that the church is not just a spiritual matter, that politics is not simply a human action of no concern to us. It may be that politics is the kingdom of the devil, but this certainly concerns us as Christians."

Charismatics are most likely to become political on matters relating to personal morality. On issues such as abortion, homosexuality, and pornography, Catholic bishops, Moral Majority, and *Charisma* seem to speak largely with one voice. When morality is broadened to include larger ethical concerns, Christians are far from agreeing that the answers are part of any "seamless garment." It is precisely on *public* issues, especially economic problems, nuclear weapons, and "national defense" at home and abroad, that the garment divides.

This division is well illustrated by differences between the charismatic Sojourners Community headed by Jim Wallis and charismatic television preacher and founder of the Christian Broadcasting Network, Pat Robertson. They share a common stance on abortion and pornography. They further share an evangelical bent to further Christianity, an acceptance of the Bible as the Word of God, as well as the charismatic belief in the power of the Holy Spirit to lead, guide, and direct human action. Their emphases and scriptural interpretations, on issues of defense, capitalism, and meeting the needs of the poor, however, are worlds apart. But their differences in perspective are due perhaps more to personal histories than to differences in charismatic theologies.

Both Wallis and Robertson brought their political positions with them as they entered the realm of charismatic Christianity. Wallis had already been involved with social activism in the late 1960s. Robertson, raised in a conservative southern milieu, followed the political direction of his father, who once represented Virginia in the United States Senate. It is a free enterprise, capitalistic adventure, and *laissez-faire* economy that has been hospitable to the rise of Robertson's Christian ministry. As Robertson views the world, communism, socialism, and big government threaten the very operation that he is using to further evangelistic efforts. Wallis, on the other hand, believes the Christian mandate emphasizes caring for the poor and mediating peace. He is sympathetic toward government efforts to relieve poverty and reduce armaments. He emphasizes social justice and believes evangelism can best be accomplished, not in an unregulated capitalistic economy, but through ministering to the material needs of the poor. Many charismatic Christians take a position between these two poles, questioning the degree to which either Robertson's or Wallis' politico-economic pronouncements are in fact biblically mandated.

While most charismatics would concur that it is important for believers to further the kingdom of God on earth, those minority involved in direct political action, especially public or institutional issues, have a different conception of what this means from those who eschew politics. As Richard Niebuhr (1937, xii) has effectively argued:

> . . . the kingdom of God had indeed been the dominant idea in American Christianity—just as the idea of the vision had been paramount in medieval faith—but it had not always meant the same thing. In the early period of American life, when foundations were laid on which we have all had to build, 'kingdom of God' meant 'sovereignty of God'; in the creative period of awakening and revival it meant 'reign of Christ'; and only in the most recent period had it come to mean 'kingdom on earth.' Yet it became equally apparent that these were not simply three divergent ideas, but that they were intimately related to one another, and that the idea of the kingdom of God could not be expressed in terms of one of them alone. . . .

All three of these meanings are found in today's religio-political scene. While the conservatives best embodied by the Moral Majority are attempting to impose their definition of the "reign of Christ" through a "re-Christianized" America, those who are involved in more liberal social action, including the National Council of Churches, desire to bring about a kind of kingdom on earth through abolition of poverty, war, and other social problems.

Charismatics are more prone to emphasize the third meaning—the "sovereignty of God"—characterized by the early historical America, but with a noteworthy addition. Most charismatics, because of their exposure to paranormal religious experiences, believe the sovereign will and power of God can be more effectively released through prayer than through political or social intervention. They are quick to cite I Timothy 2:2, urging believers to pray "for kings and all those in authority, that we may live peaceful and quiet lives." At least one national group of "prayer warriors" exists whose members gather weekly to pray for government leaders. Charismatic writer Derek Prince (1973) instructs his readers on how Christians "can change world events through the simple yet powerful tools of prayer and fasting."

Charismatics are more likely to rally behind such calls to pray for political leaders, quoting the biblical instructions for so doing, than believing political action can bring about desired results. This prayerful-ly active but politically passive position which I believe still permeates the charismatic movement is also related to the belief we are living in the last days. Shriver (1981) attributes the apolitical stance of Pentecos-tals to its teaching about the "rapture," a pre-millennarist teaching that asserts believers will be miraculously removed from the earth before the biblically foretold "time of tribulation": "In a nuclear age this is an appealing doctrine, because it not only provides a comforting interpretation of possible nuclear holocaust, but it also delivers ('raptures') those who believe into heaven before the blast. One can therefore hope that the end is coming soon, even provoke it, without fear of personal, bodily harm" (Shriver 1981, 58).

With nearly eighty years behind it, the millennarian emphasis of Pentecostalism has weakened only slightly. The doctrine is still proclaimed, often supported with interpretations of world events being filtered through the Book of Revelations. It becomes a rallying call to support missionary activity and to personal evangelism—to use these "last days to save souls." Feeding the hungry and giving drink to the thirsty is seen as a call first to care for spiritual needs. Pentecostal missionary activities are well supported by American churches and do provide for social needs both in the United States and abroad. The emphasis, unlike the controversies that have developed within the National Council of Churches, will not be political but rather "help" oriented with an eye on conversion.

Neo-Pentecostals, those remaining within mainstream churches as well as those who have converted to Pentecostalism, are of a similar mind. Some, having claimed witness to the futility of the "social gospel" to effect change, have committed themselves and their money to outreach that emphasizes conversion. Prayer and evangelism rather than political action are the twin weapons of most charismatics against world problems.

The strongest admonition against this perceived imbalance has come from the Catholic hierarchy. After noting Pope John Paul II's call to social action, Bishop William McMannis of South Bend told the 1982 Charismatic Conference:

> For charismatics, unlike for many others, prayer may be relatively easy. But "renewing the face of the earth"—the theme of your convention— reaching out an arm of charity to the destitute, crusading for justice for *women* and men—these do not come so easily. Prayer without works is dead! It is only that kind of fatal prayer in the charismatic movement that could kill it irrevocably.

This call to social action and to non-partisan political action on moral injustice issues (a stance that has been characteristic of the Catholic bishops) is being made in Catholic circles but without much impact to date.

In summary, charismatic leaders tend to avoid political endorsements and partisan politics, have little to say about social action, and tend to limit moral teachings to those hearing a call to conversion. Resources, especially time and money, are limited, and are deemed better used for changing hearts—not changing social systems. Ventures into the public sphere of political concerns have threatened division and have to date been pursued by only a small minority. Further discussion requires some consideration of charismatic ideology in relation to the political stance of some evangelicals, particularly the new Religious Right.

Ideology in Socio-Historical Context

As Kater (1982, xii) has observed, the politics of the Christian Right can only be understood in reference to its theology. With liberal politics of the recent past seen as idolatizing the government while minimizing the family, the Christian Right has sparked a voice of populist discontent to protest policies it believes counter to God's plan (Kater 1982, 11). It would be safe to say that many North American charismatics concur with the protests against a nebulous "secular humanism," the alleged demon of modern times, particularly as it infringes on privatized morality. Yet there is an underlying other-worldly ideology that persists among charismatics that causes rejection of concerns about social issues, both private and public ones (Hollen-weger 1972, 107). What Saracco (1984, 9) has recently noted about Pentecostal ideology in Central America also applies to North America:

> Another central element in Pentecostal message and ethics is a constant opposition to anything related to 'the world'. . . . This rejecting is not the first step in the promotion of a better and more just situation, but rather a leaving behind of any concern for social problems. The person is isolated from the environment from which he comes, either by spending his/her free time with church work or through a rigorous ethic which by itself breaks all connection with the world. In Pentecostal theology the social order belongs to a world that is bound to disappear and, therefore, nothing can or should be done in order to improve that which is doomed to "eternal fire." The Spirit's strength and power are not used against sinful structures that keep human beings oppressed; rather people are offered a parallel society (the Church) in which they can live fully.

This ideology, it has been noted, tends to legitimize the established order (Vidales 1978, 71) and indirectly to support positions of the Religious Right.

Most Pentecostals and neo-Pentecostals have been reluctant, as stated by former Watergate figure Charles Colson (1984), to place their faith in either the Republican or Democratic parties. Their limited efforts to tackle social problems takes a privatized, nonpolitical approach. Drug addicts, alcoholics, prisoners, and others seen in need of help are assisted but always with the focus on conversion. Conversion to the gospel is viewed as the best assistance one can offer. Groups like Teen Challenge, founded by Pentecostal minister David Wilkerson; International Prison Fellowship, by Charles Colson; or PTL Centers as promoted by charismatic Christian television stars Tammy and Jim Bakker are models of helping with the desire to give what the givers have found most meaningful in their own lives—their born-again, Spirit-filled Christianity.

Support for such activity comes from evangelicals as well as charismatics. Not all, or perhaps even the majority of born-again believers, are willing to accept the "political rebirth of American evangelicals" and its redefinition of boundaries between "morality and politics" and "religion and morality" (Wuthnow 1983, 180–81). As Liebman and Wuthnow (1983, 6–7) have noted, the New Christian Right is but one important member of the New Right—and many charismatics, especially Pentecostals, are wary of its secular ties.[1]

When they do become involved in social action, charismatics and Pentecostals are likely to offer religious, even supernatural, solutions. Conversion and Spirit baptism are believed to be powerful enough to reform hardened criminals, cure mental illness and drug addiction, and even to miraculously open doors for employment. Charismatic ideology promotes a God who is actively involved in even the most mundane affairs and who directs both ministries and ministers. Such an ideology is different from the Protestant ethic still embodied in the larger evangelical movement. As Rifkin (1979) has so astutely argued, the ideology of charismatics with their belief in "supernatural gifts of faith healing, speaking in tongues and prophecy" represents "a monumental assault on the modern age itself." Rifkin (1979, x) notes: ". . . these supernatural powers are beginning to replace science, techniques and reason as the critical reference points for interpreting one's day-to-day existence [which could] . . . provide the kind of liberating force that could topple the prevailing ethos and provide a bridge to the next age of history."

Given the basic ideological components of separatism (at least to the extent of creating alternative structures, be it through convenant communities or through superchurches designed to care for believers from cradle to grave) and the emphasis on active supernatural powers in the modern world, charismatics are not likely to follow the path suggested by Rifkin of merging their ideology with evangelical theology to produce a "New Covenant Vision." To do so would result in further accommodation and assimilation of a group that promises an ideology that has the potential of being, as we shall argue later, a world-system for religious thought. Becoming overtly political would render this charismatic potential of world appeal decidedly impotent.

Charismatics on the Central American Scene

Most of the focus thus far has been on the North American scene—and for good reason. North America has been and continues to be the life-blood of worldwide charismatic activity. This is true for Pentecostalism as well as for charismatic Catholicism that may have the potential to reshape the dominant church in Latin America. Despite the great differences between the Anglo and Latin American religious scenes, the charismatic movement has thrived in both.

In the Caribbean (Wedenoja 1980; LaRuffa 1980; Glazier 1980), in Central America (Bausett 1982; Huntington 1984 a,b), as well as in South America (Howe 1980; Norman 1981; Hollenweger 1972) missionaries of the Pentecostal faith came largely from the United States. This is also true for the charismatic gospel that has infiltrated Roman Catholicism where American missionaries more recently exported Pentecostalism for Catholic consumption (Chordas 1980). Two observations have been made repeatedly by observers of Pentecostalism south of the border. One, unlike most Protestant missionary endeavors, Pentecostalism has sought to establish indigenous churches, allowing them local autonomy. This fact has contributed to the rapid growth of the movement, making it the only viable Christian yet "non-foreign" alternative to cultural Catholicism.

The second is the nonpolitical thrust of the movement, particularly in issues that may be designated as public concerns, that has been noted repeatedly (Norman 1981; Willems 1967; Hollenweger 1972; Glazier 1980; Anderson 1979). It stands as a firm opponent to the liberation theology that has been reported on widely in the North American liberal religious press (e.g., Cox 1984). This appears to be true for the majority of Pentecostals regardless of the Latin American country under discussion and the significant differences in the spread of

Protestantism among them. Were it not for the anomalic case of Rios Montt, the charismatic former president of Guatemala, probably little question would be raised about the potential political impact of these believers. It is Rios Montt, perhaps more than any figure in Central America, who has raised questions about charismatic political potential.

The Case of Rios Montt

General Efrain Rios Montt's selection by the ruling junta as president of Guatemala in the spring of 1982 was hailed by the charismatic press in the United States as a move of God while critically evaluated by the secular media. A headline in the *Wall Street Journal* (14 April 1982) questioned, "President Rios Stirs Hope in Many Quarters, but Is He Clown or Ayatollah?" (*Charisma*, June 1982). Not surprisingly evangelical Christian reporters and Rios Montt himself blamed the American media, particularly the *New York Times* and the *Washington Post*, for his political demise seventeen months later (Minnery 1984; *Charisma*, May 1984).

While some charismatics may concur with the stance of the evangelical press, others may use the incident to reinforce the need for political neutrality. After all, if a sovereign God had placed Montt in the presidential seat, charismatic lay theology is prone to argue, only God could remove him. Most would be reticent and slow to judge his election, his presidency, or his downfall.

It is not without significance that Rios Montt, a former Catholic who converted to the California-based charismatic Church of the Word in 1977, ran for president in 1974. Although he reportedly received fifty-four percent of the popular vote, in the "aftermath" of the disputed election results ruling party leaders forced him to move to Spain as a military attaché for the Guatemalan embassy (*Charisma*, June 1982). It was after he returned to Guatemala in 1977 that he converted.

The Church of the Word was apparently not politically active when Rios Montt was asked to present himself at the palace after the 1982 coup. Upon the advice of the elders, he originally decided not to respond to the invitation. "They just weren't sure that the church should get involved" (Minnery 1982, 16). Rios Montt, a political figure before conversion, then was later seen as God's answer to Guatemala's problems when selected by the junta. It clearly was a case of *ex post facto* theologizing rather than his church's or charismatic political power that placed Rios Montt in office. As Huntington

(1984b, 24) has noted: "Rios Montt's overthrow on August 8, 1983, has not lessened the pervasive ideological influence of Guatemala's evangelicals, nor their usefullness to ruling groups. But it has dispelled the notion that they could become an active political force. They have simply gone back to their traditional 'apolitical' stance."

The case of Rios Montt may be used to illustrate the manner in which charismatics may be drawn into overt political involvement, but also the quickness with which they retreat. Accepting a charismatic gospel did not appear to alter Montt's political ideology or yearnings. His political orientation clearly was baggage brought with him into the movement from his pre-conversion days. His short-lived presidency, however, quickly was interpreted by leading charismatic magazine and popular politically-oriented television programs (especially *The 700 Club*) within a charismatic framework. God had raised up Rios Montt as his prophet for Guatemala. This interpretation, however, was quickly challenged by Rios Montt's downfall, leaving those (probably only a vocal minority) who wedded their charismatic beliefs with the political events in Guatemala to go back "to their traditional 'apolitical' stance." Rios Montt has demonstrated that charismatics are not above political entanglement, but this is not due to actively seeking political solutions and the retreat in the event of failure is quick.

The Case of Nicaragua

If Rios Montt's brief tenure as Guatemala's president reflects an anomaly to the thesis of Pentecostal-charismatic political neutrality, it is one that is more readily explained than the potentially explosive situation in Nicaragua. The Catholic church is already polarized over the Sandinista rule (NACLA, 1981), and the politically involved minority in the North American charismatic movement already reflects the division.

On the one hand, we find Sojourner's Community actively opposing American aid to the Contras who represent a counterrevolutionary force against the ruling communist power (Hollyday and Wallis 1983; Wallis 1984). On the other, we find Pat Robertson of the Christian Broadcasting Network and *The 700 Club* accusing Democratic leaders of being "naïve" when they criticize American foreign policy in Central America. *Sojourners* consistently depicts a one-sided liberal or radical stance on Nicaragua (the Sandinistas seemingly do no wrong) while Robertson's three-part series (aired July 25, 26, and 27, 1984) provided an equally one-sided conservative portrayal. Similarly conservative, although less overtly partisan reports, have appeared in *Charisma*.

If Nicaragua is indicative of a direction other Central American countries will take, more Pentecostals may be jarred into political confrontations, but such indications are very murky. *Christianity Today* (3, February 1984) reported that some eight hundred Pentecostals in Nicaragua are facing imprisonment for not registering for the draft. On the other hand, the Evangelical Press reports: "Political instability in Nicaragua has not hindered the rapid growth of the Church of God, Cleveland, Tennessee, according to a Nicaraguan delegate to the Church of God's 60th general assembly here" (*Charisma*, November 1984, 114). There are thus conflicting reports on the extent to which it is possible for religion to be apolitical in Nicaragua. The Church of God (Cleveland) has urged its ministers to exercise "great discretion in consideration of political issues," which appears to suggest remaining apolitical. For the most part, this apolitical position has "paid off" in terms of growth. Political controversies simply add another potential for division.

The situation in Nicaragua thus appears unclear. *If* (as *Charisma* and *The 700 Club* have reported) it is expected that religion either support the revolutionary government or be viewed as an enemy, the largely apolitical stance of charismatics in Nicaragua may be challenged. At present evangelicals appear to be reaping a harvest from the acrimonious split between the Catholic hierarchy and the "popular church." Evangelicals have seen their numbers soar by two-thirds since the Sandinista revolution (NACLA Report, 1984), and assumedly much of this evangelical growth is among Pentecostals. The Assemblies of God is now the second largest Protestant church in Nicaragua and growth is evident in both the Church of God (Cleveland, TN) and the International Church of the Four Square Gospel (Barrett 1982, 523). Church leaders are not eager to add a political ingredient that may adversely affect this success.

If, however, Pentecostals are forced into a political stance in Nicaragua, all indications are that, due to its conservative American evangelical support and its own social theology, it will be a conservative one. As Huntington (1984a, 10) has noted about the past: "With remarkable resilience, evangelical Protestants held to their conservative view of the world, even in the context of the increasing radicalization of Christianity during the 1960s." The political message preached is anti-communism with evangelicals representing "the last hope of freedom" (Dominguez 1984, 14). The more likely course of action, however, will be to follow the advice Paul gave to the early Roman church:

> Everyone must submit himself to the governing authorities, for there is no authority except that which God has established. The authorities that exist have been established by God. Consequently, he who rebels against the authority is rebelling against what God has instituted, and those who do so will bring judgment on themselves. For rulers hold no terror for those who do right, but for those who do wrong (Romans, 13:1–3).

This biblical stance, at least in the short run, may placate any Nicaraguan attempt to politicize Pentecostal churches.

On the Horns of A Dilemma

Unlike the separation of church and state prized by United States civil libertarians, Latin Americans historically have seen a politically active church (Mecham 1966). It was only after the Catholic church lost its favored status in one country after another that the road was paved for Protestant evangelism. Catholic clergy, however, continued in varying degrees to meddle in politics. The political neutrality and church-state separation which was a boon to evangelicalism has not been characteristic of Catholicism (Bonpane 1980). As we have already noted in Nicaragua, this has resulted in a divided Catholicism.

The division between the hierarchy and the church of the wealthy versus the church of the masses is found in other countries as well. An American priest friend who served as a missionary to El Salvador during the years Archbishop Romero gained the episcopacy and was murdered reported how Romero had been viewed as a "rich man's priest." Once he became bishop of San Salvador, however, he reportedly became sensitized to the plight of the poor. His speaking out for justice cost him his life.

The church hierarchy in many cases still upholds a conservative theology that appears to favor the landowners and rulers. Yet it is also within the Catholic church that liberation theology has developed, promising to be a Christian alternative to the appeal of Marxism (Dodson 1979–80; Costas 1982). Much of evangelical Protestantism in Latin America would share the rigid anti-communist stance of the hierarchy, a view that also reflects its North American sponsors. Since Catholicism and its hierarchy as the dominant religion has not been kind to evangelicals, a united political conservative voice is unlikely.

Moreover, an openly conservative political stance might well alienate the lower-class converts to evangelicalism.

Few Pentecostals, however, share the perspectives of liberation theologians. Its emphasis on socialism as a means to biblical justice is foreign to most American evangelicals. Its communitarian ideology is more compatible with Catholicism which has had a tradition of religious communities and teachings about the church as a "mystical body" than it has with the individualistic bent inherent in much Protestantism (Casanova, 1984). Perhaps even more importantly, liberation theology does not have a clear basis in a fundamentalist interpretation of the Bible that characterizes both Pentecostalism and neo-Pentacostalism. The Apostle Paul's instructions to the Roman Church or his admonition to Titus (Titus 3:1) reminding "the people to be subject to rulers and to authorities, to be obedient . . ." are straightforward passages. Liberation theology's curious mixture of Jesus and Marx is unlikely to attract many evangelical converts.

Whether Pentecostals can continue to ignore politics in Central America is an open question. Most certainly they will not comfortably align with those on either horn of the dilemma. Serious scholars would be wise to exert caution before heralding the saving potential of liberation theology for the masses in Latin America. There is no evidence it has any appeal for supernatural-believing Pentecostals. Pentecostals are also troubled by the poverty that engulfs so much of Central America. The unanswered question for them is how to deal with poverty and injustice without becoming politicized when supernatural solutions prove wanting.

It may be questioned whether church political involvement is desirable, necessary, or a liability in the modern world, and there is no simple answer to this query. One Catholic nun who lived in Guatemala for some years told me of a priest friend who had been murdered, reportedly for his "political activities." She assured me his "crime" was treating the poor with dignity; that made him a communist. It was of a similar injustice that Montgomery (1979, 96) noted: "Here we see the dilemma of many Latin American Protestants (and Catholics). On the one hand there is a genuine, sincere faith that is unable to escape its social consequences. On the other hand, there is a deep confusion about what this means in terms of social commitment and action."

It is unlikely, however, that any politico-religious answers will come from either Protestantism or Pentecostalism. As Casanova has effectively argued: "[I]t [Protestantism] is tied much more than Catholicism to Western civilization and to a particular stage of civilization, i.e., the bourgeois-capitalist epoch. Thus, it is less likely that Protestantism may play a creative role in any attempt to transcend the bourgeois-capitalist project of modernity" (Casanova 1984, 23).

Charismatics and a World Religious System: Summary and Conclusions

Although there are anomolies and signs of ambivalence that may dramatically force a revision of my argument at a later date, I believe the charismatic movement worldwide is characterized by political passivity. Some evidence may be presented to support a political orientation on private issues, particularly those relevant to family morals and religious freedom, but only very limited support may be found for political stands on public issues.

Given the indigenous nature of Pentecostal churches and the vast differences in the social conditions between the United States and Latin America, attributing the Latin apolitical thrust to its American origins may show a necessary but not a sufficient cause. I suggest it is the shared charismatic ideology—one that emphasizes an accessible God who intervenes in human affairs—that fosters this seemingly passive political stance. As anti-modern as this God is, He is the God of the charismatic believer—a God who provides for those who depend on Him. Testimonies of modern day healings and miracles support the plausibility structure of this decidedly anti-modern ideology. In Hunter's (1981, 6) terms this ideology may be seen as an "anthropological protest against modernity." But it appears to be an ideology with worldwide appeal, from affluent American suburbs to tiny villages of the Third World.

Perhaps it is precisely this nonpolitical orientation which allows the funeral of any politicized God (Harrington, 1982)—one that permits emphasis on meeting the anthropological need of Homo sapiens rather than the politico-social—that gives the charismatic movement its potential to spawn a universal religion. And because it strives to remain apolitical, Pentecostalism finds itself in a dialectial relationship between First and Third World cultures. Wedenoja (1980, 40) has observed the unusual interaction between these two cultures:

> While it is worthwhile to consider the effects of Western Christendom on Third World societies, we also need to ponder how the embracement and indigenization of Christianity by Third World societies will effect Western Christendom. Culture contact transforms both parties, colonizer and colonized, although we usually focus only on transformation of the

colonized. Third World Christianities may promote a new form of Christendom as we enter into the era of a global culture.

My participant observation of the missionary activities of the Assemblies of God has provided a number of illustrations about the accuracy of Wedenoja's observation as applied to Pentecostalism. The Assembly I have carefully watched for over four years, like most Assemblies of God, has a strong missionary thrust. I have noted changes in worship, belief in miracles, and attitudes about wealth as members of the Assembly have collectively and individually done missionary work in Latin America and Africa. Worship has become freer, expectation of paranormal experiences greater, and the prosperity gospel seen as an American heresy. Such missionary expeditions have deepened an awareness of the privilege of enjoying American freedoms and wealth, but they have also heightened the spiritual, personal, and nonpolitical dimensions of the Pentecostal faith.

But when forced into a political-economic stance, Pentecostalism tends toward a democratic-capitalist system. It "encourages the development of psychological traits and patterns of behavior conducive to success in a capitalist economy, including deferral of gratification, thrift and conscientious labor and exchange" (Wedenoja 1980, 40). To the extent that the modern world-capitalist economy (Wallerstein 1980) is a world-system, Pentecostalism appears to be a good religious fit as a privatized, nonpolitical meaning system for the modern world. If there is the predicted transformation into a socialist world-system, Pentecostalism (as suggested by the case of Nicaragua) may find a less hospitable milieu for its perpetuation.

At the same time, Pentecostalism has the potential to become a "revolutionary political force" that might be able to bridge a transition into a new world economic system. As a global "third force within Christendom" it may effectively provide an alternative to the universal Catholic church which has managed to speak beyond partisan politics. Unlike Catholicism, it has a renewed spiritual thrust that already challenges most "evangelical positivism" (Hunter 1983). It may possibly become that prophetic thrust in world-wide religion called for by social commentators (Webber 1982; Berger 1981; Quebedeaux 1982).

Wedenoja (1980, 42–43) provides an apt description of Pentecostalism's revolutionary potentials:

Pentecostalism is a subtle but profound revolution because it is low-key, religious and not obviously political. It should not be compared to the

American, French, Russian or Mexican revolutions but to the rise of Christianity and the Reformation. It is an ideological concomitant to modernization, which can be compared to the agricultural and industrial revolutions: . . . Pentecostalism is a revolutionary faith because it effects changes in self and the relations between self and others, which incidentally also affects the established churches, and generates an ideological force promoting corresponding changes in society, economy and polity.

Pentecostalism, itself a worldwide religious phenomenon, has already had a ripple effect in the established churches in spearheading the larger charismatic movement. Its effect on world economy and polity should also be carefully watched by social scientists.

Notes

1. Much media attention has been given to the Religious Right, but research questions the extent to which evangelical religion has been able to influence politics—or even if there is a desire to do so. In a study of evangelical pastors in the Midwest, Zwier (1982) reported that Baptist pastors were the most supportive of the Moral Majority (50%), with Lutheran, Methodist and Presbyterian pastors being much less so (12%). A decided minority (3%) felt it was acceptable to persuade people to vote for a particular candidate during a worship service. On the other hand, the overwhelming majority (96%) asserted that pastors should urge their flock to register to vote. It is this urging to vote that has helped revitalize the Christian Right as a force with evangelicals voting along class lines rather than in accord with specific perceived theological tenets. It is the socio-demographic variables that takes precedence over religious ones in shaping conservative American politics. As Shupe and Stacey (1983, 113) note:

. . . contrary to claims of fundamental preachers like Jerry Falwell, there is no evidence of a sizable constituency in support of religious involve-ment in politics. . . . Falwell and other leaders of the New Christian Right seriously overestimate the amount of agreement among sympa-thizers on the issues they hold dear.

After reviewing existing research, Guth concludes "there is little evidence of a massive new commitment of evangelicals to the ranks of Republicans or ideological conservatives" (Guth 1983, 38). If this lack of a clear linkage between politics and religion is true for the larger evangelical-fundamentalist movement where historical precedent exists for political involvements, I would suggest it is even more true for Pentecostals where politics has been historically eschewed.

References

Anderson, Robert Mapes. 1979. *Vision of The Disinherited.* New York: Oxford University Press.

Barrett, David B., ed. 1982. *World Christian Encyclopedia.* New York: Oxford University Press.

Berger, Peter. 1981. The class struggle in American religion. *Christian Century* 98, no. 6 (February 25):194.

Bonpane, Blase. 1980. The church and revolutionary struggle in Central America. *Latin American Perspectives* 25, 26 (Spring/Summer): 178–89.

Buckingham, Jamie. 1984. Endorsement dilemmas. *Charisma* (November):182.

Casanova, Jose. 1984. The politics of the religious revival. *Telos.* (Spring):3–33.

Charisma. 1982. Charismatic general rules Guatemala (June): 14.

———.1984. Nicaragua Indian faithful revolting after massacres. (June): 92, 96.

———.1984. Rios Montt says Guatemala needs pastors, not troops. (May): 98–99.

Chordas, Thomas J. 1980. Catholic Pentecostalism: A new world in a new world. *Perspectives on Pentecostalism.* Ed. S. D. Glazier, 143–76. Washington, D.C.: University Press of America.

Christianity Today. 1984. Some 800 Pentecostals in Nicaragua are facing imprisonment (February 3): 55.

Colson, Charles W. 1984. Temptations of the innocent. *Newsweek* (October 8): 10.

Costas, Orlando E. 1982. *Christ Outside The Gate.* Maryknoll, N.Y. Orbis Books.

Cox, Harvey. 1984. *Religion in a Secular City: Toward a Post Modern Theology.* New York: Simon & Schuster.

Dayton, Donald W. 1976. *Discovering an Evangelical Heritage.* New York: Harper & Row.

Dodson, Michael. 1979–80. Prophetic politics & political theory in Latin America. *Polity* 12:388–408.

Dominguez, Enrique. 1984. The great commissioner. *NACLA Report* (Jan/Feb): 11–21.

Ellul, Jacques. 1972. *The Politics of God and The Politics of Man*. Grand Rapids, MI: Eerdmans.

Glazier, Stephen D., ed. 1980. *Perspectives on Pentecostalism: Case studies from the Caribbean and Latin America*. Washington, D.C.: University Press of America.

Glazier, Stephen D. 1980. Pentecostal exorcism and modernization in Trinidad. *Perspectives on Pentecostalism*. Washington, D.C.: University Press of America: 67–80.

Guth, James L. 1983. The new Christian right. *The New Christian Right*. Eds. R.C. Liebman and Robert Wuthnow, 31–45. New York: Aldine.

Harrington, Michael. 1983.. *The Politics at God's Funeral*. New York: Penguin Books.

Hollenweger, W. J. 1972. *The Pentecostals*. Minneapolis: Augsbury.

Hollyday, Joyce and Jim Wallis. 1983. A fragile experiment. *Sojourners* (March): 8–13.

Howe, Gary Nigel. 1980. Capitalism and religion at the periphery. *Perspectives on Pentecostalism*. Ed. S.D. Glazier, 125–42. Washington, D.C.: University Press of America.

Hunter, James Davison. 1980. The new class and young evangelicals. *Review of Religious Research* (December): 155–168.

———.1981. The new religious: Demodernizing and the protest Against Modernity. *The Social Impact of New Religious Movements*. Ed. Bryan Wilson, 1–18. Barrytown, N.Y.: Unification Theological Seminary.

———.1983. *American Evangelicalism*. New Brunswick, N.J.: Rutgers University Press.

Huntington, Deborah. 1984a. The prophet motive. *NACLA Report*. (Jan/Feb): 4–10.

———.1948b. God's saving plan. *NACLA Report*. (Jan/Feb): 22–33.

Kater, John L. Jr. 1982. *Christians on the Right*. New York: The Seabury Press.

LaRuffa, Anthony L. 1980. Penecostalism in Puerto Rican society. *Perspectives on Pentecostalism*. Ed. S. D. Glazier, 49–65. Washington, D.C.: University Press of America.

Liebman, Robert C. and Robert Wuthnow, eds. 1983. *The New Christian Right*. New York: Aldine.

Lovelace, Richard. 1984. Extremism as defense? *Charisma* (November):9.

Mecham, J. Lloyd. 1966. *Church and State in Latin America*. Chapel Hill: University of North Carolina Press.

Minnery, Tom. 1984. Why we can't always trust the news media. *Christianity Today* (Jan. 13): 14–21.

Montgomery, T.S. 1979. Latin American evangelicals: Oaxtepec and beyond. *Churches and Politics in Latin America*. Ed. Daniel H. Levine, 87–107. Beverly Hills: Sage.

NACLA Report. 1981. Nicaragua, a church divided. (May/June):45–46.

_____.1984. About this issue. (Jan./Feb.)

Niebuhr, H. Richard. 1937. *The Kingdom of God in America*. New York: Harper & Row.

Noll, Mark. 1984. When 'infidels' run for office. *Christianity Today*. (October 5):20–25.

Norman, Edward. 1981. *Christianity in The Southern Hemisphere*. Oxford: Clarendon Press.

Poloma, Margaret. 1982. *The Charismatic Movement: Is There a New Pentecost?* Boston: Twayne.

Prince, Derek. 1973. *Shaping History Through Prayer and Fasting*. Old Tappan, N.J.: Revell.

Quebedeaux, Richard. 1978. *The Worldly Evangelicals*. New York: Harper and Row.

———. 1982. *By What Authority*. New York: Harper & Row.

———. 1983. *The New Charismatics II*. New York: Harper & Row.

Reese, Boyd. 1983. The new class and young evangelicals: second thoughts. *Review of Religious Research* (March): 261–67.

Rifkin, Jeremy and Ted Howard. 1979. *The Emerging Order: God in The Age of Scarcity*. New York: Putnam's Sons.

Saracco, L. and J. Norberto. 1984. The Holy Spirit and the church: Latin American Pentecostals (May) Mimeograph.

Shriver, Peggy L. 1981. *The Bible Vote*. New York: Pilgrim Press.

Shupe, Anson and William Stacey. 1983. The moral majority constituency. *The New Christian Right*. Eds. R.C. Liebman and R. Wuthnow, 103–116. New York: Aldine.

Vidales, Raul. 1978. Charisms and political action. *Charisms in The Church*. Eds. C. Duquoc and C. Floristan, 67–86. New York: Seabury.

Wallerstein, Immanuel. 1980. *The Modern World-System II: Mercantilism and The Consolidation of The European World-Economy. 1600–1750*. New York: Academic Press.

Wallis, Jim. 1984. A pledge of resistance. *Sojourners* (August):10–11.

Webber, Robert E. 1982. *The Moral Majority: Right or Wrong?* Westchester, IL: Crossway Books.

Wedenoja, William. 1980. Modernization and the Pentecostal movement in Jamaica. *Perspectives on Pentecostalism*. Ed. S.D. Glazier, 24–48. Washington, D.C.: University Press of America.

Willems, Emilio. 1967. *Followers of The New Faith*. Nashville: Vanderbilt University Press.

Wallis, Jim and Joyce Hollyday. 1983. A plea from the heart. *Sojourners* (March):3–5.

Wuthnow, Robert. 1983. Political rebirth of American evangelicals. *The new Christian Right*. Eds. R. C. Liebman and R. Wuthnow, 167–85. New York: Aldine.

Zwier, Robert. 1982. *Born-Again Politics*. Downers Grove, IL: Inter Varsity Press.

17

Egypt's Islamic Militancy Revisited

SAAD EDDIN IBRAHIM

AMONG the legacies President Muhammad Husni Mubarak inherited from his predecessor is Egypt's Islamic militants. In a macabre way Mubarak owes them his accession to power in October 1981 for they, of all Anwar Sadat's many opponents, were able to terminate his presidency by shooting him down in the midst of his army and in view of the whole world. The moment President Sadat had sought to be one of glory turned out to be one of tragic finality. Mubarak himself narrowly escaped death, and as he may wish to bury the memories of that day in October forever, so also will he probably always detest the thought of the militants as the immediate cause of bringing him to power.

The Muslim militants are still part of Egypt's political landscape. Two-and-a-half years after Sadat's assassination their grand trials are still filling the daily newspapers. To date, Mubarak has handled the issue of the militants far better than his predecessor, but the future of Islamic militancy in Egypt is uncertain.

This article sketches the story of Egypt's Islamic militancy from its beginning to the present. Mubarak has pursued a policy of moderation and accommodation, but firmness against violence, in dealing with the militants. His initial successes suggest there is a middle ground between caving into Islamic fundamentalists on the one hand, and attempting to exterminate them on the other.

353

I

April 1984 marked the tenth anniversary of the first bloody confrontation between the Sadat regime and Islamic militants in Egypt. In April 1974 a group of militants known to the Arab mass media as *Jamaat al Fonniyya al-Asskariyya* or Technical Military Academic Group (TMA) attempted a *coup d'état*. The group succeeded in taking over the Technical Military Academy in suburban Cairo in preparation for marching to the Arab Socialist Union building where Egypt's top leadership had assembled to listen to a speech by President Sadat. The attempt was foiled after eleven hours of fierce fighting which left eleven persons dead and twenty-seven wounded. Some ninety TMA members were tried; three leaders were sentenced to death and others to varying prison terms.

The decade which followed witnessed several violent confrontations between the Egyptian government and other militant Islamic groups including *Jund al-Rahman* (Soldiers of God), *Jamaat al-Muslum* (The Muslim Group), *Shabab Mohamed* (Mohamed's Youth), *al-Takfir Wa al-Hijra* (Repentence and Holy Flight) and *al-Jihad* (Holy War). The last two, especially, attracted much attention both in Egypt and elsewhere because of their size, organizational skills, and fighting tenacity. In July 1977 *Al-Takfir Wa al-Hijra* (RHF) kidnapped a former cabinet minister for religious endowments *(Awqaf)*, demanded the release of fellow detainees, then carried out its threat to kill him when the release was not obtained. A crackdown on the RHF resulted in shoot-outs around the country which left many dead and wounded. Eventually all the RHF's top leadership and some 620 members were arrested and 465 stood trial before a military court. Five leaders were sentenced to death and thirty-six received varying prison terms ranging from five years to life imprisonment.

The *Jihad* group was by far the bloodiest and most deadly in its confrontation with authorities. Despite preventive arrests of hundreds of its members by the State in September 1981, *Jihad* still had enough members and organizational capability to plan and successfully carry out an assassination plot that took the life of President Sadat on 6, October 1981. Even after a second round-up of its members in the aftermath of the assassination, *Jihad* was still able to storm the main police headquarters in the Governorate of Assyut and kill or wound ten state security men. Not until after two weeks of skirmishes around the country did the state prevail. Several hundred *Jihad* members were arrested and interrogated. Many have already been tried for involvement in the assassination of President Sadat and received sentences ranging from death to varying terms of imprisonment. As of the date of this writing, the second and third trials, involving 300 and 176 *Jihad* members respectively charged with the Assyut events and membership in an unlawful organization are still under way.

Before moving to the broader context which gave rise to these confrontations, I will sketch briefly what is known about the Muslim militants. First, they are young. Ninty percent of those engaged in the violent events were in their twenties and thirties. Second, they are highly educated. Eighty percent were either university students or university graduates. Third, they are highly motivated. Over half were students or graduates of elite colleges and/or in fields of professional specialization—medicine, engineering, pharmacy, and technical Military Academy. Forth, they are upwardly mobile. Over seventy percent are from lower-middle class, but not poor, backgrounds. Most are the first generation in their families ever to receive a higher education. Fifth, they are from rural communities or small towns. At the time they turned militant, however, they were living in Egypt's larger cities where the universities are located.

Direct empirical investigations, documents, and trial records reveal that most of the leaders of these militant groups were at one time members of the older and more established Moslem Brotherhood Society (MBS). However by the late 1960s and early 1970s they had become disillusioned with the MBS elders whom they believed had turned "soft" in the struggle for the cause of Islam. Thus, they split from MBS and formed more combative groups. The several new groups varied in organizational structure, membership-control and strategy, but all shared with MBS the goal of the application of the *Shariah* (Quranic legal code) and the establishment of an Islamic state.

II

The bloody confrontations of the 1970s were only symptomatic of a deeper crisis which has been troubling Egypt and other countries of the Arab Islam world in recent decades. Islamic resurgence has been the most dramatic response to this crisis.

A crisis, simply defined, is a complex problem to which the dominant ruling class can provide neither a persuasive understanding nor an effective solution. The ideological and spiritual reservoir, the material resources, the institutional structure, and the arsenal of skills available to the ruling elite display ineptness.

The crisis of Egypt, while age-old, flares up periodically as internal and external pressures become especially acute. The Arab defeat in 1967 at the hands of Israel represented such an acute condition. Since Egypt bore the brunt of that defeat, the crisis was bound to flare up again. For a few years after the defeat, most Egyptians hoped that Nasser's vision and feats would deliver them from the crisis. But growing numbers were plagued by doubts and with Nassar's death in 1970 the doubters grew larger in number and louder in voice.

The doubters were not of one mind regarding the solution to Egypt's problems. Some looked to the outside for salvation. Their outside was the West and Arab countries rich with the oil bounty. This group consisted largely of the affluent, old and new, who felt cramped by Nasser's vision and policies. A larger group of doubters turned to the indigenous heritage of Islam for salvation. This group also felt that Nasser had oppressed them, or at best margainalized them in the Egyptian body-politic.

President Sadat, burdened by the responsibility to dislodge the Israelies from Egyptian soil, and eager to subdue his Nasserist rivals, flirted with both groups of doubters in his early years in office. The two groups had in common varying sentiments of anti-Nasserism and hostility toward Egypt's Soviet connection and that suited Sadat very well. An impressive military performance in the October War served to consolidate Sadat's power and enhance his legitimacy. Sadat thus felt freer to pursue his only policy options.

By early 1974 Sadat threw his lot with the group that sought Egypt's salvation by opening up to the West and to the Arab rich. He moved swiftly to forge his own vision which stood on four pillars: (1) an open-door policy in economics; (2) controlled democracy in domestic politics; (3) reconciliation with Israel in regional affairs; and (4) alignment with the West (especially the United States) in global affairs.

These choices left the Islamic-oriented groups out in the cold. Most were hostile to the communist Soviets, had no love for the West, and were even more hostile toward Israel—a usurper of part of the abode of Islam. While distrustful of Nasser's brand of socialism, the Muslim militants were equally inimical to capitalism which the open-door policy was implicitly reintroducing in Egypt. The militants, like all

Muslim fundamentalists, were committed to social justice but with a conviction that it can best be attained in a truly Islamic state.

Thus, as of early 1974, Sadat's honeymoon with the Islamic militants had not only ended, but the relationship had turned sour. The Technical Military Academy (TMA) confrontation in April was an early warning and preview of things to come. Sadat's subsequent performance alienated the militants progressively. His personal lifestyle, and that of his family, reflecting an obsession with extravagance and everything Western added to their fury.

Furthermore, the yield of his four major policies was, in the eyes of the militants and others, not only meager but mostly outright negative. Tales of corruption in high places, growing disparities between the poor and the rich, and rampant inflation added moral indignation to a deeper sense of relative deprivation. Hardest hit by all this was the lower-middle class from whose ranks comes most of the Islamic militants.

From 1974 onward, the militants grew faster than any other opposition group in the country. They appropriated most of the floating dissidents among the lower-middle class youth. They were helped not only by Sadat's policy failures but also by his harassment of secular opposition—the Nasserites, the Arab nationalists, the communists, and the liberals. The militants' daring "puritanism," idealism, and sense of martyrdom attracted new members and sympathizers. An indicator of this was their landslide victories in student elections in all Egyptian universities from 1975 to 1979—a fact that led Sadat to dissolve all student unions by decree in 1979. Another telling indicator was the size and organizational sophistication of these militant groups as time went on. Despite death sentences and stiff prison terms, the numbers involved in each confrontation and the scale of violence were larger than the one before. As soon as the highly efficient state security cracked down and liquidated one group of militants, others mushroomed.

By the summer of 1981 Sadat must have recognized that most, if not all, of his policies were faltering. America was failing him and Israel was humiliating him. The economy was in trouble. Moslem-Coptic sectarian strife had reached levels unprecedented in recent memory. Even more depressing for him was the fact that the opposition parties, as well as the unorganized opposition, were taking note of his failures and were fanning public anger.

In what had come to be his favorite style of "shock-treatment," Sadat sought to preempt all his detractors with a single blow. In September

1981 he ordered the arrest and detention of nearly all the active and vocal opposition in Egypt's political community. The rest of the story is too well-known to need recounting here. Suffice it to say that of the aggrieved constituencies, only the Islamic militants, through the *Jihad* organization, struck back with vehemence and vindictiveness. Sadat paid with his life.

III

After a brief period of hesitation Mubarak evolved what appears to be a sane policy in dealing with the Muslim militants. He treats them fairly and firmly. His regime does not tolerate violation of the law or use of violence by the militants. If and when this happens, they are arrested and brought to a fair trial by their natural judges—not by military courts. These trials have been open to national and international media. Mubarak himself has abstained from comment or from interfering with due process. His aids and other government officials have also struggled to be proper in this regard.

The Mubarak regime has even taken the courageous step of opening the national mass media to the militants to present their case. Within limits, even the ones in jail pending trial have been allowed to appear on Egyptian television to debate *al Azhar Ulama* in matters of religion and Islamic jurisprudence. These debates, which sometimes have lasted for hours weekly, have helped all parties. They have clarified the issues for the public, given the Islamic establishment represented by *al-Azhar* a chance to flex its intellectual muscles and they have provided the militants with a forum to present their understanding of religion and their vision of a new and virtuous society. The careful editing of the programs never allows the militants to prevail or have the last word in the debate. But the militants have, in turn, used them skillfully. They have appeared to the public not as wild or lunatics, as Sadat tried to portray them, but as sincere and idealistic in their motives if misguided in their action. More importantly, these programs suggest to the public at large that Mubarak is fair.

Equally, other militants not implicated in the crimes, as well as other fundamentalists, now have access to the press to present their point of view. A new weekly publication, *al-Liwaa al Islami* (Islamic Banner) issued by the government's National Democratic Party (NDP) has opened its pages to them as well. Spokesmen of the Moslem Brothers have also used the uncensored pages of the opposition parties' newspapers—including the Leftist *al-Ahali.*

Unlike his provocative predecessor, Mubarak does not give the militants much room to criticize him or his family on a personal level. Mubarak's lifestyle, and that of his family, has been quite proper by Egyptian and Islamic standards. His early crackdown on government corruption helped greatly in taking the edge off the charge that the government is officiating over a *Jahiliyya* society and willfully encouraging decadence. Mubarak himself has avoided invoking religion either positively or negatively in political discourse. This is a clear departure from Sadat's proclamation to be the Faithful President *(al Rais al-Mouamen)* and Egypt to be a state of Faith and Science *(Dawlat-ul-Ilm wa il-Iman)*, when to the fundamentalists his actual practice seemed at odds with such proclamations.

All of these measures have helped to relax not only the fundamentalists but most Egyptians as well. There is decidedly less religious tension in 1984 than there was in 1981. Where there are occasional declarations of uncovering conspiratorial plans by Muslim militants to cause trouble, there has been no actual violent confrontation. On the surface, at least, Islamic militancy seems now to be leveling off or quietly going underground.

The problems which gave rise to Islamic militancy are far from over. Egypt's Islamic militancy did not arise just in response to a presidential style or a prejudiced mass media. It has arisen as one response to much deeper socio-economic grievances which we earlier termed as a multifaceted crisis. It was Sadat's inability to cope with that crisis, not his style, that was the underlying reason for the militants' wrath. His style only added fuel to their anger and passions.

The question of Mubarak's ability to address the deep grievances which gave rise to social unrest remains. And the answer to the question would appear to be that he has done some, but not enough. The four basic policies of Sadat—open-door, controlled democracy, reconciliation with Israel, and alignment with the West—are still official policy. Mubarak is trying to rationalize, streamline, and make these policies work more effectively and realistically.

The open-door is less open. The democratization process is less controlled. Mubarak is more stern with Israel. And he is not going out of his way to accommodate the United States. He has retained at least a nominal commitment to the Camp David peace process, but he seems also to recognize the limitations of this accord. He recalled Egypt's ambassador from Tel Aviv in the aftermath of Israel's invasion of Lebanon. It was a modest response, but an indication that he has no illusions about Israel's intentions. His quest to return Egypt to its "natural" circles—the Arab, Islamic, African, and nonaligned nations—is unmistakable. To be sure, Mubarak is going about this very slowly, but he has made steady progress. Egypt's return to the Islamic conference in early 1984 and his trip to Morocco are cases in point. The most successful of Mubarak's moves is his drive for gradual democratization. The margin of freedom of expression and organization is widening steadily—sometimes as a result of his initiatives and sometimes through court rulings. A telling indicator of his commitment to democratization is the fact that no single issue of opposition newspapers has been confiscated since he came to power and, further, two new political parties have been allowed (New Wafd and Umma) to organize.

The impact of all this has been to stem the growth of Islamic militancy in Egypt. Many of the previous social grievances are still there, but they are no longer expressed in passionate anger nor channeled solely through Islamic militancy. Secular outlets now exist to vent dissent. During the summer of 1984, for example, there were student uprisings in Mansura and Cairo Universities, and a workers strike in Egypt's largest tube and pipe factory in Helwan. These events were neither initiated or led by Muslim militants.

The dissidence which is still expressed in terms of politicized Islam is now channeled increasingly through the Moslem Brothers rather than the more militant splinter groups like *Jihad* and RHF. The Moslem Brothers' image has been rehabilitated in the eyes of young dissident Muslims after its leaders were jailed by Sadat in September 1981. While opting for nonviolence, these older leaders have proven to the young their unwavering faith in the cause of Islam. Released by Mubarak, these leaders have continued to stand firm in their opposition to Camp David, the excesses of the open-door policy and the American connection. Furthermore, the Moslem Brothers have normalized their relations with other secular opposition groups—including the Nasserites and the communists. In October 1983 they joined with these groups in a newly formed Committee for Defense of Democracy. More recently, some of their leaders (e.g. Sheikh Salah, Abu Ismail and Adel Eid) joined the New Wafd, an avowed secularist party. Since the Moslem Brothers do not have their own legal political party, this alliance will permit them to enter the parlimentary election process.

IV

Far from disappearing, Islamic militancy is now being integrated into the main stream of the Egyptian body-politic. Some of the militants demands have been endorsed by the Egyptian Committee for Defense of Democracy. This committee includes all opposition parties as well as the Nasserites and the communists. Cynics may write this off as political expedience, but the fact remains that on record, at least, all secular political forces in Egypt are accommodating the quest of Muslim fundamentalists for a legitimate voice in the political process.

The question for the future is not whether Islamic fundamentalism will survive. The question, rather, is will its more militant contingents return to violence as a means to express their grievances and assert their demands? The answer would appear to rest in the performance of the Mubarak regime in handling the multi-facets of Egypt's persistent crisis. Egyptians have engaged for a century in a quest for social justice, cultural authenticity, development, closer integration with its Arab-Islamic neighbors, and real independence from the world's superpowers. This quest has been frustrated over and again by their own rulers and foreign powers alike. And this is the heart of the Egyptian crisis.

Mubarak may not succeed where so many others have failed. But if his drive for greater democratization succeeds, an ever greater number of Egyptians will be struggling with the crisis and sharing responsibility for failure or success. And to the extent that he may have succeeded in calming the storm of militant Islamic fundamentalism in Egypt, he may also provide a model for other governments of Muslim peoples.

PART FIVE
CONFLICT AND
INSTITUTIONALIZATION

18

Prophets, Priests, and the Polity: European Christian Democracy In A Developmental Perspective

JOHN T. S. MADELEY

ONTEMPORARY national politics is often taken to be centrally concerned with economic matters. In the phrase of one of the founders of modern political science it is about "who gets what, when, how" (Lasswell 1936). While reference to values such as freedom, justice, and peace have continued to provide, at least at the rhetorical level, the stock-in-trade of international relations throughout the century, they or their equivalents have for much of the post-1945 period been displaced in the domestic affairs of the liberal democracies by the language and categories of interest competition.

In Europe the ideological trappings of Christian Democratic and other political traditions have tended until quite recently to be seen as little more than smoke screens obscuring the real, underlying struggle for competitive advantage among different sections of the population. An examination of the development of Christian Democracy in Europe, however, suggests, on the one hand, that this view of politics has always under-estimated the value-oriented as against the interest-oriented component in political conflict and, on the other, that its reductionist view of the nature of interests has led to a neglect of institutional as against class or group imperatives. Any major political tradition is of course an alloy of material and ideal components. It is the intention here to attempt a summary analysis of these different components as revealed by an examination of the relative roles of "prophets, priests, and politicians" in the articulation of the Christian Democratic tradition.

In 1969 a major study concluded that "religious traditions, not class, are the main social basis of parties in the Western world today" (Rose and Urwin 1909, 12). This conclusion was based on an extensive reanalysis of electoral surveys so designed as to discover the relative strength of the class, religious, ethnic, and other factors in providing cohesion to the parties' social base.

A review of Rose and Urwin's data, augmented from other sources, reveals an uneven incidence of the religious factor in West European politics (see Madeley 1982, 149–52). In the parts of Europe where Catholicism has either been dominant, or has retained the adherence of a significant minority of a country's population, religion weighs far more heavily than in the overwhelmingly Protestant countries of Scandinavia and Britain. Seventy-two percent of parties in the traditionally Catholic, or mixed-confession countries, were rated as cohesive by virtue of some factor related to religion—whether religious adherence or observance or clerical/anti-clerical attitudes. In the Protestant countries, where occupational class weighed more heavily, an almost identical proportion (71%) were found *not* to be cohesive by religion.

Despite this correlation between the strength of Catholicism and the incidence of "religion cohesive" parties, Catholicism itself could not be the only explanatory factor. Religious—and anti-religious—parties did exist among overwhelmingly Protestant populations if in lesser numbers. Nor was the presence of Christian Democratic parties very closely related to the incidence of the religious factor. Only thirteen out of a total of thirty-nine parties rated cohesive by virtue of some religious characteristic belonged to the conventional Christian Democratic category.[1] In addition the German Christian Democrats were found to be "non-cohesive" by religion while other studies have found religion to be the single best predictor of the vote even where no important Christian Democratic party exists.[2]

The Rose-Urwin study, therefore, raised a wide range of complex and often interrelated questions, which the political science literature has still not managed to investigate adequately. And such studies as have been undertaken have been relatively barren for students of the sociology of religion. More often they have been concerned with electoral behavior or patterns of political leadership and recruitment than with an enquiry into the specifically religious components of the religious factor and their insertion into the world of politics.[3]

This paper attempts to identify some of the religious components insofar as they affect the European tradition of Christian Democracy. At the most general level the focus will be on the relative role of interests as against values in the construction of the Christian Democratic tradition over time.

The term *interest* will be used here to refer to requirements for the emergence, survival, or growth of a particular institution or group. With respect to religious institutions or groups, these interests will include the basic religious freedoms of belief, assembly, and worship, access to adequate economic resources, without which the institution or group cannot support its existence, and what might be called the rights of conscience without which religious actors cannot follow the ethical requirements of their religion. Interests then are essentially self-regarding in the sense that they are cherished not for their consequences for the rest of society but for the institution or group itself.

The term *value* will be reserved for those desired ends which inherently refer to the whole of a society. Whether relative or absolute they derive not from an attachment to a particular institution or group but from an essentially disinterested conception of the ideal or the highest attainable end for society at large.

In the symbolism of this paper's title, values are the business of thinkers and visionaries—prophets—while interests are the business of those charged with responsibility for the care of institutions—priests. As is the case with all ethical religions, there is an emergent tension between the two and it is with the suppression, resolution or transcendence of this tension within European Christianity, as it has confronted the political challenges of the modern world, that this paper will deal. By examining the record of Christian Democracy and assessing its contemporary dilemmas it is hoped that some light can be shed on the conditions affecting the emergence and development of the religious factor in European politics.

In his pioneering work of thirty years ago, Fogarty identified two principal forms of Christian Democracy—what he called the *Anglo-*

Saxon and the *Continental* forms. By contrast with Continental Christian Democracy, with its overtly religious parties and strong denominational links, the Anglo-Saxon form "grew up through participation by individual Christians, each acting for himself, in any and all of those political or economic or social movements which happened to offer themselves" (Fogarty 1957, 10). With the fairly recent emergence of Christian People's parties in Scandinavia, a distinctive third form can also now be identified—one involving the existence of overtly religious parties which lack the denominational links of the Continental pattern (Madeley 1977).

All three of these species of the genus Christian Democracy have been vehicles for the political activity of Christians who have aimed "to solve—with the aid of Christian principles and 'democratic' techniques —that range of temporal problems which the Church has repeatedly and solemnly declared to lie within the supreme competence of lay society, and outside direct ecclesiastical control" (Fogarty 1957, 6). None of them however have been unaffected by the constraints and opportunities provided by contrasting patterns of church-state-society relations which have in large part determined the character and scope of priestly interest-claims and prophetic value-demands.

The Origins of Christian Democracy

Fogarty claimed that although one could trace some of its component elements far back in history—as far back doubtless as to first century Christianity—Continental Christian Democracy in its modern form had "a definite beginning" in the 1820s (Fogarty 1957, 149). In that decade there arose among liberal Catholics a number of movements that combined an attachment to Christian values with the employment of democratic means of political mobilization and opinion formation reminiscent of the full-blown Christian Democracy of the twentieth century.

It was in France that the most remarkable early statement of Christian Democratic principles occurred in the 1820s—a statement that echoed the prophetic strain of religious and social commitment which had never been completely buried beneath the institutional inertia of church establishments. Father Felicité de Lamennais was a turbulent Breton priest who abandoned his former attachment to Catholic traditionalism and the French monarchy in favor of an attempt to identify the cause of Catholicism, and of the papacy in particular, with the cause of liberty. In this his attempt failed. His newspaper, *L'Avenir* (The Future), lasted only thirteen months. A papal encyclical was issued to condemn his opinions and within a further two years he was excommunicated.

Vidler presents Lamennais as a prophetic figure in the classic mould, his profile etched all the more clearly by virtue of the confrontation which developed between him and the classic priestly figure of Pope Gregory XVI (Vidler 1954, 275–6). Lamennais believed himself charged directly by God with a mission to condemn ecclesiastical corruption and compromise and to promote a radical reorientation of the church in response to the challenge of the times. In this he pioneered many of the departures which were eventually to issue in Continental Christian Democracy. According to Fogarty, "the programme of L'Avenir anticipates in point after point that of Christian Democracy today" (Fogarty 1957, 155). At the same time, Lemannais ran up against the entrenched power of the priest-figure, the guardian of traditional doctrine, discipline and the ecclesiastical interest. In the 1830s and 1840s the confrontation resulted in the unambiguous defeat of the prophet and his witness; even his lieutenant Lacordaire, whom Irving prefers to identify as the father of French Christian Democracy, remained "a voice crying in the wilderness" (Irving 1973, 26–7).

The failure of these pioneers is of more than mere antiquarian interest. Viewed in context, their experience reflects the operation of general factors which have variously constrained and facilitated the emergence of Christian Democracy as a political tradition. It raises questions about the tension between the priestly and prophetic emphases within European Christianity at different times and the consequences for political action of various attempts to resolve or transcend this tension. These questions can, however, only be properly addressed if attention is paid to the wider context of church-state-society relations as these have developed—in particular since the French Revolution of 1789. These patterns of relations have varied widely as between different parts of Europe and different periods. Fortunately, by building on the pioneering efforts of Lipset and Rokkan and others, it is possible to develop a relatively uncontroversial account of these complex contextual factors (Lipset and Rokkan 1967).

It was the religious settlement of the seventeenth century that finally fixed the religious division of Europe which the Reformation had inaugurated. It left the Far North (principally, Scandinavia, Britain, and parts of Germany) as an almost entirely Protestant region and the counter-Reformation countries of the South as almost entirely Catholic. In between these two largely homogeneous regions was a broad belt of religiously mixed territories running from the Low Countries, through the Rhineland to Switzerland—an area which Fogarty describes as a sort of heartland of European Christianity marked ever since by relatively high levels of religious affiliation and observance.

This geographical division of Europe has even in its local detail remained remarkably intact since 1700 in spite of the changing state boundaries which have affected the political map. A second feature of the settlement after the wars of religion was the acceptance of the *cuius regio eius religio* rule whereby uniformity of religion within individual territories was legitimated. This rule meant that, until the end of the eighteenth century, at least, the secular authorities attempted to preserve approximate or complete adherence to orthodox religious observance within their jurisdiction even though the confessional character of that orthodoxy—whether Catholic, Lutheran, Calvinist, or whatever—varied from place to place. The contrasting confessional traditions each developed their own characteristic emphasis in social and political doctrine. Equally, if not more, important than doctrine for their later effect on the structuring of mass politics in the nineteenth and twentieth centuries, were the divergent patterns of relationship between church institutions, civil authority, and subject populations with their consequences for the structuring of religious interests.

In what might be called Protestant Europe—not just the Far North but also those parts of the religiously mixed belt where Protestants were in the ascendant—the church had been successfully reduced at the time of the Reformation from being the most wealthy and powerful estate of the realm to little more than the ecclesiastical arm of the royal bureaucracy. The loss of the church's wealth and independence to the crown removed an important rival to secular authority, greatly extended the scope of that authority and lent it the legitimating aura of protector of the nation's religion.

In Counter-Reformation Europe, on the other hand, the *ancien regime* alliance between throne and altar, while allowing for considerable state interference in ecclesiastical affairs, left the Catholic church relatively independent. When the French Revolution led to an attempt, not just in France but throughout continental Europe, to abolish that independence and subject the church completely to the authority of the state, a conflict broke out, the ramifications of which can still occasionally be observed in European politics. The threats to the church then and since were all the greater because of the secularism and anticlericalism of the revolutionary forces, which counterposed new political elites not only to the interests of church but also to many of the core values of traditional Catholicism.

Protestant Europe was generally spared from intra-societal conflict. The earlier integration of the church into the structure of the state and the developing national cultures had guaranteed status and monopolistic privileges to the clergy (in exchange for its loss of independence) and established elites retained at least a perfunctory loyalty to the state religion.

David Martin takes the post-1789 French experience of intransigent opposition of "massive religious beliefs, ethos and institutions confronting massive secular beliefs, ethos and institutions" as paradigmatic of conditions in Catholic Europe (Martin 1978, 7). One of the factors which gave an extra twist to this "spiral of oppositions" was the earlier intolerance of the baroque autocracies of the *ancien regime* for anti-Catholic dissent which had produced in the militant secularism of the more radical Enlightenment thinkers and activists a mirror-image of itself. When the revolution had shifted into its most violent phase traditional Catholicism had become identified as much with counter-revolutionary treason as with backwardness and superstition and the attempt was made finally to supplant it with a cult of the goddess Reason.

As de Tocqueville was to write, "the unbelievers of Europe attack the Christians as their political opponents rather than their religious adversaries: they hate the Christian religion as the opinion of a party much more than as an error of belief: and they reject the clergy less because they are the representatives of the Deity than because they are the allies of government" (Nisbet 1966, 237). The identification of the church with the political right, which was confirmed during the Bourbon Restoration in France, was a fateful legacy which has made French soil relatively infertile for the more liberal and progressive traditions of Christian Democracy.

It was against this unpropitious background then that Lamennais and Lacordaire attempted to reconcile the church to certain elements of the revolutionary tradition. Perhaps only a prophet or an impractical visionary would have tried. Their final failure occured in 1848, the year of revolutions, when the mutual antagonism of Catholicism and republicanism received powerful reinforcement. In that year Pope Pius IX, who had for the two years since his accession been regarded as a reformer with a commitment to reconciling the church to the modern world, decisively turned his back on liberalism after experiencing revolutionary violence in Rome itself. His condemnation of the ideas of the French Revolution placed the papacy in opposition to the new nation-building elite of Italy and was to lead to conflict over the

Temporal Power (an interest conflict *par excellence* not resolved until the Lateran Pacts in 1929) which bedevilled would-be Christian Democrats in that country for generations. In 1864 his *Syllabus of Errors* listed as the eightieth deviation from church teaching worthy of denunciation the view that "the Roman Pontiff can, and ought to, reconcile himself and come to terms with progress, liberalism and modern civilization." And finally six years later the first Vatican Council's declaration of the dogma of papal infallibility underscored the church's defiance of progressive opinion.

In Protestant Europe very different structures of opposition developed. Martin identified three distinct patterns of church-state-society relations, the British, Calvinist, and Lutheran (Martin 1978, 5–7). What distinguishes them all—if in varying degrees—from the French or Latin pattern, however, was the development of dissenting or nonconformist religious traditions which allowed discontent with established elites in church and state to achieve expression in religious, as against aggressively secularist, forms.

In the mixed confession areas of Europe, the relaxation of laws discriminating against Catholics added a further element of diversity to the developing religious mosaic. The introduction of religious toleration at various times—early in Britain, late in Scandinavia—was part cause and part consequence of very diverse patterns of religious cleavage. Toleration entailed a renunciation on the part of state authorities of the attempt to maintain conformity to the rites and beliefs of the established churches, even though many of the groups which took advantage of it did so in order to revive the orthodoxy which latitudinarian state churches had ceased to guard. This pluralization of the religious cultures of Protestant Europe meant that there were religious groups associated with most parts of the political spectrum. State church loyalists were generally associated with the right where the traditional connection between the church and established social elites was close, while dissident or minority religious traditions tended to gravitate to the left where their interest in the expansion of religious freedoms and securing equality of treatment and respect was served by movements committed to social, political, and economic reform as well as religious.

What Fogarty calls the Anglo-Saxon form of Christian Democracy, thus, became well-established in many parts of nineteenth-century Protestant Europe. Promotion of the interests of minority religious traditions was accomplished within and by reforming coalitions of groups where the input of specifically religious values (for example in connection with temperance campaigns or improving conditions for the developing industrial working class) could occur without the necessity for overtly religious or denominational parties arising.[4]

In Catholic Europe the need to defend church interests against what were seen as the intolerant assaults of Continental liberalism led to very different patterns of political involvement on the part of Christians.[5] In Italy, indeed, where the issue of the temporal power of the papacy was unresolved, the pope's *non expedit* encyclical of 1867 forbade Catholics to participate in electoral politics altogether. Even in those other exceptional areas such as Belgium, where in the first half of the nineteenth century relations between liberals and Catholics had been cooperative rather than conflicting, the middle and late nineteenth century revived the classic antagonism which polarized Catholics and anti-clerical liberals. In some cases the range of church interests at stake was very broad. In Switzerland the full amplitude of the conflict led in 1847 to the Catholic-Protestant *Sonderbund* war after which the defeated Catholics adopted a thorough-going anti-liberal stance. And in Germany, Bismarck's attempt in the *Kulturkampf* of the 1870s to submit the Catholics of the new Reich to the same ecclesiastical disciplines as those affecting Protestants gave a great electoral boost to the Centre party which soon became almost totally identified with Catholicism and the defense of church interests.

Elsewhere it was particularly the issue of education which gave an impetus to Catholic involvement in politics. Pius IX's Syllabus of Errors had condemned the idea that "Catholics may approve of the system of educating youth unconnected with the Catholic faith and the power of the Church." When, therefore, new state elites in the heyday of liberalism set about creating new systems of mass schooling the Catholic church found it necessary to encourage the political involvement of the faithful in order to defend and promote its interest in confessional education.

In Belgium the conflict erupted as early as 1847 and put an end to liberal-Catholic harmony. In France Napoleon III bought the support of Catholics in 1850 by granting the church extensive rights in the field of education but this only postponed until 1870 a conflict the reverberations of which continue a century later. In Austria the educational issue combined with the denunciation of a concordat and the introduction of civil marriage to push Catholics into a close alignment with the political right. In the Netherlands the 1850s inaugurated a struggle over the issue which was not resolved until 1921. It led there to the development in addition of the Calvinist

Anti-Revolutionary party which was also committed to the preservation of confessional education. The community of interest between Dutch Catholics and Calvinists against the liberals encouraged a habit of cooperation and coalition which owed little to a commonality of values between the antagonistic religious traditions.

Thus, much of continental Europe of the late nineteenth century saw the development of religious-political parties and connections whose principal object was to defend the interests of church institutions. There also emerged a great range of other confessional organizations—for employers, workers, farmers, youth, women, etc.—that served to insulate further the churches' faithful from what was seen as the baleful influence of modern secularism. For John Whyte the years 1870 to 1920 was the period when "closed" Catholicism emerged with full force—Catholic political parties were established with links to the developing Catholic social organizations and strong clerical guidance was employed to reinforce the loyalty of both to the church (Whyte 1981). The Catholic parties, and their Protestant counterparts where they existed, became the political vehicles for religious subcultures concerned to contest power with established liberal groups and, increasingly, with emerging socialist movements that usually matched where they did not out-do the liberals in anti-clericalism.

This cultural segmentation, which has distinguished continental European from Anglo-Saxon or Scandinavian politics with varying degrees of virulence ever since, in some ways inhibited and in other ways, facilitated the development of Continental Christian Democracy. Cultural segmentation inhibited the development of Christian Democracy to the extent that it reinforced anti-liberalism and in some cases aligned the religious parties or political groups to other anti-liberal groups often hostile to democracy itself let alone social and economic reform—notably as in the cases of France and Austria. Segmentation facilitated Christian Democracy also insofar as the development of confessional social organizations required lay and clerical leaders to pay attention to the demands of disadvantaged social groups. Thus working men's organizations, in particular confessional trade unions, provided a ready audience for thinkers—would-be prophets indeed—to propound schemes of social and political reform. Thus the politics of interest— both ecclesiastical and social—provided a context within which new political visions could be developed on the basis of Christian social teaching.[6]

It was particularly in the 1890s that Continental Christian Democracy began to take up the heritage of Lamennais and Lacordaire. In 1891

Pope Leo XIII addressed an encyclical specifically to French Catholics, who had only recently celebrated the Anti-Centenary of the 1789 Revolution, instructing them to recognize the legitimacy of the Third Republic and to cooperate with those moderate political forces who eschewed anti-clericalism. Despite the extraordinary bitterness of the Dreyfus affair, and the separation of church and state about a decade later, the 1890s saw the emergence of two Catholic Republican groups—the moderate Ralliement of de Mun and the more radical Sillon of Marc Sanguier. The latter figure was, like Lamennais, condemned by the church authorities in 1910. The Sillon dissolved, but not before Sanguier's influence had been widely diffused through the developing Catholic social organizations. From 1912 the small Jeune Republique organization continued the Sillon's progressive politics, if rather fitfully, through the inter-war years. But it was the Popular Democratic party, founded in 1924, that became France's first Christian Democratic party, albeit one with very limited success.

Elsewhere in Catholic Europe the 1890s saw other and sturdier departures in the direction of Christian Democracy. Leo XIII's encyclical *Rerum Novarum* (also 1891) declared papal support for the struggle for social justice against the acquisitive materialism of the capitalist, as well as the atheistic materialism of the militant socialist. Its insistence on the duty of the state to strive for the welfare of all citizens entailed a positive, rather than a merely defensive, social philosophy and this gave great encouragement to the more progressive elements in Catholic opinion.[7] Woeste, the leader of the Belgian Catholic party, was said to be "interested in nothing but increasing the budget for the Churches and the State grants to the Catholic schools," although it was clear that he strongly opposed state intervention in social and economic, as much as in church affairs. In 1896 however the new party program called for factory legislation and social insurance. In Austria the deeply conservative Catholic political movement was challenged by the emergence of Lueger's Christian Social party. Lueger was regarded by the emperor as a dangerous social revolutionary despite the fact that his urban support came principally from Vienna's petty bourgeoisie rather than from the industrial workers who flocked instead to the Social Democrats. After the First World War, however, the Social Christians' attachment to democracy was placed in considerable doubt by the actions and opinions of its leaders Seipel and Dollfuss.

In Italy two figures, Toniolo and Murri, raised the banner of Christian Democracy in the 1890s. It was only after 1918, when the pope removed the last prohibitions on Catholic participation in politics, that it was possible for Luigi Sturzo to found the Italian Popular party (PPI). Sturzo insisted that the party be both independent of church authority and uncontaminated by purely confessional or ecclesiastical interests. For him "it was dangerous to make Catholicism or the defense of ecclesiastical interests the party's ground of differentiation: for that would bring into the party Catholics unlikely to accept the social-economic or democratic program which was in fact the PPI's distinctive mark" (Fogarty 1957, 324). In this he anticipated a programmatic stance which has been characteristic of post-war Christian Democracy. But like later leaders, he found that the declaration of such a stance was insufficient to guarantee independence when the church felt its interests threatened. Despite initial electoral success, the party was effectively prevented by the church from making common cause with other anti-fascists. In 1926 it paid the penalty when it was suppressed by Mussolini.

In the mixed confession territories of Europe a more progressive strain of social Christianity also came to the fore in the last part of the nineteenth century. In Holland Msgr. Schaepman overcame the former dominance of right-wing Catholics with the support of confessional workers' associations. Among the Dutch Calvinists, meantime, the tension between socially progressive and conservative elements resulted in the latter splitting off from the Anti-Revolutionary party to form the Christian Historical Union in 1894. In Switzerland a social wing finally established itself within the (Catholic) Conservative People's party in 1919, while shortly before a small Evangelical People's party had emerged among the Protestants. In Germany the development of a social-Christian stand among Protestants was reflected in Stöcker's small Social Christian Workers' party. The much larger Catholic Centre party had from its beginning in 1870 concerned itself with the social problems created by industrialization but it was only in 1894 that a far-reaching Catholic Social Program was promulgated.

Continental Christian Democracy, unlike its Anglo-Saxon counterpart, was born out of the matrix of confessional politics. It emerged in the late nineteenth and early twentieth centuries as a politically progressive tendency on the left of parties or movements founded on the defense of ecclesiastical interests in a hostile environment—and it carried the mark of its birth. Its mission—and the message of its prophetic figures—was the creation of a sprophetic figures—was the creation of a society based on what it were distinctively Christian principles of social organization.

Its main challenge was independently to establish those principles with such clarity and force that it would not be seen, and could not be made to act, merely as another vehicle of clerical interests camouflaged in order to appeal to the spirit of the age or the fashion of the moment. Despite the parallel development of Christian social thought, few Christian Democratic parties or tendencies overcame this challenge successfully. Merkl's observation on the German Centre party is telling—"It was so faithful to the main currents of German politics . . . that it not only helped the National Liberals to write the Civil Code and supported the Kaiser's expansionism, but turned pacifist and republican after World War I, and eventually to the authoritarian right in the 1930's" (Merkl 1980, 30). However, not just in Germany but throughout Europe 1945 presented a new opportunity.

The Post-1945 Period: A New Era?

World War II was a watershed in the development of Christian Democracy in most of Europe. Not only did its eventual outcome define a new East-West division of the continent, which cross-cut the religious divisions inherited from the seventeenth century, it also created in Western Europe the conditions for a distinctively new era of Christian politics. For Christians the impact of the experience of fascism and war was perhaps as great as that of the French Revolution.[8] The involvement of believers in war-time resistance movements gave Christian Democracy's democratic credentials a new credibility among previously anti-clerical forces at a time when the great constitutional issues of church and state finally lost their political salience. The discrediting of right-wing Christian groups which had compromised themselves to fascism, particularly in Catholic Europe, facilitated the attempt of Christian Democrats to gain the leadership of the confessional movements which had survived from the inter-war period and set out a new course in the center of the political spectrum. The onset of the Cold War in the late 1940s further assisted this project by enabling Christian Democracy to present itself as the principal defender of Christian civilization and liberal democracy against a totalitarian threat from the left as much as from the right. The years immediately following World War II saw a number of important changes affecting Christian Democracy, and it is necessary briefly to review these country by country before assessing their significance.

In Germany the foundation of the inter-confessional Christian

Democratic Union (CDU) under the leadership of Adenauer marked a dramatic new beginning. As early as 1906 some leaders had been concerned to break out of the Catholic political ghetto which the Centre party had become since the *Kulturkampf*.[9] Shortly after the Nazi collapse, Catholic and Protestant groups finally combined as the old church-state issues were amicably resolved and removed from the political agenda. There remained a considerable variety of emphasis and direction on questions of social and economic policy as, for example, between rather radical Berliners, relatively progressive Rhinelanders and conservative Bavarians, the last of which founded their own sister-party, the Christian Social Union. The success of Erhard's social market policies in launching the German economic miracle soon provided a basis for unity. By 1957, assisted by the discredit of most alternatives on the right, the CDU-CSU was able to build an electoral coalition which gained over fifty percent of the votes cast. On the other hand, Adenauer's skill and success in building a classic "catch-all" party, which appealed across traditional denominational and class boundaries, raises questions about the character of German Christian Democracy.[10]

In Italy a new Christian Democratic party (*Democrazia Cristiana,* DC) emerged soon after Mussolini's fall in 1943 under the leadership of de Gasperi, the last leader of the PPI. The Lateran Pacts had, at last, resolved the problem of the Temporal Power which had previously dogged Catholic involvement in democratic politics. It was hoped that the new party would be able to make good its claim inherited from the PPI to be more than a church interest party. The countervailing strength of the secularist Communist party complicated this task, however, and the close involvement of Catholic civic committees, the clergy, the bishops and the papacy in electoral politics actually meant that the DC, in fact, became more closely tied to the church than the PPI had been (Whyte 1981, 82). Within the new party's complex factional structure autonomists and integralists, who differed over relations with the church, were (and are) to be found right across the spectrum of party opinion. Despite these strains the party enjoyed early electoral success. In 1948 the DC took over half the seats in parliament. In 1945 de Gasperi had become the first practicing Catholic to head an Italian government since the founding of the state in 1870 and the DC has remained in government ever since, albeit in coalition with various combinations of other parties.

In France Christian Democracy achieved its first and only major breakthrough with the successful launching in 1945 of the *Mouvement*

Republicain Populaire (MRP) by a group of leaders who had proven their loyalty to republican democracy in the resistance. The party adopted a rather radical program which placed great emphasis on the achievement of economic and social justice in France. In the elections of 1945 and 1946, it received support from just over a quarter of the electorate (a great advance on the three percent of votes cast for Christian Democratic candidates in 1936) and entered the government coalition where it was to remain throughout the Fourth Republic. Despite the decision to adopt a religiously neutral label it made very little impact on non-Catholic voters. Within a few years of its break-through it even lost the support of those more conservative Catholics who had supported it, in spite, rather than because of its reforming program. Much of the reason why this occurred in France, but not in Germany and Italy, was that it was possible for a respectable conserva-tive movement to develop on the right of the MRP under the leadership of de Gaulle. The Gaullists were just as reliable in church-related matters and more congenial to the majority of French Catholics with their traditional identity as religious and political conservatives. With the coming of de Gaulle's Fifth Republic in 1958 the MRP dwindled even further until in the early 1960s it sacrificed its indepen-dent identity to become just one of a number of centrist groups combined in the Democratic center.

In the smaller European democracies on the continent the changes after 1945 were less dramatic if in some cases no less interesting. In Austria the old Christian Social party was not revived. Its place was taken instead by the Austrian People's party (ÖVP) which declared itself to be a new party with "no connection with any political formation in the past" and no compromising links with the church . . . our party takes the view that religious societies, in their own interest, should not attempt to influence the current course of politics, and that it is not desirable that positions of political power should be held by ecclesiastics" *(1949 Party Programme* quoted in Fogarty 1957, 308, 315). While the bishops reciprocally announced that they and the clergy would abstain from electoral politics, the organizations of Catholic Action for which they retained some responsibility, continued to act as a transmission-belt for church interests into the political arena. With its continuing strong link to the structures of Austrian Catholi-cism the ÖVP enjoyed immediate electoral success taking almost fifty percent of the vote in 1945.

In Belgium, also, there was a change of name—from the Catholic party to the Christian Social party (PSC)—and an attempt to present itself as the promoter of Christian values rather than church interests. In the words of a spokesman in 1952:

> At the end of the war the denominational link, which arose out of the battles of the past over the schools question, seemed to Christians obsolete in the light of changing ideas, and also inadequate as a response to the general desire for the reconstruction of western civilization. Abandoning denominationalism, the Christian Social Party has adopted a common foundation on which it hopes to group, round a programme aiming at the common good, citizens without distinction of religion, class, or economic interest (Fogarty 1957, 315).

The party's electoral success was considerable, in the 1940s and 1950s taking between forty and fifty percent of voters in each election, an advance of ten percent over the Catholic party in the 1930s. On the other hand, its success in breaking its denominational links was much less. According to Whyte, the Belgian hierarchy lived up to its record as the most interventionist in Europe, particularly in the mid-1950s when the schools question reemerged. In 1958 two bishops went so far as to declare that to vote for any party other than the PSC would be gravely sinful (Whyte 1981, 89).

In Holland 1945 brought little change. The inter-war Roman Catholic States party was revived as the Catholic People's party (KVP)—the only Christian Democratic party in Europe to retain a confessional label. Its statutes declared that any citizen who agreed with its program could become a member but it remained, in effect, what its name declared it to be, the party of Dutch Catholicism. The Calvinist Anti-Revolutionary party (ARP) and Christian Historical Union (CHU) simply resumed their activities in 1945 without even changing their names—although the ARP suffered a further split on its right with the founding of the small Reformed Political League (GPV). All of the Dutch Christian parties therefore continued much as before the war and continued to serve as the political representatives of the confessional "pillars" into which Dutch society is comprehensively divided.[11] Only in the 1970s, as will be seen later, did an eventual steep decline in support lead to the establishment of an interconfessional Christian party.

Also, in Switzerland, the end of the war (in which the country had of course retained its neutrality) brought little change. The large Conservative People's party and the small Evangelical People's party continued in existence at their wonted levels of support. In 1957 the former changed its name to the Conservative Christian Social party and again in 1971 to the Christian Democratic People's party, but these changes of nomenclature were unconnected with any distinct change of orientation.

Overall, the individual changes affecting Christian Democracy on the continent of Europe, particularly in the larger countries, amounted to a sea of change as it established itself among the electorates, and in government, as the most successful cross-national political movement. Nor was this all, for in the Protestant Far North of Europe, where the old continental patterns of confessional politics had been absent for reasons already related, a new and different Christian Democratic tradition emerged. In Norway the Christian People's party, which had first emerged in 1933 in one rather remote region, achieved an electoral breakthrough at the national level in 1945. That year it took about eight percent of the votes, a figure which was to rise steadily to twelve percent in 1973. By that time its example had been followed with the founding of small sister parties in Sweden, Finland, and Denmark (see Madeley 1977, passim).

Scandinavian Christian Democracy differed from Fogarty's continental pattern. The parties were certainly religious in respect both to their programs and their bases of support. They were committed to the maintenance of religious education in the public schools and to the defense of laws which promoted their own interpretations of Christian morality (not least in the policy field of alcohol and drug abuse). And they derived their support from the fundamentalist wing of the state churches and dissenting groups, all of which had developed from waves of revivalism in the nineteenth and early twentieth centuries.

The parties were not, however, marked by a particular denominational loyalty and the leadership of the state churches tended to distance itself from them very clearly. The Scandinavian countries were, of course, overwhelmingly Lutheran in religious culture despite considerable secularization, and this fact added to the peculiarity of the new parties. In Lutheranism the separation between the worlds of religion and politics was much more distinct than was the case with the more theocratic traditions of Catholicism and Calvinism.[12] Scandinavian Christians had previously tended to spread their support among a range of parties rather in the manner of Fogarty's Anglo-Saxon pattern. Nonetheless the fact that the Norwegian party emerged onto the national stage in 1945 in order to promote particular religious values, rather than ecclesiastical interests, underlines the general point that the immediate post-war years can be seen as representing a new era for Christian Democracy.

Writing around 1954, Fogarty asked whether European Christian Democracy was, in fact, developing a "new orientation" appropriate to such a new era. He claimed that the contemporary parties had moved:

> beyond the defence of ecclesiastical interests, the affirmation of Christian principles, or even the creation of strong and stable organizations . . . Today the accent has passed from defence to attack. The problem is to find a new strategy by which the militant Christian laity, now powerful and aware of their objectives, can transform the society around them" (Fogarty 1957, 378).

It was an open question whether the traditional forms of organization on the continent which had grouped Christians together regardless of differences in social and economic policy would any longer be adequate to such a task. Even if Continental Christian Democracy had, as he argued, developed a distinctive political philosophy, it was not clear that the established parties were the best vehicle for promoting policies derived from it.

Thirty years on, it is now possible to gain a better perspective on these matters. John Whyte's recent study of Catholics in the Western democracies concludes that far from marking a breakthrough to a new pattern of politics, the years after 1945 saw the high-water mark of the development of "closed Catholicism" (Whyte 1981, 91). Despite the many new departures, in the attempts to establish a less confessional image, the actual outcome was the firmer establishment of essentially confessional parties. After the relative decline of the inter-war period, these parties enjoyed support from religious social organizations and benefited from continuing clerical interventions. Among the factors reinforcing "closed" Catholicism, Whyte notes the extension (in a number of countries) of the suffrage to women, whose antipathy to the secularist extremes of left and right added new strength to the Christian Democratic parties. In addition the continuing vitality of Catholic Action organizations, the reemergence of the educational question, for example in Belgium, and a new willingness on the part of national church hierarchies to give political guidance, all contributed to this development.

By 1960 the mainly Catholic Christian Democratic parties had all roughly approximated in their electoral reach the limits of their natural constituencies of practicing Catholics—with the exception of France where the MRP failed because of the counter-attractions of Gaullism. In Germany alone was a distinctly new pattern established after 1945. There the combination of a significant Protestant element with the cohorts of the old Centre party created an inter-confessional alliance which met with considerable electoral success. Adenauer and his party managers succeeded so well, indeed, that the CDU attracted not only the support of practicing Catholics, and many believing Protestants, but also many indifferent to religion who regarded the party (in the absence of respectable alternatives on the right) as a suitable vehicle for their own political purposes.

Since 1960, however, "Christian Democratic parties everywhere became less powerful, less confessional or both" (Whyte 1981, 100). By the mid 1970s the parties in France, Holland, and Belgium had suffered considerable electoral decline. In France, as has been noted, the MRP disappeared altogether in the 1960s. In Holland the effective halving of support for the KVP led to the establishment in 1976 of the Christian Democratic Appeal (CDA), an alliance of the three major confessional parties, the KVP, the ARP and the CHU. In Germany and Austria the Christian Democrats were ousted from government for the first time since the war in 1969 and 1970 respectively. In Luxembourg their departure from office in 1974 brought to an end a record unbroken since 1919.[13] Even in Italy, where the DC retained office, the Communist party came within two percentage points of overtaking them in 1974. Only in Switzerland, among the continental countries, did electoral support for the Christian Democrats not decline substantially.[14]

By the mid-1970s it seemed as though Continental Christian Democracy was undergoing a crisis. Having failed to adopt a new orientation of the sort Fogarty looked for it was afflicted by two problems. Firstly, there was the continuing shrinkage of the parties' core constituencies as levels of more or less orthodox religious belief and practice declined. Second, there was the new orientation among the formerly secularist parties of the left as they abandoned their anti-clericalism and bid for the support of those who retained some attachment to religion. These problems were only aggravated when issues related to religion and morality occasionally re-emerged, as was the case with abortion in Germany in 1972 and divorce in Italy in 1974. On both occasions the church again attempted to direct Catholics away from supporting parties and candidates who favored the liberalization of the law only to find that its interventions were both resented as improper and ignored as inconvenient.

Irving claimed in 1979 that the late 1970s had brought a revival of fortunes to the Christian Democratic parties (Irving 1979, 254). Concerned as he was only with the parties in countries of the European Community, he did not refer to the establishment of new parties in Spain and Portugal whose electoral success, after the collapse of dictatorship in those countries also provided some support for his view. It should be added that their success has more recently been quite overshadowed by the even greater success of socialist parties. Even if the late 1970s and early 1980s has seen a levelling off in the decline of Christian Democracy, rather than a revival, the factors which Irving mentions in order to explain it are of interest:

> In the light of the energy crisis of the mid-1970s, inflation, relatively high unemployment . . . and sporadic outbursts of urban terrorism, there was a revival of interest in the "old" Christian Democratic values—pragmation, class reconciliation, *concertation*, concern for the security of the individual and even European integration (ibid).

It is now necessary, in conclusion, to discuss the extent to which such values represent the input into politics of a distinctively Christian impulse.

CONCLUSION

> The widely varying empirical stands which historical religions have taken in the face of political action have been determined by the entanglement of religious organisations in power interests and in struggles for power, by the always unavoidable collapse of even the highest states of tension with the world in favour of compromises and relativities . . . (Weber in Gerth and Mills, 1948, 337).

Modern liberal democracies impose on their citizens the responsibility of making political choices—choices between personalities, parties, and programs which usually present themselves in complex combinations. For the ideal Christian citizen these choices are complicated rather than simplified by the consideration of how, if at all, his or her Christianity should affect them. The same applies, only with greater force, to the Christian politician who bears the responsibility of helping to assemble the "packages" between which ordinary citizens choose. In the words of one author, "the problem is to derive a programme from the general Christian apprehension of reality or to establish a link between the two" (War 1979, 11). Or as the historian of Switzerland's political parties puts it more sharply, "What political options will a party have that has inscribed on its banner not the interests of the farmers, the workers or industry but pre-eminently, always and everywhere the interests of God? It can be conceded that it will have many options but one of the most essential tasks will always be to find out what are the true interests of God that one wishes to represent" (Gruber 1966, 166).

In terms of the usages adopted earlier, the "interests of God" embrace not only the interests *propria dicta*, which priests have historically guarded, but also the values which have been the particular concern of prophets. The record of European Christian Democracy since the nineteenth century shows that it has been the priest who has succeeded most consistently in identifying "the interests of God." By stressing the need to defend and promote the interests of the church as the institutional embodiment of God's people, the priest has been able to bracket out more difficult questions of theology and political philosophy, which the prophet has been unavoidably stuck with. The latter's task of deriving a distinctive and compelling social or political message from the values of Christianity has been made the more difficult by virtue of the fact that a wide variety of contrasting political traditions can claim, even in a secular age, to be inspired by the common heritage of those values.

When, particularly in the nineteenth century, great issues of church and state occupied center-stage, the Christian politician's problem of translating his religious loyalties and world-view into political positions scarcely arose. The priest's cry of the church in danger directed his attention forcibly to the defense of church interests. Questions of the specificity and relevance of Christian values could be held in the background. It was even possible for Christians to differ widely on such matters as long as the commonality of church interest provided a positive basis for unity.

However, since 1945 the problem has become acute. Direct church interest issues have generally been resolved. Taking positions on those which do recur has progressively ceased to provide an adequate basis for maintaining the cohesion of parties which must address an agenda of political questions made all the more wide-ranging and complex by the enormously greater scope and reach of the modern state.

In only one area has the new agenda of European politics led to a simplification of the Christian Democratic politician's problem. As continuing secularization has raised the question of removing the inherited bias of legal systems in favor of traditional Christian conceptions of morality, Christians have been reminded of certain value commitments which continue to distinguish them from many of their more secular fellow-citizens. In this, again, it is the priest rather than the prophet whose voice is most often heard—this time in defense not so much of a church interest (although one is indirectly involved insofar as the legalization of actions condemned by the church tends to undermine church discipline), as of the church's tradition of moral teaching and the values it encapsulates.

In continental Europe, this new salience of "politics of morality" has not always had the consequence of increasing the cohesion of the parties as attitudes even among the decreasing numbers of practicing Christians have become less strict. In Scandinavia, on the other hand, the emergence of these issues in countries where the established churches' privileged status had not previously fostered the development of confessional politics, the new moral-political questions have, along with older issues such as temperance, actually led to the emergence of a new brand of Christian Democracy.

There is no doubt that Christian Democracy has its own characteristic doctrines derived and developed in particular from the Catholic church's long and rich tradition of social teaching. Even the succession churches of the Reformation have carried over elements of this teaching. Most authors have little difficulty in identifying the principal features of this body of theory. A large part of Fogarty's study was concerned with a lengthy description and discussion of personalism—as distinct from individualism—and of a particular form of pluralism—in contrast to collectivism—(Fogarty 1957, 15–145). Irving identified three basic principles or underlying themes in Christian Democratic thinking which help to make it a distinctive political phenomenon: (1) Christian principles, (2) democracy, and (3) integration—the last of which refers to both class and transnational reconciliation (Irving, 1979b, 54). And Pridham, in turn, focused on six *leitmotifs:* (1) anti-communism, (2) democracy, (3) European unity, (4) traditional Roman Catholic values, (5) social progress; and (6) economic liberalism (Pridham 1976, 150–3).

A number of points emerge from these different treatments of Christian Democratic theory. First, it amounts more to a "world of ideas" (Fogarty) or a "mentality" (Irving) than a strict, ideological system. Second, however characteristic the various elements and their mode of expression, commitment to them often fails to distinguish

Christians from most other liberal democrats. In Fogarty's words they have tended to become "part of the common fund on which Western democrats of all ideologies draw" (Fogarty 1957, 392). And third, Christian Democratic doctrine is so elastic as to legitimate any one of a number of conflicting policies on major contemporary issues. For Heidenheimer this was both a short-run advantage and a long-term handicap:

> [The] relationship between an underlying set of moral values and an extremely elastic fund of working doctrines makes Christian Democracy an adaptable force within a stable political system. But its lack of ideological focus also imposes limits. The more the situation calls for fundamental, independent political initiatives or radical change the less likely is Christian Democracy to be able to provide leadership (Heidenheimer 1960, 17).

The conservative orientation of Christian Democracy at the level of theory has furthermore been buttressed by considerations of party strategy. The historian of Italy's PPI observed that the adoption of a political program committing a party to a large number of detailed long-term policy objectives "pays less well than to create a nucleus of strength and to set out with this to win power, adapting the program from hour to hour, without fear of inconsistency, to the changing moods of the electorate and the needs of the battle for power" (Jacini quoted in Fogarty 1957, 16).

This judgment reflects rather neatly, if somewhat cynically, one of the tactical desiderata of politicians who have shown great acumen and achieved great success in making Christian Democratic parties preeminently parties of government. Once power has been achieved, moreover, party managers have been constrained by the breadth of the social bases of support insofar as these span many social groups with divergent and conflicting interests. In this context, the stress on class reconciliation can be seen as being as much of a tactical necessity as an ideologically motivated goal. In most continental parties, and notoriously Italy's DC, the internal strains created by this diversity has been reflected in internal factional divisions which have occasionally had the effect of paralyzing party leaderships. Such situations indicate the weakness of prophets and even priests when the politicians are so heavily engaged.

For Weber "the religion of brotherliness has always clashed with the orders and values of this world and, the more consistently its demands have been carried through, the sharper the clash has been" (Gerth and

Mills 1948, 330). In terms of this view of the prophetic, impetus inherent in Christianity European Christian Democracy has been a broken reed. Its record has illustrated well "the entanglement of religious organisations in power interests" and the "collapse . . . in favor of compromises and relativities" referred to in the quotation at the head of this conclusion. The electorally most successful parties have proved truly inadequate vehicles for the prophet, if trusty chariots for the priest and the politician.

Notes

1. Other parties that were found to be cohesive by virtue of a positive identification with a religious characteristic were the Unionist and Nationalist parties of Northern Ireland and the neo-fascist MSI in Italy.
2. See, for example, Michelat, G. and Simon, M. 1977 for a study which confirms earlier findings in the case of France.
3. A conspicious exception to this is Whyte 1981.
4. Scandinavia provides the most striking examples of this outside Britain. See Madeley 1977 and 1982.
5. Fogarty stresses the illiberal intolerance of Continental Liberalism (with a capital L). See, for example, Fogarty 1957, 152.
6. For the interesting case of Germany see Buchheim 1953.
7. In this Pope Leo XIII should, like his successor John XXIII seventy years later, be reckoned among the "prophets" of Christian Democracy. Other popes have tended to be "priests"—or even politicians.
8. Some authors refer to a mood of religious revival in parts of Europe after the end of the war. See, for example, Pridham 1977, 22.
9. It was in 1906 that Julius Bachem published a famous article with the title "Wir Missen ans dem Turm heraus"—"we must come down out of our tower," or, as Fogarty translates it more freely, "we must fight in the open field."
10. Bryan Wilson, for example, claimed "It would be hard to say in exactly what policies the Christian Democrats in Germany (CDU) were specifically Christian" (Wilson 1966, 59).
11. The most influential work on the "pillarisation"–verzuiling–of Dutch society is Lijphart 1975.
12. On the contrasts between Catholicism, Calvinism and Lutheranism, and their differential propensity to generate religious political parties, see Lipset 1968, 219–23.
13. The absence of any mention of Luxemburg hitherto is due to the

paucity of information. The relevant party contested elections under the name Party of the Right up to 1945 when it changed its name to the Christian Social Party.

14. In Norway the increase in Christian People's Party support to 12% in 1973 can be seen as resulting from a windfall consequent on the virtual demise of the Liberal party in that year.

References

Buchheim, K. 1953. *Geschichte der Christlichen Parteien in Deutschland*. Munich: Kösel Verlag.

Fogarty, M.P. 1957. *Christian Democracy in Western Europe 1820–1953*. London: Routledge and Kegan Paul.

Gerth, H.H. and C.W. Mills. 1948. *From Max Weber*. London: Routledge and Kegan Paul.

Gruber, C. 1966. *Die Politischen Parteien der Schweiz im Zweiten Weltkrieg*. Vienna: Europa.

Heidenheimer, A.J. 1966. *Adenauer and The CDU*. The Hague: Jijhoff.

Irving, R.E.M. 1973. *Christian Democracy in France*. London: Allen & Unwin.

Irving, R.E.M. 1979a. *The Christian Democratic Parties of Western Europe*. London: Allen & Unwin.

Irving, R.E.M. 1979b. Christian democracy in post-war Europe: Conservatism writ-large or distinctive political phenomenon? *West European Politics* 2, no.1.

Lasswell, H. 1936. *Politics: Who Gets What, When, How*. New York: McGraw Hill.

Lasswell, H. and A. Kaplan. 1950. *Power and Society: A Framework for Political Inquiry*. New Haven: Yale University Press.

Lijphart, A. 1975. *The Politics of Accommodation*. Berkeley: University of California Press.

Lipset, S.M. 1960. *Political Man*. London: Mercury.

Lipset, S.M. and Rokkan, S. 1967. *Party Systems and Voter Alignments*. New York: Free Press.

Lipset, S.M. 1968. *Revolution and Counter-Revolution*. New York: Anchor Books.

Madeley, J.T.S. 1977. Scandinavian Christian democracy: Throwback or portent? *European Journal of Political Research* 5.

Madeley, J.T.S. 1982. Politics and the pulpit: The case of Protestant Europe. In *Religion in West European Politics*. Ed. S. Berger. London: Frank Cass.

Martin, D. 1978. *A General Theory of Secularization*. Oxford: Blackwell.

Merkl, P.H. 1980. West Germany. *Western European Party Systems*. London: Free Press.

Michelat, G. and M. Simon. 1977. Religion, class and politics. *Comparative Politics*. 10, no.1.

Nisbet, R.A. 1966. *The Sociological Tradition*. London: Heinemann.

Pridham. G. 1976. Christian democracy in Italy and West Germany: A comparative analysis. In *Social and Political Movements in Western Europe*. Ed. Kolinsky, M. and W. Paterson. London: Croom Helm.

Pridham, G. 1977. *Christian Democracy in Western Germany*. London: Croom Helm.

Rose, R. and D. Urwin. 1969. Social cohesion, political parties and strains in regimes. *Comparative Political Studies* 2. no.1.

Vidler, A. 1954. *Prophecy and Papacy*. London: SCM.

Ward, W.R. 1979. *Theology, Sociology and Politics*. Berne: Peter Lang.

Whyte, J.H. 1981. *Catholics in Western Democracies*. Dublin: Gill and Macmillan.

Wilson, B. 1966. *Religion in a Secular Society*. London: Watts.

19

Some Elementary Forms of Authority and Fundamentalist Politics

JOHN H. SIMPSON

DURING roughly the past twenty-five years American society has been generous in the provision of grist for the intellectual mills of the sociology of religion. The increasing importance of Orthodoxy in the Jewish community at, perhaps, the expense of liberal Reform Judaism, the impact of Vatican II upon a gentrified American Roman Catholicism, and the growth of Pentecostalism and Neo-fundamentalism among Protestants represent major shifts away from the religious "normalcy" of the post-World War II period as documented and celebrated by Will Herberg (1960) in *Protestant-Catholic-Jew*. While not always directly involved, religion was certainly implicated in the movement for civil rights, the emergence of countercultures in the 1960s, and the protest against the United States' involvement in Vietnam. During the 1970s analyses of the so-called "new religions" launched a considerable number of scholarly careers while, more recently, research on televangelism and the incursion of fundamentalism into national politics have occupied a prominent place on the sociology of religion agenda.

Perhaps, no event or movement associated with religion in the past

The author wishes to thank John T.S. Madeley and Margaret M. Poloma for helpful comments.

twenty-five years engendered more surprise than the emergence of right-wing Protestantism in the political arena in the late 1970s. What seemed to be irrelevant to public life since the repeal of Prohibition in 1933 and especially so during the heady, libertine days of the counter-cultural 1960s, namely, a politics focusing on personal morality, was suddenly an important force to be reckoned with in 1980. This chapter attempts to account for that phenomenon.

A repectable body of well–documented research now exists on the organizational, cultural, and micro-political factors associated with the rise to political prominence in recent years of the neo-fundamentalists (see, e.g., Liebman and Wuthnow 1983; and Bromley and Shupe 1984). Also, there is a firmly established tradition in political sociology identified most prominently with the work of Seymour Martin Lipset (1968) and concerned with the important relations between political parties, voting behavior, and religion that have existed since the founding of the Republic. Furthermore, Lipset (see Lipset and Raab 1978) has written extensively on the tie between right-wing Protestant-ism and right-wing politics. While not denying the usefulness of these various literatures for understanding the details of contemporary Moral Majority politics and the broader scope of the religion-politics nexus in American society, this paper seeks an understanding of the fundamental properties of a society which encourage and support a politics of morality. In this context, "fundamental" refers to the criteria of parsimony and adequacy. What is sought, in other words, is the minimal set of properties that are necessary to explain the occurrence of the politics of morality. While the primary referent is American society, the analytic focus is explicitly comparative since the argument can only be valid if the properties of American society that support and encourage a politics of morality are absent in comparable societies where right-wing Protestantism plays no important role in the political arena.

After some introductory remarks on the theoretical and methodolog-ical scope of the article, substantive discussion begins with a considera-tion of church-state relations in the United States and, more specifically, with a consideration of the ambiguity of that country's wall of separation between church and state. Volunteerism and the absence of an aristocratic tradition, it is argued, are the key elements that encourage organizational formation encompassing ideas and doctrines including socio-moral religious notions. The politics of morality in American society, then, is founded on: (1) the general societal tendency to form autonomous organizations whose interests are defined in terms of particular doctrines or ideas, and (2) the likelihood that interests will be pursued in the open political arena. The ambiguity of the wall of separation between church and state arises from the presence of socio-moral interests in the political arena, interests that, in fact, are ultimately generated and sustained in sectarian or denominational milieux. I shall contend that these arguments can be generalized into a typification of the basis for societal authority.

The argument is then made that societal authority patterns are, essentially, independent of the phenomenon of modernization, thus suggesting that fundamentalist politics is not a function of modernization. In pursuit of this thesis, two basic authority codes are identified— the *ex parte* and the *ex toto*. It is argued that fundamentalist politics is more likely to arise in a society where the *ex parte* code holds sway than where the *ex toto* code governs action. Finally Canada and the United States are compared with reference to the *ex toto/ex parte* distinction. The absence of the politics of morality in the national political arena in Canada lends support to the conceptual argument developed here.

Theoretical and Methodological Scope Conditions

Formulated in the most general terms the analytic task here is to account for cross-societal variation in the relationship between power and culture. There are two premises—one theoretical, the other methodological—narrowing the scope of my argument within that diffuse problematic. It is assumed that at the societal level polity and culture are institutionally differentiated. With reference to religion this means that primary secularization has occurred. Religion is differentiated, autonomous, and organizationally distinct and, therefore, the empirical relationship between religion and politics is, at least in principle, problematic and variegated.

There are civilizational boundaries that must be respected in applying the theoretical perspective put forward here. These are boundaries that arise out of the scope condition requiring the existence of primary secularization, i.e., the differentiation of polity and religion. From its inception, the realms of God and Caesar in Christianity have had separate standing. Even in the extreme case of caesaropapism an absolute monarch exercised control over an institution (the church) that was recognized as not coincident with the state. Furthermore, whatever the empirical relationships have been between church and state there has never been an ideal requirement associated with the foundation of Christianity that the church and state should be one.

Such is not the case for Islam for, as Cragg (1969, 77) points out, the idea that "the fundamental axiom of Islamic existence, namely that the state is the sign and surety of the faith and the faith is the ground and seal of the state" has never ceased to hold normative sway even though it proved impossible after 750 A.D. ". . . to preserve effective unity through tumultuous centuries and across three continents. . . ." There would seem to be little doubt that resurgent Islam in the twentieth century derives at least part of its inspiration from the "fundamental axiom of Islamic existence" which makes no distinction between church and state. The theoretical perspective put forward here, then, does not encompass so-called Islamic fundamentalism or, indeed, any society where primary secularization is not normative.

Methodologically the paper rests on the axiomatic yet frequently disregarded principle that the understanding and explanation of social phenomena begin with the observation of the conditions, features, and circumstances associated with both the presence and the absence of a particular social phenomenon. "Thick description" of "local knowledge" in Geertz's (1983; 1973) terms illuminates the specifics of a *case*. Theoretical understanding, however, begins with the comparison of *cases* (Simpson 1983, 349). An explanation for the contemporary incidence of fundamentalist politics, then, must account for both its appearance in some societies and its absence in others.

Two preliminary observations follow from the premises outlined above. First, the various accounts of the rise of the Moral Majority/New Christian Right in the United States that have appeared in the literature so far are, in themselves, merely descriptive. Thus, no choice can be made on grounds of explanatory adequacy between such arguments as cultural persistence and change (Wuthnow 1983), resource mobilization (Hadden 1984), or status enhancement (Simpson 1985a, 1983) because those arguments are no more than descriptions of the intertwined moments of a complex social phenomenon occurring within the bounds of a single society. They, therefore, beg the questions: What are the contextual antecendent conditions underlying the ideological formulations, resource flows, and the search for social reevaluation that accompany and drive contemporary fundamentalist politics in the United States? Furthermore, is the absence or impotence of fundamentalist politics in other comparable units of the world system associated with the absence of the contextual conditions found in the United States?

Secondly, as hinted at by the use of the phrase "contextual conditions," the perspective developed in this paper asserts the primacy of structure or relations between units in a system as the locus of explanation. Therefore, it is assumed that processes, as such, do not constitute explanatory antecedent conditions. Thus, revitalization and dedifferentiation which have been invoked as explanations for fundamentalist politics are viewed herein as descriptions of the dynamic status of a system and not as explanations for that status (e.g., Lechner 1983).

Finally, by way of introduction I note that the perspective presented in this paper explicitly rejects modernization or the encounter with modernity as the source of fundamentalist politics as postulated by some (e.g., Hunter 1983). Thus, the advent of industrialization, mass education, the mass media, and, in general, increases in societal complexity are side-stepped in the search for an adequate explanation for fundamentalist politics. The reason for this tack is spelled out below. At the same time, however, it is not denied that the differential intra-societal impact of modernization in general and education in particular may perform the function of stimulating and fixing the individual propensities, social locations, and organizational contexts supporting fundamentalist politics. Whether a given society will, in fact, produce and sustain fundamentalist politics is not, however, derivable from the consequences of modernization nor, for that matter, from the persistence of tradition as that is commonly understood.

In certain respects this paper is a journey into the wilderness. For once the notion is abandoned, as it is here, that some purchase can be gained on explaining, say, the Moral Majority phenomenon in the United States with reference to an internal perspective alone, then the question of a suitable comparative framework is raised immediately. With few notable exceptions that question has not been raised in a grand manner within the contemporary circle of those doing the sociology of religion (Martin 1978). The reasons for this are not completely clear, but I venture to say that it has something to do with an abandonment in the sociology of religion of the problem foci of general sociological theory. For where sensitivity to general sociological theory is in evidence among those who do the sociology of religion, there is also a concomitant sensitivity to the efficacy of comparative analysis for the solution of problems in the sociology of religion and, more generally, in the sociology of culture.

This paper, then, describes a comparative "ballpark" within which explanations for phenomena and, especially, social movement phenomena that are of interest to contemporary practitioners of the sociology of religion can be located. While the link between fundamentalism and politics is of particular concern in the present context there is no reason to believe that the theoretical "ballpark" is not also a suitable location for understanding other phenomena. Thus Bergesen has recently explained the cross-national incidence of political witchhunts—for example, McCarthyism and the Chinese Cultural Revolution—using a theoretical perspective that is closely related to the formulation in this paper.[1]

The Wall of Separation: Rock or Sand?

As a point of departure I begin with an observation on the classical *locus in quo* of the problematic addressed herein, i.e., church-state relations. Recent scholarly opinion underscores the point that from an historical perspective the "dual non-competence of the state and religion with regard to one another" in the United States has been and remains ambiguous (Bergeson 1984; Demerath and Williams 1984, 3).[2] Nowhere is that ambiguity better illustrated than in the double-irony that disestablishment emerged in the post-colonial period from a milieu of establishment at the state level while the current undergirding of religion as, say, in the Supreme Court's 1984 creche decision occurs at a time "when the nation is arguably more secular than ever before in its history" (Demerath and Williams 1984, 6). The relatively recent oscillation under the pressure of political expedience between John F. Kennedy's disavowal in 1960 of the propriety of *any* relationship between religion and government and Ronald Reagan's statement in 1984 that religion needs the help of government clearly suggests that the grounds for the ambiguity in the wall of separation do not lie in the framing of the principle or, even, ultimately in its judicial interpretation but rather in the nature of the society, itself, and especially, its political arena.

Given the legal specification of the church-state institutional relationship, what societal features render the wall of separation ambiguous? I suggest that there are two—one linked to the organizational nature of the society (voluntarism) and the other linked to the stratification system (absence of an aristocratic tradition). Those characteristic features of American society are, of course, fundamental considerations in Tocqueville's classic analysis contrasting America and Europe. In the present context the task is to describe their peculiar admixture and complementarity in order to understand the wall of separation and its relation to fundamentalist politics in America.

Tocqueville, it will be recalled, asserted that in "no country in the world has the principle of association been more successfully used . . . than America . . . In the United States, associations are established to promote . . . public safety, commerce, industry, morality, and religion. There is no end which the human will despairs of attaining through the combined power of individuals united into a society . . ." (Tocqueville 1956, 95–6).

But it was not, simply, the number and variety of voluntary organizations outside the bounds of the state that impressed Tocqueville. It was also the fact that associations formed around the assent "which a number of individuals give to certain *doctrines.*" Thus, Tocqueville sharply contrasted association in America for the purpose of developing and promoting ideas, norms, and values ("doctrines") with what he understood the goal of association to be in Europe at the time: to forge "a weapon which is to be hostilely fashioned, and immediately tried in the conflict [against the state]." In Europe, he says, an association "is, in fact, an army . . . In America, there are factions, but no conspiracies" (1956, 98).

Central to Tocqueville's discussion, then, in his emphasis on the proliferation of associations in America organized to express "doctrines" and influence public opinion. Ideas, themselves, are the basis for association and, in that sense, the society is "idealistic." Raw interests, too, have been and are a basis for organization in American society and its history is not bereft of examples of the perception of conspiracy by the government. Nevertheless, Tocqueville's characterization rings true. In that regard there is, perhaps, no better testimony than Parson's insistence in *The Structure of Social Action* (1937) nearly one-hundred years after *Democracy in America* was written that the theory of action begins with the normatively oriented actor. When relativized to American society, Parson's analysis is seen for what it is, at least, and, perhaps, at most—a theory of action in the context of association on the basis of "doctrines."

While voluntary association or organization is a defining modality of American society, its peculiar potency in the American context arises, I believe, from another feature of the society that unleashes the principle and allows it free rein. I refer to the absence of an aristocratic tradition. Aristocracy in the West was founded, essentially, on the control of land through force of arms. The dependence of all upon land for subsistence in the formative period, its control by a few, and the transmission of control through inheritance provided the model for an impermeable social boundary uncrossable by any means except, of course, forcible expropriation. Thus, the presence of an aristocratic tradition creates the sense of firmly bounded niches in a stratification system, niches within which, in an absolute sense, one lives and moves. That sense tends to persist long after an aristocracy either ceases to be empowered or unchallenged in hegemonic control, such as in France and England.

In the United States the model of the aristocratic boundary never gained a secure foothold, the South notwithstanding. (The Civil War resulted in the degentrification of the South and not in the destruction of a landed aristocracy embedded in a system of feudal tenure dependent upon the military control of the planter's domain.) In the absence of an aristocratic tradition, a social model of penetrable boundaries became ascendant. This is not to say that American society does not provide for its members, as all societies do, a sense of "us" vs. "them" based on the differential distribution of social and economic desiderata (Ossowski 1963). However, what is at stake is the *finality* of that sense and the contention here is that the sense of "us" vs. "them" is less final in American society than elsewhere. This contention, it should be noted, is analytically independent of mobility rates based, as it is, upon a cultural model of the nature of social boundaries in a stratification system and not on aggregated empirical evidence which may, in fact, be unknown to most members of a population.

While organization around ideas and permeable social boundaries are analytically distinct features that could exist, one without the other in any society, it is the presence of these elements in combination that produces the organizationally dense public arena observed in America. The "active society" exists because there is, ultimately, no fundamental limitation imposed by a social model of impenetrable boundaries upon the autonomous organization of ideas, that is, organization for the purpose of implementing an idea (Etzioni 1968). The probability of an organization forming for *any purpose,* then, is higher in American society than elsewhere and it is higher because the stratification system or, more precisely, the cultural definition of stratification boundaries provides a social model underwriting the notion of relatively unfettered opportunity as, for example, in the Horatio Alger myth. In this regard it is worth noting that sociological perspectives which turn on the notion of actors encountering a multiplicity of organized purposes in their lives or are in some sense "pragmatic" may, perhaps, be relativized to the American context (Swanson 1967; 1960; Simpson 1984; Winter 1984).[3]

Considering the separation of church and state in the context of the American propensity to organize ideas and interests sheds further light on the ambiguity of the wall of separation. It is clear that while the legal institutional barrier of separation does exist, it imposes no limitation on the organization of religious ideas and, furthermore, it does not preclude the expression of those ideas as interests in the political arena. (What it does preclude is a fundamental institutional rearrangement whereby the state would be bound in the service of the interests of some religious group or denomination.)

But why are organized ideas including religious ideas likely to end up in the publically visible political arena in America? The answer, at least in part, is that there is virtually no sphere of public administration apart from politics in the United States. Not only do constitutionally underwritten structures and populist traditions encourage bringing special interests to the attention of public officials but they also compel them to make bargains and compromises. Government, in other words, is open to direct penetration by any defined and organized interest (Banfield and Wilson 1963, 1). The case is different in other democracies. In Canada and the United Kingdom, for example, the administrative apparatus of government (the civil service) operates behind the shield of cabinet and is, therefore, only indirectly penetrable by organized interests.

Given the bias of American society in the direction of embedding ideas and interests in autonomous groups that further a cause and the penetrability of government by special interests, it is not surprising that religious ideas are expressed, organized, and cast into the political arena. The ambiguity of the wall of separation between church and state, then, is derived (at least in part) from the capacity of the society to organize and reorganize itself in terms of "leading" ideas which may, on occasion, be religious ideas or ideas derived from religion and whose expression in politics is encouraged by the structure of the system itself. At the same time, the constitutionally established church-state boundary prevents a fundamental rebuilding of the wall even in the face of strident political pressure, at least so far.

These conclusions, I will argue, can be generalized and recast into a characterization of the primordial warrants that imbue action with authority in a society. Such warrants typify the relationship between acting units and, especially, the relationship between the governing center of a society and its members. In the final analysis, it is these warrants or elementary forms of authority that condition the likelihood that the politics of morality will appear in a society. However, before putting that case I will argue that modernization cannot explain fundamentalist politics because it is not a correlate of authority systems.

Side-Stepping Modernization: The Persistence of Authority

Over forty years ago Shumpeter asked:

> . . . whether the economic interpretation of history is more than a convenient approximation which must be expected to work less satisfactorily in some cases than it does in others. *Social structure, types and attitudes are coins that do not readily melt* [emphasis added]. Once they are formed they persist, possibly for centuries, and since different structures and types display different degrees of this ability to survive, we almost always find that actual groups and national behavior more or less departs from what we should expect it to be if we tried to infer it from the dominant forms of the productive process (1950, 12–13).

While Shumpeter attacked the Marxian doctrine of a tight correspondence between social structure and forms of the productive process, free-world theoreticians in the post-World War II period gave birth to a no less restricted correlative perspective by proposing a correspondence between economic development and the presence of a democratic polity. The two modernizations (economic and political) were indissolubly linked, especially in the work of Lipset (1980). Polity became the generative substructure and the inevitability of socialism was replaced by the necessity of democracy if modernization were to be achieved.

More recently it has become clear that the model of institutional "looseness" proposed by Shumpeter in his debate with the Marxists characterizes as well the economy-polity linkage within the context of modernization/industrialization. For as Baum (1980, 61–118) puts it in his trenchant critique of the literature ". . . the available evidence is pretty conclusive: industrialism is not associated with democracy. However 'systematic' modernizing change and its products may be . . . in other respects the universal transformation of an agrarian and/or commercial economy into an industrial one does not impact uniformly on politics. Autocracy as well as democracy are forms compatible with industrial society."

Baum's conclusion does not mean, however, that no inter-institutional consistencies exist in the context of modernization. What is rejected is the notion of invariant correlations between polities and indices of modernization, e.g., literacy and education, energy consumption, rates and forms of communication through the mass media, etc. What is, clearly, not rejected is the hypothesis that continuity can exist in the command or authority systems underlying the organizational structures embodying political and economic institutions. Consistency, then, may be glimpsed in the similarity of cross-institutional authority patterns which appear to be impervious to the overlay of modernization.

For example, the Japanese system of group management, recently discovered by business writers in the West and thought by some to be the source of the Japanese economic miracle, on examination reveals those structural characteristics that have typified the exercise of authority in Japanese society for a long time and, certainly, since before the advent of World War II (e.g., Nakane 1970). Furthermore, close scrutiny of Japanese political parties (Richardson 1974) and that country's government agencies (Johnson 1978) exposes no crucial departures from the model of authority in industrial organizations. Thus, despite the imposition of democracy and the development of, arguably, the most advanced economy in the world, Japan remains, in the colorful words of one observer, the "land of the perpetual Geisha and eternal Samurai" (Toynbee 1984, 19) engrossed in an entanglement of relationships that any pre-war visitor would instantly recognize.

That authority patterns persist in the midst of the transformations of modernity is a working hypothesis that does seem to account for the lack of convergence between industrialization, on the one hand, and the form of regimes on the other hand. Baum, in fact, has taken the argument a step further and proposed a neo-Parsonian explanation for the persistence of the range of authority patterns found in the modern West. For my purposes here that argument can be bracketed. My concern is to establish a linkage between authority patterns and political expression in the first instance while leaving open the question of the "ultimate" explanation for that linkage. However, it should be noted that whatever the explanation for the linkage might be, it does not appear to lie within the scope of modernization theory since the phenomenon addressed by that consideration is not, on the fact of the evidence, a covariate of authority systems. In short, modernization can be side-stepped in the search for an adequate explanation for fundamentalist politics.

Authority Codes and Political Expression

The theoretical perspective used to establish a tie between forms of authority and political expression is derived from the work of Swanson (1971; 1967; 1960) and of Baum's (1980) adaptation of Swanson's analytic system. Swanson proposes the existence of a number of "constitutional" possibilities specifying the range of stable corporate decision-making patterns that can arise in any collectivity. Any collectivity from an informal periodic gathering of friends to a nation-state may, in principle, be mapped into one of Swanson's constitutional categories.

The types of constitutional possibilities proposed by Swanson can be explicated with reference to two considerations: the notion of *association* and the notion of *system*. Any collectivity, according to Swanson, has both associative and systemic features characterizing the action of units in the collectivity. As participants in an association, the members of a collectivity will try to use the collective relationship to further their private or special interests. At the same time, acting units must take into consideration the interests of the system itself. That is, units must act to maintain the collectivity by serving its needs. When participants in a collectivity act on behalf of their own interests they bear the status of an *agent*. *"Constitutional systems vary in the formal recognition they provide for this distinction"* (Swanson 1971, 162-Emphasis added).

Baum, in fact, argues that variation over constitutional systems in the recognition of the constituent body/agent distinction congeals around two distinct poles. Furthermore, he contends that the two poles typify not simply the organizational characteristics of a collectivity—that is, the manner in which units are linked one to another and to a center—but also distinct codes which, as Robertson (1980, 223) puts it, in the most general sense specify "ground rules of social interaction . . . [basic] cultural models . . . modes of legitimization . . . [and] the extra-societal warrants" that by their immanence in action justify the claim that an authoritative act has occurred. Baum labels one code *ex parte* and the other *ex toto*.

The *ex parte* and *ex toto* codes arise as the only possible solution (in an ideal-typical sense) to the central dilemma of politics. Any government, Baum argues, depends upon the support of organized legitimate social interests that pursue diverse and, often, conflicting purposes. At the same time, the government must assert its *raison d'être:* the existence of a common interest transcending all particular group interests. The endemic dilemma of politics exists because a choice must be made between the purposes of organized private interests and the purposes of the system, itself, *and both must be served.*

The dilemma is solved in any particular polity by granting ascendance to either the interests of constitutional bodies (the parts of society) or to the purposes of system agents (representing the whole of society) while recognizing that the interests and purposes of both constituent bodies and agents are legitimate and necessary aspects of the collective enterprise. Where ascendance is granted to constituent bodies, the *ex parte* code provides the warrant for authoritative action and common purposes arise out of a negotiated social order derived from the direct interaction of society's more real constituent parts. On the other hand, where ascendance is granted to the agents of a collectivity, the *ex toto* code provides the warrant for authoritative action, a greater reality is attributed to what all have in common than to the diverse purposes of constituent groups, and the common purpose is an immanent given that must be awakened.

Regarding politics in societies governed by *ex parte* and *ex toto* codes, we might expect the following in terms of the way in which interests are factored into the political process. In the *ex parte* case there is an aggregate multiplicity of interests any one of which may precipitate the formation of an autonomous group. Becoming organized itself confers legitimacy. As organized interests proceed upward through the system, conflict is generated, and there is a public sense of "withoutness" seeking redress. Success comes about when social, economic, or legal desiderata—real or symbolic—are redistributed in favor of the organized interest.

In the *ex toto* case, on the other hand, the fact of organization does not invoke either the stamp of autonomy or automatic legitimacy. That only comes about, paradoxically, where an interest is incorporated into "the system." There is a bias favoring the articulation of interests from above and a tendency to deem a cause successful where its proponents (but not necessarily their ideas formulated as interests) have been absorbed into the structure of power. In the *ex toto* case interests tend either to disappear into a black-hole of "withiness" or to remain forever on the margins cast in the role of a petulant child.

Considering, then, the difference between societies governed by *ex parte* and *ex toto* codes, fundamentalist politics or the politics of morality is more likely to appear in the former than in the latter simply on the grounds that an interest on the periphery has a greater chance of becoming autonomously organized and politically effectual in an *ex parte* society than in an *ex toto* society.[4]

Canada and the United States

The purpose of this article has been to propose a theoretical framework for understanding fundamentalist politics in cross-cultural perspectives. Further insight into the theoretical abstractions may be gained from a brief comparison of Canada and the United States. Despite great similarity between the two nations—democratic regimes, similar sources of colonization and immigration, a similar range of religious denominations and groups, similar positions on the modernization scale, and enormous cultural interpenetration through the mass media —the politics of morality has failed to appear in the contemporary Canadian political arena. Can that absence be attributed to a difference in the authority systems of the two North American neighbors?

At the heart of the distinction between the *ex toto* and *ex parte* authority codes lies a difference in emphasis on collective purposes as opposed to the purposes of the members of a collectivity. In an *ex toto* system collective purposes are ascendant while in the *ex parte* case the purposes of individual units are paramount. That Canada and the United States differ in terms of those emphases is a conclusion which is consistent with Lipset's comparative analysis of the two nations (Lipset 1985; 1968, 31–63). According to Lipset, Canada's value system emphasizes a collective orientation while that of the United States encourages self-orientation. He attributes this difference and other value differences, as well, to Canada's "counterrevolutionary past, a continuing need to differentiate itself from the United States, the influence of monarchical institutions, a dominant Anglican religious tradition, and a less individualistic and more governmentally controlled frontier expansion than was present on the American frontier" (1968, 33). Concrete evidence for Canada's collective orientation is found in, among other things, significant government roles in health and hospital insurance programs, publically funded family allowances granted to all mothers, and widespread public ownership of major utilities and industrial enterprises.

Comparing the two nations in terms of religion, Lipset notes that evangelicals gained the upper hand in the United States soon after the Revolution. The rise of the Baptists and Methodists which had no establishment roots contrasted with the leading roles played by the

Anglican and Roman Catholic churches in Canada which had existed for centuries in a milieu of close association between throne and altar. While church establishment on the British model disappeared in Canada long ago, religion always has been less explicitly separated from the national community and its purposes than in the United States. There the practice of religion may at times be linked to the social health of the Republic but religion is not constrained or encouraged to pursue specific state goals. In Canada, on the other hand, religion has been and continues to be viewed as an institutional sector that, at a minimum, must not run counter to national purposes. This difference is well-illustrated by the regulation of broadcasting and its impact upon religious broadcasting in the two countries.

In the United States the Federal Communication Commission (FCC) freely grants broadcasting licenses to religious groups and denominations. Unlike the FCC, the Canadian Radio-Television and Telecommunications Commission (CRTC) will not license stations that intend to broadcast particular sectarian viewpoints or serve a special sector rather than community interests as a whole. Thus, a few years ago the fundamentalist Family Radio Group was denied a license. More recently, Crossroads Christian Communications, an organization controlled by the Canadian Pentecostal televangelist, the Reverend David Mainse, was denied a satellite broadcasting license. These denials were consistent with the past history of broadcasting regulation in Canada through which the potentially divisive impact of sectarian religious expression has always been curbed (Simpson 1985).

That a fundamentalist politics of morality has not appeared in Canada may, in part, be due to the demographics of religious preference in Canada. About forty percent of the church members in the United States are sectarian Protestants. About nine to twenty-two percent of the Canadian population fall into the same category (Simpson and McLeod 1985). Hence, the base for a Moral Majority-type political movement is not as large in Canada as it is in the United States. But even if it were it is doubtful that socio-moral issues would receive much attention in Canada because their emergence in the political arena would surely be interpreted as an attempt by English-speaking Protestants to impose their mores on the entire nation in violation of the historic accommodation between Francophone Roman Catholics and Anglophones on which Canada is founded. That accommodation demands close attention to the common purposes that define Canada's nationhood.

In fact, it can be argued that the regional, linguistic, ethnic, religious, and cultural diversity of the Canadian mosaic requires a continuous and visible emphasis on collective purposes in order to counterbalance the centrifugal forces that constantly tug at Canadian unity. Historically, the interests of the major churches in Canada—Anglican, Roman Catholic, the United Church of Canada—have been identified with those purposes and have been factored into the political process through formal and informal channels of representation and communication. On the other hand, sectarian interests remain outside the networks of influence, excluded by the fear that inclusion would sow the seeds of disunity. That exclusion, in the final analysis, eliminates the possibility of a politics of morality emerging in the contemporary Canadian political arena.

Conclusion

In sum, I have argued here that societal authority patterns are fundamentally independent of so-called modernization phenomenon. The obvious implication is that fundamentalist politics as found in the United States are not a simple function of modernization. The argument here distinguished between *ex parte* and *ex toto* authority codes, postulating that fundamentalist-style politics are more likely to arise in a society where the *ex parte* code holds sway (and independent interest group formation finds fewer obstacles) than where the *ex toto* code governs activism. The main point is both comparative and political–sociological: In the United States, with its political tradition of *ex parte* societal authority, a politics of morality has been allowed (even encouraged) to exist and flourish; in the Canadian political arena, on the other hand, the absence of a politics of morality can be explained by that country's *ex toto* societal authority.

Notes

1. See, for example, the classics: Guy E. Swanson, *The Birth of the Gods* (Ann Arbor: University of Michigan Press, 1960); Guy E. Swanson, *Religion and Regime* (Ann Arbor: University of Michigan Press, 1967); and the more recent Roland Robertson and Burkart Holzner, eds. *Identity and Authority: Explorations in the Theory of Society* (New York: St. Martin's, 1980).
2. The quotation is from Carroll J. Bourg, "Politics and Religion," *Sociological Analysis* 41, no. 4 (1981): 300.
3. The argument that the probability of an organization forming for any purpose is higher in American society than elsewhere is sup-

ported by the following observation: In Canada which, of all the countries of the world, most nearly resembles the United States there are approximately 11,000 associations. That figure includes associations at the local, provincial, national, and international levels. In the United States there are 18,000 associations at the national level alone. See Akey (1985) and Land and Gallagher (1984).

4. A test of this conclusion would require holding constant across societies the extent to which personal morality involving, especially, conflict items such as abortion or homosexuality is deemed to make a real difference in the vitality and strength of a society.

References

Akey, Denise S., ed. 1985. *Encyclopedia of Associations*. 19th ed. Detroit: Gale Research.

Banfield, Edward C. and James Q. Wilson. 1963. *City Politics*. Cambridge: Harvard University Press and M.I.T. Press.

Baum, Rainer C. 1980. Authority and identity: The case for evolutionary invariance. In *Identity and Authority: Explorations in the Theory of Society*. Ed. Roland Robertson and Burkart Holzner, 61–118. New York: St. Martin's.

Bergesen, Albert. 1984. *The Sacred and the Subversive: Political Witch-hunts as National Rituals*. Monograph Series, no. 4. Storrs, Connecticut: Society for the Scientific Study of Religion.

Cragg, Kenneth. 1969. *The House of Islam*. Belmont, Calif.: Dickenson.

Demerath, N.J. III and Rhys H. Williams. 1984. A mythical past and uncertain future. *Society* 21, no. 4: 3–10.

Etzioni, Amitai. 1968. *The Active Society: A Theory of Societal and Political Processes*. London: Collier-Macmillan.

Geertz, Clifford. 1973. *The Interpretation of Cultures*. New York: Basic Books.

———. 1983. *Local Knowledge: Further Essays in Interpretive Anthropology*. New York: Basic Books.

Hadden, Jeffrey K. 1984. Televangelism and the future of American politics. In *New Christian Politics*. Ed. David G. Bromley and Anson Shupe, 151–65. Macon, Ga.: Mercer University Press.

Herberg, Will. 1960. *Protestant-Catholic-Jew*. Rev. ed. Garden City, N. Y.: Doubleday Anchor.

Hunter, James Davison. 1983. *American Evangelicalism: Conservative Religion and the Quandary of Modernity*. New Brunswick, N. J.: Rutgers University Press.

408 JOHN H. SIMPSON

Johnson, Chalmers A. 1978. *Japan's Public Policy Companies*. Washington, D.C.: American Enterprise Institute.
Land, Brian and Diane Gallagher, eds. 1984. *Directory of Associations in Canada/Repertoire des Associations du Canada*. 5th ed. Toronto: Micromedia Limited.
Lechner, Frank J. 1983. Fundamentalism and sociocultural revitalization. Paper read at the annual meeting of the Society for the Scientific Study of Religion, 4–6 November, Knoxville, Tennessee.
Liebman, Robert C. and Robert Wuthnow, eds. 1983. *The New Christian Right*. New York: Aldine.
Lipset, Seymour Martin. 1960. *Political man*. New York: Doubleday.
———. 1968. *Revolution and Counterrevolution: Change and Persistence in Social Structures*. New York: Basic Books.
———. 1985. Canada and the United States: The cultural dimension. *Canada and the United States*. Ed. Charles F. Doran and John H. Sigler. Englewood Cliffs, N.J. and Scarborough, Ont.: Prentice-Hall. Forthcoming.
Lipset, Seymour Martin and Earl Rabb. 1978. *The Politics of Unreason: Right-Wing Extremism in America, 1790–1977*. 2d ed. Chicago: University of Chicago Press.
Martin, David. 1978. *A General Theory of Secularization*. New York: Harper & Row.
Nakane, Chie. 1970. *Japanese Society*. Berkeley: University of California Press.
Parsons, Talcott. 1937. *The Structure of Social Action*. New York: McGraw-Hill.
Ossowski, Stanislaw. 1963. *Class Structure in the Social Consciousness*. Trans. Sheila Patterson. New York: The Free Press of Glencoe.
Richardson, Bradley M. 1974. *The Political Culture of Japan*. Berkeley: University of California Press.
Robertson, Roland. 1980. Aspects of identity and authority in sociological theory. In *Identity and Authority: Explorations in the Theory of Society*. Ed. Roland Robertson and Burkart Holzner, 218–65, New York: St. Martin's Press.
Robertson, Roland and Burkart Holzner, eds. 1980. *Identity and Authority: Explorations in the Theory of Society*. New York: St. Martin's Press.
Schumpeter, Joseph A. 1950. *Capitalism, Socialism and Democracy*. 3d ed. New York: Harper & Row.
Simpson, John H. 1983. Power transfigured: Guy Swanson's analysis of religion. *Religious Studies Review* 9, no. 4: 349–52.

———. 1983. Moral issues and status politics. In *The New Christian Right*. Ed. Robert C. Liebman and Robert Wuthnow, 187–205. New York: Aldine.

———. 1984. High gods and the means of subsistence. *Sociological Analysis* 45 no. 3: 213–22.

———. 1985a. Status inconsistency and moral issues. *Journal for the Scientific Study of Religion* 24, no. 2.

———. 1985b. Federal regulation and religious broadcasting in Canada and the United States. *Canadian Issues* 7.

Simpson, John H. and Henry G. MacLeod. 1985. The politics of morality in Canada. In *Religious Movements: Genesis, Exodus, and Numbers*. Ed. Rodney Stark. New York: Paragon House. Forthcoming.

Swanson, Guy E. 1960. *The Birth of the Gods*. Ann Arbor: University of Michigan Press.

———. 1967. *Religion and Regime*. Ann Arbor: University of Michigan Press.

———. 1971. An organizational analysis of collectivities. *American Sociological Review* 36: 607–23.

Tocqueville, Alexis de. 1956. *Democracy in America*. Ed. Richard D. Heffner. New York: New American Library.

Toynbee, Polly, 1984. I have rarely seen a bleaker society, more competitive, more full of fierce social pressures. *Manchester Guardian Weekly* 131, no. 2 (July 8): 19.

Winter, J. Alan. 1984. Toward a fuller version of Swanson's sociology of religion. *Sociological Analysis* 45, no. 3: 205–11.

Wuthnow, Robert. 1983. The political rebirth of American evangelicals. *The New Christian Right*. Ed. Robert C. Liebman and Robert Wuthnow, 168–85. New York: Aldine.

20

Protestantism and Politics in Scotland and Ulster

STEVE BRUCE

Introduction

IT is commonly known that Scotland and Ulster are similar in their religion and politics, and yet little effort has been directed to a systematic comparison of religious conflicts in the two countries. This paper is one of a series of comparative studies of Protestant politics and aims to identify those features of the Scottish setting which have contributed to a muting of the same sectarian conflict so prevalent in Ulster.[1]

Geographical proximity underlies the complex inter-connections of Scottish and Ulster history. Constant migration of populations across the short sea crossing has meant that few events or processes in one setting have failed to produce some complementary event or process in the other. The Protestants who settled the northeastern part of Ireland in the seventeenth century were mainly Scots, and they took with them the reformed Presbyterianism of the Scottish church. Until the early nineteenth century the Ulster Presbyterians were formally under the authority of the Scottish church. Scotland was used as a refuge on more than one occasion by Ulster Presbyterians escaping persecution by the Anglican elite in Ireland (Stewart 1950; Reid 1853; Loughridge 1984).

Both provinces share a common relationship with the center of power in the United Kingdom. Both have an identity distinct from that of England, and they have maintained some structures of autonomy, but both are peripheries dependent on, and controlled by, London. Interestingly, this is subjectively appreciated not only by Ulster Protestants but also by Northern Irish Catholics. A 1978 survey showed that, while only forty-three percent of Ulster Protestants and thirty-three percent of Catholics think themselves similar to the English, eighty-two percent and fifty-seven percent respectively think themselves similar to the Scots (Browne 1983, 12).

Both provinces at times have seen considerable conflict between Protestants and Catholics. Both had anti-Catholic political parties and the main vehicle for popular Protestantism—the Orange Order—has its largest memberships in Ulster and Scotland.

Yet in 1982 the Pope, who—according to the doctrines of classic Presbyterianism is the "anti-Christ"—visited England, Wales *and* Scotland but *not* Northern Ireland. And for all the sound and fury that greeted the initial announcement of the papal visit, there was almost no opposition to the arrival on the sacred soil of reformed Scotland of the head of the "Mother of Harlots."

It is now obvious that while one can still see obscenities aimed at the Pope sprayed on walls in Glasgow, and while the two main Glasgow football teams—Celtics and Rangers—are still seen to be Catholic and Protestant, respectively, anti-Catholicism is no longer a major social force in Scotland. For all its similarities with Ulster, Scotland has developed in the direction of the modern secular society in which religious affiliation is treated as a private matter, a concern only for the individual and the family. It no longer plays a major part in informing social and political debates. In the following pages I analyze the reasons for this development.

Protestants and Catholics in Ulster

Since the early Middle Ages, the native Irish population was Roman Catholic. The Protestants in Ireland came from two sources; settlers from England who were mainly Episcopalian and settlers from Scotland who were Presbyterian, all of whom had been given grants of land by the British government. From the early eighteenth century there was a social structure resembling a three-layer sandwich. The elite stratum was made up of Anglo-Irish and Episcopalians (as were many of their agricultural laborers). The Roman Catholic natives were generally the lowest class, and the Scots settlers came to form a middle layer of more prosperous farmers caught between the elites and the native population.

At various points in the eighteenth century it seemed possible that the Presbyterian Scots-Irish could be led by some radical ministers into an alliance with the Roman Catholic Irish against the Anglo-Irish elite. However, the growth of nationalism and its development into a "home rule" movement was accompanied by conflict, sometimes in the form of large-scale massacres of people, which convinced the Presbyterians that their best interests lay in casting their lot with the elite. In return the British government gradually removed the restrictions on the Presbyterians and opened the way for the growth of a shared Protestant identity.

The simplification of the triad of Catholic, Episcopalian, and Presbyterian into a dyad of Protestant and Catholic can be conveniently illustrated with two points. When in the 1820s the British government planned to disestablish the Episcopalian Church of Ireland (which after all had only the support of a small part of the population), leading Presbyterian ministers opposed the move on the grounds that there should be an established Protestant church, even if it was the "wrong" Protestant church (Holmes, 1981). At the same time, large numbers of Presbyterians joined the Orange Order, a fraternal organization that had its roots in conflicts between the native Irish and the settlers and which had previously been overwhelmingly Episcopalian (Gray, 1977; Senior, 1966).

The move from triad to dyad was hastened by the partial success of the nationalist movement which despite the abortive 1916 rising gained independence for twenty-six countries of Ireland. The Protestants in the northeast resisted pressure to leave Britain and were permitted their own "state" in a smaller version of the old province of Ulster. Large numbers of Episcopalians and Presbyterians left what became the Free State (later the Republic of Ireland) and moved either to the British mainland or to Northern Ireland. Those who remained have gradually been eroded by the Roman Catholic church's insistence that the children of mixed marriages be raised as Catholics. At partition in 1921, some sixteen percent of the population of the south were Protestants. This figure has now shrunk to approximately two percent (Lyons, 1979).

The general point to be drawn from this extremely condensed history is that since the middle of the seventeenth century there has been general competition between the Roman Catholic natives and the Protestant settlers. Given that the conflict began in an era when ethnic identities were profoundly informed by religious beliefs and values, the history of the conflict has only served to increase the importance of religion in social, economic and political relations.[2] The Scots settlers (who, with the rise of the nationalist movement, became more and more the core of Protestantism) came to Ireland with a strong shared religious identity and framed their confrontations with the natives (who shared a commitment to the one form of Christianity most antagonistic to Calvinist Presbyterianism) in religious terms. They had their religious identities reinforced by the persecutions of first the Anglo-Irish elites and then the increasingly confident Roman Catholic population.

Nothing symbolizes this more clearly than the resource the Ulster Protestants fell back on when they wished to symbolize their resistance to the home rule movement; they modelled their protest on the "Solemn League and Covenant" of the old Scots Presbyterians.[3] Throughout their sojourn in Ireland, the Ulster Presbyterians have seen themselves as a persecuted religious minority. At times of crises, it is to their religious traditions that they have returned. Irrespective of whether or not they have in reality been engaged in a holy war, that is how they view their history. Periodic actions of the Roman Catholic church have done nothing to undermine that world-view. When the constitution of the Republic was accepted in 1937, it included not only a territorial claim to the whole of the island but also an assertion that the Roman Catholic church had a special status in the Irish state.

Ulster Protestant unity was stabilized through Protestants of all denominations joining the fraternal Orange Order and the formation of the Ulster Unionist party (over which the Order had considerable control). Possible divisions within the Protestant community were prevented from developing by a combination of the Unionist elites' ability either actually or symbolically to reward working class Protestants and the ever-present dual threat from the south and from the nationalists within. For the churches and for the Unionist party the period from 1921 to the onset of the present "Troubles" in 1969 was one of remarkable unity and cohesion.[4]

Protestants and Catholics in Scotland

Scotland has always been divided. For convenience, people think of the division as north and south although a more accurate geography would identify the parts as east and west. The lowlands rapidly adopted the principles of the Reformation and became Protestant. The highlands, their social development considerably affected by poor land and worse communications, remained pagan, Episcopalian, or Roman Catholic.

Such separate development was brought to an end by the supporters of the Hanoverian monarchy and the Protestant faith who reacted to the highlanders' Jacobite rebellions in 1715 and 1745 by engaging in deliberate social reconstruction (Bruce, 1983a). The symbols of the old feudal highland culture were outlawed, the clan chiefs were stripped of their powers, and roads were built to encourage the assimilation of the highlands to the lowland culture and economy. Thus, by 1790 there existed a strongly Protestant lowlands and a reluctantly Protestant highlands with some pockets of Episcopalian and Roman Catholic support mostly in Banff, Buchan, and some of the Western Isles.

By 1890, however, there were large numbers of Irish Roman Catholics immigrants in the Western lowlands. Economic hardship had been the main push factor, and the demand for labor either to work in the growing Scottish industries or to replace Scots who had moved into those industries was the main pull (Handley, 1983, 1945; Piggott, 1979).

The arrival of a large number of Roman Catholics provided most of the raw material for anti-Catholicism. The catalyst of prejudice came also from Ireland for not all of the migrants were Catholics. A small but significant proportion were Protestants and they had already acquired a practical anti-Catholicism in the Orange Order. Thus there had emerged the basic elements for conflict: two ethnically distinct populations in competition, identified by different and opposed religions.

Two additional points can be made here. The first is that the Irish Roman Catholics were "especially" Catholic. The old Scots Catholics of Banff and Buchan, on the other hand, had become quite "Protestant" (or in Catholic terms, Jansenist). Indeed, their styles of worship were almost puritan. They had more lay participation and were less dominated by their priests. The Irish Catholics, especially those from the poorer rural areas, were subservient to their clergy, not surprising given that most of them were at best semi-literate, and the local priest was often the only person with any claims to a high social status. The variety of Catholicism brought to Scotland by the Irish immigrants in the middle of the nineteenth century was a throwback to the styles of the Counter-Reformation and offended the old Scots Catholics almost as much as the Protestants.

The second point is that the arrival of the Irish coincided with the great wave of urban expansion and industrialization. The certainties of rural life were replaced by the harsh cruelties of hurriedly thrown up cities. The Scots Protestants made a simple equation: the Irish and the problems of industrialization had arrived at the same time, therefore the problems were caused by the Irish. A particular source of conflict for workers in Ayrshire and Lanarkshire was the role of the Irish as scab labor in industrial disputes in the 1820s (Campbell, 1979). The Irish came in at the bottom of the labor market, leaving the native Protestants in control of the skilled trades and as the main supporters of the early union activity, thus creating a dimension of conflict which persisted into this century.[5]

One brief example of anti-Catholic activism will make the general point about the social location of support for militant Protestantism. In 1829, the British government decided to remove most of the legal obstacles to Roman Catholics enjoying full citizenship. This caused a major outcry from the Scots. Public meetings and petitions became the order of the day. But a close examination of who most vigorously protested against the emancipation of Catholics brings some important points to light. If one looks at the churches, one finds that generally the more conservative Presbyterian churches were most vocal in their opposition, but there was also a regional bias. The Glasgow Presbytery of the Church of Scotland was more opposed to emancipation than was the Edinburgh Presbytery; that is, the churches on the West lowlands coast were more anti-Catholic than those on the East coast. The other major source of opposition was the skilled working class. Many of the organizations that represented skilled craftsmen petitioned against the Emancipation Act but again this is compounded by a regional influence: more protests came from those areas with large Irish populations than from those on the East coast (Muirhead, 1973).[6]

Protestant Divisions and the Scottish Acceptance of Catholics

In the brief history of the Ulster Protestants, I suggested that the history of conflict between Presbyterians and Episcopalians with the Roman Catholic natives forced the two former groups into a shared Protestant identity. While there were splits from the main body of Ulster Presbyterianism and the formation of small denominations outside that tradition, there were only two main Presbyterian churches and these united in 1840.

In contrast, the history of Scottish Presbyterianism until the end of the nineteenth century was one of division (Drummond and Bulloch,

1973). The reasons for these divisions need not concern us here but their existence had profound consequences for undermining opposition to Roman Catholicism. At the time when the "threat" from the Irish immigrants was at its height, the largest Presbyterian body, the established Church of Scotland, was in the throes of a major conflict about the relationship between church and state. Although the arrival on the British throne of the Protestant Hanoverian monarchy had formally guaranteed the Presbyterian structure of the Church in Scotland, the local democracy of the church had been undermined by the restoration of patronage. The major landowners (who effectively paid for the church) were given back the right to appoint their own nominees as ministers over the wishes of the congregation. In theological terms this meant the evangelicals had less power than the moderates whose emphasis on good works rather than personal salvation was more appealing to a class which had little commitment to piety. The conflict between the evangelicals and moderates raged from the 1830s until 1843 when the evangelicals withdrew, taking one third of the church with them, to form the Free Church of Scotland.

With Presbyterianism being such an important part of Scottish culture and the Church of Scotland being one of the few national Scottish institutions left after the Union of the Crowns and the shift of political power to London, the division of the Kirk was a passionate concern for a very large part of the population. In this respect, it diverted attention from relations with Roman Catholics. Furthermore, it hastened secularization. While there was one national church, it was quite reasonable for the church, funded by the major ratepayers, to organize not only religion but also education and social welfare provision, such as it was. The growth of the Seceder Presbyterians, formed in 1733 already undermined the national status of the Kirk. The formation of the Free Church killed it. The consequence was *de facto* pluralism. The various Presbyterian groupings were unable to attack convincingly the rights of Roman Catholics while simultaneously defending their own rights to full religious, civil, and political liberties.[7]

The next stage in the religious development of Scotland was the extension of secularization into the churches. The lowland Presbyterians spent the last half of the nineteenth century adopting various rationalistic rewritings of their faith. This was the case even for the Free Church which had been formed as a conservative schism (Drummond and Bulloch 1975; Maclaren 1974). Only in the highlands of Scotland, finally converted to evangelical Protestantism a hundred years later than the lowlands, did an evangelical Protestant culture endure. The increasing rationalism of the lowland churches permitted a series of reunions and the recreation of a dominant Presbyterian church, but it was one formed in an ecumenical climate. Whereas the increasing harmony of the Ulster Protestants was produced as a reaction to a sense of threat, the cohesion of the Scottish Presbyterians was a result of the erosion of distinctive religious beliefs. Hence it did not form the basis for coherent anti-Catholicism.

Scottish Protestant Politics in the 1930s

Throughout the turbulent period of Irish politics leading up to partition and the creation of the Free State, events in Ireland produced only faint resonances in Scotland. When Carson formed his Ulster Volunteer Force to resist home rule, a company was raised in Glasgow. But the most successful Scottish Protestant political movements were indigenous and owed nothing to the Ulster situation.

In 1920 Alexander Ratcliffe, a railway clerk, formed his Scottish Protestant League in Edinburgh, but had little impact until he moved his headquarters to Glasgow in 1930. While in Edinburgh he won election to the School Board on the platform of repealing the 1918 Education Act, which brought the Catholic and Episcopalian schools into the national system. But this was accomplished at the costs of giving those churches control over the hiring of teachers and of religious education, and of forcing local authorities reluctantly to take over the costs of denominational schools. It is important to note that Ratcliffe, although supported by a substantial popular vote, was entirely powerless on the Board because the Church of Scotland, and other ministers refused to support his anti-Catholic motions.[8]

The move to Glasgow took Ratcliffe into a more fruitful environment. In 1931 he and the SPL's full-time worker were elected to the council for Dennistoun and Dalmarnock respectively. The following year, the SPL took 11.7 percent of the total vote and gained a third seat. In 1933 four more Protestants were elected as the League took twenty-three percent of the vote.

The League quickly collapsed. When Ratcliffe came up for reelection at the end of his three-year term, he was opposed by a popular candidate who had been on the council before, now standing as an independent conservative. The three socialist candidates stood down, and there was a straight fight which Ratcliffe narrowly lost. Four of the

League councilors defected, claiming that Ratcliffe was dictatorial, but a major part of the problem was that the League did not have a coherent political platform. Its members agreed that they did not like Catholics, but beyond that they had little in common. At the elections, the League took conservative votes and some labor votes. In the council, four of the representatives usually voted with the conservatives and the other three normally voted with the socialists: hardly the recipe for a coherent political party. And in common with all new parties in first-past-the-post elections, the League won many votes but few seats, and many of its "experimental" supporters abandoned it.

The League emerged at a time when the socialists were unpopular and divided and when the conservatives were a byword in municipal corruption. Ratcliffe's populism drew initial support, but the League had neither the organization nor the ideology to produce a politics which could have survived the concerted attacks from almost every organization in Glasgow. Ratcliffe was attacked by every other party, but, most importantly, he was criticized by the leaders of the Orange Order who preferred to support mainstream Unionist candidates. Furthermore, he was rejected by the churches.

A similar story can be told for the Protestant Action Society (PA) led by John Cormack. Cormack was in the League but left to lead his own grouping which promised "applied muscular Christianity," and developed something of a reputation for street violence. As with the League, PA won its first seat when its leader was elected in 1934, quickly gained a number of other seats, and then went into an electoral decline which was only halted by the World War II postponing local elections. At the first elections after the war, Protestant Action was reduced to Cormack and one other councilor who called himself an independent. In contrast to the League, PA was less overtly religious and had more working class support. Also in contrast to the League, it was more conservative. While Ratcliffe's populism tended to the left, Cormack's favored the right-wing.

The important general point about the SPL and PA is that they came to the fore during a period of general political transition in Scotland. The labor movement was divided between three parties: Communist, Labour, and Independent Labour; and the conservatives who, in local elections, called themselves Moderates or Progressives were steadily losing support. Support for the SPL and PA can be seen as a temporary resting place on the road from conservative to Labour. When the first national elections were held after the war, there was a massive swing to

Labour which had now consolidated into one major party. At the local government level, conservatives were pushed out of power. In sum, the temporary success of the SPL and PA parties owed more to confusion in the other parties and the growing support for the labor movement than it did to the actual appeal of anti-Catholicism.

The Ulster Crisis

Militant Protestantism in Scotland was firmly in the doldrums from the 1930s until 1968 when the instability in Northern Ireland gave Protestants a new issue. Local branches of the Ulster paramilitary organizations (the Ulster Volunteer Force and the Ulster Defence Association) were formed and Pastor Jack Glass came to prominence as a local spokesman for militant Protestantism (Bruce 1983b).

But a number of factors point to the general unpopularity in Scotland of a militant Protestant response to the Ulster crisis. The first is the failure of the paramilitaries. Examination of their activities makes it clear that they had some initial popular support among the working class of the lowlands for their fund-raising for Ulster loyalist prisoners' families and similar work. But once they moved into collecting weapons and committing offenses in Scotland, their support dwindled and the lack of enthusiasm for such activity was reinforced by the decision of the Scottish legal establishment to make an example of anyone involved in political violence. Polls in the Glasgow elections show that Glass had some support but not enough to mean anything. For example, in 1970 he took 6.9 percent of the vote in the Bridgeton constituency; in 1982 he took 1.3 percent of the vote in the Hillhead byelection, and in the regional council elections the same year only 6.7 percent of the voters in the Bellahouston Mosspark ward supported him.

Again one sees the pattern that runs through this account: the overwhelming opposition of the Scottish Protestant elites, especially the leadership of the Church of Scotland, to militant Protestantism. There are almost no Kirk ministers who are active supporters of the Orange Order. Furthermore a number of Presbyterians have passed anti-Orange Order motions. When the Pope came to Scotland there was no major move in the Kirk to prevent the Moderator meeting the "anti-Christ" beneath the statue of John Knox. If anything, the Ulster crisis has paralyzed militant Protestantism. A few militant Protestants see it as an object lesson in what happens when one lets Roman

Catholics get out of hand. The rest of the population sees it as an example of what happens when one mixes religion and politics.

Explaining Scottish Development

The first obvious difference between Scotland and Ulster is the greater secularization of the former. Whether one considers the involvement of individuals in organized expressions of religiosity,[9] or the impact of the religious values on the general culture and polity, the conclusion has to be that Scotland is less religious than Northern Ireland. But this suggests a tautology, i.e., we are explaining the decline of anti-Catholicism in Scotland by arguing that religion matters less. To avoid that pitfall we need to explain why religion matters less in Scotland. Part of that explanation involves elements particular to Protestant-Catholic conflict. But there is a more general element. It is well-recognized that modernization and pluralism undermine religiosity (Berger 1982; Wilson 1976; 1982). Scotland is far more integrated into the British economy and into European culture than is Northern Ireland. Thus, even if relations with Catholics had not been an issue in either contest, one would have expected Scotland to be the more secular.

However, if we concentrate on relations between Protestants and Catholics, the key difference between Scotland and Ulster can be found in the combination of internal fragmentation with the absence of external threat. Following Durkheim, Simmel, and Coser on the social functions of conflict, I would argue that cohesion is created and maintained by a people feeling threatened by some alien group (Durkheim 1975; Simmel 1956; Coser 1965). We thus need first to consider why the Protestants of Scotland felt less threatened by the Roman Catholic population than did their counterparts in the northeast of Ireland.

The Irish Catholics in Scotland: In the first place there were not *that* many Catholics in Scotland. The best figures available suggest that the Catholics formed 9.2 percent of the population of Scotland in 1878, rising gradually to 13.7 percent in 1931 and 15.9 percent in 1977 (McRobert, 1979). In contrast, if one takes Ireland as a whole, Catholics form the vast majority of the population and in Northern Ireland, as constituted since 1926, more than a third of the population is Catholic (Compton 1982).

Second, the total impact of the Irish Catholic immigrants on

Scotland was considerably reduced by their settlement in certain regions. Basically, they concentrated where industry was developing: Ayrshire, Lanarkshire, Glasgow, Dunbarton, the Lothians, and Edinburgh. Even within this area, the distribution was uneven. While Catholics formed 25.3 percent of the population of Strathclyde Region in 1977, they were only 10.1 percent of Lothian Region (McRoberts 1979, 240). Although Catholics were strongest in the most populous parts of Scotland, important organizations such as the Church of Scotland and the Free Church had a national structure, which although skewed towards population concentration, was slow to adapt to movements of people. Thus in the period from 1890 to 1930—the crucial time for the career of anti-Catholicism—relations with Catholics were not a practical issue for most ministers of the churches.

Third, the Irish Catholics in Scotland flirted with Irish politics, but generally they settled to regard themselves as Scots. While they acted to preserve their own religion and culture, they did not maintain a distinctive Catholic politics (Gallagher 1981). Unlike the Ulster setting, there was no move to take the Protestants of Scotland into another political formation. Hence the only way in which they could be seen as a "threat" was if it were supposed that they would change dramatically the nature of Scotland from within and not many Scots, even those of a conservative Protestant faith, were convinced that they posed such a threat. What is of particular importance is that a specificially Catholic party along the lines of the European Christian Democratic parties, was not formed.[10] Instead Catholics became active in the secular labor movement and in what became the Labour party.[11] This meant that a neat alignment of religion and politics could only be created if all or most Protestants supported the Unionist and later Conservative parties. But the development of politics in Scotland had created a strong link between the evangelicals of the Free Church and the Liberals. Although this was gradually eroded, it did prevent an easy association of conservative Protestants with the Conservative party. Furthermore, the Conservatives in Scotland have retained far longer than their English counterparts an image of being a hunting, shooting, and fishing party (Harvie 1977, Ch.5; Kellas 1975, Ch.6). What lingering attachment the Protestant working class might have had to the Tories has been destroyed by the collapse of Scottish heavy industry which is, rightly or wrongly, blamed on Conservative economic policies.

To summarize, the Catholic presence in Scotland did not offer good evidence of a significant "threat" to the Scottish Protestants,[12] and hence did not act as a counter to the fragmentation which already existed and which *increased* between 1870 and the present. In contrast, relations between Protestants and Catholics in Ireland caused an increase in Protestant cohesion. Whereas there was considerable conflict between the Ulster Presbyterians and the more "Anglo" Irish of the Church of Ireland during eighteenth and early nineteenth century, reaction to Catholic demands for emancipation and, later, home rule, brought Protestants in Ulster together.

Scottish Protestant fragmentation: There were also a number of sources of fragmentation in Scottish Protestant culture.

First, the topography of the highlands delayed its development so that it was always out of step with lowland Scotland. When the lowlands were Protestant, the highlands were Catholic and Episcopalian. By the time the highlands had been converted to Calvinism, the lowlands had become secularized and the dominant form of Protestantism, for those who still had any form, was moderate, rational, and ecumenical. In language, custom, social relations, and economy the two parts of Scotland have been so different as to challenge the usefulness of regarding the area north of the Solway sands and the Tweed as one country.

Second, as mentioned, Scottish Protestants spent most of the nineteenth century arguing with each other and produced a *de facto* pluralism which hastened secularization.

Third, Protestant divisions might have been partly healed had there been a "pork barrel" to bribe dissenters, and the power to punish those who could not be sweetened. But Scotland was impotent. Since the Union of the Crowns, real power has rested in London. The elites therefore tended to see London and cosmopolitan values as their main point of reference. The limited number of members of the elite who wished to maintain the Protestant ascendency did not have the power to fulfill their ambitions. Further, they had nothing to offer the Protestant working classes. In contrast, the Unionist elite in Ulster could make major concessions to the working class. They legalized the popular militias as the Special Constabulary (Farrell 1983) and they discriminated in housing and local employment policy (Buckland 1979).

Fourth, the final contrast concerns the implications of the political impotence of Scotland. The Ulster Unionists were popular enough to resist being incorporated in a united Ireland, and for almost fifty years they had considerable control over many areas of life in Northern Ireland. Although subordinate to the British parliament at Westminster, the devolved parliament at Stormont could make its own policy on local government, employment, housing, education, and policing. It was thus in a position to create policy in precisely those areas which would best serve to alienate the Catholic minority. The continued alienation of the Catholic minority then acted as a constant local reminder of the dangers to the Protestants of incorporation into a united Ireland and therefore maintained the religious and cohesion of the Protestant population.

Scotland did not have that degree of control over its own affairs. The only Scottish institution that still had some influence was the church and it was divided. The Scottish Unionists could not offer much to militant Protestants because they were a small part of a party which represented England and Wales as well as Scotland. An example of their powerlessness was the failure of two Scots Unionist members of parliament—Sprot (North Lanarkshire) and McInnes Shaw (Renfrew) —to have Scotland made exempt from the provisions of the Catholic Relief Bill.[13] Scottish matters generally (let alone relations with Catholics which were only a concern for *part* of Scotland) had little impact on the British parties. Taking the other side of the coin, voters in Scotland knew that there was little point in electing anti-Catholic politicians such as Ratcliffe or Cormack to Westminster.[14] What could one or even ten militant Protestants in Westminster have achieved?

The Elements of Religio-Ethnic Conflict

One very simple generalization can be drawn from the comparison of religious politics in Ulster and Scotland: one needs an ideological element—a theory of the virtues of one's own people and the vices of some other group—and one needs actual competition between the two populations. This does not mean that one requires actual competition between *every member* of both populations. The proposition is not refuted by pointing out that racist attitudes can be held by white citizens in parts of America that have hardly ever seen a black person. The "actual" conflict can be fixed and made real for members of a society who themselves have not participated in the competition by the transmission of experiences through various media. Nonetheless, a sustained absence of actual competition for a large part of a population will reduce the plausibility and importance of the experience of the rest. This simple proposition explains the collapse of anti-Catholicism in Scotland and, by simple reversal, the maintenance of anti-Catholicism in Ulster.

The highlands of Scotland retained a Calvinist evangelical Protestant faith but did not engage in any of the expressions of practical anti-Catholicism. The Orange Order, the main organization for popular anti-Catholicism, has never had any support from above the highland line. The highlanders had the theology but no Irish Catholic immigrants.

The lowlands of Scotland were already well on their way to being a secular society by the time the Irish Catholics arrived in any great numbers. The main churches had either abandoned evangelical Protestantism or, even if they maintained it, had accepted (as an unintended consequence of their own divisions) pluralism. Of crucial importance is the observation that, as in most other societies, the urban working class of the lowlands, the very people who were in day to day competition with the Irish Catholics, were not "theologically" Protestant. The proleteriat of Glasgow experienced the actual competition with Catholics, but it lacked the ideological element.

The consequence of this is best seen if one moves from large-scale generalization to actual individuals and social movement organizations. Modern militant Protestant leaders in Glasgow such as Jack Glass and David Cassells (the local representative of Ian Paisley's Free Presbyterian Church of Ulster) are constrained by the absence of a general evangelical culture amongst those Protestants who are prepared to campaign against Roman Catholics. They are forced to distance themselves from the supporters of the Orange Order and the recent paramilitary Protestant groups because they know (and their critics are quick to remind them) that the average Orangeman is not an evangelical, is not "born again," is not a total abstainer, and does not keep the sabbath. Lowland militant Protestant leaders are forced to distance themselves from the only constituency which shares their willingness to protest against Catholics because that constituency possesses none of the other characteristics of evangelical Protestantism.

In sum, this analysis of Protestant politics in Scotland and Ulster suggests that progress in theorizing about religious conflict can be made by concentrating on: (1) the degree to which religion plays a part in the shared ethnic identities of the populations at the time they come into contact; (2) the extent to which conflict between the populations reinforces the part played by religious elements in the ethnic identity; and (3) the degree to which the populations involved have the power to act in support of their own interests. These are, admittedly, broadly sketched factors. That as yet we can do little more than simply enumerate them in value-added fashion shows both the relative neglect that sociological theorizing about religious politics and conflict has suffered and the task of more refined comparative analysis ahead.

Notes

1. The Scottish material used in this paper is reported at length in Bruce (1985). The research was funded by the Economic and Social Research Council and the Queen's University of Belfast and I am grateful to both institutions. The best parts of my analyses have been produced in collaboration with Professor Roy Wallis with whom I have written two companion pieces (Wallis and Bruce, forthcoming; Wallis, Bruce and Taylor, forthcoming).

2. Hickey (1984) has an excellent brief review of various explanations of the Northern Ireland conflict and argues well for the centrality of religious differences.

3. The old Scots Presbyterians were fond of encapsulating their views of the proper relationship between God, the church and the state in "covenants." Unlike the Africaners who were fond of the covenant as a metaphor, the Scots actually wrote and signed such documents. On the first covenant of 1643, see: Burleigh (1973, 224–5).

4. The desire for unity and consolidation following the trauma of partition can be seen in the broad church support for the religious revivals inspired by W.P. Nicholson in the late twenties and in the failure of the Davey heresy trial to produce a serious division in the Presbyterian Church. The conservatives charged Professor J. Ernest Davey of the Presbyterian Theological College with the heresy of "modernism" in 1927. They failed to win their case and a handful withdrew to form what became the Evangelical Presbyterian Church. In the more conducive climate of the turmoil of the "troubles," Ian Paisley led a similar and far more successful schism.

5. On the relative positions of Protestants and Catholics in the labor market in the Vale of Leven—an area representative of the industrialized west coast—see: Gallacher (1982).

6. There is one vital qualification to the observation that the more conservative Presbyterian churches were most opposed to emancipation, and that concerns the stance of Thomas Chalmers. Chalmers was a rising star on the evangelical wing of the Church of Scotland and in 1843 he led the evangelicals out of the Kirk and into the Free Church of Scotland. A simple association of Presbyterian orthodoxy and opposition to the emancipation of Catholics would suggest that Chalmers should have been leading the forces of

reaction—and many of his supporters expected just that—but Chalmers sided publicly with the enlightened sections of the Edinburgh middle class. This refusal of the leading members of the bourgeoisie to support the Protestant protests was the first obvious sign of what was later to become very clear: the elites were not interested in promoting sectarian tension.

7. Reasonable estimates of sizes of the various churches in the 1850's are as follows: Established Church of Scotland: 260,000; Free Church: 190,000; United Presbyterians (the heirs of the Seceders): 143,000; Episcopal Church in Scotland: 56,000; Reformed Presbyterians (Covenanters): 6,000; Roman Catholics: 146,000. There were also small representations of all the English dissenter churches. See: Currie, Gilbert and Horsley (1977) and McRoberts (1979).

8. A similar combination of popular support and political impotence was the lot of the Reverend James McB. Brisby. Brisby was an Ulsterman who started his own congregation in Glasgow sometime shortly after the start of the century. He campaigned against "papal aggression," edited and printed his own *Scottish Protestant Review,* and was involved in the formation of the Glasgow company of Carson's Ulster Volunteer Force, which he served as Chaplain. He was regularly elected to the Glasgow School Board on a "no popery" ticket, usually coming second to the United Free Church minister James Barr who was later socialist MP for Motherwell. (The United Free Church was produced by a union of the liberal wing of the Free Church and the United Presbyterians in 1900. The conservatives, mainly highlanders, continued in the Free Church). Despite his considerable popular support he was unable to have any effect on educational policy because his anti-popery platform was rejected by the official Church of Scotland and United Free Church representatives, who normally supported the Roman Catholic Church representatives.

9. The church membership figures for the 'non-Roman Catholic' population of Scotland and Ulster suggest that in 1970 only about 27% of the adults claimed to be church members. The comparable figure for Ulster is around 70%. For most recent reliable estimates, see: Brierley (1983;1984).

10. The idea of a Catholic centrist party was floated in 1911 by Hugh Murnin, a Catholic mineworkers organizer who was the socialist incumbent for the Stirling and Falkirk Burghs Westminster seat when Ratcliffe made his 1929 bid for parliament. Murnin never

pursued the idea and continued to work in that section of the labor movement which became the Parliamentary Labour Party.

11. The alignment of Roman Catholics on the left of center is a common pattern explored by David A. Martin (1978). A possibility that, to my knowledge, has not been explored is that militant Protestantism ends up on the right because it reacts to the Catholic alignment with the left rather than because it has a natural tendency to be conservative.

12. Of course, the absence of strong evidence for a significant threat is no obstacle to people claiming that there is such a threat. They need simply argue that there is a *secret* conspiracy. Nonetheless, it seems reasonable sometimes to use the absence of strong evidence to explain why such conspiracy theories do not become "popular."

13. The amendment was supported by only 22 votes and the Bill was passed without dissension on 15 March 1926.

14. Both stood for Westminster but at the wrong times. Ratcliffe contested Stirling and Falkirk Burghs in 1929, before the League's successes in the Glasgow Council elections. Cormack did not have a chance to contest a Westminster seat until 1945 and by then the PAS had passed its peak. Ratcliffe came third with 21.3% of the poll to the 47.5% of the socialist Hugh Murnin and the 31.3% of the Unionist candidate. When Cormack contested Leith he got only 7.8% of the total 2,493 votes. Yet, less than two years later, when he stood for re-election to the council, more than 5,000 people from South Leith (which was about a third of the Westminster Leith constituency) voted for him. One might note that the same problem of regionalism has dogged the Scottish and Welsh Nationalist Parties and the short-lived Scottish Labour Party.

References

Berger, P.L. 1982. *The Heretical Imperative*. London: Collins.

Brierley, P. 1983. *The United Kingdom Christian Handbook*. London: MARC Europe.

———. 1984. *The United Kingdom Christian Handbook: 1985/86 edition*. London: MARC Europe.

Browne, E. Moxon. 1983. *Nation, Class and Creed in Northern Ireland*. Aldershot: Gower Publishing.

Bruce, S. 1983a. Social change and collective behaviour: the revival in eighteenth century Ross-shire. *British Journal of Sociology*. 34(4): 554–72.

———. 1983b. Ideology and isolation: a failed Scots Protestant movement. *Archives de Sciences Sociales des Religions.* 56(1): 147–59.

———. 1985. *No Pope of Rome: Anti-Catholicism in Modern Scotland.* Edinburgh: Mainstream.

Buckland, P. 1979. *The Factory of Grievances: Devolved Government in Northern Ireland, 1921–39.* Dublin: Gill and Macmillan.

Burleigh, J.H.S. 1973. *A Church History of Scotland.* London: Oxford University Press.

Campbell, A.B. 1979. *The Lanarkshire Miners: A Social History of Their Trade Unions, 1775–1874.* Edinburgh: John Donald.

Compton, P.A. 1982. The demographic dimension of integration and division in Northern Ireland. *Integration and Division: Geographical Perspectives on the Northern Ireland Problem.* Ed. F.P.W. Boal and J.N.H. Douglas. 75–104. London: Academic Press.

Coser, L. 1965. *The Functions of Social Conflict.* London: Routledge Kegan Paul.

Currie, R. A. Gilbert and L. Horsley, 1977. *Churches and Churchgoers: Patterns of Church Growth in the British Isles Since 1700.* Oxford: Clarendon Press.

Drummond, A.L. and J. Bulloch. 1973. *The Scottish Church, 1688–1843.* Edinburgh: St. Andrew Press.

———. 1975. *The Church in Victorian Scotland, 1843–1874.* Edinburgh: St. Andrew Press.

Durkheim, E. 1975. *Suicide.* London: Routledge Kegan Paul.

Gallacher, R. 1982. The Vale of Leven; 1914–75: Changes in working class organization and action. *Capital and Class in Scotland.* Ed. T. Dickson, 186–211. Edinburgh: John Donald.

Gallagher, T. 1981. Catholics in Scottish politics. *Bulletin of Scottish Politics.* (Spring): 21–43.

———. 1984. Scotland, Britain and conflict in Ireland. *Terrorism in Ireland.* Ed. Y. Alexander and A. O'Day, 53–72. London: Croom Helm.

Gray, T. 1972. *The Orange Order.* London: Bodley Head.

Handley, J. 1938. *The Irish in Modern Scotland.* Cork: Cork University Press.

———. 1945. *The Irish in Scotland.* Cork: Cork University Press.

Harvie, C. 1977. *Scotland and Nationalism: Scottish Society and Politics, 1707–1977.* London: George Allen and Unwin.

Hickey, J. 1984. *Religion and the Northern Ireland Problem.* Dublin: Gill and Macmillan.

Holmes, R.F. 1981. *Henry Cooke.* Belfast: Christian Journals Ltd.

Kellas, J. 1982. *The Scottish Political System*. Cambridge: Cambridge University Press.

Loughridge, A. 1984. *The Covenanters in Ireland*. Belfast: Cameron Press.

Lyons, F.S. 1979. The silent minority: Southern Ireland Protestantism, 1921–1972. *The Month*. 12: 233–39; 273–79.

MacLaren, A.A. 1974. *Religion and Social Class: the Disruption Years in Aberdeen*. London: Routledge Kegan Paul.

McRoberts, D.A. 1979. *Modern Scottish Catholicism, 1878–1978*. Glasgow: Burns.

Martin, D.A. 1978. *A General Theory of Secularization*. Oxford: Basil Blackwell.

Muirhead, I.A. 1973. Catholic emancipation: Scottish reactions in 1829. *Innes Review*: 26–42.

Piggott, C.A. 1979. *A Geography of Religion in Scotland*. Ph.D. diss., Edinburgh University, Edinburgh.

Reid, J.S. 1854. *History of the Presbyterian Church in Ireland*. London: Whitaker.

Stewart, D. 1950. *The Seceders in Ireland*. Belfast: Presbyterian Historical Society.

Wallis, R. and S. Bruce. n.d. Sketch for a theory of conservative Protestant politics. *Social Compass*. Forthcoming.

Wallis, R., S. Bruce and D. Taylor, n.d. *"No surrender": Paisleyism and the Politics of Ethnic Identity*. Forthcoming.

Wilson, B.R. 1976. *Contemporary Transformations of Religion*. London: Oxford University Press.

———. 1982. *Religion in Sociological Perspective*. London: Oxford University Press.

21

Prophecy and Ecstacy: Religion and Politics in the Caribbean

STEPHEN D. GLAZIER

Introduction

HANS Baer (1983, 8) in his study of the black spiritual movement, contends that all black religions "exist in a state of tension with the larger society." This same statement could have been made for almost all Caribbean religions in the early part of this century. However, over the past thirty years a number of Caribbean religions have attempted to make peace with the political establishments of their respective islands. We can no longer look at Caribbean religions as "religions of protest" or as "religions of the oppressed." Many religions, formerly classified as "religions of the oppressed," have joined the political and economic elites.

Each Caribbean religion seems to have followed a different pattern in adapting to its political environment. Some Caribbean religions have attempted to influence party platforms or to influence candidate selection. A number of Caribbean religious leaders have attempted to influence their members to vote for one party rather than another. In my research I noted that most religious leaders—of both folk religions and established denominations—expressed some party preference. This is of great interest because much of the literature on Caribbean folk religions stresses that these groups are either at odds with the political system or apolitical.

Just as it is difficult to make general statements about political activism (or the lack of such activity) among Caribbean religions, it is also very difficult to make sweeping generalizations about church-state relations in the region. Some groups, such as the Presbyterians and Methodists (from whom one might expect harmonious relations with the state) have been at the center of church-state tensions. Other groups traditionally characterized as vehicles of protest, such as Ras Tafari and vodun, have established harmonious relations. If nothing else, one might conclude that church-state relations in the Caribbean are unpredictable. In each group's history it is possible to find evidence for both hostility toward and cooperation with the state.

In this presentation I will discuss religion and politics (with a major focus on church-state relations) in three Caribbean religions: Ras Tafari, vodun, and the Spiritual Baptists. I did not choose these religions because they are the most important of Caribbean religions. In terms of numbers that title belongs to Pentecostalism and Roman Catholicism, still dominant forces in island life—even on English–speaking islands such as Trinidad and Jamaica (Glazier 1980a, 67–80). I chose these three religions because they have received widespread attention from American, European, and Caribbean scholars and are consequently among the best documented of Caribbean religions. Also, these religions have been most often cited in support of the deprivation and protest hypotheses.

It is important to recognize that, in many respects, anthropologists and sociologists have failed to come to terms with contemporary Caribbean religions. When scholars such as an anthropologist I.M. Lewis use the Spiritual Baptists, vodun, or Ras Tafari to illustrate general theories of religion and protest or religion and deprivation, they often base their interpretations on data collected thirty years ago.[1] Yet many changes have taken place in both Caribbean religions and Caribbean societies over the past thirty years. Frequently, these changes have been ignored in the study of Caribbean religions.

Ras Tafari

Rasta, largely due to the widespread influence of reggae music, is perhaps the best known of the religions I shall consider. It is difficult to estimate the number of adherents to the religion because they refuse to be counted either officially or unofficially, although Leonard Barrett

(1977, 2) and Klaus de Albuquerque (1979, 234) estimate their numbers in the hundreds of thousands. This, I feel, may be an exaggeration. Nevertheless, their influence far exceeds their numbers both in Jamaica and elsewhere in the Caribbean.

The movement traces its history to several native preacher-leaders— Leonard Howell, Joseph Hibbert, Archibald Dunkley, Paul Earlington, Vernal Davis, Ferdinand Richetts, and Robert Hinds.[2] These leaders, each working in isolation from the others, came to the conclusion that Haile Selassie, then enthroned as Ethiopian emperor, was "the Lion of Judah" who would lead blacks in the promised land—Africa.

There were many precursors to the "Back to Africa" movement in Jamaica. Among the best documented are Bedwardism of the 1920s and Garveyism of the late 1920s and 1930s. But Garvey, a native of Jamaica, found his greatest following not in Jamaica but in the streets of New York City.

Rasta is by no means an organized, hierarchical, or uniform movement. As in all three religions to be considered in this presentation, there are no formal creeds, few written texts, and no seminaries to enforce orthodoxy. Because adherents share so few beliefs and values, it is not possible for Ras Tafarians to present a uniform front in their political actions in the same way as well organized, cohesive groups such as the New Religious Right in the United States. Nevertheless, there are shared values, and some Rastas are both willing and able to act upon these values when they feel that their interests are threatened.

The case of Rasta is particularly fascinating from the standpoint of church-state relations. More than any other Caribbean religion it is Ras Tafarianism which is said to typify a "religion of the oppressed." Still, anthropologists such as George Eaton Simpson, Klaus de Albuquerque, Rex Nettleford, Yoshiko Nagashima, Leonard Barrett, and Claudia Rogers report instances of increased political action. It has been suggested that during Michael Manley's term as prime minister, government officials frequently consulted with Ras Tafarian leaders prior to setting policy. It is unclear whether consultations with Rasta leaders has continued under the Seaga government, although informants insisted to me that it had. George Eaton Simpson (1983), in a recent paper on Ras Tafarianism and the concept of justice, suggests that Rastas are becoming an important part of the Jamaican political establishment. Other scholars have suggested, perhaps facetiously, that in the Manley government Rastas *were* the political establishment.

Politics are not new to the Rastas. In the formative years of the Ras Tafarian movement fifty years ago the basic struggles of rural Jamaicans were over land, rent, and taxes. According to most scholars of the movement it was these struggles, and pressures from the police, which gave rise to the millenarian visions of the early Ras Tafarians. The idea of black domination, a prominent aspect of Rastafarian millenarian ideology, may have been an important factor in occasioning labor uprisings in 1938 (Hill 1981, 30–71). Although individual Rasta leaders continue to advocate violence as a legitimate response to social evils and have played a prominent role in a number of recent riots in Kingston, their pronouncements are no longer tied to a millenarian vision. For many activists, black domination is not seen as a realistic goal. On the other hand, many conservatives within the faith believe that black rule will come eventually, but through proper adherence to ritual form and traditional doctrine, not political action.

During the religion's formative years, Ras Tafarians belonged to small, autonomous groups that were augmented by persons who attended the meetings or sympathized with the sentiments and aims of the movement. Simpson (1983, 4) reports that in these early years *ganja* (marijuana) was not smoked and that beards and dreadlocks were a less prominent feature of the movement than they later became. This is of interest because today *ganja* and dreadlocks are considered by many to be key elements of Rasta identity. Simpson asserts that in its beginnings Ras Tafarians were bitter about "racialism" and about class differences in Jamaican society. They railed against the "white man" and the "black traitors"—politicians, the police, clergymen, landholders, teachers, business and professional people who were said to have mistreated and misled the people.

In a paper published over thirty years ago, Simpson (1955, 168–70) enumerated seven basic Ras Tafarian beliefs: (1) black people were exiled to the West Indies because of their moral transgressions; (2) the wicked white man is inferior to black people; (3) the Jamaican situation is hopeless; (4) Ethiopia is heaven; (5) Haile Selassie is the living God; (6) the Emporer of Ethiopia will arrange for all expatriated persons of African descent to return to their homeland; (7) black people will obtain revenge by compelling white people to serve them.

Today, he reports, Ras Tafarianism is much more heterogeneous than it was in the 1950s. Different sub-groups stress different elements of the original creed, and some important modifications are discernible. For example, the death of Haile Selassie has raised significant questions about Selassie's role in the movement. There is less emphasis on Ethiopia and more on pan-Africanism.

Doctrines concerning the white man have also undergone some

changes. According to Father Joseph Owens (1982, 60–1), a long-time, sympathetic observer of the movement, "notwithstanding certain statements with apparently racist import, the essence of Rastafarian teaching is that all races are basically equal." Moreover, Owens contends that the Rasta claim that they are the chosen people of God does not signify superiority as much as it dictates a prophetic role and puts them in the service of all nations. Many Rastas, he asserts, are willing to admit that there is good and bad in all races, and that anyone who confesses Rasta's divinity is gladly welcomed into their midst, no matter what race or color. On the basis of my own experiences in the region, this would seem to be the case. Also, many of the leading scholars of Ras Tafarianism—with the notable exception of Leonard Barrett—are white and claim to have experienced little difficulty in being accepted by members of the religion. For example, I personally found it easier to gain acceptance among the Rastas than among some Pentecostal groups.

Barry Chevannes (1978, 1–17) has contended that as various revival religions began to decline in the mid-1950s, many former revivalists were attracted to Ras Tafari.[3] The movement has grown rapidly and, at the same time, become more complex. Adherents and sympathizers have extended throughout all levels of society. Repatriation to Africa has received less attention in some groups, and there has been greater stress on themes of black power and black cultural ascendency.

At the same time Ras Tafari has played an important role in the development of Jamaican popular music—vocal and instrumental. It is frequently portrayed as the music of the oppressed. But not all Rasta music is music of protest. Reggae contains caustic social commentary but also celebrates Jamaican heroes, freedom, and, of course, *ganja*.

Nagashima (1984) suggests that many fundamentalists within the movement have great difficulty accepting reggae music as genuine. It is seen as denigration of the faith by a growing minority of conservative, and increasingly apolitical, brethren. His conclusion is that the message of Ras Tafarian music is far from clear. While conservatives favor chants over musical forms like reggae, their influence on reggae is nonetheless pervasive.

According to Campbell (1980), by the mid-1970s Ras Tafari had become the culture and/or counterculture of a sizeable percentage of the Jamaican population. Whereas the movement had earlier been considered subversive and a force to be eliminated, Nettleford (1982, xviii) and a number of other observers suggest that Jamaicans of all social classes have come to accept some aspects of the Rastafarian vision. This resulted in what he calls "tactical accommodation." For example, while some Rastas see themselves as fighters against oppression, others believe that peaceful living will bring about a victory against evil. By adopting this philosophy many Rastas have made a fragile peace with the Jamaican power structure.

Vodun

Vodun, the Afro-Catholic folk religion of Haiti, combines an impressive continuity with ancestral African elements and a remarkable openness to change, whether from innovation or borrowing. Like many Caribbean religions, it appears to be both heterodox and orthodox. Although its origins may have been with the oppressed, in recent years many vodun centers have been identified closely with the Duvalier regime—a tradition begun by Papa Doc Duvalier and continued by his son.

African dances were performed by slaves in the western part of the island of Hispaniola as early as the seventeenth century, but Leyburn (1971) refers to the period 1730 to 1790, when African slaves were imported in increasing numbers, as vodun's formative period. It was at this time that religious beliefs of the Dahomeans, Senegalese, Congolese, Yoruba, and other Africans were combined with selected ideas concerning Catholic saints to form the complex religious syncretism we now call vodun.

The central focus of vodun, in all its manifestations, is devotion to the *loa* or dieties. Many *loa,* including all important members of the vodun pantheon, are said to be of African origin. This is reflected in their names: Damballah, Ezilie, Obatala, Legba, Ogun, Shango, and so on. Confusion in beliefs surrounding these deities is due in part to contradictions in the Dahomean religious system as it was taken over by the Haitians as well as to the addition of the Yoruba pantheon to the Dahomean religious system.

The relationship between devotees and *loa* is thought to be a contractual one. If one is scrupulous in the performance of offerings and ceremonies, the *loa* will be generous in their aid. If one neglects the *loa,* one cannot expect their favors and even risks their wrath. It is widely believed that neglect of one's *loa* will result in sickness, the death of relatives, crop failure, and other misfortunes. In this respect, vodun is a personal religion. Relations with the *loa* are first and foremost an individual responsibility. Nevertheless, it is the public vodun ceremonies which have received the bulk of scholarly attention, and it is public (as opposed to private) ritual that gives vodun its potential political impact.

The case of Haitian vodun politics is even less clear-cut than that of Ras Tafari. But there is considerable evidence that vodun—at least in major urban centers—is moving in some of the same accomodative directions as Rasta. Both vodun and Rasta are heterogeneous, acephalous movements. Vodun, however, is tied to specific localities within Haiti while Rasta—which has spread to Antigua, Dominica, Grenada, Trinidad, St. Thomas, St. Kitts, Guyana, London, and Paris—has become international in scope (Campbell 1980, 47–48).

The parochialism of vodun also affects its structural position in Haitian society. It is possible, however, to make statements about specific congregations or specific leaders. Individual leaders in the cult are more consistent in their political activities over time than leaders of the two other groups dealt with in this presentation. This may be because vodun leaders are associated with particular locations and continue to be associated with that same location throughout their religious careers. Even when a vodun priest travels to another country, he is thought to represent, in descending order of importance, his center, his village, his region, and his nation (Glazier 1983b, 322).

Vodun has no well-defined body of doctrine and most priests of the faith hardly trouble themselves with theological speculations (Simpson 1980, 187). Nor is there a formal mythology on which to base a theological system, and as Erika Bourguignon (1982, 291–2), one of the foremost scholars of vodun, points out, traditions vary from family to family and cult house to cult house and contact with spirits is direct and intimate. It is primarily through dreams and possession-trance that spirits reveal themselves to humans.

Despite this lack of systemization—and in some cases because of it—Haitian vodun contains a strict moral code which supports many of the underlying assumptions of the Haitian social and political structures. For example, Simpson states that the *loa* "do not condone criminal acts, and a *loa* may reprimand or punish his servant for behavior which his relatives and neighbors regard as reprehensible. . . . They [*loa*] provide supernatural sanction for such mores as taboos on murder, incest, theft, and the showing of disrespect for the old" (Simpson 1980, 191–2). Obedience and respect for seniority, whether of age or hierarchy, is the primary moral law and punishment for its infraction is swift.

It should be stressed that the basic beliefs of vodun are not limited to cult adherents. Even those who reject vodun and practice a "pure"

Catholicism or have converted to Protestantism accept the reality status of vodun spirits. Thus, when vodun spirits are used as mechanisms of social control their influence is not limited to the faithful but extends to almost the entire society.

Most importantly, many Haitians believe that those who control the spirit world should also control the social and political worlds as well. Haitians assert that vodun can be used as a stepping stone in the climb to political power, and many successful Haitian politicians—including Haiti's "President for Life" Baby Doc Duvalier—are said to maintain active connections with the cult. Most Port-au-Prince vodun centers contain special seats for honored guests, especially visiting political leaders, and many centers also maintain a special seat for Baby Doc himself, should he desire to attend services. Of course, Duvalier's seat is usually empty, but there is always at least one government minister or a member of the secret police in attendance (personal communication, Leslie G. Desmangles). It is frequently alleged that many Port-au-Prince *houngans* (ritual priests) work as informants for Baby Doc's personal police force (an organization considered to be at the epitome of Haitian political power). It is also pointed out that some *houngans* experience little difficulty obtaining private audiences with the president, something less easily accomplished by the rest of the population.

While a student at the Haitian Bureau of Ethnography, the senior Duvalier (Francois) studied vodun and made personal acquaintance with many of its most accomplished practitioners. He was able to construct a credible (for its time) ethnography of the vodun belief system and maintained contacts developed during his fieldwork for the rest of his life. These contacts are said to have been continued by Duvalier's son. While the junior Duvalier does not claim to have studied vodun, it is assumed that the father passed on much of his knowledge to the son and that many of the most powerful *houngans* in Haiti are on Jean-Claude's payroll. This may not be an accurate assumption, but, as with any belief system, it need not be true to influence political reality.

As Sereno (1948, 15–31) has pointed out, religions like vodun are essentially conservative. They provide an outlet for aggression in societies that allow for very little direct expression of aggression, and, at the same time, serve to legitimate the economic and political structures of the islands. Haitians believe that all power and wealth are fundamentally unjust because all wealth and power can only be obtained by unjust means, i.e., sorcery or vodun (Beck 1976, 23–33). In a society of limited goods such as Haiti there can be no such thing as "deserved" wealth. If one gets ahead, it is because he or she has advanced at the expense of his or her neighbors. Thus, in the eyes of many Haitians, the fact that the Duvaliers rose to such a high position and have been able to maintain that position is proof that they practiced vodun. Even if the senior Duvalier had had no connections with *houngans,* many Haitians would have assumed that he did.

Haiti is a large country by Caribbean standards, and, as noted previously, vodun is very much a localized religion. How then, can alleged connections with a few vodun centers in the capital city serve to consolidate political power over so vast an area? As mentioned, there is a great deal of heterodoxy within the religion, especially when one considers rural centers. But even when vodunists emphasize variation within their faith, they recognize a hierarchy of power and prestige. *Houngans* in urban centers (and especially in the capital city of Port-au-Prince) are accorded higher status and assumed to be more powerful than *houngans* in outlying areas; therefore, even though Duvalier is not seen as having direct ties to the rural enters, he is seen as having the most powerful *houngans* (and *loa*) on his side.

Unlike Ras Tafari, vodun is not a prophetic religion (at least not as this term is usually understood in the sociology of religion). Religious leaders do not often make public pronouncements. The principle duty of the *houngan* is to facilitate spirit possession in others; that is, to allow them to serve as mouthpieces for the gods. *Houngans* are rarely possessed during their own ceremonies.

One way in which the role of the *houngan* is prophetic, however, is that it is the *houngan* who differentiates "true" and "false" prophecy. Many lesser *loa* impersonate high ranking members of the vodun pantheon, and it is the *houngan's* job to decide whether participants are possessed by a god or an imposter. In this capacity they do serve something of a prophetic role, although it is indirect.

The Spiritual Baptists

The Spiritual Baptists are an international religious movement with congregations in St. Vincent (where some Baptists claim the faith originated), Trinidad and Tobago[4] (where I did the bulk of my fieldwork), Grenada, Guyana, Venezuela, Toronto and New York City. There are a number of religious groups on other islands whose rituals are similar to those of the Baptists (e.g., the "Tieheads" of Barbados and the so-called "Spirit Baptists" of Jamaica), but Trinidad Baptists do not consider these others to be part of their religion and do not participate in joint worship, pilgrimages, missions, and other services with members of these other groups.

Like the other religions considered here, Baptist membership is predominantly black, and, like many other Afro-Caribbean religions, the Spiritual Baptists started out as a "religion of the oppressed." In recent years, however, congregations in Trinidad have attracted membership among middle class blacks as well as sizeable numbers of wealthy East Indians, Chinese, and creoles. Over the past ten years, membership has remained stable at about ten thousand.

Many Trinidadians confuse Spiritual Baptists with an African-derived cult known as Shango (a possession cult somewhat similar to vodun in Haiti) and assume that Spiritual Baptist and Shango rituals are identical. Members of these faiths, however, do not share this confusion, and a large number of Spiritual Baptists condemn Shango rituals as "heathen worship." Shangoists, for their part, claim that Spiritual Baptists copy their ideas and try to steal their power. On more than one occasion during my fieldwork, Baptist leaders picketed Shango centers prior to Shango ceremonies.

In examining the relationships between Spiritual Baptist churches and Shango centers, four distinct types of organization may be discerned: (1) Spiritual Baptist churches with Shango connections; (2) Spiritual Baptist churches with no Shango connections; (3) Shango centers with Spiritual Baptist connections; and (4) Shango centers without Spiritual Baptist connections. These distinctions reflect ways in which members of these religions think of themselves. Are they, for example, Spiritual Baptists who also "do" Shango or Shangoists who also "do" Baptist work?

Both the Spiritual Baptists and Shango are syncretic (Glazier 1985a, 49–62). A major difference in Shango and Baptist belief systems is that Baptist rituals are directed toward their version of the Holy Trinity, while Shango rituals are directed toward African or African-derived gods. Spiritual Baptists are ostensibly Christians and, in the words of one informant, "don't worship them others." This is not to say that Baptists do not believe in the existence of African gods. A majority of Spiritual Baptists do believe in the power of Shango deities, but do not feel that African gods should be venerated.

Although the Spiritual Baptists and Shango are clearly separate ritual traditions, they are interrelated on a number of levels. Their memberships overlap. I would estimate that about eighty percent of all Shangoists in Trinidad also participate in Baptist services and about forty percent of all Baptists also participate in Shango. There are, of course, degrees of participation. For example, not all leaders in the former religion are necessarily officials in the latter and vice versa.

Individual Baptist churches vary considerably in their attitudes toward major institutions in Trinidadian society. Some church leaders, for example, actively support the government, while other church leaders claim that the Baptists are constantly persecuted by the government. Those leaders who claim to be persecuted make much of a 1917 ordinance introduced in the Legislative Council to ban the faith. As a result of the ordinance, the faith was officially banned between 1917 and 1953.

On the other hand, leaders who do not believe that the faith has been subject to persecution point out that the ban was never rigidly enforced and that it did little to slow the spread of the Baptist religion. For example, the Baptist church at Belmont, alleged to be the target of the original ordinance, continued to hold weekly services throughout the entire period of the ban. Moreover, during the entire period of the ban not a single church was closed nor was a single Baptist leader imprisoned. Some Baptist leaders contend that other Baptist leaders like to exaggerate the degree of government persecution because Baptists associate prestige with martyrdom.

Early researchers present a very different picture. Herskovits and Herskovits (1947, 343) reported very strained relations between Baptist churches and the government during the time of their fieldwork. In 1939 two separate charges against Baptist churches were lodged. The government fined the church leader and the man on whose land the Baptist meeting had been held. (According to a prominent Spiritual Baptist archbishop similar fines were imposed in 1940, 1941, and 1945; however, I have gone over the church records and have not been able to verify his assertion.)

Many Spiritual Baptist leaders are quite active politically, and over the past ten years more than fifteen church leaders have run for public office. In two cases during my fieldwork candidates ran as Spiritual Baptists emphasizing their church positions in newspapers and radio advertisements. Although both candidates failed to be elected, this is a far cry from the lack of political ambition that would have been predicted for a so-called "ecstatic" religion.

The most recent area of church-state contention pertains to a central ritual in the faith—the mourning ceremony.[5] The concept of mourning has a very different meaning among the Spiritual Baptists than it has in many other religious traditions. Among Baptists, it does not relate directly to death and bereavement, but is an elaborate ritual involving fasting, lying on a dirt floor, and other deprivations. The major purpose of the rite, according to most informants, is to discover one's "true" ranking within the church hierarchy.

The state has argued that Baptist leaders should be held responsible for the physical well-being of mourners. Mourning rites are believed to have curative powers, and because so many participants enter the rite in an unhealthy state, every two or three years someone dies during the ordeal, resulting in a government inquiry. Government prosecutors assert that poor diet and damp conditions in the mourning room are contributing factors to mourners' deaths. Baptists leaders, they contend, must refuse to allow participation by individuals believed to be too weak to withstand the rigors of the ceremony.

Leaders defend themselves in such cases by claiming that they take every possible precaution to insure the mourner's survival. This is very difficult for them to prove, and many leaders interpret government charges as evidence of government persecution. They claim that someone in "high places" is trying to discredit them.

A further complication is that the late prime minister of Trinidad and Tobago (Dr. Eric Williams) was himself believed to have been a Baptist. I have been unable to determine the prime minister's true status within the faith. But then again, Williams's "true" religious preferences are of minor importance to this discussion. The most important thing is that many Baptists believed that he was a member. (Though it is significant that Williams made no attempt to deny such claims.)

It is possible to overplay the relationship between the late Dr. Williams and the Spiritual Baptists. I have seen newspaper and popular accounts that portray the relations between the Baptists and the Peoples' National Movement (William's party) as one of the dominant forces in Trinidadian politics during the late 1960s and early 1970s. A majority of these stories appeared in scandal sheets such as *The Bomb* (Trinidad's equivalent of the *National Inquirer*) and sought to portray Dr. Williams as a mysterious, reclusive, Howard Hughes-like figure. His Baptist connections were usually cited as further evidence of the prime minister's intellectual, moral, and emotional decay.

Since the Baptists are relatively small in number, not especially wealthy as a group, and, as noted, many Baptists are apolitical or at least anti-PNM, their significance may have been greatly exaggerated by the press. On the other hand, academic researchers have tended to underplay the group's political impact.

Meanwhile Baptist leaders are not shy about expressing themselves on public matters. Spiritual Baptist leaders do occasionally take on the prophetic role. Prophecy occurs in two contexts: (1) regular worship, and (2) "on mission." In the context of regular worship all high ranking members of the faith are expected to offer some prophetic utterances. A majority of these statements are confined to church affairs, but, on occasion, Baptist leaders will also offer political commentary. During the last general election in Trinidad and Tobago a number of sermons were devoted to the PNM platform and the worthiness of Prime Minister Williams's likely successor, George Chambers. In the middle of one service a prominent church member leaped from her chair and spoke in tongues for several minutes. The paramount leader of the church later informed church members that the message the Holy Spirit had given was "Get out and vote for the PNM!" This message was seen as inappropriate by many church members.

Most high ranking church members go "on mission" twice each year. Generally one receives a call to go "on mission" to a particular place or to address a particular person. These calls often appear in a vision or dream, but some Baptists go "on mission" first and hope that a vision will be received later. In either case, missions usually entail a journey of considerable distance, and it is believed that the further one has traveled, the more important one's message. For example, every autumn a contingent of Trinidad Spiritual Baptists go "on mission" to Grenada or St. Vincent to warn the people there that their respective islands will be washed away in a great hurricane if they do not turn from their evil ways. In Grenada, several Baptists preached extensively against the regime of former Prime Minister Eric Gairy. One Baptist leader in Curepe (Trinidad) even claimed that it was his preaching that eventually led to Gairy's undoing.

Discussion and Conclusions

As is evident from the above discussion, the relationship between religion and politics in the Caribbean is extremely complex. It is not easily accounted for in terms of protest, deprivation, or, as Frances Mischel (1959) has suggested, alternate systems of prestige. All religions, it seems, have the potential to enhance the status of their members; for example, in the United States, a man who is not able to become president of his company may obtain satisfaction by becoming the chair of the board of deacons at his church. This does not mean that if he had become president of his company, he would not have continued his struggle for a position on the board of deacons. The problem of status enhancement and alternate systems of prestige is much more complex than Mischel has described it. Even Ras Tafari, the Caribbean religion that once came closest to Lanternarri's (1963) definition of a "religion of the oppressed," no longer fits Lanternarri's definition.

Many changes have taken place in Caribbean societies over the past thirty years. A large number of Jamaicans, Trinidadians, and, to a lesser extent, Haitians have experienced upward mobility. This has been especially true in Trinidad, thanks, in part, to the recent oil boom. One of the goals of my fieldwork among Trinidad's Spiritual Baptists has been to examine the consequences of affluence for a religious group whose primary appeal had previously been among the poor. What happens when a religion of the oppressed joins the establishment? This same question has been asked by other researchers on other islands. For example, Claudia Rogers (1978), in her study of Jamaican Ras Tafari, questions whether Rasta will be able to survive its many successes. She points out that as Rastas have gained media access and have been portrayed not as dangerous to Jamaican society but as its potential saviors, opposition to Rasta has shifted and membership recruitment has become much more difficult. Recruitment has also become a problem for some Port-au-Prince *houngans*. Desmangles (personal communication) suggests that some Haitians do not attend certain vodun centers due to some centers' alleged associations with the secret police. It is difficult to recruit among the oppressed when the oppressed are afraid to attend services monitored by the establishment.

A critical methodological problem in the study of Caribbean religions is that of selecting a unit of analysis. Because all three religions studied lack denominational chains of command, one cannot make statements about church-state relations in the same way that one might make statements about, say, the Roman Catholic church or Presbyterianism. The most accurate statements refer to individual churches and their leaders—not denominations or denominational organizations. To examine faiths such as Rasta or vodun or the Spiritual Baptists as if they were unified denominations on the North American model is to present an overly coherent picture of an incredibly fragmented situation.

Another problem is that outdated theoretical models abound in the study of Caribbean religions. For example, foreign scholars are not alone in advocating protest models. Many native researchers accept as an article of faith that Caribbean folk religions serve as vehicles of protest against white rule. They contend that now that white rule—or at least overt white rule—has ended in the region, these religions should decline. When non-native researchers point out that these religions are growing or at least maintaining stable memberships, such conclusions are not well received.

There is, in addition, considerable resentment of foreign scholars who attempt to study Caribbean folk religions. This bias should be honestly admitted and confronted. Caribbean sociologists and anthropologists understandably feel that they should be the experts on Caribbean religions, but they do not assign high priority to conducting basic research on the topic. For example, it should be a fairly simple matter to gather accurate—or at least better—statistical data on the religions covered in this presentation, and Caribbean researchers are in a much better position to do this type of research than outsiders. Yet in the ten years I have researched the area no native scholar has published such a census. What statistical data we possess on these movements is taken almost exclusively from American and British sources.

Last, the changing status of Caribbean religions has also changed their once prophetic role. Caribbean religious leaders are discovering, like religious leaders throughout history, that one cannot have it both ways. If one chooses to support the power structure it becomes difficult to recruit among those who do not participate in the power structure. This need not lead to a decline in membership or influence. My experiences among Spiritual Baptist leaders causes me to conclude that for many Caribbean religious leaders the benefits of alliance with the power structure far exceed the potential disadvantages, including the possible loss of lower class members.

Notes

1. A prime example is Ioan M. Lewis, *Ecstatic Religions: An Anthropological Study of Spirit Possession and Shamanism* (Middlesex, England: Penguin, 1971); For a critique see, Stephen D. Glazier, "Religion and Contemporary Religious Movements in the Caribbean," *Sociological Analysis* 41, no. 3 (1980): 181–83.
2. These leaders are discussed in Yoshiko S. Nagashima, *Rastafarian Music in Contemporary Jamaica: A Study of Socioreligious Music of the Rastafarian Movement in Jamaica* (Tokyo: Institute for the Study of Languages and Cultures of Asia and Africa, 1984), 13. See also, M. G. Smith, Roy Augier, and Rex Nettleford, *A Report on the Rastafari Movement in Kingston, Jamaica* (Kingston: Institute of Social and Economic Research, University College of the West Indies, Mona, 1960).
3. Chevannes argues that it is class interests which make it possible for

Rastas to transcend race, not, as Father Owens asserts, the essence of Rasta teachings concerning the equality of the races.

4. Research in Trinidad was conducted during the summers of 1976, 1977, 1978, 1979, and 1982. It was sponsored, in part, by grants from the University of Connecticut Research Foundation. For more information on the Baptists see my *Marchin' the Pilgrims Home: Leadership and Decision-Making in an Afro-Caribbean Faith* (Westport, Conn.: Greenwood, 1983).

5. For a detailed description of the mourning ceremony see my "Mourning in the Afro-Baptist Tradition," (Glazier 1985b). A number of scholars have interpreted the mourning ceremony as a form of sensory deprivation. A survey of the literature is contained in Ward and Beaubrun (1979).

References

Albuquerque, Klaus de. 1979. The future of the Rastafarian movement. *Caribbean Review* 8 (4).

Baer, Hans A. 1983. *The Black Spiritual movement: A Religious Response to Racism*. Knoxville: University of Tennessee Press.

Barrett, Leonard. 1977. *The Rastafarians: The Dreadlocks of Jamaica*. Kingston: Sangster's Book Stores.

Beck, Jane C. 1976. The implied Obeah man. *Western Folklore* 20: 23–33.

Bourguignon, Erika. 1982. Ritual and myth in Haitain *Vodoun*. *African Religious Groups and Beliefs*. Ed. S. Ottenberg. Meerut: Archana.

———. 1983. Religion and justice in Haitian *Vodoun*. Paper presented at the annual meeting of the Society for the Scientific Study of Religion, Knoxville, Tenn.

Campbell, Horace, 1980. The Rastafarians in the eastern Caribbean. *Caribbean Quarterly* 26: 42–61.

Chevannes, Barry. 1977. The literature of Rastafari. *Social and Economic Studies* 26: 239–62.

———. 1978. Revivalism: A disappearing religion. *Caribbean Quarterly* 24: 1–17.

Glazier, Stephen D. 1980a. Pentecostal exorcism and modernization in Trinidad, West Indies. *Perspectives on Pentecostalism: Case Studies From the Caribbean and Latin America*. Washington, D.C.: University Press of America.

———. 1980b. Religion and contemporary religious movements in the Caribbean: A report. *Sociological Analysis* 41: 181–83.

446   STEPHEN D. GLAZIER

————. 1980c. Commentary on Ward and Beaubrun. *Journal of Psychological Anthropology* 3: 231–33.

————. 1983a. *Marchin' the Pilgrims Home: Leadership and Decision-making in an Afro-Caribbean Faith.* Westport, Conn.: Greenwood.

————. 1983b. Caribbean pilgrimages: A typology. *Journal for the Scientific Study of Religion* 22: 316–25.

————. 1985a. Syncretism and separation: Ritual change in an Afro-Caribbean faith. *Journal of American Folklore* 98: 49–62.

————. 1985b. Mourning in the Afro-Baptist tradition: A comparison of Trinidad and the American South. *The Southern Quarterly* 23:141–56.

Herskovits, Melville J. and Frances S. Herskovits. 1947. *Trinidad Village.* New York: Alfred A. Knopf.

Hill, Robert A., 1981. Dread history: Leonard Howell and millenarian visions in early Rastafari religions in Jamaica. *Epoche* 9: 30–71.

Lantenarri, Vittorio. 1963. *The Religions of the Oppressed: A Study of Modern Messianic Cults.* New York: Alfred A. Knopf.

Leyburn, James G. 1971. *The Haitian People.* New Haven: Yale University Press.

Lewis, Ioan M. 1971. *Ecstatic Religion: An Anthropological Study of Spirit Possession and Shamanism.* Middlesex, England: Penguin.

Mintz, Sidney and Richard Price. 1976. *An Anthropological Approach to the Afro-American Past: A Caribbean perspective.* ISHI Occasional Papers in Social Change no. 2. Philadelphia: Institute for the Study of Human Issues.

Mischel, Frances. 1959. *A Shango Group and the Problem of Prestige in Trinidadian Society.* Unpublished Ph. D. Diss., Ohio State University, Columbus.

Nagashima, Yosahiko S. 1984. *Rastafarian Music in Contemporary Jamaica.* Tokyo: Institute for the Study of Languages and Cultures of Asia and Africa.

Nettleford, Rex. 1982. Intro. *Dread: The Rastafarians of Jamaica* by J. Owens. London: Heinemann.

Nicholas, Tracy. 1979. *Rastafari: A Way of Life.* Garden City, N.Y.: Anchor Doubleday.

Owens, Joseph. 1982. *Dread: The Rastafarians of Jamaica.* London: Heinemann.

Rogers, Claudia. 1978. Social transformation in Jamaica: The internal dynamics of the Rastafarian movement. Paper presented at the annual meeting of the Caribbean Studies Association. Fort-de-France, Martinique.

Sereno, Renzo. 1948. Obeah, magic and social structure in the Lesser Antilles. *Psychiatry* 11: 15–31.

Simpson, George Eaton. 1955. The Ras Tafari movement in Jamaica: A study of race and class conflict. *Social Forces* 34, no. 2: 168–70.

————. 1980. *Religious Cults of the Caribbean: Trinidad, Jamaica and Haiti*. Rio Piedras, P. R.: Institute of Caribbean Studies.

————. 1983. Religion and justice: Some reflections on the Ras Tafari movement in Jamaica. Paper presented at the annual meeting of the Society for the Scientific Study of Religion, Knoxville, Tenn.

Smith, M. G., Roy Augier, and Rex Nettleford. 1960. A Report on the Rastafari movement in Kingston, Jamaica. Kingston: ISER.

Ward, Colleen and Michael Beaubrun. 1979. Trance induction and hallucination in Spiritual Baptist mourning. *Journal of Psychological Anthropology* 2: 279–88.

Contributors

Karol H. Borowski, Director, Massachusetts Institute for Social Studies, Boston, Massachusetts

Steve Bruce, Department of Social Studies, The Queen's University, Belfast, Northern Ireland

Randall Collins, Editor, *Sociological Theory,* San Diego, California

Cromwell S. Crawford, Professor of Religious Studies, University of Hawaii, Honolulu, Hawaii

John L. Esposito, Chairman, Department of Religious Studies, College of Holy Cross, Worcester, Massachusetts

Frank K. Flinn, Consultant in Forensic Theology, St. Louis, Missouri

William R. Garrett, Chairman and Professor of Sociology, St. Michael's College, Winooski, Vermont

Stephen D. Glazier, Assistant Professor of Sociology, Connecticut College, New London, Connecticut

Jeffrey K. Hadden, Professor of Sociology, University of Virginia, Charlottesville, Virginia

Paget Henry, Assistant Professor of Sociology, University of Virginia, Charlottesville, Virginia

Saad Eddin Ibrahim, Professor of Sociology, American University in Cairo, Cairo, Egypt

Theodore E. Long, Chairman and Associate Professor of Sociology, Washington and Jefferson College, Washington, Pennsylvania

John T. S. Madeley, Lecturer, Department of Government, London School of Economics, London, England

Zulkarnaina M. Mess, Department of Malay Studies, University of Malaya, Kuala Lumpur, Malaysia

Michael L. Mickler, Ph.D. Candidate, Graduate Theological Union, Berkeley, California

Jerry G. Pankhurst, Assistant Professor of Sociology, Wittenberg University, Springfield, Ohio

W. Barnett Pearce, Chairman and Professor of Communication Studies, University of Massachusetts, Amherst, Massachusetts

Margaret M. Poloma, Professor of Sociology, Department of Sociology, University of Akron, Akron, Ohio

Roland Robertson, Professor of Sociology, University of Pittsburgh, Pittsburgh, Pennsylvania

Wade Clark Roof, Professor of Sociology, University of Massachusetts, Amherst, Massachusetts

Nader Saiedi, Assistant Professor of Sociology, University of California, Los Angeles, California

Anson Shupe, Associate Professor of Sociology, University of Texas, Arlington, Texas

John H. Simpson, Director, Centre for Religious Studies, University of Toronto, Toronto, Canada

Index

The numbers in **bold face** refer to pages written by the person indexed, while that person may also be referred to within those same pages. The numbers in parenthesis refer to chapter footnotes which appear on that page. The letter *n* refers to a footnote on that page. Spellings which are apparently preferred are followed, whereas a different spelling may appear on specific pages; alternative spellings were not intentionally indexed.

Abduh, Muhammed 156
Abdulhamid 187
Abrahamian, Ervand 170 (32)
Abu Bakar 201
Abu Ismail 360
Abu-Lughod, Ibrahim 215, 219
Aczel, Gyorgy 274, 303
Adel Eid 360
Adenauer, Konrad 378
Aflaq, Michel 159, 169 (12)
Ahlstrom, Sydney E. 28–32
Ahmad H. Sakr 220
Ahmad Ibrahim 199, 219
Ahmad Lutfi al-Sayyid 169 (6)
Ahmad, Al-e 171
Ahmad, Aziz 168 (4), 171
Ahmad, Khurshid 171
Ahmad, Muhammad 312
Akey, Denise S. 407
Akhavi, Shahrough 171

al-Banna, Hasan 160–161, 169 (16)
al-Bazzaz, Iraqi Abd al-Rahman 148, 169 (10)
al-Husrim, Sati 169 (9)
al-Husti, Sati 157–158
al-Maraghi, Mustafa 158
al-Nasser, Abd 160–162
al-Quaddafi, Muammar 162–165, 167, 170 (20)
al-Sadat, Anwar 161
al-Sayyuid, Lutfi 157
al-Shahid 161
al-Sibaii, Mustapha 161, 165, 169 (19)
Albania 293–294 (table)
Albuquerque, Klaus de 445
Alexander VII 310
Alexander, Stella 273, 303
Alexander, Y. 428
Algar, Hamid 184, 193 (1)
Allende, Salvador 79

449

Aly, Abd al-Moneim Said 170 (29)
Anderson, Robert Mapes 340, 349
Anderson, G. 150
Anderson, Lisa 170 (24)
Anderson, Perry 90 (5), 100
Ansari, Murtaza 185
Appiah-Kubi, Kofi 121 (23)
Apter, David E. 38, 49
Aquinas, Thomas 324–325
Aristotle 179
Arjomand, Said 146, 149
Arroyo, Alberto 329n
Arslan, Amir Shaykh 158
Asad, Muhammad 171
Asahi Nenkan 251
Ashaari, Uztaz 207
Asoka, Emperor 264
Aspaturian, Vernon V. 272, 303
Assman, Hugo 121 (22)
Augier, Roy 444 (2), 447
Ayoub, Muhammad 170 (25), 171 (36)

Baer, Hans A. 438, 445
Baerwald, Hans H. 245, 251–2
Bakar, Abu 212
Bakker, Jim 25, 27
Banfield, Edward C. 399, 407
Banisadr, Abul Hasan 167, 171
Baptist Union of Romania 293–294
    (table)
Barnes, Douglas F. 8, 17
Barrett, David B. 136, 293–294 (table),
    306, 330, 343, 349
Barrett, Leonard E. 150, 431–432, 434,
    445
Barth, Karl 308, 325–6
Bass, Jerry 204, 209, 219
Bastide, Roger 100
Bauer, Raymond 279, 304
Baum, Rainer C. 96, 100, 400, 402, 407
Bausett 340
Bayat, Mangol 170 (32)
Baytar, Salah al-Din 159
Beasely, W.G. 252
Beaubrun, Michael 445 (5), 447
Beck, Jane C. 437, 445
Beeson, Trevor 273, 303
Beig, Ahman 177
Belden, Jack 326
Bell, Daniel 120 (11)
Bellah, Robert N. 198, 219, 252
Bendix, Reinhard 38, 49

Benedict, Pope 310
Bensman, Joseph 39, 49
Berger, Peter L. 8, 17, 107, 113, 120
    (13), 121 (28), 215, 219, 349, 420,
    427
Berger, S. 389
Bergesen, Albert 396, 407
Berman, Marshall 219
Bernard, Lewis 194 (13)
Bernstein, Basil 192, 194
Berryman, Phillip 77, 198 (3), 200
Bhutto, Zulfikar Ali 146
Biao, Lin 317
Bird, Thomas E. 227, 231
Bismarck 373
Biswas, D.K. 68 (5)
Blacker, Carmen 251
Blaker, Michael K. 244–245, 251–252
Boal, F.P.W. 428
Bociurkiw, B.R. 304–305
Boff, Leonardo 121 (34), 122 (47)
Bonino, Jose 148, 150
Bonpane, Blase 344, 349
Borowski, Karol H. xxii–xxiii, **221–232**,
    231, 447
Bourguignon, Erika 436, 445
Brannen, Noah S. 237, 239–240, 243,
    247, 250 (3), 351
Brett, Cecil 2432, C. 251
Brierley, P. 427
Brill, E.J. 252
Brisby, James McB 426 (8)
Bromley, David G. xii, xviii, 32, 34, 241,
    251, 407
Brown, J.F. 304
Browne, E. Moxon 411, 427
Bruce, Steve xxvii, 414, **410–429**, 425
    (1), 427, 447
Bruneau, Thomas 98 (2), 99 (10), 100
Buchheim, K. 389
Buckingham, Jamie 68, 332, 349
Buckland, P. 422, 428
Bulgaria 293–294 (table)
Bulloch, J. 415, 416, 428
Bundy, David 309, 326
Burghs, Falkirk 427 (14)
Burke, Edmund 53–54
Burkett, Randall K. 49
Burleigh, J.H.S. 425 (3), 428
Burman, Debajuoti 68 (7)
Butterfield, Fox 317, 319, 326
Butterworth, Charles E. 170 (28)

Calvinist Calvinism 21, 25
Camara, Dom Helder 122 (45)
Campbell, A.B. 415, 428
Campbell, Horace 434, 436, 445
Campbell, R. 172, 205, 219
Carpini, Giovanni de Plano 3–9
Carside, Roger 307
Casanova, Jose 345–346, 349
Cass, Frank 389
Cassells, David 424
Cassirer, Ernst 120 (9)
Castro, Americo 30, 80, 100, 103
Ceausescu, Nicolae 298
Ch'en, Kenneth 257, 267, 270 (2)
Chadwick, Henry 255–256, 270
Chakravarti, S.C. 68 (11)
Chalmers, Thomas 425–426 (6)
Chance, Norman A. 326
Chand, Tara 69 (31)
Chandler, Ralph Clark 32 (5)
Chen Zemin 323–324, 326
Cheng Ho 199
Chevannes, Barry 434, 445
Chiang Kai-Shek 213
Chordas, Thomas J. 340, 349
Christian Brethren 293–294 (table)
Churchill, Winston 38
Clark, Charles Allen 48, 309, 326
Cleary, Edward L. 82, 98 (3), 100
Clement XI 310
Cohen, D.L. 35, 49
Cohn, Norman 324, 326
Cole, Juan R. 165, 185, 194
Collet, Sophia D. 68 (5)
Collins, Randall xxiii, 254–271, 447
Colson, Charles W. 333, 339, 349
Compton, P.A. 428
Cone, James 150
Confucius 319
Cormack, John 418, 423, 427 (14)
Corvino, Giovanni de Monte 310
Coser, Lewis A. 274, 303, 420, 428
Costas, Orlando E. 329n, 344, 349
Cox, Harvey 116, 118–119, 121 (20),
    340, 349
Cragg, Kenneth 407 168 (3), 394, 407
Crawford, Cromwell S. xix, 52–69, 447
Crawford, J. 69 (36)
Crecelius, Daniel 169 (14)
Cronen, Vernon E. 220
Cronon, David E. 41, 44–49
Cserhati, Jozef 274, 303
Cuddihy, John Murray 30, 32

Cudsi, Alexander S. 170 (27), 171
Currie, R.A. Gilbert 426 (7), 428
Curtis, Gerlad L. 243–244, 252
Czechoslovakia 293–294 (table)

D'Antonio, William V. 97 (2), 98 (2),
    (6), 100–101
Dahrendorf, Ralf 275, 303
Darwin, Charles 20–21
Dator, James Allen 241–244, 252
Datta, K.K. 68 (1)
Davey, J. Ernest 425 (4)
Davies, James C. 38, 49
Davis, Kortright 150
Davis, Lenwood G. 49
Davis, Vernal 432
Davis, Winston 244, 247–248, 252
Dayton, Donald W. 331, 349
de Albuquerque, Klaus 432
de Gaulle, Charles 38, 379
de Graveve, Frank 310, 326
de Gruchy, John W. 121 (233)
de Jaegher, Raymond J. 315, 326
de Nobili, Roberrto 310
Dekmejian, R. Hrair 170 (26)
Demerath, III, N.J. 396, 407
Deng Xiaoping 314, 317–319, 326
Desmangles, Leslie G. 437
Dessouki, Ali E. Hillal 170 (24–25,
    27–29), 171
Dickson, T. 428
Din din Ali 199
Ding Xiaoping 307
Dodson, Michael 99 (7), 100, 344, 349
Dominquez, Enrique 344, 349
Domoulin, Heinrich 257, 271
Donohue 169 (5–6, 9, 12, 15–16, 19),
    170 (20, 27), 171 (34)
Doran, Charles F. 408
Douglas, J.N.H. 428
Douglas, Mary 33, 219
Drummond, A.L. 415, 416, 428
Drury, John 100, 102
Dulles, Avery 308, 326
Dumont, Louis 270 (4), 271
Dumoulin, Heinrich 241, 350 (3), 252,
    271
Dunkley, Archibald 136, 432
Duquoc, C. 351
Durkheim, Emile 88, 192, 194, 428
Dussel, Enrique 98 (3–4), 100
Duvalier, Francois 435, 437
Duvalier, Jean-Claude 437–438

Eagleson, John 98 (2–3), 100–102, 121
  (22)
Earlington, Paul 432
Eisenhower, Dwight D. 38
Eisenstadt, S.N. 50
Ellison, Marvin M. 121 (29)
Ellul, Jacques 334, 350
Ellwood, Jr., Robert S. 236, 239,
  250(6), 251 (7), 252
Elvin, Mark 267, 271
Enayat, Hamid 171, 183, 193 (3), 195
Erskine, Noel 134, 150
Esposito, John L. xxi, 168 (1, 4), 169
  (5–6), 9, 12, 14–16, 19), 153–172,
  170 (20, 25, 28), 171 (34), 447
Etzioni, Amitai 398, 407
Evangelical Church of Czech Brethren
  293–294 (table)
Evangelical Church of the Augsburg
  Confession 293–294 (table)
Evangelical Lutheran Church 293–294
  (table)

Fagan, Richard 38, 50
Falwell, Jerry xviii, 21, 25, 27, 32 (8),
  118
Fanon, Frantz 138, 150
Fazlur, Rahman 193 (6)
Federation of Evangelical Churches
  293–294 (table)
Fernbach, David 120 (11)
Feuer, Lewis S. 194 (7), 195
Fischoff, E. xxix, 17
Flake, Carol 24, 33
Flinn, Frank K. xxiv, 307–328, 447
Floristan, C. 351
Fogarty, M.P. 368–369, 376, 386,
  379–382, 389
Foster, Bruce 34
Frank, Andre Gunder 212 (30)
Frei Montalva, Edwando 100
Freire, Paulo 101
Friedland, William H. 37–38, 50
Friedrichs, Robert W. xi, xviii
Friere, Paulo 76–77
Fromm, Eric 194 (12), 195
Fuller, Peter 199 (5), 201

Gairy, Eric 442
Galilea, Segundo 122 (46)
Gallagher, R. 421, 428 425 (5), 428
Gallagher, T. 428
Gallup, Jr., George 219
Gandhi, Mohandas K. xix, 38

Ganguli, P.O. 68 (5), 69 (34)
Garrett, William R. xx, 103–122, 447
Garside, Roger 307, 317, 320, 326
Garvey, Amy Jacques 50
Garvey, Marcus xix, 36, 40–47,
  135–136
Gauhar, Altaf 171
Gautama Buddah 270 (4)
Geertz, Clifford 394, 407
German Democratic Republic 293–294
  (table)
Gerth, Hans H. xviii, 17, 328, 338,
  384
Gibellini, Rosina 121 (21)
Gierek, Edward 224
Gilbert, A. 426 (7)
Givant, Michael 39, 49
Glaser, Barney G. 36, 50
Glass, Jack 419, 424
Glazier, Stephen D. xxvii, 169 (6), 329n,
  340–350, 431, 436, 430–447, 444
  (1) , 445 (5), 446–447
Glemp, Cardinal 228, 281
Glock, Charles Y. 34
Gluckmann, Max 326
Gordon, Charles G. 312
Gottel, Gerard 49 (1)
Graham, Billy, xxiv
Gray, Francine 120 (1)
Gray, T. 412, 428
Gregory, Rose 186, 195
Greinacher, Norbert 122 (46)
Gruber, C. 385, Gserhati, Jozsef 303
Guha, Rajani Kanta 59 (17)
Guth, James L. 350
Gutiérrez, Gustavo 76–77, 79, 83, 101,
  113, 117, 121 (21, 33), 141, 150
Gyorgy, Andrew 303–305

Habermas, Jurgen 125, 150
Haddad, Yvonne 169 (18), 172
Hadden, Jeffrey K. xi–xxix, 32 (7), 33,
  120 (16), 329n, 394, 407, 447
Haile Selassie 135, 137, 432–433
Haim, Sylvia 169 (10)
Hall, B. Welling 274, 303
Halliday, Fred 193 (2), 195
Hamid, Idris 134, 150
Hammond, Phillip E. xii–xiii, xviii, 29,
  33, 216, 219
Hanafi, Hassan 166, 172
Handley, J. 414, 428
Handy, Robert T. 20, 33
Hanhardt, Jr., Arthur M. 274, 304

Hank, Li Poh 199
Hardie, John B. 172
Hargrove, Barbara 4, 17
Harrell, Jr., David E. 33
Harrington, Michael 346, 350
Harris, C.P. 169 (17), 172
Harris, Jo Ann 49 (1)
Harris, Marvin 263, 271
Harvie, C. 421, 428
Hastings, Lord 54, 62
Hatch, Orrin 24
Heffner, Richard D. 409
Hegel, G.F. 97. 179, 316–317
Heidenheimer, A.J. 387, 389
Helms, Jesse 25
Henderson, A.M. xviii, 17
Hendricks, John Stephen 26, 33
Hendricks, Tyler 326–328
Heneghan, Thomas E. 274, 304
Henry, Paget xx, **123–150**, 447
Herberg, Will 391, 407
Herskovits, Frances S. 440, 446
Herskovits, Melville J. 440, 446
Hibbert, Joseph 432
Hickey, J. 428, 425 (2), 428
Hill, Jr., Samuel S. 32 (4), 33, 433
Hill, Robert A. 446
Hindi, Ahman Khan 177
Hinds, Robert 136, 432
Hinton, William 307, 314–316, 318,
    324, 326
Hitam, Datuk Musa 214
Hitchins, Keith 274, 304
Hitler, Adolf 38. 198
Hj. Mohd. Din bin Ali 219
Hoare, Quinton 120 (11)
Hobbes, Thomas 324
Hodgson, Marshall G. S. 178–176, 180,
    195
Hollenweger, W.J. 338, 340, 350
Hollyday, Joyce 342, 350–351
Holmes, R.F. 412, 428
Holzner, Burkhart 100, 407–408
Horsley, L. 428 426 (7), 428
Hourani, Albert 168 (2–3), 172,
    180–182, 193 (5), 195
Howard, Ted 351
Howe, Gary Nigel 348, 350
Howell, Leonard 136, 432
Hoxha, Enver 273
Hsia, Adrian 316–317, 327
Huai Jui 324
Hung Hsiu-ch'uan 310

Hungary 293–294 (table)
Hunter, James Davidson 32 (9), 33,
    217–219, 331, 346–347, 350, 395,
    407
Huntington, Deborah 340–343, 350
Husain, Imam M. 169 (17), 172, 190
Hussein, Taha 157, 169 (6), 213
Hussite Church 293–294 (table)

Ibrahim Abu-Lughod 219
Ibrahim, Anwar 166, 206–207
Ibrahim, Saad Eddin xxv, **353–361**, 447
Ikado, Fujo 244, 252
Ikeda, Daisaku 241
Inda, Caridad 101
Inkeles, Alex 279, 304
Iqbal, Muhammad 168 (4), 172
Irving, R.E.M. 286, 384, 389
Iskandar Shah 199

Jacuet, Constance 33, 387
Jiang Peifen 324, 327
Jiang Wenhan 313, 315, 317, 327
John Paul II 222, 227, 299, 337, 411
Johnson, Chalmers A. 242, 246, 401,
    425 (6)
Johnson, Harry M. 17
Jones, A.H.M. 54, 256, 271
Jorstad, Erling 33
Josei, Toda 238–239, 243
Joshi, V.C. 69 (323)

Kahn, Genghis 309
Kangxi, Emperor 310
Kaplan, A. 389
Kater, Jr., John L. 338, 350
Keddie, Nikki R. 168 (2), 172, 187, 193
    (4), 195
Kellas, J. 421, 429
Kennedy, John Fitzgerald 9, 396
Kenyatta, Jomo 48
Khan, Sayyid Ahmad 168 (4)
Khomeini, Ayatollah Ruhullah xiii,
    xxi–xxii, 164–167, 172, 183–189,
    194 (9), 195
Kierkegaard, Sören 134, 150
Kim Il Sung 38
King, Robert R. 48, 274, 304
Kirk, Irina 280, 304
Kloczowski, Jerzy 230, 232
Knox, John 419
Kolinsky, M. 390
Korbonski, Andrzej 232, 274, 304

Kovats, Charles E. 274, 304
Kovrig, Bennett 174, 304
Kuebman, R.C. 351
Kuhn, Thomas S. xi, xviii

Lacordaire 364, 369, 371
Lamb, Matthew L. 121 (21)
Lamennais, Felicite de 368, 371, 374
Land, Brian 407–8
Lane, Christel 274, 304
Lane, Dermot A. 120 (15)
Lantenarri, Vittorio 443, 446
LaRuffa, Anthony L. 340, 350
Lasswell, H. 365, 389
Latourette, Kenneth Scott 309, 327
Laurentin, Rene 121 (31)
Lechner, Frank J. 395, 408
Lee Meng Ng 312–313, 327
Leiden, Neth 252
Lenin, V.I. 38, 109, 113, 319
Leo XIII 375
Lernoux, Penny 78, 101
Levine, Daniel H. 100–101, 251
Lewis, Ioan M. 431, 444 (1), 446
Lewy, Guenter xv, xviii, 169 (14)
Leyburn, James G. 435, 446
Lianzuo, Wang 315
Liebman, Robert C. xviii, 33, 339, 350, 352, 392, 408–409
Lijphart, A. 389
Lincoln, Abraham 52
Lipp, Wolfgang 40–41, 45, 50
Lipset, Seymour Martin 102, 369, 389, 392, 400, 404, 408
Liss, Sheldon B. 98 (5), 101
Liu Shaoqi 316–318
Locke, John 324
Lofland, John 36, 50
Long, Theodore E. xvi, xviii, 3–17, 447
Longimel, André de 310
Loughridge, A. 418, 429
Lovelace, Richard 333, 350
Lu Weidu 319, 327
Lyons, F.S. 412, 429

MacLaren, A.A. 416, 429
MacLeod, Henry G. 409
Macnaghten, Francis 63
Madeley, John T.S. xxvi, 365–390, 389, 391n, 447
Maduro, Otto 65, 101
Magata, Judith 220
Mahathir 201–202, 204, 220

Mainse, David 405
Majka, Jozef 228, 232
Majumdar, J.K. 69 (19)
Majumdar, R.C. 68 (1)
Makisuchi, Tsunesaburo 238
Malik, Hafeez 180. 195
Manley, Michael 432
Mannheim, Karl 116, 122 (37)
Mansor Shah 199
Mao Zedong (Tse-Tung) 38, 327, 310, 312, 314–316, 318–321
Maraldo, John C. 252
Marsden, George M. 20–21, 32 (3), 33
Marshall, Jr., R.H. 305
Martin, David A. 41, 48, 95, 101, 277, 296, 304, 371–372, 390, 395, 408, 427 (11), 429
Martin, Tony 50
Martindale, D. xx, 17
Marty, Martin E. xviii, 20, 33
Marx, Karl 106–107, 115, 316, 319
Matthews, Jay 317, 327
Matthews, Linda 317, 327
Mawdudi, Mawlana Abul Ala 157, 169 (5), 172
Mayer, Ann 170 (24)
Mayer, N. Zald 304
Mazarin, Cardinal 262
McCann, Dennis 77, 98 (3), 101
McCarthy, John D. 278, 304
McClelland, David 174, 195
McGovern, Arthur F. 121 (32)
McGuire, Meredith 4, 17
McKinney, William 27, 33
McLellan, David 120 (10)
MacLeod, Henry G., 405, 409
McMannis, William 337
McRoberts, D.A. 420–421, 429, 426 (7), 429
Mecham, J. Lloyd 344, 350
Meerson-Aksyonov, Mikhail 280
Menashri, David 187
Mencken, H.L. 26
Merad, Ali 170 (27)
Merelman, R.M. 43, 50
Merkl, P.H. 377, 390
Mess, Zulkarnaina xxii, 196–220, 448
Meyendorff, John 302, 304
Michelat, G. 390
Michnik, Adam 230, 232
Mickler, Michael L. xix, 35–51, 448
Mindszenty, Cardinal 287
Mill, James 53–54

Mills, C.W. 384–388, 389
Minnery, Tom 341, 351
Mintz, Sidney 446
Miranda, Jose 101, 142, 150
Mischel, Frances 442, 446
Mitchell, Richard P. 169 (17), 172
Mohamad Abu Bakar 220
Mondale, Fritz 332
Monino, Jose Miguez 121 (32)
Montgomery, T.S. 351
Montt, Efrain Rio xxv, 349, 341–342
Moon, Sun Myung xix, 36, 40–48
Morioka, Kiyomi 252
Morrision, Robert 308
Mortimer, Edward 172, 184, 195
Morton, H.W. 305
Mubarak, Muhammad Hujn: 353,
   358–361
Mubarak, Hosn: xxv
Muhahidin-i-Khalq 166
Muhammad Ali 17, 183
Muirhead, I.A. 415, 429
Muller, Alois 122 (46)
Mullins, Nicholas C. xi, xviii
Münzer, Thomas 116
Murnin, Hugh 426 (11, 14)
Musaad, I. 168 (3)
Muslims 293–294 (table)
Mussolini, Benito 376, 378
Muthchler, David E. 86, 101

Nag, Kalidaw 68 (7)
Nagashima, Yoshiko S. 432, 434, 444
   (2), 446
Nagata, Judith 206, 208, 218 (3)
Naidu, Sarojini 59 (30)
Naipul, V.S. 129, 209, 220
Naisbitt, John xii, xviii
Nakane, Chie 401, 408
Napoleon III 176, 373
Nasser, Gamal Abdul 176, 356
Neely, Alan 98 (4), 101
Nettl, J.P. 101
Nettleford, Rex 432, 434, 444 (2),
   446-7
Neuhaus, Richard John 31, 33
Newell, William H. 252
Nichiren, 236–238
Nicholas, Tracy 446
Nichols, R.L. 305
Nickolson, W.P. 425 (4)
Niebuhr, Richard 339, 351
Nisbet, R.A. 390

Nkrumah, Kwame 38, 48
Noll, Mark 333, 351
Norbeck, Edward 248, 252
Norberto, J. 351
Norman, Edward 98 (4), 99 (10), 101,
   340, 351
Novak, Michael 89, 102
Nyomavky, Joseph 38, 50

O'Day, A. 428
Oestreicher, Paul 274, 305
Orthodox 293–294 (table)
Ossowski, Stanislaw 398, 408
Ottenberg, S. 445
Owens, Joseph 150, 434 446

Paisley, Ian 424–425 (4)
Palmer, Spencer J. 309, 327
Palmerston, Lord 312
Pankhurst, Jerry G. xxiv, 221, **272–306,**
   305, 448
Pano, Nicholas C. 273, 305
Parsons, Talcott xviii, 17, 271, 408
Passin, Herbert 244
Paterson, W. 390
Patterson, Sheila 129, 408
Paul V, Pope 310
Pearce, W. Barnett xxii, **196–220,** 220,
   448
Pegis, Anton C. 325
Pentecostal Churches 293–294 (table)
Perinbanayagan, R.S. 38, 50
Petersen, David L. 6, 17
Phillips, Kevin 24, 33
Pickering, W.S.F. 88, 102
Piggott, C.A. 414, 429
Pike, Fredrick B. 98 (2), 99 (6),
   100–101
Pius IX 371, 373, 375
Pius XII 315
Piwowarski, Wladyslaw 229, 232
Poland 293–294 (table)
Poloma, Margaret M. xxv, **329–352,**
   391n, 448 351, 448
Pomian-Srzednicki, Maciej 221, 232
Popieluszko, Jerzy 228
Powell, Adam Clayton 50
Powell, David 41, 274, 305
Price, Richard 446
Pridham, G. 390
Prifti, Peter 273, 305
Prince, Derek 336, 351
Protestants 293–294 (table)

Qaddafi, Muammar xxi
Quebedeaux, Richard 331, 347, 351
Quinley, Harold C. 34
Quinn, Laura 153n
Qutb, Sayyid 161, 165, 172

Rabb, Earl 392, 408
Rahman, Fazlur 178, 191, 195
Rahman, Tunku Abdul 202
Raina, Peter 224, 232
Rajana, Eini Watavabe 247, 252
Rakowska-Harmstone, Teresa 272,
    303–305
Ramet, Pedro 273, 305
Ramos, Mura Bergman 101
Ratcliffe, Alexander 417–418, 426 (10,
    14)
Ratman, K.J. 38, 50
Ray, Niharranjan 69 (34)
Raychaudhuri, H.C. 68 (1)
Reagan, Ronald 18, 24, 111, 332–334,
    396
Reese, Boyd 331, 351
Reformed Christian Church 293–294
    (table)
Reformed Church of Hungary 293–294
    (table)
Reformed Church of Romania 293–294
    (table)
Regan, Daniel 216, 220
Reid, Gilbert 312, 410
Reid, J.S. 429
Remington, Robin Alison 273, 305
Ricci, Matteo 308–310, 319
Richardson, Bradley M. 401
Richelieu, Cardinal 262
Richetts, Ferdinand 432
Ricouer, Paul 130, 150
Rida, Rashid 156
Rifkin, Jeremy 339–340, 351
Ritzer, George xi, xviii
Roberts, Keith A. 4, 17
Robertson, Pat xix–xx, xxv, 25, 27, 335,
    342
Robertson, Roland 73–102, 100–102,
    120 (3), 329n, 402, 407–408, 448
Robinson, H. Wheeler 69 (37)
Rogers, Claudia 432, 443, 446
Roggendorf, Joseph 248, 252
Rokkan, S. 369, 389
Roman Catholics 293–294 (table)
Romania 293–294 (table)
Romero, Archbishop 344

Roof, Wade Clark xviii–xix, 18–34, 33,
    449
Rose, R. 366, 390
Roth, G. xxix, 17
Rothenberg, Joshua 274, 305
Rouleau, F.A. 310, 320, 327
Rousseau, Jean Jacques 105, 107–109,
    115, 118, 120 (8)
Roy, Ram Mohan 52–69
Ruggieri, Michaele 310
Runciman, W.G. 38, 50
Rustow, Dankwart A. 38, 50

Sachedina, Abdul Aziz 170 (32)
Sacks, M.P. 305
Sadat, Anwar 354–358
Sadra, Mulla 179
Saiedi, Nader xxi–xxii, 173–195, 448
Sakr, Ahmad H. 210, 220
Samuels, Richard J. 245–246, 252
Sandoval, Moises 91, 102
Sanguier, Marc 375
Saniel, Josefa M. 252
Sansom, George 261, 271
Saracco, L. 339, 351
Sarkar, Sumit 69 (32)
Schafly, Phyllis 24
Scharper, Philip 89 (2), 100–102
Schimmel, Anne Marie 178, 195
Schlesinger, Arthur 50
Schmitt, Karl M. 102
Schram, Stuart 38, 50
Schumpeter, Joseph A. 408
Seal, Brajendranath 58 (11)
Segundo, Juan Luis 77, 79, 102, 113,
    121 (21), 142, 150
Selover, Thomas 313, 327
Sereno, Renxzo 437, 447
Shaltut, Shaykh Mahumud 160, 169 (15)
Shariati, Ali 166–167, 171 (34), 172,
    183, 194 (8), 195
Shaull, Richard 101, 121 (33)
Shaw, McInnes 423
Shils, Edward 38–39, 50
Shoup, Paul 272, 305
Shriver, Peggy L. 331, 336–337, 351
Shumpeter, Joseph A. 400, 408
Shupe, Jr., Anson D. xi–xxix, 32 (10),
    33–34, 120 (17), 235–253, 251-2,
    312, 327, 351, 407, 448
Sigler, John H. 408
Simmel, Georg 195, 277, 428
Simon, M. 390

Simpson, George Eaton 432–433, 436, 447
Simpson, John H. XXVI, 28, 33. **391–409**, 448
Sims, Janet L. 48–49
Slovak Evangelical Church of the Augsburg Confession 293–294 (table)
Smith, Bardwell L. xiv, xviii
Smith, Brian H. 88, 90, 99 (6–8), 102
Smith, Donald Eugene xiii–xv, xviii, 169 (14)
Smith, M.G. 444 (2), 447
Smith, Vincent A. 68 (2)
Smith, W.C. 172
Sohn, Rudolph 36
Solzhenitsyn, Aleksandr 287
Southern, R.W. 268, 271
Speer, James A. 23, 32 (5), 34
Spence, Jonathan D. 319, 328
Stacey, William A. xii, xviii, 32 (18), 33, 120 (17), 351
Stackhouse, Max L. 121 (19), 122 (36)
Stalin, Jozef 190, 279
Stark, Rodney 31 (10), 34, 409
Stauffer, Milton T. 313, 328
Stavrou, T.G. 305
Stevens-Arroyo, Anthony M. 102
Stewart, D. 410. 429
Stransku, T. 150
Straus, Leo 120 (7)
Strauss, Anselm L. 36, 50
Strong, J.W. 304–305
Sturzo, Luigi 376
Sun Yat Sen 310
Sutherland, James 69 (28)
Swaggert, Jimmy 27
Swann, Charles E. XII, xviii, 32 (7), 120 (16)
Swanson, Guy E. 399, 401, 408–409
Swatos, Jr., William H. 38, 50

T'ai P'ing 311–312
T'ien Wang 312
Tabari, Azar 194 (18), 195
Talmon, J.L. 103–105
Tasker, Rodney 212, 220
Taussig, Michael T. 100 (12), 102
Taylor, D. 425 (1), 429
Tillich, Paul 130, 150
Ting, H.K. 315, 317–320, 322–324, 326–328
Tipton, Stephen M. 33, 219
Tocqueville, Alexis de 397, 409

Toffler, Alvin xii, xviii
Tokes, R.L. 305
Tonnies, Bernhard 273, 305
Torres, Camilo 79
Torres, Sergio 98 (3), 100, 102, 121 (22–23)
Toynbee, Polly 401, 409
Troll, Christian W. 168 (4), 172
Tu Shihua 328
Tucker, Robert C. 38, 5050
Turabi, Hassan 166, 170 (30)
Turner, Victor 328

Uchida, Mitsura 245, 252
Ul-Haq, Zia 167
Ulc, Otto 305
Urwin, D. 366, 390
USSR 293–294 (table)

Valignano, Alessandro 310
Vallier, Ivan 84–86, 90–92, 102
Vidales, Raul 338, 351
Vidler, A. 390
Viguerie, Richard 24
Vilder, A. 369, 390
Vinson, Donald E. 38, 50
Voll, John O. 145, 150, 172, 174, 177, 195
von der Mehden, Fred R. 170 (31)
von Vorys, Karl 198, 202, 220

Wagner, Peter 329n
Walesa, Lech 226, 281
Wallace, Anthony F.C. 220, 247, 253
Wallerstein, Immanuel 87, 102, 174, 195, 347, 351
Wallis, Jim 329n, 335, 342, 350–351
Wallis, Roy xxv, 250 (4), 253, 425 (1), 429
Waliullah, Shah 176
Walters, Philip 273, 288, 306
Ward, Caroline 274, 306
Ward, Colleen 447
Ward, W.R. 390
Ware, Timothy 302, 306
Washington, Booker T. 41
Webber, Robert E. 347, 351
Weber, Max xviii, xxix, 3–17, 36–39, 51, 111, 121 (10), 138, 235, 262–263, 270 (2), 271, 312, 328, 384, 387
Wedenoja, William 340, 346–347, 352
Welch, Alfred T. 172
Wellesley, Lord 60

Wenhan, Jiang 310
Wenner, Manfred W. 170 (29)
Weschler, Lawrence 225, 232
Weyrich, Paul 24
White, Theodore H. 318, 328
Whyte, John H. 374, 378, 380, 382–383, 390
Wiatr, Jerzy 222, 231 (1)
Wickeri, J. 326
Wilkerson, David 339
Willems, Emilio 340, 351
Williams, Eric 441–442
Williams, Rhys H. 396, 407
Willner, Ann Ruth 38, 51
Willner, Dorothy 38, 51
Wilson, Bryan R. xxiii, xxix, 4, 35, 38, 40, 51, 93, 102, 219, 249, 253, 350, 390, 399, 429
Wilson, James Q. 407
Wilson, John 17
Winter, J. Alan 399, 409
Wojtyla, Cardinal 229

Woodward, Jr., Ralph Lee 102
Wren, Christopher S. 319, 328
Wright, Arthur F. 271
Wuthnow, Robert 31 (1), 33, 339, 350–352, 392, 394, 408–409
Wuzong, Emperor 309
Wyszynski, Cardinal 229, 282

Xie, Moses P. 317

Yaozong, Wu 313
Yeganeh, Nahid 194 (10), 195
Yi He Tuan 308
Yugoslavia 293–294 (table)

Zald, Mayer 278
Zhao Fusan 311, 313–314, 328
Zhao Puchu 320
Zhou Enlai 313, 315
Zia, General Mohammed 146
Zwier, Robert 352